Mathematical Finance

Volume I

Mathematical Finance
Volume I

Edited by **Isabelle Maxwell**

Clanrye International
New Jersey

Published by Clanrye International,
55 Van Reypen Street,
Jersey City, NJ 07306, USA
www.clanryeinternational.com

Mathematical Finance: Volume I
Edited by Isabelle Maxwell

International Standard Book Number: 978-1-63240-337-7 (Hardback)

Printed in China.

Contents

Preface

At a very basic level, Mathematical Finance is an area of applied mathematics, which deals with financial markets. Instead of treating Mathematics and Finance as two separate disciplines, Mathematical Finance is a unique field, which converges the two dynamic subjects. Also known as Quantitative Finance, Mathematical Finance overlaps majorly with the field of Computational Finance.

An important highlight of this subject is the integration of practical domains of mathematics with a comprehensive knowledge of both the theory and practical applications of modern finance. One of the key theorems in this subject is arbitrage-free pricing with the Black–Scholes equation and formula among the crucial results.

Mathematical Finance is emerging as an interesting area of research. Increasingly sophisticated mathematical models and derivative pricing strategies have been developed in this discipline. A lot of exciting work is happening on mathematical modelling and computational methods in finance. Issues relevant to regulatory issues such as funding valuation, counterparty credit risk and collateral modelling are also being studied and researched. Topics on quantitative modelling such as optimization, simulation, statistics are also being researched extensively.

I wish to thank all the contributors who've allowed us to publish their studies on mathematical finance in this book.

Editor

VaR-Optimal Risk Management in Regime-Switching Jump-Diffusion Models

Alessandro Ramponi
Department of Economics and Finance, University of Roma Tor Vergata, Roma, Italy

ABSTRACT

In this paper we study a classical option-based portfolio strategy which minimizes the Value-at-Risk of the hedged position in a continuous time, regime-switching jump-diffusion market, by using Fourier Transform methods. However, the analysis of this hedging strategy, as well as the computational technique for its implementation, is fairly general, *i.e.* it can be applied to any dynamical model for which Fourier transform methods are viable.

Keywords: Regime Switching Jump-Diffusion Models; Value at Risk; Risk Management; Fourier Transform Methods

1. Introduction

In this paper we study a classical hedging policy based on options followed by an institutional manager whose aim is to minimize the Value-at-Risk of a position in a regime-switching jump-diffusion market. Although sharply criticized for the lack of sub-additivity and its inability to quantify the severity of an exposure to rare events, VaR has been adopted as a benchmark in the financial industry and for regulatory purposes. It plays a central role in banking regulation and internal risk management, mainly due to its simplicity. The analysis of this hedging strategy has been initiated by [1] a decade ago for a portfolio made by a risky asset following a lognormal random dynamic, and hence analytically solved in a Black-Scholes setting. More recently, it has been considered for a bond portfolio in [2,3]. By taking the VaR as the risk measure for potential losses L of a portfolio, we hedge the risky position by buying a fraction h of a put option with maturity T and strike price K: but what K and h? By fixing a hedging constraint, the corresponding (constrained) optimality condition involves quantiles computations and derivative pricing. Both steps can be efficiently faced with the Fourier transform technique, under historical and risk-neutral probability respectively.

The dynamic model we consider for the risky position is $S(t)=S_0 e^{X(t)}$, where $X(t)$ is specified on a filtered probability space as a jump-diffusion whose parameters change over time, driven by a continuous time and stationary Markov Chain on a finite state space $\mathcal{S}$, representing the unobserved *state of the world*. In fact, empirical studies on the behavior of financial markets show the ability of regime-switching models to capture some peculiarities in the observed data, as firstly highlighted in the seminal paper by Hamilton [4]. Since then, there has been a growing effort in applying switching models to a wide class of financial and/or economic problems. On the other hand, the necessity of including jumps in the underlying models to provide better representation of their dynamical properties is widely recognized (see e.g. [5]). Empirical stylized facts about observed data, such as volatility clustering and heavy tails, are then well captured by regime-switching jump-diffusions which turns out to be an appealing and flexible class of dynamic models. The computation of quantiles in regime-switching models has been considered by several authors mainly in discrete-time setting (see e.g. [6,7] and ref. therein). Here we consider this problem in the continuous time framework in which the required computations can be very efficiently implemented with the help of Fourier Transform methods (see e.g. [8]). The use of this kind of technique for the analytical calculation of VaR has been considered in Duffie and Pan [9] in terms of the Fourier inversion of the characteristic function. The use of Generalized Fourier Transform and the FFT algorithm is more recent: see Le Courtois and Walter [10], Kim *et al.* [11] and Scherer *et al.* [12].

The paper is organized as follows: we firstly derive the optimality conditions for the VaR minimizing strategy (Section 2) and then (Section 3) we introduce the regime-switching dynamic model, its generalized characteristic function and the change-of-measure result for switching from the historical to the risk-neutral probability. Finally, in Section 4 we specify the Fourier Transform technique for calculating quantiles and put/call option prices and report some numerical experiments to show the impact of jumps and regime-switching on the optimal hedging strategy.

Some final comments can be briefly outlined. Firstly, the analysis of the hedging strategy is fairly general, that is it can be applied to any dynamical model for which Fourier transform methods are viable, for example it can be extended to Variance-Gamma or Bates models. Furthermore, besides the choice of different dynamic models, it would be interesting to consider alternative risk measures, such as the Conditional Value at Risk (CVaR). This is certainly less commonly used in finance industry, but it is widely used in insurance industry being a coherent, convex and stable risk measure (see [13]).

2. VaR and Optimal Risk Management

Given a confidence level $\alpha \in (0,1)$, the set of ϵ-quantiles of the random variable Y is the interval $\left[q_\alpha^-(Y), q_\alpha^+(Y)\right]$ where $q_\alpha^-(Y) = \inf\{q \in \mathbb{R} \mid P(Y \le q) \ge \alpha\}$ and $q_\alpha^+(Y) = \inf\{q \in \mathbb{R} \mid P(Y \le q) > \alpha\}$. For a random variable having continuous and strictly increasing distributions function $F_Y(y)$, $q_\alpha^-(Y) = q_\alpha^+(Y) \equiv q_\alpha(Y) = F_Y^{-1}(\alpha)$, *i.e.* it solves the equation $\mathbb{P}(Y \le q_\alpha(Y)) = \alpha$.

Here we take the portfolio loss L to describe a financial position in a fixed time interval and, in order to simplify notations, we assume in this section that L has a continuous and strictly increasing distributions function. The Value-at-Risk at level α is defined as

$$\mathrm{VaR}_\alpha(L) \equiv \inf\{q \in \mathbb{R} \mid P(L \le q) > \alpha\}.$$

Let S_t be the value of the risky asset, $t \in [0,T]$ and r be the risk-free rate, that without loss of generality we consider fixed in the period: we define the loss at time 0 of such a position as $L^u = S_0 - \mathrm{e}^{-rT} S_T$ implying $\mathrm{VaR}_\alpha(L^u) = S_0 - \mathrm{e}^{-rT} q_{1-\alpha}(S_T)$. Let us now consider a classical hedging problem in which an institution has an exposure to a risky asset S_t and decide to hedge such an exposure in the interval $[0,T]$ by buying a fraction $h \in [0,1]$ of an European put option on the asset with maturity T and strike price K. Analogously to the situation considered in [1], we take as the hedged position the portfolio composed by the risky asset and the put option: the loss of the hedged portfolio at time 0 is therefore $L^{h,K} = S_0 + h\Pi_0^P(K,T) - \mathrm{e}^{-rT}\left(S_T + h(K - S_T)^+\right)$, where $\Pi_t^P(K,T)$ is the price of the put option at time t. By defining the strictly increasing function $g(u) = u - h(u - \bar{K})^+ + h\Pi_0^P(K,T)$, where $\bar{K} = S_0 - \mathrm{e}^{-rT} K$, it is immediately seen that $L^{h,K} = g(L^u)$; therefore

$$\mathrm{VaR}_\alpha(L^{h,K}) = g(\mathrm{VaR}_\alpha(L^u)) = \mathrm{VaR}_\alpha(L^u) + h\Pi_0^P(K,T) - \mathrm{e}^{-rT} h(K - q_{1-\alpha}(S_T))^+.$$

Let us firstly notice that if $K \le q_{1-\alpha}(S_T)$, then $\mathrm{VaR}_\alpha(L^{h,K}) > \mathrm{VaR}_\alpha(L^u)$ since $\Pi_0^P(K,T) > 0$. Hence, given the budget constraint C, the optimal hedging strategy is specified by the following problem:

$$\begin{cases} \min\limits_{K,h}\left\{\mathrm{VaR}_\alpha(L^u) + h\Pi_0^P(K,T) - \mathrm{e}^{-rT} h(K - q_{1-\alpha}(S_T))\right\} \\ h\Pi_0^P(K,T) = C, \\ h \in (0,1], \ K > q_{1-\alpha}(S_T). \end{cases} \tag{1}$$

Since $h = C/\Pi_0^P(K,T)$, the optimality first order condition for K is given by the following non-linear equation:

$$\Pi_0^P(K,T) = (K - q_{1-\alpha}(S_T))\frac{\partial}{\partial K}\Pi_0^P(K,T). \tag{2}$$

Assuming that (2) has a solution $K^* > q_{1-\alpha}(S_T)$ and the twice differentiability of the price functional we can prove that this is actually a minimum since

$$\frac{\partial^2 \mathrm{VaR}_\alpha(L^{h,K})}{\partial K^2} = \frac{\mathrm{e}^{-rT} C(K^* - q_{1-\alpha}(S_T))}{\Pi^P(K^*,T)^2} \times \frac{\partial^2 \Pi^P}{\partial K^2}(K^*,T) > 0$$

by the convexity of the price functional w.r.t. the strike. Correspondingly, the optimal amount of the hedging put option is

$$h^* = \frac{C}{\Pi_0^P(K^*,T)}. \tag{3}$$

We now assume the following:

Assumption 2.1. The price of the put option can be represented as the discounted expected value of the payoff at time T under a risk-neutral measure $\mathbb{Q}$:

$$\Pi_t^P(K,T) = \mathrm{e}^{-rT}\mathbb{E}^{\mathbb{Q}}\left[(K - S_T)^+\right].$$

Furthermore, let $F_S(s) = \mathbb{Q}(S_T \le s)$ be the cumulative distribution function (cdf) of the random variable S_T under such a measure: hence

$$\Pi_t^P(K,T) = \mathrm{e}^{-rT}\int_0^{+\infty}(K - s)^+ \,\mathrm{d}F_S(s) = \mathrm{e}^{-rT}\left(K\mathbb{Q}(S_T \le K) - \int_0^K s\,\mathrm{d}F_S(s)\right)$$

and

$$\frac{\partial}{\partial K}\Pi_t^P(K,T)=\mathrm{e}^{-rT}\mathbb{Q}(S_T\le K).$$

We can finally prove the following property:

Proposition 2.1. If $K^*>q_{1-\alpha}(S_T)$, then

$\mathrm{VaR}_\alpha\left(L_0^{h^*,K^*}\right)<\mathrm{VaR}_\alpha\left(L^u\right)$.

Proof. Since K^* and h^* are characterized through (2) and (3), we get

$$\begin{aligned}&\mathrm{VaR}_\alpha\left(L_0^{h^*,K^*}\right)\\&=\mathrm{VaR}_\alpha\left(L^u\right)\\&+\frac{C}{\Pi_t^P(K^*,T)}\left(\Pi_t^P(K^*,T)-\mathrm{e}^{-rT}\left(K^*-q_{1-\alpha}(S_T)\right)\right)\\&=\mathrm{VaR}_\alpha\left(L^u\right)\\&+\frac{C}{\Pi_t^P(K^*,T)}\left(K^*-q_{1-\alpha}(S_T)\right)\left(\frac{\partial}{\partial K}\Pi_t^P(K^*,T)-\mathrm{e}^{-rT}\right).\end{aligned}$$

From Assumption 2.1, we have

$$\frac{\partial}{\partial K}\Pi_t^P(K,T)-\mathrm{e}^{-rT}=\mathrm{e}^{-rT}\left(\mathbb{Q}(S_T\le K)-1\right)<0.$$

Therefore

$$\begin{aligned}&\mathrm{VaR}_\alpha\left(L_0^{h^*,K^*}\right)=\mathrm{VaR}_\alpha\left(L^u\right)\\&+\frac{C}{\Pi_t^P(K^*,T)}\left(K^*-q_{1-\alpha}(S_T)\right)\mathrm{e}^{-rT}\left(\mathbb{Q}(S_T\le K^*)-1\right)\\&<\mathrm{VaR}_\alpha\left(L^u\right).\end{aligned}$$

Remark 2.1. Notice that the optimality condition (2) under Assumption 2.1 simplifies to

$$\frac{1}{\mathbb{Q}(S_T\le K)}\int_{-\infty}^{K}s\mathrm{d}F_S^Q(x)=q_{1-\alpha}(S_T) \qquad (4)$$

and depends on both the objective and the risk neutral distributions $\mathbb{P}$ and $\mathbb{Q}$. Furthermore, it easily seen that the l.h.s. is equal to the conditional expectation $\mathbb{E}^Q[S_T\mid S_T\le K]$ which is an increasing function of K bounded by $\mathbb{E}^{\mathrm{Q}}[S_T]$. Therefore, (4) has a unique solution if and only if $q_{1-\alpha}(S_T)<\mathbb{E}^{\mathrm{Q}}[S_T]$.

3. Regime-Switching Jump Diffusions and Measure Change

Let us consider on a filtered probability space $(\Omega,\mathcal{F},\mathcal{F}_t,\mathbb{P})$ a stochastic process of the form $S_t=S_0\mathrm{e}^{X_t}$, $S_0>0$, modeling the value, of a risky asset for $t\in[0,T]$. We consider a jump-diffusion setting in which the jump process is described as a marked point process (MPP), that is a random measure $p(dy,dt)$ characterized by the intensity process $\lambda_t(dy)$, the parameters of which are driven by a finite state and continuous time Markov chain. So, let $\alpha(t)$ be a continuous time, homogeneous and stationary Markov Chain on the state space $\mathcal{S}=\{1,2,\cdots,M\}$ with generator $H\in\mathbb{R}^{M\times M}$: the elements h_{ij} of the matrix H are positive numbers such that $\sum_{j\ne i,j=1}^{M}h_{ij}=-h_{ii}$, for $i=1,\cdots,M$. Furthermore, $\mu:\mathcal{S}\to\mathbb{R}$, $\sigma:\mathcal{S}\to\mathbb{R}$ and $\gamma:E\times\mathcal{S}\to\mathbb{R}$ are given functions, $(E,\mathcal{E})$ being the measurable mark space. Without loss of generality, we can assume in the following $E\subseteq\mathbb{R}$. In a given interval $0\le t\le T$, we consider the dynamic

$$\begin{aligned}dX(t)&=\left(\mu(\alpha(t))-\frac{1}{2}\sigma^2(\alpha(t))\right)dt+\sigma(\alpha(t))dW(t)\\&+\int_E\gamma\left(y,\alpha(t^-)\right)p^\alpha(dy,dt),\ X(0)=0,\end{aligned} \qquad (5)$$

where $W(t)$ is a standard brownian motion and $p^\alpha(dy,dt)$ is a MPP characterized by the intensity $\lambda_t^\alpha(dy)\equiv\lambda(\alpha)m(\alpha,dy)$. Here $\lambda(\cdot)$ represents the (regime-switching) intensity of the Poisson process N_t, while $m(\cdot,dy)$ are a set of probability measures on E, one for each state (regime) $i\in\mathcal{S}$. The function $\gamma(y,\alpha)$ represents the jump amplitude relative to the mark y in regime α. The couple $(\lambda(\alpha),m(\alpha,dy))$ is called the $(\mathbb{P},\mathcal{F}_t)$*-local characteristic* of $p^\alpha(ds,dy)$. Furthermore $\int_0^t\int_E\mathcal{H}(y,s)\left(p^\alpha(dy,ds)-\lambda_s^\alpha(dy)ds\right)$ is a martingale for a suitable class of processes $\mathcal{H}$ (see [14]),

$$q^\alpha(dy,dt)=p^\alpha(dy,dt)-\lambda\left(\alpha(t^-)\right)m\left(\alpha(t^-),dy\right)dt$$

being the compensated process.

Throughout the paper we assume that the processes $\alpha(\cdot)$ and $W(\cdot)$ are independent, $W(\cdot)$ and $p^\alpha(dy,dt)$ are conditionally independent given $\alpha(t)$ and that $\mathbb{E}\left[\mathrm{e}^{\gamma(Y,\alpha)}\right]=\int_E\mathrm{e}^{\gamma(y,\alpha)}m(\alpha,dy)$ is finite for each regime α. An application of the generalized Ito's Formula gives the corresponding jump-diffusion SDE for the asset price

$$\begin{aligned}&\frac{dS(t)}{S(t^-)}\\&=\mu(\alpha(t))dt+\sigma(\alpha(t))dW(t)\\&+\int_E\left(\mathrm{e}^{\gamma(y,\alpha(t-))}-1\right)p^\alpha(dy,dt)\\&=\left[\mu(\alpha(t))+\lambda(\alpha(t))\kappa(\alpha(t))\right]dt\\&+\sigma(\alpha(t))dW(t)+\int_E\left(\mathrm{e}^{\gamma(y,\alpha(t-))}-1\right)q^\alpha(dy,dt),\end{aligned} \qquad (6)$$

with $S(0)=S_0$ and $\kappa(\alpha)=\mathbb{E}\left[\mathrm{e}^{\gamma(Y,\alpha)}-1\right]$.

Measure changes. An absolutely continuous transformation of measures in a jump-diffusion setting allows to change the intensities of the MPP and the Markov chain in addition to the translation of the Wiener process (see [14]). It results convenient to represent the underlying Markov chain itself as the MPP $\upsilon(dt,dz)$ with finite mark space $(\mathrm{S},\mathcal{P}(\mathrm{S}))$, $\mathrm{S}=\{z=(i,j): i\neq j,\ i,j\in\{1,2,\cdots,M\}\}$ and $\mathcal{P}(\mathrm{S})=2^{\mathrm{S}}$: the compensator is

$$\lambda_{\upsilon}(\alpha(t-),dz)=\sum_{i\neq j} h_{ij}\mathbb{I}_{\{\alpha(t-)=i\}}\epsilon_{(i,j)}(dz) \tag{7}$$

$\epsilon_{(i,j)}(dz)$ being the Dirac measure. Consequently, let $\vartheta_t(\alpha)$ be a square integrable predictable processes, $h_t(\alpha,y)$ a non-negative function such that $\int_E h_t(\alpha,y)\,m(\alpha,dy)=1,\ \forall t\in[0,T]$ and let $\psi(\alpha)$ and $\Phi(z)$ be strictly positive functions defined on $\mathcal{S}$ and S, respectively. We can define a new measure $\mathbb{Q}$ on the measurable space by setting

$$\begin{cases} dW_t^{Q} = dW_t - \vartheta_t(\alpha(t))dt \\ q^{Q,\alpha}(dt,dy) = p(dt,dy)-\psi(\alpha(t))\lambda(\alpha(t))h_t(\alpha(t),y)m(\alpha(t),dy)dt \\ \lambda_{\upsilon}^{Q}(\alpha,dz)=\Phi(z)\lambda_{\upsilon}(\alpha,dz). \end{cases} \tag{8}$$

Besides the translation of the Wiener process W_t, we perform a change in the intensity of the MPP giving the compensated process $q^{Q,\alpha}(dt,dy)$ with $(\mathbb{Q},\mathcal{F}_t)$-local characteristic $(\psi(\alpha(t))\lambda(\alpha(t)),h_t(\alpha(t),y)m(\alpha(t),dy))$ and a change of the intensity of the Markov chain which under $\mathbb{Q}$ has generator $H^{Q}=\{h_{ij}^{Q}\}$ where

$$h_{ij}^{Q}=\Phi(i,j)h_{ij},\quad h_{ii}^{Q}=-\sum_{k=1,k\neq i}^{M}\Phi(i,k)h_{ik},\quad i=1,\cdots,M.$$

By taking the Radon-Nikodym derivative

$$\begin{aligned} L_t = \exp\Big(& -\frac{1}{2}\int_0^t \vartheta_s(\alpha(s))^2\,\mathrm{d}s+\int_0^t\vartheta_s(\alpha(s))\mathrm{d}W_s^{Q}+\int_0^t(1-\psi(\alpha(s))\lambda(\alpha(s)))\mathrm{d}s \\ & +\int_0^t\int_E \log(\psi(\alpha(s))h_t(\alpha(s),y))p(ds,dy)+\int_0^t\int_{\mathrm{S}}(1-\Phi(z))\lambda_{\upsilon}(\alpha(t-),dz)\mathrm{d}s+\int_0^t\int_{\mathrm{S}}\log(\Phi(z))\upsilon(ds,dz)\Big) \end{aligned} \tag{9}$$

and supposing that $\mathbb{E}^{\mathbb{P}}[L_t]=1$ for $t\in[0,T]$, we have a probability measure $\mathbb{Q}$ on $\mathcal{F}$ equivalent to $\mathbb{P}$ with $d\mathbb{Q}=L_T d\mathbb{P}$, under which

$$\begin{aligned} \frac{dS(t)}{S(t^-)} &= \left[\mu(\alpha(t))+\sigma(\alpha(t))\vartheta_t(\alpha(t))+\psi(\alpha(t))\lambda(\alpha(t))\kappa^{Q}(\alpha(t))\right]dt \\ & +\sigma(\alpha(t))dW^{Q}(t)+\int_E\left(\mathrm{e}^{\gamma(y,\alpha(t-))}-1\right)q^{Q,\alpha}(dy,dt), \end{aligned} \tag{10}$$

where $\kappa^{Q}(\alpha)=\mathbb{E}^{Q}\left[\mathrm{e}^{\gamma(Y,\alpha)}-1\right]$ (see [14]).

In order to price derivatives under the model (6) we need to specify a risk-neutral or martingale measure, that is a measure under which the discounted price process $\mathrm{e}^{-rt}S_t$ is a martingale. This is done by taking

$$\vartheta(\alpha)\equiv\frac{r-\mu(\alpha)-\psi(\alpha)\lambda(\alpha)\kappa^{Q}(\alpha)}{\sigma(\alpha)} \tag{11}$$

from which we finally get the risk-neutral dynamic for the underlying

$$\begin{aligned} \frac{dS(t)}{S(t^-)} &= r dt+\sigma(\alpha(t))dW^{Q}(t) \\ & +\int_E\left(\mathrm{e}^{\gamma(y,\alpha(t-))}-1\right)q^{Q,\alpha}(dy,dt) \\ &= \left[r-\psi(\alpha(t))\lambda(\alpha(t))\kappa^{Q}(\alpha(t))\right]dt \\ & +\sigma(\alpha(t))dW^{Q}(t)+\int_E\left(\mathrm{e}^{\gamma(y,\alpha(t-))}-1\right)p^{Q,\alpha}(dy,dt). \end{aligned} \tag{12}$$

Correspondingly, for the process $X(t)$ we have

$$\begin{aligned} & dX(t) \\ &= \left[r-\frac{1}{2}\sigma^2(\alpha(t))\right]dt+\sigma(\alpha(t))dW^{Q}(t) \\ & +\int_E\gamma(y,\alpha(t^-))q^{Q,\alpha}(dy,dt) \\ &= \left[r-\frac{1}{2}\sigma^2(\alpha(t))-\psi(\alpha(t))\lambda(\alpha(t))\kappa^{Q}(\alpha(t))\right]dt \\ & +\sigma(\alpha(t))dW^{Q}(t) \\ & +\int_E\gamma(y,\alpha(t^-))p^{Q,\alpha}(dy,dt). \end{aligned} \tag{13}$$

The measure transformation defined by (8) through (9) preserves the probability structure of the stochastic process $X(t)$ under both $\mathbb{P}$ and $\mathbb{Q}$. It worth noting that we can specify infinitely many equivalent measures $\mathbb{Q}$. In practice, the usual way to select one of the equivalent measures is to calibrate the model to a set of observed data.

GFT for regime-switching jump-diffusions. In order to apply Fourier methods, we need to calculate the Fourier transform $\phi_X(z)$ of our process. Since we have to consider the process X_T under two different measure, we derive its characteristic function for the following general dynamic

$$dX(t)=\xi(\alpha(t))dt+\sigma(\alpha(t))dW(t) \\ +\int_E \gamma(y,\alpha(t^-))p(dy,dt), \quad (14)$$

with $(\bar{\lambda}(\alpha),\bar{m}(\alpha,dy))$ local characteristic, and Markov chain generator Q. In [8] it was proved the following

Proposition 3.1. Let $\phi_j(z)=\mathbb{E}\left[e^{iz\gamma(Y(j),j)}\right]$ be the generalized Fourier transform of the jump magnitude under the given measure. Then, by letting

$$\vartheta_j(z)=z\xi(j)+\frac{1}{2}iz^2\sigma^2(j)-i\bar{\lambda}(j)(\phi_j(z)-1) \quad (15)$$

and $\tilde{\vartheta}_i(z)=\vartheta_j(z)-\vartheta_M(z)$, we have

$$\phi_T(z)=e^{i\vartheta_M(z)T}\left(\mathbf{1}'\cdot e^{(Q'+i\,\mathrm{diag}(\tilde{\vartheta}_1(z),\cdots,\tilde{\vartheta}_{M-1}(z),0))T}\cdot\mathbb{I}(0)\right) \\ =\mathbf{1}'\cdot e^{(Q'+i\,\mathrm{diag}(\tilde{\vartheta}_1(z),\cdots,\tilde{\vartheta}_{M-1}(z)))T}\cdot\mathbb{I}(0), \quad (16)$$

where $\mathbf{1}=(1,\cdots,1)'\in\mathbb{R}^{M\times1}$,

$\mathbb{I}(0)=\left(\mathbb{I}_{\alpha(0)=1},\cdots,\mathbb{I}_{\alpha(0)=M}\right)'\in\mathbb{I}^{M\times1}$ and Q' is the transpose of Q.■

Different models can be recovered with simple linear constraints on the full parameter set of our model (RSJDM) (6), (12), $\xi_i,\sigma_i,\lambda_i,h_{ij}$, $i,j=1,\cdots,M$. This follows by noticing that if $\xi(i)=\xi,\sigma(i)=\sigma$, $\lambda(i)=\lambda$ and $\phi_i(z)=\phi(z)$ we are implicitly assuming a unique regime so recovering the well-known characteristic function of the (single-regime) jump-diffusion dynamic $\phi_T(z)=\exp\left(z\xi+\frac{1}{2}iz^2\sigma^2-i\lambda(\phi(z)-1)\right)$

which includes the standard geometrical Brownian motion (GBM) $(\lambda=0)$, the Merton jump-diffusion models (JDM); furthermore, if $\lambda_i=0$ we get the regime-switching version of GBM (RSGBM).

The evaluation of the characteristic function requires to compute matrix exponentials for which efficient numerical techniques are available; conversely, the case $M=2$ can be considered explicitly (see [8] and the references therein).

4. Computing Results

In order to implement the optimal hedging strategy, we need to evaluate the VaR of the risky asset and the value of a put option. Both steps can be efficiently faced by means of Fourier methods. In this section we firstly outline such a technique and then we apply it to study numerically a model with two regimes and gaussian jumps.

4.1. Fourier Methods

Fourier transform methods are efficient techniques emerged in recent years as one of the main methodology for the evaluation of derivatives. Here we consider the technique introduced in [15] which consider the generalized Fourier transform with respect to the trigger parameter characterizing the payoff.

More formally, let $\Pi(S,K)$ be the payoff at maturity of the derivative: for example, $\Pi(S,K)=(K-S)^+$ is the payoff of the put option. The no-arbitrage price is therefore given by

$$\Pi_0=e^{-rT}\mathbb{E}^{\mathbb{Q}}\left[\Pi(S_T,K)\right].$$

Due to the exponential structure of the underlying dynamic $S_t=S_0\exp(X_t)$, it is convenient to represent the payoff with respect to the new variables $\log(S)=X+\log(S_0)\equiv x$ and $\log(K)\equiv k$, in such a way

$\Pi(S,K)=\Pi(\exp(X+\log(S_0)),\exp(k))\equiv\Pi(x,k)$.

Therefore, let us denote with $\Pi(x,k)$ an arbitrary payoff function and with $\hat{\Pi}_x(z)$ its generalized Fourier transform (GFT) w.r.t. k, that is

$$\hat{\Pi}_x(z)=\int_{\mathbb{R}}e^{izk}\Pi(x,k)dk,\ z\in\mathbb{C};$$

under proper regularity conditions about the payoff and the Fourier transform of the underlying dynamic variables (see e.g. [16]), it can be proved that

$$e^{rT}\Pi_0=\frac{1}{2\pi}\int_{i\nu-\infty}^{i\nu+\infty}e^{-izk}\mathbb{E}^{\mathbb{Q}}\left[\hat{\Pi}_{X(T)+\log(S_0)}(z)\right]dz$$

in some strip of $\mathbb{C}$. Let us consider the *payoff* functions $\Phi_1(x,k)=(e^k-e^x)^+$, and $\Phi_2(x,k)=\mathbb{I}_{\{x\le k\}}$, in such a way $\Pi_0^P(\kappa,T)=e^{-rT}\mathbb{E}^{\mathbb{Q}}\left[\Phi_1(X_T+\log(S_0),k)\right]$ and $\mathbb{P}\{S_T\le v\}=\mathbb{P}\{X_T\le k\}=\mathbb{E}\left[\Phi_2(X_T,k)\right]$, with $k=\log(v/S_0)$. Their GFT w.r.t. the trigger parameter k are

$$\hat{\Phi}_1(x,z)=\frac{e^{x(1+iz)}}{iz-z^2},\ \nu>1\ \text{and}\ \hat{\Phi}_2(x,z)=\frac{i}{z}e^{ixz},\ \nu>0$$

respectively. Hence we get the formulas

$$\Pi_0^P(k,T)=e^{-rT}\frac{e^{\nu k}S_0^{1-\nu}}{\pi} \\ \cdot\Re\left(\int_0^{+\infty}e^{-iu(k-\log(S_0))}\frac{\phi_X^{\mathbb{Q}}(u+i(\nu-1))}{\nu^2-u^2-\nu+iu(1-2\nu)}du\right),\nu>1 \quad (17)$$

and

$$\mathbb{P}\{S_T \le v\} = \frac{(v/S_0)^{\nu}}{\pi} \Re\left(\int_0^{+\infty} e^{-iu\log(v/S_0)} \frac{\phi_X^{\mathbb{P}}(u+i\nu)}{\nu - iu} du \right), \quad \nu > 0 \tag{18}$$

$\phi_X^{\mathbb{Q},\mathbb{P}}(z) = \mathbb{E}^{\mathbb{Q},\mathbb{P}}\left[e^{izX_T}\right]$ being the (generalized) Fourier transform, or characteristic function, of the random variable X_T under the appropriate measure. If this is a regular functions in a properly defined strip of $\mathbb{C}$, the transform method can be applied in both cases (see [16]). Since under the Assumption (2.1) the optimality condition is

$$\left(K - q_{1-\alpha}(S_T)\right) = \frac{\Pi_0^P(K,T)}{\frac{\partial}{\partial K}\Pi_0^P(K,T)} \equiv \frac{\Pi_0^P(K,T)}{e^{-rT}\mathbb{Q}(S_T \le K)}.$$

the optimal hedging strategy is then implemented by running twice a root search algorithm to find the values

1) q^* such that

$$\frac{(q^*/S_0)^{\bar{\nu}}}{\pi} \Re\left(\int_0^{+\infty} e^{-iu\log(q^*/S_0)} \frac{\phi_X^{\mathbb{P}}(u+i\bar{\nu})}{\bar{\nu} - iu} du \right) = \alpha, \quad \bar{\nu} > 0; \tag{19}$$

2) K^* such that

$$\left(K^* - q^*\right) = \frac{S_0 \Re\left(\int_0^{+\infty} e^{-iu\left(\log(K^*/S_0)\right)} \frac{\phi_X^{\mathbb{Q}}(u+i(\nu-1))}{\nu^2 - u^2 - \nu + iu(1-2\nu)} du \right)}{\Re\left(\int_0^{+\infty} e^{-iu\left(\log(K^*/S_0)\right)} \frac{\phi_X^{\mathbb{Q}}(u+i(\bar{\nu}-1))}{\bar{\nu} - iu} du \right)}, \quad \nu > 1, \bar{\nu} > 0. \tag{20}$$

Numerical quadrature must be used for integral evaluation. Alternatively the FFT algorithm can be used to efficiently approximate integrals (see [16]) and then a standard root-finding routine will find the required solutions.

4.2. Some Numerical Results

We report some numerical results about the valuation of the optimal hedging strategy in the regime-switching jump-diffusion framework. An extended set of results can be found in [17]. All numerical procedures were implemented in the MatLab© framework. A standard root-search algorithm was used to solve Equations (19) and (20), with $\nu = 2$ and $\bar{\nu} = 1$, together with the Gauss-Lobatto quadrature for approximating the corresponding integrals. Few milliseconds were needed to get the required quantities on an Intel© Core i5.

We consider a two-state regime switching version of the jump-diffusion model with gaussian jumps $Y(i) \sim \mathcal{N}(a_i, b_i)$, $i = 1,2$, characterized by the parameters $\sigma_i, \lambda_i > 0$ and $\mu_i, i = 1,2$. The two state Markov chain $\alpha(t)$ has generator $Q = \begin{pmatrix} -q_1 & q_1 \\ q_2 & -q_2 \end{pmatrix}$.

The first issue we consider is the reduction of risk obtained by implementing the optimal hedging strategy in the RSJD framework. The risk reduction percentage $R = 1 - \frac{\mathrm{VaR}_\alpha\left(L_0^{h^*,K^*}\right)}{\mathrm{VaR}_\alpha\left(L^u\right)}$ evaluated for different set of parameters range from 4.39% up to 58%, meaning that the strategy is effective in reducing the portfolio VaR, even in presence of jumps and regime-switching. On the other hand, by changing the value of some relevant parameters inside each model (GBM, JD, RSGBM, RSJD) the profile of the hedging portfolio VaR can change significantly. Hence we face the following issue: what is the effect of a wrong model specification which discards regime switchings and jumps, when they are indeed present in the market, and consider the simpler GBM model? In order to explore the model sensitivity of the optimal hedging strategy, we implemented the following exercise. We firstly fixed a RSJD model by choosing a complete set of parameters. Then we generated a set of call/put prices on which we calibrate the GBM model, finding the volatility $\hat{\sigma}_{GBM}$ with a constrained non-linear least-squares algorithm: hence we run the optimal hedging strategy obtaining K^*_{GBM}, h^*_{GBM} and correspondingly the minimal VaR, VaR^*_{GBM}. We finally calculated the probability

$$\beta_{RSJD} = \mathbb{P}\left(L^{K^*,h^*} \ge \mathrm{VaR}^*_{GBM}\right)$$

under the RSJD model. This step requires to evaluate the integral in (18): as before, we use a Gauss-Lobatto quadrature algorithm. Results are shown in **Tables 1** and **2**.

Table 1. Optimal hedging strategy $(K^*, h^*, \mathrm{VaR}^*)$ under the simulated true model (first column), the fitted GBM model (second column—estimated volatility) and the corresponding value of β_{RSJD}. Here $\sigma_1 = 0.3$, $\sigma_2 = 0.05$, $\lambda_1 = 2$, $\lambda_2 = 0.8$, $a_1 = 0.0$, $a_2 = 0.0$, $b_1 = 0.08$, $b_2 = 0.15$, $q_1 = 1$, $q_2 = 0.2$; furthermore $r = 0.5\%$, $\alpha = 0.01$ and the budget constraint is $C = 0.1$.

	Optimal strategy RSJD	Optimal strategy GBM $(\hat{\sigma})$	β_{RSJD}
T = 0.5	64.7442, 0.7197, 37.0189	65.6191, 0.8433, 35.3880 (0.2905)	0.0132
T = 1	55.5928, 0.6165, 47.1767	57.1579, 0.7644, 44.4718 (0.2689)	0.0148
T = 3	41.6851, 0.5294, 62.3356	43.5664, 0.7382, 58.6379 (0.2254)	0.0157

Table 2. Optimal hedging strategy $(K^*, h^*, \mathrm{VaR}^*)$ under the simulated true model (first column), the fitted GBM model (second column—estimated volatility) and the corresponding value of β_{RSJD}. Here $\sigma_1 = 0.3$, $\sigma_2 = 0.05$, $\lambda_1 = 2$, $\lambda_2 = 0.8$, $a_1 = 0.05$, $a_2 = -0.3$, $b_1 = 0.08$, $b_2 = 0.15$, $q_1 = 1$, $q_2 = 0.2$; furthermore $r = 0.5\%$, $\alpha = 0.01$ and the budget constraint is $C = 0.01$.

	Optimal strategy RSJD	Optimal strategy GBM $(\hat{\sigma})$	β_{RSJD}
T = 0.5	61.1841, 0.0581, 45.2341	63.3076, 0.0816, 41.3746 (0.3137)	0.0166
T = 1	45.8347, 0.0833, 60.5069	52.7089, 0.0744, 52.6106 (0.3047)	0.0255
T = 3	18.8056, 0.4015, 83.7630	32.7103, 0.0797, 72.5986 (0.2930)	0.0640

Table 3. Optimal hedging strategy $(K^*, h^*, \mathrm{VaR}^*)$ under the simulated true model (first column), the fitted GBM model (second column—estimated volatility) and the corresponding value of β_{RSJD}. Here $\sigma_1 = 0.27$, $\sigma_2 = 0.13$, $\lambda_1 = 6.8$, $\lambda_2 = 0.8$, $a_1 = -0.13$, $a_2 = -0.34$, $b_1 = 0.08$, $b_2 = 0.15$, $q_1 = 6.5$, $q_2 = 0.002$; furthermore $r = 0.5\%$, $\alpha = 0.01$ and the budget constraint is $C = 0.01$.

	Optimal strategy RSJD	Optimal strategy GBM $(\hat{\sigma})$	β_{RSJD}
T = 0.5	38.3721, 0.2497, 66.0564	60.0168, 0.0785, 44.8655 (0.3479)	0.1165
T = 1	26.6034, 0.4103, 76.3270	49.4859, 0.0737, 55.8926 (0.3320)	0.1304
T = 1.5	19.6884, 0.6506, 81.8069	41.9632, 0.0741, 63.4963 (0.3291)	0.1430

Notice that even when the optimal strategies are similar, the probability that the portfolio loss exceeds the (optimal) VaR is greater than the fixed level $\alpha = 0.01$. Of course this behavior depends on the choice of the parameters, but the underestimation produced by a wrong model choice can be quite severe: see **Table 3**, where parameters from a real data set were used (see [8]).

REFERENCES

[1] D. H. Ahn, J. Boudoukh, M. Richardson and R. F. Whitelaw, "Optimal Risk Management Using Options," *Journal of Finance*, Vol. 54, No. 1, 1999, pp. 359-375.

[2] J. Annaert, G. Deelstra, D. Heyman and M. Vanmaele, "Risk Management of a Bond Portfolio Using Options," *Insurance: Mathematics and Economics*, Vol. 41, No. 3, 2007, pp. 299-316.

[3] F. Antonelli, A. Ramponi and S. Scarlatti, "Option Based Risk Management of a Bond Portfolio under Regime Switching Interest Rates," *Decisions in Economics and Finance*, 2011.

[4] J. Hamilton, "A New Approach to the Economic Analysis of Non Stationary Time Series and the Business Cycle," *Econometrica*, Vol. 57, No. 2, 1989, pp. 357-384.

[5] R. Cont and P. Tankov, "Financial Modelling with Jump Processes," Chapman & Hall, CRC Press, Boca Raton, 2003.

[6] R. Kawata and M. Kijima, "Value at Risk in a Market Subject to Regime Switching," *Quantitative Finance*, Vol. 7, No. 6, 2007, pp. 609-619.

[7] A. Taamouti, "Analytical Value-at-Risk and Expected Shortfall under Regime-Switching," *Finance Research Letters*, Vol. 6, No. 3, 2009, pp. 138-151.

[8] A. Ramponi, "On Fourier Transform Methods for Regime-Switching Jump-Diffusions and the Pricing of Forward Starting Options," *International Journal of Theoretical and Appplied Finance*, Vol. 15, No. 5, 2012, 26 p.

[9] D. Duffie and J. Pan, "Analytical Value-at-Risk with Jumps and Credit Risk," *Finance and Stochastics*, Vol. 5, No. 2, 2001, pp. 155-180.

[10] O. Le Courtois and C. P. Walter, "A Study on Value-at-Risk and Lévy Processes," 2009. http://ssrn.com/abstract=1598360

[11] Y. S. Kim, S. T. Rachev, M. L. Bianchi and F. J. Fabozzi, "Computing VaR and AVaR in Infinitely Divisible Distributions," *Probability and Mathematical Statistics*, Vol. 30, No. 2, 2010, pp. 223-245.

[12] M. Scherer, S. T. Rachev, Y. S. Kim and F. J. Fabozzi, "A FFT-Based Approximation of Tempered Stable and Tempered Infinitely Divisible Distributions," 2009. http://www.ams.sunysb.edu/~rachev/publication/StandardTSDistr_20100306final.pdf

[13] P. Artzner, F. Delbaen, J. Eber and D. Heath, "Coherent Measures of Risk," *Mathematical Finance*, Vol. 9, No. 3, 1999, pp. 203-228.

[14] W. J. Runggaldier, "Jump-Diffusion Models," In: S.T. Rachev, Ed., *Handbook of Heavy Tailed Distributions in Finance*, Elesevier/North-Holland, Amsterdam, 2003, pp. 169-209.

[15] P. Carr and D. B. Madan, "Option Valuation Using the Fast Fourier Transform," *Journal of Computational Finance*, Vol. 2, No. 4, 1999, pp. 61-73.

[16] R. W. Lee, "Option Pricing by Transform Methods: Extensions, Unifications and Error Control," *Journal of Computational Finance*, Vol. 7, No. 3, 2004, pp. 51-86.

[17] A. Ramponi, "Computing Quantiles in Regime-Switching Jump-Diffusions with Application to Optimal Risk Management: A Fourier Transform Approach," arXiv: 1207.6759, 2012.

2

Optimal Investment under Price and Wage Uncertainty*

Jinwu Huang
School of Finance, Shanghai University of Finance and Economics, Shanghai, China

ABSTRACT

The effects of future output price uncertainty and wage uncertainty on a firm's investment decision are examined in this paper, by assuming the competitively risk-neutral firm maximizes the expected value of the sum of discounted cash flows. We find that the optimal investment behavior is such that the expected proportional growth rate of investment is invariant over time, although there exists a tradeoff between the effects of the two uncertainty on firm's investment because the shift in output price has positive effects on firm's investment, whereas the shift in wage has negative impacts on firm's investment. And what's more important, fluctuations in output price and wage are correlated so that changes in output price tend to be accompanied by changes in wage.

Keywords: Optimal Investment; Output Price; Wage Rate; Uncertainty

1. Introduction

During the past decades, many scholars studied the effects of uncertainty on a firm's input and output decisions. Regarding to this topic, one can see references we enumerate at the end of the paper and etc. Within those papers, considerable results and conclusions have been achieved. For example, Hartman [1] examined the impacts that increased uncertainty in future output prices, wage rates and investment costs has on the quantity of investment undertaken by a firm, and pointed out current investment doesn't decrease with increased uncertainty in future output prices as well as wage rates, and invariant to increased uncertainty in future investment costs. The sign of the investment-uncertainty relationship is negative, and that the quantitative negative impact is substantially greater in industries dominated by small firms are shown in Ghosal and Lougani [2] by studying the impact of profit uncertainty on investment and whether or not this response is different in industries that are dominated by small firms versus those that are dominated by relatively larger firms. These results are robust to accounting for potential endogeneity of the uncertainty measure, alternate procedures for measuring uncertainty, and alternate ways of segmenting industries into small-and-large firm groups. In Peeters [3], empirical results proved that both demand and price uncertainty correlate significantly with corporate investment, and that output price uncertainty depresses investment in Belgium and Spain. Applying dynamic panel data methods, Temple, *et al.* [4] found that all sources of uncertainty exert a considerable negative impact on investment while financial factors may be important in some industries. Bloom offered a structural framework to analyze the impact of these uncertainty shocks and built a model with a time-varying second moment, which is numerically solved and estimated using firm-level data in Bloom [5]. The parameterized model demonstrated higher uncertainty causes firms to temporarily pause their investment and hiring, and the increased volatility from the shock induces an overshoot in output, employment, and productivity. Thus, uncertainty shocks generate short sharp recessions and recoveries. In Lee and Shin [6], they discovered that in the absence of fixed adjustment cost, a higher labor share strengthens the positive relationship between investment and uncertainty, whereas in the presence of a lumpy adjustment cost, optimal investment will drop to zero as uncertainty increases if labor share is low, but will increase if labor share is high. Both the case in which the firm faces an uncertain price in a perfectly competitive commodity market and the case in which the firm faces an uncertain downward sloping demand function are studied in Nielsen [7], the results showed higher expected price increases optimal output, and a quantity setting policy implied a tendency towards smaller quantities and higher price, while on the contrary, a price setting policy implied a tendency towards lager quantities and lower price, than under certainty.

Besides, Lucas and Prescott [8] made an extension of "cost-of-adjustment" type investment theory to situations involving demand uncertainty, and determined the time

*This work is supported by Research Innovation Foundation of Shanghai University of Finance and Economics under Grant No. CXJJ-2011-336.

series behavior of investment, output, and price in a competitive industry with a stochastic demand. The effects of demand and cost uncertainty on a firm's investment, output and pricing decisions are examined in Pindyck [9], the conclusion suggested the desired capital stock and output level will be higher/lower if marginal adjustment costs are rising at an increasing/decreasing rate, under the condition that demand shifts stochastically. At the same time, when the marginal adjustment costs of a risk-averse firm rise at an increasing or constant rate, uncertainty will increase the desired capital stock and output. Furthermore, the effects of stochastic fluctuations in factor costs are the same as demand fluctuations on a firm's behavior. And what's more important, these results are robust and consistent whether a firm is competitive or monopolistic. In particular, Abel [10] demonstrated the results of Hartman [1] continue to hold using the stochastic specification of Pindyck [9] and the analysis of Pindyck's applies to a so called "target" investment rate which is not optimal in general, by developing a special case of the model in Pindyck's to verify the effects of output price uncertainty on investment decision for a risk-neutral competitive firm with convex adjustment costs. Abel and Eberly [11] extended the theory of investment under uncertainty to incorporate fixed costs of investment, a wedge between purchase price and sale price of capital, and potential irreversibility of investment. They found investment is a nondecreasing function of shadow price of installed capital, and the optimal rate of investment relies on the value of shadow price relative two critical values. By using information on the subjective probability distribution of future demand for firm's products, Guiso and Parigi [12] investigated the effects of uncertainty on the investment decisions of some Italian firms. The results suggest uncertainty weakens the response of investment to demand, and the negative effects of uncertainty on investment can't be explained by uncertainty proxying for liquidity constraints. In Bloom, *et al.* [13], they showed that with (partial) irreversibility higher uncertainty reduces the responsiveness of investment to demand shocks, and uncertainty increases real option values making firms more cautious when investing or disinvesting, which confirmed both numerically for a model with adjustment costs and time-varying uncertainty. And so on(See [14-27]).

Ultimately, it's worth mentioning that the shortcoming of Pindyck [9] is that it didn't derive an expression for the optimal rate of investment in the general model, but analyzed it by stochastic phase diagram approach instead, of which the problem is that it's unreasonable for a firm to be on the locus with zero expected change in investment, even in the long-run. In view of this, we construct a concrete case can be solved explicitly herein. In addition, our model is an extension to that in Abel [10], since we take output price uncertainty and wage rate uncertainty into account simultaneously, rather than consider output price uncertainty only. Evidently, it's sensible and logical to consider the price uncertainty and wage uncertainty together because fluctuations in output price tend to be accompanied by variations on wage in general, that is, changes in output price and wage are correlated.

The major contributions, in brief, of this paper relative to existing literatures are, on the one hand, an explicit solution is derived and firm's investment behavior is analyzed qualitatively and quantitatively rather than just qualitatively, on the other hand, both price and wage uncertainty are taken into account reasonably and simultaneously rather than consider the price uncertainty only. What's more important, so far to our knowledge, the question we discussed in the paper is still open. As we expected, our conclusion is consistent with that in Abel [10], which shows that the optimal investment behavior is such that the expected proportional rate of change of investment is constant over time. The remaining of this paper is organized as follows. In Section 2, we describe our model at length. Section 3 analyzes the effects of uncertainty on investment. Finally, conclusion is presented in Section 4.

2. Model Description

In this section, we will introduce the model again in detail for the sake of intactness, although it's a special case of the model in Pindyck [9], and is an extension to the model in Abel [10]. For our purpose, we give hypothesis as below.

(H_1) The firm is risk-neutral and competitive with strictly quasi-concave production function as well as with convex costs of adjustment function. But for simplicity and operability, production function is adopted by Cobb-Douglas type, namely

$$F(K,L) = AK^{\omega}L^{1-\omega}, \quad 0<\omega<1,$$

where, K and L are respectively capital stock and labor, and A denotes technology. Without loss of generality, we normalize A to unit one hereafter, *i.e.*, $A=1$. It's obviously that $F(K,L)=K^{\omega}L^{1-\omega}$ satisfies the conditions of quasi-concave, *i.e.*,

$F_K, F_L>0, F_{KK}, F_{LL}<0, F_{KL}=F_{LK}>0, F_{KK}F_{LL}-F_{KL}^2\geq 0$

And the convex costs of adjustment function is adopted by the form as $C(I)=\upsilon I^{\zeta}, \upsilon>0$ is the purchase price of one unit capital(equipment), $\zeta>1$ is the constant elasticity, and I is the gross investment. As many literatures suggested previously, $C(I)$ confirms with $C(0)=0$ and $C(I)>0, C'(I)>0, C''(I)>0$, for any $I>0$. Note that the convexity of the adjustment costs function $C(I)$ implies that it is more costly to increase capital stock quickly than slowly.

(H_2) Capital accumulation equation at time t is defined by

$$\dot{K}_t = I_t - \delta K_t, \tag{1}$$

here, $0 < \delta < 1$ is the depreciation rate.

(H_3) The stochastic behavior of output price *p* and of wage rate *w* at time *t* follows geometric Brownian motion, that is

$$dp_t / p_t = \nu_1 dt + \sigma_1 dW_1, \tag{2}$$

$$dw_t / w_t = \nu_2 dt + \sigma_2 dW_2, \tag{3}$$

where, W_1 and W_2 are two Wiener processes with zero mean and unit variance, $\nu_1, \nu_2, \sigma_1, \sigma_2$ are all non-zero constants. As a matter of fact, ν_1 and ν_2 can be regarded as inflation rates. Besides, we set

$$E[dW_1 dW_2] = \rho_{12} dt, \tag{4}$$

here, $0 \le \rho_{12} \le 1$ is the instantaneous correlation coefficient for the two Wiener processes W_1 and W_2. E is the expectation operator.

For a risk-neutral and competitive firm, its objective is to maximize the expected present value Ψ of cash flow by selecting labor L and investment I. Mathematically, the optimal problem can be described as

$$\begin{aligned}&\Psi(K_t, p_t, w_t)\\ &= \max_{L_s, I_s} E_t \int_t^\infty \left(p_s K_s^\omega L_s^{1-\omega} - w_s L_s - \upsilon I_s^\zeta \right) e^{-\beta(s-t)} ds,\\ &\forall s \ge t,\end{aligned}$$

subject to constraints in (1)-(4). Of course, discount rate $\beta > 0$ is set to be constant here.

Remark 1. *In Pindyck* [9], *the general model can be rewritten as*

$$\begin{aligned}&\max_{L_s, I_s} E_t \int_t^\infty \left(p_s F(K_s, L_s) - w_s L_s - C(I_s) \right) e^{-\beta(s-t)} ds,\\ &\forall s \ge t,\end{aligned}$$

subject to (1) *and* $dp = \mu_1(p) dW_1, dw = \mu_2(w) dW_2$, *where,* $F(K, L)$ *is a general production function with strictly quasi-concavity and* $C(I)$ *is a general adjustment-cost function with convexity, and* $\mu_1(p), \mu_2(w)$ *are two functions respectively with respect to* p, w. *In the general case, Pindyck did not obtain an explicit solution for the optimal investment, but analyzed the firm's investment behavior qualitatively by using stochastic phase diagram approach instead. However, our model will collapse to the the special case expressed in Abel* [10] *by setting* $\nu_1 = 0$ *as well as* $\nu_2 = 0, \sigma_2 = 0$, *i.e., the wage is non-stochastic. In this special case, Abel derived an explicit solution and found the optimal investment rate is such that the expected proportional rate of change of investment is a non-zero constant over time.*

Remark 2. *We argue that it is not nonsense to assume that the wage rate follows a stochastic process in reality. Also, it's feasible in practice. For example, Hartman* [14] *has considered the wage rate as a random variable and perfect results have been achieved. Differently, however, we here need not presume that the distribution of price* p_t *and of wage rate* w_t *are independent, which was proposed in Hartman's. Conversely, the dependence of them is allowed in our paper. Fortunately, we will prove later that this case is feasible too. Alternatively, it's logical to think wage rate changes with the fluctuation of output price. Indeed, by supposing that the firm's goal is to pursuit the maximum profit, then, at least in the short-run, the employers would cut back their costs by reducing wage rate if the price of output falls due to some reasons. By contrary, if the price of output rises, then the firm would raise the wage rate to make employees work harder to produce more.*

It's not difficult to prove that $\Psi(K_t, p_t, w_t)$, reduced by Ψ hereafter, obeys formula

$$\begin{aligned}\beta \Psi dt = \max\left(p_t K_t^\omega L_t^{1-\omega} - w_t L_t - \upsilon I_t^\zeta \right) dt\\ + E_t(d\Psi).\end{aligned} \tag{5}$$

Straightforwardly, the left-hand side of (5) can be regarded as the total mean return desired by the firm over the time interval *dt*, if the firm requires a mean return rate β. On the contrary, the right-hand side of (5) is the whole return expected by the firm, which is the sum of cash flow and expected capital gain or loss $E_t(d\Psi)$. In other words, optimality means the desired mean return is equal to the expected return.

Now, we will derive the expression of the optimal investment rate I_t step by step. To begin, we present the following Proposition 1.

Proposition 1. *The firm's optimal rate of investment* I_t *can be expressed as*

$$I_t = \left(\frac{\chi_1 p_t^{1/\omega} w_t^{(\omega-1)/\omega}}{\chi_2 \upsilon \zeta} \right)^{1/(\zeta-1)}, \tag{6}$$

where

$$\begin{aligned}\chi_1 &= \omega(1-\omega)^{(\omega-1)/\omega},\\ \chi_2 &= \beta + \delta - \frac{\nu_1 + (\omega-1)\nu_2}{\omega}\\ &\quad - \frac{(1-\omega)\left(\sigma_1^2 + \sigma_2^2 - 2\sigma_1\sigma_2\rho_{12}\right)}{2\omega^2}.\end{aligned} \tag{7}$$

It is clear to see from (6) *that the optimal rate of investment* I_t *does not depend on* K_t, *but increases with* p_t, *decreases with* w_t, *since* $0 < \omega < 1, \zeta > 1$.

Proof. First of all, we claim that Itô's Lemma is applicable under the hypothesis $(H_1)-(H_3)$. Thus, applying Itô's Lemma to calculate the capital gain or loss $d\Psi$, we have

$$\begin{aligned} d\Psi &= \Psi_K dK_t + \Psi_p dp_t + \Psi_w dw_t \\ &+\Psi_{KK}(dK_t)^2/2 + \Psi_{pp}(dp_t)^2/2 + \Psi_{ww}(dw_t)^2/2 \\ &+\Psi_{pK}(dp_t)(dK_t) + \Psi_{wK}(dw_t)(dK_t) \\ &+\Psi_{pw}(dp_t)(dw_t). \end{aligned} \tag{8}$$

Inserting (1)-(4) into (8), meanwhile recalling that $Et(dW) = (dt)^2 = (dt)(dW) = 0$ and $(dW)^2 = dt$ for any standard Wiener process W, we get

$$\begin{aligned} E_t(d\Psi) &= \big((I_t - \delta K_t)\Psi_K + v_1 p_t \Psi_p + v_2 w_t \Psi_w \\ &+ \sigma_1^2 p_t^2 \Psi_{pp}/2 + \sigma_2^2 w_t^2 \Psi_{ww}/2 + \sigma_1\sigma_2\rho_{12} p_t w_t \Psi_{pw}\big) dt. \end{aligned} \tag{9}$$

Substituting (9) into (5), we obtain

$$\begin{aligned} \beta\Psi &= \max\big(p_t K_t^{\omega} L_t^{1-\omega} - w_t L_t - \upsilon I_t^{\zeta} + (I_t - \delta K_t)\Psi_K \\ &+ v_1 p_t \Psi_p + v_2 w_t \Psi_w + \sigma_1^2 p_t^2 \Psi_{pp}/2 \\ &+ \sigma_2^2 w_t^2 \Psi_{ww}/2 + \sigma_1\sigma_2\rho_{12} p_t w_t \Psi_{pw}\big). \end{aligned} \tag{10}$$

By simple computation, it yields

$$\begin{aligned} &\max_{L_t} = \left(p_t K_t^{\omega} L_t^{1-\omega} - w_t L_t\right) = \chi_1 p_t^{1/\omega} w_t^{(\omega-1)/\omega} K_t, \\ &\chi_1 = \omega(1-\omega)^{(\omega-1)/\omega}. \end{aligned} \tag{11}$$

Notice that, $\chi_1 p_t^{1/\omega} w_t^{(\omega-1)/\omega}$ is the marginal revenue product of capital.

Next, differentiating the right-hand side of (10) with respect to I_t, there holds

$$\upsilon\zeta I_t^{\zeta-1} = \Psi_K. \tag{12}$$

An economic interpretation can be seen straightly from (12), *i.e.*, the optimal investment rate is such that the marginal cost of investment equals the marginal valuation of capital. Plugging (11) and (12) into (10), we have

$$\begin{aligned} \beta\Psi &= \chi_1 p_t^{1/\omega} w_t^{(\omega-1)/\omega} K_t + \chi_3 \Psi_K^{\zeta/(\zeta-1)} - \delta K_t \Psi_K \\ &+ v_1 p_t \Psi_p + v_2 w_t \Psi_w + \sigma_1^2 p_t^2 \Psi_{pp}/2 \\ &+ \sigma_2^2 w_t^2 \Psi_{ww}/2 + \sigma_1\sigma_2\rho_{12} p_t w_t \Psi_{pw}, \end{aligned} \tag{13}$$

where

$$\chi_3 = \upsilon(\zeta-1)(\upsilon\zeta)^{\zeta/(1-\zeta)}, \text{ and } \chi_1 \text{ as in (7).} \tag{14}$$

It's well known that we can rewrite (12) and (13) as a nonlinear second-order partial differential equation, despite such equations are unsolvable in general case. But fortunately, an explicit solution can be derived herein due to our assumptions. Note that we can strictly prove that there exists a Ψ to satisfy the nonlinear second-order partial differential equation given by (12) and (13) together. The argument process, however, is not the emphasis in the paper. Hence, we omit the details here. Now that the solution Ψ exists and taking the form of (12) and (13) into account, we guess the form of Ψ as

$$\Psi = \lambda_1 p_t^a w_t^b K_t + \lambda_2 p_t^m w_t^n, \tag{15}$$

where, $\lambda_1, \lambda_2, a, b$ and m, n are all undetermined coefficients.

In terms of (15), it yields

$$\begin{aligned} \Psi_K &= \lambda_1 p_t^a w_t^b, \\ \Psi_{pw} &= ab\lambda_1 p_t^{a-1} w_t^{b-1} K_t + mn\lambda_2 p_t^{m-1} w_t^{n-1}, \end{aligned} \tag{16}$$

$$\begin{aligned} \Psi_p &= a\lambda_1 p_t^{a-1} w_t^b K_t + m\lambda_2 p_t^{m-1} w_t^n, \\ \Psi_{pp} &= a(a-1)\lambda_1 p_t^{a-2} w_t^b K_t \\ &+ m(m-1)\lambda_2 p_t^{m-2} w_t^n, \end{aligned} \tag{17}$$

$$\begin{aligned} \Psi_w &= b\lambda_1 p_t^a w_t^{b-1} K_t + n\lambda_2 p_t^m w_t^{n-1}, \\ \Psi_{ww} &= b(b-1)\lambda_1 p_t^a w_t^{b-2} K_t \\ &+ n(n-1)\lambda_2 p_t^m w_t^{n-2}. \end{aligned} \tag{18}$$

Lastly, applying method of undetermined coefficients, and combining (13) as well as (16)-(18), it's not difficult to get

$$\begin{aligned} \Psi &= \frac{\chi_1}{\chi_2} p_t^{1/\omega} w_t^{(\omega-1)/\omega} K_t \\ &+ \chi_4 p_t^{\zeta/\omega(\zeta-1)} w_t^{\zeta(\omega-1)/\omega(\zeta-1)}, \end{aligned} \tag{19}$$

where

$$\chi_4 = \frac{2\chi_3(\chi_1/\chi_2)^{\zeta/(\zeta-1)}}{2\beta - 2\frac{(v_1 - v_2 + \omega v_2)\zeta}{\omega(\zeta-1)} - \frac{(\omega+\zeta-\omega\zeta)\zeta\sigma_1^2 + (\omega^2-\omega-\omega\zeta+\zeta)\zeta\sigma_2^2 + 2\rho_{12}(\omega-1)\zeta^2\sigma_1\sigma_2}{\omega^2(\zeta-1)^2}},$$

χ_1, χ_2 as in (7),and χ_3 as in (14).

Following (12) and (19), we see immediately that

$$I_t = \left(\frac{\chi_1 p_t^{1/\omega} w_t^{(\omega-1)/\omega}}{\chi_2 \upsilon\zeta}\right)^{1/(\zeta-1)}, \chi_1, \chi_2 \text{ as in (7)} \tag{20}$$

Obviously, some results can be obtained directly from (19) and (20). The firm's value , for instance, is a linear function of the capital stock K_t. The optimal rate of investment It does not depend on K_t, but increases with p_t, decreases with w_t, since $0 < \omega < 1, \zeta > 1$.

3. The Effects of Uncertainty on Investment

We will analyze the qualitative effects of price and wage uncertainty on investment in this section, for given the current level of output price p_t, and of wage rate w_t.

Proposition 2. *If* $\varepsilon_1^2+\varepsilon_2^2>2\rho_{12}\left(\sqrt{(\sigma_1^2+\varepsilon_1^2)(\sigma_2^2+\varepsilon_2^2)}-\sigma_1\sigma_2\right)$, *then the increases in uncertainty of output price and of wage rate together will have positive effects on the optimal investment rate* I_t. *Conversely, if* $\varepsilon_1^2+\varepsilon_2^2<2\rho_{12}\left(\sqrt{(\sigma_1^2+\varepsilon_1^2)(\sigma_2^2+\varepsilon_2^2)}-\sigma_1\sigma_2\right)$, *then the increases in the two uncertainty will have negative effects on the optimal rate of investment. Particularly, there will be no effects of shifts in uncertainty on the investment so long as* $\varepsilon_1^2+\varepsilon_2^2=2\rho_{12}\left(\sqrt{(\sigma_1^2+\varepsilon_1^2)(\sigma_2^2+\varepsilon_2^2)}-\sigma_1\sigma_2\right)$. *Here,* $\varepsilon_1^2,\varepsilon_2^2$ *are respectively the fluctuations in uncertainty* σ_1^2,σ_2^2, *which associate with* p_t, w_t, *correspondingly.*

Proof. As a matter of fact, in order to analyze the effects of uncertainty on investment behavior, we just need to determine the effects of uncertainty on $\xi_t=\frac{\chi_1}{\chi_2}p_t^{1/\omega}w_t^{(\omega-1)/\omega}$, because I_t relies on ξ_t only. To this end, taking the expression of ξ_t,χ_1,χ_2 into account, we only require focusing on the change of $\sigma_1^2+\sigma_2^2-2\sigma_1\sigma_2\rho_{12}$. By simple analysis, we see the changes in uncertainty of output price and of wage rate together will result in a rising in the optimal investment rate I_t if

$$\sigma_1^2+\varepsilon_1^2+\sigma_2^2+\varepsilon_2^2-2\rho_{12}\left(\sqrt{(\sigma_1^2+\varepsilon_1^2)(\sigma_2^2+\varepsilon_2^2)}\right)>\sigma_1^2+\sigma_2^2-2\sigma_1\sigma_2\rho_{12},$$

i.e., $\varepsilon_1^2+\varepsilon_2^2>2\rho_{12}\left(\sqrt{(\sigma_1^2+\varepsilon_1^2)(\sigma_2^2+\varepsilon_2^2)}-\sigma_1\sigma_2\right)$. Similarly, the changes in the two uncertainty will lead to a falling in the optimal rate of investment if Specially, as long $\varepsilon_1^2+\varepsilon_2^2<2\rho_{12}\left(\sqrt{(\sigma_1^2+\varepsilon_1^2)(\sigma_2^2+\varepsilon_2^2)}-\sigma_1\sigma_2\right)$. Specially, as long as $\varepsilon_1^2+\varepsilon_2^2=2\rho_{12}\left(\sqrt{(\sigma_1^2+\varepsilon_1^2)(\sigma_2^2+\varepsilon_2^2)}-\sigma_1\sigma_2\right)$, then there will be no effects of changes in uncertainty on the investment behavior.

Remark 3. *Certainly, the conclusion above will hold as long as* $\zeta>1$, *but no matter the marginal adjustment cost function is convex* $(\zeta>2)$, *concave* $(\zeta<2)$, *or linear* $(\zeta=2)$.

Subsequently, we will explain the effects of uncertainty on investment. To achieve this goal, it's a good choice to simulate the idea in Abel [10]. As mentioned in (11), $\chi_1 p_t^{1/\omega}w_t^{(\omega-1)/\omega}$ is the marginal revenue product of capital(M_t hereafter), thus

$$E_t(M_s)=\chi_1E_t\left(p_s^{1/\omega}w_s^{(\omega-1)/\omega}\right)=\chi_1p_t^{1/\omega}w_t^{(\omega-1)/\omega}\exp\left\{\left(\frac{v_1+(\omega-1)v_2}{\omega}+\frac{(1-\omega)(\sigma_1^2+\sigma_2^2-2\sigma_1\sigma_2\rho_{12})}{2\omega^2}\right)(s-t)\right\}. \tag{21}$$

Here, we used (2)-(4) to get the second equality. Naturally, the expected present value of the marginal revenue product of capital is $\int_t^\infty E_t(M_s)\exp(-(\beta+\delta)(s-t))\mathrm{d}s$. Inserting (21) into this integral directly, we see that the integral is actually equal to ξ_t, this indicates $\xi_t=\frac{\chi_1}{\chi_2}p_t^{1/\omega}w_t^{(\omega-1)/\omega}$ is the expected present value of the marginal revenue product of capital $\chi_1p_t^{1/\omega}w_t^{(\omega-1)/\omega}$. Hence, we can say that the uncertainty affects investment by means of influencing the expected value of future marginal revenue product of capital.

Finally, the dynamic behavior of investment will be explored at the end of this section.

Proposition 3. *The optimal investment behavior is such that the expected proportional growth rate of investment(non-zero in general) is constant over time.*

Proof. Applying Itô's Lemma to $\xi_t=\frac{\chi_1}{\chi_2}p_t^{1/\omega}w_t^{(\omega-1)/\omega}$, it yields

$$\frac{d\xi_t}{\xi_t}=\frac{1}{\omega}\frac{dp_t}{p_t}+\frac{\omega-1}{\omega}\frac{dw_t}{w_t}+\frac{1-\omega}{2\omega^2}\left(\frac{dp_t}{p_t}\right)^2+\frac{1-\omega}{2\omega^2}\left(\frac{dw_t}{w_t}\right)^2+\frac{\omega-1}{\omega^2}\frac{dp_t}{p_t}\frac{dw_t}{w_t}. \tag{22}$$

Substituting (2)-(4) into (22), it's easily to obtain

$$\frac{1}{dt}E_t\frac{d\xi_t}{\xi_t}=\frac{v_1+(\omega-1)v_2}{\omega}+\frac{(1-\omega)(\sigma_1^2+\sigma_2^2-2\sigma_1\sigma_2\rho_{12})}{2\omega^2}. \tag{23}$$

Applying Itô's Lemma to (20), there holds

$$\frac{dI_t}{I_t}=\frac{1}{\omega(\zeta-1)}\frac{dp_t}{p_t}+\frac{\omega-1}{\omega(\zeta-1)}\frac{dw_t}{w_t}+\frac{1+\omega-\omega\zeta}{2\omega^2(\zeta-1)^2}\left(\frac{dp_t}{p_t}\right)^2+\frac{(1-\omega)(1+\omega\zeta-2\omega)}{2\omega^2(\zeta-1)^2}\left(\frac{dw_t}{w_t}\right)^2+\frac{\omega-1}{\omega^2(\zeta-1)^2}\frac{dp_t}{p_t}\frac{dw_t}{w_t}. \tag{24}$$

Substituting (2)-(4) into (24), it's easily to get

$$\frac{1}{dt}E_t\frac{dI_t}{I_t}=\frac{v_1+(\omega-1)v_2}{\omega(\zeta-1)}+\frac{(1+\omega-\omega\zeta)\sigma_1^2+(1-\omega)(1+\omega\zeta-2\omega)\sigma_2^2-2(\omega-1)\sigma_1\sigma_2\rho_{12}}{2\omega^2(\zeta-1)^2}. \tag{25}$$

So far, from (23) and (25), we observe that both the expected growth rate of marginal revenue product of capital and the expected proportional growth rate of investment are constants over time, neither they depends on output price or wage. Simultaneously, it's clearly to see the two expected growth rates are zero in the case without uncertainty.

4. Concluding Remarks

The objective of this paper is to analyze the effects of uncertainty on a competitively risk-neutral firm's investment decision. By referring the methods presented in Abel [10] and Pindyck [9], we find that given the current output price and wage rate, then the fluctuations in uncertainty of output price and of wage rate together will result in positive impacts on the optimal investment rate I_t if $\varepsilon_1^2+\varepsilon_2^2>2\rho_{12}\left(\sqrt{(\sigma_1^2+\varepsilon_1^2)(\sigma_2^2+\varepsilon_2^2)}-\sigma_1\sigma_2\right)$, whereas the fluctuations in uncertainty will lead to negative impacts on the optimal rate of investment if $\varepsilon_1^2+\varepsilon_2^2<2\,\rho_{12}\left(\sqrt{(\sigma_1^2+\varepsilon_1^2)(\sigma_2^2+\varepsilon_2^2)}-\sigma_1\sigma_2\right)$, and there won't have any effects of fluctuations in uncertainty on the investment so long as $\varepsilon_1^2+\varepsilon_2^2>2\rho_{12}\left(\sqrt{(\sigma_1^2+\varepsilon_1^2)(\sigma_2^2+\varepsilon_2^2)}-\sigma_1\sigma_2\right)$, where $\varepsilon_1^2,\varepsilon_2^2$ are changes in uncertainty of output price σ_1^2 and of wage rate σ_2^2, respectively.

The expected growth rate of marginal valuation of capital and of investment are both invariant over time. And moreover, by observing (23) and (25) carefully, we see that the expected growth rate of marginal valuation of capital multiplies the elasticity of investment with respect to marginal valuation of capital, $1/(\zeta-1)$, is equal to the expected growth rate of investment when the marginal adjustment costs function is linear, *i.e.*, $\zeta=2$. As to the convex marginal adjustment costs function and the concave type, the relationship between the two expected growth rates are uneasy to determine, which is unlike the case demonstrated in Abel [10].

We remark that it's unnecessary to confine the production function to Cobb-Douglas type, and strictly speaking, the argument presented in the paper can be applied to any production function obeys homogeneous of degree one. Besides, we derived our results without considering whether the marginal revenue product of capital is convex, concave or linear, which is different from Pindyck [9]. Self-evidently, our model will collapse to the one in Abel [10], if set v_1 to be zero and assume the wage rate w_t without uncertainty.

At last, we mention the major contribution of this paper. For one thing, an explicit solution is derived and firm's investment behavior is analyzed qualitatively and quantitatively rather than just qualitatively. For another thing, both price and wage uncertainty are examined simultaneously since fluctuations in output price tend to be accompanied by fluctuations in wage, rather than consider the price uncertainty only. What's more important, so far to our knowledge, the question we discussed in the paper is still open.

5. Acknowledgements

The author would like to express his sincere thanks to the anonymous referees for their helpful comments and suggestions, which greatly improved the presentation of this paper. The author also would like to thank the editors for their help.

REFERENCES

[1] R. Hartman, "The Effects of Price and Cost Uncertainty on Investment," *Journal of Economic Theory*, Vol. 5, No. 2, 1972, pp. 258-266.

[2] V. Ghosal and P. Lougani, "The Differential Impact of Uncertainty on Investment in Small and Large Businesses," *Review of Economics and Statistics*, Vol. 82, No. 2, 2000, pp. 338-349.

[3] M. Peeters, "Does Demand and Price Uncertainty Affect Belgian and Spanish Corporate Investment?" *Recherches Economiques de Louvain*, Vol. 67, No. 3, 2001, pp. 235-255.

[4] P. Temple, G. Urga and C. Driver, "The Influence of Uncertainty on Investment in the UK: A Macro or Micro Phenomenon?" *Scottish Journal of Political Economy*, Vol. 48, No. 4, 2001, pp. 361-382.

[5] N. Bloom, "The Impact of Uncertainty Shocks," *Econometrica*, Vol. 77, No. 3, 2009, pp. 623-685.

[6] J. Lee and K. Shin, "The Role of Variable Input in the Relationship between Investment and Uncertainty," *American Economic Review*, Vol. 90, No. 3, 2001, pp. 667-680.

[7] N. C. Nielsen, "The Price and Output Decisions of the Firm under Uncertainty," *Swedish Journal of Economics*, Vol. 77, No. 4, 1975, pp. 459-469.

[8] R. E. Lucas and E. C. Prescott, "Investment under Uncertainty," *Econometrica*, Vol. 39, No. 5, 1971, pp. 659-681.

[9] R. S. Pindyck, "Adjustment Costs, Uncertainty, and the Behavior of the Firm," *American Economic Review*, Vol. 72, No. 3, 1982, pp. 415-427.

[10] A. B. Abel, "Optimal Investment under Uncertainty," *American Economic Review*, Vol. 73, No. 1, 1983, pp. 228-233.

[11] A. B. Abel and J. C. Eberly, "A Unified Model of Investment under Uncertainty," *American Economic Review*, Vol. 84, No. 5, 1994, pp. 1369-1384.

[12] L. Guiso and G. Parigi, "Investment and Demand Uncertainty," *Quarterly Journal of Economics*, Vol. 114, No. 1, 1999, pp. 185-227.

[13] N. Bloom, S. Bond and J. Van-Reenen, "Uncertainty and Investment Dynamics," *Review of Economics Studies*, Vol. 74, No. 2, 2007, pp. 391-415.

[14] R. Hartman, "Adjustment Costs, Price and Wage Uncertainty, and Investment," *Review of Economic Studies*, Vol. 40, No. 2, 1973, pp. 259-267.

[15] R. Bachmann, S. Elstner and E. Sims, "Uncertainty and Economic Activity: Evidence from Business Survey Data," NBER Working Paper, No. 16143, 2010. http://www.nber.org/papers/w16143

[16] N. Bloom, "Uncertainty and the Dynamics of R&D," *American Economic Review*, Vol. 97, No. 2, 2007, pp. 250-255.

[17] A. Carruth, A. Dickerson and A. Henley, "What Do We Know about Investment under Uncertainty?" *Journal of Economic Surveys*, Vol. 14, No. 2, 2000, pp. 119-153.

[18] T. Dunne and X. Y. Mu, "Investment Spikes and Uncertainty in the Petroleum Refining Industry," *Journal of Industrial Economics*, Vol. 58, No. 1, 2010, pp. 190-213.

[19] J. P. Gould, "Adjustment Costs in the Theory of Investment of the Firm," *Review of Economic Studies*, Vol. 35, No. 1, 1968, pp. 47-55.

[20] R. Hartman, "Factor Demand with Output Price Uncertainty," *American Economic Review*, Vol. 66, No. 4, 1976, pp. 675-681.

[21] M. Kurz and M. Motolese, "Endogenous Uncertainty and Market Volatility," *Journal of Economic Theory*, Vol. 17, No. 4, 2001, pp. 497-544.

[22] J. A. List and M. S. Haigh, "Investment under Uncertainty: Testing the Options Model with Professional Traders," *The Review of Economics and Statistics*, Vol. 92, No. 4, 2010, pp. 974-984.

[23] R. E. Lucas, "Adjustment Costs and the Theory of Supply," *Journal of Political Economy*, Vol. 75, No. 4, 1967, pp. 321-334.

[24] R. S. Pindyck, "Irreversibility, Uncertainty, and Investment," *Journal of Economic Literature*, Vol. 29, No. 3, 1991, pp. 1110-1148.

[25] R. S. Pindyck, "Investments of Uncertain Cost," *Journal of Financial Economics*, Vol. 34, No. 1, 1993, pp. 53-76.

[26] R. S. Pindyck, "A Note on Competitive Investment under Uncertainty," *American Economic Review*, Vol. 83, No. 1, 1993, pp. 273-277.

[27] E. Zabel, "Multiperiod Monopoly under Uncertainty," *Journal of Economic Theory*, Vol. 5, No. 3, 1972, pp. 524-536.

An Empirical Study of Option Prices under the Hybrid Brownian Motion Model

Hideki Iwaki[1], **Lei Luo**[2]
[1]Faculty of Business Administration, Kyoto Sangyo University, Kyoto, Japan
[2]Finance Division, Citigroup Global Markets Japan, Tokyo, Japan

ABSTRACT

In this paper, we mainly discuss an empirical study of option prices under the hybrid Brownian motion model developed by [1]. In a specific case of parameters, we have a simple transition probability density function that has a fat-tailed feature as time passes. We show some empirical evidences that the feature of the model reflects the real market price movements in Japanese stock market. Furthermore, we make a performance comparison between the hybrid model and the BS model using Nikkei 225 call options. In general our results show that the hybrid model is slightly better than the BS model.

Keywords: Hybrid Brownian Motions; Fat-Tailed Properties; Non-Normal Distribution; Empirical Studies; Nikkei 225 Index Options

1. Introduction

Measuring the risk of financial assets and pricing the financial instruments such as options are very important for financial institutions and other companies. In this area, the normal distribution is commonly used as a distribution of stock return and the Black-Scholes (BS) model based on the normal distribution is mostly used in practice. But fat-tailed and non-normal distributions of stock return are shown by plenty of empirical evidences. As early as 60s, [2,3] suggested the use of heavy tailed distributions to describe daily returns. Reference [4] compared the stable distribution and t-distribution for stock prices of United States. Reference [5] presented an empirical evidence of the normal inverse Gaussian distribution and t-distribution in the European market. As to Japanese market, [6] extensively studied on a Pearson type distribution and made an empirical study in Japanese stock market.

The financial crisis of 2007-2009 made it clear that the extreme movements of stock return were much more likely than normal distribution. After the financial crisis the world financial market has become more and more turbulent. European sovereign debt crisis is getting worse and the governors of EU are trying to solve the problem. The companies in Japan also suffered the loss from aftermath of the earthquake in northern Japan in March 2011.

Based on the facts mentioned above, we need a new approach which reflects the fat-tailed property to evaluate financial assets and instruments. In the paper, we investigate validity of a stochastic differential equation (SDE) that is a hybrid of arithmetic and geometric Brownian motion introduced by [1]. They made an analysis on a model of the market that involves two types of market participants such as fundamental traders and technical traders. Through the analysis they pointed out that the log-return approximately follows such a hybrid Brownian motion.

When we specify some parameter values, we can explicitly derive a transition probability density and the variance of its distribution is increasing exponentially as time passes. This special case might reflect the real market movements in short term especially in some situations like financial crises. We have fitted the model to the Japanese stock market. We show the distribution can describe the market well compared with normal distribution if we focus on the short term or daily.

A well-known empirical bias associated with the BS model is the volatility smile which is shown by [7] etc. The volatility is assumed to be constant in the BS model, but realized volatility of underlyings actually rise and fall over time. Corresponding to the observed volatility fluctuation, [8] introduced a stochastic volatility model and [9] gave a closed-form solution for option pricing under the stochastic volatility model. Reference [10] has made a thorough empirical study about the performance of the stochastic volatility model. When volatility is merely a function of the current asset level and time, we have a local volatility model which is a useful simplification of the stochastic volatility model. The local volatility model is developed by [11]. The hybrid model is a kind of local volatility models.

To show the performance of the hybrid model in option pricing empirically, we compare the performance between the hybrid model and the BS model using Nikkei 225 index options. Since we cannot get a closed-form option pricing formula under the hybrid model, we implement the risk neutral option pricing by applying a trinomial tree method. We compare two models in an in-sample parameter estimation and an out-of-sample pricing performance. Our empirical evidence indicates that generally the hybrid model is slightly better than the BS model.

The rest of the paper is organized as follows. Section 2 introduces the hybrid Brownian motion model and its special case. We can use this special case to describe the turbulent financial environments. Section 3 discusses fat-tailed property of the model. If we focus on distributions of daily returns, we can find that the model can fit the market data well. Section 4 shows the results of our empirical studies on comparison of option pricing under the hybrid model with that under the BS model and discusses some performance issues. Section 5 is our conclusion.

2. The Hybrid Brownian Motion

2.1. A General Model

We consider a market containing a stock with share price S_t at time $t \geq 0$. The log-return X_t is given by $X_t = \log(S_t/S_0)$. Reference [1] introduced a hybrid SDE mixing both arithmetic and geometric Brownian motions to describe fluctuation of X_t. They make a model of market with two different types of agents. One set of agents consists of fundamental traders acting independently of the current value of X_t. The other set consists of technical traders that trade based on the historical values $\{X_s \mid 0 \leq s \leq t\}$. They show that after some appropriate linearization and approximation, the aggregation of those two type trader's impacts on the log-return of stock prices leads to a general form of the hybrid SDE;

$$\mathrm{d}X_t = (\mu_1 - \mu_2 X_t)\mathrm{d}t + \sigma_1 \mathrm{d}W_{1t} + \sigma_2 X_t \mathrm{d}W_{2t}, \qquad (1)$$

where μ_1, μ_2, σ_1 and σ_2 are constants, and where W_{1t} and W_{2t} are standard Brownian motions. In Equation (1), the part of the arithmetic Brownian motion is related to the fundamental trades. On the other, the part of the geometric Brownian motion is related to the technical trades. We can of course reduce it to an SDE with a single noise term. If ρ is the infinitesimal correlation coefficient between the two Brownian motions, then we can rewrite the SDE as

$$\mathrm{d}X_t = (\mu_1 - \mu_2 X_t)\mathrm{d}t + \sqrt{\sigma_1^2 + X_t^2\sigma_2^2 + 2\rho\sigma_1 X_t \sigma_2^2}\,\mathrm{d}W_t. \qquad (2)$$

The model has five parameters σ_1, σ_2, μ_1, μ_2 and ρ. We can explain them intuitively. σ_1 is the fundamental volatility related to the economy. σ_2 is the investor volatility related to the market confidence of investors. μ_1 is the drift related to the economy itself. μ_2 is the drift controlled by the investor sentiment. ρ represents the relationship between the two volatilities above.

2.2. A Special Case

Although there might be some positive or negative relationship between W_1 and W_2, investors cannot get the accurate information about the relationship because of information asymmetry in the financial market. They might just react randomly to the price of stock. So it might be reasonable to assume $\rho = 0$. μ_1 also has minor influence to analyze the model especially for a short term. Thus we adopt such a special case that $\rho = \mu_1 = 0$. Under the special case, [1] show the variance $V(X_t)$ can be written in such a tractable form that

$$V(X_t) = \frac{\sigma_1^2}{\sigma_2^2(\nu-2)}\left[1 - \mathrm{e}^{-\sigma_2^2(\nu-2)t}\right]$$

$$\sim \sigma_1^2 t - \frac{\mu_1}{\mu_2}\sigma_1^2\sigma_2^2(\nu-2)t^2 + O(t^3),$$

where

$$\nu = 1 + \frac{2\mu_2}{\sigma_2^2}.$$

ν plays an essential dynamic role. Assuming the condition $\nu = 0$, we can find that the variance grows exponentially as time passes. It makes fatten the tails of distribution of X_t. Under the assumption that $\nu = 0$ we can simplify Equation (2) as

$$\mathrm{d}X_t = \frac{\sigma_2^2}{2}X_t\mathrm{d}t + \sqrt{\sigma_1^2 + X_t^2\sigma_2^2}\,\mathrm{d}W_t. \qquad (3)$$

We observe the momentum property from Equation (3). Since $-\mu_2$ in the general model is substituted by $\sigma_2^2/2$, the positive (negative) return will try to bring a positive (negative) return next day. This mean-reversion condition in turn allows an equilibrium to establish. In general, the transition probability density of X_t is an integral of a hyper-geometric function of complex parameters. However [1] show that under this special case with $\nu = 0$, the transition probability density $f(x,t)$ of X_t is explicitly given by

$$f(x,t) = \frac{1}{\sqrt{2\pi t\left(\sigma_1^2 + \sigma_2^2 x^2\right)}} \times \exp\left\{\frac{1}{2}\sigma_2^2 t\left[\sinh^{-1}\left(\sigma_2 x/\sigma_1\right)\right]^2\right\}. \quad (4)$$

We note that we do not have any closed form transition probability density except for this special case.

3. An Evidence of a Fat-Tailed and Non-Normal Distribution

We show evidence such that logarithmic returns of Nikkei 225 index follow a fat-tailed and non-normal distribution. We use daily closing prices of Nikkei 225 index from January 04, 2008 to September 30, 2011 which corresponds to 915 observations. **Figure 1** shows normal QQ-plots for the corresponding logarithmic returns. For the Nikkei 225 index distribution, both tails are heavier than the Gaussian.

Since our main interest is in the tails of the distributions, we use graphical logarithmic left and right tail tests employed by [5] to examine the fit in the tails. The graphical tests were performed as follows. Let $F(x)$ denote the estimated cumulative distribution function of the fitted distribution, computed by numerical integration of Equation (4), and $(X_1,\cdots,X_N)$ the order statistic of the historical data. A plot of $\log(F(X_t))$ against X_t superimposed onto a plot of $\log(1/(N+1))$ against X_t shows the left tail fit for the fitted distribution, and a plot of $\log(1-F(X_t))$ against X_t superimposed onto a plot of $\log((N+1-t)/(N+1))$, the right tail fit.

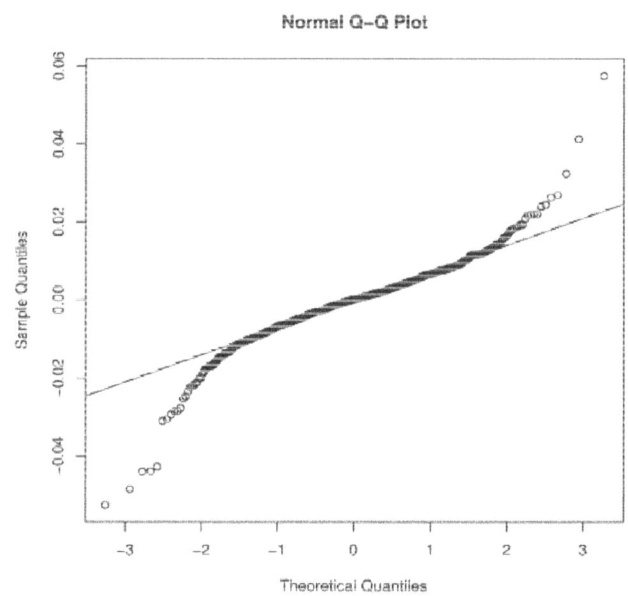

Figure 1. QQ-plots for log returns of Nikkei 225 index.

Figure 2 shows the plots. The upper panel in the figure shows the left tail fit, and the lower panel the right tail fit. The circles correspond to the empirical data, the line plotted around the circles corresponds to the distribution Equation (4), and the line deviating from the circles corresponds to the normal distribution. We can find the distribution Equation (4) fits the index daily return quite well.

4. Option Pricing and Empirical Tests

4.1. An Numerical Approach for Option Pricing

As we discussed in the previous sections, the hybrid model has some good features to describe the financial market. In some situations the pricing of options based on this model might be better than the traditional pricing based on the BS model. Since we cannot find a closed form option pricing formula under the hybrid model, we use a trinomial tree pricing method to derive the prices of European call options.

We assume that there exists a constant instantaneous risk-free rate r and there does not exist any arbitrage opportunities. Let us define

$$Y_t = \mathrm{e}^{-rt} S_t,\ t \in [0,T].$$

By Ito's lemma, we have

$$\mathrm{d}Y_t = \mathrm{e}^{-rt}\sigma\left(\mathrm{e}^{rt}Y_t, t\right)\mathrm{d}\tilde{W}_t,\ t\in[0,T];\ Y_0 = S_0,$$

where

$$\sigma(S,t) = S\sqrt{\sigma_1^2 + \left(\ln\left(S/S_0\right)\sigma_2\right)^2},$$

and where $\tilde{W}_t$ denotes the Wiener process under the risk neutral probability measure.

We construct a trinomial tree as follows. Parting period $[0,T]$ into N parts and $\Delta t = T/N$. For every node

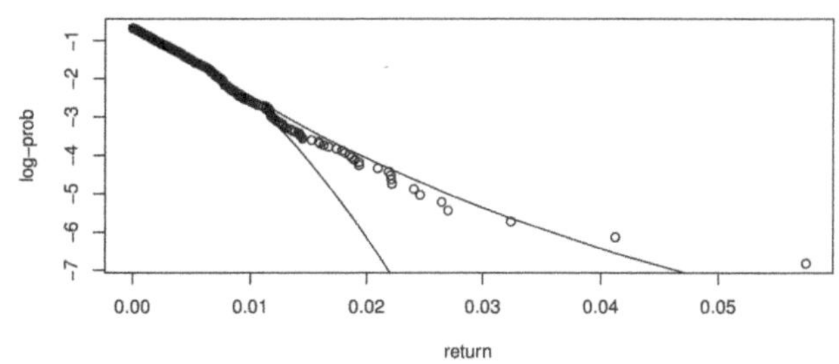

Figure 2. Left and right tail plots for Nikkei 225 index.

(n,i), $n=0,1,\cdots,N; i=0,\pm1,\pm2,\cdots$, the value of $Y(t)$ is given by

$$y(n,i)=S_0+i\Delta y$$

with a constant Δy. We set $\Delta y=\sigma(e^{rT}S,t)S\sqrt{3\Delta t}$ to satisfy such constraints that every transition probability $p(n;i,j)$ must be positive and that $\Delta y\to 0 (N\to\infty)$.

$Y(t)$ jumps from (n,i) to three nodes;

$$(n+1,i+j(n,i)),(n+1,i),(n+1,i-j(n,i)).$$

Here the width of jump $j(n,i)$ is given by

$$j(n,i)=\left[\frac{e^{-rt}\sigma(e^{rn\Delta t}y(n,i),n\Delta t)}{\Delta y}\sqrt{\Delta t}\right]+1,$$

where $[a]$ means the largest integer less than or equal to a. At each node (n,i), the risk-neutral transition probability $p(n;i,j)$ is given by

$$p(n;i,j)=\begin{cases}1-\dfrac{e^{-2rt}\sigma^2(e^{rn\Delta t}y(n,i),n\Delta t)\Delta t}{j^2(n,i)(\Delta y)^2} & \text{if } j=i,\\ \dfrac{e^{-2rt}\sigma^2(e^{rn\Delta t}y(n,i),n\Delta t)\Delta t}{j^2(n,i)(\Delta y)^2} & \text{if } j=i\pm j(n,i),\\ 0 & \text{otherwise.}\end{cases}$$

Since the option price at the maturity is given by $C(N,j)=\max\{y(N,j)e^{rT}-K,0\}$, where K denotes the strike price, and the risk-neutral transition probability has been calculated at every node, the current option price $C(0,0)$ can be derived by cal- culating backwards from the final nodes to the initial node $(0,0)$.

4.2. Data Description

We use Nikkei 225 index call option prices for the empirical study. Options written on this index are the most actively traded European type contracts in Japan. We use daily closing prices of the premiums during October 2011. We also adopt three month TIBOR as the risk-free rate. For the simplicity we don't adjust for dividends. We divide the option data into several categories according to either the moneyness or the term to expiration. As to the moneyness, we classify an option contract as at-the-money (ATM) if $0.97<S/K<1.03$, out-of-the-money (OTM) if $S/K\le 0.97$, in-the-money (ITM) otherwise. As to the term to expiration, we classify an option contract as short-term if $T<60$ days, medium-term if $60\le T<180$, long-term otherwise. Since the long term option contracts are traded scarcely, we exclude them from the test.

4.3. Parameter Estimation and In-Sample Fit

In this section, we make some performance tests by comparing option pricing under the hybrid model with that under the BS model. We follow the approach taken by [10]. In order to apply the hybrid model for option pricing, we need to estimate the model parameters. Strike price K and time to maturity T are specified in the contract. We also know spot price S and interest rate r from the market. However, since structural parameters σ_1 and σ_2 are unobservable, we estimate them as follows. First collect N prices of Nikkei 225 index call options on a given day in October 2011. For each $n=1,\cdots,N$, let T_n and K_n be respectively the time to maturity and the strike price of the n-th option. Let $\hat{C}_n(t,T_n,K_n)$ denote the observed market price and $C_n(t,T_n,K_n)$ be the model price. For each n, we define a function of σ_1 and σ_2 by

$$\epsilon_n(\sigma_1,\sigma_2)=\hat{C}_n(t,T_n,K_n)-C_n(t,T_n,K_n).$$

Then we estimate the parameters so as to minimize the sum of squared errors;

$$\min_{\sigma_1,\sigma_2}\sum_{n=1}^{N}\left|\epsilon_n(\sigma_1,\sigma_2)\right|^2. \quad (5)$$

We employed the function optim in the R software to implement the minimization in Equation (5). Daily averages of the estimated parameters are reported in **Table 1** followed by the standard errors in the parentheses. SSE denotes the total sum of squared errors and $\overline{SSE}$ denotes an average of SSE in the sample period.

In general we can find the hybrid model improves the goodness of fit. In most of the trading days, the values of σ_1 are similar in two models and those of σ_2 are very small near to zero. It might indicate that the option prices are mostly determined by the BS model. This is not surprising because the most of the financial institutions quote the prices based on the BS model. We can find that the standard errors of σ_2 are significantly greater than those of σ_1. This may be explained as follows. In different days there are different market conditions not reflected in the BS model but described by σ_2. The values of σ_2 in the short term are larger than those in the long term. This is consistent with that the price feedback in volatility becomes larger and larger as time passes. SSE of the hybrid model in the short term is better than that in the long term because option prices with the short term are affected heavily by the volatility fluctuations and the hybrid model can consider this kind of effect in option pricing. The performance among the out-of-the-money options is not as good as predicted, regardless to the time to maturities. However, we note that most of out-of-the-

Table 1. Estimated parameters and in-sample fit.

Parameters	All Options		Short-term		Medium-term	
	BS	Hybrid	BS	Hybrid	BS	Hybrid
σ [a]	0.238 (0.031)		0.252 (0.038)		0.232 (0.028)	
σ_1		0.237 (0.031)		0.250 (0.039)		0.231 (0.029)
σ_2		0.081 (0.254)		0.453 (0.700)		0.096 (0.297)
SSE	47,557	47,196	17,138	16,926	26,588	26,328
$\overline{SSE}$	1056	1048	613	605	1499	1485
Parameters	**OTM**		**ATM**		**ITM**	
	BS	Hybrid	BS	Hybrid	BS	Hybrid
σ	0.216 (0.026)		0.247 (0.033)		0.298 (0.053)	
σ_1		0.215 (0.027)		0.243 (0.036)		0.251 (0.049)
σ_2		0.089 (0.277)		0.534 (0.942)		2.459 (1.479)
SSE	1672	1600	2263	2168	14,406	8307
$\overline{SSE}$	59	56	275	264	1379	836

[a] σ denotes the volatility of the BS model.

money options are relatively long maturities.

4.4. Out-of-Sample Performance

We have shown that the in-sample fit of the hybrid model is generally better than that of the BS model. However we could think that the improvement of the performance might be due to increase of number of the parameters. To deal with this concern, we next examine pricing performance of each model in the out-of-sample. In each day in October 2010, we first estimate the required parameters using the previous day's option prices by the same method used in the in-sample fit, and then we use them as inputs to compute current day's model-based option prices. We measure the performance of each model by calculating the residual sum of squares.

Our result is shown in **Table 2**. Generally the hybrid model is slightly better than the BS model. Among others, the hybrid model of options in-the-money outperforms the BS model obviously. This might be due to the same reason as the results of the in-sample test since almost all the options in-the-money belong to the short-term category. However, since σ_2 changes significantly in day-to-day trading, the estimations may over-fit the prices of next day. Especially, both prices of the short-term options and those of at-the-money are affected by the most recent market changes. This may cause the performance of the hybrid model not to be better than expected.

5. Conclusions

In this paper we have made an empirical test of option pricing under the hybrid Brownian motion model introduced by [1]. In a specific case of parameters of the model, the variance grows exponentially and shows a fat-tailed property as time passes. These features of the model reflect the real market movements especially in some situations like financial crisis or some event driven by fluctuation. We have fitted the model to Japanese stock market. We have also implemented the performance comparison between the hybrid model and the BS model in two aspects as in-sample parameter estimation and out-of-sample pricing prediction.

Our empirical evidence indicates that generally the hybrid model is slightly better than the BS model. Since the actual pricing of options in the market is based on the

Table 2. Out-of-sample pricing errors.

	All Options		Short-term		Medium-term	
	BS	Hybrid	BS	Hybrid	BS	Hybrid
SSE	58,292	58,246	20,565	20,583	33,870	33,774
$\overline{SSE}$	1297	1296	733	733	1935	1932
	OTM		ATM		ITM	
	BS	Hybrid	BS	Hybrid	BS	Hybrid
SSE	3646	3638	4928	4962	32,995	25,793
$\overline{SSE}$	128	127	627	632	3082	2468

BS model, it is reasonable that the BS model fits the market data moderately. So it might be difficult to dominate the BS model remarkably. But if we can improve the algorithm of pricing method under the hybrid model, it might be possible to get better results. Furthermore, although we have made an empirical test using a special case of the hybrid model explained in Section 2.2 for the computational convenience, we might try to make similar tests using the general model of the hybrid Brownian motion in the near future.

6. Acknowledgements

Hideki Iwaki is supported in part by Grant-in-Aid for Scientific Research (C) No. 22530310, Japan Society for the Promotion of Science.

REFERENCES

[1] W. T. Shaw and M. Schofield, "A Model of Returns for the Post-credit-crunch Reality: Hybrid Brownian Motion with Price Feedback," *Quantitative Finance*, 2012, pp. 1-24.

[2] B. Mandelbrot, "The Variation of Certain Speculative Prices," *Journal of Business*, Vol. 36, No. 4, 1963, pp. 394-419.

[3] E. F. Fama, "The Behavior of Stock-market Prices," *Journal of Business*, Vol. 38, No. 1, 1965, pp. 34-105.

[4] R. C. Blattberg and H. J. Gonedes, "A Comparison of the Stable and Student Distributions as Statistical Models for Stock Prices," *Journal of Business*, Vol. 47, No. 2, 1974, pp. 244-280.

[5] K. Aas and I. H. Haff, "The Generalized Hyperbolic Skew Student T-distribution," *Journal of Financial Econometrics*, Vol. 4, No. 2, 2006, pp. 275-309.

[6] Y. Nagahara, "Non-Gaussian Distribution for Stock Returns and Related Stochastic Differential Equation," *Asia-Pacific Financial Markets*, Vol. 3, 1996, pp. 121-149.

[7] M. Rubinstein, "Nonparametric Tests of Alternative Option Pricing Models Using All Reported Trades and Quotes on the 30 Most Active CBOE Options Classes from August 23, 1976 through August 31, 1978," *Journal of Finance*, Vol. 40, No. 2, 1985, pp. 455-480.

[8] J. Hull and A. White, "The Pricing of Options on Assets with Stochastic Volatilities," *Journal of Finance*, Vol. 42, No. 2, 1987, pp. 281-300.

[9] S. Heston, "A Closed-Form Solution for Options with Stochastic Volatility with Applications to Bond and Currency Options," *Review of Financial Studies*, Vol. 6, No. 2, 1993, pp. 327-343.

[10] G. Bakshi, C. Cao and Z. Chen, "Empirical Performance of Alternative Option Pricing Models," *Journal of Finance*, Vol. 52, No. 5, 1997, pp. 2003-2049.

[11] B. Dupire, "Pricing with a Smile," *Risk*, Vol. 7, 1994, pp. 18-20.

4

How Do Principal-Agent Effects in Delegated Portfolio Management Affect Asset Prices?

Petter N. Kolm
Courant Institute of Mathematical Sciences, New York University, New York, USA

ABSTRACT

We investigate the impact of delegated portfolio management on asset prices in a noisy rational equilibrium model. Asset prices in our model are linear in fund managers' private signals and in realized supply shocks. We show that equilibrium expected returns 1) decrease as the proportion of fund managers increase in the economy; 2) decrease as the precision of fund managers' signals increase' and 3) increase as the fund managers' contingent fees increase.

Keywords: Delegated Portfolio Management; Portfolio Choice; Asset Pricing; Noisy Rational Expectations Equilibrium

1. Introduction

Today, most investors delegate their investment decisions to financial professionals. For example, equity holdings through delegated management (such as pension funds and mutual funds) in the US market have increased from 7.2 percent in 1950 to more than 49 percent in 2002, whereas the proportion held directly by individuals has decreased from about 90 percent to slightly below 40 percent over the same period [1].

In his presidential address, Allen [2] provides reasons why investors delegate the portfolio decision process: 1) professional investment analysis possesses economies of scale; 2) investors may recognize their own limited knowledge and capacity for information dissemination/processing and therefore hire a professional manager; and 3) a professional manager might be able to steer free from the behavioral biases that individual investors otherwise have been shown to be susceptible to.

However, financial institutions and professional fund managers are influenced by incentives that are not fully captured by standard models in finance[1,2]. Therefore, the significant increase of ownership of equities under delegated management raises the question: how does this form of ownership affect asset prices?

In behavioral models of asset pricing, people have nonstandard preferences and/or form beliefs that are not based on rational information processing[3]. However, by turning to professional managers an investor faces an agency problem. Delegated investing implies that relative asset prices depend on the utility functions of agents, not the utility functions of investors. Because of asymmetric information and different incentives present in delegated decision making, the utility functions of agents are different from the ones of consumers.

There are several differences between the delegated portfolio management problem considered here and the standard agency problem: 1) the delegated portfolio management problem is one of *information acquisition* rather than direct performance. Consequently, in the delegated portfolio management problem the fund manager exerts effort to obtain a private (noisy) signal, and thereafter makes portfolio decisions based on the signal received. 2) Contrary to a typical agency problem where the agent *only* chooses whether or not to take action and *cannot* influence the size/strength of his response, the fund manager has full discretion in his portfolio decisions and controls both return and variance of the portfolio.

The dominant portion of the theoretical literature in

[1]See, for example, [3].

[2]We note that most mutual fund shareholders own their funds through financial intermediaries such as a professional financial advisor, defined contribution retirement plan, brokerage firm, banks, insurance company or mutual fund supermarket. The mutual fund holdings of individuals that are held *directly* with the fund company have decreased from 28 percent in 1982 to about 15 percent in 2003 (see, [4]). However, this "double" or "nested" agency situation is outside the scope of this paper.

[3]For a survey of behavioral finance, see [5].

delegated management focuses on partial equilibrium settings represented by a game between an investor (principal) and a portfolio manager (agent) where asset prices and returns are taken as given. However, an important aspect of delegated portfolio management concerns the impact of this agency relationship on asset prices. Indeed, the type of compensation contracts or incentives agreed upon between investor and manager influence the equilibrium at the aggregate level. For example, if fund managers underperform relative to their peer group (or some other benchmark) investors may transfer their capital to a better performing fund (fund chasing). This mechanism typically results in fund managers being afraid of taking too much risk relative to the peer group. They may end up investing in similar stocks to their peers; driving up the prices of these "peer group popular" stocks and driving down the prices of "peer group unpopular" stocks. These types of effects have been studied to some extent in the literature, see for example, [6-14].

This paper studies how delegated portfolio management affects asset prices. Our model is inspired by the single-security *noisy rational expectations equilibrium* of [15-17]. It is also related to the models of [18,19].

The outline of this paper is as follows. In section 2, we introduce a simple economy with two risky assets and a risk-free bond with two types of agents, fund managers and investors, both with CARA preferences – but with different final wealth. Fund managers receive a private noisy signal about future payoffs of the risky assets whereas investors only have access to the public information and information revealed from asset prices in equilibrium. Then, in Sections 3 and 4, we derive the portfolio decisions and demand functions for each agent, and show that the noisy rational expectation equilibrium exists where asset prices are linear in fund managers' signals and in realized supply shocks. We discuss the impact of delegated portfolio management on the equilibrium risk premiums and on the cross-section of returns. Section 5 concludes and provides possible extensions of this model.

2. Model

The noisy rational expectations framework of [15-17] inspires our model. This framework centers on the idea that uninformed agents use the equilibrium asset price as an informative signal about asset returns and extract some of the information that the informed agents possess.

2.1. Economy and Preferences

We consider a two period model where market participants choose their portfolio allocation "today" ($t = 0$) and assets are liquidated and paid off "tomorrow" ($t = 1$). The economy consists of a continuum of two groups of agents: investors and fund managers. Investors endowed with an initial wealth of W_0 can choose either to manage their portfolio themselves or delegate the investment decision to a fund manager. Fund managers have no independent wealth and are not allowed to borrow. We assume there are as many fund managers as there are delegating investors and that each delegating investor is matched with one fund. After investors make the decision to self-manage or to delegate, the proportion of fund managers and self-managing investors are μ and $1-\mu$, respectively. We will refer to these two groups as the "fund managers" and the "investors"; and we use superscript M for fund managers and I for investors to distinguish functions and variables that are specific to these two groups.

We assume all agents in our model have CARA preferences with risk aversion parameter ρ, so that the expected utility of a final payoff of W becomes

$$E\left(u(W)\right) = E\left(-\exp(-\rho W)\right).$$

2.2. Asset Structure

There are three assets in the economy, a risk-free bond and two risky assets. The bond, normalized to have a price of 1 at $t = 0$, yields a certain gross return of R at $t = 1$ and has perfect elastic supply. The two risky assets have a price at $t = 0$ of p_i with independent random payoffs at $t = 1$ of p_i with mean $\bar{P}_i$ and precision γ_{P_i}; that is

$$P_i \sim N\left(\bar{P}_i, \gamma_{P_i}^{-1}\right)$$

where $i = 1, 2$[4]. We assume that markets clear. Then, as we will see, the prices today of the risky assets can be determined endogenously. The per capita supplies of the risky assets are independent and normally distributed,

$$X_i \sim N\left(\bar{X}_i, \gamma_{X_i}^{-1}\right)$$

where $\bar{X}_i > 0$. The supply is never observed, but agents who possess information, as defined below, can back it out from equilibrium prices. We interpret this random supply as the presence of noise traders in the economy and remark that 1) the role of random supply shocks is to prevent information from being fully revealing to uninformed agents; and 2) a positive expected per capita supply implies that in equilibrium, some agents will hold the risky assets.

2.3. Information Structure

[4]In our setup rational expectations equilibrium prices of risky assets are independent of each other, and no cross-security information aggregation is present. In other words, there is no difference between single-security equilibrium prices (as in [16]), and the multi-security equilibrium prices (as in [20]). In future work we intend to generalize this model. We provide a discussion of these extensions in Section 5.

All agents in our economy have a common prior distribution of the final payoffs of the risky assets. However, at t=0 fund managers obtain independent and normally distributed private signals for each asset[5]

$$S_i = P_i + \varepsilon_i$$

where

$$\varepsilon_i \sim N\left(0, \gamma_{S_i}^{-1}\right).$$

this signal is unobservable to investors. They know only that fund managers have superior information in terms of them receiving a normally distributed signal on each risky asset in the economy.

2.4. Fund Manager Compensation.

Fund managers' final wealth depends on their compensation. Today, the most common compensation of professional managers is a fixed percentage of the portfolio value. For example, fees earned by mutual fund managers are proportional to assets under management[6]. For hedge funds, it is more common that compensation schemes reward managers by the portfolio's total return in absolute terms or relative to a particular benchmark. The compensation may also feature a floor or a cap, often based on the value of assets under management[7].

In this paper we use the linear compensation contract defined by a pair (f, k), where f is the fixed fee paid to the fund manager regardless of portfolio performance and k, $0 \le k \le 1$, the fraction of the final portfolio value paid to the fund manager[8]. We will refer to the fraction k as the "contingent fee." In other words, if W is the final portfolio value then the linear contract implies a compensation to the fund manager of

$$W^M = f + kW .$$

Consequently, the final wealth of the delegating investor becomes

$$W^{DI} = (1-k)W - f .$$

3. Portfolio Choice

Given the model set up described in the previous section, next we determine agents' demand functions and then solve for equilibrium.

We denote by $\lambda^a = \left(\lambda_b^a, \lambda_1^a, \lambda_2^a\right)$, $a = I, M$, the demands of an agent a, where λ_b^a and $\left(\lambda_1^a, \lambda_2^a\right)$ are his allocations to the risk-free bond and the two risky assets, respectively. Since asset returns and payoffs in our model are normally distributed, the expected utility for agent a with a final payoff of W^a can be expressed as

$$E\left(W^a \middle| I^a\right) - \rho \mathrm{Var}\left(W^a \middle| I^a\right).$$

The budget constraint for self managing investors is

$$W_0 = \lambda_b^I + \lambda_1^I p_1 + \lambda_2^I p_2 ,$$

and their final payoff is the random variable

$$W^I = \lambda_b^I R + \lambda_1^I P_1 + \lambda_2^I P_2 .$$

Substituting the budget constraint into investors' final payoff gives

$$W^I = W_o R + \lambda_1^I \left(P_1 - Rp_1\right) + \lambda_2^I \left(P_2 - Rp_2\right).$$

Similarly, fund managers' final payoff becomes

$$W^M = f + k\left(W_o R + \lambda_1^M \left(P_1 - Rp_1\right) + \lambda_2^M \left(P_2 - Rp_2\right)\right).$$

3.1. Fund Manager Demand

Maximizing the expected utility of the fund managers' final payoff, their demand functions become

$$\lambda_i^M = \frac{E\left(P_i \middle| s_i\right) - Rp_i}{k\rho \mathrm{Var}\left(P_i \middle| s_i\right)} .$$

Calculating the conditional expectation and variance by Bayes' rule, we obtain

$$E\left(P_i \middle| s_i\right) = \frac{\overline{P}_i \gamma_{P_i} + s_i \gamma_{S_i}}{\gamma_{P_i} + \gamma_{S_i}},$$

and

$$\mathrm{Var}\left(P_i \middle| s_i\right) = \left(\gamma_{P_i} + \gamma_{S_i}\right)^{-1} .$$

After substituting these expressions into the fund managers demand function, we get

$$\lambda_i^M = \frac{P_i \gamma_{P_i} + s_i \gamma_{S_i} - Rp_i \left(\gamma_{P_i} + \gamma_{S_i}\right)}{k\rho} .$$

We observe that the fund managers' demand increases when the contingent fee k (the proportion of final portfolio value received by fund managers as compensation)

[5] We ignore any costs for the informative signals in this paper. Nevertheless, introducing a convex cost does not significantly change our results.

[6] According to [21] only about 1.7 percent of US mutual funds used fulcrum fees in 1999. Reference [22] identified fulcrum fees in only 27 of 370 funds studied; the remaining funds charged a fixed fraction of assets under management.

[7] By the 1970 amendment to the Investment Company Act of 1940, mutual funds must use a form of incentive fee known as a ''fulcrum fee.'' The (symmetric) incentive fee centers around a benchmark, increases the fees for performance above the benchmark, and decreases the fees for performance below the benchmark. In practice, the size of the incentive fees has a floor and cap. In contrast, the (asymmetric) incentive fee structure used by hedge funds and other private partnerships is typically non-negative, has a high watermark, uses zero (or cash) as a reference benchmark, and does not have a cap.

[8] For expositional simplicity, we assume that the contract has been chosen such that the fund managers' participation constraint (e.g. a constraint of the form $E\left(u\left(W^M\right)\right) \ge u_o \ge 0$) is satisfied. We do this to avoid having to distinguish between the two different cases of the Karush-Kuhn-Tucker conditions in which the constraint is either binding or non-binding at the optimum.

decreases. Intuitively, the contingent fee changes fund managers' risk aversion from ρ to $k \cdot \rho$, and thus fund managers are expected to trade more aggressively when their contingent compensation is smaller. The fund manager demand function also captures the case when fund managers do not receive signals; setting $\gamma_{S_i} \equiv 0$ in the expression above yields

$$\lambda_i^M = \frac{\left(\bar{P}_i - Rp_i\right)\gamma_{P_i}}{k\rho}.$$

3.2. Investor Demand

Similar to fund managers, investors' demand functions take the form

$$\lambda_i^I = \frac{E\left(P_i | I^I\right) - Rp_i}{\rho \mathrm{Var}\left(P_i | I^I\right)}$$

where I^I denotes the information set available to investors. While investors do not observe the private signals available to fund managers, they condition upon that in equilibrium market prices convey information. With the knowledge that fund managers have private signals and their associated distributions, investors rationally infer how these signals will affect the demands of the fund managers and consequently also equilibrium prices. In order to learn from prices, the investors must conjecture a price function and, in the rational expectations equilibrium, this conjecture must be correct. We assume investors conjecture the linear price function

$$p_i = a_i \bar{P}_i + b_i s_i - c_i x_i + d_i \bar{X}_i$$

where s_i and x_i are the signal and the supply for assets *i*, and the coefficients a_i, b_i, c_i and d_i are determined in equilibrium[9].

To calculate the expectation and the variance conditional on the conjectured price, we first introduce the random variable Z_i defined by

$$Z_i = \frac{p_i - a_i \bar{P}_i + \bar{X}_i\left(c_i - d_i\right)}{b_i} = s_i - \frac{c_i}{b_i}\left(x_i - \bar{X}_i\right).$$

Since the only uncertainty in this random variable stems from p_i, we note that conditioning on Z_i is equivalent to conditioning on the price conjecture. We observe that

$$Z_i \sim N\left(P_i, \gamma_{Z_i}^{-1}\right)$$

where

$$\gamma_{Z_i}^{-1} = \gamma_{S_i}^{-1} + \left(\frac{c_i}{b_i}\right)^2 \gamma_{X_i}^{-1},$$

and therefore by Bayes' rule

[9]A direct application of the standard noisy rational expectations equilibrium framework of [16] and [15] proves the existence of this linear price function.

$$E\left(P_i | Z_i\right) = \frac{\bar{P}_i \gamma_{P_i} + Z_i \gamma_{Z_i}}{\gamma_{P_i} + \gamma_{Z_i}},$$

and

$$\mathrm{Var}\left(P_i | Z_i\right) = \left(\gamma_{P_i} + \gamma_{Z_i}\right)^{-1}.$$

Substituting this into the investors' demand functions yields

$$\lambda_i^I = \frac{\bar{P}_i \gamma_{P_i} + Z_i \gamma_{Z_i} - Rp_i\left(\gamma_{P_i} + \gamma_{Z_i}\right)}{\rho}.$$

4. Equilibrium Prices and Demands

Here, we establish equilibrium prices for our model and derive some implications of such prices. In particular, we discuss how the delegated portfolio management industry affects the equity premium and the cross-section of returns. We also look at how changes in the economic environment and the information structure impact investor and fund manager demands. We start with our main result in this section, Proposition 1.

Proposition 1: Given the three asset economy described above with a fraction of μ fund managers under contract (*f*, *k*) and a fraction of 1-μ investors, then there exists a noisy rational expectations equilibrium at time $t = 0$ such that asset prices are given by

$$p_i = a_i \bar{P}_i + b_i s_i - c_i x_i + d_i \bar{X}_i$$

where $i = 1,2$ and

$$a_i = \frac{\gamma_{P_i}\left(\mu + k(1-\mu)\right)}{h_i}$$

$$b_i = \frac{\gamma_{S_i} + k(1-\mu)\gamma_{Z_i}}{h_i}$$

$$c_i = \frac{\rho k\left(1 + \frac{k(1-\mu)\gamma_{Z_i}}{\mu \gamma_{S_i}}\right)}{h_i}$$

$$d_i = \frac{\rho k^2 (1-\mu)\gamma_{Z_i}}{\mu \gamma_{S_i} h_i}$$

$$h_i = R\left(\mu\left(\gamma_{P_i} + \gamma_{S_i}\right) + k(1-\mu)\left(\gamma_{P_i} + \gamma_{Z_i}\right)\right)$$

Finally, the precision of Z_i is

$$\gamma_{Z_i}^{-1} = \frac{1}{\gamma_{S_i}^{-1} + \left(\frac{k\rho}{\mu \gamma_{S_i}}\right)^2 \gamma_{X_i}^{-1}}.$$

Proof: First, we note that market clearing implies that

$$\mu \lambda_i^M + (1-\mu)\lambda_i^I = x_i.$$

Substituting fund managers' and investors' demand functions, we obtain

$$\mu\frac{\bar{P}_i\gamma_{P_i}+s_i\gamma_{S_i}-Rp_i\left(\gamma_{P_i}+\gamma_{S_i}\right)}{k\rho}$$
$$+(1-\mu)\frac{\bar{P}_i\gamma_{P_i}+Z_i\gamma_{Z_i}-Rp_i\left(\gamma_{P_i}+\gamma_{Z_i}\right)}{\rho}=x_i$$

Substituting

$$Z_i=s_i-\frac{c_i}{b_i}\left(x_i-\bar{X}_i\right)$$

and solving for p_i yields

$$p_i=h_i^{-1}\left\{\left\{\bar{P}_i\gamma_{P_i}\left(\mu+k(1-\mu)\right)+s_i\left(\mu\gamma_{S_i}+k(1-\mu)\gamma_{Z_i}\right)\right.\right.$$
$$\left.-x_i\left(k\rho+k(1-\mu)\gamma_{Z_i}\frac{c_i}{b_i}+s_i\gamma_{S_i}\right)+\bar{X}_i\left(k(1-\mu)\gamma_{Z_i}\frac{c_i}{b_i}\right)\right\}$$

We observe it must hold that

$$\frac{c_i}{b_i}=\frac{k\rho+k(1-\mu)\gamma_{Z_i}\frac{c_i}{b_i}}{\mu\gamma_{S_i}+k(1-\mu)\gamma_{Z_i}},$$

from which it follows that

$$k\rho=\mu\gamma_{S_i}\frac{c_i}{b_i}.$$

Therefore,

$$\frac{c_i}{b_i}=\frac{k\rho}{\mu\gamma_{S_i}}$$

and

$$\gamma_{Z_i}^{-1}=\gamma_{S_i}^{-1}+\left(\frac{k\rho}{\mu\gamma_{S_i}}\right)^2\gamma_{X_i}^{-1}$$

The proposition now immediately follows.

The next proposition summarizes some properties of the equilibrium prices established in Proposition 1.

Proposition 2: The equilibrium expected return on the risky assets are given by

$$E\left(P_i-Rp_i\right)=\frac{\rho k\bar{X}_i}{\mu\left(\gamma_{P_i}+\gamma_{S_i}\right)+k(1-\mu)\left(\gamma_{P_i}+\gamma_{Z_i}\right)}.$$

Furthermore, we have that

1) Equilibrium expected returns are decreasing functions in the proportion of fund managers μ in the economy, that is

$$\frac{\partial E\left(P_i-Rp_i\right)}{\partial\mu}<0;$$

2) Equilibrium expected returns are increasing functions in the risk aversion parameter ρ, that is

$$\frac{\partial E\left(P_i-Rp_i\right)}{\partial\rho}>0;$$

3) Equilibrium expected returns are decreasing functions in the precision γ_{S_i} of the fund managers' signal, that is

$$\frac{\partial E\left(P_i-Rp_i\right)}{\partial\gamma_{S_i}}<0;$$

4) Equilibrium expected returns are decreasing functions in the precision γ_{P_i} of the assets' payoff, that is

$$\frac{\partial E\left(P_i-Rp_i\right)}{\partial\gamma_{P_i}}<0;$$

5) Equilibrium expected returns are increasing functions in the fraction k of the final portfolio value paid to the fund manager, that is

$$\frac{\partial E\left(P_i-Rp_i\right)}{\partial k}>0;$$

and

6) Equilibrium expected returns are not affected by changes in the precision γ_{X_i} of the assets' supply, that is

$$\frac{\partial E\left(P_i-Rp_i\right)}{\partial\gamma_{X_i}}=0.$$

Proof: Using equilibrium prices from Proposition 1, we have

$$E\left(P_i-Rp_i\right)=\bar{P}_i\left(1-Ra_i-Rb_i\right)+R\bar{X}_i\left(c_i-d_i\right)$$
$$=R\frac{\rho k\bar{X}_i}{h_i}$$

since

$$c_i-d_i=\frac{\rho k}{h_i}$$

and

$$1-Ra_i-Rb_i=0.$$

The proofs of (a)-(f) are similar. Here we show (a): It's easy to see that $\gamma_{Z_i}<\gamma_{S_i}$ for all admissible values of k and μ. In other words, the precision of the signals investors infer are always smaller than the signals fund managers receive. Consequently,

$$k\left(\gamma_{P_i}+\gamma_{Z_i}\right)<\gamma_{P_i}+\gamma_{S_i}.$$

We emphasize that Proposition 2 implies a positive risk premium for the risky assets. In particular, since these assets are risky, agents demand compensation for holding them in equilibrium. The risk premium decreases as the fraction of fund managers increases (part (a)) because fund managers are more informed and their information is partly revealed in equilibrium.

Jagannathan, McGrattan and Scherbina [23] show that the equity premium has declined significantly since the 1970s. They estimate the premium averaged around 7 percent during the period 1926-70 and thereafter decreased to about 0.7 percent. The authors argue that it is difficult to rationalize a shrinking equity premium by a permanent shift in investor preferences. Instead, they suggest that institutional changes occurred in the US stock market that causes a permanent shift in stock returns. Fama and French [24] reach similar conclusions. Through a dividend growth model, they show that the equity premium has shrunk from about 4.17 percent during the period 1872-1950, to about 2.55 percent for the half-century 1951-2000. We understand these views as consistent since delegated management in the US market increased from 7.2 percent in 1950 to more than 49 percent in 2002. At the same time, the proportion of investments held directly by individuals decreased from about 90 percent to slightly below 40 percent [1].

Proposition 2 also holds implications for the cross-section of returns. In particular, all else equal, the equilibrium risk premium is higher for the asset where the precision of fund managers' *signals* is lower (part (c)) or where *fund investment* is lower (part (a)). This can be interpreted in several different ways. For example, the largest fund managers tend to focus their research on the subset of stocks where capacity and liquidity are sufficiently high (typically, large-cap stocks) thereby being able to acquire more precise signals for these stocks.

The results from Proposition 2 are consistent with the empirical findings of [25] who argue that the demand pressure for risky assets (in particular large-cap stocks) is a direct consequence of the growth of institutional investors. They also show from their data that the last decade's decrease in the small-cap premium is due to the same effect. Lakonishok, Shleifer and Vishny [3] suggest that pension fund managers are biased towards "glamour" stocks, that is, stocks that are easy to justify buying. Glamour stocks with proven track records of consistent earnings growth may attract investors because nobody would doubt them as "good" companies. In our model, we can loosely interpret glamour stocks as assets where fund managers' signals and assets' payoffs have higher precision. They suggest further that the increased demand for equity by institutions and unsophisticated individuals who equate profitability with potential capital gains have made these stocks overpriced. In our simple set up, we can derive the following relationship between fund manager and investor demands:

Proposition 3: Suppose λ_i^M and λ_i^I denote fund manager and investor demands for asset i as derived above. Then, the average difference in demand is positive and given by

$$E\left(\lambda_i^M-\lambda_i^I\right)=\frac{\overline{X}_i\left(\gamma_{P_i}+\gamma_{S_i}-k\left(\gamma_{P_i}+\gamma_{Z_i}\right)\right)}{\mu\left(\gamma_{P_i}+\gamma_{S_i}\right)+k(1-\mu)\left(\gamma_{P_i}+\gamma_{Z_i}\right)}.$$

Proof: Direct calculation shows that

$$E\left(\lambda_i^M-\lambda_i^I\right)=\frac{1}{k\rho}\left\{\overline{P}_i\left(\gamma_{P_i}+\gamma_{Z_i}-k\left(\gamma_{P_i}+\gamma_{Z_i}\right)\right)-Rp_i\left(\gamma_{P_i}+\gamma_{S_i}-k\left(\gamma_{P_i}+\gamma_{Z_i}\right)\right)\right\}.$$

Using the equilibrium price from Proposition 1, we have

$$E\left(Rp_i\right)=R\left(\left(a_i+b_i\right)\overline{P}_i+\overline{X}_i\left(d_i-c_i\right)\right).$$

Now, observing that

$$a_i+b_i=\frac{1}{R}$$

and

$$d_i-c_i=-\frac{\rho k}{h_i}$$

the proposition follows.

We note the average difference in demand between fund managers and investors is a decreasing function in the fraction μ of fund managers in the economy and fund managers' contingent fee k. In particular, this difference decreases from

$$\frac{\overline{X}_i}{\mu}\ (\text{for } k=0)$$

to

$$\frac{\overline{X}_i\left(\gamma_{S_i}+\gamma_{Z_i}\right)}{\mu\left(\gamma_{S_i}+\gamma_{Z_i}\right)+\gamma_{P_i}+\gamma_{Z_i}}\quad(\text{for } k=1).$$

the high fund manager demand for low compensation levels (small k) raises the question of leverage. From the perspective of an investor in a fund, it makes sense to impose some form of leverage constraints. We note that, in practice, mutual funds are subject to short selling and borrowing/margin constraints that naturally limit fund manager demand.

In this model, demand differences occur because fund managers and investors do not have the same beliefs about assets' expected return and variance. In contrast, in the incomplete market model of [26], different demands arise because not all agents are aware of all assets in the economy. Here, both fund managers and investors hold the same assets and thus bear idiosyncratic risk, but choose to do so in different proportions. If we take into consideration that fund managers will overweight stocks with "good" prospects and underweight them with "bad" prospects, then since the investors will hold the remainder, they will end up underweighting "good" stocks and overweighting "bad" stocks.

5. Conclusions and Extensions

The model presented in this paper is inspired by the single-security noisy rational expectations equilibrium of [15-17]. It is also related to [18,19]. Our main contribution is in using a noisy rational expectations equilibrium framework to study the impact of delegated portfolio management on asset prices.

Using an exponential-normal set up, we modeled a simple economy consisting of two types of agents, fund managers and investors. Fund managers were assumed to receive a private noisy signal about future payoffs of the risky assets, whereas investors only have access to the public information and information revealed from asset prices in equilibrium. Our main findings are as follows:

1) We proved that a partially revealing equilibrium exists where asset prices are linear in fund manager signals and in realized supply shocks.

2) Studying the impact on equilibrium expected returns from delegated portfolio management, we showed that these risk premiums: a) decrease as the proportion of fund managers increase in the economy; b) decrease as the precision of fund managers' signals increase; and c) increase as the fund managers' contingent fees (the fraction of the final portfolio value paid to the fund manager as compensation) increase.

3) The result under 2) b) has some implications for the cross-section of returns. All else being equal, the equilibrium risk premium is higher for assets where the precision of fund managers' signals is lower. This we can interpret, for example, in the following way: when the largest fund managers focus their research on the subset of stocks where capacity and liquidity are sufficiently high (typically, large-cap stocks) they acquire more precise signals for these stocks. Through their higher demand in these assets, asset prices increase thereby decreasing future returns.

4) Due to asymmetric information, fund managers and investors hold the same stocks, but with different exposure to idiosyncratic risk. In particular, the average difference in fund manager and investor demands for a particular asset is positive, and is a decreasing function in the fraction of fund managers in the economy and the fund managers' contingent fee.

In closing, we discuss several possible extensions.

5.1. Distributional Assumptions

In our framework we assumed that payoffs of the risky assets and fund managers' signals are independent and identically distributed—that is, all risk is idiosyncratic. A natural extension is to introduce correlations between assets and between signals. There are several directions in which this can be done. Following [20], one can assume that asset payoffs are distributed normally and satisfy a general variance-covariance matrix and that private signals are simply risky asset payoffs plus noise. One can then proceed as proposed in [27] by positing a factor model setting where noisy signals are available to fund managers for these systematic factors. Unfortunately, these two frameworks allow for explicit closed form solutions for equilibrium prices only in special cases.

One way to proceed is to use a set up like the working paper of [28]. They investigate the effects of private information and diversification on risk premiums in a noisy rational expectations model where payoffs of the risky assets obey a factor structure and private signals, These provide information on both systematic factors and idiosyncratic risks. One obtains solutions for equilibrium prices in this multi-asset exponential-normal framework.

5.2. Finite and Infinite Asset Economies

Under homogeneous beliefs/information the implications of risk premiums are known from arbitrage pricing theory (APT). Under asymmetric information, the impact of private signals on risk premiums in large economies are less understood. Delegated portfolio management provides a natural mechanism with which fund managers incorporate private signals into the economy. It may be of interest to study an extension of the factor model discussed in the previous paragraph where the number of assets approaches infinity. Then one might determine the conditions that lead to linear pricing relationships.

5.3. Investment Decisions

In our simple model we made the assumption that investors decide either to delegate or self-manage their portfolio. In practice, this is an unrealistic assumption. Investors typically hold a proportion of their investments in delegated mutual funds and another in self-managed stocks.

5.4. Heterogeneity

For simplicity, we have assumed all agents are homogeneous and thus have identical risk aversion. Preliminary results, not reported here, show the basic results from this model carry over to a heterogeneous economy.

5.5. Participation, Short Selling and Borrowing/Margin Constraints

We assumed that fund managers' participation constraints are satisfied. As observed in Sections 3 and 4, fund manager demand increases as the contingent compensation k decreases. To keep their risk exposure constant as contingent compensation decreases, fund managers will increase their leverage. Since most funds (for example, mutual funds) are subject to short selling and borrowing/margin constraints, incorporating these in a model (to limit fund manager demand) seems a natural extension. However, these constraints lead to nonlinear equilibrium prices that must be solved by numerical techniques (see, for example, the noisy rational expectations model in [29]).

5.6. Information Costs and the Size of the Delegated Portfolio Management Business

Precise information comes at a cost. A natural extension is first to model the cost of information acquisition in our model and endogenize this decision by solving for the optimal signal acquiring strategy as a function of contingent fees and other parameters (for the single risky asset case, see for example, [17]). Next, one might solve for the fraction of fund managers in the economy endogenously.

This would be particularly interesting in a multi-asset economy—where assets and signals are correlated—in which information is more expensive for certain types of assets, and could produce new understandings of delegated portfolio management on the cross-section of returns. This might also provide a greater comprehension of why so many different mutual funds and mutual fund families are available in the marketplace. In a setting of this type, we might even examine the relationship between fund specialization and contingent fees.

5.7. Incomplete Market Economies

It may also be interesting to study a multi-security model with uninformed (or irrational) investors and rational fund managers. Uninformed investors consider a small part of the investable universe in the sense of [26], and calculate their demands conditional on the prices they observe *only* on these assets. Fund managers, on the other hand, condition on all available assets and therefore benefit from cross-security aggregation. This model would exploit the differences between multi-security equilibrium prices, obtained along the lines of [20] and single-security equilibrium prices derived in this paper.

5.8. Sharing of Information

We observe in the marketplace that many larger mutual fund companies offer a whole menu of mutual funds in different flavors. In order to better understand the relationship between mutual funds in a fund family, one must model how they share information: 1) in which cases do fund managers share information; 2) do they collude in determining management fees; and 3) what is the optimal equilibrium relationship between contingent fees and the size of mutual fund families?

REFERENCES

[1] NYSE, "Institutional Investors," Factbook, New York Stock Exchange, New York, 2003.

[2] F. Allen, "Do Financial Institutions Matter?" *Journal of Finance*, Vol. 56, No. 4, 2001, pp. 1165-1175.

[3] J. Lakonishok, A. Shleifer and R. W. Vishny, "The Structure and Performance of the Money Management Industry," *Microeconomics*, Vol. 1992, 1992, pp. 339-391.

[4] Investment Company Institute, "Ownership of Mutual Funds through Professional Financial Advisers," *Research Fundamentals*, Vol. 14, No. 3, 2005.

[5] N. Barberis and R. Thaler, "A Survey of Behavioral Finance," In: G. M. Constantinides, M. Harris and R. M. Stulz, Eds., *Handbook of the Economics of Finance*, Elsevier Science, Oxford, 2004, pp. 1051-1121.

[6] D. S. Scharfstein and J. C. Stein, "Herd Behaviour and Investment," *American Economic Review*, Vol. 80, No. 3, 1980, pp. 465-479.

[7] D. W. Diamond and R. E. Verrecchia, "Optimal Managerial Contracts and Equilibrium Security Prices," *Journal of Finance*, Vol. 37, No. 2, 1982, pp. 275-287.

[8] R. T. Ramakrishnan and A. V. Thakor, "Moral Hazard, Agency Costs, and Asset Prices in a Competitive Equilibrium," *Journal of Financial and Quantitative Analysis*, Vol. 17, No. 4, 1982, pp. 503-532.

[9] R. T. Ramakrishnan and A. V. Thakor, "The Valuation of Assets under Moral Hazard," *Journal of Finance*, Vol. 39, No. 1, 1984, pp. 229-238.

[10] N. Arora and H. Ou-Yang, "Explicit and Implicit Incentives in a Delegated Portfolio Management Problem: Theory and Evidence," Unpublished, 2001.

[11] E. Goldman and S. L. Slezak, "Delegated Portfolio Management and Rational Prolonged Mispricing," *Journal of Finance*, Vol. 58, No. 1, 2003, pp. 283-311.

[12] H. Ou-Yang, "Optimal Contracts in a Continuous-Time Delegated Portfolio Management Problem," *Review of Financial Studies*, Vol. 16, No. 1, 2003, pp. 173-208.

[13] B. Cornell and R. Roll, "A Delegated-Agent Asset-Pricing Model," *Financial Analysts Journal*, Vol. 61, No. 1, 2005, pp. 57-69.

[14] S. A. Ross, "Markets for Agents: Fund Management," In: B. N. Lehmann, Ed., *Legacy of Fischer Black*, University Press, Oxford 2005, pp. 96-124.

[15] S. J. Grossman and J. E. Stiglitz, "On the Impossibility of Informationally Efficient Markets," *American Economic Review*, Vol. 70, No. 3, 1980, pp. 393-408.

[16] M. F. Hellwig, "On the Aggregation of Information in Competitive Markets," *Journal of Economic Theory*, Vol. 22, 1980, pp. 477-498.

[17] R. E. Verrecchia, "Information Acquisition in a Noisy Rational Expectations Economy," *Econometrica*, Vol. 50,

No. 6, 1982, pp. 1415-1430.

[18] M. O'Hara, "Presidential Address: Liquidity and Price Discovery," *Journal of Finance*, Vol. 58, No. 4, 2003, pp. 1335-1354.

[19] D. Easley and M. O'Hara, "Information and the Cost of Capital," *Journal of Finance*, Vol. 59, No. 4, 2004, pp. 1553-1583.

[20] A. R. Admati, "A Noisy Rational Expectations Equilibrium for Multi-Asset Securities Markets," *Econometrica*, Vol. 53, No. 3, 1985, pp. 629-658.

[21] E. J. Elton, M. J. Gruber and C. R. Blake, "Incentive Fees and Mutual Funds," *Journal of Finance*, Vol. 58, No. 2, 2003, pp. 779-804.

[22] J. H. Golec, "Empirical Tests of a Principal-Agent Model of the Investor-Investment Advisor Relationship," *Journal of Financial and Quantitative Analysis*, Vol. 27, No. 1, 1992, pp. 81-95.

[23] R. Jagannathan, E. R. McGrattan and A. Scherbina, "The Declining US Equity Premium," *Federal Reserve Bank of Minneapolis Quarterly Review*, Vol. 24, No. 4, 2000, pp. 3-19.

[24] E. F. Fama and K. R. French, "The Equity Premium," *Journal of Finance*, Vol. 57, No. 2, 2002, pp. 637-659.

[25] P. A. Gompers and A. Metrick, "Institutional Investors and Equity Prices," *Quarterly Journal of Economics*, Vol. 116, No. 1, 2001, pp. 229-259.

[26] R. C. Merton, "A Simple Model of Capital Market Equilibrium with Incomplete Information," *Journal of Finance*, Vol. 42, No. 3, 1987, pp. 483-510.

[27] A. R. Admati, "On Models and Measures of Information Asymmetries in Financial Markets," PhD, Yale University, New Haven, 1982.

[28] J. Hughes and J. Liu, "Private Information, Diversification and Asset Pricing," Unpublished, 2005.

[29] E. Ozdenoren and K. Yuan, "Feedback Effects and Asset Prices," *Journal of Finance*, Vol. 63, No. 4, 2006, pp. 1939-1975.

5

Is the Driving Force of a Continuous Process a Brownian Motion or Fractional Brownian Motion?

Xinbing Kong[1], Bingyi Jing[2,3], Cuixia Li[3*]
[1]School of Management, Fudan University, Shanghai, China
[2]Department of Mathematics, Hong Kong University of Science and Technology, Hong Kong, China
[3]School of Mathematics and Statistics, Lanzhou University, Lanzhou, China

ABSTRACT

Itô's semimartingale driven by a Brownian motion is typically used in modeling the asset prices, interest rates and exchange rates, and so on. However, the assumption of Brownian motion as a driving force of the underlying asset price processes is rarely contested in practice. This naturally raises the question of whether this assumption is really appropriate. In the paper we propose a statistical test to answer the above question using high frequency data. The test can be used to validate the assumption of semimartingale framework and test for the existence of the long run dependence captured by the fractional Brownian motion in a parsimonious way. Asymptotic properties of the test statistics are investigated. Simulations justify the performance of the test. Real data sets are also analyzed.

Keywords: Itô Semimartingale; Fractional Brownian Motion

1. Introduction

There has been extensive literature in using Itô's semimartingale driven by a Brownian motion to model the asset prices, interest rates and exchange rates, since the seminal work by [1-3]. Statistical inference of Itô's semimartingales is also investigated by many authors, including [4-7] among others.

However, the assumption of Brownian motion as a driving force of the underlying asset price processes is rarely contested statistically. This naturally raises the question of whether this assumption is really appropriate. If not, what alternative can one use in place of Brownian motion? In this paper, we will focus on the use of more general fractional Brownian motion as a driving force if the usual Brownian motion is not appropriate.

The failure of models based on (conditional) uncorrelated increments to describe certain financial data sets has been observed since [8] and [9]. In their works, significant long run dependence was found. To take the long run dependence into account in modeling financial data, [10] proposed to replace Brownian motion with fractional Brownian motion. Using Wavelet method, [11] studied the fractal dimension of the S&P 500 data sampled every minute. They found empirically that the Hurst parameter of the S&P 500 data was significantly above the efficient market value $H = 1/2$ and began to approach that level around 1997. They attributed the trend to the increase in internet trading. [12] investigated the theoretical variational properties of continuous-time processes driven by a fractional Brownian motion using high frequency data.

Before moving on, we define a fractional Brownian motion with Hurst parameter $H \in (0,1)$, which is given by

$$B_t^H = c\left[\int_{-\infty}^{0}\left\{(t-s)^{H-1/2} - (-s)^{H-1/2}\right\}\mathrm{d}W_s + \int_0^{\infty}\left((t-s)^{+}\right)^{H-1/2}\mathrm{d}W_s\right], \quad (1)$$

for $t \geq 0$, where W is a standard Brownian motion with $W_0 = 0$, x^+ and x^- are the positive and negative parts of x, and

$$c^{-2} \equiv (2H)^{-1} + \int_0^{\infty}\left((1+v)^{H-1/2} - v^{H-1/2}\right)^2 \mathrm{d}v.$$

Note that B^H reduces to a standard Brownian motion when $H = 1\ 2$, and otherwise B^H becomes a self-similar process with (long run) dependence when $H \neq 1\ 2$;

*Corresponding author.

the latter property is very attractive in financial models.

The purpose of this paper is to develop some tests to see whether the driving force is a Brownian motion or a true fractional Brownian motion. In terms of the Hurst parameter, this can be formulated as

$$H_0 : H = 1/2 \qquad v.s. \qquad H_1 : H \neq 1/2. \qquad (2)$$

We introduce a method to test (2) based on the asymptotic normality of the ratio of two realized power variations with different sampling frequencies.

If a test rejects H_0, then a fractional Brownian motion will be used in modeling. One problem of using the integral process driven by a fractional Brownian motion is the admission of arbitrage when the integral is defined in a pathwise Stieltjes way, in [13]. The theory of modeling using fractional Brwonian motion was renewed after the work of [14] in which a new type of integration based on the Wick product was introduced. If the new Wick type integration is adopted, [15] proved that the fractional Black-Scholes market has no arbitrage opportunities. However, it is hard to give economic interpretations to trading strategies using the Wick type integration, in [11]. In [11,] the pathwise Stieltjes integration was suggested although arbitrage opportunities of [13]'s type exist. They argued that strategies to make gains with no risk involve exploiting the very fine-scale properties of the process' trajectories. The ability of a trader to implement this type of strategy is likely to be hindered by market frictions, such as transaction costs and minimum amount of time between two consecutive transactions. Indeed [16] showed that by introducing a minimal amount of time between two consecutive transactions, arbitrage opportunities are ruled out from a geometrical fractional Brownian motion.

In this paper, we will implement the pathwise Stieltjes integration that has good interpretations in defining a self-financing strategy. Using high frequency data, our test could give insight into 1) whether the underlying dynamic shows long run dependence; 2) whether the underlying dynamic is a semimartingale; and 3) how rough is the underlying dynamics in terms of its Hurst parameter, e.g., is it $> 1/2$?

The paper is organized as follows. In Section 2, we give some preliminaries and assumptions. Test statistic is given in Section 3. Main results are also presented in Section 3. Simulations are run in Section 4. Section 5 is devoted to real data analysis. Section 6 discusses some future problems. Technical proofs are postponed to the Appendices.

We assume that the observations are

$$\left\{X_{t_i}; 0 \leq i \leq n\right\}, \quad 0 = t_0 \leq \cdots t_i \leq \cdots t_n = T.$$

For simplicity, we further assume that

$$\left\{X_{t_i}, 0 \leq i \leq n\right\}$$

are equally spaced, that is,

$$\Delta_n := t_i - t_{i-1} = T/n.$$

We denote the ith one-step increment by

$$\Delta_i^n X = X_{t_i} - X_{t_{i-1}}.$$

Mathematically, high frequency data set means that $n \to \infty$ for fixed T. Although in theory we will consider the limiting case where $\Delta_n = 0$, in practice Δ_n is strictly positive but close to 0.

2. Preliminaries and Assumptions

2.1. Properties of Fractional Brownian Motion

Throughout this paper, we define $\mathscr{F}_t$ as the natural filtration of W for $t \geq 0$, and $\mathscr{F} = \mathscr{F}_T$. The B^H given in (1) has the following useful properties:

- It is a semimartingale only if $H = 1/2$.
- It is a zero-mean Gaussian process with

$$E\left|B_t^H - B_s^H\right|^2 = |t-s|^{2H}$$

and

$$\rho_H(j) := E\left[B_1^H\left(B_{j+1}^H - B_j^H\right)\right] = \frac{1}{2}\left[(j+1)^{2H} + (j-1)^{2H} - 2j^{2H}\right].$$

- For $n \in Z$, $\left\{B_{n+1}^H - B_n^H\right\}_{n=1}^{\infty}$ is a stationary series.
- B^H is $(H-\epsilon)$-Hölder continuous for any $\epsilon > 0$. Hence B^H has finite $1/(H-\epsilon)$th-variation where the qth-variation of a process Z is defined as

$$v_q(Z,[s,t]) = \sup_{\pi}\left(\sum_{i=1}^{n}\left|Z_{t_i} - Z_{t_{i-1}}\right|^q\right)^{1/q}$$

where the supremum is taken over all partition π of $[s,t]$.

Let σ be a positive process adapted to $\mathscr{F}_t$, the integral process, $\int_0^t \sigma_s dB_s^H$ be defined as the pathwise Riemann-Stieltjes integral. By Young's inequality, c.f. [12], the discretization error of the integral process could be controlled by

$$\left|\int_s^t (\sigma_u - \sigma_s) dB_u^H\right| \leq c_{a,b} v_a(\sigma,[s,t]) v_b(B^H,[s,t]), \quad a.s. (3)$$

where

$$c_{a,b} = \sum_{n=1}^{\infty} n^{-(1/a+1/b)}.$$

So to make the right side of (3) finite, $1/a + H > 1$, *i.e.*, σ could at most have finite $1/(1-H)$th power variation.

2.2. Model Assumptions

As studied in [12], [17] and the references therein, we

assume that the model is a simple continuous process of the following integral form

$$X_t = X_0 + \int_0^t \sigma_s \mathrm{d}B_s^H, \tag{4}$$

where X_0 is the initial value. We make the following assumptions on the diffusive coefficients.

Assumption 1: *σ is a locally bounded càdlàg processes.*

Assumption 2: *σ is an α-Hölder continuous process with $\alpha > 1 - H$.*

3. Test Statistics

Our test is based on power variational property of X:

$$V(p,\Delta_n) = \sum_{i=1}^{n} |\Delta_i^n X|^p.$$

Under Assumptions 1-2, it can be shown

$$\Delta_n^{1-pH} V(p,\Delta_n) \to^P m_p \int_0^T |\sigma_s|^p \, \mathrm{d}s, \tag{5}$$

where m_p is some constant depending only on p. Since the right side of (5) is unknown, one could use the two-time scale technique as used in [18] to define the test statistic as follows,

$$U(p) := \frac{V(p,k\Delta_n)}{V(p,\Delta_n)}, \tag{6}$$

where

$$V(p,k\Delta_n) = \sum_{i=1}^{[n/k]} |\Delta_{ki-k+1}^n X + \cdots + \Delta_{ki}^n X|^p := \sum_{i=1}^{[n/k]} |\Delta_{i,k}^n X|^p. \tag{7}$$

It is worthy of noticing that [4] proposed a test statistic of the same form as (6) in the context of testing for the presence of jumps within the semi-martingale framework.

Now we state our main results.

Theorem 1: *Under Assumptions* 1-2, *we have*

1) $U(p) \to^P k^{pH-1}$,

2) if $\alpha > 1/2$ and $H < 3/4$,

$$\Delta_n^{-1/2}\left(U(p) - k^{pH-1}\right) \to G, \quad \text{stably}$$

where G is a centered Gaussian random variable conditional on $\mathscr{F}$ with the conditional variance

$$u_T^2 = M_p(k)\frac{A(2p)_T}{\left(A(p)_T\right)^2},$$

where

$$A(l)_T = \int_0^T |\sigma_s|^l \, \mathrm{d}s$$

and

$$M_p(k) = \frac{\left(k^{2(pH-1)} + k^{2(pH-1/2)}\right)v_1^2 - 2k^{2(pH-3/4)}(cor)^2}{m_p^2},$$

where

$$m_l = E|\mathcal{N}(0,1)|^l,$$

$$v_1^2 = m_{2p} - m_p^2 + 2\sum_{j\ge1}\left(\gamma_p\left(\rho_H(j)\right) - \gamma_p(0)\right)$$

where

$$\gamma_p(x) = \left(1-x^2\right)^{p+1/2} 2^p \sum_{k=0}^{\infty} \frac{(2x)^{2k}}{\pi(2k)!}\Gamma\left(\frac{p+1}{2}+k\right)$$

with $\Gamma(x)$ be the Gamma function, and $(cor)^2$ is a constant dependent on H.

Remark 1

- Under H_0, the condition $\alpha > 1/2$ could be weakened, actually, σ could be semimartingales driven by Brownian motion where paths of σ are

$$\left(\frac{1}{2} - \epsilon\right)\text{-Hölder}$$

continuous, c.f. [19].

- From Part 1 of Theorem 1, an estimator of H can be given by

$$\hat{H} = \left(1 + \frac{\log U(p)}{\log k}\right)\Big/ p.$$

The behavior of $U(p)$ depends on H, and so can be used as a test statistic. From the above theorem, $U(p)$ is asymptotically normal with unknown conditional variance u_T^2 under $H_0: H = 1/2$. By (5), a consistent estimator of u_T^2 under H_0 is

$$\hat{u}_T^2 = M_p(k)\frac{\hat{A}(2p)_T}{\left(\hat{A}(p)_T\right)^2},$$

where

$$\hat{A}(l)_T = \Delta_n^{1-l/2} V(l,\Delta_n)/m_l.$$

From Theorem 1, we reject H_0 if

$$\left|U(p) - k^{p/2-1}\right| > \sqrt{\Delta_n} z_{\alpha/2} \hat{u}_T,$$

where $z_{\alpha/2}$ satisfies

$$P\left(\mathcal{N}(0,1) > z_{\alpha/2}\right) = \alpha/2.$$

By Theorem 1 and (5), we have

Theorem 2: *Under the assumptions in Part 2 of Theorem 1, we have*

$$P\left(\text{Reject } H_0 \middle| H_0\right) \to \alpha,$$

and

$$P\left(\text{Reject } H_0 \middle| H_1\right) \to 1.$$

Therefore, our test is of asymptotic size α with asymptotic power one.

4. Simulation Studies

4.1. Assessment of the Size

In assessing the performance of the size of the test, we draw 5000 samples of size n from the following stochastic volatility process driven by a Brownian motion

$$\mathrm{d}X_t = \sigma_t \mathrm{d}W_t$$

with

$$\sigma_t = v_t^{1/2}, \quad \mathrm{d}v_t = \kappa(\eta - v_t)\mathrm{d}t + \gamma v_t^{1/2}\mathrm{d}B_t,$$

and $E[\mathrm{d}W_t \mathrm{d}B_t] = \rho \mathrm{d}t$. We take $\eta = 1/16$, $\gamma = 0.5$, $\kappa = 5$, $\rho = -0.5$. Set the time horizon to be $T = 1$ (day) consisting of 6.5 trading hours.

We use two different sample sizes, $n = 511, 1023$. **Figure 1** shows the histograms of the test statistics under $H_0 : H = 1/2$. The histograms imply that the normal approximation matches well the sampling distribution of the test statistics $U(2)$ under H_0.

Take the nominal level $\alpha = 5\%$. The dot-dashed curve in **Figure 2** gives the empirical sizes of the test based on $U(2)$ against ρ when $n = 511$, from which we see that the type I error probabilities are well controlled.

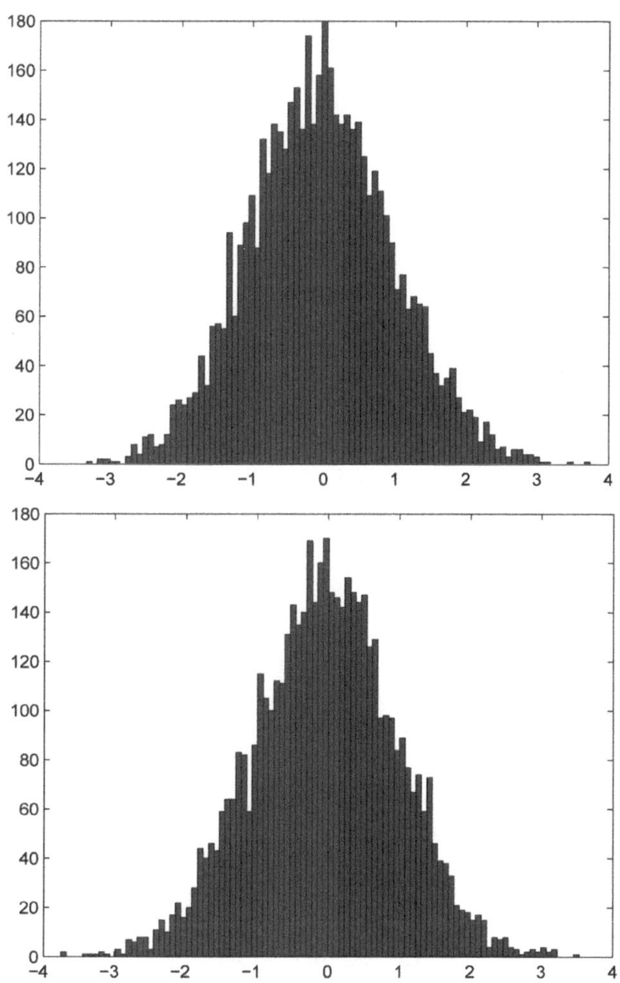

Figure 1. Histograms of the test statistics under H_0: $n = 511$ in the left panels; $n = 1023$ in the right panels.

4.2. Assessment of the Power

We simulate only the geometric fractional Brownian motion for 5000 times, c.f. [20], *i.e.*,

$$\mathrm{e}^{X_t} = \mathrm{e}^{\mu t + \sigma B_t^H},$$

where μ and σ are two constants. We take $\mu = 0$ and σ around $\sqrt{\eta} = \sqrt{1/16}$, in order to be comparable to the data generating process used in the assessment of the size. We set $n = 511$. The simulations when $n = 1023$ was also done but will not be listed here to save space. The conclusions are the same as those given below.

Table 1 gives the averaged $U(2)$ over 5000 repetitions. From the table, whatever the values of H and σ, they are very close to k^{pH-1} and here $k = 2$, $p = 2$. **Table 2** reports the empirical power of the test based on $U(2)$. We make the following remarks.

- The powers are insensitive to different values of σ's.
- The powers grow bigger as H moves away from $1/2$, and the test is very powerful especially when $|H - 1/2| \geq 0.1$.

5. Real Data Analysis

We now implement our test to some real data sets. The first three data sets are from the New York Stock Exchange. Another two data sets, SZ000002 and SH000001, are from the Shenzhen Stock Exchange and Shanghai Stock Exchange of China, respectively.

We use the stock price records of Microsoft (MSFT) in the trading days: Nov. 1, and Dec. 1., 2000, and that of Dell Company (DELL) in Dec. 1, 2011. All data sets are from the TAQ database. For prices recorded simultaneously, we use the average. To weaken the po-ssi-ble effect from microstructure noise, we sparsely sample observations and the sample sizes for the aforementioned three trading days are 448, 568 and 528, respectively. If i.i.d. microstructure noises are assumed, then the microstructure noise would drive $U(2)$ to $1/2$ as $n \to \infty$

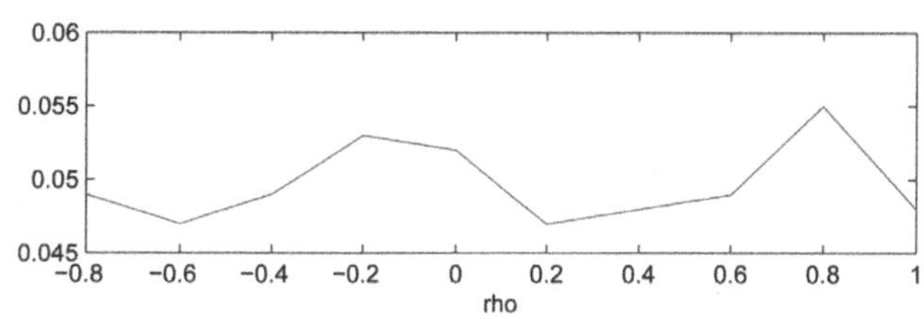

Figure 2. Empirical sizes of the test based on $U(2)$ against ρ.

Table 1. Averaged $U(2)$ over different H and σ.

H & σ	0.1	0.2	0.25	0.3	0.4	0.5	2^{2H-1}
0.1	0.576	0.575	0.574	0.575	0.574	0.574	0.574
0.2	0.660	0.660	0.660	0.659	0.659	0.659	0.660
0.3	0.758	0.759	0.756	0.757	0.758	0.758	0.758
0.4	0.869	0.869	0.870	0.869	0.870	0.868	0.871
0.6	1.146	1.145	1.146	1.146	1.147	1.147	1.149
0.7	1.314	1.315	1.314	1.315	1.315	1.313	1.320

Table 2. Empirical powers of the test based on $U(2)$ over different H and σ.

H & σ	0.1	0.2	0.25	0.3	0.4	0.5
0.1	1.000	1.000	1.000	1.000	1.000	1.000
0.2	1.000	1.000	1.000	1.000	1.000	1.000
0.3	0.976	0.973	0.977	0.974	0.971	0.974
0.4	0.558	0.562	0.554	0.555	0.552	0.572
0.425	0.367	0.366	0.372	0.353	0.366	0.367
0.45	0.208	0.203	0.197	0.199	0.191	0.195
0.55	0.202	0.199	0.199	0.199	0.204	0.208
0.575	0.406	0.408	0.400	0.409	0.414	0.400
0.6	0.655	0.640	0.645	0.653	0.660	0.663
0.7	0.997	0.998	0.998	0.998	0.998	0.999
0.8	1.000	1.000	1.000	1.000	1.000	1.000
0.9	1.000	1.000	1.000	1.000	1.000	1.000

if $k = 2$. The results shown later demonstrate that the sparse sampling is effective since all estimated $U(2)$ of all real data sets are away from $1/2$. Finally, we take logarithm of the sparsely sampled prices and use the log prices to calculate the test statistics. We set $T = 1$ (day) consisting of 6.5 hours of trading time.

The test statistics and an estimate of the Hurst parameter are provided in **Table 3**. $U(2)$ is given in (3.5) with $p = 2$, its studentized form is given by t. Seen from the table, our test do not reject the use of Brownian motion as the driving force for all three data sets at the significance level of 5%.

Next, we analyze the stock price records of SZ000002 and SH000001. Prices are recorded from 9:25 am - 15:00 pm in the trading day Jan. 1, 2004. **Figure 3** displays the log prices against the time. An obvious dependence structure among returns is observed in both plots which demonstrates strong dependence between (log) returns.

Test statistics and estimates of the Hurst parameters of the log price dynamics of these two stocks are given in **Table 4**. The sample sizes of SZ000002 and SH000001 are respectively 356 and 394. Seen from **Table 4**, we have the following observations:

- Although we do not reject H_0 for SZ000002, minor evidences of the departure of the driving force from the Brownian motion are seen.
- Strong evidence against the Brownian motion as the driving force are shown for SH000001.
- In contrast to **Table 3**, it looks that the dynamics of the two Chinese stocks deviate from semimartingales driven by the Brownian motion much while semimartingales driven by the Brownian motion are still good approximation to the three U.S. stocks. This is in fact to be expected since the New York Stock Exchange is a far more efficient market than the Shenzhen Stock Exchange and Shanghai Stock Exchange.

6. Discussions

In this paper, we develop test to check whether the driving force of continuous integral processes with drift is a Brownian motion or a fractional Brownian motion. There is little literature in this direction, and there are some interesting future research directions. Here are a couple of examples.

1) It is commonly accepted that jumps exist in price processes, which has been well studied in the literature. So it is of interest to extend our results to process with jump components. Here, the truncated power variation as in [21], should prove useful, and the results in this paper may still hold true for appropriate choice of p.

2) The effect of the microstructure noise to the test statistics will also be investigated in the future work.

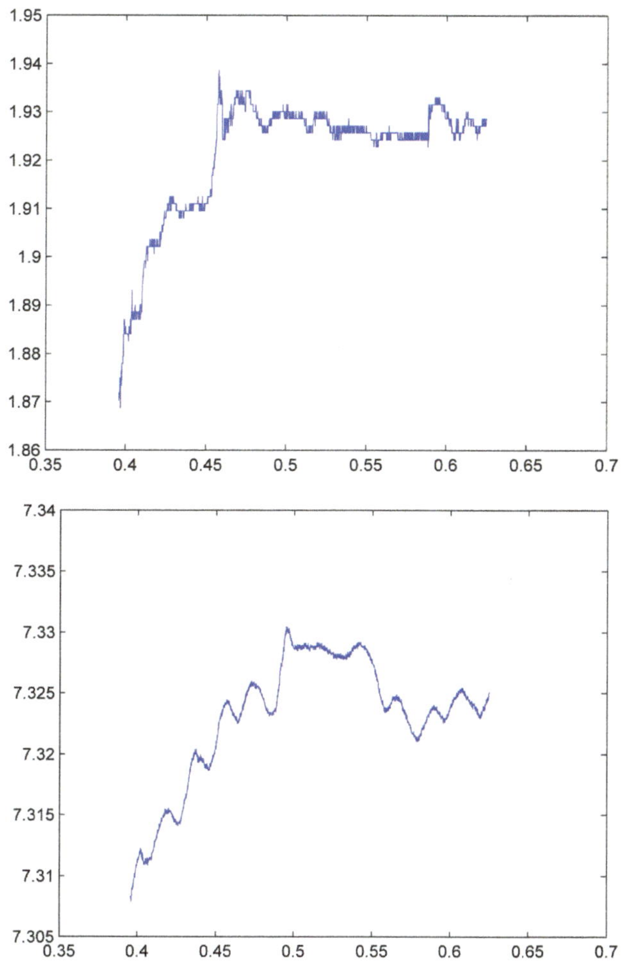

Figure 3. Plots of the Prices of SZ000002 (left panel) and SH000001 (right panel) against Time.

Table 3. Test Statistics and Estimate of the Hurst Parameter.

Date & Statistics	$U(2)$	t	$\hat{H}$
Nov. 1, 2000 (MSFT)	0.96	−0.35	0.4678
Dec. 1, 2000 (MSFT)	0.96	−0.36	0.4739
Dec. 1, 2011 (DELL)	0.95	−0.60	0.4594

Table 4. Test Statistics and Estimate of the Hurst Parameter, $n = 356$ (SZ000002) and $n = 394$ (SH000001).

Date & Statistics	$U(2)$	t	$\hat{H}$
Jan. 2, 2004 (SZ000002)	1.13	0.91	0.58
Jan. 2, 2004 (SH000001)	1.30	3.79	0.69

Asymptotically, the microstructure noise would drive $U(p)$ to $1/k$. Multi scale technique or pre-averaging method would serve as good ways to eliminate the effect of the microstructure noise first, c.f. [18] and [22]. Many theoretical works and practical analyses can be done along this line.

5. Acknowledgements

The authors would like to thank the editor, an associate editor and referees for their constructive suggestions that improved this paper considerably. Kong's work is supported in part by the NSF China (11201080) and the Humanity and Social Science Youth Foundation of Chinese Ministry of Education (12YJC910003), and in part by the Fundamental Research Funds for the Central Universities (FDU20520133198). Jing's research is supported by Hong Kong RGC Grants HKUST6019/10P, HKUST-6019/12P, HKUST6022/13P, and in part by the Fun-14 damental Research Funds for the Central Universities, Research Funds of Renmin University of China (Grant no. 10XNL007), and by NSF China (Grant no. 71071010). Li's work is supported by the NSF China (11301236) and the Fundamental Research Funds for the Central Universities (lzujbky-2012-179), and in part by the NSF China (41271038).

REFERENCES

[1] F. Black and M. Scholes, "The Pricing of Options and Corporate Liabilities," *Journal of Political Economy*, Vol. 81, No. 3, 1973, pp. 133-155.

[2] J. Hull and A. White, "Pricing Interest Rate Derivative Securities," *Review of Financial Studies*, Vol. 3, No. 4, 1990, pp. 573-592.

[3] S. Heston, "A Closed-From Solution for Options with Stochastic Volatility with Applications to Bond and Currency Options," *Review of Financial Studies*, Vol. 6, No. 2, 1993, pp. 327-343.

[4] Y. Aït-Sahalia and J. Jacod, "Testing for Jumps in a Discretely Observed Process," *The Annals of Statistics*, Vol. 37, No. 1, 2009, pp. 184-222.

[5] Y. Aït-Sahalia and J. Jacod, "Is Brownian Motion Necessary to Model High Frequency Data?" *The Annals of Statistics*, Vol. 38, No. 5, 2010, pp. 3093-3128.

[6] O. E. Barndorff-Nielsen and N. Shephard, "Econometrics of Testing for Jumps in Financial Economics Using Bipower Variation," *Journal of Financial Econometrics*, Vol. 2, No. 1, 2006, pp. 1-48.

[7] V. Todorov and G. Tanchen, "Activity Signature Functions for High-Frequency Data Analysis," *Journal of Econometrics*, Vol. 154, No. 2, 2010, pp. 125-138.

[8] M. T. Greene and B. D. Fielitz, "Long term Dependence in Common Stock Returns," *Journal of Financial Economics*, Vol. 4, No. 3, 1977, pp. 339-349.

[9] B. B. Mandelbrot, "When Can Price Be Arbitraged Efficiently? A Limit to the Validity of the Random Walk and Martingale Models," *Review of Economic Statistics*, Vol.

53, No. 3, 1971, pp. 225-236.

[10] N. J. Cutland, P. E. Kopp and W. Willinger, "Stock Price Returns and the Joseph Effect: A Fractal Version of the Black-Scholes Model," *Progress in Probability*, Vol. 36, 1995, pp. 327-351.

[11] E. Bayraktar, H. V. Poor and R. Sircar, "Estimating the fractal Dimension of the S&P 500 Index Using Wavelet Analysis," *International Journal of Theoretical and Applied Finance*, Vol. 7, No. 5, 2004, pp. 615-643.

[12] J. Corcuera, D. Nualart and J. Woerner, "Power Variation of Some Integral Fractional Processes," *Bernoulli*, Vol. 12, No. 4, 2006, pp. 713-735.

[13] L. Rogers, "Arbitrage with Fractional Brownian Motion," *Mathematical Finance*, Vol. 7, No. 1, 1997, pp. 95-105.

[14] T. E. Duncan, Y. Hu and B. Pasik-Duncan, "Stochastic Calculus for Fractional Brownian Motion," *SIAM Journal on Control and Optimization*, Vol. 38, No. 1, 2000, pp. 582-612.

[15] B. Oksendal and Y. Hu, "Fractional White Noise and Applications to Finance," *Infinite Dimensional Analysis, Quantum Probability and Related Topics*, Vol. 6, No. 1, 2000, pp. 1-32.

[16] P. Cheridito, "Arbitrage in Fractional Brownian Motion Models," *Finance and Stochastics*, Vol. 7, No. 4, 2003, pp. 533-553.

[17] S. Si, "Two-Step Variations for Processes Driven by Fractional Brownian Motion with Applications in Testing for Jumps form the High Frequency Data," Ph.D. Thesis, University of Tennessee, Knoxville, 2009.

[18] L. Zhang, P. A. Mykland and Y. Ait-Sahalia, "A Tale of Two Time Scales: Determining Integrated Volatility with Noisy High-Frequency Data," *Journal of the American Statistical Association*, Vol. 100, No. 472, 2005, pp. 1394-1411.

[19] O. E. Barndorff-Nielsen, S. Graversen, J. Jacod and N. Shephard, "A Central Limit Theorem for Realized Power and Bipower Variations of Continuous Semi Martingales," *From Stochastic Calculus to Mathematics*, 2006, pp. 33-68.

[20] D. Nualart, "Stochastic Calculus with Respect to the Fractional Brownian Motion and Applications," *Contemporary Mathematics*, Vol. 336, 2003, pp. 3-39.

[21] C. Mancini, "Estimating the Integrated Volatility in Stochastic Volatility Models with Lévy Type Jumps," Technical Report, University di Firenze, Firenze, 2004.

[22] J. Jacod, Y. Li, P. A. Mykland, M. Podolskij and M. Vetter, "Microstructure Noise in the Continuous Case: The Pre-Averaging Approach," *Stochastic Processes and Their Applications*, Vol. 119, No. 7, 2009, pp. 2249-2276.

Appendix A: Proofs of Main Theorems

By the standard localization method, it suffices to prove the main results under the following strengthened assumptions.

Assumption 3: σ *is a bounded process.*

In the sequel, C will stand for a constant that may take different values at different appearance.

Proof of Theorem 1 Let

$$\xi_n = \Delta_n^{1-pH} V(p,\Delta_n) - m_p \int_0^T |\sigma_s|^p \, ds$$

$$\zeta_n = (k\Delta_n)^{1-pH} V(p,k\Delta_n) - m_p \int_0^T |\sigma_s|^p \, ds.$$

Simple algebras yield

$$\Delta_n^{-1/2}\left(\frac{V(p,k\Delta_n)}{V(p,\Delta_n)} - k^{pH-1}\right) = \Delta_n^{-1/2} k^{(pH-1)} (\zeta_n - \xi_n) / \left(\Delta_n^{1-pH} V(p,\Delta_n)\right).$$

Then Theorem 1 is a straightforward consequence of Proposition 1 of which the proof is given later in *Appendix B*.

Proposition 1: *Under Assumptions* 1-3, *if* $\gamma > 1/4$, $\alpha > 1/2$ *and* $H < 3/4$, *then we have*

$$\left[B_T^H, \Delta_n^{-1/2}(\xi_n, \zeta_n)\right] \to \left[B_T^H, (z_1, z_2)\right]$$

stably, where (z_1, z_2) is a centered bivariate Gaussian random vector conditional on $\mathscr{F}$ with

$$E\left(z_1^2 \middle| \mathscr{F}\right) = v_1^2 \int_0^T |\sigma_s|^{2p} \, ds,$$

$$E\left(z_2^2 \middle| \mathscr{F}\right) = k v_1^2 \int_0^T |\sigma_s|^{2p} \, ds,$$

$$E\left(z_1 z_2 \middle| \mathscr{F}\right) = k^{1/2} (cor)^2 \int_0^T |\sigma_s|^{2p} \, ds.$$

Proof of Theorem 2 The first convergence is a consequence of Theorem 1. Now we prove the second convergence. Under H_1,

$$\hat{A}(l)_T = O_P\left(\Delta_n^{l(H-1/2)}\right)$$

and $\hat{u}_T = O_P(1)$. Therefore we further have

$$U(p) - k^{p/2-1} \to^P k^{pH-1} - k^{p/2-1}$$

and $\sqrt{\Delta_n} z_{\alpha/2} \hat{u}_T = o_P(1)$. By the rejection rule, the second convergence is proved.

Appendix B: Proof of Proposition 1

To prove Proposition 1, we need the following lemma.

Lemma 1

$$(cor)^2 =: \mathrm{Cov}\left\{\sqrt{n}\left(\Delta_n^{1-pH}\sum_{i=1}^{n}|\Delta_i^n|^p - m_p\right), \sqrt{n/k}\left((k\Delta_n)^{1-pH}\sum_{i=1}^{[n/k]}|\Delta_{i,k}^n|^p - m_p\right)\right\}$$

$$= \frac{1}{\sqrt{k}}\sum_{j=1}^{k}\left[\gamma_p\left(k^{-H}\left(\rho_H(k-j)+\cdots+\rho_H(1-j)\right)\right)\right]$$

$$+ \frac{1}{\sqrt{k}}\sum_{j=1}^{k}\sum_{l=1}^{\infty}\left[2\gamma_p\left(k^{-H}\left(\rho_H(kl+k-j)+\cdots+\rho_H(kl+1-j)\right)\right) - \gamma_p(0)\right].$$

Proof. For simple, denote

$$U = B_{k(i-1)+j}^H - B_{k(i-1)+j-1}^H$$

and

$$V = k^{-H}\left(B_{kl}^H - B_{kl-k}^H\right).$$

Then, we have

$$EU = EV = 0, \quad EU^2 = EV^2 = 1,$$

and

$$\frac{\Delta_i^n B^H}{\Delta_n^H} =^d B_i^H - B_{i-1}^H, \quad \frac{\Delta_{i,k}^n B^H}{\Delta_n^H} =^d B_{ki}^H - B_{ki-k}^H.$$

Then,

$$E[UV] = E\left[\left(B_{k(i-1)+j}^H - B_{k(i-1)+j}^H\right)\left(k^{-H}\left(B_{kl}^H - B_{kl-k}^H\right)\right)\right]$$

$$= k^{-H} E\left[\left(B_{k(i-1)+j}^H - B_{k(i-1)+j-1}^H\right)\left(\left(B_{kl}^H - B_{kl-1}^H\right)+\cdots+\left(B_{kl-k+1}^H - B_{kl-k}^H\right)\right)\right]$$

$$= k^{-H}\left[\rho_H(kl-ki+k-j)+\cdots+\rho_H(kl-ki+1-j)\right].$$

Now, for $(cor)^2$, we have

$$(cor)^2 = E\left[\frac{n}{\sqrt{k}}\left(\Delta_n\sum_{i=1}^{n}\left|V_i^H - B_{i-1}^H\right|^p - m_p\right)\left(k^{1-pH}\Delta_n\sum_{i=1}^{[n/k]}\left|B_{ki}^H - B_{ki-k}^H\right|^p - m_p\right)\right]$$

$$= k^{\frac{1}{2}-pH}\Delta_n E\left[\left(\sum_{i=1}^{[n/k]}\sum_{j=1}^{k}\left|B_{k(i-1)+j}^H - B_{k(i-1)+j-1}^H\right|^p\right)\left(\sum_{l=1}^{[n/k]}\left|B_{kl}^H - B_{kl-k}^H\right|^p\right)\right] - \frac{n}{\sqrt{k}}m_p^2$$

$$= \sqrt{k}\Delta_n E\left[\left(\sum_{i=1}^{[n/k]}\sum_{j=1}^{k}|U|^p\right)\left(\sum_{l=1}^{[n/k]}|V|^p\right)\right] - \frac{n}{\sqrt{k}}m_p^2$$

$$= \sqrt{k}\Delta_n\left[\sum_{i=1}^{[n/k]}\sum_{j=1}^{k}E\left(|U|^p|V|^p + 2\sum_{i=1}^{[n/k]}\sum_{l=i+1}^{[n/k]}\sum_{j=1}^{k}E|U|^p|V|^p\right)\right] - \frac{n}{\sqrt{k}}m_p^2$$

$$= \sqrt{k}\Delta_n\left[\sum_{i=1}^{[n/k]}\sum_{j=1}^{k}\gamma_p\left[k^{-H}\left(\rho_H(k-j)+\cdots+\rho_H(1-j)\right)\right]\right] - \frac{n}{\sqrt{k}}m_p^2$$

$$+ \sqrt{k}\Delta_n\left[2\sum_{i=1}^{[n/k]}\sum_{l=i+1}^{[n/k]}\sum_{j=1}^{k}\gamma_p\left[k^{-H}\left(\rho_H(kl-ki+k-j)+\cdots+\rho_H(kl-ki+1-j)\right)\right]\right]$$

$$= \frac{1}{\sqrt{k}}\sum_{j=1}^{k}\gamma_p\left[k^{-H}\left(\rho_H(k-j)+\cdots+\rho_H(1-j)\right)\right] - \frac{n}{\sqrt{k}}m_p^2$$

$$+ 2\sqrt{k}\Delta_n\left[\sum_{i=1}^{[n/k]}\sum_{l=1}^{[n/k]-i}\sum_{j=1}^{k}\gamma_p\left[k^{-H}\left(\rho_H(kl+k-j)+\cdots+\rho_H(kl+1-j)\right)\right]\right]$$

$$= \frac{1}{\sqrt{k}}\sum_{j=1}^{k}\gamma_p\left[k^{-H}\left(\rho_H(k-j)+\cdots+\rho_H(1-j)\right)\right] - \frac{n}{\sqrt{k}}m_p^2$$

$$+ 2\sqrt{k}\Delta_n\left[\sum_{l=1}^{[n/k]-1}\sum_{i=1}^{[n/k]-l}\sum_{j=1}^{k}\gamma_p\left[k^{-H}\left(\rho_H(kl+k-j)+\cdots+\rho_H(kl+1-j)\right)\right]\right]$$

$$= \frac{1}{\sqrt{k}}\sum_{j=1}^{k}\gamma_p\left[k^{-H}\left(\rho_H(k-j)+\cdots+\rho_H(1-j)\right)\right] - \frac{1}{\sqrt{k}}\sum_{j=1}^{k}\sum_{l=1}^{[n/k]-1}\gamma_p(0)$$

$$+ \frac{2}{\sqrt{k}}\sum_{j=1}^{k}\sum_{l=1}^{[n/k]-1}\left[(1-lk\Delta_n)\gamma_p\left[k^{-H}\left(\rho_H(kl+k-j)+\cdots+\rho_H(kl+1-j)\right)\right]\right].$$

when we fixed k, $k\Delta_n \to 0$, then we have

$$(cor)^2 = \frac{1}{\sqrt{k}}\sum_{j=1}^{k}\left[\gamma_p\left[k^{-H}\left(\rho_H(k-j)+\cdots+\rho_H(1-j)\right)\right]\right.$$

$$\left. + \sum_{l=1}^{\infty}2\gamma_p\left(k^{-H}\left(\rho_H(kl+k-j)+\cdots+\rho_H(kl+1-j)\right)-\gamma_p(0)\right)\right].$$

Proof of Proposition 1: Recall that

$$X_t = X_0 + \int_0^t \sigma_s \mathrm{d}B_s^H .$$

For simplicity, we assume that $T = 1$ which implies that $\Delta_n = 1/n$. Then by the extended Wold device, see e.g. Lemma 4.32 in [17], it suffices to show that for any $(c_1, c_2) \in R^2$,

$$\left(B_1^H, c_1\sqrt{n}\xi_n + c_2\sqrt{n/k}\zeta_n\right) \to^L \left(B_1^H, \tilde{\sigma}\int_0^1 |u_s|^p \,\mathrm{d}W_s\right), \quad (8)$$

where,

$$\tilde{\sigma}^2 = c_1^2 v_1^2 + c_2^2 v_1^2 + 2c_1c_2(cor)^2 .$$

Rewrite the left side of (8) as

$$\left(B_1^H, c_1\sqrt{n}\left(\frac{1}{n}\frac{1}{\left(\frac{1}{n}\right)^{pH}}\sum_{i=1}^{[n/k]}\sum_{j=1}^{k}\left|\Delta_{k(i-1)+j}^n X\right|^p - m_p\int_0^1|\sigma_s|^p\,\mathrm{d}s\right) + c_2\sqrt{\frac{n}{k}}\left(\frac{1}{\frac{n}{k}}\frac{1}{\left(\frac{k}{n}\right)^{pH}}\sum_{i=1}^{[n/k]}\left|\Delta_{i,k}^n X\right|^p - m_p\int_0^1|\sigma_s|^p\,\mathrm{d}s\right)\right).$$

For any $m \geq n$ we write

$$c_1\sqrt{m}\left(\frac{1}{m}\frac{1}{\left(\frac{1}{m}\right)^{pH}}\sum_{i=1}^{[m/k]}\sum_{j=1}^{k}\left|\Delta_{k(i-1)+j}^{m}X\right|^{p} - m_p\int_0^1|\sigma_s|^p\,\mathrm{d}s\right) = c_1\sqrt{m}\left(A^{(m)} + B^{(n,m)} + C^{(n,m)} + D^{(m)}\right)$$

and

$$c_2\sqrt{\frac{m}{k}}\left(\frac{1}{\frac{m}{k}}\frac{1}{\left(\frac{k}{m}\right)^{pH}}\sum_{i=1}^{[m/k]}\left|\Delta_{i,k}^{m}X\right|^{p} - m_p\int_0^1|\sigma_s|^p\,\mathrm{d}s\right) = c_2\sqrt{\frac{m}{k}}\left(\bar{A}^{(m)} + \bar{B}^{(n,m)} + \bar{C}^{(n,m)} + \bar{D}^{(m)}\right),$$

where

$$A^{(m)} = \frac{1}{m}\frac{1}{\left(\frac{1}{m}\right)^{pH}}\sum_{i=1}^{[m/k]}\sum_{j=1}^{k}\left(\left|\Delta_{k(i-1)+j}^{m}X\right|^{p} - \left|\sigma_{\frac{k(i-1)+j-1}{m}}\Delta_{k(i-1)+j}^{m}B^{H}\right|^{p}\right),$$

$$\begin{aligned}B^{(n,m)} = {} & \frac{1}{m}\frac{1}{\left(\frac{1}{m}\right)^{pH}}\sum_{i=1}^{[m/k]}\sum_{j=1}^{k}\left|\sigma_{\frac{k(i-1)+j-1}{m}}\Delta_{k(i-1)+j}^{m}B^{H}\right|^{p} - \frac{1}{m}\sum_{i=1}^{[m/k]}\sum_{j=1}^{k}m_p\left|\sigma_{\frac{k(i-1)+j-1}{m}}\right|^{p} \\ & - \frac{1}{m}\frac{1}{\left(\frac{1}{m}\right)^{pH}}\sum_{l=1}^{[n/k]}\sum_{j=1}^{k}\left(\left|\sigma_{\frac{k(i-1)+j-1}{n}}\right|^{p} - \left|\sigma_{\frac{kl-k}{n}}\right|^{p}\right)\sum_{i\in I_n(l)}\left|\Delta_{k(i-1)+j}^{m}B^{H}\right|^{p} + \frac{1}{n}\sum_{l=1}^{[n/k]}\sum_{j=1}^{k}m_p\left(\left|\sigma_{\frac{k(i-1)+j-1}{n}}\right|^{p} - \left|\sigma_{\frac{kl-k}{n}}\right|\right)^{p} - C^{(n,m)},\end{aligned}$$

$$C^{(n,m)} = \frac{1}{m}\frac{1}{\left(\frac{1}{m}\right)^{pH}}\sum_{l=1}^{[n/k]}\sum_{j=1}^{k}\left|\sigma_{\frac{kl-k}{n}}\right|^{p}\sum_{i\in I_n(l)}\left|\Delta_{k(i-1)+j}^{m}B^{H}\right|^{p} - \frac{1}{n}\sum_{l=1}^{[n/k]}\sum_{j=1}^{k}m_p\left|\sigma_{\frac{kl-k}{n}}\right|^{p},$$

$$D^{(m)} = \frac{1}{m}\sum_{i=1}^{[m/k]}\sum_{j=1}^{k}m_p\left|\sigma_{\frac{k(i-1)+j-1}{m}}\right|^{p} - m_p\int_0^1|\sigma_s|^p\,\mathrm{d}s, \quad \text{and} \quad \bar{A}^{(m)} = \frac{1}{\frac{m}{k}}\frac{1}{\left(\frac{k}{m}\right)^{pH}}\sum_{i=1}^{[m/k]}\left(\left|X_{\frac{ki}{m}} - X_{\frac{ki-k}{m}}\right|^{p} - \left|\sigma_{\frac{ki-k}{m}}\left(B_{\frac{ki}{m}}^{H} - B_{\frac{ki-k}{m}}^{H}\right)\right|^{p}\right),$$

$$\begin{aligned}\bar{B}^{(n,m)} = {} & \frac{1}{\frac{m}{k}}\frac{1}{\left(\frac{k}{m}\right)^{pH}}\sum_{i=1}^{[m/k]}\left|\sigma_{\frac{ki-k}{m}}\left(B_{\frac{ki}{m}}^{H} - B_{\frac{ki-k}{m}}^{H}\right)\right|^{p} - \frac{1}{\frac{m}{k}}\sum_{i=1}^{[m/k]}m_p\left|\sigma_{\frac{ki-k}{m}}\right|^{p} \\ & - \frac{1}{\frac{m}{k}}\frac{1}{\left(\frac{k}{m}\right)^{pH}}\sum_{l=1}^{[n/k]}\left|\sigma_{\frac{kl-k}{n}}\right|^{p}\sum_{i\in I_n'(l)}\left|B_{\frac{ki}{m}}^{H} - B_{\frac{ki-k}{m}}^{H}\right|^{p} + \frac{1}{\frac{n}{k}}\sum_{l=1}^{[n/k]}m_p\left|\sigma_{\frac{kl-k}{n}}\right|^{p},\end{aligned}$$

$$\bar{C}^{(n,m)} = \frac{1}{\frac{m}{k}}\frac{1}{\left(\frac{k}{m}\right)^{pH}}\sum_{l=1}^{[n/k]}\left|\sigma_{\frac{kl-k}{n}}\right|^{p}\sum_{i\in I_n'(l)}\left|B_{\frac{ki}{m}}^{H} - B_{\frac{ki-k}{m}}^{H}\right|^{p} - \frac{1}{\frac{n}{k}}\sum_{l=1}^{[n/k]}m_p\left|\sigma_{\frac{kl-k}{n}}\right|^{p},$$

$$\bar{D}^{(m)} = \frac{1}{\frac{m}{k}}\sum_{i=1}^{[m/k]}m_p\left|\sigma_{\frac{ki-k}{m}}\right|^{p} - m_p\int_0^1|\sigma_s|^p\,\mathrm{d}s, \quad \text{with} \quad I_n(l) = \left\{i \,\middle|\, \frac{k(i-1)+j}{m} \in \left(\frac{k(l-1)+j-1}{n}, \frac{k(i-1)+j}{n}\right]\right\}, \quad l > 1;$$

$$I_n'(l) = \left\{i \,\middle|\, \frac{ki}{m} \in \left(\frac{kl-k}{n}, \frac{kl}{n}\right]\right\}, \quad l > 1.$$

Then the left side of (8) is equal to

$$\left(c_1\sqrt{m}A^{(m)}+c_2\sqrt{\frac{m}{k}}\bar{A}^{(m)}\right)+\left(c_1\sqrt{m}B^{(n,m)}+c_2\sqrt{\frac{m}{k}}\bar{B}^{(n,m)}\right)+\left(c_1\sqrt{m}C^{(n,m)}+c_2\sqrt{\frac{m}{k}}\bar{C}^{(n,m)}\right)+\left(c_1\sqrt{m}D^{(m)}+c_2\sqrt{\frac{m}{k}}\bar{D}^{(m)}\right).$$

From the proof of Theorem 4 in [12], we know that all terms are negligible in probability except for

$$\left(c_1\sqrt{m}C^{(n,m)}+c_2\sqrt{\frac{m}{k}}\bar{C}^{(n,m)}\right)=\sum_{l=1}^{[n/k]}\left[c_1Y_{n,m}^l+c_2\bar{Y}_{n,m}^l\right]\left|\sigma_{\frac{kl-k}{n}}\right|^p,$$

where,

$$Y_{n,m}^l=\sum_{j=1}^{k}\left[\frac{1}{\sqrt{m}}\frac{1}{\left(\frac{1}{m}\right)^{pH}}\sum_{i\in I_n(l)}\left|\Delta_{k(i-1)+j}^m B^H\right|^p-\frac{\sqrt{m}m_p}{n}\right],$$

$$\bar{Y}_{n,m}^l=\frac{1}{\sqrt{\frac{m}{k}}}\frac{1}{\left(\frac{k}{m}\right)^{pH}}\sum_{i\in I'_n(l)}\left|B_{\frac{ki}{m}}^H-B_{\frac{ki-k}{m}}^H\right|^p-\frac{\sqrt{\frac{m}{k}}m_p}{\frac{n}{k}}.$$

From Lemma 1, we have for fixed n, as a vector,

$$\left\{c_1Y_{n,m}^l+c_2\bar{Y}_{n,m}^l\right\}_{l=1}^{[n/k]}\to\bar{\sigma}\left(W_{\frac{kl}{n}}-W_{\frac{kl-k}{n}}\right)_{l=1}^{[n/k]}$$

stably as $m\to\infty$, where

$$\bar{\sigma}^2=c_1^2v_1^2+c_2^2v_1^2+2c_2c_2\left(cor\right)^2.$$

So, we have that for any $\mathcal{F}_1$-measurable random variables,

$$\left|\sigma_{\frac{kl-k}{n}}\right|^p,\ l=1,\cdots,[n/k],$$

as $m\to\infty$,

$$\left(\left|\sigma_{\frac{kl-k}{n}}\right|^p,c_1Y_{n,m}^l+c_2\bar{Y}_{n,m}^l\right)_{1\le l\le[n/k]}\to^L\left(\left|\sigma_{\frac{kl-k}{n}}\right|^p,\bar{\sigma}\left(W_{\frac{kl}{n}}-W_{\frac{kl-k}{n}}\right)\right)_{1\le l\le[n/k]},$$

where W is a Brownian motion independent of $\mathcal{F}_1$.

Hence,

$$c_1\sqrt{m}C^{(n,m)}+c_2\sqrt{\frac{m}{k}}\bar{C}^{(n,m)}\to\bar{\sigma}\sum_{l=1}^{[n/k]}\left|\sigma_{\frac{kl-k}{n}}\right|^p\left(W_{\frac{kl}{n}}-W_{\frac{kl-k}{n}}\right)$$

stably, as m tends to infinity. On the other hand,

$$\sum_{l=1}^{[n/k]}\left|\sigma_{\frac{kl-k}{n}}\right|^p\left(W_{\frac{kl}{n}}-W_{\frac{kl-k}{n}}\right)$$

converges uniformly in probability to $\int_0^1|\sigma_s|^p\,dW_s$ as n tends to infinity. This implies, by letting first m and then n tend to infinity, that

$$c_1\sqrt{m}C^{(n,m)}+c_2\sqrt{\frac{m}{k}}\bar{C}^{(n,m)}$$

converges in distribution to

$$\bar{\sigma}\int_0^1|\sigma_s|^p\,dW_s$$

stably.

Note that

$$\bar{\sigma}^2=(c_1,c_2)\begin{pmatrix}v_1^2 & (cor)^2\\(cor)^2 & v_1^2\end{pmatrix}(c_1,c_2)^{\mathrm{T}}=\tilde{\sigma}^2,$$

which completes the proof of (8).

6

Further Results for General Financial Equilibrium Problems via Variational Inequalities

Annamaria Barbagallo[1], Patrizia Daniele[2], Mariagrazia Lorino[2], Antonino Maugeri[2], Cristina Mirabella[2]
[1]Department of Mathematics and Applications "R. Caccioppoli", University of Naples "Federico II", Naples, Italy
[2]Department of Mathematics and Computer Science, University of Catania, Catania, Italy

ABSTRACT

This paper is the sequel of the previous papers [1] and [2]. More precisely, we study the regularity of the solutions of the evolutionary variational inequality governing the general financial evolutionary problem. Specifically we obtain that such a solution is continuous and Lipschitz continuous with respect to time and we illustrate the achieved result through numerical examples. Moreover the numerical examples enables us to understand the behaviour of the financial equilibrium and the impact of the components of the model on the financial equilibrium.

Keywords: Financial Problem; Equilibrium Condition; Variational Inequality Formulation; Lagrange Variables; Deficit Formula; Balance Law; Liability Formula; Continuity; Lipschitz Continuity

1. Introduction

In the previous papers [1] and [2], a general equilibrium model of financial flows and prices is considered. The model is assumed evolving in time. The equilibrium conditions are considered in dynamic sense and the governing variational inequality formulation is presented. Precisely, the variational inequality we are working with is the following one:

$$\text{Find}\left(x^*,y^*,r^*\right)\in\prod_{i=1}^{m}P_i\times\mathcal{R}:$$

$$\sum_{i=1}^{m}\int_0^T\left\{\sum_{j=1}^{n}\left[-\frac{\partial u_i\left(t,x_i^*(t),y_i^*(t)\right)}{\partial x_{ij}}-\left(1-\tau_{ij}(t)\right)r_j^*(t)\right]\times\left[x_{ij}(t)-x_{ij}^*(t)\right]\right.$$

$$\left.+\sum_{j=1}^{n}\left[-\frac{\partial u_i\left(t,x_i^*(t),y_i^*(t)\right)}{\partial y_{ij}}+\left(1-\tau_{ij}(t)\right)r_j^*(t)\left(1+h_j(t)\right)\right]\times\left[y_{ij}(t)-y_{ij}^*(t)\right]\right\}\mathrm{d}t$$

$$+\sum_{j=1}^{n}\int_0^T\sum_{i=1}^{m}\left\{\left(1-\tau_{ij}(t)\right)\left[x_{ij}^*(t)-\left(1+h_j(t)\right)y_{ij}^*(t)\right]+F_j(t)\right\}\times\left[r_j(t)-r_j^*(t)\right]\mathrm{d}t\geq 0,$$

$$\forall(x,y,r)\in\prod_{i=1}^{m}P_i\times\mathcal{R},$$

where P_i is the set of feasible assets and liabilities for each sector $i=1,\cdots,m$ given by

$$P_i=\left\{\left(x_i,y_i\right)\in L^2\left([0,T],\mathbb{R}^{2n}\right):\sum_{j=1}^{n}x_{ij}(t)=s_i(t),\text{ a.e. in }[0,T],\right.$$

$$\left.\sum_{j=1}^{n}y_{ij}(t)=l_i(t)\text{ a.e. in }[0,T],\quad x_i(t)\geq 0,y_i(t)\geq 0,\text{ a.e. in }[0,T]\right\},$$

$s_i(t)$ is the total financial volume held by sector i as assets, $l_i(t)$ is the total financial volume held by sector i as liabilities, $-u_i(t, x_i(t), y_i(t))$ is a measure of the risk of the financial agent, $\tau_{ij}(t)$ is the tax rate levied on sector i's net yield on financial instrument j, $h_j(t) \in L^\infty([0,T])$ is a nonnegative function, $F_j(t)$ is the portion of financial transaction per unit employed to cover the expenses of the financial institutions, $\mathcal{R}$ is the set of feasible instrument prices given by

$$\mathcal{R} = \{ r \in L^2([0,T], \mathbb{R}^n) : \underline{r}_j(t) \le r_j(t) \le \overline{r}_j(t),, \\ j = 1, \cdots, n, \text{a.e. in } [0,T] \},$$

where $\underline{r}$ and $\overline{r}$ are assumed to be in $L^2([0,T], \mathbb{R}^n)$.

Setting, for the sake of simplicity,

$$v = (x, y, r) = \left((x_{ij})_{\substack{i=1,\cdots,m \\ j=1,\cdots,n}}, (y_{ij})_{\substack{i=1,\cdots,m \\ j=1,\cdots,n}}, (r_j)_{j=1,\cdots,n} \right);$$

$$A : L^2([0,T], \mathbb{R}^{2mn+n}) \to L^2([0,T], \mathbb{R}^{2mn+n})$$

defined as:

$$A(t,v) = \left(\left[-\frac{\partial u_i(t,x,y)}{\partial x_{ij}} - (1 - \tau_{ij}(t)) r_j(t) \right]_{\substack{i=1,\cdots,m \\ j=1,\cdots,n}}, \right.$$

$$\left[-\frac{\partial u_i(t,x,y)}{\partial y_{ij}} + (1 - \tau_{ij}(t))(1 + h_j(t)) r_j(t) \right]_{\substack{i=1,\cdots,m \\ j=1,\cdots,n}}, \quad (1)$$

$$\left. \left[\sum_{i=1}^{m} (1 - \tau_{ij}(t)) (x_{ij}(t) - (1 + h_j(t)) y_{ij}(t)) \right]_{j=1,\cdots,n} \right)$$

$$\mathbb{K} = \{ v = (x, y, r) \in L^2([0,T], \mathbb{R}^{2mn+n}) : \\ x(t) \ge 0, \ y(t) \ge 0, \text{ a.e. in } [0,T], \\ \sum_{j=1}^{n} x_{ij}(t) = s_i(t), \sum_{j=1}^{n} y_{ij}(t) = l_i(t), \text{a.e. in } [0,T], \quad (2) \\ \forall i = 1, \cdots, m, \\ \underline{r}(t) \le r(t) \le \overline{r}(t), \text{ a.e. in } [0,T] \},$$

then variational inequality (1) becomes the problem:

$$\text{Find } v^* = (x^*, y^*, r^*) \in \mathbb{K} : \langle A(t, v^*), v - v^* \rangle \ge 0, \\ \forall v \in \mathbb{K}.$$

Variational inequality (1) proved to be a very useful tool which enables us to study the financial equilibrium of an economy evolving in time and in the previous papers [1] and [2] the authors provided an interesting and useful output as the *deficit formula*, a general *balance law* and the *liability formula* which could be of great importance for the theory of equilibrium problems evolving in time. For the reader's convenience we recall such important formulas:

1) **Deficit formula**

$$\sum_{i=1}^{m} (1 - \tau_{ij}(t)) \left[x_{ij}^*(t) - (1 + h_j(t)) y_{ij}^*(t) \right] \\ + F_j(t) + \rho_j^{(2)*}(t) = \rho_j^{(1)*}(t), \quad \forall j = 1, \cdots, n,$$

where $\rho_j^{(1)*}(t)$ and $\rho_j^{(2)*}(t)$ are the Lagrange variables associated to the price bounds:

$$\left. \begin{aligned} \rho_j^{(1)*}(t)(\underline{r}_j(t) - r_j^*(t)) &= 0, \\ \rho_j^{(2)*}(t)(r_j^*(t) - \overline{r}_j(t)) &= 0, \end{aligned} \right. \quad \forall j = 1, \cdots, n.$$

The meaning of $\rho_j^{(1)*}(t)$ is that it represents the deficit per unit whereas $\rho_j^{(2)*}(t)$ is the positive surplus per unit;

2) **Balance law**

$$\sum_{i=1}^{m} l_i(t) = \sum_{i=1}^{m} s_i(t) - \sum_{i=1}^{m} \sum_{j=1}^{n} \tau_{ij}(t) \left[x_{ij}^*(t) - y_{ij}^*(t) \right] \\ - \sum_{i=1}^{m} \sum_{j=1}^{n} (1 - \tau_{ij}(t)) h_j(t) y_{ij}^*(t) \\ + \sum_{j=1}^{n} F_j(t) - \sum_{j=1}^{n} \rho_j^{(1)*}(t) + \sum_{j=1}^{n} \rho_j^{(2)*}(t);$$

3) **Liability formula**

$$\sum_{i=1}^{m} l_i(t) = \frac{1}{(1 - \theta(t))(1 + i(t))} \\ \cdot \left\{ (1 - \theta(t)) \sum_{i=1}^{m} s_i(t) + \sum_{j=1}^{n} F_j(t) - \sum_{j=1}^{n} \rho_j^{(1)*}(t) + \sum_{j=1}^{n} \rho_j^{(2)*}(t) \right\},$$

where $\theta(t)$ and $i(t)$ are the averages of $\tau_{ij}(t)$ and $h_j(t)$, namely $\theta(t) = \frac{\sum_{i=1}^{m} \sum_{j=1}^{n} \tau_{ij}(t)}{mn}$ and $i(t) = \frac{\sum_{j=1}^{n} h_j(t)}{n}$, respectively.

These suggested formulas could be of topical utility for the management of the world economy and to this aim in [2] the authors give some suggestions for the achievement of the world financial equilibrium and for finding the necessary way to follow in order to reach an improvement of the economy. It is worth reminding such suggestions:

Proposition 1.1 *When the prices are minimal, namely they coincide with the floor prices, the economy collapses.*

Proposition 1.2 *Minimal prices imply the increase in the public debt.*

Proposition 1.3 *Minimal prices produce an economic recession. There is no incentive to the economic efforts.*

Proposition 1.4 *Even if it could be shocking, the*

development of the economy and of the employment results from an increase in the prices.

The value of these propositions can be realized by taking into account that the increase in prices indicated in Proposition 1.4 has been forecasted many months before (June 2011) it happened in our days.

Moreover, in [2] an "Evaluation Index", that we denoted by $E(t)$, has been introduced as a useful and simple tool for the evaluation of an economy, given by

$$E(t)=\frac{\sum_{i=1}^{m} l_i(t)}{\sum_{i=1}^{m}\tilde{s}_i(t)+\sum_{j=1}^{n}\tilde{F}_j(t)},$$

where we set

$$\tilde{s}_i(t)=\frac{s_i(t)}{1+i(t)},\quad \tilde{F}_j(t)=\frac{F_j(t)}{1+i(t)-\theta(t)-\theta(t)i(t)}.$$

We remark that if $E(t)$ is greater or equal to 1 the evaluation of the financial equilibrium is positive (better if $E(t)$ is proximal to 1) whereas if $E(t)$ is less than 1 the evaluation of the financial equilibrium is negative.

The aim of this paper is to provide new theoretical and numerical results about solutions of financial equilibrium problems. In particular, we will prove a continuity result with respect to time of the solution, namely:

Theorem 1.1 *Let* $s\in C^0([0,T],\mathbb{R}^m)$, *let* $l\in C^0([0,T],\mathbb{R}^n)$, *let* $\underline{r},\bar{r}\in C^0([0,T],\mathbb{R}^n_+)$ *and let* $A\in C^0([0,T],\mathbb{R}^{2mn+n})$ *be a strongly monotone map, namely there exists* $\alpha>0$ *such that, for* $t\in[0,T]$,

$$\langle A(t,v_1)-A(t,v_2),v_1-v_2\rangle\ge\alpha\|v_1-v_2\|^2,$$
$$\forall v_1,v_2\in\mathbb{R}^{2mn+n}.$$

Then variational inequality (1) admits a unique continuous solution.

Furthermore, we prove the following Lipschitz continuity result:

Theorem 1.2 *Let* $A\in C^0([0,T],\mathbb{R}^{2mn+n})$ *be strongly monotone, namely there exists* $\alpha>0$ *such that, for* $t\in[0,T]$,

$$\langle A(t,v_1)-A(t,v_2),v_1-v_2\rangle\ge\alpha\|v_1-v_2\|^2,$$
$$\forall v_1,v_2\in\mathbb{R}^{2mn+n};$$

Lipschitz continuous with respect to v, namely there exists $\beta>0$ such that, for $t\in[0,T]$

$$\|A(t,v_1)-A(t,v_2)\|\le\beta\|v_1-v_2\|,\ \forall v_1,v_2\in\mathbb{R}^{2mn+n};$$

and Lipschitz continuous with respect to t, namely there exists $M>0$ such that, for $t_1,t_2\in[0,T]$,

$$\|A(t_1,v)-A(t_2,v)\|\le M\|v\||t_1-t_2|,\ \forall v\in\mathbb{R}^{2mn+n}.$$

Let $s,l:[0,T]\to\mathbb{R}^m$ be two Lipschitz continuous functions and let $\underline{r},\bar{r}:[0,T]\to\mathbb{R}^n$ be two Lipschitz continuous functions. Then, the unique financial equilibrium solution $v^*=(x^*,y^*,r^*)$ is Lipschitz continuous in $[0,T]$. Moreover, let $t_1\ne t_2$, the following estimate holds:

$$\frac{\|v^*(t_2)-v^*(t_1)\|^2}{|t_2-t_1|^2}\le\gamma\left(\|v^*\|^2_{C^0([0,T],\mathbb{R}^{2mn+n})}+L^2\right), \quad (3)$$

where $\gamma=\gamma(\alpha,\beta,M,T,L)$ and

$$L=\sup_{\substack{t_1,t_2\in[0,T]\\ t_1\ne t_2}}\left\|\frac{P_{\mathbb{K}(t_2)}(z)-P_{\mathbb{K}(t_1)}(z)}{t_2-t_1}\right\|.$$

The continuity and Lipschitz continuity of solutions to financial equilibrium problems is a very important property for applications. Indeed, it is fundamental to establish numerical approximate solutions. Such numerical solutions can be obtained making use of a modified version of the algorithms (see for instances [3-7]). It is worth remarking that the Lipschitz continuity allows us to calculate the error in approximating the solution.

In order to clearly illustrate theoretical results, some significant examples are provided and, in such a way, the impact that the components of the model have on the equilibrium are highlighted.

It is worth mensioning that even in this case variational inequalities are able to express the time-dependent equilibrium conditions. Then, applying delicate tools of nonlinear analysis (see [8-11]), it is possible to prove existence results and qualitative analysis. For other economic problems where the time plays an important role we refer to the papers devoted to the Walrasian equilibrium problem [12-15], to the oligopolistic market equilibrium problem [16,17], to the weighted traffic equilibrium problem [18,19], and to [20].

The paper is organized as follows. In Section 2 we present the general financial model. In Section 3 we study the continuity results of the solution to the variational inequality which characterizes the financial model. In Section 4 we provide a Lipschitz continuity result for the solution. Finally, in Section 5 we propose a numerical examples from which we deduce that the solution, computed by means of the direct method (see [21]), is Lipschitz continuous.

2. The Model

We consider a financial economy consisting of m sectors, with a typical sector denoted by i, and of n instruments, with a typical financial instrument denoted by j, in the time interval $[0,T]$. Let $s_i(t)$ denote the total financial volume held by sector i at time t as assets, and let $l_i(t)$ be the total financial volume held by sector i at time t as liabilities. Then, unlike previous papers (see [22-27]), we allow markets of assets and liabilities to have different investments $s_i(t)$ and $l_i(t)$, respectively. Since we are working in the presence of uncertainty and of risk perspectives, the volumes $s_i(t)$ and $l_i(t)$ held by each sector cannot be considered stable with respect to time and may decrease or increase depending on unfavorable or favorable economic conditions. At time t, we denote the amount of instrument j held as an asset in sector i's portfolio by $x_{ij}(t)$ and the amount of instrument j held as a liability in sector i's portfolio by $y_{ij}(t)$. The assets and liabilities in all the sectors are grouped into the matrices

$$x(t)=\begin{bmatrix} x_1(t) \\ \vdots \\ x_i(t) \\ \vdots \\ x_m(t) \end{bmatrix}=\begin{bmatrix} x_{11}(t) & \dots & x_{1j}(t) & \dots & x_{1n}(t) \\ \vdots & \ddots & \vdots & \ddots & \vdots \\ x_{i1}(t) & \dots & x_{ij}(t) & \dots & x_{in}(t) \\ \vdots & \ddots & \vdots & \ddots & \vdots \\ x_{m1}(t) & \dots & x_{mj}(t) & \dots & x_{mn}(t) \end{bmatrix}$$

and

$$y(t)=\begin{bmatrix} y_1(t) \\ \vdots \\ y_i(t) \\ \vdots \\ y_m(t) \end{bmatrix}=\begin{bmatrix} y_{11}(t) & \dots & y_{1j}(t) & \dots & y_{1n}(t) \\ \vdots & \ddots & \vdots & \ddots & \vdots \\ y_{i1}(t) & \dots & y_{ij}(t) & \dots & y_{in}(t) \\ \vdots & \ddots & \vdots & \ddots & \vdots \\ y_{m1}(t) & \dots & y_{mj}(t) & \dots & y_{mn}(t) \end{bmatrix}.$$

We denote the price of instrument j held as an asset at time t by $r_j(t)$ and the price of instrument j held as a liability at time t by $(1+h_j(t))r_j(t)$, where h is a nonnegative function defined into $[0,T]$ and belonging to $L^\infty([0,T])$. We introduce the term $h_j(t)$ because the prices of liabilities are generally greater than or equal to the prices of assets so that we can describe, in a more realistic way, the behaviour of the markets for which the liabilities are more expensive than the assets. In such a way, this paper appears as an improvement in various directions of the previous ones [22-27]. We group the instrument prices held as assets into the vector $r(t)=[r_1(t), r_2(t),\cdots, r_i(t),\cdots, r_n(t)]^{\mathrm{T}}$ and the instrument prices held as liabilities into the vector

$$\begin{aligned}&(1+h(t))r(t)\\&=\big[(1+h_1(t))r_1(t),(1+h_2(t))r_2(t),\cdots,\\&\quad (1+h_i(t))r_i(t),\cdots,(1+h_n(t))r_n(t)\big]^{\mathrm{T}}\end{aligned}$$

In our problem the prices of each instrument appear as unknown variables. Under the assumption of perfect competition, each sector will behave as if it has no influence on the instrument prices or on the behaviour of the other sectors.

In order to express the time-dependent equilibrium conditions by means of an evolutionary variational inequality, we choose as a functional setting the very general Lebesgue space $L^2([0,T],\mathbb{R}^p)$. Then, the set of feasible assets and liabilities for each sector $i=1,\cdots,m$, is P_i.

Now, in order to improve the model of competitive financial equilibrium described in [1], we consider the possibility of policy interventions in the financial equilibrium and incorporate them in form of taxes and price controls.

To this aim, denote the ceiling price associated with instrument j by $\overline{r}_j$ and the nonnegative floor price associated with instrument j by $\underline{r}_j$, with $\overline{r}_j(t)>\underline{r}_j(t)$, a.e. in $[0,T]$. The meaning of the constraint $\underline{r}_j(t)\le r_j(t)$ a.e. in $[0,T]$ is that to each investor a minimal price $\underline{r}_j$ for the assets held in the instrument j is guaranteed, whereas each investor is requested to pay for the liabilities not less than the minimal price $(1+h_j)\underline{r}_j$. Analogously each investor cannot obtain for an asset a price greater than $\overline{r}_j$ and as a liability the price cannot exceed the maximum price $(1+h_j)\overline{r}_j$.

Denote the given tax rate levied on sector i's net yield on financial instrument j, as τ_{ij}. Assume that the tax rates lie in the interval $[0,1)$ and belong to $L^\infty([0,T])$. Therefore, the government in this model has the flexibility of levying a distinct tax rate across both sectors and instruments.

Let us group the instrument ceiling prices $\overline{r}_j$ into the column vector $\overline{r}(t)=[\overline{r}_1(t),\cdots,\overline{r}_i(t),\cdots,\overline{r}_n(t)]^{\mathrm{T}}$, the instrument floor prices $\underline{r}_j$ into the column vector $\underline{r}(t)=[\underline{r}_1(t),\cdots,\underline{r}_i(t),\cdots,\underline{r}_n(t)]^{\mathrm{T}}$, and the tax rates τ_{ij} into the matrix

$$\tau(t)=\begin{bmatrix} \tau_{11}(t) & \dots & \tau_{1j}(t) & \dots & \tau_{1n}(t) \\ \vdots & \ddots & \vdots & \ddots & \vdots \\ \tau_{i1}(t) & \dots & \tau_{ij}(t) & \dots & \tau_{in}(t) \\ \vdots & \ddots & \vdots & \ddots & \vdots \\ \tau_{m1}(t) & \dots & \tau_{mj}(t) & \dots & \tau_{mn}(t) \end{bmatrix}.$$

The set of feasible instrument prices is $\mathcal{R}$.

In order to determine for each sector i the optimal composition of instruments held as assets and as liabilities, we consider, as usual, the influence due to risk-aversion and the process of optimization of each sector in the financial economy, namely the desire to maximize the value of the asset holdings and to minimize the value of liabilities. Then, we introduce the utility function $U_i(t,x_i(t),y_i(t),r(t))$, for each sector i, in this way

$$\begin{aligned}&U_i(t,x_i(t),y_i(t),r(t))=u_i(t,x_i(t),y_i(t))\\&+\sum_{j=1}^{n} r_j(t)(1-\tau_{ij}(t))\big[x_{ij}(t)-(1+h_j(t))y_{ij}(t)\big],\end{aligned}$$

where the term $-u_i(t, x_i(t), y_i(t))$ represents a measure of the risk of the financial agent and

$r_j(t)(1-\tau_{ij}(t))[x_i(t)-(1+h_j(t))y_i(t)]$ represents the value of the difference between the asset holdings and the value of liabilities. We suppose that the sector's utility function $U_i(t, x_i(t), y_i(t))$ is defined on $[0,T]\times\mathbb{R}^n\times\mathbb{R}^n$, is measurable in t and is continuous with respect to x_i and y_i. Moreover we assume that $\partial u_i/\partial x_{ij}$ and $\partial u_i/\partial y_{ij}$ exist and that they are measurable in t and continuous with respect to x_i and y_i. Further, we require that $\forall i=1,\cdots,m$, $\forall j=1,\cdots,n$, and a.e. in $[0,T]$ the following growth conditions hold true:

$$|u_i(t,x,y)| \le \alpha_i(t)\|x\|\|y\|, \quad \forall x, y \in \mathbb{R}^n, \tag{4}$$

and

$$\left|\frac{\partial u_i(t,x,y)}{\partial x_{ij}}\right| \le \beta_{ij}(t)\|y\|, \qquad \left|\frac{\partial u_i(t,x,y)}{\partial y_{ij}}\right| \le \gamma_{ij}(t)\|x\|, \tag{5}$$

where α_i, β_{ij}, γ_{ij} are non-negative functions of $L^\infty([0,T])$. Finally, we suppose that the function $u_i(t,x,y)$ is concave.

In order to determine the equilibrium prices, we establish the equilibrium condition which expresses the equilibration of the total assets, the total liabilities and the portion of financial transactions per unit F_j employed to cover the expenses of the financial institutions including possible dividends, as in [1]. Hence, the equilibrium condition for the price r_j of instrument j is the following:

$$\sum_{i=1}^{m}(1-\tau_{ij}(t))[x_{ij}^*(t)-(1+h_j(t))y_{ij}^*(t)] + F_j(t)\begin{cases}\ge 0 & \text{if } r_j^*(t)=\underline{r}_j(t)\\ =0 & \text{if } \underline{r}_j(t)<r_j^*(t)<\overline{r}_j(t)\\ \le 0 & \text{if } r_j^*(t)=\overline{r}_j(t)\end{cases} \tag{6}$$

In other words, the prices are determined taking into account the amount of the supply, the demand of an instrument and the charges F_j, namely if there is an actual supply excess of an instrument as assets and of the charges F_j in the economy, then its price must be the floor price. If the price of an instrument is greater than $\underline{r}_j(t)$, but not at the ceiling, then the market of that instrument must clear. Finally, if there is an actual demand excess of an instrument as liabilities and of the charges F_j in the economy, then the price must be at the ceiling.

Now, we can give different but equivalent equilibrium conditions, each of which is useful to illustrate particular features of the equilibrium.

Definition 2.1 *A vector of sector assets, liabilities and instrument prices* $(x^*(t), y^*(t), r^*(t)) \in \prod_{i=1}^{m} P_i \times \mathcal{R}$ *is an equilibrium of the dynamic financial model if and only if* $\forall i=1,\cdots,m$, $\forall j=1,\cdots,n$, *and a.e. in* $[0,T]$, *it satisfies the system of inequalities*

$$-\frac{\partial u_i(t,x^*,y^*)}{\partial x_{ij}} - (1-\tau_{ij}(t))r_j^*(t) - \mu_i^{(1)*}(t) \ge 0, \tag{7}$$

$$-\frac{\partial u_i(t,x^*,y^*)}{\partial y_{ij}} + (1-\tau_{ij}(t))(1+h_j(t))r_j^*(t) - \mu_i^{(2)*}(t) \ge 0, \tag{8}$$

and equalities

$$x_{ij}^*(t)\left[-\frac{\partial u_i(t,x^*,y^*)}{\partial x_{ij}} - (1-\tau_{ij}(t))r_j^*(t) - \mu_i^{(1)*}(t)\right] = 0, \tag{9}$$

$$y_{ij}^*(t)\cdot\left[-\frac{\partial u_i(t,x^*,y^*)}{\partial x_{ij}} + (1-\tau_{ij}(t))(1+h_j(t))r_j^*(t) - \mu_i^{(2)*}(t)\right] = 0, \tag{10}$$

where $\mu_i^{(1)*}(t), \mu_i^{(2)*}(t) \in L^2([0,T])$ are Lagrange functions, and verify conditions (6) a.e. in $[0,T]$.

Let us explain the meaning of the above conditions. To each financial volumes s_i and l_i held by sector i, we associate the functions $\mu_i^{(1)}(t), \mu_i^{(2)}(t)$, related, respectively, to the assets and to the liabilities and which represent the "equilibrium disutilities" per unit of the sector i. Then, (7) and (9) mean that the financial volume invested in instrument j as assets x_{ij}^* is greater than or equal to zero if the j-th component $-\frac{\partial u_i(t,x^*,y^*)}{\partial x_{ij}} - (1-\tau_{ij}(t))r_j^*(t)$ of the disutility is equal to $\mu_i^{(1)}(t)$, whereas if $-\frac{\partial u_i(t,x^*,y^*)}{\partial x_{ij}} - (1-\tau_{ij}(t))r_j^*(t) > \mu_i^{(1)}(t)$, then $x_{ij}^*(t)=0$. The same occurs for the liabilities and the meaning of (6) is already illustrated.

The functions $\mu_i^{(1)}(t)$ and $\mu_i^{(2)}(t)$ are Lagrange functions associated a.e. in $[0,T]$ with the constraints $\sum_{j=1}^{n} x_{ij}(t) - s_i(t) = 0$ and $\sum_{j=1}^{n} y_{ij}(t) - l_i(t) = 0$, respectively. They are unknown a priori, but this fact has no influence because we will prove in the following theorem that Definition is equivalent to a variational inequality in which $\mu_i^{(1)}(t)$ and $\mu_i^{(2)}(t)$ do not appear.

Theorem 2.1 *A vector* $(x^*,y^*,r^*)\in\prod_{i=1}^m P_i\times\mathcal{R}$ *is a dynamic financial equilibrium if and only if it satisfies variational inequality* (1).

Moreover, we recall the result about Lagrange multipliers (see [2]):

Theorem 2.2 *Let* $(x^*,y^*,r^*)\in\prod_{i=1}^m P_i\times L^2([0,T],\mathbb{R}_+^n)$ *be a solution to variational inequality* (1). *Then there exist*

$$\lambda^{(1)*},\lambda^{(2)*}\in L^2([0,T],\mathbb{R}_+^{mn}),$$
$$\mu^{(1)*},\mu^{(2)*}\in L^2([0,T],\mathbb{R}_+^{m}),$$
$$\rho^{(1)*},\rho^{(2)*}\in L^2([0,T],\mathbb{R}_+^{n})$$

such that a.e. in $[0,T]$,

$$\begin{gathered}-\frac{\partial u_i(t,x^*(t),y^*(t))}{\partial x_{ij}}\\-(1-\tau_{ij}(t))r_j^*(t)-\lambda_{ij}^{(1)*}(t)-\mu_i^{(1)*}(t)=0,\\\forall i=1,\cdots,m,\ \forall j=1,\cdots,n,\\-\frac{\partial u_i(t,x^*(t),y^*(t))}{\partial y_{ij}}+(1-\tau_{ij}(t))(1+h_j(t))r_j^*(t)\\-\lambda_{ij}^{(2)*}(t)-\mu_i^{(2)*}(t)=0,\\\forall i=1,\cdots,m,\ \forall j=1,\cdots,n,\\\sum_{i=1}^m(1-\tau_{ij}(t))\left[x_{ij}^*(t)-(1+h_j(t))y_{ij}^*(t)\right]\\+F_j(t)+\rho_j^{(2)*}(t)=\rho_j^{(1)*}(t),\quad\forall j=1,\cdots,n,\end{gathered}\tag{11}$$

$$\left.\begin{aligned}\lambda_{ij}^{(1)*}(t)x_{ij}^*(t)=0,\\\lambda_{ij}^{(2)*}(t)y_{ij}^*(t)=0,\end{aligned}\right.\quad\forall i=1,\cdots,m,\ \forall j=1,\cdots,n,\tag{12}$$

$$\left.\begin{aligned}\mu_i^{(1)*}(t)\left(\sum_{j=1}^n x_{ij}^*(t)-s_i(t)\right)=0,\\\mu_i^{(2)*}(t)\left(\sum_{j=1}^n y_{ij}^*(t)-l_i(t)\right)=0,\end{aligned}\right.\quad\forall i=1,\cdots,m,\tag{13}$$

$$\left.\begin{aligned}\rho_j^{(1)*}(t)\left(\underline{r}_j(t)-r_j^*(t)\right)=0,\\\rho_j^{(2)*}(t)\left(r_j^*(t)-\overline{r}_j(t)\right)=0.\end{aligned}\right.\quad\forall j=1,\cdots,n,\tag{14}$$

3. Continuity Results for Financial Equilibrium Solutions

In order to show the continuity result for the financial equilibrium problem, first of all, let us recall the well-known property of set convergence due to K. Kuratowski (see [28]), that is a generalization of the classical Hausdorff definition of a metric for the space of closed subsets of a (compact) metric space.

Let (X,d) be a metric space and let $\{K_n\}_{n\in\mathbb{N}}$ be a sequence of subsets of X. Recall that

$d-\underline{\lim}_n K_n=$

$\{x\in X:\exists\{x_n\}_{n\in\mathbb{N}}$ eventually in K_n such that $x_n\xrightarrow{d}x\}$

$d-\overline{\lim}_n K_n=$

$\{x\in X:\exists\{x_n\}_{n\in\mathbb{N}}$ frequently in K_n such that $x_n\xrightarrow{d}x\}$

where *eventually* means that there exists $\delta\in\mathbb{N}$ such that $x_n\in K_n$ for any $n\geq\delta$, and *frequently* means that there exists an infinite subset $N\subseteq\mathbb{N}$ such that $x_n\in K_n$ for any $n\in N$. Finally we can remind the set convergence in Kuratowski's sense.

Definition 3.1 *We say that* $\{K_n\}_{n\in\mathbb{N}}$ *converges to some subset* $K\subseteq X$ *in Kuratwoski's sense, and we briefly write* $K_n\to K$, *if* $d-\underline{\lim}_n K_n=d-\overline{\lim}_n K_n=K$. *Thus, in order to verify that* $K_n\to K$, *it suffices to check that*

(K1) $K\subseteq d-\underline{\lim}_n K_n$, *i.e.* for any $x\in K$, there exists a sequence $\{x_n\}_{n\in\mathbb{N}}$ converging to x in X such that x_n lies in K_n for all $n\in\mathbb{N}$;

(K2) $d-\overline{\lim}_n K_n\subseteq K$, *i.e.* for any subsequence $\{x_n\}_{n\in\mathbb{N}}$ converging to x in X, such that x_n lies in K_n for all $n\in\mathbb{N}$, then the limit x belongs to K.

Now, let us prove that the set of feasible vectors satisfies the property of the set convergence in Kuratowski's sense.

Proposition 3.1 *Let* $s\in C^0([0,T],\mathbb{R}^m)$, *let* $l\in C^0([0,T],\mathbb{R}^m)$, *let* $\underline{r},\overline{r}\in C^0([0,T],\mathbb{R}_+^n)$ *and let* $\{t_k\}_{k\in\mathbb{N}}\subseteq[0,T]$ *be a sequence such that* $t_k\to t\in[0,T]$, *as* $k\to+\infty$. *Then, the sequence of sets*

$$\begin{aligned}&\mathbb{K}(t_k)\\&=\{v(t_k)=(x(t_k),y(t_k),r(t_k))\in\mathbb{R}^{2mn+n}:\\&\quad x_{ij}(t_k)\geq0,\ y_{ij}(t_k)\geq0,\ \forall i=1,\cdots,m,\ j=1,\cdots,n,\\&\quad\sum_{j=1}^n x_{ij}(t_k)=s_i(t_k),\ \sum_{j=1}^n y_{ij}(t_k)=l_i(t_k),\ \forall i=1,\cdots,m,\\&\quad\underline{r}_j(t_k)\leq r_j(t_k)\leq\overline{r}_j(t_k),\ \forall j=1,\cdots,n\},\end{aligned}$$

$\forall k\in\mathbb{N}$, converges to

$$\begin{aligned}\mathbb{K}(t)=\{&v(t)=(x(t),y(t),r(t))\in\mathbb{R}^{2mn+n}:\\&x_{ij}(t)\geq0,\ y_{ij}(t)\geq0,\ \forall i=1,\cdots,m,\ j=1,\cdots,n,\\&\sum_{j=1}^n x_{ij}(t)=s_i(t),\ \sum_{j=1}^n y_{ij}(t)=l_i(t),\ \forall i=1,\cdots,m,\\&\underline{r}_j(t)\leq r_j(t)\leq\overline{r}_j(t),\ \forall j=1,\cdots,n\},\end{aligned}$$

as $k \to +\infty$, in Kuratowski's sense.

Proof In order to prove that the sequence $\{\mathbb{K}(t_k)\}_{k\in\mathbb{N}}$ converges to $\mathbb{K}(t)$ in Kuratowski's sense, for any sequence $\{t_k\}_{n\in\mathbb{N}} \subseteq [0,T]$ such that $t_k \to t \in [0,T]$, as $k \to +\infty$, it is enough to show that conditions (K1) and (K2) hold.

Let $v(t) = (x(t), y(t), r(t)) \in \mathbb{K}(t)$ be fixed and let us consider the sequence

$\{v(t_k)\}_{k\in\mathbb{N}} = \{(x(t_k), y(t_k), r(t_k))\}_{k\in\mathbb{N}}$, such that

$\forall i = 1,\cdots,m$, $\forall j = 1,\cdots,n$, $\forall k \in \mathbb{N}$,

$$x_{ij}(t_k) = x_{ij}(t) + \frac{s_i(t_k) - s_i(t)}{n},$$

$$y_{ij}(t_k) = y_{ij}(t) + \frac{l_j(t_k) - l_j(t)}{n},$$

and $\forall j = 1,\cdots,n$, $\forall k \in \mathbb{N}$,

$$r_j(t_k) = \underline{r}_j(t_k) + \min\{r_j(t) - \underline{r}_j(t), \overline{r}_j(t_k) - \underline{r}_j(t_k)\}.$$

Let us verify that $v(t_k) \in \mathbb{K}(t_k)$, $\forall k \in \mathbb{N}$. Taking into account that

$$\lim_{k\to+\infty} x_{ij}(t_k) = \lim_{k\to+\infty}\left(x_{ij}(t) + \frac{s_i(t_k) - s_i(t)}{n}\right) = x_{ij}(t) \ge 0,$$

$$\lim_{k\to+\infty} y_{ij}(t_k) = \lim_{k\to+\infty}\left(y_{ij}(t) + \frac{l_j(t_k) - l_j(t)}{m}\right) = y_{ij}(t) \ge 0,$$

there exist two index ν_1 and ν_2 such that for $k > \nu_1$ we get

$$x_{ij}(t_k) \ge 0, \ \forall i = 1,\cdots,m, \forall j = 1,\cdots,n,$$

and for $k > \nu_2$ we have

$$y_{ij}(t_k) \ge 0, \ \forall i = 1,\cdots,m, \forall j = 1,\cdots,n.$$

Since $\min\{r_j(t) - \underline{r}_j(t), \overline{r}_j(t_k) - \underline{r}_j(t_k)\} \ge 0$, $\forall k \in \mathbb{N}$, it results $r_j(t_k) \ge \underline{r}_j(t_k)$, $\forall k \in \mathbb{N}$. Moreover, being

$\min\{r_j(t) - \underline{r}_j(t), \overline{r}_j(t_k) - \underline{r}_j(t_k)\} \le \overline{r}_j(t_k) - \underline{r}_j(t_k)$,

$\forall k \in \mathbb{N}$, it follows $r_j(t_k) \le \overline{r}_j(t_k)$, $\forall k \in \mathbb{N}$. Finally, it results

$$\lim_{k\to+\infty} r_j(t_k) = \lim_{k\to+\infty}\left[\underline{r}_j(t_k) + \min\{r_j(t) - \underline{r}_j(t), \overline{r}_j(t_k) - \underline{r}_j(t_k)\}\right] = r_j(t), \quad \forall j = 1,\cdots,n.$$

Then we can consider a sequence $\{v(t_k)\}_{k\in\mathbb{N}}$ such that for $k > \nu = \max\{\nu_1, \nu_2\}$, $\forall i = 1,\cdots,m$, $\forall j = 1,\cdots,n$,

$$x_{ij}(t_k) = x_{ij}(t) + \frac{s_i(t_k) - s_i(t)}{n},$$

$$y_{ij}(t_k) = y_{ij}(t) + \frac{l_j(t_k) - l_j(t)}{m},$$

$$r_j(t_k) = \underline{r}_j(t_k) + \min\{r_j(t) - \underline{r}_j(t), \overline{r}_j(t_k) - \underline{r}_j(t_k)\},$$

and for $k < \nu$, $\forall i = 1,\cdots,m$, $\forall j = 1,\cdots,n$,

$$v(t_k) = P_{\mathbb{K}(t_k)} v(t),$$

where $P_{\mathbb{K}(t_k)}(\cdot)$ denotes the Hilbertian projection on $\mathbb{K}(t_k)$.

We have $\lim_{n\to+\infty} v(t_n) = v(t)$ and for $n > \nu_j$

$$\sum_{j=1}^{n} x_{ij}(t_n) = \sum_{j=1}^{n}\left[x_{ij}(t) + \frac{s_i(t_k) - s_i(t)}{n}\right] = s_i(t_k),$$

$$\sum_{j=1}^{n} y_{ij}(t_n) = \sum_{j=1}^{n}\left[y_{ij}(t) + \frac{l_i(t_k) - l_i(t)}{n}\right] = l_i(t_k).$$

Then the first condition has been shown.

For the second one, let $\{v(t_n)\}_{n\in\mathbb{N}}$ be a fixed sequence, with $v(t_n) = (x(t_n), y(t_n), r(t_n)) \in \mathbb{K}(t_n)$, $\forall n \in \mathbb{N}$, such that $x(t_n) \to x(t)$ in $\mathbb{R}^{mn}$, $y(t_n) \to y(t)$ in $\mathbb{R}^{mn}$, $r(t_n) \to r(t)$ in $\mathbb{R}^n$. We want to prove that $v(t) = (x(t), y(t), r(t)) \in \mathbb{K}(t)$. Since $v(t_n) = (x(t_n), y(t_n), r(t_n)) \in \mathbb{K}(t_n)$, $\forall n \in \mathbb{N}$, it results

$$x(t_n) \ge 0, \forall n \in \mathbb{N}, \tag{15}$$

$$y(t_n) \ge 0, \forall n \in \mathbb{N}, \tag{16}$$

$$\underline{r}(t_n) \le r(t_n) \le \overline{r}(t_n), \forall n \in \mathbb{N}. \tag{17}$$

Passing to the limit as $n \to +\infty$ in (15), (16) and (17), we obtain

$$x(t) \ge 0,$$

$$y(t) \ge 0,$$

$$\underline{r}(t) \le r(t) \le \overline{r}(t).$$

Then $v(t) \in \mathbb{K}(t)$.

The claim is, now, achieved.□

For what follows, it is convenient to recall that variational inequality (1) can be rewritten in the equivalent parameterized form:

$$\left\langle A(t, v^*(t)), v - v^*(t)\right\rangle \ge 0, \quad \forall v \in \mathbb{K}(t), t \in [0,T], \tag{18}$$

where the constraint set $\mathbb{K}(t)$, $t \in [0,T]$, is a closed convex and nonempty subset of $\mathbb{R}^n$, $A:[0,T]\times\mathbb{R}^{2mn+n} \to \mathbb{R}^{2mn+n}$ is a mapping and $\langle\cdot,\cdot\rangle$ denotes the scalar product in $\mathbb{R}^n$. Moreover, we recall that under general assumptions existence theorems have been proved in [2] (see Section 6).

Taking into account the general continuity result for solutions to parameter variational inequalities in reflexive Banach spaces (see [29], Theorem 4.1) and Proposition, we obtain Theorem 1.1 of Section 1.

Theorem 1.1 *Let* $s \in C^0([0,T],\mathbb{R}^m)$, *let* $l \in C^0([0,T],\mathbb{R}^m)$, *let* $\underline{r},\overline{r} \in C^0([0,T],\mathbb{R}^n_+)$ *and let* $A \in C^0([0,T],\mathbb{R}^{2mn+n})$ *be a strongly monotone map, namely there exists* $\alpha > 0$ *such that, for* $t \in [0,T]$,

$$\langle A(t,v_1)-A(t,v_2),v_1-v_2\rangle \geq \alpha\|v_1-v_2\|^2,$$

$$\forall v_1,v_2 \in \mathbb{R}^{2mn+n}.$$

Then variational inequality (1) admits a unique continuous solution.

4. Lipschitz Continuity Result

The aim of this section is to provide a Lipschitz continuity result for the financial equilibrium solution. For this reason, we recall a general result proved in [30] for the solutions to the parameterized variational inequality (18). More precisely, the following result holds (see [30], Theorem 1):

Theorem 4.1 *Let* A *be strongly monotone, Lipschitz continuous with respect to* v, *Lipschitz continuous with respect to* t, *and there exists* $\kappa \geq 0$ *such that, for* $t_1,t_2 \in [0,T]$,

$$\left\|P_{\mathbb{K}(t_1)}(z)-P_{\mathbb{K}(t_2)}(z)\right\| \leq \kappa|t_1-t_2|, \forall z \in \mathbb{R}^{2mn+n},$$

where $P_{\mathbb{K}(t)}(z) = \arg\min_{v\in\mathbb{K}(t)}\|z-v\|$, $t \in [0,T]$, denotes the projection onto the set $\mathbb{K}(t)$. Then, the unique solution $v^*(t)$, $t \in [0,T]$, to (18) is Lipschitz continuous in $t \in [0,T]$, $t_1 \neq t_2$, the following estimate holds:

$$\frac{\left\|v^*(t_2)-v^*(t_1)\right\|}{|t_2-t_1|} \leq \gamma\left(\|v^*\|^2_{C^0([0,T],\mathbb{R}^{2mn+n})} + \sup_{\substack{t_1,t_2\in[0,T]\\ t_1\neq t_2}}\left\|\frac{P_{\mathbb{K}(t_2)}(z)-P_{\mathbb{K}(t_1)}(z)}{t_2-t_1}\right\|^2\right)^{\frac{1}{2}},$$

where $\gamma = \gamma(\alpha,\beta,M,T,L)$.

For the sake of simplicity, we set

$$L = \sup_{\substack{t_1,t_2\in[0,T]\\ t_1\neq t_2}}\left\|\frac{P_{\mathbb{K}(t_2)}(z)-P_{\mathbb{K}(t_1)}(z)}{t_2-t_1}\right\|.$$

Before applying the previous result to our dynamic financial equilibrium problem, it is necessary to estimate the variation rate of projections onto time-dependent constraint set $[\mathcal{P}_{\mathbb{K}}]$ describing the problem. It is useful to note that $\mathbb{K}(t)$ can be rewritten as the Cartesian product of the following set:

$$\mathbb{K}_1(t) = \left\{x(t) \in \mathbb{R}^{mn} : x_{ij}(t) \geq 0, \forall i = 1,\cdots,m,\ j = 1,\cdots,n, \sum_{j=1}^{n} x_{ij}(t) = s_i(t), \forall i = 1,\cdots,m\right\}$$

$$\mathbb{K}_2(t) = \left\{y(t) \in \mathbb{R}^{mn} : y_{ij}(t) \geq 0, \forall i = 1,\cdots,m,\ j = 1,\cdots,n, \sum_{j=1}^{n} y_{ij}(t) = l_i(t), \forall i = 1,\cdots,m\right\}$$

$$\mathbb{K}_3(t) = \left\{r(t) \in \mathbb{R}^n : \underline{r}_j(t) \leq r_j(t) \leq \overline{r}_j(t), \forall j = 1,\cdots,n\right\},$$

namely

$$\mathbb{K}(t) = \mathbb{K}_1(t)\times\mathbb{K}_2(t)\times\mathbb{K}_3(t).$$

Making use of Proposition 1 in [30], we can show that assuming $s_i(t)$, $t \in [0,T]$, is Lipschitz continuous with Lipschitz constant L_i^1, for $i = 1,\cdots,m$, it results

$$\left\|P_{\mathbb{K}_2(t_2)}(z)-P_{\mathbb{K}_1(t_1)}(z)\right\| \leq \sqrt{n}\sum_{i=1}^{m} L_i^1|t_1-t_2|. \quad (19)$$

Moreover, under the assumption that $l_i(t)$, $t \in [0,T]$, is Lipschitz continuous with Lipschitz constant L_i^2, for $i = 1,\cdots,m$, we have

$$\left\|P_{\mathbb{K}_2(t_2)}(z)-P_{\mathbb{K}_1(t_1)}(z)\right\| \leq \sqrt{n}\sum_{i=1}^{m} L_i^2|t_1-t_2|. \quad (20)$$

Now, taking into account Proposition 4.1 in [31] and assuming that $\underline{r}_j(t)$ and $\overline{r}_j(t)$, $t \in [0,T]$, are Lipschitz continuous with Lipschitz constants $\underline{L}_j^3$ and $\overline{L}_j^3$, respectively, for $j = 1,\cdots,n$, we can prove

$$\left\|P_{\mathbb{K}_3(t_2)}(z)-P_{\mathbb{K}_3(t_1)}(z)\right\| \leq L^3|t_1-t_2|, \quad (21)$$

where $L^3 = \max_{j=1,\cdots,n}\left(\overline{L}_j^3+\underline{L}_j^3\right)$.

We can conclude that

Proposition 4.1 *Let* $t_1,t_2 \in [0,T]$, *let* $s,l:[0,T]\to\mathbb{R}^m$ *be two Lipschitz continuous functions and let* $\underline{r},\overline{r}:[0,T]\to\mathbb{R}^n$ *be two Lipschitz continuous functions. Let* z *be an arbitrary point in* $\mathbb{R}^{mn}$. *Then it results to be*

$$\left\|P_{\mathbb{K}_2(t_2)}(z)-P_{\mathbb{K}_1(t_1)}(z)\right\| \leq L|t_2-t_1|,$$

where L is the positive constant as in (3).

As a consequence, it results

$$\frac{\left\|P_{\mathbb{K}(t_2)}(z)-P_{\mathbb{K}(t_1)}(z)\right\|}{|t_2-t_1|} \leq L.$$

Hence, applying Theorem 4.1, we get the following result.

Theorem 1.2 *Let* $A \in C^0([0,T],\mathbb{R}^{2mn+n})$ *be strongly monotone (with constant* α*), Lipschitz continuous with* *respect to* x *(with constant* β*), Lipschitz continuous with respect to* t *(with constant* M*), and let* $s,l:[0,T]\to\mathbb{R}^m$ *be two Lipschitz continuous functions and let* $\underline{r},\overline{r}:[0,T]\to\mathbb{R}^n$ *be two Lipschitz continuous functions. Then, the unique financial equilibrium solution* $v^*=(x^*,y^*,r^*)$ *is Lipschitz continuous in* $[0,T]$*. Moreover, let* $t_1\neq t_2$*, the following estimate holds:*

$$\frac{\left\|v^*(t_2)-v^*(t_1)\right\|^2}{|t_2-t_1|^2}\le\gamma\left(\left\|v^*\right\|^2_{C^0\left([0,T],\mathbb{R}^{2mn+n}\right)}+L^2\right),$$

where $\gamma=\gamma(\alpha,\beta,M,T,L)$.

5. Some Numerical Examples

Let us study some numerical financial examples in which we consider as the risk aversion function the one suggested by H.M. Markowitz in [32] and [33], which expresses at each instant $t\in[0,T]$ the risk aversion by means of variance-covariance matrices denoting the sector's assessment of the standard deviation of prices for each instrument. We will see that the solutions of the examples are regular and we illustrate the impact of the components of the model on the financial equilibrium, especially for what regards F_1 and F_2 and the deficit and the surplus.

Let us consider an economy with two sectors and two financial instruments, as shown in **Figure 1**, but this setting is not restrictive since we can consider a general economy by an iteration of this significant case, and assume that the variance-covariance matrices of the two sectors are the following:

$$Q^1(t)=\begin{bmatrix}1&0&-0.5t&0\\0&1&0&0\\-0.5t&0&1&0\\0&0&0&1\end{bmatrix},$$

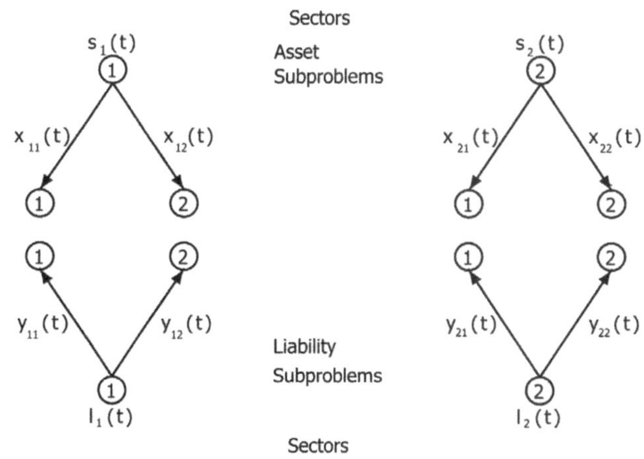

Figure 1. Two sectors and two financial instruments network a.e. in [0,1].

$$Q^2(t)=\begin{bmatrix}1&0&0&0\\0&1&-0.5t&0\\0&-0.5t&1&0\\0&0&0&1\end{bmatrix}.$$

Let us choose as the feasible set

$$\begin{aligned}\mathbb{K}=\{&(x_{11}(t),x_{12}(t),x_{21}(t),x_{22}(t),y_{11}(t),y_{12}(t),\\&y_{21}(t),y_{22}(t),r_1(t),r_2(t))\in L^2([0,1],\mathbb{R}^{10}):\\&x_{11}(t)+x_{12}(t)=3t+1,\ \text{a.e. in }[0,1],\\&x_{21}(t)+x_{22}(t)=t+4,\ \text{a.e. in }[0,1],\\&y_{11}(t)+y_{12}(t)=t+2,\ \text{a.e. in }[0,1],\\&y_{21}(t)+y_{22}(t)=t+3,\ \text{a.e. in }[0,1],\\&x_{11}(t),x_{12}(t),x_{21}(t),x_{22}(t)\ge0,\ \text{a.e. in }[0,1],\\&y_{11}(t),y_{12}(t),y_{21}(t),y_{22}(t)\ge0,\ \text{a.e. in }[0,1],\\&0\le r_1(t)\le4t+3,\ \ \text{a.e. in }[0,1],\\&0\le r_2(t)\le7t+8,\text{ a.e. in }[0,1]\}.\end{aligned}$$

The variational inequality

$$\begin{aligned}&\int_0^1\sum_{i=1}^2\sum_{j=1}^2\left[2\left(\left(Q^i_{(11)j}(t)\right)^T\cdot x_i^*(t)+\left(Q^i_{(21)j}(t)\right)^T\cdot y_i^*(t)\right)-\left(1-\tau_{ij}(t)\right)r_j^*(t)\right]\\&\qquad\times\left[x_{ij}(t)-x_{ij}^*(t)\right]\\&+\sum_{i=1}^2\sum_{j=1}^2\left[2\left(\left(Q^i_{(12)j}(t)\right)^T\cdot x_i^*(t)+\left(Q^i_{(22)j}(t)\right)^T\cdot y_i^*(t)\right)+\left(1-\tau_{ij}(t)\right)r_j^*(t)\left(1+h_j(t)\right)\right]\\&\qquad\times\left[y_{ij}(t)-y_{ij}^*(t)\right]\\&+\sum_{j=1}^2\left[\sum_{i=1}^2\left(1-\tau_{ij}(t)\right)\left(x_{ij}^*(t)-\left(1+h_j(t)\right)y_{ij}^*(t)\right)+F_j(t)\right]\times\left[r_j(t)-r_j^*(t)\right]\mathrm{d}t\ge0,\\&\forall(x,y,r)\in\mathbb{K},\end{aligned}$$

which expresses the financial equilibrium conditions, becomes

$$\begin{aligned}&\int_0^1\{[2x_{11}^*(t)-ty_{11}^*(t)-(1-\tau_{11}(t))r_1^*(t)](x_{11}(t)-x_{11}^*(t))+[2x_{12}^*(t)-(1-\tau_{12}(t))r_2^*(t)](x_{12}(t)-x_{12}^*(t))\\&+[2x_{21}^*(t)-(1-\tau_{21}(t))r_1^*(t)](x_{21}(t)-x_{21}^*(t))+[2x_{22}^*(t)-ty_{21}^*(t)-(1-\tau_{22}(t))r_2^*(t)](x_{22}(t)-x_{22}^*(t))\\&+[2y_{11}^*(t)-tx_{11}^*(t)+(1+h_1(t))(1-\tau_{11}(t))r_1^*(t)](y_{11}(t)-y_{11}^*(t))\\&+[2y_{12}^*(t)+(1+h_2(t))(1-\tau_{12}(t))r_2^*(t)](y_{12}(t)-y_{12}^*(t))\\&+[2y_{21}^*(t)-tx_{22}^*(t)+(1+h_1(t))(1-\tau_{21}(t))r_1^*(t)](y_{21}(t)-y_{21}^*(t))\\&+[2y_{22}^*(t)+(1+h_2(t))(1-\tau_{22}(t))r_2^*(t)](y_{22}(t)-y_{22}^*(t))\\&+[(1-\tau_{11}(t))x_{11}^*(t)+(1-\tau_{21}(t))x_{21}^*(t)-(1+h_1(t))[(1-\tau_{11}(t))y_{11}^*(t)+(1-\tau_{21}(t))y_{21}^*(t)]+F_1(t)](r_1(t)-r_1^*(t))\\&+[(1-\tau_{12}(t))x_{12}^*(t)+(1-\tau_{22}(t))x_{22}^*(t)-(1+h_2(t))[(1-\tau_{12}(t))y_{12}^*(t)+(1-\tau_{22}(t))y_{22}^*(t)]+F_2(t)]\\&(r_2(t)-r_2^*(t))\}\,dt\ge 0,\quad \forall(x,y,r)\in\mathbb{K}.\end{aligned}\tag{22}$$

Following the direct method (see [21]) in order to find the solution, we can derive from the constraints of the convex set $\mathbb{K}$ the values of some variables in terms of the others, namely we obtain, a.e. in $[0,1]$,

$$x_{12}(t)=3t+1-x_{11}(t),\quad x_{22}(t)=t+4-x_{21}(t),$$
$$y_{12}(t)=t+2-y_{11}(t),\quad y_{22}(t)=t+3-y_{21}(t).$$

Then, setting

$$\begin{aligned}\tilde{\mathbb{K}}=\{&(x_{11},x_{21},y_{11},y_{21},r_1,r_2)\in L^2([0,1],\mathbb{R}^6):\\&0\le x_{11}(t)\le 3t+1,\ 0\le x_{21}(t)\le t+4,\ \text{a.e. in }[0,1]\\&0\le y_{11}(t)\le t+2,\ 0\le y_{21}(t)\le t+3,\ \text{a.e. in }[0,1]\\&0\le r_1(t)\le 4t+3,\ 0\le r_2(t)\le 7t+8,\ \text{a.e. in }[0,1]\},\end{aligned}$$

variational inequality (22) can be expressed in the equivalent form:

$$\begin{aligned}&\int_0^1\{[4x_{11}^*(t)-ty_{11}^*(t)-(1-\tau_{11}(t))r_1^*(t)+(1-\tau_{12}(t))r_2^*(t)-6t-2](x_{11}(t)-x_{11}^*(t))\\&+[4x_{21}^*(t)+ty_{21}^*(t)-(1-\tau_{21}(t))r_1^*(t)+(1-\tau_{22}(t))r_2^*(t)-2t-8](x_{21}(t)-x_{21}^*(t))\\&+[4y_{11}^*(t)-tx_{11}^*(t)+(1+h_1(t))(1-\tau_{11}(t))r_1^*(t)-(1+h_2(t))(1-\tau_{12}(t))r_2^*(t)-2t-4](y_{11}(t)-y_{11}^*(t))\\&+[tx_{21}^*(t)+4y_{21}^*(t)+(1+h_1(t))(1-\tau_{21}(t))r_1^*(t)-(1+h_2(t))(1-\tau_{22}(t))r_2^*(t)-t^2-6t-6](y_{21}(t)-y_{21}^*(t))\\&+[(1-\tau_{11}(t))x_{11}^*(t)+(1-\tau_{21}(t))x_{21}^*(t)-(1+h_1(t))((1-\tau_{11}(t))y_{11}^*(t)+(1-\tau_{21}(t))y_{21}^*(t))+F_1(t)](r_1(t)-r_1^*(t))\\&+[-(1-\tau_{12}(t))x_{11}^*(t)-(1-\tau_{22}(t))x_{21}^*(t)+(1+h_2(t))((1-\tau_{12}(t))y_{11}^*(t)+(1-\tau_{22}(t))y_{21}^*(t))\\&+(1-\tau_{12}(t))(3t+1-(1+h_2(t))(t+2))+(1-\tau_{22}(t))[t+4-(1+h_2(t))(t+3)]+F_2(t)](r_2(t)-r_2^*(t))\}\,dt\ge 0,\\&\forall(x,y,r)\in\tilde{\mathbb{K}}.\end{aligned}$$

Let us set

$$\Gamma_1=4x_{11}^*(t)-ty_{11}^*(t)-(1-\tau_{11}(t))r_1^*(t)+(1-\tau_{12}(t))r_2^*(t)-6t-2,$$

$$\Gamma_2=4x_{21}^*(t)+ty_{21}^*(t)-(1-\tau_{21}(t))r_1^*(t)+(1-\tau_{22}(t))r_2^*(t)-2t-8,$$

$$\Gamma_3=4y_{11}^*(t)-tx_{11}^*(t)+(1+h_1(t))(1-\tau_{11}(t))r_1^*(t)-(1+h_2(t))(1-\tau_{12}(t))r_2^*(t)-2t-4,$$

$$\Gamma_4=tx_{21}^*(t)+4y_{21}^*(t)+(1+h_1(t))(1-\tau_{21}(t))r_1^*(t)-(1+h_2(t))(1-\tau_{22}(t))r_2^*(t)-t^2-6t-6,$$

$$\Gamma_5=(1-\tau_{11}(t))x_{11}^*(t)+(1-\tau_{21}(t))x_{21}^*(t)-(1+h_1(t))((1-\tau_{11}(t))y_{11}^*(t)+(1-\tau_{21}(t))y_{21}^*(t))+F_1(t),$$

$$\begin{aligned}\Gamma_6=&-(1-\tau_{12}(t))x_{11}^*(t)-(1-\tau_{22}(t))x_{21}^*(t)+(1+h_2(t))((1-\tau_{12}(t))y_{11}^*(t)+(1-\tau_{22}(t))y_{21}^*(t))\\&+(1-\tau_{12}(t))(3t+1-(1+h_2(t))(t+2))+(1-\tau_{22}(t))(t+4-(1+h_2(t))(t+3))+F_2(t).\end{aligned}$$

As the first step of the direct method suggests, let us search solutions obtained from the system

$$\begin{cases}\Gamma_1 = 4x^*_{11}(t) - ty^*_{11}(t) - (1-\tau_{11}(t))r^*_1(t) + (1-\tau_{12}(t))r^*_2(t) - 6t - 2 = 0\\ \Gamma_2 = 4x^*_{21}(t) + ty^*_{21}(t) - (1-\tau_{21}(t))r^*_1(t) + (1-\tau_{22}(t))r^*_2(t) - 2t - 8 = 0\\ \Gamma_3 = 4y^*_{11}(t) - tx^*_{11}(t) + (1+h_1(t))(1-\tau_{11}(t))r^*_1(t) - (1+h_2(t))(1-\tau_{12}(t))r^*_2(t) - 2t - 4 = 0\\ \Gamma_4 = tx^*_{21}(t) + 4y^*_{21}(t) + (1+h_1(t))(1-\tau_{21}(t))r^*_1(t) - (1+h_2(t))(1-\tau_{22}(t))r^*_2(t) - t^2 - 6t - 6 = 0\end{cases}$$

We get the values of the variables x_{ij} and y_{ij} in terms of τ_{ij}, r_j and h_j, namely

$$\begin{cases}x^*_{11}(t) = \frac{1}{16-t^2}\left\{2t^2 + 28t + 8 + r_1(t)(1-\tau_{11}(t))\left[4 - t(1+h_1(t))\right] + r_2(t)(1-\tau_{12}(t))\left[-4 + t(1+h_2(t))\right]\right\},\\ x^*_{12}(t) = \frac{1}{16-t^2}\left\{-3t^3 - 3t^2 + 20t + 8 - r_1(t)(1-\tau_{11}(t))\left[4 - t(1+h_1(t))\right] - r_2(t)(1-\tau_{12}(t))\left[-4 + t(1+h_2(t))\right]\right\},\\ x^*_{21}(t) = \frac{1}{16-t^2}\left\{-t^3 - 6t^2 + 2t + 32 + r_1(t)(1-\tau_{21}(t))\left[4 + t(1+h_1(t))\right] - r_2(t)(1-\tau_{22}(t))\left[4 + t(1+h_2(t))\right]\right\},\\ x^*_{22}(t) = \frac{1}{16-t^2}\left\{2t^2 + 14t + 32 - r_1(t)(1-\tau_{21}(t))\left[4 + t(1+h_1(t))\right] + r_2(t)(1-\tau_{22}(t))\left[4 + t(1+h_2(t))\right]\right\},\\ y^*_{11}(t) = \frac{1}{16-t^2}\left\{6t^2 + 10t + 16 + r_1(t)(1-\tau_{11}(t))\left[t - 4(1+h_1(t))\right] - r_2(t)(1-\tau_{12}(t))\left[t - 4(1+h_2(t))\right]\right\},\\ y^*_{12}(t) = \frac{1}{16-t^2}\left\{-t^3 - 8t^2 + 6t + 16 - r_1(t)(1-\tau_{11}(t))\left[t - 4(1+h_1(t))\right] + r_2(t)(1-\tau_{12}(t))\left[t - 4(1+h_2(t))\right]\right\},\\ y^*_{21}(t) = \frac{1}{16-t^2}\left\{2t^2 + 16t + 24 - r_1(t)(1-\tau_{21}(t))\left[t + 4(1+h_1(t))\right] + r_2(t)(1-\tau_{22}(t))\left[t + 4(1+h_2(t))\right]\right\},\\ y^*_{22}(t) = \frac{1}{16-t^2}\left\{-t^3 - 5t^2 + 24 + r_1(t)(1-\tau_{21}(t))\left[t + 4(1+h_1(t))\right] + r_2(t)(1-\tau_{22}(t))\left[t + 4(1+h_2(t))\right]\right\}.\end{cases}$$

For the sake of simplicity, we assume

$$h_1(t) = 2t, \qquad h_2(t) = t.$$

We get

$$\begin{cases}x^*_{11}(t) = \frac{1}{16-t^2}\left\{2t^2 + 28t + 8 + r_1(t)(1-\tau_{11}(t))(4 - t - 2t^2) + r_2(t)(1-\tau_{12}(t))(t^2 + t - 4)\right\},\\ x^*_{12}(t) = \frac{1}{16-t^2}\left\{-3t^3 - 3t^2 + 20t + 8 - r_1(t)(1-\tau_{11}(t))(4 - t - 2t^2) - r_2(t)(1-\tau_{12}(t))(t^2 + t - 4)\right\},\\ x^*_{21}(t) = \frac{1}{16-t^2}\left\{-t^3 - 6t^2 + 2t + 32 + r_1(t)(1-\tau_{21}(t))(2t^2 + t + 4) - r_2(t)(1-\tau_{22}(t))(-t^2 - t - 4)\right\},\\ x^*_{22}(t) = \frac{1}{16-t^2}\left\{2t^2 + 14t + 32 - r_1(t)(1-\tau_{21}(t))(2t^2 + t + 4) + r_2(t)(1-\tau_{22}(t))(-t^2 - t - 4)\right\},\\ y^*_{11}(t) = \frac{1}{16-t^2}\left\{6t^2 + 10t + 16 + r_1(t)(1-\tau_{11}(t))(-7t - 4) - r_2(t)(1-\tau_{12}(t))(3t + 4)\right\},\\ y^*_{12}(t) = \frac{1}{16-t^2}\left\{-t^3 - 8t^2 + 6t + 16 - r_1(t)(1-\tau_{11}(t))(-7t - 4) + r_2(t)(1-\tau_{12}(t))(3t + 4)\right\},\\ y^*_{21}(t) = \frac{1}{16-t^2}\left\{2t^2 + 16t + 24 - r_1(t)(1-\tau_{21}(t))(-9t - 4) + r_2(t)(1-\tau_{22}(t))(5t + 4)\right\},\\ y^*_{22}(t) = \frac{1}{16-t^2}\left\{-t^3 - 5t^2 + 24 + r_1(t)(1-\tau_{21}(t))(-9t - 4) - r_2(t)(1-\tau_{22}(t))(5t + 4)\right\}.\end{cases}$$

In the following, we study various examples of financial equilibrium for which the deficit (namely $\rho_j^{(1)*}$) and surplus (namely $\rho_j^{(2)*}$) are different from zero in certain time intervals. Such examples depend on the choose of suitable values of the data. In the first example, we consider values of τ_{ij} such that

$$\max\left\{\frac{22t^2+27t-4}{(4t+3)(7t+4)},\frac{5t^3+7t^2+7t-4}{(4t+3)(2t^2+t-4)}\right\}\le\tau_{11}(t)$$
$$\le\min\left\{\frac{8t^3+8t^2-41t-20}{(4t+3)(2t^2+t-4)},\frac{-t^3+20t^2+43t+28}{(4t+3)(7t+4)}\right\},$$
$$\max\left\{\frac{8t^3+8t^2+5t-20}{(4t+3)(2t^2+t+4)},\frac{34t^2+27t-12}{(4t+3)(9t+4)}\right\}\le\tau_{21}(t)$$
$$\le\min\left\{\frac{7t^3+4t^2+21t+44}{(4t+3)(2t^2+t+4)},\frac{-t^3+31t^2+43t+36}{(4t+3)(9t+4)}\right\},$$

as **Figures 2** and **3** show.

In particular, we assume

$$\tau_{11}(t)=\frac{t+1}{2},\quad \tau_{12}(t)=3t,$$
$$\tau_{21}(t)=t,\quad \tau_{22}(t)=\frac{5t+1}{2}.$$

There exist $t_1\in]0.650,0.652[$ and $t_2\in]0.975,0.977[$, such that the vector

$$\begin{cases} x_{11}^*(t)=\dfrac{8t^4+2t^3-19t^2+57t+28}{2(16-t^2)},\\ x_{12}^*(t)=\dfrac{-8t^4-8t^3+17t^2+39t+4}{2(16-t^2)},\\ x_{21}^*(t)=\dfrac{-8t^4-3t^3-15t^2+9t+44}{16-t^2},\\ x_{22}^*(t)=\dfrac{8t^4+2t^3+11t^2+7t+20}{16-t^2},\\ y_{11}^*(t)=\dfrac{28t^3+21t^2-5t+20}{2(16-t^2)},\\ y_{12}^*(t)=\dfrac{-30t^3-25t^2+37t+44}{2(16-t^2)},\\ y_{21}^*(t)=\dfrac{36t^3+9t^2-15t+12}{16-t^2},\\ y_{22}^*(t)=\dfrac{-37t^3-12t^2+31t+36}{16-t^2},\\ r_1^*(t)=4t+3,\\ r_1^*(t)=0, \end{cases}$$

is solution of the variational inequality in the interval $]t_1,t_2[$, because x_{ij}^*, y_{ij}^* fulfil the constraints and

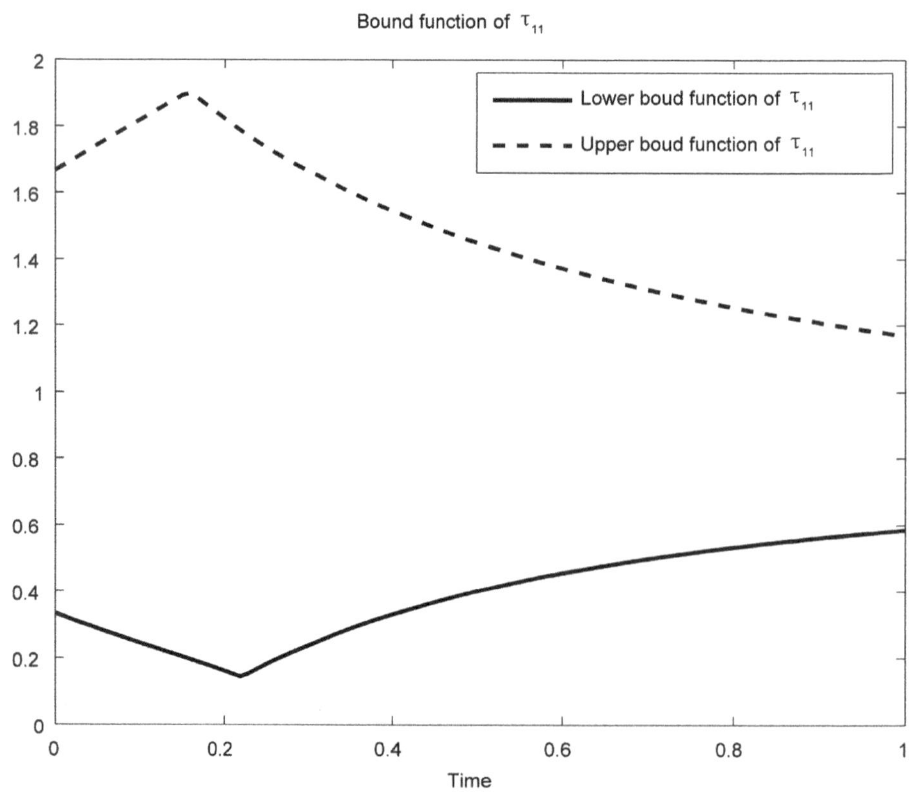

Figure 2. Bound functions of τ_{11}.

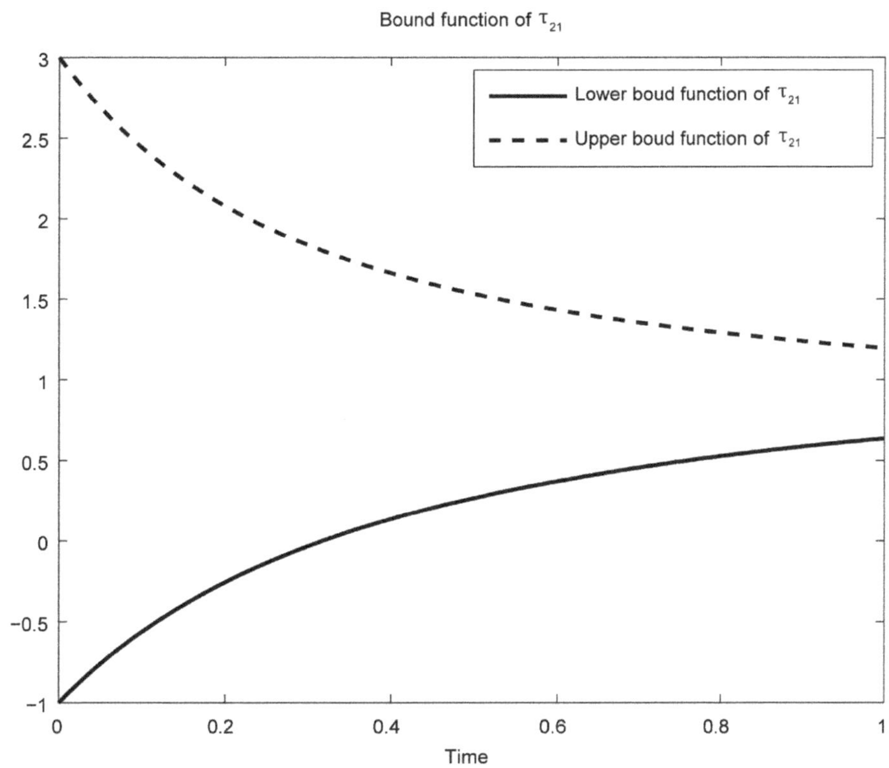

Figure 3. Bound functions of τ_{21}.

$$\Gamma_5 = \frac{184t^5 - 36t^4 - 145t^3 - 14t^2 - 57t + 68}{2\left(16 - t^2\right)} + F_1(t) < 0,$$

$$\Gamma_6 = \frac{-291t^5 - 329t^4 + 123t^3 + 423t^2 + 98t - 56}{2\left(16 - t^2\right)}$$

$$+F_2(t) > 0,$$

for $F_1(t)$ small enough and for any $F_2(t)$ non negative. In fact, if we consider

$$\gamma_5 = \frac{184t^5 - 36t^4 - 145t^3 - 14t^2 - 57t + 68}{2\left(16 - t^2\right)},$$

$$\gamma_6 = \frac{-291t^5 - 329t^4 + 123t^3 + 423t^2 + 98t - 56}{2\left(16 - t^2\right)},$$

we obtain that they are negative and positive respectively, as it can be verified in **Figure 4** where the graphs of the numerators are represented.

Let us remember that, by virtue of Theorem 2.2, $\forall j = 1,2$, the following relationships are satisfied

$$\begin{aligned} &\rho_j^{(1)*}(t)\left(\underline{r}_j(t) - r_j^*(t)\right) = 0, \\ &\rho_j^{(2)*}(t)\left(r_j^*(t) - \overline{r}_j(t)\right) = 0; \end{aligned} \tag{23}$$

$$\begin{aligned} &\sum_{i=1}^{2}\left(1 - \tau_{ij}(t)\right)\left[x_{ij}^*(t) - \left(1 + h_j(t)\right)y_{ij}^*(t)\right] \\ &+F_j(t) + \rho_j^{(2)*}(t) = \rho_j^{(1)*}(t). \end{aligned} \tag{24}$$

Taking into account that, in our case,

$$r_1^*(t) = 4t + 3 = \overline{r}_1(t),$$

$$r_2^*(t) = 0 = \underline{r}_2(t),$$

from (23), we obtain

$$\rho_1^{(1)*}(t) = 0, \ \rho_1^{(2)*}(t) \geq 0,$$

$$\rho_2^{(2)*}(t) \geq 0, \ \rho_2^{(2)*}(t) = 0.$$

So, from (24), we get

$$\rho_1^{(2)*}(t) = -\Gamma_5 > 0,$$

$$\rho_2^{(1)*}(t) = \Gamma_6 > 0,$$

provided that $F_1(t)$ is small enough and for any $F_2(t)$ non negative.

The importance of this example remains in the fact that, in the interval $]t_1, t_2[$, for $F_1(t)$ small enough, price r_1^* is maximum and the financial market has a surplus given by

$$\rho_1^{(2)*}(t)\overline{r}_1(t)$$

$$= -\Gamma_5 \overline{r}_1(t)$$

$$= \frac{-736t^6 - 408t^5 + 688t^4 + 491t^3 + 270t^2 - 101t - 204}{2\left(16 - t^2\right)}$$

$$-F_1(t)(4t + 3).$$

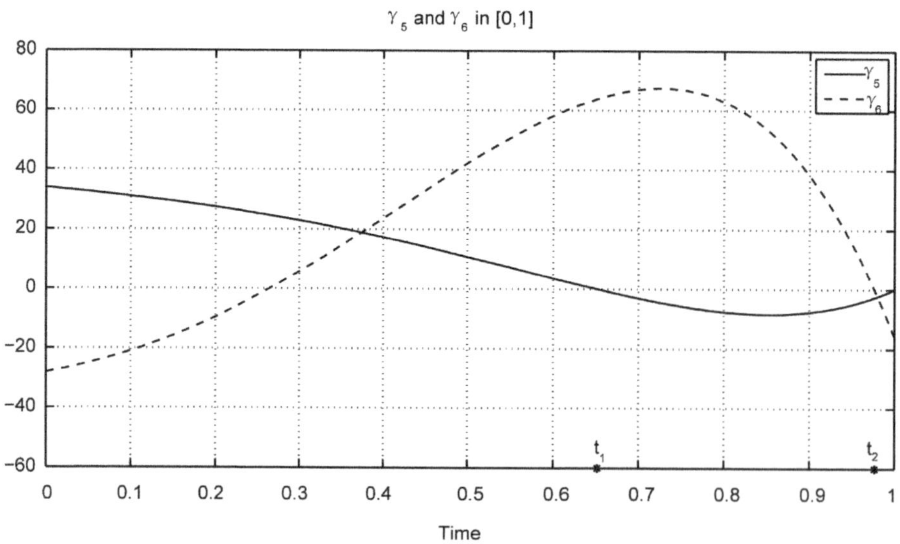

Figure 4. γ_5 **and** γ_6 **in** $[0,1]$.

Whereas, for the instrument $j=2$, we have minimal price and the deficit is given by

$$\rho_2^{(1)*}(t)\underline{r}_2(t)=\Gamma_6\underline{r}_2(t)=0.$$

Now, we would like to calculate the Evaluation Index for this financial problem. More precisely, we have

$$\theta(t)=\frac{7t+1}{4},\quad i(t)=\frac{3}{2}t,$$

$$\sum_{i=1}^{2} l_i(t)=2t+5,\quad \sum_{i=1}^{m} s_i(t)=4t+5,$$

$$\sum_{i=1}^{2}\tilde{s}_i(t)=\frac{\sum_{i=1}^{2} s_i(t)}{1+i(t)}=\frac{2(4t+5)}{2+3t},$$

$$\sum_{j=1}^{2}\tilde{F}_j(t)=\frac{\sum_{j=1}^{2}F_j(t)}{(1+i(t))(1-\theta(t))}=\frac{8(F_1(t)+F_2(t))}{(3-7t)(2+3t)}.$$

As a consequence, the Evaluation Index is given by:

$$E(t)=\frac{2t+5}{\frac{2(4t+5)}{2+3t}+\frac{8(F_1(t)+F_2(t))}{(3-7t)(2+3t)}}$$

$$=\frac{1}{1+\frac{8(F_1(t)+F_2(t))-t(6t+11)(3-7t)}{(3-7t)(2t+5)(2+3t)}}.$$

In the interval $\left[0,\frac{3}{7}\right[$, if

$$8(F_1(t)+F_2(t))\le t(6t+11)(3-7t)$$

the economy has a positive average evaluation. The same situation happens if

$$8(F_1(t)+F_2(t))\ge t(6t+11)(3-7t)$$

in the interval $\left]\frac{3}{7},1\right]$ (where $3-7t<0$).

Now let us consider the case where the values of τ_{ij} are such that

$$\max\left\{\frac{7t^3+17t^2+8t-24}{(7t+8)(t^2+t-4)},\frac{t^3+29t^2+46t+16}{(7t+8)(3t+4)}\right\}\le\tau_{12}(t)$$

$$\le\min\left\{\frac{10t^3+18t^2-40t-40}{(7t+8)(t^2+t-4)},\frac{27t^2+62t+48}{(7t+8)(3t+4)}\right\},$$

$$\max\left\{\frac{8t^3+21t^2+34t}{(7t+8)(t^2+t+4)},\frac{t^3+40t^2+68t+8}{(7t+8)(5t+4)}\right\}\le\tau_{22}(t)$$

$$\le\min\left\{\frac{7t^3+17t^2+50t+64}{(7t+8)(t^2+t+4)},\frac{37t^2+84t+56}{(7t+8)(5t+4)}\right\},$$

as **Figures 5** and **6** show.

In particular, we assume

$$\tau_{11}(t)=3t,\quad \tau_{12}(t)=-\frac{1}{5}t+\frac{6}{5},$$

$$\tau_{21}(t)=t,\quad \tau_{22}(t)=-\frac{1}{5}t+\frac{6}{5}.$$

There exist $t_3\in]0.946,0.948[$ and $t_4\in]0.997,0.999[$, such that the vector

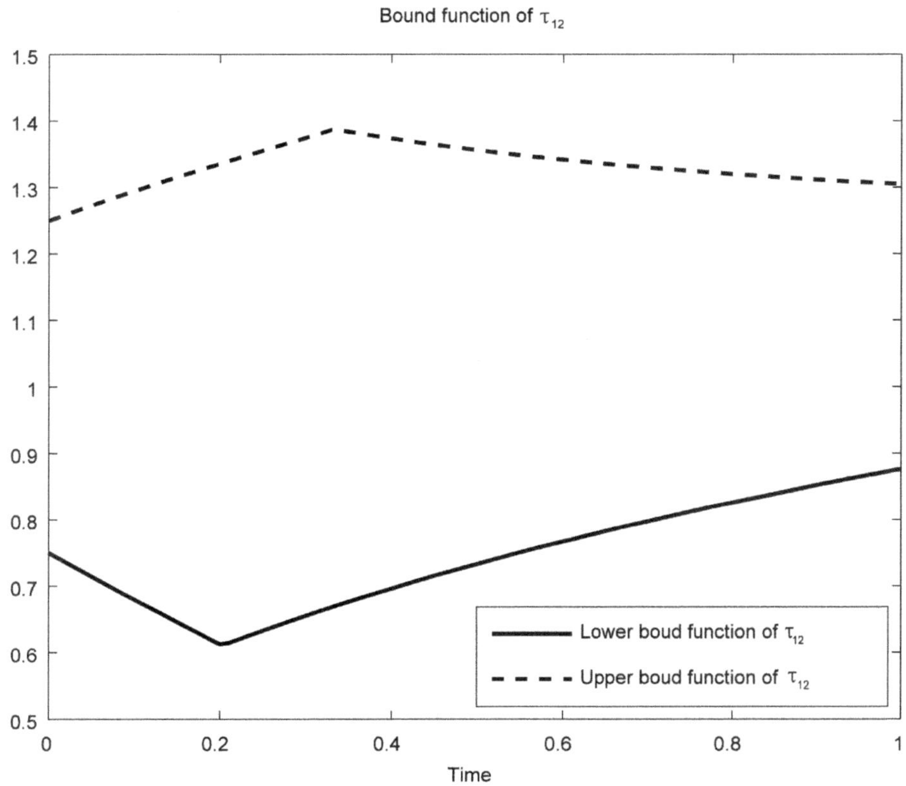

Figure 5. γ_5 **and** γ_6 **in** $[0,1]$.

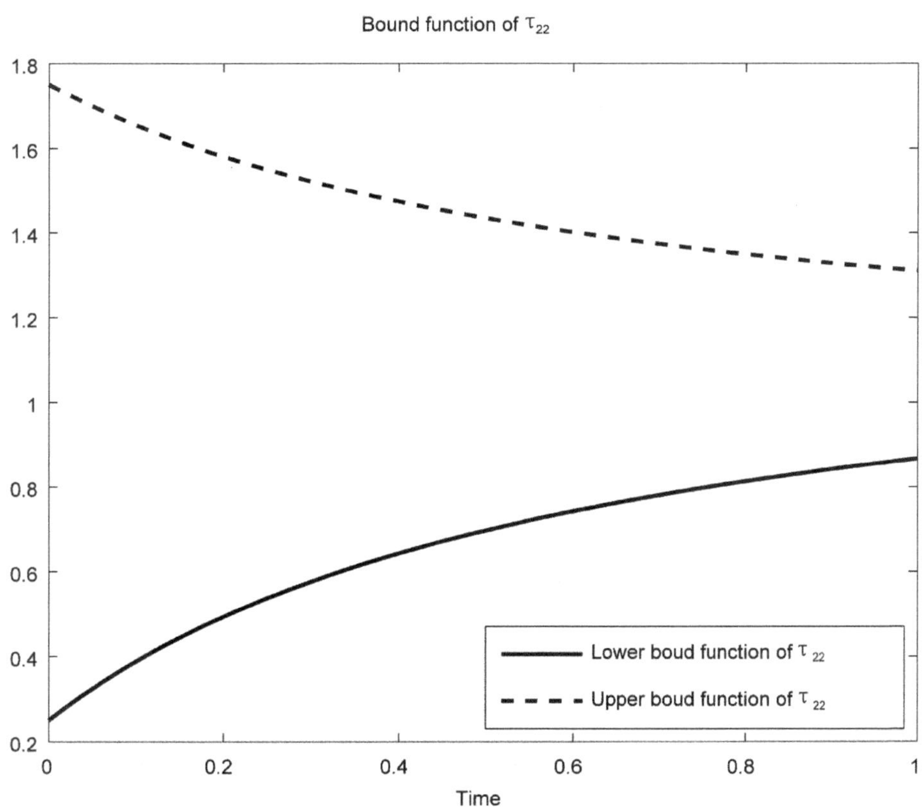

Figure 6. γ_5 **and** γ_6 **in** $[0,1]$.

$$\begin{cases} x_{11}^*(t)=\dfrac{7t^4+8t^3-25t^2+128t+72}{5(16-t^2)}, \\ x_{12}^*(t)=\dfrac{-7t^4-23t^3+20t^2+112t+8}{5(16-t^2)}, \\ x_{21}^*(t)=\dfrac{-7t^4-13t^3-51t^2+14t+192}{5(16-t^2)}, \\ x_{22}^*(t)=\dfrac{7t^4+8t^3+31t^2+66t+128}{5(16-t^2)}, \\ y_{11}^*(t)=\dfrac{21t^3+61t^2+30t+48}{5(16-t^2)}, \\ y_{12}^*(t)=\dfrac{-26t^3-71t^2+50t+62}{5(16-t^2)}, \\ y_{21}^*(t)=\dfrac{35t^3+43t^2+44t+88}{5(16-t^2)}, \\ y_{22}^*(t)=\dfrac{-40t^3-58t^2+36t+152}{5(16-t^2)}, \\ r_1^*(t)=0, \\ r_2^*(t)=7t+8, \end{cases}$$

is solution of the variational inequality in the interval $]t_3,t_4[$, because x_{ij}^*, y_{ij}^* fulfil the constraints and

$$\Gamma_5=\frac{182t^5+427t^4+351t^3-128t^2-380t+128}{5(16-t^2)}$$
$$+F_1(t)>0,$$
$$\Gamma_6=\frac{66t^5+114t^4-86t^3-266t^2+44t+128}{25(16-t^2)}+F_2(t)<0,$$

for any $F_1(t)$ non negative and for $F_2(t)$ small enough. In fact, if we consider

$$\gamma_5=\frac{182t^5+427t^4+351t^3-128t^2-380t+128}{5(16-t^2)},$$

$$\gamma_6=\frac{66t^5+114t^4-86t^3-266t^2+44t+128}{25(16-t^2)},$$

we obtain that they are positive and negative respectively, as it can be verified in **Figures 7** and **8** where the graphs of the numerators are represented in detail.

If we remember that, in this case,

$$r_1^*(t)=0=\underline{r}_1(t),$$
$$r_2^*(t)=7t+8=\overline{r}_2(t),$$

from (23), we obtain

$$\rho_1^{(1)*}(t)\ge 0,\ \rho_1^{(2)*}(t)=0,$$
$$\rho_2^{(1)*}(t)=0,\ \rho_2^{(2)*}(t)\ge 0.$$

So, from (24), we get

$$\rho_1^{(1)*}(t)=\Gamma_5>0,$$
$$\rho_2^{(2)*}(t)=-\Gamma_6>0,$$

provided that $F_2(t)$ is small enough and for any $F_1(t)$ non negative.

In this situation, we can assert that, in the interval $]t_3,t_4[$, for the instrument $j=1$, we have minimal price and the deficit is given by

$$\rho_1^{(1)*}(t)\underline{r}_1(t)=\Gamma_5\underline{r}_1(t)=0.$$

Whereas, for $F_2(t)$ small enough, price r_2^* is maximum and the financial market has a surplus given by

$$\rho_2^{(2)*}(t)\overline{r}_2(t)=-\Gamma_6\overline{r}_2(t)=\frac{-462t^6-605t^5+514t^4+2550t^3+1820t^2-1248t-1024}{25(16-t^2)}-F_2(t)(7t+8).$$

Now let us proceed to the calculation of the Evaluation Index. We have

$$\theta(t)=\frac{9t+6}{10},\quad i(t)=\frac{3}{2}t,$$

$$\sum_{i=1}^{2} l_i(t)=2t+5,$$

$$\sum_{i=1}^{m} s_i(t)=4t+5,$$

$$\sum_{i=1}^{2}\tilde{s}_i(t)=\frac{\sum_{i=1}^{2}s_i(t)}{1+i(t)}=\frac{2(4t+5)}{2+3t},$$

$$\sum_{j=1}^{2}\tilde{F}_j(t)=\frac{\sum_{j=1}^{2}F_j(t)}{(1+i(t))(1-\theta(t))}=\frac{20(F_1(t)+F_2(t))}{(4-9t)(2+3t)}.$$

Then the Evaluation Index is

$$E(t)=\frac{2t+5}{\dfrac{2(4t+5)}{2+3t}+\dfrac{20(F_1(t)+F_2(t))}{(4-9t)(2+3t)}}$$
$$=\frac{1}{1+\dfrac{20(F_1(t)+F_2(t))-t(6t+11)(4-9t)}{(4-9t)(2+3t)(2t+5)}}.$$

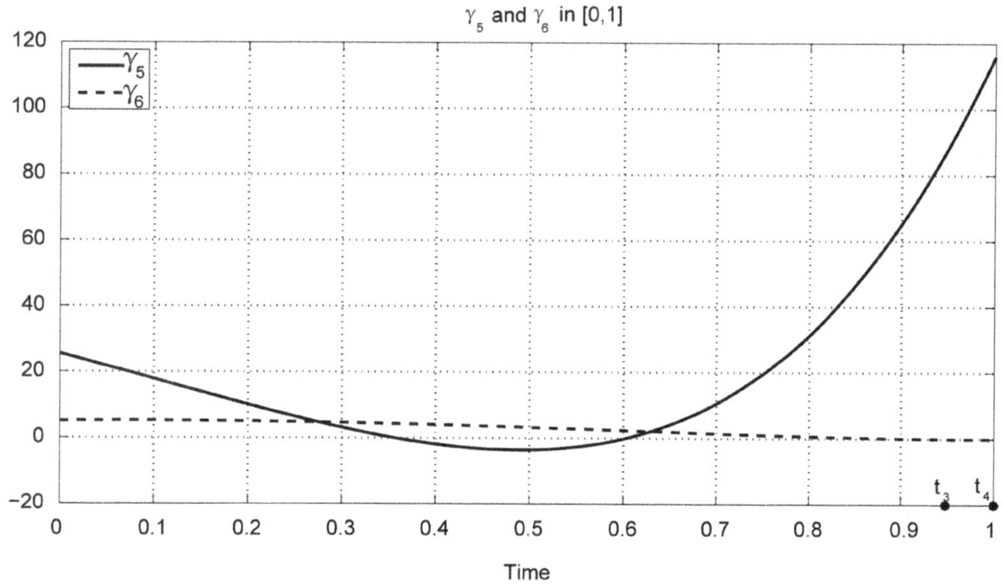

Figure 7. γ_5 **and** γ_6 **in** $[0,1]$.

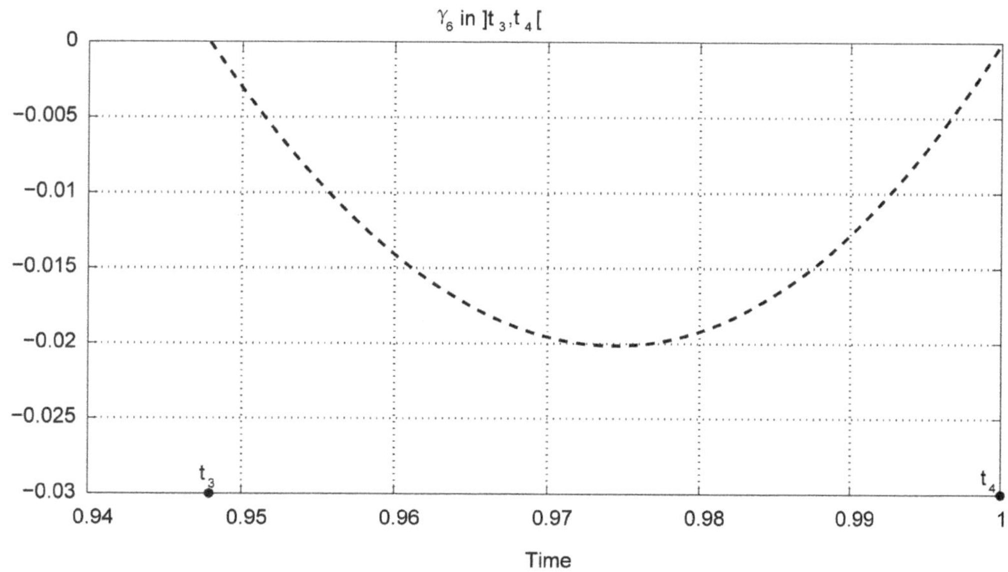

Figure 8. γ_5 **and** γ_6 **in** $[0,1]$.

As a consequence, in the interval $\left[0,\frac{4}{9}\right[$, if

$$20\left(F_1(t)+F_2(t)\right)\le t(6t+11)(4-9t)$$

the economy has a positive average evaluation. The same situation happens if

$$20\left(F_1(t)+F_2(t)\right)\ge t(6t+11)(4-9t)$$

in the interval $\left]\frac{4}{9},1\right]$ (where $4-9t<0$). From this example we see that we can get useful information from the $E(t)$, which requires simple calculations.

Now, we would like to study another example in which we assume

$$\tau_{11}(t)=3t,\quad \tau_{12}(t)=-t+1,$$

$$\tau_{21}(t)=t,\quad \tau_{22}(t)=-\frac{1}{2}t+\frac{1}{2}.$$

Under these assumptions, there exist $t_5\in\left]0,638;0,640\right[$ and $t_6\in\left]0,997;0,999\right[$, such that the vector

$$\begin{cases} x_{11}^*(t) = \dfrac{2t^2+28t+8}{16-t^2}, \\ x_{12}^*(t) = \dfrac{-3t^3-3t^2+20t+8}{16-t^2}, \\ x_{21}^*(t) = \dfrac{-t^3-6t^2+2t+32}{16-t^2}, \\ x_{22}^*(t) = \dfrac{2t^2+14t+32}{16-t^2}, \\ y_{11}^*(t) = \dfrac{6t^2+10t+16}{16-t^2}, \\ y_{12}^*(t) = \dfrac{-t^3-8t^2+6t+16}{16-t^2}, \\ y_{21}^*(t) = \dfrac{2t^2+16t+24}{16-t^2}, \\ y_{22}^*(t) = \dfrac{-t^3-5t^2+24}{16-t^2}, \\ r_1^*(t) = 0, \\ r_2^*(t) = 0, \end{cases}$$

is solution of the variational inequality in the interval $]t_5, t_6[$, because x_{ij}^*, y_{ij}^* fulfil the constraints and

$$\Gamma_5 = \frac{41t^4+95t^3+40t^2-60t}{16-t^2} + F_1(t) > 0,$$

$$\Gamma_6 = \frac{3t^5+19t^4+11t^3-7t^2-18t+8}{2(16-t^2)} + F_2(t) > 0,$$

for $F_1(t)$ and $F_2(t)$ non negative. In fact, if we consider

$$\gamma_5 = \frac{41t^4+95t^3+40t^2-60t}{16-t^2},$$

$$\gamma_6 = \frac{3t^5+19t^4+11t^3-7t^2-18t+8}{2(16-t^2)},$$

we obtain that they are both positive, as it can be verified in **Figure 9** where the graphs of the numerators are represented.

We observe that, in our case

$$r_1^*(t) = 0 = \underline{r}_1(t),$$

$$r_2^*(t) = 0 = \underline{r}_2(t),$$

so, from (23), it follows that

$$\rho_1^{(1)*}(t) \geq 0, \ \rho_1^{(2)*}(t) = 0,$$

$$\rho_2^{(1)*}(t) \geq 0, \ \rho_2^{(2)*}(t) = 0.$$

Then, from (24), we obtain

$$\rho_1^{(1)*}(t) = \Gamma_5 > 0,$$

$$\rho_2^{(1)*}(t) = \Gamma_6 > 0,$$

for any $F_1(t)$ and $F_2(t)$ non negative.

As consequence of the meaning of $\rho_j^{(i)*}$, in the interval $]t_5, t_6[$, for both the instruments, we have minimal price and the deficit is given, respectively, by

$$\rho_1^{(1)*}(t)\underline{r}_1(t) = \Gamma_5 \underline{r}_1(t) = 0,$$

$$\rho_2^{(2)*}(t)\underline{r}_2(t) = \Gamma_6 \underline{r}_1(t) = 0.$$

As regards the calculation of the Evaluation Index, we have

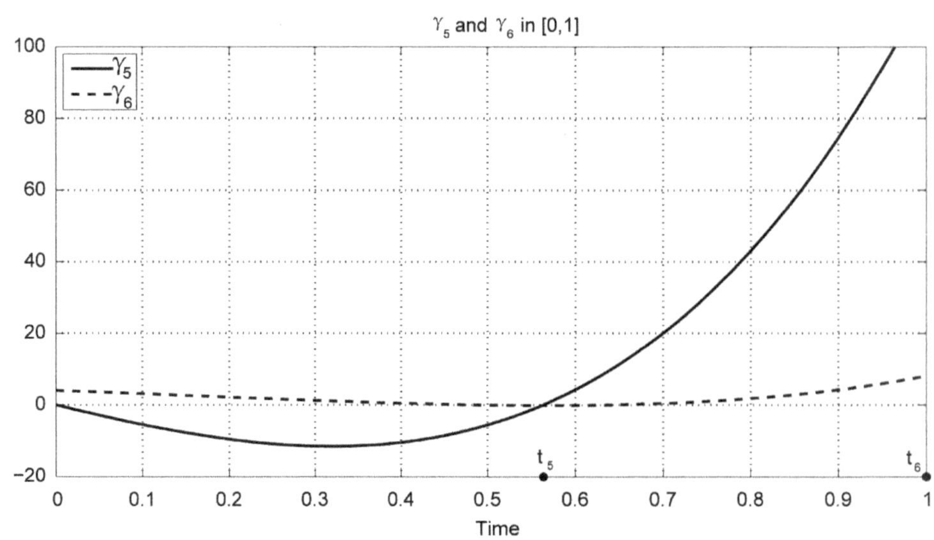

Figure 9. γ_5 **and** γ_6 **in** $[0,1]$.

$$\theta(t)=\frac{5t+3}{8},\quad i(t)=\frac{3}{2}t,$$

$$\sum_{i=1}^{2} l_i(t)=2t+5,\quad \sum_{i=1}^{m} s_i(t)=4t+5,$$

$$\sum_{i=1}^{2}\tilde{s}_i(t)=\frac{\sum_{i=1}^{2}s_i(t)}{1+i(t)}=\frac{2(4t+5)}{2+3t},$$

$$\sum_{j=1}^{2}\tilde{F}_j(t)=\frac{\sum_{j=1}^{2}F_j(t)}{(1+i(t))(1-\theta(t))}=\frac{16(F_1(t)+F_2(t))}{5(1-t)(2+3t)}.$$

As a consequence, the Evaluation Index is

$$E(t)=\frac{2t+5}{\frac{2(4t+5)}{2+3t}+\frac{16(F_1(t)+F_2(t))}{5(1-t)(2+3t)}}$$
$$=\frac{1}{1+\frac{16(F_1(t)+F_2(t))-\frac{1}{6}t(6t+11)(1-t)}{5(1-t)(2+3t)(2t+5)}}.$$

Then, in the interval $[0,1[$, if

$$16(F_1(t)+F_2(t))\le\frac{1}{6}t(6t+11)(1-t)$$

the economy has a positive average evaluation because $1-t<0$. From this example we see that it is easier to achieve financial balance if τ_{ij} and h_j are more or less equal.

REFERENCES

[1] A. Barbagallo, P. Daniele and A. Maugeri, "Variational Formulation for a General Dynamic Financial Equilibrium Problem. Balance Law and Liability Formula," *Nonlinear Analysis: Theory, Methods & Applications*, Vol. 75, No. 3, 2012, pp. 1104-1123.

[2] A. Barbagallo, P. Daniele, S. Giuffrè and A. Maugeri, "Variational Approach for a General Financial Equilibrium Problem: the Deficit Formula, the Balance Law and the Liability Formula, a Path to the Economy Recover," Submitted.

[3] A. Barbagallo, "Degenerate Time-Dependent Variational Inequalities with Applications to Traffic Equilibrium Problems," *Computational Methods in Applied Mathematics*, Vol. 6, No. 2, 2006, pp. 117-133.

[4] A. Barbagallo, "Regularity Results for Time-Dependent Variational and Quasi-Variational Inequalities and Application to Calculation of Dynamic Traffic Network," *Mathematical Models and Methods in Applied Sciences*, Vol. 17, No. 2, 2007, pp. 277-304.

[5] A. Barbagallo, "Regularity Results for Evolutionary Nonlinear Variational and Quasi-Variational Inequalities with Applications to Dynamic Equilibrium Problems," *Journal of Global Optimization*, Vol. 40, No. 1-3, 2008, pp. 29-39.

[6] A. Barbagallo, "Existence and Regularity of Solutions to Nonlinear Degenerate Evolutionary Variational Inequalities with Applications to Traffic Equilibrium Problem," *Applied Mathematics and Computation*, Vol. 208, No. 1, 2009, pp. 1-13.

[7] A. Barbagallo, "On the Regularity of Retarded Equilibria in Time-Dependent Traffic Equilibrium Problems," *Nonlinear Analysis*, Vol. 71, No. 12, 2009, pp. e2406-e2417.

[8] P. Daniele and S. Giuffrè, "General Infinite Dimensional Duality and Applications to Evolutionary Network Equilibrium Problems," *Optimization Letters*, Vol. 1, No. 3, 2007, pp. 227-243.

[9] P. Daniele, S. Giuffré and A. Maugeri, "Remarks on General Infinite Dimensional Duality with Cone and Equality Constraints," *Communications in Applied Analysis*, Vol. 13, No. 4, 2009, pp. 567-578.

[10] P. Daniele, S. Giuffrè, G. Idone and A. Maugeri, "Infinite Dimensional Duality and Applications," *Mathematische Annalen*, Vol. 339, No. 1, 2007, pp. 221-239.

[11] A. Maugeri and F. Raciti, "Remarks on Infinite Dimensional Duality," *Journal of Global Optimization*, Vol. 46, No. 4, 2010, pp. 581-588.

[12] M. B. Donato, M. Milasi and C. Vitanza, "Dynamic Walriasian Price Equilibrium Problem: Evolutionary Variational Approach with Sensitivity Analysis," *Optimization Letters*, Vol. 2, No. 1, 2008, pp. 113-126.

[13] M. B. Donato, M. Milasi and C. Vitanza, "Quasi-Variational Approach of a Competitive Economic Equilibrium Problem with Utility Function: Existence of Equilibrium," *Mathematical Models and Methods in Applied Sciences*, Vol. 18, No. 3, 2008, pp. 351-367.

[14] M. B. Donato, A. Maugeri, M. Milasi and C. Vitanza, "Duality Theory for a Dynamic Walrasian Pure Exchange Economy," *Pacific Journal of Optimization*, Vol. 4, No. 3, 2008, pp. 537-547.

[15] M. B. Donato, M. Milasi and C. Vitanza, "A New Contribution to a Dynamic Competitive Equilibrium Problem," *Applied Mathematics Letters*, Vol. 23, No. 2, 2010, pp. 148-151.

[16] A. Barbagallo and M.-G. Cojocaru, "Dynamic Equilibrium Formulation of Oligopolistic Market Problem," *Mathematical and Computer Modelling*, Vol. 49, No. 5-6, 2009, pp. 966-976.

[17] A. Barbagallo and A. Maugeri, "Duality Theory for the Dynamic Oligopolistic Market Equilibrium Problem," *Optimization*, Vol. 60, No. 1-2, 2011, pp. 29-52.

[18] S. Giuffrè and S. Pia, "Weighted Traffic Equilibrium Problem in Non Pivot Hilbert Spaces," *Nonlinear Analy-*

sis, Vol. 71, No. 12, 2009, pp. e2054-e2061.

[19] A. Barbagallo and S. Pia, "Weighted Variational Inequalities in Non-Pivot Hilbert Spaces with Applications," *Computational Optimization and Applications*, Vol. 48, No. 3, 2011, pp. 487-514.

[20] S. Giuffrè, G. Idone and S. Pia, "Some Classes of Projected Dynamical Systems in Banach Spaces and Variational Inequalities," *Journal of Global Optimization*, Vol. 40, No. 1-3, 2008, pp. 119-128.

[21] A. Maugeri, "Convex Programming, Variational Inequalities and Applications to the Traffic Equilibrium Problem," *Applied Mathematics & Optimization*, Vol. 16, No. 2, 1987, pp. 169-185.

[22] P. Daniele, "Variational Inequalities for Evolutionary Financial Equilibrium," In: A. Nagurney, Ed., *Innovations in Financial and Economic Networks*, Edward Elgar Publishing, Cheltenham, 2003, pp. 84-108.

[23] P. Daniele, "Variational Inequalities for General Evolutionary Financial Equilibrium," In: F. Giannessi and A. Maugeri, Eds., *Variational Analysis and Applications*, Springer Verlag, New York, 2005, pp. 279-299.

[24] P. Daniele, "Evolutionary Variational Inequalities Applied to Financial Equilibrium Problems in an Environment of Risk and Uncertainty," *Nonlinear Analysis*, Vol. 63, No. 5-7, 2005, pp. 1645-1653.

[25] P. Daniele, "Dynamic Networks and Evolutionary Variational Inequalities," Edward Elgar Publishing, Chentelham, 2006.

[26] P. Daniele, "Evolutionary Variational Inequalities and Applications to Complex Dynamic Multi-Level Models," *Transportation Research Part E*, Vol. 46, No. 6, 2010, pp. 855-880.

[27] P. Daniele, S. Giuffrè and S. Pia, "Competitive Financial Equilibrium Problems with Policy Interventions," *Journal of Industrial and Management Optimization*, Vol. 1, No. 1, 2005, pp. 39-52.

[28] K. Kuratowski, "Topology," Academic Press, New York, 1966.

[29] A. Barbagallo and M.-G. Cojocaru, "Continuity of Solutions for Parametric Variational Inequalities in Banach Space," *Journal of Mathematical Analysis and Applications*, Vol. 351, No. 2, 2009, pp. 707-720.

[30] A. Maugeri and L. Scrimali, "Global Lipschitz Continuity of Solutions to Parameterized Variational Inequalities," *Bollettino Unione Matematica Italiana*, Vol. 2, No. 9, 2009, pp. 45-69.

[31] A. Barbagallo and R. Di Vincenzo, "Lipschitz Continuity and Duality for Dynamic Oligopolistic Market Equilibrium Problem with Memory Term," *Journal of Mathematical Analysis and Applications*, Vol. 382, No. 1, 2011, pp. 231-247.

[32] H. M. Markowitz, "Portfolio Selection," *The Journal of Finance*, Vol. 7, No. 1, 1952, pp. 77-91.

[33] H. M. Markowitz, "Portfolio Selection: Efficient Diversification of Investments," Wiley, New York, 1959.

7

Weather Derivatives with Applications to Canadian Data

Anatoliy Swishchuk, Kaijie Cui
Department of Mathematics and Statistics, University of Calgary, Calgary, Canada

ABSTRACT

We applied two daily average temperature models to Canadian cities data and derived their derivative pricing applications. The first model is characterized by mean-reverting Ornstein-Uhlenbeck process driven by general Lévy process with seasonal mean and volatility. As an extension to the first model, Continuous Autoregressive (CAR) model driven by Lévy process is also considered and calibrated to Canadian data. It is empirically proved that the proposed dynamics fitted Calgary and Toronto temperature data successfully. These models are also applied to derivation of an explicit price of CAT futures, and numerical prices of CDD and HDD futures using fast Fourier transform. The novelty of this paper lies in the applications of daily average temperature models to Canadian cities data and CAR model driven by Lévy process, futures pricing of CDD and HDD indices.

Keywords: Weather Derivatives; Mean-Reverting Process; Lévy Process; Continuous Autoregressive Model; Fast Fourier Transform

1. Introduction

Over the last decade, weather derivatives have emerged as an attractive and interesting new derivative class for risk management and other related fields. Since the purpose of weather derivatives is to allow businesses and other organizations to insure themselves against fluctuations in the weather, a number of insurance, reinsurance companies, banks, hedge funds and energy companies have set up weather trading desks. It is obvious that there are close connections between energy and weather, for example, a natural gas distributor may want to buy weather derivatives to ensure profits in case of a warm winter in which consumers will buy less gas for heating purpose. Hence, weather derivatives will provide a financial instrument for companies or organizations to avoid some unzealous impact of the "bad" weather effects and control the weather risks. Also, additional instruments for hedging in the energy markets require quantitative models of both energy and weather derivatives included.

The weather derivatives market, in which contracts written on weather indices was firstly appeared Over-the-counter (OTC) in July 1996 between Aquila Energy and Consolidated Edison Co. from United States. After that, companies accustomed to trading weather contracts based on electricity and gas prices in order to hedge their price risks realized by weather during the end of 1990s and the beginning of 2000s. Consequently, the market grew rapidly and expanded to other industries and to Europe and Japan. Reported from Weather Risk Management Association (WRMA), an industry body that represents the weather market, recently, the total notional value of the global weather risk market has reached $11.8 billion in last year. With geographic expansion, the OTC market boosted nearly 30% in last year. In this article, we will concentrate on the futures market of temperature derivatives found at the Chicago Mercantile Exchange (CME), which is one of the largest weather derivatives trading platforms. Up to now, the CME has weather futures and options traded based on a range of weather indices for 47 cities from United States, Canada, Europe, Australia and Asia.

As a common sense, weather affects different entities in different ways. In order to hedge these different types of risks, weather derivatives are written on different types of weather variables or weather indices. The most commonly used weather variable is the temperature. Widely used temperature indices include cumulative average temperature (CAT), heating degree days (HDD) and cooling degree days (CDD). They are originated from the energy industry, and designed to correlate well with the local demands for heating or cooling. CAT are defined as the sum of the daily average temperature over the period $[\tau_1, \tau_2]$ of the contract, the index $\mathrm{CAT} := \sum_{t=\tau_1}^{\tau_2} T(t) = \int_{\tau_1}^{\tau_2} T(t)\mathrm{d}t$ where $T(t)$ is the daily average temperature. It is mainly used in Europe and Canada. In winter, HDD are used to measure the demand for heating, *i.e.* they are a measure of how cold the weather is and usually used in United States, Europe, Canada and Australia. In contrast, CDD are used in summer to measure the demand of energy used for cooling and a measure of how hot the weather is. They are usually used in United States, Canada and Australia. The definitions for HDD and CDD are given by

$\text{HDD} := \max\left(T(t)-c,0\right)$ and $\text{CDD} := \max\left(c-T(t),0\right)$,

where the threshold c takes value of $65^{\circ}\text{F}(18^{\circ}\text{C})$.

The pricing of a given weather derivative by calculating the expected value of its appropriately discounted payoff is inherently related to weather forecasting and simulation (see Zeng [1] and Cao and Wei [2]). The conventional approach is to identify the probability distribution of the associated index at maturity, and then integrate the payoff of the derivative with respect to it. Dornier and Queruel [3] characterized weather dynamics by mean-reverting Itô diffusions, driven by a standard Brownian motion, and then resorted to Monte Carlo simulation. Davis [4] used the geometric Brownian motion to model the accumulated HDDs (or CDDs). Brody *et al.* [5] proposed to replace the traditional Brownian motion by a fractional Brownian motion, leading to a fractional Ornstein-Uhlenbeck, allowing incorporate a long memory effect. Benth [6] used the Fourier transformation technique to get the explicit expressions of European and average type of weather contracts, and also showed the pricing formulas satisfy certain Black-Scholes PDE. Benth and Šaltytė-Benth [7] proposed an Ornstein-Uhlenbeck model with seasonal mean and volatility, where the residuals are generated by the class of generalized hyperbolic Lévy process rather than Brownian motion family. The process they used is a flexible class of Lévy process capturing the semi-heavy tails and skewness properties of residuals. A similar model driven by Brownian motion was applied for pricing CAT, HDD and CDD futures in Benth and Šaltytė-Benth [8], they also gave discussions about options written upon these futures. Benth *et al.* [9] generalized the analysis in the above OU model to higher-order (with lag p) Continuous-time Autoregressive models with seasonal variance for the temperature, and they found the choice of $p = 3$ turns out to be sufficient to explain the temperature dynamics in Stockholm, Sweden by calibrating the model to more than 40 years of daily observations. More recently, Zapranis and Alexandridis [10] began proposing using a time dependent speed of mean reversion parameter in the Ornstein-Uhlenbeck model and use neural networks to estimate the parameters.

The remaining of this article is organized as follows: In Section 2, we firstly apply existed Lévy driven mean-reverting model to the modeling of temperature index of Canadian temperature data, and then present Lévy driven CAR model and its application to Canadian data. In Section 3, we develop the futures pricing techniques with respect to weather futures of CAT, CDD and HDD based on the established two models. Finally, in Section 4, we illustrate the concluding remarks and some possible future research in this direction.

2. Modeling of Weather Index

2.1. Lévy Driven Ornstein-Uhlenbeck Model

As our first proposed model, consider the weather index $T(t)$, which is the daily average temperature (DAT). We suppose the DAT has a generalization of the dynamics:

$$dT(t) = ds(t) + \kappa\left(T(t) - s(t)\right)dt + s(t)dL(t), \quad (1)$$

where $s(t)$ is the seasonal mean level across years given days and κ is the speed in which $T(t)$ revert to $s(t)$. $\sigma(t)$ is assumed to be a measurable and bounded function represents the seasonal volatility of temperature. $L(t)$ is cádlág, adapted, real valued Lévy process with independent, stationary increments and stochastically continuous. For formal definition of Lévy process, we refer the reader to the introduction paper by Papapantoleon [11]. This model was firstly introduced by Dornier and Queruel [3] with Brownian motion. We will firstly apply this model with Lévy process to Canadian temperature data.

From Equation (1), we can directly use Itô formula for semimartingales to get the explicit solution

$$\begin{aligned} T(t) = {} & s(t) + \left(T(0) - s(0)\right)\mathrm{e}^{\kappa t} \\ & + \int_0^t \sigma(u)\mathrm{e}^{\kappa(t-u)}\mathrm{d}L(u). \end{aligned} \quad (2)$$

For the purpose of fitting this model to our daily average temperatures, we reformulate Equation (2) by subtracting $T(t)$ from $T(t+1)$,

$$\begin{aligned} \Delta T(t) = {} & \Delta s(t) - \left(1 - \mathrm{e}^{\kappa}\right)\left(T(t) - s(t)\right) \\ & + \mathrm{e}^{\kappa}\int_t^{t+1} \sigma(u)\mathrm{e}^{\kappa(t-u)}\mathrm{d}L(u) \end{aligned} \quad (3)$$

with the notation $\Delta X(t) := X(t+1) - X(t)$. The stochastic integral could be approximated by

$$\begin{aligned} \Delta T(t) = {} & \Delta s(t) - \left(1 - \mathrm{e}^{\kappa}\right)\left(T(t) - s(t)\right) \\ & + \mathrm{e}^{\kappa}\sigma(t)\Delta L(t). \end{aligned} \quad (4)$$

Adding $T(t) - s(t) :\stackrel{\sim}{=} \overline{T}(t)$ to both sides

$$\overline{T}(t+1) = \mathrm{e}^{\kappa}\overline{T}(t) + \mathrm{e}^{\kappa}\sigma(t)\varepsilon(t). \quad (5)$$

If we define $\overline{\varepsilon} := \mathrm{e}^{\kappa}\sigma(t)\varepsilon(t)$, we will have the following three parts for modeling $T(t)$ step by step:

$$T(t) \Leftrightarrow s(t) + c(t) + \overline{\varepsilon}(t), \quad (6)$$

where $s(t)$ is the seasonal component, $c(t)$ is the cyclical component derived from Equation (5), and $\overline{\varepsilon}(t)$ is the stochastic part.

The data sets we are going to analyse include daily average temperatures (measured in centigrade) from Calgary, AB and Toronto, ON in Canada. The choice of these two cities is intuitively based on the location and importance of these cities. These data are provided by the Canadian National Climate Data and Information Archive (NCDIA) over a period ranging from January 1st 2001 to January 1st 2011, resulting in 3652 records for each city. For simplicity, the measurement on each February 29th was removed from the sample in each leap year to equalize the length of each year.

2.1.1. Linear Trend

Empirically, the daily average temperature should have an increasing trend due to some reasons such as global warming, green-house effect and so on. However, from **Figure 1**, we cannot verify significant linear trends for both data sets. The slopes for linear fitting of Calgary and Toronto are 1.346×10^{-4} and 1.806×10^{-4} respectively. A potential explanation to this is that our sample size is reasonably small with a period of 10 years data. Larger sample size will show us relatively more significant increasing trend using least square fit. Hence, at this stage we will ignore the linear trend, and keep a constant mean level in the seasonal trend.

2.1.2. Seasonal Trend

In order to model the seasonality pattern, we use the trigonometric function with the form

$$s(t)=a_0+a_1\sin\left(\frac{2\pi}{365}(t-t_0)\right), \qquad (7)$$

where a_0 is the mean level, a_1 is amplitude of the mean. The period of the oscillations is one year (365 days neglecting leap year), so the weight $\omega=\frac{2\pi}{365}$. t_0 represents the phase angle. The results of parameters estimation using least square method are reported in **Table 1**.

2.1.3. Cyclical Component

To remove the adjacent correlation in the time series, make the time series stationary, we model the cyclical component by recursive regression based on Equation (5). The cyclical component $c(t)$ can be modeled by:

$$c(t)=e^{\kappa}\overline{T}(t)=e^{\kappa}\left(T(t)-s(t)\right), \qquad (8)$$

The results of e^{κ} estimated implicitly by an autoregressive model and corresponding R^2 are given in **Table 2**.

The autocorrelation function (ACF) plots for the squared residuals in **Figure 2** clearly reveal seasonality of correlation for both cities. In the squared residuals ACF plots, the autocorrelation violated 95% interval for lots of lags, and the wave for the ACF is a sign of seasonal pattern.

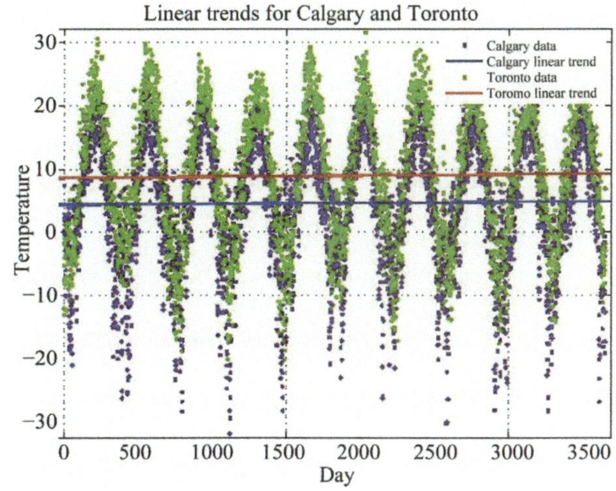

Figure 1. Linear trends of Calgary and Toronto.

Table 1. Estimated parameters for seasonal function.

Parameters	Calgary	Toronto
a_0	4.614	8.924
a_1	−12.03	−13.67
t_0	−72.85	−67.83
R^2	0.6753	0.8331

Table 2. Estimated parameters in regression.

Parameters	Calgary	Toronto
e^{κ}	0.7858	0.7018
R^2	0.6172	0.4924

2.1.4. Seasonal Volatility

We consider the seasonal pattern in the residual after removing the cyclical component as the seasonal volatility. The motivation behind seasonal volatility is straight forward. The temperature appears bigger variation in the winter and smaller variation in the summer. By Equation (5), the random term has the form $e^{\kappa}\sigma(t)\varepsilon(t)$. To get the seasonal volatility $\sigma(t)$, we have the following methods:

- Organize the data into 365 groups, one for each day of the year;
- Find the means of the squared data in each group. These means are crude estimation for the expected squared data. $\sigma^2(t)=E\left[\left(\sigma(t)\varepsilon(t)\right)^2\right]$;
- To smooth the estimation, first way is trying the smoothing technique. In details, we could take logarithm of the estimation and use moving average method to smooth the crude estimation. Then the smoothed estimation of $\sigma^2(t)$ could be get by ex-

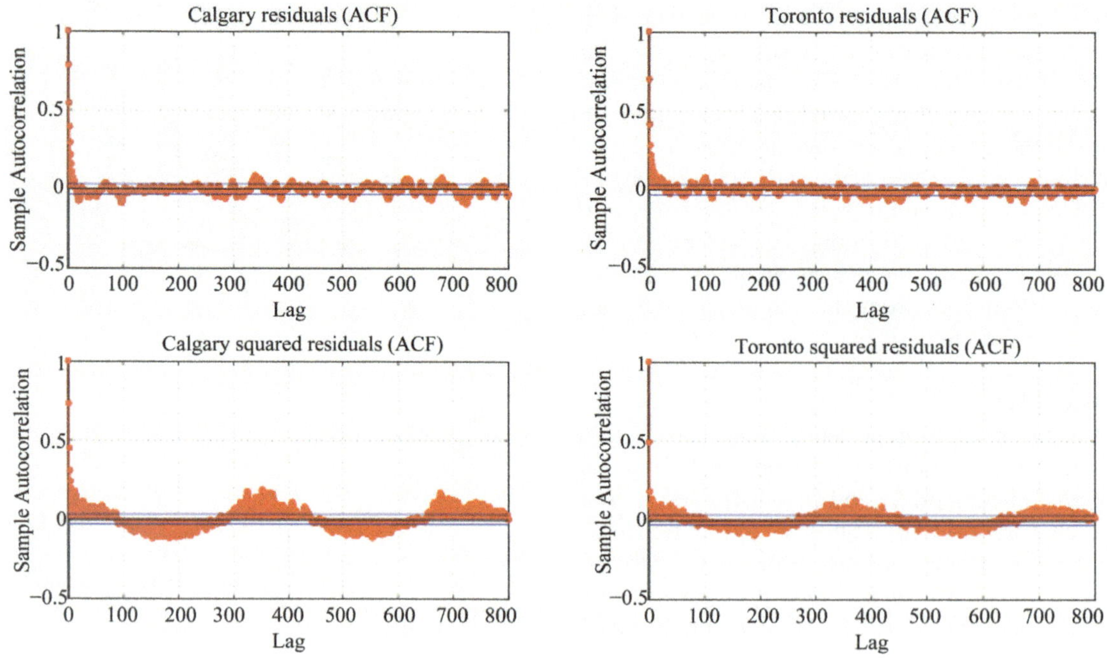

Figure 2. Empirical ACF after regression.

ponentiation of the result. Alternatively, use the truncated Fourier series (9) to fit the estimation from previous two steps. The Fourier series will indicate the presence of different cycles in $\sigma(t)$ as a deterministic function.

$$\sigma(t) = c_1 + \sum_{i=1}^{N} \left(c_{2i} \sin(iwt) + c_{2i+1} \cos(iwt) \right) \quad (9)$$

Figure 3 shows the fitted and smoothed $\sigma(t)$ by three days moving average technique. More average smoothing range will make the estimation smoother, but for our Canadian temperature study, the variation of the temperature in more days would be relatively larger than that of three days. Hence, the choice of three days moving average makes sense for both the smoothing and accuracy purpose.

After removing the estimated seasonal volatility, the ACF for the data and squared data are plotted in **Figure 4**. It shows that the seasonality pattern is completely removed from the squared data.

On the other hand, we also tried the way of fitting the crude seasonal volatility by truncated Fourier series with other three. The values of the estimated parameters are given in **Table 3**.

Corresponding fitted results are shown in **Figure 5**.

Again, the seasonal pattern in the ACF plot was removed from **Figure 6**. So, we could find that both methods can model the seasonal volatility appropriately.

2.1.5. Random Noise

Then we head to fit the random part $\varepsilon(t)$ remained from above. The classical literatures of temperature modeling suggest the random noise are independent and identically normal distributed, (see Dornier and Queruel [3], Alaton *et al.* [12]). However, we could see from the QQ-plot and normal fit of the random noise for our data, the normal distributed random noise may lead misdescription to the data. Moreover, modeling of random noise using Gaussian process is not always the case.

Table 3. Truncated fourier series parameters.

	c_1	c_2	c_3	w
Calgary	4.424	1.633	0.1912	0.0167
Toronto	4.33	1.082	0.2108	0.0153

Instead, we try to apply the generalized hyperbolic family process to model the random part for our data, based on Benth and Šaltytė-Benth [7]. As the name suggests, it is super-class of processes such as normal-inverse Gaussian, variance-gamma, hyperbolic and so on. This will allow the family better capture the features of the data set and relatively easy to analyze from the Lévy properties it holds.

The generalized hyperbolic distribution is an infinitely divisible distribution which can be defined with the density function

$$\begin{aligned} & gh(x;\lambda,\alpha,\beta,\delta,\mu) \\ & = a(\lambda,\alpha,\beta,\delta)\left(\delta^2+(x-\mu)\right)^{2(\lambda-1/2)/2} \\ & \times K_{\lambda-1/2}\left(\alpha\sqrt{\delta^2+(x-\mu)^2}\right)\exp\left(\beta(x-\mu)\right) \end{aligned}$$

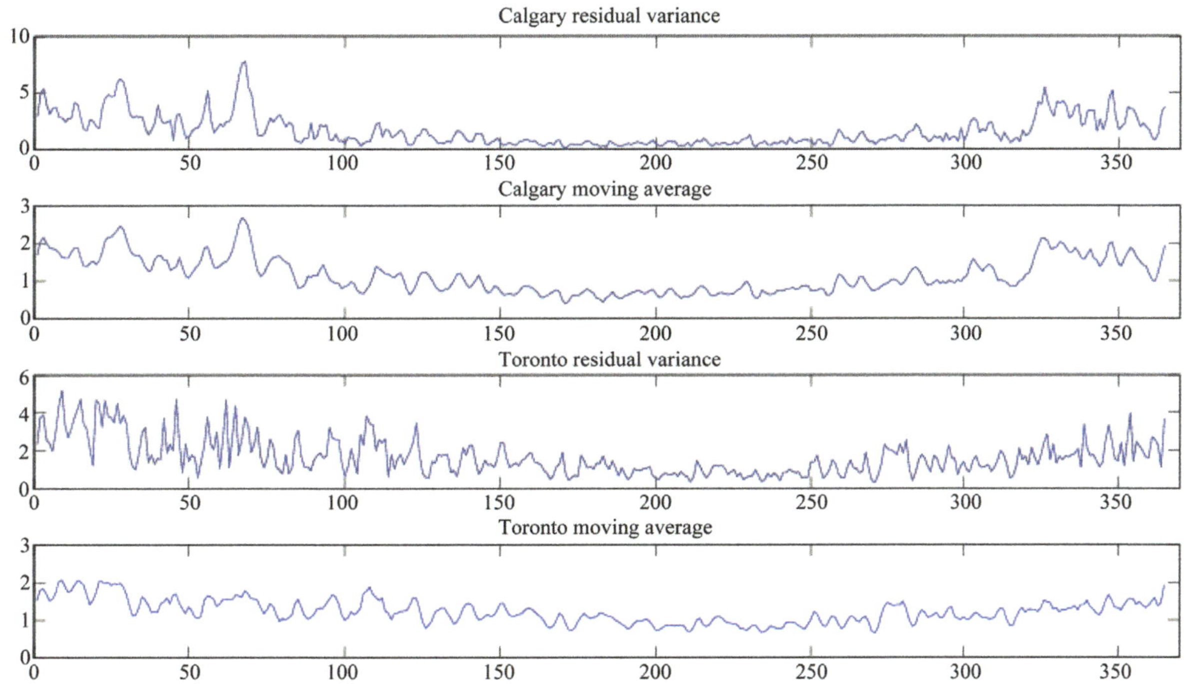

Figure 3. Empirical and smoothed seasonal variation.

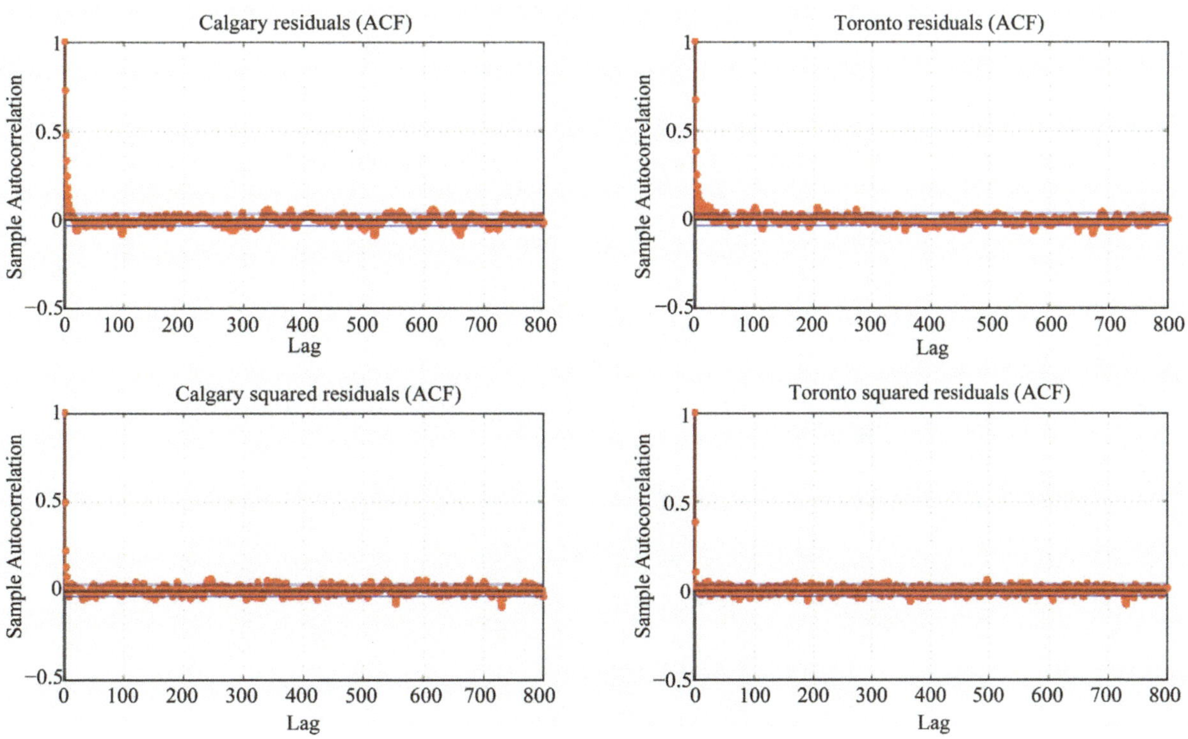

Figure 4. ACF after removing seasonal variation.

$$a(\lambda,\alpha,\beta,\delta)=\frac{\left(\alpha^2-\beta^2\right)^{\lambda/2}}{\sqrt{2\pi}\alpha^{\lambda-1/2}\delta^{\lambda}K_{\lambda}\left(\delta\sqrt{\alpha^2-\beta^2}\right)}$$

where K_s is modified Bessel function of the third kind with index s. Parameters of the generalized hyperbolic distribution can be estimated by maximum likelihood method. In detail, for a vector of observations $x=\{x_1,\cdots,x_n\}$, the maximum likelihood estimate of the parameters $\theta=(\lambda,\alpha,\beta,\delta,\mu)$ can be obtained by maxi-

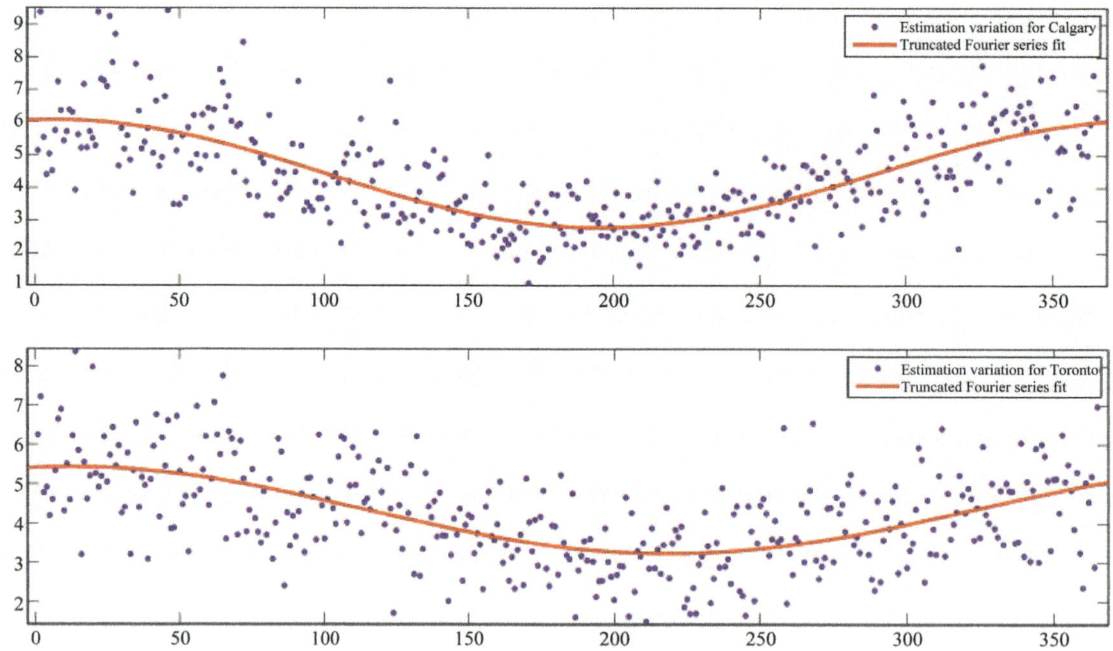

Figure 5. Fit of volatility by truncated Fourier series.

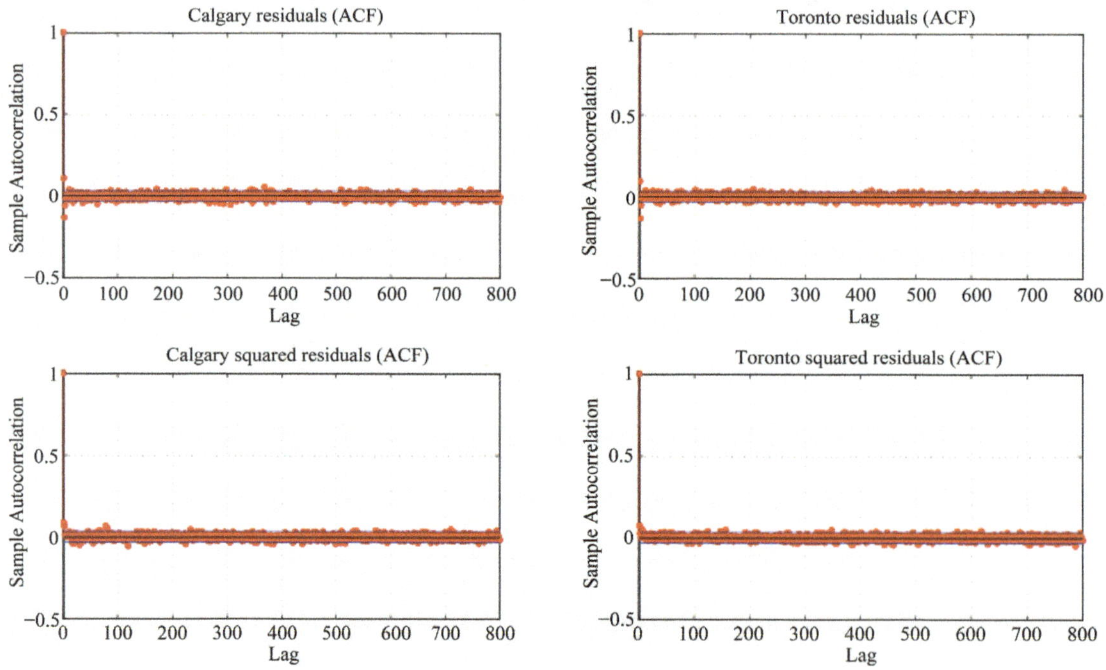

Figure 6. ACF after removing seasonal variation.

mizing the log-likelihood function for generalized hyperbolic distribution:

$$L(x;\theta) = \log(a) + \frac{\lambda - 1/2}{2}\sum_{i=1}^{n}\log\left(\delta^2 + (x_i - \mu)^2\right) \times \sum_{i=1}^{n}\log\left(K_{\lambda-\frac{1}{2}}\left(\alpha\sqrt{\delta^2 + (x_i - \mu)^2}\right)\right) + \beta(x_i - \mu).$$

McNeil *et al.* [13] described a modified EM method, which is called multi-cycle, expectation, conditional estimation (MCECM) algorithm to optimize the log-likelihood function. We use this algorithm written as "ghyp" package in "R" to estimate parameters. Estimated parameters are presented in **Table 4**.

In order to check the goodness of fitting, we simulated a series of generalized hyperbolic distributed random

Table 4. Estimations of generalized hyperbolic parameters.

	λ	α	β	δ	μ
Calgary	27.55	26.50	−21.70	0.72	5.39
Toronto	16.81	31.33	24.82	7.49	−10.96

variables using estimated parameters, and plotted the empirical cumulative distribution function, then compared with our residual observations' empirical cumulative distribution function plot. The results are shown in **Figure 7**. The result implies our calibration to the model is reasonably fair for Canadian data.

2.2. Lévy Driven Continuous-Time AR Model

Another suitable class of stochastic process we could use to analyze the evolution of temperature is an extension of the previous OU process to the multi-factor OU process. The model is called Continuous-time Autoregressive (CAR) model, which is also a subclass of the general Continuous-time Autoregressive Moving-average (CAR-MA) model introduced by Brockwell and Marquardt [14]. The intuition behind using this model is the temperature memory is consistent with high-order AR model, and the seasonality of mean and volatility is also involved in the model. In other words, the CAR model combine the mean-reverting property of OU process and the memory of AR model together to better capture the features of temperature.

Followed by the classical stochastic assumption, suppose given a probability space $(\Omega, \mathbf{F}, \mathbf{P})$. Let $Y(t)$ be a stationary solution to the stochastic differential equation in $\boldsymbol{R}^p$ for $p \geq 1$.

$$\alpha(D)Y(t) = \sigma(t)DL(t), \tag{10}$$

where the operator D denotes the differential operator with respect to t, $\alpha(D) = D^p + \alpha_1 D^{p-1} + \cdots + \alpha_p$ is the p-order differential operator and $\{L(t), t \geq 0\}$ is 1-dim Lévy process. Let $\boldsymbol{X}(t)$ be a column vector defined as

$$\boldsymbol{X}(t) = (X_1(t), X_2(t), \cdots, X_p(t))'.$$

We could also rewrite the Equation (10) in the state-space form.

$$Y(t) = \boldsymbol{e}_1' \cdot \boldsymbol{X}(t) := X_1(t), \tag{11}$$

$$d\boldsymbol{X}(t) = A\boldsymbol{X}(t)dt + \boldsymbol{e}_p \sigma(t) dL(t), \tag{12}$$

$$A = \begin{pmatrix} 0 & 1 & 0 & \cdots & 0 \\ 0 & 0 & 1 & \cdots & 0 \\ \vdots & \vdots & \vdots & \ddots & \vdots \\ 0 & 0 & 0 & \cdots & 1 \\ -\alpha_p & -\alpha_{p-1} & -\alpha_{p-2} & \cdots & -\alpha_1 \end{pmatrix}, \boldsymbol{e}_p = \begin{pmatrix} 0 \\ 0 \\ \vdots \\ 0 \\ 1 \end{pmatrix}.$$

The vector $\boldsymbol{X}(t) \in \boldsymbol{R}^p$ is usually recognized as state vector. The standard deviation of the noise is described by a continuous function $\sigma(t) > 0$, we usually refer the

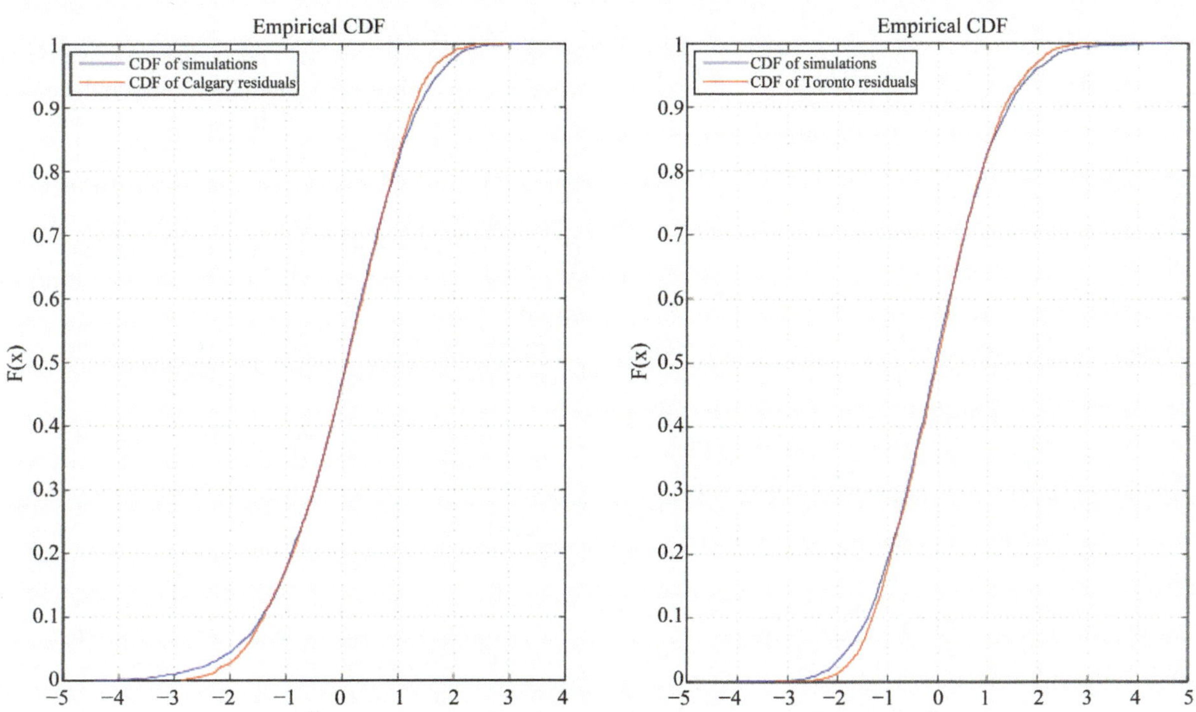

Figure 7. CDF of simulated series and observations.

function $\sigma(t)$ as the volatility of the process $Y(t)$. The constant p denotes the order of the CAR model.

Assume additionally the seasonal function $\Lambda(t):[0.T]\mapsto \boldsymbol{R}$ is bounded and continuously differentiable on t. The temperature dynamics is formulated by:

$$T(t)=\Lambda(t)+Y(t), \tag{13}$$

where $Y(t)$ is the first entry of the state vector $\boldsymbol{X}(t)$ in Equation (11). Note that for Equation (12), since we have the function $\Lambda(t)$ to capture the deterministic temperature level, the OU process should ideally revert to zero. This is the main reason we have only the mean-reverting rate A but without level in dynamic of $\boldsymbol{X}(t)$.

Again, by using the Itô lemma for semimartingale, the explicit solution for the stochastic differential Equation (12) has the form

$$\boldsymbol{X}(t)=\mathrm{e}^{At}\mathbf{X}(0)+\int_0^t \mathrm{e}^{A(t-u)}\boldsymbol{e}_p\sigma(u)\mathrm{d}L(u). \tag{14}$$

If we construct the expectation of the Wiener-Lévy integral in Equation (14) equals to zero (it is obviously true for the Itô integral in the special case), once all eigenvalues of the matrix A have negative real parts, the process $\boldsymbol{X}(t)$ then have a mean equal to zero. We could still use simple intuition to have the idea, when eigenvalues of the matrix A have negative real parts and take $t\to+\infty, \mathrm{e}^{At}\to 0,$ then the expectation goes to zero. This result implies the temperature dynamic on average will mainly depend on the seasonal function $\Lambda(t)$ by Equation (13).

Notice that we could have a link point of view to this CAR model from the previous OU model. Consider CAR(1) model as an example. In this case, $p=1$ in Equation (12), the matrix A will simply becomes a constant $-\alpha_1$. The process $X_1(t)=Y(t)$, and by Equation (14), the temperature dynamics

$$T(t)=\Lambda(t)+\mathrm{e}^{-\alpha_1 t}X_1(0)+\int_0^t \mathrm{e}^{-\alpha_1(t-u)}\sigma(u)\mathrm{d}L(u).$$

Our proposed CAR model is therefore consistent with the single-factor OU model and also satisfies the requirements of regression and mean-reverting properties. For simplicity of estimation, we connect our CAR model to the classical AR model. Benth *et al.* [15] (Lemma 10.2) provided an explicit way to find the relation between the coefficients α_i in CAR model and b_i in AR model by induction as

$$\begin{aligned}&\sum\nolimits_{k=0}^{p}(-1)^k c_k^p X_1(t+p-k)=-\sum\nolimits_{q=1}^{p}\alpha_{p-q+1}\\&\sum\nolimits_{k=0}^{q-1}(-1)^k c_k^{q-1}X_1(t+q-1-k)\end{aligned} \tag{15}$$

with coefficients $c_k^q=c_{k-1}^{q-1}+c_k^{q-1},\ k=1,\cdots,p-1,\ q\geq 2,$ and initially $c_0^q=c_q^q=1, q=0,\cdots,p.$

Next, we will recap the calibration procedure to the same empirical Canadian daily average temperature data based on the CAR model.

2.2.1. Linear and Seasonal Trend

As we did for OU model in Section 2.1.2., we could combine the linear and seasonal trend in the OU model to construct the seasonal function $\Lambda(t)$ in CAR model as

$$\Lambda(t)=a_0+a_1t+a_2\sin\left(\frac{2\pi}{365}(t-t_0)\right). \tag{16}$$

The coefficients for trigonometric function in Equation (16) play the same role in Equation (7). Followed by the description of linear trend in Section 2.1.2., we eliminated the linear part in $\Lambda(t)$ again for CAR model, and the fitted results for seasonal part are the same to that in **Table 1**.

2.2.2. Cyclical Component

The PACF plots in **Figure 8** clearly show that the evolution of detrended temperature $Y(t)$ could be modeled by the classical AR(3) model. Motivated by the PACF plots, by Equation (15), we have $b_1=3-\alpha_1$, $b_2=2\alpha_1-\alpha_2-3,\ \ b_3=\alpha_2+1-\alpha_1-\alpha_3.$

The estimated parameters are outlined in **Table 5**.

PACF plots in **Figure 9** show the significant correlation in the first three lags is removed by regression, but still a distinct seasonality in the ACF plots of squared residuals.

2.2.3. Seasonal Volatility

For the CAR model, we will apply the truncated Fourier series in Equation (9) to model the seasonal volatility. We choose the degree $N=1$ in Equation (9), since there is no significant improvement for the result by adding degree. The fitted parameters are shown in **Table 6**.

In **Figure 10** we present the empirical $\sigma(t)$ and fitted $\sigma(t)$, both of them show that the fluctuation in the cold season are considerably larger than that of the mild season.

Figure 11 tells us that seasonal pattern in the squared residual is removed successfully.

Table 5. Estimations of cyclical component.

	b_1	b_2	b_3
Calgary	0.9520	−0.2796	0.0967
Toronto	0.8243	−0.2373	0.1059

Table 6. Truncated Fourier series parameters.

	c_1	c_2	c_3	w
Calgary	13.13	8.529	0.6149	0.01636
Toronto	9.712	4.307	0.6857	0.01491

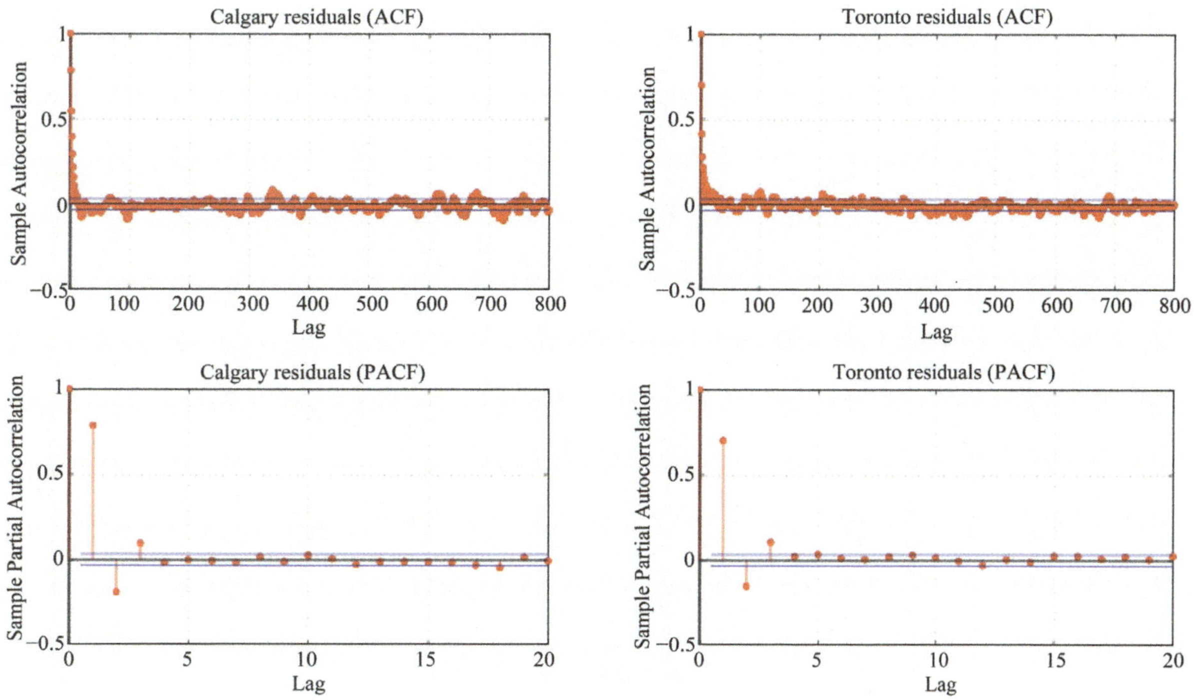

Figure 8. Empirical ACF and PACF.

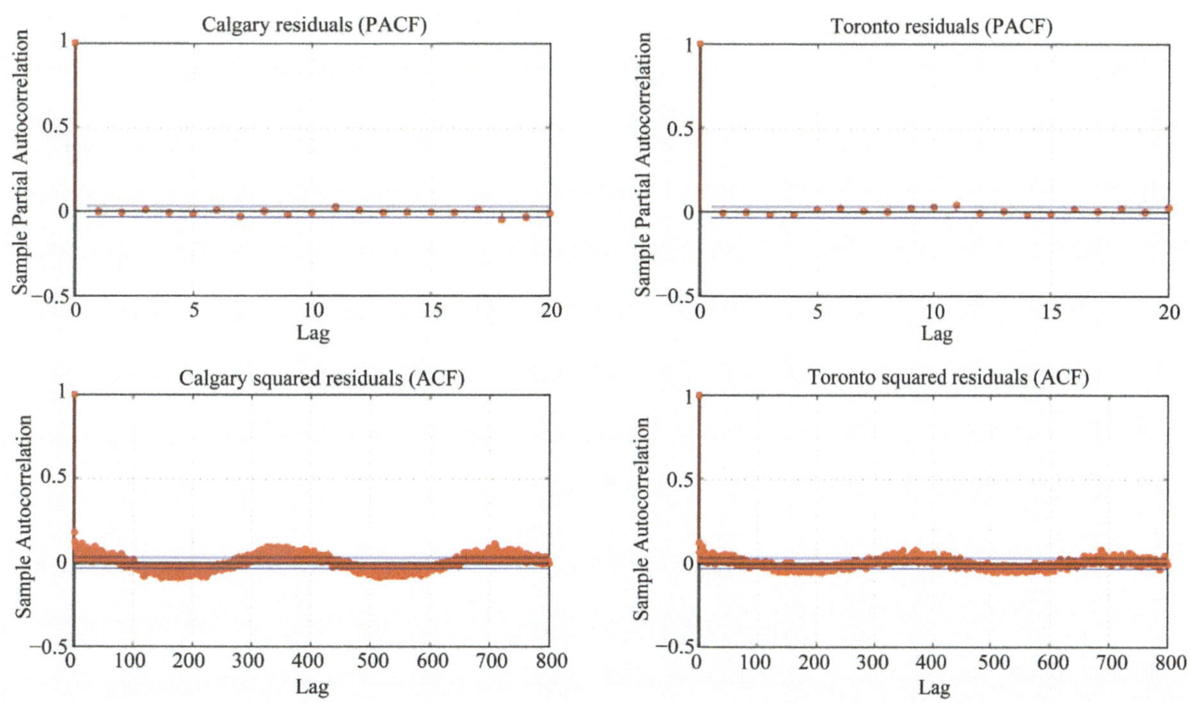

Figure 9. Empirical ACF and PACF.

2.2.4. Random Noise

We try again apply the generalized hyperbolic process to model our random noise part. The method is the same to that for OU model. **Table 7** shows the fitted parameters for our Canadian cities data.

Also as we did for OU model, we simulated a series of generalized hyperbolic random variables with estimated parameters, then compare the empirical CDF with that of historical data in **Figure 12**. The empirical CDF coincides with simulated CDF almost perfectly, so we may expect this model fairly well describe our Canadian temperature data.

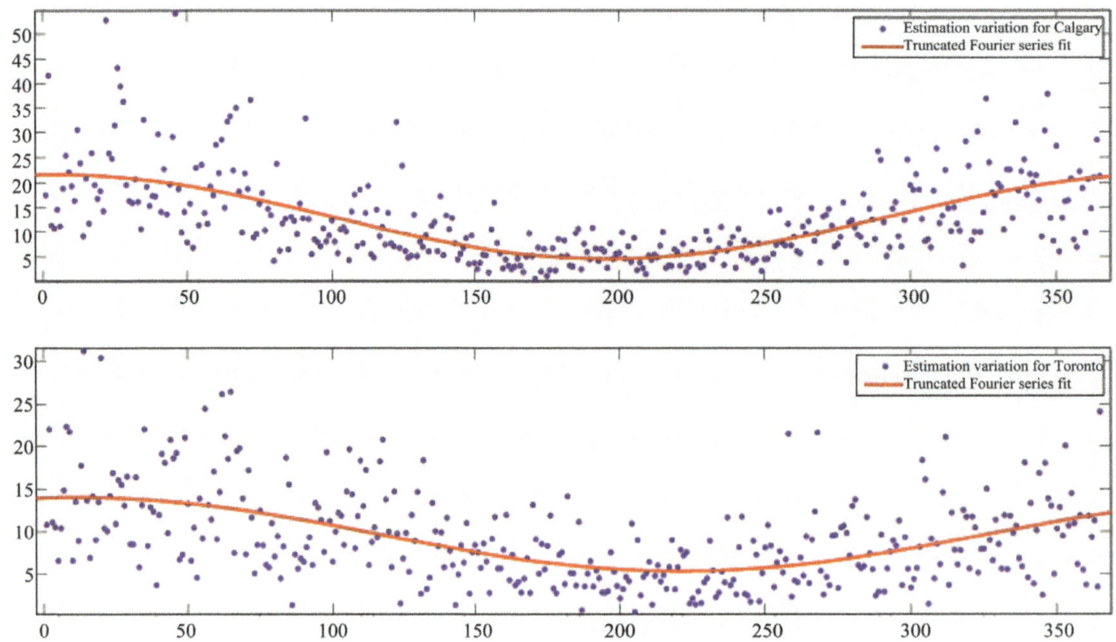

Figure 10. Empirical and fitted seasonal volatility.

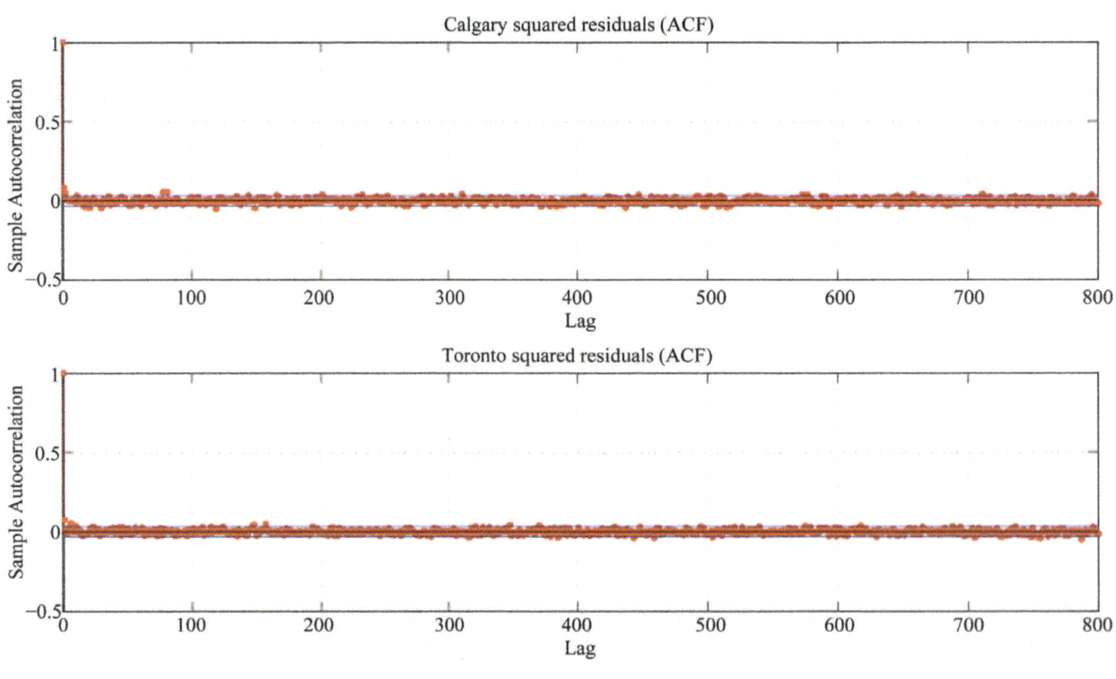

Figure 11. Empirical ACF plot of squared residuals.

3. Pricing of Weather Derivatives

In this section, we will derive the temperature futures prices written on CAT, CDD and HDD, which constitute the three main classes of future products at CME market.

3.1. Future Pricing of Lévy Driven OU Model

Consider the price dynamic of future written on CAT over specific time period $[\tau_1, \tau_2]$, with $\tau_1 < \tau_2$. Firstly, assume the daily average temperature follows stochastic differential Equation (1) with $L(t)$ being Lévy process and constant continuously compounding interest rate r. The future price at time $0 \le t \le \tau_1$ based on CAT under risk-neutral probability measure Q will be $\mathcal{F}_t$ adapted stochastic process $F_{\text{CAT}}(t, \tau_1, \tau_2)$ satisfying

$$e^{-r(\tau_2 - t)} \mathrm{E}^Q \left[\int_{\tau_1}^{\tau_2} T(u) \mathrm{d}u - F_{\text{CAT}}(t, \tau_1, \tau_2) \mid \mathcal{F}_t \right] = 0. \quad (17)$$

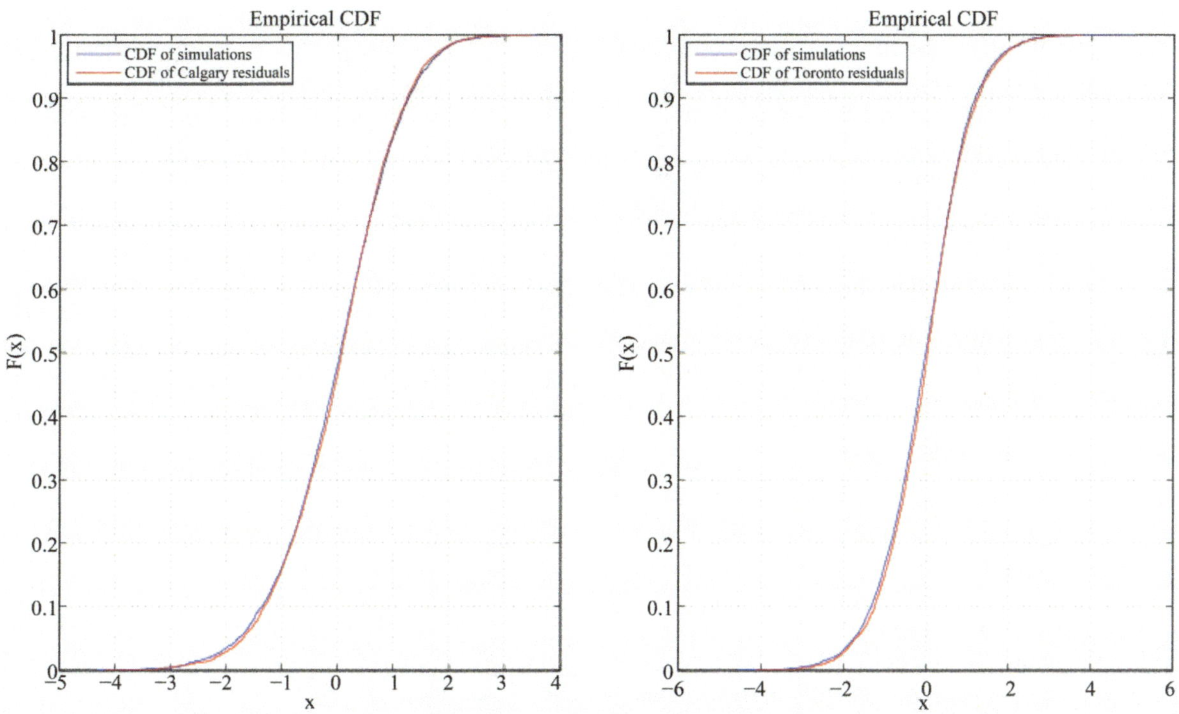

Figure 12. Empirical ACF plot of squared residuals.

Table 7. Estimations of generalized hyperbolic parameters.

	λ	α	β	δ	μ
ryCalga	8.65	4.28	−1.00	0.59	1.02
Toronto	4.24	2.95	−0.12	0.41	0.13

By adaption of the stochastic process $F_{\text{CAT}}(t,\tau_1,\tau_2)$ with respect to measure Q, the future price

$$F_{\text{CAT}}(t,\tau_1,\tau_2) = \mathrm{E}^Q\left[\int_{\tau_1}^{\tau_2} T(u)\mathrm{d}u \mid \boldsymbol{F}_t\right]. \quad (18)$$

To derive the explicit future price in Equation (18), we need to specify a risk-neutral probability measure Q. However, the commodity market is typical incomplete market, since most of commodity trades impose big transaction and storage cost. For our case, the underlying temperature is even not possible to be stored and traded. These features break down the classical hedging approach used to derive the unique fair price of derivatives. Because of the incompleteness of the temperature market, any probability measure Q being equivalent to the real measure P is a risk-neutral measure. Next, following the analysis in Benth and Šaltytė-Benth [16], we will specify a class of risk-neutral measure via Esscher transform. Before using the Esscher transform, we need an integrable condition for the Lévy measure to ensure the existence of moments of underlying asset process.

Condition 1. [Benth *et al.* ([15], p. 74)] $\exists k > 0$ such that the Lévy measure v satisfies the integrable condition

$$\int_{|z|\geq 1} |z|^k \, v(\mathrm{d}z) < \infty \quad (19)$$

almost surely.

The constant k determines the order of the moment that is finite for the underlying process. With this condition, we recap the following results from several sources that we will use in our further analysis (see Section 3.2).

Lemma 1. [Benth and Šaltytė-Benth [16]] Let function $f:[0,t]\mapsto \boldsymbol{R}$ be a bounded and measurable function and Condition 1 holds for $k := \sup_{s\in[0,t]}|f(s)|$, then

$$\mathrm{E}\left[\exp\left(\int_0^t f(s)\mathrm{d}L(s)\right)\right] = \exp\left(\int_0^t \psi(f(s))\mathrm{d}s\right), \quad (20)$$

where $\psi(u) = \eta(-\mathrm{i}u)$ is the cumulant function of the Lévy process $L(t)$, $\eta(u)$ is the Lévy symbol defined by map $\boldsymbol{R}\mapsto\boldsymbol{C}$ such that the characteristic function of the Lévy process $\phi(u) = \mathrm{e}^{\eta(u)}$.

Now assume $\theta:[0,T]\mapsto\boldsymbol{R}$ is a measurable and bounded function. Let us consider the stochastic process

$$Z_t^\theta = \exp\left(\int_0^t \theta(s)\mathrm{d}L(s) - \int_0^t \psi(\theta(s))\mathrm{d}s\right). \quad (21)$$

The probability measure Q^θ can be defined by the Esscher transform

$$Q^\theta(A) = \mathrm{E}\left[1_A Z_T^\theta\right], \quad (22)$$

where 1_A is the indicator function over a probability space A. Obviously this measure is equivalent to the real measure P, and transformed from the probability measure P, so an equivalent risk-neutral measure. A way to get a more flexible class of equivalent martingale measure is to use time varying θ when fitting the observed forward curve. Note that the market price of risk is represented by θ in this case.

Then, consider the existence of the fair forward price dynamics $F_{\text{CAT}}(t,\tau_1,\tau_2)$ given by Equation (18). We need to have another condition such that

$\mathrm{E}^Q\left[\int_{\tau_1}^{\tau_2} T(t)\,\mathrm{d}t \mid \boldsymbol{F}_t\right]$ is finite almost surely.

Condition 2. [Benth and Šaltytė-Benth [16]] Assume a constant k satisfies $k = 1+\sup_{s\in[0,T]}|\theta(s)|$ such that Condition 1 holds, then the price dynamics

$\mathrm{E}^Q\left[\int_{\tau_1}^{\tau_2} T(t)\,\mathrm{d}t \mid \boldsymbol{F}_t\right] < \infty$ almost surely.

With the existence of explicit risk-neutral probability measure and fair pricing technique, we could derive the following results for the future price written on CAT.

Lemma 2. [Benth and Šaltytė-Benth [7]] Given a measurable and bounded function $f(t)$, the expectation of Lévy integral under risk-neutral measure over $[\tau_1,\tau_2]$ is

$$\mathrm{E}^Q\left[\int_{\tau_1}^{\tau_2} f(t)\,\mathrm{d}t \mid \boldsymbol{F}_{\tau_1}\right] = \int_{\tau_1}^{\tau_2} f(t)\psi'(\theta(t))\,\mathrm{d}t.$$

With these lemmas, we could get the explicit formula for the future price written on CAT.

Theorem 1. [Benth and Šaltytė-Benth [7]] The future price $F_{\text{CAT}}(t,\tau_1,\tau_2)$ at time $t \le \tau_1 < \tau_2$ written on CAT index is given by

$$\begin{aligned} &F_{\text{CAT}}(t,\tau_1,\tau_2) \\ &= \int_{\tau_1}^{\tau_2} s(u)\,\mathrm{d}u + \kappa^{-1}\left(T(t)-s(t)\right)\left(\mathrm{e}^{\kappa(\tau_2-t)} - \mathrm{e}^{\kappa(\tau_1-t)}\right) \\ &\quad + \kappa^{-1}\int_t^{\tau_2} \sigma(u)\left(\mathrm{e}^{\kappa(\tau_2-u)}-1\right)\psi'(\theta(u))\,\mathrm{d}u \\ &\quad - \kappa^{-1}\int_t^{\tau_1} \sigma(u)\left(\mathrm{e}^{\kappa(\tau_1-u)}-1\right)\psi'(\theta(u))\,\mathrm{d}u. \end{aligned}$$

Next, for pricing of CDD and HDD futures, recall that the CDD and HDD over a measurable time $[\tau_1,\tau_2]$ is

$$\text{CDD}: \int_{\tau_1}^{\tau_2} \max\left(T(t)-c,0\right)\mathrm{d}t = \int_{\tau_1}^{\tau_2} \left(T(t)-c\right)^+ \mathrm{d}t;$$

$$\text{HDD}: \int_{\tau_1}^{\tau_2} \max\left(c-T(t),0\right)\mathrm{d}t = \int_{\tau_1}^{\tau_2} \left(c-T(t)\right)^+ \mathrm{d}t.$$

Before introduce the pricing technique for the CDD and HDD future, we should notice that there is a parity relation between futures prices of CAT, CDD and HDD. This relation will help us to get one of future price of CDD or HDD, once we have the CAT future price and the other one of them.

Theorem 2. [Benth *et al.* ([15], p. 279)] The relation between futures prices of CAT, CDD and HDD is

$$F_{\text{CDD}} + F_{\text{HDD}} = c(\tau_2-\tau_1) - F_{\text{CAT}}. \quad (23)$$

With this theorem, we will focus on the pricing of CDD future, but the pricing technique for CDD future is also analogously applicable to HDD future.

Based on risk-neutral pricing theory, the CDD future price satisfies

$$\mathrm{e}^{-r(\tau_2-t)}\mathrm{E}^Q \cdot\left[\int_{\tau_1}^{\tau_2}\left(T(u)-c\right)^+\mathrm{d}u - F_{\text{CDD}}(t,\tau_1,\tau_2) \mid \boldsymbol{F}_t\right] = 0$$

with risk-free interest rate r and risk-neutral measure Q. Given the risk-neutral measure derived from Esscher transform, since the CDD future under the measure is adapted, the risk-neutral CDD future price is derived as

$$F_{\text{CDD}}(t,\tau_1,\tau_2) = \mathrm{E}^Q\left[\int_{\tau_1}^{\tau_2}\left(T(u)-c\right)^+\mathrm{d}u \mid \boldsymbol{F}_t\right], \quad (24)$$

Theorem 3. [Benth and Šaltytė-Benth [7]] For $X(\tau) := \int_0^\tau \sigma(t)\mathrm{e}^{\kappa(\tau-t)}\mathrm{d}L(t)$, $\mathrm{E}^Q\left[\exp\left(\mathrm{i}\lambda X(\tau)\right)\right] = \exp\left(\Psi(\lambda)\right)$, the logarithm of characteristic function $\Psi(\lambda)$ of $X(\tau)$ under measure Q^θ is given by

$$\begin{aligned} \Psi(\lambda) &= \int_0^\tau \psi\left(\lambda\sigma(t)\mathrm{e}^{\kappa(\tau-t)} - \mathrm{i}\theta(t)\right)\mathrm{d}t \\ &\quad - \int_0^\tau \psi\left(-\mathrm{i}\theta(t)\right)\mathrm{d}t, \end{aligned} \quad (25)$$

where ψ is the cumulant generating function of $L(1)$.

This theorem provides us a way to get the characteristic function of Lévy integral of the type $X(\tau)$ under the risk-neutral measure Q^θ. With the characteristic function, the pricing approach we could try is using the celebrated Fourier inversion theorem to get the numerical probability density function of $X(\tau)$ under Q^θ measure, and then using the density function to price CDD future.

Theorem 4. (Fourier Inversion Theorem) [Hewitt and Stromberg ([17], p. 409)] Let $F(x)$ denote the cumulative density function of random variable $X(\tau)$, the corresponding probability density function $f(x)$ is integrable in Lebesgue sense, *i.e.* $f(x)\in L$. The characteristic function of $X(\tau)$ is defined as $\phi(t) = \int_{-\infty}^{+\infty}\mathrm{e}^{\mathrm{i}tx}f(x)\,\mathrm{d}x \in L$. Then,

$$\begin{aligned} f(x) &= \frac{1}{2\pi}\int_{-\infty}^{+\infty}\mathrm{e}^{-\mathrm{i}tx}\phi(t)\,\mathrm{d}t \\ &= \frac{1}{\pi}\int_0^{+\infty}\mathrm{e}^{-\mathrm{i}tx}\phi(t)\,\mathrm{d}t. \end{aligned} \quad (26)$$

To calculate the probability density function from characteristic function, consider the density $f(x)$ and the discrete Fourier transform (DFT) $X_k = \sum_{n=0}^{N-1} x_n \mathrm{e}^{-\mathrm{i}k\frac{2\pi}{N}n}$. We could use the trapezoid rule to approximate the integral in Equation (26).

$$f(x)=\frac{1}{\pi}\int_0^{+\infty}\mathrm{e}^{-\mathrm{i}tx}\phi(t)$$
$$=\frac{1}{\pi}\left(\frac{\mathrm{e}^{-\mathrm{i}t_0x}\phi(t_0)+\mathrm{e}^{-\mathrm{i}t_Nx}\phi(t_N)}{2}+\sum_{k=1}^{N-1}\mathrm{e}^{-\mathrm{i}t_kx}\phi(t_k)\Delta t\right) \quad (27)$$
$$\approx\frac{1}{\pi}\sum_{k=0}^{N-1}\delta_k\mathrm{e}^{-\mathrm{i}t_kx}\phi(t_k)\Delta t,$$

where $\delta_k=\begin{cases}1/2, & k=0;\\ 1, & \text{otherwise.}\end{cases}$ The last step of approximation is because when we take t_k to be large enough, $t_k\to\infty$, $\mathrm{e}^{-\mathrm{i}t_Nx}\psi(t_N)\to 0$. The purpose to have the upper bound of summation as $N-1$ is to match with the form of DFT.

Now we propose an approach to calculate the probability density function analytically based on the construction of Choudakis [18]. Note that the application of DFT will result in a set of integral approximation which have the form of Equation (27) based on $x_j, j=0,\cdots,N-1$. Let $\eta=\Delta t$, then $t_k=\eta k$. For the return values x_j, these values are setting to be also equidistant with the grid spacing λ. By contrasting Equation (27) and DFT, we have $\lambda\eta=\frac{2\pi}{N}\Rightarrow\lambda=\frac{2\pi}{\eta N}$.

Then set the return grids

$$x_j=-b+\lambda j, j=0,\cdots,N-1, \quad (28)$$

where b is a parameter to control the return range. For the center returns around zero, we could set $b=\frac{\lambda N}{2}$. With these settlements, from Equation (27), the probability density function has the form

$$f(x_j)\approx\frac{1}{\pi}\sum_{k=0}^{N-1}\delta_k\mathrm{e}^{-\mathrm{i}\eta k(-b+\lambda j)}\phi(\eta k)$$
$$=\sum_{k=0}^{N-1}\frac{1}{\pi}\delta_k\mathrm{e}^{\mathrm{i}\eta kb}\mathrm{e}^{-\mathrm{i}k\frac{2\pi}{N}j}\phi(\eta k) \quad (29)$$
$$=\sum_{k=0}^{N-1}f_k\mathrm{e}^{-\mathrm{i}j\frac{2\pi}{N}k},$$

where $f_k=\frac{1}{\pi}\delta_k\mathrm{e}^{\mathrm{i}\eta kb}\phi(\eta k)\eta, j=0,\cdots,N-1$. This summation has the form of DFT, could be computed efficiently.

Theorem 5. Numerically, the CDD future

$$F_{\mathrm{CDD}}(t,\tau_1,\tau_2)=\sum_{\tau_1}^{\tau_2}\sum_{x_k\ge d}\left[x_k+\left(s(u)+\left(T(0)-s(0)\right)\mathrm{e}^{\kappa u}-c\right)\right]f(x_k,u)\Delta u$$

where $d=c-s(u)+\left(T(0)-s(0)\right)\mathrm{e}^{\kappa u}$, $f(x_k,u)$ is given by Equation (29) and x_k are constructed by Equation (28) in the approach of fast Fourier transform.

Proof. Recall the CDD future is priced by Equation (24). By Fubini theorem, the definition of expectation and property of Riemann integral,

$$F_{\mathrm{CDD}}(t,\tau_1,\tau_2)$$
$$=\int_{\tau_1}^{\tau_2}\mathrm{E}^{Q}\left[\left(X(u)+\left(s(u)+\left(T(0)-s(0)\right)\mathrm{e}^{\kappa u-c}\right)\right)^+\mid\boldsymbol{F}_t\right]\mathrm{d}u$$
$$=\sum_{u=\tau_1}^{\tau_2}\mathrm{E}^{Q}\left[\left(X(u)+\left(s(u)+\left(T(0)-s(0)\right)\mathrm{e}^{\kappa u-c}\right)\right)^+\mid\boldsymbol{F}_t\right]\Delta u$$
$$=\sum_{u=\tau_1}^{\tau_2}\sum_{x_k\ge d}\left[x_k+\left(s(u)+\left(T(0)-s(0)\right)\mathrm{e}^{\kappa u}-c\right)\right]f(x_k,u)\Delta u$$

3.2. Future Pricing of Lévy Driven CAR Model

Now we assume the temperature dynamic follows Lévy driven CAR model, introduced by Equations (11) and (12). The risk-neutral measure Q^θ is given by Equation (22), and the Existences of futures prices for CAT, CDD and HDD are preserved under Condition 2.

Based on the derivation of futures prices of CAT, CDD and HDD indices under Lévy driven OU model, we have the following results for the futures prices of these indices under the Lévy driven CAR model.

Lemma 3. The cumulated temperature on the time interval $[\tau_1,\tau_2]$ under Lévy driven CAR model is

$$\int_{\tau_1}^{\tau_2}T(t)\mathrm{d}t$$
$$=\int_{\tau_1}^{\tau_2}\Lambda(t)\mathrm{d}t+\boldsymbol{e}_1'A^{-1}\left(\mathrm{e}^{A\tau_2}-\mathrm{e}^{A\tau_1}\right)\boldsymbol{X}(0)+\boldsymbol{e}_1'A^{-1}$$
$$\times\int_0^{\tau_2}\left[\mathrm{e}^{A(\tau_2-t)}-\mathrm{e}^{A(\tau_1-t)}1_{[0,\tau_1]}(t)-1_{[\tau_1,\tau_2]}(t)\right]\boldsymbol{e}_p\sigma(t)\mathrm{d}L(t).$$

Proof. Integrating the original Equation (12) over the time interval $[\tau_1,\tau_2]$, we have

$$\boldsymbol{X}(\tau_2)-\boldsymbol{X}(\tau_1)=A\int_{\tau_1}^{\tau_2}\boldsymbol{X}(t)\mathrm{d}t+\boldsymbol{e}_p\int_{\tau_1}^{\tau_2}\sigma(t)\mathrm{d}L(t).$$

Then, by using the solution of Lévy stochastic model, Equation (14), Equations (11) and (13),

$$\int_{\tau_1}^{\tau_2}\left(T(t)-\Lambda(t)\right)\mathrm{d}t$$
$$=\int_{\tau_1}^{\tau_2}\boldsymbol{e}_1'\boldsymbol{X}(t)\mathrm{d}t=\boldsymbol{e}_1'\int_{\tau_1}^{\tau_2}\boldsymbol{X}(t)\mathrm{d}t$$
$$=\boldsymbol{e}_1'A^{-1}\left(\boldsymbol{X}(\tau_2)-\boldsymbol{X}(\tau_1)-\boldsymbol{e}_p\int_{\tau_1}^{\tau_2}\sigma(t)\mathrm{d}L(t)\right)$$
$$=\boldsymbol{e}_1'A^{-1}\left(\left(\mathrm{e}^{A\tau_2}-\mathrm{e}^{A\tau_1}\right)\boldsymbol{X}(0)+\int_0^{\tau_2}\mathrm{e}^{A(\tau_2-t)}\boldsymbol{e}_p\sigma(t)\mathrm{d}L(t)\right.$$
$$\left.-\int_0^{\tau_2}\mathrm{e}^{A(\tau_1-t)}\boldsymbol{e}_p\sigma(t)\mathrm{d}L(t)-\int_{\tau_1}^{\tau_2}\boldsymbol{e}_p\sigma(t)\mathrm{d}L(t)\right).$$

So, the result is proved. □

Theorem 6. The future price of CAT

$$F_{\text{CAT}}(t,\tau_1,\tau_2) = \int_{\tau_1}^{\tau_2} \Lambda(u)\mathrm{d}u + e_1' A^{-1}\left(e^{A(\tau_2-t)} - e^{A(\tau_2-t)}\right)X(t) + e_1' A^{-1}\int_t^{\tau_2}\left(e^{A(\tau_2-u)}-1\right)e_p\sigma(u)\psi'(\theta(u))\mathrm{d}u - e_1' A^{-1}\int_t^{\tau_1}\left(e^{A(\tau_1-u)}-1\right)e_p\sigma(u)\psi'(\theta(u))\mathrm{d}u.$$

Proof. By Equation (18), we could use Lemma 3 to expand each term separately, and then use Lemma 2 to get the final explicit formula. □

For CDD or HDD futures pricing, by using Theorem 3, the characteristic function of $\int_0^\tau e_p\sigma(t)e^{A(\tau-t)}\mathrm{d}L(t)$ could be found as $\exp(\Psi(\lambda))$ where

$$\Psi(\lambda) = \int_0^\tau \psi\left(\lambda e_1' e^{A(\tau-t)} e_p\sigma(t) - \mathrm{i}\theta(t)\right)\mathrm{d}t - \int_0^\tau \psi(-\mathrm{i}\theta(t))\mathrm{d}t.$$

Then, followed by the approach in the OU model, we have

Theorem 7. Numerically, the CDD future price

$$F_{\text{CDD}}(t,\tau_1,\tau_2) = \sum_{\tau_1}^{\tau_2}\sum_{x_k \ge d}\left[x_k + \left(\Lambda(u) + e_1' e^{Au} X(0) - c\right)\right] f(x_k,u)\Delta u,$$

where $f(x_k,u)$ is given by Equation (29) and x_k are constructed by Equation (28) in the approach of fast Fourier transform to compute $f(x_k,u)$

The proof of this theorem is similar to that of Theorem 5.

4. Summary, Conclusion and Future Work

This paper investigates the problem of modeling and pricing weather derivatives and their application to Canadian data. We have shown that two models, including Ornstein-Uhlenbeck model and Continuous-time Autoregressive model, both driven by Lévy process are fairly suitable to capture the evolution of Canadian cities temperature. Also, based on these two models, we derived approaches for risk-neutral prices of future contracts written on CAT, CDD and HDD.

For the Ornstein-Uhlenbeck model, we followed the analysis developed in Benth and Šaltytė-Benth [7], and calibrated the model to empirical study of our Canadian temperature data. As an extension, we derived a numerically explicit pricing formula for futures written on CDD and HDD futures. For the Continuous-time Autoregressive model, we extended the original model introduced by Benth *et al.* [15] to the one with Lévy process as the random variable instead of Brownian motion. And we also, calculated the explicit formulas for futures written on CAT, CDD and HDD indices under the structure. We would like to mention that our approaches and results could be applied to other temperature data set rather than Canadian ones with some modifications and adjustments.

This work can be extended in several ways. For instance, based on our empirical studies of Canadian data, the volatility possesses significant seasonal behaviour under the existed models. One could consider using regime-switching techniques to model this seasonal volatility under the structure of the established models in this paper. For instance, depending on the local appearance of the weather in Canadian cites, one can intend to use two-state Markov chain for modeling of Calgary's volatility and four-state one for Toronto's.

As an application to risk management in industries, we could also consider the dynamic hedging strategy of other futures by using weather future. Take the energy futures for example, if we consider a portfolio at time t containing one unit of energy (e.g. heating oil) future F_E and β_t units of weather futures F_W, both with maturity at time *T*. Assume the portfolio has value $\Pi(t)$ at time t, then

$$\Pi(t) = e^{-r(T-t)}\left[F_E(t) + \beta_t F_W(t)\right].$$

If the portfolio is self-financing, the change in this portfolio in a small amount of time dt is given by

$$d\Pi(t) = r\Pi(t)dt + e^{-r(T-t)}\left[dF_E(t) + \beta_t dF_W(t)\right].$$

Assume the energy future and weather future followed by a model we have built in this paper, the future hedge ratio

$$\beta_t = -\frac{dF_E(t)}{dF_W(t)}.$$

In this case, the stochastic component of portfolio vanishes and the portfolio value is hedged. Thus, in order to hedge an energy future, we can short β_t shares of weather futures and the portfolio is hedged dynamically.

Future discussion about this idea will be centered on two viewpoints. Firstly, further research need to be done for the dynamics of energy future and weather future. As such, explicit dynamic hedging conclusion regarding to hedging risks of energy commodities could be founded. The other point of view is allowing other closely related derivatives to be involved into the constructing of portfolio. For instance, we could also take the newly burgeoning carbon dioxide derivatives into account in the portfolio. These considerations will be a comprehensive tool to integrate into hedging of energy commodities' risks.

REFERENCES

[1] L. Zeng, "Weather Derivatives and Weather Insurance: Concept, Application and Analysis," *Bulletin of the Ame-*

rican Meteorological Society, Vol. 81, No. 9, 2000, pp. 2075-2081.

[2] M. Cao and J. Wei, "Pricing the Weather," *Risk Magazine*, May 2000, pp. 67-70.

[3] F. Dornier and M. Queruel, "Caution to the Wind," *Energy and Power Risk Management*, 2000, pp. 30-32.

[4] M. H. A. Davis, "Pricing Weather Derivative by Marginal Value," *Quantitative Finance*, Vol. 1, No. 3, 2001, pp. 305-308.

[5] D. C. Brody, J. Syroka and M. Zervos, "Dynamical Pricing of Weather Derivatives," *Quantitative Finance*, Vol. 2, No. 3, 2002, pp. 189-198.

[6] F. E. Benth, "On Arbitrage-Free Pricing of Weather Derivatives Based on Fractional Brownian Motion," *Applied Mathematical Finance*, Vol. 10, No. 4, 2003, pp. 303-324.

[7] F. E. Benth and J. Šaltytė-Benth, "Sthochastic Modeling of Temperature Variations with a View towards Weather Derivatives," *Applied Mathematical Finance*, Vol. 12, No. 1, 2005, pp. 53-85.

[8] F. E. Benth and J. Šaltytė-Benth, "The Volatility of Temperature and Pricing of Weather Derivatives," *Quantitative Finance*, Vol. 7, No. 5, 2007, pp. 553-561.

[9] F. E. Benth, J. Šaltytė-Benth and S. Koekebakker, "Putting a Price on Temperature," *Scandinavian Journal of Statistics*, Vol. 34, No. 4, 2007, pp. 746-767.

[10] A. D. Zapranis and A. Alexandridis, "Modeling the Temperature Time-Dependent Spped of Mean Reversion in the Context of Weather Derivatives Pricing," *Applied Mathematical Finance*, Vol. 15, No. 4, 2008, pp. 355-386.

[11] A. Papapantoleon, "An Introduction to Lévy Processes with Applications in Finance," Lecture Notes, Berlin, 2008. http://page.math.tu-berlin.de/~papapan/papers/introduction.pdf

[12] P. Alaton, B. Djehiche and D. Stillberger, "On Modeling and Pricing Weather Derivatives," *Applied Mathematical Finance*, Vol. 9, No. 8, 2002, pp. 1-20.

[13] A. J. McNeil, R. Frey and P. Embrechts, "Quantitative Risk Management: Concepts, Techniques and Tools," Princeton University Press, Princeton, 2005.

[14] P. J. Brockwell and T. Marquardt, "Lévy-Driven and Fractionally Integrated ARMA Processes with Continuous Time Parameter," *Statistica Sinica*, Vol. 15, No. 2, 2005, pp. 477-494.

[15] F. E. Benth, J. Šaltytė-Benth and S. Koekebakker, "Stochastic Modeling of Electricity and Related Markets," World Scientific Press, The Singapore City, 2008.

[16] F. E. Benth and J. Šaltytė-Benth, "The Normal Inverse Gaussian Distribution and Spot Price Modeling in Energy Markets," *International Journal of Theoretical Applied Finance*, Vol. 7, No. 2, 2004, pp. 177-192.

[17] E. Hewitt and K. R. Stromberg, "Real and Abstract Analysis: A Modern Treatment of the Theory of Functions of a Real Variable," Springer-Verlag, Berlin, 1965.

[18] K. Chourdakis, "Option Pricing Using the Fractional FFT," *Journal of Computational Finance*, Vol. 8, No. 2, 2004, pp. 1-18.

8

Exploiting Market Integration for Pure Alpha Investments via Probabilistic Principal Factors Analysis

George Tzagkarakis[1], Juliana Caicedo-Llano[1,2], Thomas Dionysopoulos[3]
[1]Eonos Investment Technologies, Paris, France
[2]University of Evry-Val-d'Essone, Evry, France
[3]Axianta Research, Nicosia, Cyprus

ABSTRACT

In this paper, a long-short beta neutral portfolio strategy is proposed based on earnings yields forecasts, where positions are modified by accounting for time-varying risk budgeting by employing an appropriate integration measure. In contrast to previous works, which primarily rely on a standard principal component analysis (PCA), here we exploit the advantages of a probabilistic PCA (PPCA) framework to extract the factors to be used for designing an efficient integration measure, as well as relating these factors to an asset-pricing model. Our experimental evaluation with a dataset of 12 developed equity market indexes reveals certain improvements of our proposed approach, in terms of an increased representation capability of the underlying principal factors, along with an increased robustness to noisy and/or missing data in the original dataset.

Keywords: Market Integration; Risk budgeting; Probabilistic Principal Component Analysis

1. Introduction

Markets constitute a highly dynamically evolving universe, which undergoes through distinct time periods, and reacts in diverse conditions and phenomena, thus, monitoring the opportunities which appear for investors during these periods is of significant importance. An approach to take this behavior into account in asset management is to exploit the importance of the market factor to explain expected returns. More specifically, the part of the variance related to the global market component of risk can be considered as a proxy of market integration. In this context, integration implies that all barriers are eliminated and therefore risk premia associated with global factors are identical in any of such markets.

Construction of optimal portfolios by accounting not only for the diversification across assets, but also across time, attracted the interest of the research community during the last decades [1-4]. In a recent work [5], an alternative way of taking the time-varying risk aversion of the investor into account was proposed. More specifically, a simple and easily implemented two-stage process was introduced, where optimal weights are determined first by suitable optimization techniques and then the weights are adjusted according to a suitable integration measure.

By adopting the same assumptions as in [5], based on the capital asset-pricing model (CAPM) [6], a portfolio can be decomposed in two individual components, namely, the *beta* component and the *alpha* component. The beta component corresponds to the part exposed to market risk, while here we consider alpha as the portfolio's return generated by a risk exposure unrelated to the market risk, where the market portfolio is an international portfolio. A pure alpha strategy is employed, which is not related to the market risk.

The developed strategy is based on the intuition that if global factors determine strongly the excess returns, then less alpha opportunities are left for long-short investors. It is then straightforward to use market integration as a guide for risk-budgeting decisions. Indeed, one would expect that an investment manager would allocate more risk to those decisions that he is most confidence in, rather than to those he feels less certain about.

The standard *principal component analysis* (PCA) was employed in [5] as a method to construct a measure of integration based on the average percentage of variance explained by the first principal factor. However, the standard PCA approach may suffer from several drawbacks, such as, the sensitivity to outliers, the inaccuracy in case of noisy data, or when the original data are corrupted with missing values. In this study, we overcome these limitations by measuring integration in the framework of *probabilistic PCA* (PPCA) [7]. More specifically, the principal factors are extracted based on an associated probabilistic model for the observed data, as well as for the potential noise which may corrupt the data. Then, a simple correlation-based integration measure is employed, which is related to the market risk component, while being highly robust in case of noisy data and/or missing values in the original time-series. In addition, this process is carried out in overlapping time-windows to manage risk through time, in conjunction with an adaptation of our long-short weights at each date in a way such that when markets are strongly integrated, a more conservative position is taken, thus, protecting our strategy from the risk we would face during periods of high integration, when markets tend to exhibit a strong directional trend.

The rest of the paper is organized as follows: Section 2 introduces the main principles of PPCA and analyzes in detail the proposed methodology for portfolio optimization. In Section 3, an experimental evaluation of the proposed approach is performed on a set of 14 developed equity markets, while Section 4 concludes and gives directions for further extensions.

2. Market Integration via PPCA

Market integration is a fundamental concept in financial economics [8,9]. Especially for investors, integration would provide a broader range of available assets and lower risk premia, but at the cost of fewer diversification opportunities. Markets are *internationally integrated* if the reward for risk is identical regardless the market one trades in. Previous works [10,11] exploited an increase in the common component of equity returns data as an indication of higher integration, although such approaches do not measure market integration in the strict sense.

Motivated by [12], where several distinct measures of market co-movements were analyzed, a simple, though still efficient, integration measure is designed by extracting the main factors explaining the cross-sectional equity returns in terms of the average percentage of variance explained by the first significant principal components. However, the performance of the standard PCA may deteriorate in several cases, such as, the presence of a noisy behavior in the original data, and/or the case where a portion of the original data values may be missing or we don't have access to. The recently introduced framework of PPCA [7] is capable of overcoming such limitations, and it is exploited in our proposed market integration measure to build portfolios for pure alpha investors.

2.1. Linear Multiple Factor Structure

In the subsequent analysis, we consider an ensemble of M time-series $\boldsymbol{r}_m, m=1,\cdots,M,$ each one with N observations representing equity returns. This ensemble is assumed to follow a linear multiple factor structure, as follows:

$$\boldsymbol{r}_{m,t} = E_m + \sum_{l=1}^{L} b_{ml} \boldsymbol{f}_{l,t} + \epsilon_{m,t}, t=1,\cdots,N, \quad (1)$$

where L is the number of common factors, which capture the systematic component of risk, E_m denotes the expected return on the m-th asset, $\boldsymbol{f}_{l,t}$ is the realization at time t of the l-th common factor, b_{ml} is the sensitivity of the m-th asset to the movements of the l-th factor, and $\epsilon_{m,t}$ denotes the noise term. The assumption for a linear multiple factor structure yields that the factors can be estimated by employing a principal component analysis, in our case working in a probabilistic framework.

2.2. Probabilistic PCA

In this section, the main principles of PPCA are introduced in brief. A remarkable feature of the typical PCA is the absence of an associated probabilistic model for the observed data. A probabilistic formulation of PCA is obtained from a Gaussian latent-variable model, with the principal axes emerging as maximum-likelihood (ML) estimates. Moreover, the latent-variable formulation results naturally in an iterative, and computationally efficient, expectation-maximization (EM) algorithm for performing PPCA.

A further motivation is that PPCA is characterized by some additional practical advantages: a) the probabilistic model offers the potential to extend the scope of standard PCA. For instance, multiple PPCA models may be combined as a *probabilistic mixture*, increasing the explanatory power of the principal factors, while also PPCA projections can be obtained in case of *missing observations*, and b) along with its use as a dimensionality reduction technique, PPCA can be employed as a general Gaussian density model. The benefit of doing this is that ML estimates for the parameters associated with the covariance matrix can be computed efficiently from the data principal components. Potential applications include detection and classification of abnormal changes, which may be further employed as an alerting mechanism for an investment manager. This later observation is left as a separate thorough study.

Let $\boldsymbol{X}^{\mathrm{T}} = \left[\boldsymbol{r}_1,\cdots,\boldsymbol{r}_M\right]$ be the $N \times M$ data matrix whose columns are the observed time-series. A latent-variable model aims to relate an M-dimensional observation vector (rows of $\boldsymbol{X}^{\mathrm{T}}$) to a corresponding K-dimensional vector of latent (or unobserved) variables (rows of $\boldsymbol{Y}^{\mathrm{T}}$) as follows:

$$\boldsymbol{X}^{\mathrm{T}} = \boldsymbol{Y}^{\mathrm{T}}\boldsymbol{W}^{\mathrm{T}} + \mathbf{1}_{N\times1}\boldsymbol{\mu}^{\mathrm{T}} + \mathbf{1}_{N\times1}\boldsymbol{\eta}^{\mathrm{T}}, \quad (2)$$

where $\boldsymbol{Y}^{\mathrm{T}}$ is the $N \times K(K \le M)$ matrix of latent variables, $\boldsymbol{W}$ denotes a $M \times K$ linear mapping between the original space and the space of latent variables, $\mathbf{1}_{N\times1}$ is a vector of all ones, $\boldsymbol{\mu}^{\mathrm{T}}$ is an M-dimensional parameter vector, which permits the model to have non-zero mean, and $\boldsymbol{\eta}^{\mathrm{T}}$ is an M-dimensional vector, which stands for the measurement error or the noise corrupting the observations.

In the following, let $\boldsymbol{x}^{\mathrm{T}}, \boldsymbol{y}^{\mathrm{T}}$ denote an arbitrary row of the matrices $\boldsymbol{X}^{\mathrm{T}}$ and $\boldsymbol{Y}^{\mathrm{T}}$, respectively. Working in a probabilistic framework, we make the following assumptions for the parameters contained in Equation (2):

- The latent variables are independent and identically distributed (i.i.d.) Gaussians with unit variance, that is, $\boldsymbol{y}^{\mathrm{T}} \sim \mathcal{N}(0, \boldsymbol{I})$, where $\boldsymbol{I}$ is the identity matrix.
- The error (or noise) model is isotropic Gaussian, that is, $\boldsymbol{\eta}^{\mathrm{T}} \sim \mathcal{N}(0, \sigma^2 \boldsymbol{I})$.
- By combining the above two assumptions with Equation (2), a Gaussian distribution is also induced for the observations, namely, $\boldsymbol{x}^{\mathrm{T}} \sim \mathcal{N}(\boldsymbol{\mu}^{\mathrm{T}}, \boldsymbol{C})$, where the observation covariance model is given by $\boldsymbol{C} = \boldsymbol{W}\boldsymbol{W}^{\mathrm{T}} + \sigma^2 \boldsymbol{I}$.

From the above we deduce that the model parameters can be determined by ML via an iterative procedure. We also emphasize that the subspace defined by the ML estimates of the columns of $\boldsymbol{W}$ will not correspond, in general, to the principal subspace of the observed data.

The isotropic Gaussian noise model, in conjunction with Equation (2), yields that the conditional probability distribution of $\boldsymbol{x}^{\mathrm{T}}$ given $\boldsymbol{y}^{\mathrm{T}}$ is as follows:

$$\boldsymbol{x}^{\mathrm{T}} \left| \boldsymbol{y}^{\mathrm{T}} \sim \mathcal{N}\left(\boldsymbol{y}^{\mathrm{T}}\boldsymbol{W}^{\mathrm{T}} + \boldsymbol{\mu}^{\mathrm{T}}, \sigma^2 \boldsymbol{I}\right)\right.. \quad (3)$$

Then, the associated log-likelihood function is given by

$$\mathcal{L} = -\frac{N}{2}\left(M \ln(2\pi) + \ln(|\boldsymbol{C}|) + \operatorname{tr}\left(\boldsymbol{C}^{-1}\boldsymbol{\Sigma}_X\right)\right), \quad (4)$$

where $|\boldsymbol{A}|$ and $\operatorname{tr}(|\boldsymbol{A}|)$ denote the determinant and the trace, respectively, of a matrix $\boldsymbol{A}$, and the sample covariance matrix is given by

$$\boldsymbol{\Sigma}_X = \frac{1}{N-1}\sum_{n=1}^{N}\left(\boldsymbol{x}_n^{\mathrm{T}} - \boldsymbol{\mu}^{\mathrm{T}}\right)^{\mathrm{T}}\left(\boldsymbol{x}_n^{\mathrm{T}} - \boldsymbol{\mu}^{\mathrm{T}}\right), \quad (5)$$

with $\boldsymbol{x}_n^{\mathrm{T}}$ denoting the n-th observation (row of $\boldsymbol{X}^{\mathrm{T}}$). Notice also that the ML estimate for $\boldsymbol{\mu}^{\mathrm{T}}$ is given by the sample mean of the data. Finally, the estimates for the probabilistic principal components, that is, the columns of $\boldsymbol{W}$ and the noise variance σ^2, are obtained by iterative maximization of Equation (4):

$$\sigma_{ML}^2 = \frac{1}{M-K}\sum_{j=K+1}^{M}\lambda_j, \quad (6)$$

$$\boldsymbol{W}_{ML} = \boldsymbol{E}_K\left(\boldsymbol{\Lambda}_K - \sigma_{ML}^2 \boldsymbol{I}\right)^{1/2}\boldsymbol{R}, \quad (7)$$

where the K columns of the $M \times K$ matrix $\boldsymbol{E}_K$ are the principal eigenvectors of $\boldsymbol{\Sigma}_X$, with corresponding eigenvalues $\lambda_j, j = 1, \cdots, K$, constituting the $K \times K$ diagonal matrix $\boldsymbol{\Lambda}_K$, and $\boldsymbol{R}$ is an arbitrary $K \times K$ orthogonal rotation matrix. In practice, $\boldsymbol{R}$ is ignored by simply setting $\boldsymbol{R} = \boldsymbol{I}$. Finally, the $N \times K$ matrix $\boldsymbol{P}$ whose columns are the probabilistic principal factors is simply obtained by projecting the data matrix on the probabilistic principal components, that is,

$$\boldsymbol{P} = \boldsymbol{X}^{\mathrm{T}}\boldsymbol{W}_{ML}. \quad (8)$$

2.3. Integration Measure via 2nd-Order Statistics

One of the main aspects of the proposed approach is the *time-varying* management of the risk, through an integration measure based on second-order statistics, which is applied on overlapping time-windows. More specifically, let h denote the window length and s the step size. Then, the integration measure we use at time t, G_t, is defined as

$$G_t = \frac{1}{M}\sum_{m=1}^{M}\hat{\rho}^2\left(\boldsymbol{r}_{m,[t-h,t]}, \boldsymbol{P}_{1,[t-h,t]}\right), \quad (9)$$

where $\hat{\rho}^2(\cdot,\cdot)$ is the squared correlation between two variables, $\boldsymbol{P}_{1,[t-h,t]}$ denotes the first principal factor extracted by applying PPCA in the time window $[t - h, t]$, and $\boldsymbol{r}_{m,[t-h,t]}$ is the vector of returns of the m-th asset during the time interval $[t - h, t]$. The integration measure is computed by rolling the time window every s time steps, where the time-scale depends on our specific needs (e.g., daily, weekly, monthly).We interpret the periods when the returns are highly correlated to the first probabilistic principal component to be periods of high integration. We emphasize again that measuring and monitoring integration is crucial in the pure alpha framework, since a high integration period nominates decisions for decreased risk to be taken. Moreover, since our data have only equity indexes we can use this measure toassess integration assuming that most of the times equity markets are positively correlated.

2.4. Optimal Portfolio Strategies

2.4.1. Optimal Long-Short Portfolios

The construction of an optimal portfolio entails a mean-variance optimization over an ensemble of assets expected returns and a covariance matrix. For this purpose, accurate prediction of returns and covariances are required, with the former one, that is, the forecast of returns, being the most challenging part.

Concerning the estimationof the sample covariance matrix, an initial estimate is computed for each time window $[t - h, t]$, which is then corrected using shrinkage (Stein's estimator) [13,14] to improve the out-of-sample performance and reduce the estimation risk.

Market neutral portfolios are portfolios uncorrelated with the market, delivering positive returns. This is only possible through the use of short sales, the optimization program will return the long and short positions, with the additional property of being *beta neutral*. Among the advantages of market neutral investing, is its ability to enhance the performance of any index portfolio by combining an alpha strategy with an equity index. Our goal is to build a zero-beta portfolio by determining optimal long and short positions, under the constraint that portfolio's beta should be equal to zero.

According to modern portfolio theory, an investor is interested in maximizing his utility $\mathrm{U}(\boldsymbol{w})$, associated with a portfolio p, with $\boldsymbol{w}$ being an M-dimensional vector of weights (one weight per asset). The vector of optimal weights is obtained by solving the following optimization problem:

$$\boldsymbol{w}^* = \arg\max_{w} \mathrm{U}(\boldsymbol{w}) \tag{10}$$

$$= \arg\max_{w}\left(E\{r_p\} - \zeta Var\{r_p\}\right), \tag{11}$$

where $E\{r_p\} = \boldsymbol{w}^{\mathrm{T}} z$ is the expected return of our portfolio, with z being the vector of expected excess returns of the assets, $Var\{r_p\} = \boldsymbol{w}^{\mathrm{T}}\hat{\boldsymbol{\Sigma}}\boldsymbol{w}$ is the portfolio's variance, with $\hat{\boldsymbol{\Sigma}}$ being the estimated covariance matrix of the returns, and σ_0^2 is the desired portfolio's variance. In Equation (11), ζ is a regularization parameter representing the investor's level of risk aversion. In order to eliminate the exposure to the market or main factor, a beta constraint should be introduced:

$$\boldsymbol{\beta}_p = \boldsymbol{w}^{\mathrm{T}}\boldsymbol{\beta} = \boldsymbol{0}$$

where $\boldsymbol{\beta}$ is the M-dimensional vector of assets' beta values calculated with an *equally weighted index* (EWI) as the market, and $\boldsymbol{\beta}_p$ the portfolio's beta. The constraint of zero portfolio's beta yields an optimal portfolio which is not exposed to market risk. Motivated by [15], where it was shown that the principal orthogonal linear factor dominating the equity returns is highly correlated to an EWI, we justify the consistency of employing probabilistic principal factors to quantify co-movements among the distinct assets.

In addition, the EWI assumption results in the following simple expression for the vector of assets' betas:

$$\boldsymbol{\beta} = \frac{\boldsymbol{\Sigma}\boldsymbol{1}_{M\times 1}}{\boldsymbol{1}_{M\times 1}^{\mathrm{T}}\boldsymbol{\Sigma}\boldsymbol{1}_{M\times 1}}, \tag{12}$$

where $\boldsymbol{1}_{M\times 1}$ is the M-dimensional vector of all ones.

We modify the approach introduced by [5] where earning yields are used to estimate the expected returns and a beta neutral portfolio is constructed, we suggest building a portfolio strategy based on a *minimum variance portfolio*, which does not require an estimate of expected returns. We have analyzed the properties of the beta-neutral portfolio, which is a portfolio uncorrelated with the main factor explaining the returns of the set of assets in the system. We argue that this portfolio should be similar to a minimum variance portfolio. In fact, a beta neutral portfolio should neutralize the exposure to the principal factor or market factor, while a minimum variance portfolio will be the result of a mix of assets mainly related to the smallest risk factors. We can therefor build a minimum variance portfolio, which has been studied by other authors who argue that it is a more stable strategy than the full mean-variance optimization, in part because it does not rely on an estimate of expected returns.

In the case of a minimum variance portfolio, the objective function is modified such that only the risk part is optimized. The optimization problem in this case is then:

$$\boldsymbol{w}^* = \arg\min_{w}\left(Var\{r_p\}\right). \tag{13}$$

As we mentioned above, we expected that the selected assets in the optimal minimal variance portfolios correspond to those highly related to the smallest factors and, in the same way, the market neutral portfolios will be composed of assets not highly related to the main factor, therefore related to factors of lower risk. The construction of portfolios with minimum variance is therefore an indirect way to build an alpha strategy.

2.4.2. Adjustment of Optimal Weights

Having calculated the optimal weights (long and short positions) by solving the optimization problem expressed by Equations (11) and (13), the second stage aims in adapting these weights so as to keep a constant risk through the strategy or to achieve a time-varying risk allocation. Two adjustmentsare considered: 1) reduction of the exposure to the market and enforcement to constant volatility of our portfolio for the initial strategy, and 2) adaptation of the corresponding weights by employing the values of the computed integration measure G_t for the scaled strategies.

As mentioned before, one the main purposes for monitoring the degree of integration through time is to warn investors for periods of high integration, where fewer opportunities are left to generate alpha, and thus, they should take more conservative decisions.

The approach introduced in [5] was the first attempt to account for time variations of a risk budgeting rule, which is of significant importance. This, in conjunction with the robustness of the extracted probabilistic principal factors against potentially distinct noise levels across time or among different assets, as well as the inherent property to account for corrupted values in the original data, make our proposed portfolio construction method even more powerful when compared with the method introduced in [5].

More specifically, the integration measure G_t, given by Equation (9), is employed to decide for the units of risk, which could be taken at each period of time.The rule we propose for the adaptation of the weights $\boldsymbol{w}$ is as follows: for small integration values, the portfolio is allowed to have the maximum risk exposure, which is equivalent to using the optimal weights obtained from the solution of the optimization problem defined by Equation (11). On the other hand, for high integration values, the risk is reduced by reducing the weights of every position proportionally to its integration value.

The vector of optimal weights $\boldsymbol{w}^*$ is scaled by an appropriate scaling factor resulting in the following scaled weights

$$\boldsymbol{w}_S^* = \left(1 - \frac{\bar{G}_t - G_{\min}}{G_{\max}}\right)\boldsymbol{w}^*, \tag{14}$$

where $\bar{G}_t$ is the integration value at time t after removing the mean computed over all the overlapping windows, so as to use the same thresholds for the whole time period of study. The lower and upper bounds of the integration, $G_{\min}$ and $G_{\max}$, respectively, are thresholds which specify when the integration is low, and therefore higher possibilities to generate alpha exist, and when the integration reaches an upper limit, above which there are very few chances to generate alpha. Equation (14) implies that the optimal weights $\boldsymbol{w}^*$ are modified linearly for integration values ranging in the interval $[G_{\min}, G_{\max}]$, while for integration values larger than $G_{\max}$ the weights are set equal to zero and for integration values smaller than $G_{\min}$ the optimal weights are left unchanged. In practice, the values of the two thresholds $G_{\min}$ and $G_{\max}$ can be set based on the quantiles of the distribution of the historical integration measure.

3. Experimental Evaluation

The proposed PPCA-based approach to analyze a dataset is used to measure integration and build alpha generating portfolio strategies for a set of financial data. We analyzed a group of 12 developed equity markets (Australia, Canada, France, Germany, Hong Kong, Japan, Singapore, Spain, Sweden, Switzerland, United Kingdom, and USA), for which liquid index futures contracts are available in order to enable short positions in the portfolio strategies.

Closing prices at a daily frequency for the main futures indexes of each country have been collected, expressed in local currency, covering the period between January 2001 and January 2013. The use of data in local currencies can be advantageous in terms of diversification of international portfolios, however any undesired exposure to a specific currency can be hedge using several methods which do not need to be considered in this study.

During the selected time period, all markets had undergone through the two main markets crisis of recent years: the IT-bubble and the subprimes and debt crisis. Both crises are followed by a recovery period, thus, offering a good opportunity to study integration and long-term portfolio strategies. We note also that, in order to emphasize the short-run movements of the data, the relative change between consecutive time instants is used. This can be measured by computing the first difference of the natural logarithm (dlog) of the time-series samples. Thus, a preprocessing step is applied on the original ensemble of the M time-series as follows:

$$\tilde{\boldsymbol{r}}_{m,t} = \ln\left(\boldsymbol{r}_{m,t}\right) - \ln\left(\boldsymbol{r}_{m,t-1}\right), m = 1, \cdots, M. \tag{15}$$

Besides, to overcome the limitation of significantly different variances or expression in different units (as it is the case in our dataset with the different currencies) between the several time-series, a further normalization to zero mean and unit variance of the dlog time-series is performed. The performance of the proposed method is evaluated for a window length $h = 250$ and step-size $s = 25$.

3.1. Performance Measures

To analyze the risk-adjusted performance of the different portfolio strategies we use three different indicators [16]: 1) the Sharpe ratio (SR), 2) the Sortino ratio (SoR) and 3) the maximum drawdown (MDD). For all these three measures we define r_P as the portfolio's return and r_F as the return of a risk free asset.

The Sharpe ratio is defined as the ratio of the average excess return of an asset over the risk-free rate and the volatility of this excess return:

$$\text{SR} = \frac{E\{r_P - r_F\}}{\sigma(r_P)}. \tag{16}$$

This ratio is the most common risk-adjusted performance measure used in financial studies. Its main drawback is that it is only useful for symmetrical distributions of returns.

The Sortino ratio is a variation of the Sharpe ratio, where the return is adjusted by the downside volatility, the volatility calculated only with negative returns. The Sortino ratio is defined as

$$\text{SoR} = \frac{E\{r_P - r_F\}}{\sigma(r_P^+)}. \tag{17}$$

Since it takes into account the skewness of the distribution of returns, it would therefore be a better risk-adjusted performance indicator for payoffs with higher downside risk.

The maximum drawdown, which is defined as the maximum cumulated continuous loss over a given period, measures the degree of extreme losses. We also present the ratio of the maximum drawdown divided by the volatility, which indicates the degree of extreme loss in terms of the standard deviation of the returns. In particular, a lower maximum drawdown could be associated with lower overall risk. Moreover, this ratio standardizes the

MDD measure in order to make it possible to compare payoffs with different volatilities.

3.2. Extraction of Probabilistic Principal Factors

In this section, the characteristics of the probabilistic principal factors extracted with PPCA are exhibited for the complete dataset. **Figure 1** shows the correlation coefficients for the 12 market indexes from the initial data set. As it can be seen, all markets are positively correlated, with the highest correlation appearing between the CF1 and GX1 indexes compared to Z1 and ES1 indexes.

For a visual inspection of the difference between the principal components extracted with PCA and PPCA, **Figure 2** shows the loadings of the original data $\tilde{X}^{\mathrm{T}}$ in the space of the first two principal components, for the whole time period. We observe that the effect of the probabilistic approach for the specific dataset results in a scaling and rotation of the principal axes, when compared with the typical PCA. Concerning the discriminative capability of both PCA and PPCA, at least for the first two principal components, the same behavior is observed, that is, the second principal components can be used to split the original variables (indexes) into the same two subsets.

However, one of the major advantages of PPCA, in contrast to PCA, is its ability to estimate simultaneously the underlying noise variance σ^2. This feature can be very important for further processing, such as, for designing adaptive and more accurate predictors of the local or global trends, by taking into account the spurious variations caused by the underlying noise. In **Figure 3**, the time-varying estimated noise variance is shown for (h, s) = (250, 25). As it can be seen, large variations of the estimated noise variance appear across time, thus, revealing the significance of its accurate estimation for further actions, such as, trend estimation and forecasting. Moreover, interestingly, the noise variance acquires its local

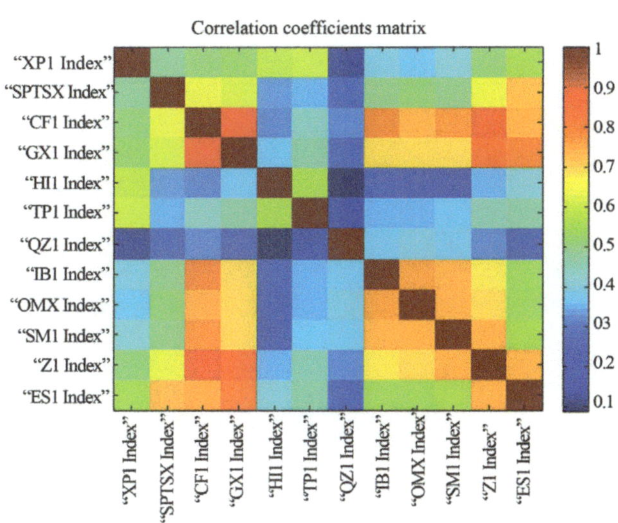

Figure 1. Correlation coefficient matrix of the 12 indexes.

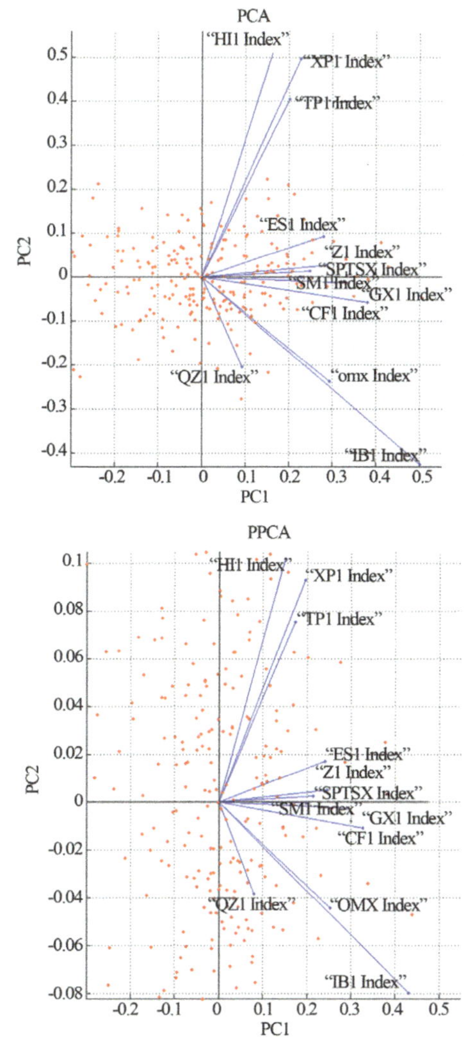

Figure 2. PCs for each variable (index) and PC score for each observation.

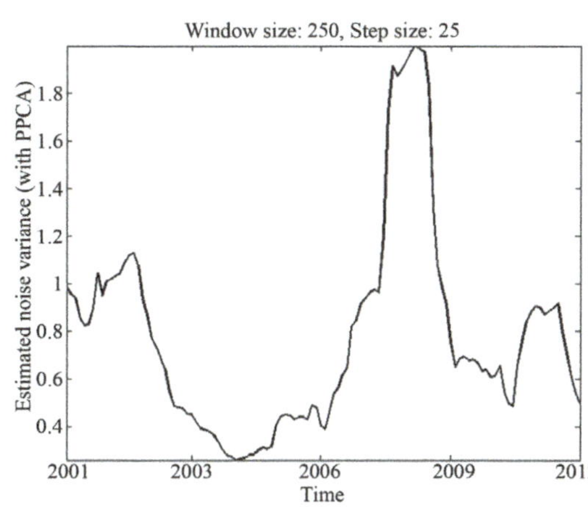

Figure 3. Estimated noise variance for (*h*, *s*) = (250, 25).

maximum values in periods close to the periods of crises.

Concerning the evolution of the integration measure G_t, **Figure 4** shows the values of G_t for the PCA and PPCA, for $(h, s) = (250, 25)$. As it can be seen, the dominant principal component extracted by both PCA and PPCA results in the same mean squared correlations with the 12 market indexes. This was expected, since from **Figure 2**, PPCA results in scaled and slightly rotated principal components.

Although the integration measure defined by Equation (9) results in similar values for both PCA and PPCA, we emphasize once again the superiority of our PPCA-based approach, which is also capable of monitoring the time-varying behavior of the underlying noise component, as well as its robustness against corrupted data, as it will be shown experimentally in a subsequent section.

3.3. Long-Short Strategies Payoffs

In this section, the efficiency of the proposed optimal portfolio construction method is evaluated. More specifically, the portfolio positions are calculated as the minimum variance optimal weights. Besides, the risk is controlled after each optimization by adjustment of the weights to a target volatility of 10%. As our optimized portfolio has long and short positions, it is possible to decrease (increase) the overall portfolio risk by reducing (enlarging) each position by a given proportion.

In the optimization process, the matrix $\hat{\Sigma}$ is used, which is obtained from a historical covariance matrix adjusted with a shrinkage method. We build a minimum variance portfolio at each estimation date with the shrunk covariance matrix estimated from the matrix of excess returns for each window. The proposed strategy has a Sharpe ratio of 0.20%, a Sortino ratio of 0.35%, and a maximum drawdown of 44.3%. The results are summarized in **Table 1**.

Integration is calculated for rolling windows of one year length ($h = 250$) every 25 observations. As we mentioned before, we have observed that high integration allows very few opportunities to generate alpha. This is illustrated in **Figure 5**, which shows the time-relation between our proxy of market integration and the minimum variance strategy.

We observe that the strategy suffers during periods of high integration of the equity markets. In addition, integration spikes during periods of crisis, which make this information useful to adjust the total risk taken at each date.

We construct a scaling factor for our long-short weights-based on the level of integration in order to structure a downside protection that alerts during periods of high integration, when the market is highly drifted and there are few possibilities of alpha generation. The idea is to transform the integration measure, which is a variable defined in the range [0,1], where 1 indicates perfect integration and 0 indicates no integration, into a variable defined in the same range but where 1 indicates that the optimal weights from the optimization should be considered and 0 indicates that no risk should be taken.

Three simple scaling methods are employed to transform the integration level: 1) $\left(1-\bar{G}_t\right)$, 2) using Equation (14), for levels of G_t between $G_{\min}$ and $G_{\max}$ and outside their

Table 1. Risk adjusted performance measures.

		Scaled by integration strategies		
	MV	$(1 - G_t)$	$(1 - (G_t - G_{min})/G_{max})$	$\left(1-G_t^{det}\right)$
Return	2.02	1.20	2.53	2.25
Volatility	10.22	4.74	5.90	4.07
SR	0.20	0.25	0.43	0.55
SoR	0.35	0.39	0.44	0.21
MDD	−44.33	−18.36	−22.75	−14.96
MDD/S	−4.34	−3.87	−3.85	−3.68

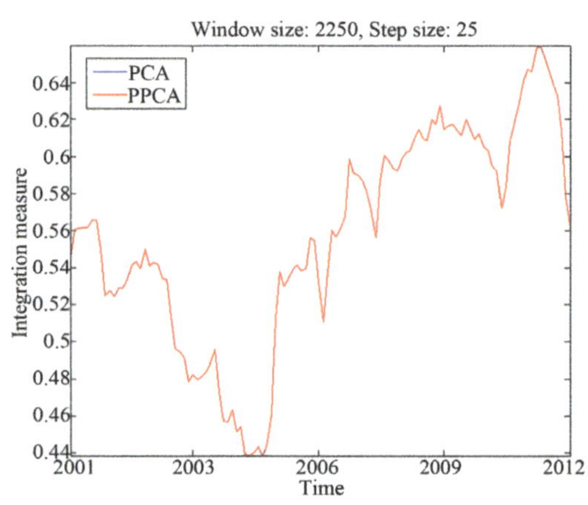

Figure 4. Integration measure G_t for PCA and PPCA, with $(h, s) = (250, 25)$.

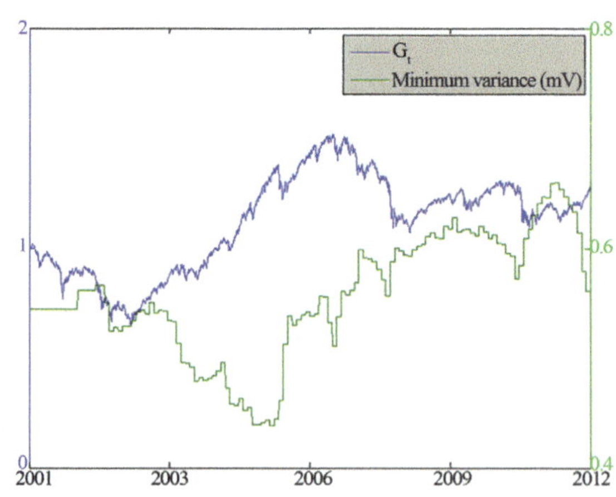

Figure 5. Minimum variance strategy and integration.

range we set the levels equal to 0 for $G_t > G_{\max}$ and equal to 1 for $G_t < G_{\min}$, and 3) $\left(1-G_t^{det}\right)$,where G_t^{det} is the *linearly de-trended* series of G_t. The optimal weights are scaled according to these three methods and the performance of each strategy is computed. For the second scaling method, we set the parameters $G_{\min}$ to be the 20th percentile of G_t observed up to the estimation point and $G_{\max}$ to be equal to the 80th percentile that we consider a high level of integration.

The average value of G_t for the whole period of study is 0.56. The minimum $G_{\min}$ for the whole series of observations is 0.43 and $G_{\max}$ is 0.66. We compare the basic minimum variance strategy with the different proposed strategies with the risk adjusted by integration. Sharpe ratios improve from 0.2 to 0.41 on average for the scaled strategies. The Sortino ratio is equal to 0.35 for the basic strategy and does not change on average for the risk budgeting strategies. However, it is different for each of the three scaling methods. The ratio of maximum drawdown over volatility varies from 4.34 to 3.80, resulting in a 0.54 improvement of standard deviation.

The best of the three scaling methods is shown to be the third one, which improves the Sharpe ratio of the standard minimum variance strategy from 0.20 to 0.55 and the ratio of maximum drawdown over volatility from 4.34 to 3.68, while the size of the extreme loss of the strategy is reduced by 0.66 standard deviations. All the above results are summarized in **Table 1**.

It is also important to note that all the scaled strategies have improved the risk-adjusted performance indicators. As a general conclusion we see that the use of a time-varying risk budgeting, based on an integration measure expressed in terms of the dominant probabilistic principal factor, improves the payoff of the basic minimum variance strategy with the protection against loses during certain critical periods.

Figure 6 presents the basic minimum variance portfolio strategy compared to the improved by integration scaling strategies. We observe that the risk-budgeting strategies are characterized by reduced levels of risk during the periods of high integration, which was exactly our desired goal.

3.4. Performance of PPCA with Missing Data

In this section, we study the robustness and efficiency of PPCA to extract the dominant principal factors, and subsequently to calculate the integration measure G_t in case of missing data. This is often the case when we don't have full access to some closing values of the market indexes, or when those values may be hidden on purpose. We emphasize that, in contrast to previous approaches, it is not required to fill in the missing data, but PPCA proceeds by fitting the remaining data with a probabilistic model. This capability is not available with the standard PCA, which would need the reconstruction of the missing observations in some way, prior to the construction of the optimal portfolio. We also note that the advantage of PPCA to extract accurately the principal factors to be used for the calculation of the associated integration measure in case of missing data cannot be incorporated in the current portfolio optimization strategy. The reason is that, apart from the integration measure, the proposed risk-budgeting strategies also employ the full data prior to the current date, which requires filling in the missing data. However, the design of appropriate strategies without necessitating the recovery of missing values is left as a separate study.

In order to evaluate the efficiency of PPCA to extract principal factors and estimate accurately the underlying noise variance in case of missing data, a varying percentage $\theta \in \{10\%,\cdots,50\%\}$ of missing elements from the original log-returns matrix $\boldsymbol{X}^{\mathrm{T}} = \left[\tilde{\boldsymbol{r}}_1,\cdots,\tilde{\boldsymbol{r}}_M\right]$ is ignored uniformly at random.

Figure 7 shows first that the PPCA-based approach is robust in estimating accurately the variance of the underlying noise component, even in the extreme scenario of 50% of missing values. Finally, and most importantly, **Figure 8** verifies the efficiency of the proposed simple integration measure between the given market indexes and the dominant probabilistic principal factor, even for an extreme situation of missing observations at the order of 40% of the original data.

4. Conclusions and Future Work

In this paper, we introduced a portfolio optimization method for pure alpha investments, by exploiting a market integration measure based on second-order statistics between the original data and the dominant probabilistic principal factor. The proposed time-varying risk-budgeting strategies were characterized by reduced levels of risk during the periods of high integration, thus, verifying the efficiency of our method to be used as an alerting

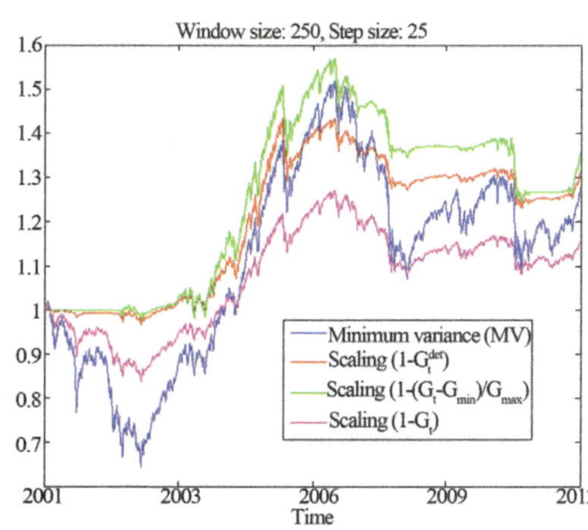

Figure 6. Minimum variance strategy compared to scaled strategies with the integration measure G_t based on PPCA.

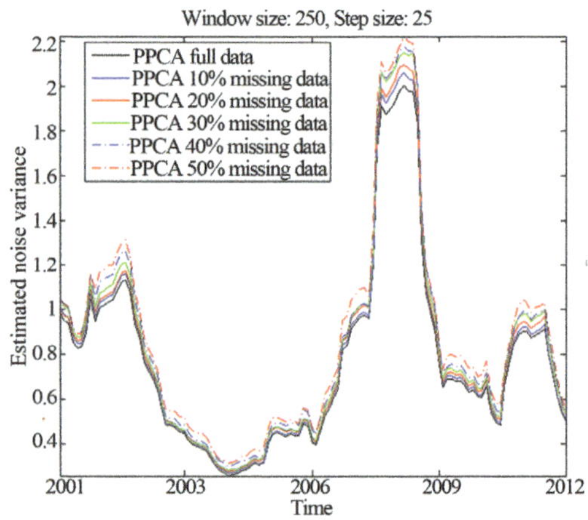

Figure 7. Estimated noise variance for (*h*, *s*) = (250, 25), and for a varying percentage of missing observations $\theta \in \{10\%, \cdots, 50\%\}$.

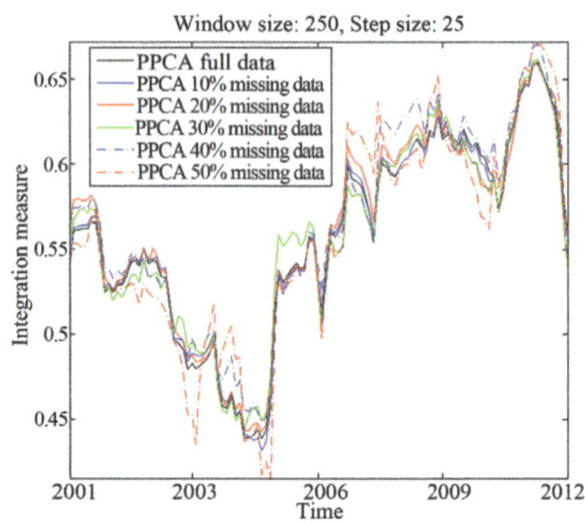

Figure 8. Integration measure G_t for PPCA, with (*h*, *s*) = (250, 25), and for a varying percentage of missing observations $\theta \in \{10\%, \cdots, 50\%\}$.

mechanism for pure alpha investors.

As a future work, the time-varying estimated noise variance, which is a byproduct of the method presented in this study, will be further exploited to design efficient algorithms for estimating and predicting local and global trends, by taking into account the spurious variations caused by the underlying noise component. Moreover, due to the market-neutral property, which is inherent in our method, the proposed alpha strategy will be combined with an index portfolio (or any other portfolio strategy) to achieve an overall increase of the portfolio optimization performance.

REFERENCES

[1] R. Merton, "Lifetime Portfolio Selection under Uncertainty: The Continuous Time Case," *Review of Economics and Statistics*, Vol. 51, No. 3, 1969, pp. 247-257.

[2] J. Campbell and L. Viceira, "Consumption and Portfolio Decisions when Expected Returns Are Time Varying," *Quarterly Journal of Economics*, Vol. 114, No. 2, 1999, pp. 433-495.

[3] R. Bansal, M. Dahlquist and C. Harvey, "Dynamic Trading Strategies and Portfolio Choice," *NBER Working Paper*, 2004.

[4] M. Brandt and P. Santa-Clara, "Dynamic Portfolio Selection by Augmenting the Asset Space," *Journal of Finance*, Vol. 61, No. 5, 2006, pp. 2187-2217.

[5] J. Caicedo-Llano and T. Dionysopoulos, "Market Integration: A Risk-Budgeting Guide for Pure Alpha Investors," *Journal of Multinational Financial Management*, Vol. 18, No. 4, 2008, pp. 313-327.

[6] W. Sharpe, "Capital Asset Prices: A Theory of Market Equilibrium under Conditions of Risk," *Journal of Finance*, Vol. 19, No. 3, 1964, pp. 425-442.

[7] M. Tipping and C. Bishop, "Probabilistic Principal Component Analysis," *Journal of the Royal Statistical Society, Series B*, Vol. 61, Pt. 3, 2002, pp. 611-622.

[8] M. Gordon, "The Investment, Financing, and Valuation of the Corporation," *American Economic Review*, Vol. 52 No. 5, 1962.

[9] J. Campbell and Y. Hamao, "Predictable Stock Returns in the United States and Japan: A Study of Long-Term Capital Market Integration," *Journal of Finance*, Vol. 47, No. 1, 1992, pp. 43-69.

[10] G. Bekaert and C. Harvey, "Time Varying World Market Integration," *Journal of Finance*, Vol. 50, No. 2, 1995, pp. 403-444.

[11] M. Fratzscher, "Financial Market Integration in Europe: On the Effects of EMU on Stock Markets," ECB, Vol. 48, 2001.

[12] J. Caicedo-Llano and C. Bruneau, "Co-movements of International Equity Markets: A Large-Scale Factor Model Approach," *Economics Bulletin*, Vol. 29, No. 2, 2009, pp. 1466-1482.

[13] P. Jorion, "International Portfolio Diversification with Estimation Risk," *Journal of Business*, Vol. 58, No. 3, 1985, pp. 259-278.

[14] M. Daniels and R. Kass, "Shrinkage Estimators for Covariance Matrices," *Biometrics*, Vol. 57, No. 4, 2001, pp. 1173-1182.

[15] S. Heston, K. Rouwenhorst and R. Wessels, "The Structure of International Stock Returns and the Integration of Capital Markets," *Journal of Empirical Finance*, Vol. 2, No. 3, 1995, pp. 173-197.

[16] J. Campbell and R. Shiller, "Valuation Ratios and the Long-Run Stock Market Outlook: An Update," *Cowles Foundation Discussion Papers*, 2001.

9

A Simple Method to Price Window Reset Options

Yi-Long Hsiao
Department of Finance, National Dong Hwa University, Hualien, Chinese Taipei

ABSTRACT

A window reset option is a kind of reset options with continuous reset constraints. The issue is very important for applying to employee stock options in finance or reservation options on truck-only toll lanes in traffic management. Our contribution of this study is that we proposed an accurate and simple method to price window reset options. The option price is formulated as the solution of a boundary value problem of the Black-Scholes PDE. The problem is then transformed into an initial-boundary value problem of the heat equation. Then Green's function is applied to solve the heat equation problem. Finally, the option price is calculated numerically. A numerical example and some discussions are presented in this paper.

Keywords: Window Reset Option; Black-Scholes PDE; Boundary Integral Method; Green's Function

1. Introduction

A reset option is a path-dependent derivative whose payoff depends on the historical prices of underlying assets. The strike price can be adjusted according to pre-specified conditions during the specified discrete monitoring dates or a continuous period. The main function of the reset clause is to protect investors from downside risk that affects the underlying prices during bear or uncertain financial markets.

A window reset option is a reset option with a continuous reset period which is called the reset window. The strike price of a window reset option is reset to a prespecified level provided the underlying asset price being below the reset threshold during the pre-specified window period. This study presents a simple and effective method for pricing window reset options under Black-Scholes economy assumptions.

Derivatives with reset clauses are extremely popular. For example, the Chicago Board Options Exchange (CBOE) and the New York Stock Exchange (NYSE) traded the S&P 500 index put warrants with a three-month reset period in 1996. In June 1997, Morgan Stanley issued a warrant containing a reset clause on the Hong Kong stock market [1]. Furthermore, Grand Cathay Securities issued six American-style reset warrants listed on the Taiwan Stock Exchange from 1998 to 1999, all of which were multiple reset warrants that possessed multiple reset prices during the reset period.

Since Black and Scholes [2] and Merton [3] developed the option valuation formula, the Black-Scholes model has become the mainstream framework for option pricing. Most researchers have proposed various pricing methods for the valuation of reset options with discrete monitoring dates. Gray and Whaley [4,5] studied the S&P 500 index reset put warrant and obtained a closed-form solution for a reset warrant with a single reset date. Cheng and Zhang [1] evaluated a reset option with multiple discrete reset dates. They obtained a closed-form solution by using probability method. Liao and Wang [6] built on the work of Cheng and Zhang [1] and used multiple normal distribution functions to price a reset option. Dai, Fang and Lyuu [7] studied the analytics for geometric average trigger reset options. Hsiao, Wang and Chen [8] priced an arithmetic average reset option using the Green function method.

In recent years, it became more and more popular for companies to issue employee stock options with reset constraints on a lock-up period. When the employee stock option is embedded with a continuous reset period, it is called the window reset option. However, there are few studies about pricing continuous reset options since there is no closed-form exact solution for the valuation of window reset options. Liao and Wang [6] formulated the price of a continuous reset option to be equal to the difference between the prices of a down-and-out barrier option with an original strike price and a down-and-in barrier option with a reset strike price. Their method can't solve the valuation of window reset options, since the method is useful only when the end of reset date is the maturity of the contract.

Our contribution of this study is that we proposed an accurate and simple method to formulate window reset option as the solution to a boundary value problem of the

Black-Scholes PDE. The problem was simplified into an initial-boundary value problem of a heat equation. The solution could be represented explicitly via a boundary integral representation [9]. Additionally, if we change the reset clauses to a barrier condition, the method can also apply to solve window barrier options [10]. Finally, the numerical integration is employed to calculate the option price. An example of a window reset option is presented to demonstrate the influence of different levels of stock volatility on option prices.

The rest of this paper is organized as follows. The window reset option is detailed in Section 2. In Section 3, we formulate the mathematical model, while in Section 4, we transform it into a boundary value problem of the heat equation. The boundary integral representation of the solution is then obtained. Next, in Section 5 we present a numerical example. Finally, in the last section there are conclusions and discussions.

2. Window Reset Options

A window reset option is a reset option with a partial continuous reset window. The strike price of a window reset option is reset to a new level if the price of underlying asset is below the threshold at a pre-specific period. This period is called the reset window. The path of stock value will determine the strike price of the option. In this article, the period, the strike price and the reset level are denoted by $[t_0, t_1]$, E and αE respectively. The reset price is assumed to be the same as the reset level. Therefore, at expiration T, the option price $C(s,T)$ is

$$C(s,T) = \begin{cases} s - E^*, & \text{if } s \geq E^* \\ 0, & \text{if } s < E^* \end{cases} \tag{1}$$

where $E^* = \begin{cases} E, & \text{if } s > \alpha E \quad \text{for all } t \in (t_0, t_1) \\ \alpha E, & \text{if } s \leq \alpha E \quad \text{for some } t \in (t_0, t_1) \end{cases}$.

3. Mathematical Model

In this section, we establish the mathematical model for a window reset option. Under the Black-Scholes [2] economy assumptions, when the stock price, s, follows a geometric Brown motion, the price of the option, C, must satisfy the Black-Scholes PDE as follows:

$$\frac{1}{2}\sigma^2 s^2 C_{ss} + r_f s C_s + C_t = r_f C \tag{2}$$

where σ is the stock's volatility, r_f is the risk-free interest rate, and t is the time.

At the end of the reset window, the strike price is determined. Thus, by the Black-Scholes formula, the price has to be

$$C(s,t) = sN(d_1) - Ee^{-r_f \cdot (T-t)} N(d_2), \text{ for } s > \alpha E \tag{3}$$

where $N(.)$ is the standard normal cumulative distribution function,

$$d_1 = \frac{\ln\left(\frac{s}{E}\right) + \left(r_f - \frac{\sigma^2}{2}\right)(T-t)}{\sigma\sqrt{T-t}}, \quad d_2 = d_1 - \sigma\sqrt{T-t}.$$

Let $C_1(s,t)$ denote the option price with strike E and $C_2(s,t)$ with strike αE. Then the formulae for $C_1(s,t)$ and $C_2(s,t)$ are as follows:

$$C_1(s,t) = sN(d_{11}) - Ee^{-r_f \cdot (T-t)} N(d_{12}) \tag{4}$$

where $d_{11} = \dfrac{\ln\left(\frac{s}{E}\right) + \left(r_f - \frac{\sigma^2}{2}\right)(T-t)}{\sigma\sqrt{T-t}}$,

$d_{12} = d_{11} - \sigma\sqrt{T-t}$.

$$C_2(s,t) = s\,N(d_{21}) - \alpha E e^{-r_f \cdot (T-t)} N(d_{22}) \tag{5}$$

where $d_{21} = \dfrac{\ln\left(\frac{s}{\alpha E}\right) + \left(r_f - \frac{\sigma^2}{2}\right)(T-t)}{\sigma\sqrt{T-t}}$,

$d_{22} = d_{21} - \sigma\sqrt{T-t}$.

During the reset window, if the stock price has touched the reset level, the strike price is reset to αE and never changes until expiration. In this situation, the option price can be expressed by the Black-Scholes formula, *i.e.* $C(s,t) = C_2(s,t)$. Thus, we only need to evaluate the option price $C(s,t)$ before the stock price touches the reset level during the window. The option price $C(s,t)$ fulfills the Black-Sholes Equation (2). When the stock price touches the reset level, the price $C(s,t) = C_2(s,t)$. If the stock prices do not touch the reset level through the window, at the end of the window, the price has to be $C_1(s,t)$. Therefore

$$C(\alpha E, t) = C_2(\alpha E, t) = C_b(t), t \in (t_0, t_1), \tag{6}$$

and

$$C(s, t_1) = C_1(s, t_1) = C_0(s), s > \alpha E \tag{7}$$

In the domain of $s > \alpha E$ and $t \in (t_0, t_1)$. Equation (2) is the PDE, Formula (6) is the boundary condition and Formula (7) is the initial condition.

4. Variables Transformation and Integral Representation

In this section, we employ a variables transformation to simplify the boundary value problem established in the last section. After the variables transformation as in Equation (8), the Black -Scholes PDE will be simplified into the homogeneous heat equation as Equation (9), and the time variables, t_0, t_1, and T will be transformed into time to maturity as τ_0, τ_1, and 0.

Let

$$\begin{cases} \tau = T - t \\ x = \ln s + \left(r_f - \dfrac{\sigma^2}{2} \right)\tau \\ u\left(x(s),\tau\right) = e^{r_f \cdot \tau} C\left(s, T-\tau\right) \end{cases} \quad (8)$$

The Black-Scholes PDE becomes

$$\frac{\sigma^2}{2} u_{xx} = u_\tau \quad (9)$$

The boundary condition becomes:

$$u\left(B(\tau),\tau\right) = C_b\left(T-\tau\right)\cdot e^{r_f \cdot \tau},$$

where $B(\tau) = \ln(\alpha E) + \left(r_f - \dfrac{\sigma^2}{2} \right)\tau$, $\tau_1 \le \tau \le \tau_0$.

The initial condition becomes

$$u(x,\tau_1) = C_0\left(e^{x - \left(r_f - \frac{\sigma^2}{2}\right)\tau_1} \right)\cdot e^{rf\cdot\tau_1}, \text{ for}$$

$$x > \ln(\alpha E) + \left(r_f - \frac{\sigma^2}{2} \right)\tau_1 .$$

The transformed boundary value problem is an initial-boundary value problem of the heat equation. The solution to the problem can be represented by Shen and Wang [9].

Let $u_b(\tau) = C_b\left(T-\tau\right)\cdot e^{r_f \cdot \tau}$,

$u_0(x) = C_0\left(e^{x - \left(r_f - \frac{\sigma^2}{2}\right)\tau_1} \right)\cdot e^{rf\cdot\tau_1}$ and

$\dfrac{\partial}{\partial x} u\left(B(\tau),\tau\right) = f(\tau)$.

$$\begin{aligned} u(x_0,\tau_0) = & -\frac{\sigma^2}{2}\int_{\tau_1}^{\tau_0} f(\tau) G\left(B(\tau),\tau; x_0,\tau_0\right)\mathrm{d}\tau \\ & + \frac{\sigma^2}{2}\int_{\tau_1}^{\tau_0} u_b(\tau) G_x\left(B(\tau),\tau; x_0,\tau_0\right)\mathrm{d}\tau \\ & + \int_{\tau_1}^{\tau_0} u_b(\tau) G\left(B(\tau),\tau; x_0,\tau_0\right) B'(\tau)\mathrm{d}\tau \\ & + \int_{B(\tau_1)}^{\infty} u_0(x) G\left(x,\tau_1; x_0,\tau_0\right)\mathrm{d}x \end{aligned} \quad (10)$$

where $B(\tau) = \ln(\alpha E) + \left(r_f - \dfrac{\sigma^2}{2} \right)\tau$, $\tau_1 \le \tau \le \tau_0$.

The function $G(.)$ is a fundamental solution of the heat equation. The formula (10) is called the integral representation of the heat equation. There exists a fundamental solution G such that G is banished on the boundary $B(\tau)$, *i.e.* $G\left(B(\tau),\tau;\bar{x},\bar{\tau}\right) = 0$. The fundamental solution G is called Green's function with boundary $B(\tau)$.

$$\begin{aligned} G\left(x,\tau;\bar{x},\bar{\tau}\right) = & \frac{H(\bar{\tau}-\tau)}{\sqrt{2\pi\sigma_2^2(\bar{\tau}-\tau)}}\left\{ \exp\left[-\frac{(x-\bar{x})^2}{2\sigma_2^2(\bar{\tau}-\tau)} \right] \right. \\ & \left. - \exp\left[-\frac{(x-2b_1+\bar{x})^2}{2\sigma_2^2(\bar{\tau}-\tau)} + \alpha \right] \right\} \end{aligned} \quad (11)$$

where b_1 is the transformed reset threshold at $\bar{\tau}$,

$$b_1 = \ln(\alpha E) + \left(r_f - \frac{\sigma^2}{2} \right)\bar{\tau}, \quad \alpha = \frac{2\left(r_f - \frac{\sigma^2}{2} \right)(b_1 - \bar{x})}{\sigma^2}.$$

$H(\tau_0 - \tau)$ is the Heaviside step function and is defined in Equation (12).

$$H(\tau_0-\tau) = \begin{cases} 1, & \text{if } \tau_0 - \tau \ge 0 \\ 0, & \text{if } \tau_0 - \tau < 0 \end{cases} \quad (12)$$

The partial derivative of the Green function about the variable x is as follows.

$$\begin{aligned} & G_x\left(x,\tau;\bar{x},\bar{\tau}\right) \\ = & \frac{H(\bar{\tau}-\tau)}{\sqrt{2\pi\sigma^2(\bar{\tau}-\tau)}}\left\{ \exp\left[-\frac{(x-\bar{x})^2}{2\sigma^2(\bar{\tau}-\tau)} \right]\left(\frac{\bar{x}-x}{\sigma^2(\bar{\tau}-\tau)} \right) \right. \\ & + \exp\left[-\frac{(x-2b_1+\bar{x})^2}{2\sigma^2(\bar{\tau}-\tau)} + \frac{2\left(r_f - \frac{\sigma^2}{2} \right)(b_1-\bar{x})}{\sigma^2} \right] \\ & \left. \cdot \left(\frac{x-2b_1+\bar{x}}{\sigma^2(\bar{\tau}-\tau)} \right) \right\} \end{aligned} \quad (13)$$

When we use the characteristics of the Green function at the boundary condition, we can further simplify the integral representation (10) to equation (14). Therefore, we substitute Green's function with boundary $B(\tau)$ into the integral representation (10), and the integral representation is as follows.

$$\begin{aligned} u(\bar{x},\bar{\tau}) = & \int_{B(\tau_1)}^{\infty} u_0(x) G\left(x,\tau_1;\bar{x},\bar{\tau}\right)\mathrm{d}x \\ & + \frac{\sigma^2}{2}\int_{\tau_1}^{\bar{\tau}} u_b(\tau) G_x\left(B(\tau),\tau;\bar{x},\bar{\tau}\right)\mathrm{d}\tau \end{aligned} \quad (14)$$

where $B(\tau) = \ln(\alpha E) + \left(r_f - \dfrac{\sigma^2}{2} \right)\tau$, $\tau_1 \le \tau \le \tau_0$, and $\bar{\tau} \in [\tau_1, \tau_0]$. The solution u is expressed explicitly in formula (14).

The first term of Equation (14) is the contribution of initial data, and it can be calculated easily via Simpson's rule. The second term of Equation (14) is the contribution of boundary data, and we use the Gaussian quadrature[1], which is a simile accurate method to approach the

[1]David Kincaid and Ward Chency [11], "Numerical Analysis," Brooks/Code Publishing Company, Pacific Grove, p. 460.

solution of the integration, to calculate it as follows:

$$\int_{\tau_1}^{\bar{\tau}} u_b\left(B(\tau),\tau\right)G_x\left(B(\tau),\tau;\bar{x},\bar{\tau}\right)\mathrm{d}\tau$$
$$=\sum_{i=1}^{n} u_b\left(\xi_i\right)\cdot\int_{\tau_1+(i-1)\Delta\tau}^{\tau_1+i\Delta\tau} G_x\left(B(\tau),\tau;\bar{x},\bar{\tau}\right)\mathrm{d}\tau$$
$$\approx\sum_{i=1}^{n}\left\{u_b\left(\xi_i\right)\cdot\frac{\Delta\tau}{18}\left[5G_x\left(B\left(\xi_i-h\sqrt{\frac{3}{5}}\right),\xi_i-h\sqrt{\frac{3}{5}};\bar{x},\bar{\tau}\right)\right.\right.$$
$$+8G_x\left(B(\xi_i),\xi_i;\bar{x},\bar{\tau}\right)$$
$$\left.\left.+5G_x\left(B\left(\xi_i+h\sqrt{\frac{3}{5}}\right),\xi_i+h\sqrt{\frac{3}{5}};\bar{x},\bar{\tau}\right)\right]\right\} \tag{15}$$

where $\Delta\tau=\frac{\bar{\tau}-\tau_1}{n}$, $h=\frac{\Delta\tau}{2}$, $\xi_i=\tau_1+(i-0.5)\Delta\tau$, $i=1,2,\cdots,n$.

Thus, we obtain the transformed valuation of window reset option, $u(x_0,\tau_0)$. The option price is

$$C(s_0,t_0)=u(x_0,\tau_0)\cdot\mathrm{e}^{-r_f\cdot\tau_0} \tag{16}$$

where $\tau_0=T-t_0$ and $x_0=\ln(s_0)+\left(r_f-\frac{\sigma^2}{2}\right)\tau_0$.

5. Numerical Example

Considering a window reset option, the original strike price E = 100, the reset rate $\alpha=90\%$, the risk-free rate r_f = 0.02. Option life begins at time t_0. The reset period is the interval $[t_0, t_1]$, $t_1 = t_0 + 0.25$ year. The time to maturity of the contract is $T = t_0 + 1$ year. The accuracy, calculation time and numerical orders of option price with respect to the volatilities 0.25, 0.5 and 0.75 are showed in **Table 1-3**. The integration results would be accurate at least to the fourth decimal place in all tables. If we double the partition numbers, the calculation time increases around four folds. It shows that our method is useful to price the window reset option.

On the other hand, we compare the valuation of window reset option with different volatility to vanilla option in **Figures 1-3**. The value of a window reset option increases with the current stock price. **Figure 4** presents the differences between the value of a vanilla option and a window reset option with stock volatility 0.25, 0.5, 0.75 respectively. We can tell that the difference is significant when the volatility of stock price is at a low level and the current stock price is close to the reset threshold αE, 90. When the volatility of stock price is low, the difference curve varies violently and decreases quickly to zero in **Figure 4**.

Table 1. The accuracy of the option pricing with the volatility 0.25.

Partition Number of x	Partition Number of τ	Option Price	Calculation Time (s)	Numerical Order
64	512	12.4423302951149	0.000	3.9551
128	1024	12.4423213941089	0.062	3.8256
256	2048	12.4423208239143	0.218	3.4641
512	4096	12.4423207845684	0.921	2.8854
1024	8192	12.4423207811784	3.978	2.6252
2048	16384	12.4423207807338	15.558	*
4096	32768	12.4423207806478	60.057	*

Note: The current stock price S_0 = 100, the original strike price E = 100; the reset rate α = 90%; the risk-free rate r_f = 0.02; option life begins at time t_0; the reset window is from t_0 to $t_1 = t_0 + 0.25$; time to maturity $T = t_0 + 1$.

Table 2. The accuracy of the option pricing with the volatility 0.5.

Partition Number of x	Partition Number of τ	Option Price	Calculation Time (s)	Numerical Order
64	512	23.1489383687899	0.015	3.9807
128	1024	23.1489197908478	0.047	3.9125
256	2048	23.1489186179280	0.265	3.6968
512	4096	23.1489185409322	1.186	3.2252
1024	8192	23.1489185351864	4.695	2.8503
2048	16384	23.1489185345938	17.318	*
4096	32768	23.1489185344984	71.911	*

Note: The current stock price S_0 = 100, the original strike price E = 100; the reset rate α = 90%; the risk-free rate r_f = 0.02; option life begins at time t_0; the reset window is from t_0 to $t_1 = t_0 + 0.25$; time to maturity $T = t_0 + 1$.

Table 3. The accuracy of the option pricing with the volatility 0.75.

Partition Number of x	Partition Number of τ	Option Price	Calculation Time (s)	Numerical Order
64	512	32.6615235692113	0.000	3.9985
128	1024	32.6614991873055	0.062	3.9496
256	2048	32.6614976653689	0.281	3.8135
512	4096	32.6614975675389	1.284	3.4598
1024	8192	32.6614975607290	4.976	3.0694
2048	16384	32.6614975601293	18.814	*
4096	32768	32.6614975600482	80.230	*

Note: the current stock price $S_0 = 100$, the original strike price $E = 100$; the reset rate $\alpha = 90\%$; the risk-free rate $r_f = 0.02$; option life begins at time t_0; the reset window is from t_0 to $t_1 = t_0 + 0.25$; time to maturity $T = t_0 + 1$.

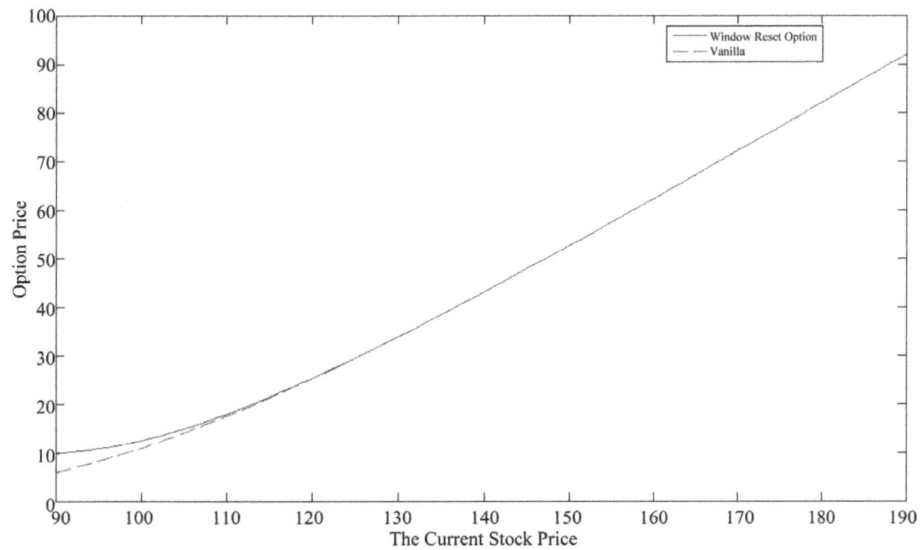

Figure 1. The valuation of a vanilla option and window reset option with a stock volatility 0.25 under different stock prices. Note: The original strike price $E = 100$; the reset rate $\alpha = 90\%$; the risk-free rate $r_f = 0.02$; option life begins at time t_0; the reset window is from t_0 to $t_1 = t_0 + 0.25$; time to maturity $T = t_0 + 1$.

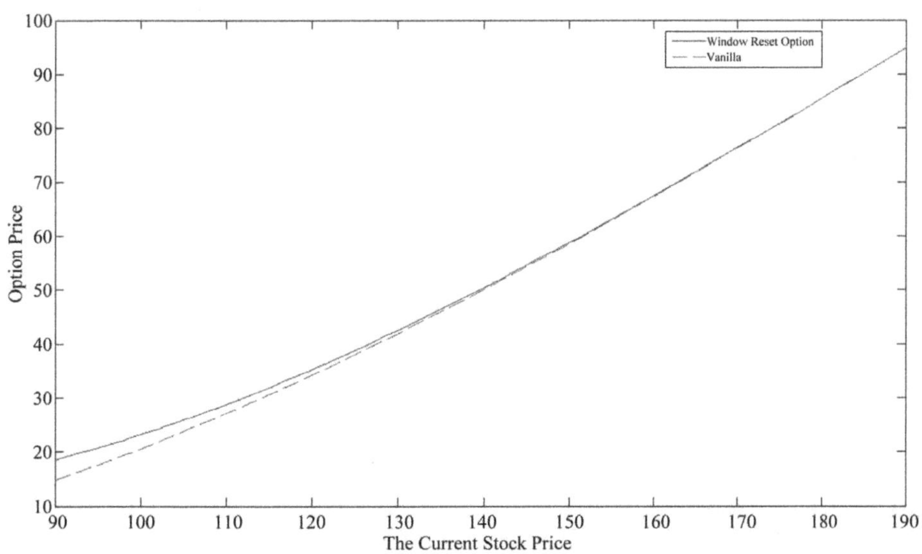

Figure 2. The valuation of the vanilla option and window reset option with a stock volatility 0.5 under different stock prices. Note: The original strike price $E = 100$; the reset rate $\alpha = 90\%$; the risk-free rate $r_f = 0.02$; option life begins at time t_0; the reset window is from t_0 to $t_1 = t_0 + 0.25$; time to maturity $T = t_0 + 1$.

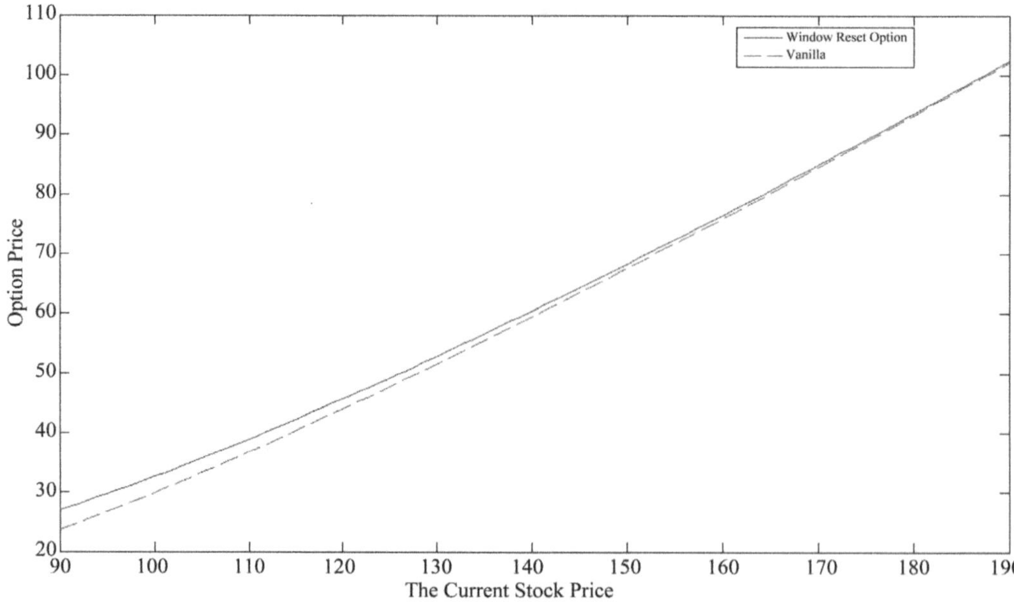

Figure 3. The valuation of the vanilla option and window reset option with a stock volatility 0.75 under different stock prices. Note: the original strike price E = 100; the reset rate α = 90%; the risk-free rate r_f = 0.02; option life begins at time t_0; the reset window is from t_0 to $t_1 = t_0 + 0.25$; time to maturity $T = t_0 + 1$.

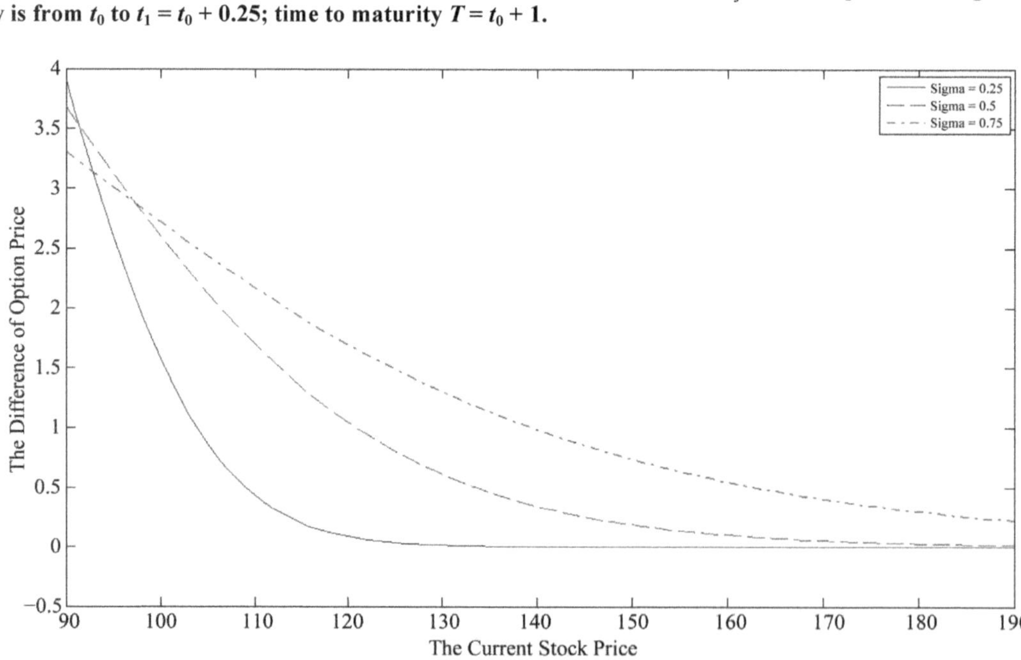

Figure 4. The difference between a vanilla option and window reset option with stock volatility 0.25, 0.5, 0.75 under different stock prices. Note: the original strike price E = 100; the reset rate α = 90%; the risk-free rate r_f = 0.02; option life begins at time t_0; the reset window is from t_0 to $t_1 = t_0 + 0.25$; time to maturity $T = t_0 + 1$.

6. Conclusions and Discussions

Emerging derivatives are more and more popular in recent years. In this paper, we focus on the valuation of a window reset option which is a kind of reset options with continuous reset constraints. The issue is very important for applying to employee stock options in finance or reservation options on truck-only toll lanes in traffic management. Our contribution of this study is that we proposed an accurate and simple method to price window reset options. We use the efficient integral representation of PDE to present the valuation of window reset option and use the numerical method, Simpson's rule and Gauss integral method, to calculate it.

Our pricing method is useful to obtain accurate numerical results fast. The difference between a vanilla option and a window reset option is significant when the stock volatility is at a low level and the current stock price is close to the reset threshold. In our numerical example, when the current stock price is about more than twofolds standard deviations, the price of window reset option is close to the value of vanilla option. The numerical result is related to the reset period and the volatility of stock price, since a short reset period or a low level of stock volatility will decrease the effect of the reset constraints. Therefore, the price difference volatilizes when the stock volatility is at a low level as shown in **Figure 4**.

REFERENCES

[1] W. Cheng and S. Zhang, "The Analytics of Reset Options," *Journal of Derivatives*, Vol. 8, No. 1, 2000, pp. 59-71.

[2] F. Black and M. Scholes, "The Pricing of Options and Corporate Liabilities," *The Journal of Political Economy*, Vol. 81, No. 3, 1973, pp. 637-654.

[3] R. C. Merton, "Theory of Rational Option Pricing," *Bell Journal of Economics and Management Science*, Vol. 4, No. 1, 1973, pp. 141-183.

[4] S. Gray and R. Whaley, "Valuing S&P 500 Bear Market Reset Warrants with A Periodic Reset," *Journal of Derivatives*, Vol. 5, No. 1, 1997, pp. 99-106.

[5] S. Gray and R. Whaley, "Reset Put Options: Valuation, Risk Characteristics, and an Application," *Australian Journal of Management*, Vol. 24, No. 1, 1999, pp. 1-20.

[6] S.-L. Liao and C.-W. Wang, "The Valuation of Reset Options with Multiple Strike Resets and Reset Dates," *The Journal of Futures and Markets*, Vol. 23, No. 1, 2003, pp. 87-107.

[7] T. S. Dai, Y. Y. Fang and Y. D. Lyuu, "Analytics for Geometric Average Trigger Reset Options," *Applied Economics Letters*, Vol. 12, No. 13, 2005, pp. 835-840.

[8] Y. L. Hsiao, A. M. L. Wang and C. Y. Chen, "Pricing an Arithmetic Average Reset Option Using the Green Function Method," *Asia Pacific Management Review*, 2011.

[9] S. Y. Shen and A. M. L. Wang, "On Stop-Loss Strategies for Stock Investments," *Applied Mathematics and Computation*, Vol. 119, No. 2-3, 2001, pp. 317-337.

[10] Y.-L. Hsiao, "Closed-Form Approximate Solutions of Window Barrier Options with Term-Structure Volatility and Interest Rates Using the Boundary Integral Method," *Journal of Mathematical Finance*, Vol. 2, No. 4, 2012, pp. 291-302.

[11] D. Kincaid and W. Chency, "Numerical Analysis," Brooks/Code Publishing Company, Pacific Grove, 1991, p. 460.

10

Rentiers and Workers-Capitalists in a Non-Classical Model

Romar Correa
Department of Economics, University of Mumbai, Mumbai, India

ABSTRACT

We separate the "rentier" portion of the budget constraint of the representative agent from the "income-plus-distributed profits" segment. The former's wealth consists exclusively of returns on government bonds, the latter's wealth is wage income from working for firms plus the distributed profits of the latter. The non-neoclassical element is the non-imposition of the market-clearing assumption. The Barro-Ricardo theorem only applies to rentiers. The level of activity is shown to depend on the level of employment along with a set of parameters that capture the imperfect competition of the model.

Keywords: Financial Wealth; Competition; Public Works

1. Introduction

The financial crisis originating in the US of A was sufficient but not necessary to heighten protests against the representative agent that underlies the new classical (Keynesian) model that still holds sway over the profession. Franklin Fisher, Alan Kirman and many others have long established that the foundations of that fiction in pure theory are shaky. Still, while our model below can be regarded as part of the agent-based modeling response to the DSGE, we do not tamper with the elements of the maximand like discount rates and time horizons. Instead, we differentiate the interest-income and wage-cum-profits components in the right-hand side of the budget constraint of the representative agent. However, an important assumption we drop is that markets clear continuously.

The strategy is motivated by the increased financial layering that has begun to permeate economies beginning with the United States. The counterpart has been the constriction of the production of goods and services. Hein [1] has emphasised the increasing rate of return on bonds and the escalating potential for wealth- and debt-based consumption trajectories.

In the next section we work with a dynamic general equilibrium model with monetary-financial foundations. Two sharp results are discussed, one pertaining to the finance-government policy nexus, the second to the production of goods and services. A final section is an overview of the theorems.

2. The Institutional Framework and Results

Outside of the United States, structural models with price-setting agents have long been staple fare. For instance, Benassy [2,3], has developed a framework that includes both price and quantity setting by households and firms. Agents are infinitely-lived households (rentiers and workers-capitalists), firms, and government. Households are indexed by $i \in [0,1]$, and firms by $j \in [0,1]$. As workers, households provide different qualities of labour. They set the corresponding wage, W_i. There is a homogenous consumption good (output) and differentiated intermediate goods indexed by $j \in [0,1]$. A one-to-one correspondence between intermediate good and firm j exists. CES aggregators will be used in the noncompetitive account below.

The price of output is P. At the present time t, it is produced by competitive firms endowed with the following technology,

$$Y_t = \left(\int_0^1 Y_{jt}^{\theta} \mathrm{d}j \right)^{\theta} \tag{1}$$

Firm j produces its intermediate good using quantities of different types of labour i, N_{ijt}. It is characterized by a production function with the usual properties,

$$Y_{jt} = F\left(N_{jt}\right) \quad (2)$$

where N_{jt}, a scalar index is deduced from the N_{ij}s by an aggregator function

$$N_{jt} = \left(\int_0^1 N_{ijt}^{\nu} \mathrm{d}i\right)^{1/\nu} \quad (3)$$

Firm j seeks to maximize its profits

$$\Pi_{jt} = \int_{s=t}^{\infty} \left(P_{jt}Y_{jt} - \int_0^1 W_{it}N_{ijt}\mathrm{d}i\right)\mathrm{d}t \quad (4)$$

The worker-household attempts to maximize her intertemporal utility function given by

$$U_{it} = \left(\int_{s=t}^{\infty} \mathrm{e}^{\beta(s-t)}\left(\log C_{it} - V(N_{it}\right)\mathrm{d}t\right) \quad (5)$$

where V is a disutility function.

In time period t, household i sets its wage and supplies a total quantity of labour

$$N_{it} = \int_0^1 N_{ijt}\mathrm{d}j \quad (6)$$

In addition, all profits are distributed to households. So, worker i's share of profits is

$$\Pi_{it} = \int_0^1 \Pi_{jt}\mathrm{d}j \quad (7)$$

From the above, worker i consumes C_{it} and the surplus is "wealth", Ω_{is+1}, carried over to the next period, integrating over all time periods from the present,

$$\int_{s=t}^{\infty} \Omega_{is+1} = \int_{s=t}^{\infty} \left(W_{is}N_{is} + \Pi_{is} - P_sC_{is}\right) \quad (8)$$

Taking the limit of the expression as $t \to \infty$, and imposing the transversality condition,

$$W_{it}N_{it} + \Pi_{it} = \int_{s=t}^{\infty} \left(P_{is}C_{is}\right)\mathrm{d}s \quad (9)$$

Benassy (2002, 75-76) derives the following objective demand curves addressed to firm j and household i in period t.

$$Y_{jt} = \left(\frac{P_{jt}}{P_t}\right)^{-1/(1-\theta)} Y \quad (10)$$

$$N_{it} = \left(\frac{W_{it}}{W_t}\right)^{-1/(1-\nu)} \int_0^1 F^{-1}\left(Y_{jt}\right)\mathrm{d}j \quad (11)$$

where

$$P_t = \left(\int_0^1 P_{jt}^{-\theta/(1-\theta)}\mathrm{d}j\right)^{-\theta/(1-\theta)} \quad (12)$$

and

$$W_t = \left(\int_0^1 W_{it}^{-(1-\nu)/\nu}\right)^{-(1-\nu)/\nu} \quad (13)$$

A worker-household will now choose its wage, labour supply, and consumption to maximize (5) subject to (8) and (10). The first-order conditions yield the intertemporal Euler condition for the worker,

$$P_{s+1}C_{is+1} = \beta P_sC_{is} \quad (14)$$

and

$$\frac{\nu}{P_tC_{it}} = \frac{V'\left(N_{it}\right)}{W_{it}} \quad (15)$$

$$\frac{W_{it}}{P_t} = \theta F'\left(N_t\right) \quad (16)$$

We turn to the rentier. Her felicity function is identical to (5) but without the element representing the work-leisure tradeoff. The rentier has positive holdings of government bonds, B_{it}, inherited from the past. The current stock can also be negative which means that the rentier is borrowing from the government. The latter case might be regarded as a "bonds-in-advance" constraint without requiring the holder to spend the amount on current consumption. The absence of cash in what follows is justified by history. Central Banks rose from the pool of commercial banks and have recently begun to return to these origins. Bills of exchange slowly took on a fiat character. In the current period the rentier consumes and is taxed. Like the worker, the rentier consumes but, unlike the worker, only she pays tax T_{it}. Rentier i's wealth, then, is

$$\Omega_{it} = B_{it} \quad (17)$$

The wealth transferred to the next period is

$$\Omega_{is+1} = \left(1+i_s\right)B_{is} - P_sC_{is} - P_sT_{is} \quad (18)$$

In a manner identical to the derivation of Equation (9) for the consumer, summing over all periods from t to infinity and imposing the transversality condition, we get

$$B_{it} = \int_{s=t}^{\infty} \left(P_sC_{is} + P_sT_{is}\right)\mathrm{d}s \quad (19)$$

The government budget constraint mirrors the budget constraint of the rentier,

$$\Omega_{s+1} = \left(1+i_s\right)\Omega_s - P_sT_s \quad (20)$$

Once more integrating forward and imposing a terminal-value condition, we derive

$$B_t = \int_{s=t}^{\infty} \left(P_sT_s\right)\mathrm{d}s \quad (21)$$

Combining (19) and (21), rentier consumption is

$$\int_{s=t}^{\infty} \left(P_s C_{is}\right) \mathrm{d}s = 0 \tag{22}$$

The result can be summarized thus

Proposition 1. *Ricardian equivalence is equivalent to "the euthanasia of the rentier".*

In an essay "Economic Possibilities for our Grandchildren" written in 1930, Keynes looked forward to the "euthanasia of the rentier". His economic framework was built around decent work and employment and he had little sympathy for those who consumed without working. The equivalence result highlights the importance of "financial wealth taxation" rather than the undifferentiated lump-sum taxation of the standard model. Direct taxes are disapproved off anywhere as they allegedly load the work-leisure choice in favour of the latter. This microeconomic theorem does not apply to the rentier choice problem. Secondly, it is also irrelevant to the aggregate of choices in a macroeconomic model. Taxes on wealth (in this sense) and financial transactions continue to excite academic and popular debate. According to Moe [4], the result is consistent with consensus macroeconomics outside the mainstream. On the one hand, the monetary and the fiscal authorities are supposed to coordinate on policies to achieve full employment. Secondly, steeply progressive taxation might be returning to the models. The circular flow of goods and services and money requires distributed profits so that workers-consumers can spend their incomes and recycle them back to firms. High wages contribute to that end.

Aggregate consumption, then, is just Equation (9), the consumption of workers-capitalists,

$$\int_{s=t}^{\infty} P_s C_s = W_s N_s + \Pi_s \tag{23}$$

The intertemporal Euler condition for the rentier is more familiar,

$$P_{s+1} C_{is+1} = \beta\left(1+i_s\right) P_s C_{is} \tag{24}$$

Combining the two Euler conditions (14) and (22), we get the aggregate first-order condition

$$P_{s+1} C_{s+1} = \left[\beta + \beta\left(1+i_s\right)\right] P_s C_s \tag{25}$$

Alpha will turn out to be a multiplier where $\alpha \stackrel{\text{def}}{=} \left[\beta + \left(1+i_s\right)\right]$.

The level of activity is given by the first-order conditions (15) and (16) along with $Y_t = F\left(N_t\right)$ and the aggregate budget constraints (19) and Euler Equation (24). The national income identity $P_t Y_t = W_t N_t + \Pi_t$ is used. In combination, this gives

$$Y_t = \frac{1}{1-\alpha}\left(\theta \nu F'\left(N_t\right) V'\left(N_t\right)\right) \tag{26}$$

In words,

Proposition 2. *Output is independent of government.*

The result can be viewed from opposite ends. On the one hand, with the coefficients theta and nu, it makes the case for vibrant markets. They are the "degrees of monopoly" held by firms and workers. As the elasticities approach unity, they approach the competitive outcome and increase output. Thus, freedom of entry and exit must be encouraged and monopolies, other than natural and public, discouraged. Trade unions, in the sense of blocking outsiders and fixing wages, are a thing of the past anyway. The model can be developed to include vigorous bargaining over productivity gains by small firms and groups of workers. At the same time, the letter N in the numerator of the expression suggests Keynes rather than Keynesians. The latter are associated with G, government expenditure, which is conspicuously absent. Keynes wrote of public works and not fiscal policy. When output is at a less-than-full-employment level, the task of the government is to set out a schedule of projects that can employ able and willing hands at a dignified wage.

3. Conclusions

We develop a demand-determined model. The model dichotomises into a monetary-financial and a real sector. Over thirty years ago, Barro posed the question whether government bonds were net wealth and answered in the negative. The reason is that rational consumers would discount the present value of the wealth with the own-lifetime taxes they would have to pay on it. Therefore, present consumption equals present income. However, when present income is the return on government securities, the rentier vanishes. The Barro-Ricardo result can be interpreted as a balanced-budget case for confiscatory taxes on wealth. This does not mean that production and employment are outside government purview. Local governments can work through the intermediation of local banks to generate private-public participation in local projects.

REFERENCES

[1] E. Hein, "Finance-Dominated Capitalism and Redistribution of Income: A Kaleckian Perspective," Working Paper No. 746, Levy Economics Institute of Bard College, New York, 2013.

[2] J.-P. Bénassy, "The Macroeconomics of Imperfect Competition and Nonclearing Markets," The MIT Press, Cambridge, 2002.

[3] J.-P. Bénassy, "Money, Interest, and Policy," The MIT

Press, Cambridge, 2007.

[4] T. G. Moe, "Marriner S. Eccles and the 1957 Treasury-Federal Reserve Accord: Lessons for Central Bank Independence," Working Paper No. 747, Levy Economics Institute of Bard College, New York, 2013.

Optimal Portfolio Strategy with Discounted Stochastic Cash Inflows

Charles I. Nkeki
Department of Mathematics, Faculty of Physical Sciences, University of Benin,
Benin City, Nigeria

ABSTRACT

This paper examines optimal portfolios with discounted stochastic cash inflows (SCI). The cash inflows are invested into a market that is characterized by inflation-linked bond, a stock and a cash account. It was assumed that inflation-linked bond, stock and the cash inflows are stochastic and follow a standard geometric Brownian motion. The variational form of Merton portfolio strategy was obtained by assuming that the investor chooses constant relative risk averse (CRRA) utility function. The inter-temporal hedging terms that offset any shock to the SCI were obtained. A closed form solution to our resulting non-linear partial differential equation was obtained.

Keywords: Optimal Portfolio; Stochastic Cash Inflows; Inflation-Linked Bond; Variational Form; Intertemporal Hedging Terms

1. Introduction

This paper consider the optimal portfolio strategies with valuing expected discounted cash inflows. It was assumed that the underlying assets and cash inflow process follow a standard geometric Brownian motion. The investment of the investor's SCI into a cash account, an inflation-linked bond and a stock was considered. The SCI and stock price were correlated with inflation and stock market risk.

In a related literature, [1] studied an optimal investment problem in a continuous-time framework where the interest rate follows the Cox-Ingersoll-Ross dynamics. They obtained a closed form solution for the optimal investment strategy under a complete market framework. They assumed that the investor chooses CRRA utility function. [2] considered the process of finding the optimal portfolio, optimal consumption and the efficient frontier for a small agent in an economy. They also considered financial market that composed of two sources of uncertainties: an m-dimensional Brownian motion and a continuous time Markov chain. They found theoretically, that the regimes of an economy have a significant impacts on the portfolio and consumption decision as well as on the efficient frontier of a small investor. [3] studied the present value and overcome the difficulty of independence by reversing the order of the cash flow. He found that similar recursive formulas for the present value is also applicable to the future value of the expected returns. [4] considered the problem of constructing a portfolio of finitely many assets whose returns are described by a discrete joint distribution. They proposed a new portfolio optimization model involving stochastic dominance constraints on the portfolio return. [5] studied how portfolio composition changes with individual wealth. [6] considered the present value of expected future contribution into the pension fund. [7] investigated the stochastic dynamics of depository financial institution assets, liabilities and capital under the influence of macroeconomic factors. They adopted dynamic programming techniques in their optimization process. They provided an analysis of the economic aspects of the depository financial institution modeling. [8] studied a portfolio problem of a fund manager who wants to maximize the expected utility of his terminal wealth in a complete financial market. He found that the optimal portfolio is formed by three components: a speculative, an hedging, and a preference-free hedging component. He obtained a close form solution to the asset allocation problem. [9] considered the optimal portfolio selection problem with portfolio constraints. They derived the general utility function using the martingale approach. They found that using CRRA utility function, optimal policies can be obtained explicitly when there are minimum capital requirements. ([10,11]) studied the optimal portfolio management in the accumulation phase of a defined contribution pension scheme. They obtained portfolio values with hedging strategies for a pension plan member. In this paper, we consider the optimal portfolio and investment strategies involving cash inflow valuation over time. We obtain explicitly, analytical solution to our resulting HJB equation. The risk-free rate is assume to be deterministic.

The remaining parts of the paper is structured as follows: In Section 2, we described the structure of the financial market; In Section 3, we consider the dynamics of the discounted present value of expected SCI process; In Section 4, we consider the wealth process of the investor; In Section 5, we consider the valuation of the discounted present value of expected SCI process of the investor as well as the sensitivity of the present value of the SCI; In Section 6, we consider the optimization program and optimal portfolio and optimal solution of the investor's wealth using CRRA utility function; Section 7 concludes the paper.

2. The Model

Let (Ω, F, P) be a probability space. Let $\mathrm{F}(F)=\{F_t : t\in[0,T]\}$, where $F_t=\sigma(S(s),I(s):s\le t)$. The Brownian motions $W(t)=(W^I(t),W^S(t))$ is a 2-dimensional process, defined on a given filtered probability space $(\Omega,F,\mathrm{F}(F),\mathrm{P})$, $t\in[0,T]$, where P is the real world probability measure, t the time period, T the terminal time period, $W^I(t)$ is the Brownian motion with respect to source of uncertainty arising from inflation and $W^S(t)$ is the Brownian motion with respect to source of uncertainty arising from the stock market. It is assumed that the market is arbitrage-free, complete and continuously open between time period 0 and T.

Financial Model

The dynamics for the cash account with the price $Q(t)$ at time t is given by

$$\begin{aligned} \mathrm{d}Q(t)&=rQ(t)\mathrm{d}t,\\ Q(0)&=1; \end{aligned} \tag{1}$$

where r is the short term interest rate. The stock price $S(t)$ at time t is given by the dynamics:

$$\begin{aligned} \mathrm{d}S(t)&=S(t)(\mu\mathrm{d}t+\sigma_1\cdot\mathrm{d}W(t)),\\ S(0)&=s_0; \end{aligned} \tag{2}$$

where, μ is the expected growth rate of stock price, $\sigma_1=\left(\rho\sigma_S,\sigma_S\sqrt{1-\rho^2}\right)$ and $0<\rho<1$. σ_S is the volatility of stock. The price of the inflation-linked bond $B(t,I(t))$ is given by the dynamics:

$$\begin{aligned} \mathrm{d}B(t,I(t))&=B(t,I(t))\left[(r+\sigma_I\theta_I)\mathrm{d}t+\sigma_B\cdot\mathrm{d}W(t)\right],\\ B(0,I(0))&=b; \end{aligned} \tag{3}$$

where, $\sigma_B=(\sigma_I,0)$ is the volatility of inflation-linked bond, θ_I is the market price of inflation risk, $I(t)$ is the inflation index at time t and has tha dynamics:

$$\mathrm{d}I(t)=qI(t)\mathrm{d}t+\sigma_I I(t)\mathrm{d}W^I(t),$$

where q is the expected rate of inflation, which is the difference between nominal interest rate, r real interest rate $\bar{r}$ and σ_I is the volatility of inflation index. Since the market is complete, we have that

$$\Sigma:=\begin{pmatrix}\sigma_B\\ \sigma_1\end{pmatrix}=\begin{pmatrix}\sigma_I & 0\\ \rho\sigma_S & \sigma_S\sqrt{1-\rho^2}\end{pmatrix}, \tag{4}$$

$$\lambda:=(\sigma_I\theta_I,\mu-r)'. \tag{5}$$

Therefore, the market price of market risk is given by

$$\theta:=\Sigma^{-1}\lambda=\begin{pmatrix}\theta_I\\ \theta_S\end{pmatrix}=\begin{pmatrix}\theta_I\\ \dfrac{\mu-r-\rho\sigma_S\theta_I}{\sigma_S\sqrt{1-\rho^2}}\end{pmatrix}, \tag{6}$$

where, θ_S is the market price of stock market risk. The exponential process $Z(t):=\exp\left(-\theta'\cdot W(t)-\frac{1}{2}\|\theta\|^2 t\right), 0\le t\le T$, is assumed to be a martingale. We now define the state-price density function by

$$\Lambda(t):=\frac{Z(t)}{Q(t)}=Z(t)\exp(-rt),$$
$$0\le t\le T.$$

3. Dynamics of Stochastic Cash Inflows

The dynamics of the stochastic cash inflows with price process, $D(t)$ is given by

$$\begin{aligned} \mathrm{d}D(t)&=D(t)(k\mathrm{d}t+\sigma_D'\cdot\mathrm{d}W(t)),\\ D(0)&=D_0; \end{aligned} \tag{7}$$

where, $\sigma_D=\left(\sigma_1^D,\sigma_2^D\right)'$ is the volatility of the cash inflows and k is the expected growth rate of the cash inflows. σ_1^D is the volatility arising from inflation and σ_2^D is the volatility arising from the stock market. **Figure 1** presents the simulated diffusion paths of (7).

Figure 1 was obtained by setting $k=0.099$, $\sigma_1^D=0.25$, $\sigma_2^D=0.36$, $D_0=100$, $dt=\frac{t-t_0}{nt}$, $t=10$, $t_0=0$ and $nt=1000$.

Applying It$\hat{o}$ lemma to (7), we obtain

$$D(t)=D_0\exp\left(\left(k-\frac{1}{2}\|\sigma_D\|^2\right)t+\sigma_D'\cdot W(t)\right). \tag{8}$$

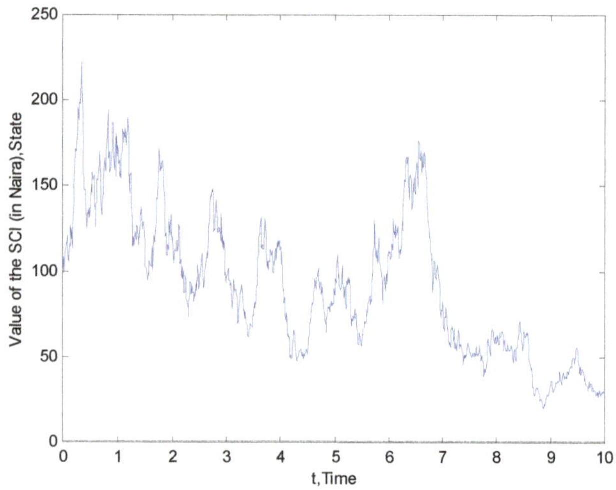

Figure 1. Simulated diffusion paths of the stochastic cash inflows.

4. The Wealth Process

Let $X(t)$ be the wealth process and

$\Delta(t) = (\Delta_I(t), \Delta_S(t))'$ be the portfolio value at time t, where $\Delta_I(t)$ is the portfolio value in inflation-linked bond and $\Delta_S(t)$ is the portfolio value in stock at time *t*. Then, $\Delta_0(t) = 1 - \Delta_I(t) - \Delta_S(t)$ is the portfolio value in cash account at time t. Therefore, the dynamics of the wealth process is given by

$$\begin{aligned} dX(t) &= X(t)\Delta_S(t)\frac{dS(t)}{S(t)} \\ &+ X(t)\Delta_I(t)\frac{dB(t,I(t))}{B(t,I(t))} \\ &+ X(t)(1-\Delta_I(t)-\Delta_S(t))\frac{dQ(t)}{Q(t)} + D(t)dt, \\ X(0) &= x. \end{aligned} \tag{9}$$

Substituting (1), (2) and (3) into (9), we obtain

$$\begin{aligned} dX(t) &= (X(t)(r+\lambda\cdot\Delta(t)) + D(t))dt \\ &+ X(t)(\Sigma\Delta(t))'\cdot dW(t), \\ X(0) &= x. \end{aligned} \tag{10}$$

5. The Discounted Value of SCI

In this section, we determine the value of expected discounted SCI.

Definition 1:

The discounted value of the expected future SCI is defined as

$$\Psi(t) = E_t\left(\int_t^T \frac{\Lambda(u)}{\Lambda(t)} D(t)\mathrm{d}u\right) \tag{11}$$

where, $E_t = E(\cdot \mid F_t)$ is the conditional expectation with respect to the Brownian filtration $\{F_t\}_{t\geq 0}$ and $\Lambda(t) = Z(t)\exp(-rt)$ is the stochastic discount factor which adjusts for nominal interest rate and market price of risks for stock and inflation-linked bond.

Proposition 1:

Suppose $\Psi(t)$ is the discounted value of the expected future SCI, then

$$\Psi(t) = \frac{D(t)(\exp((k-r-\sigma_D\cdot\theta)(T-t))-1)}{k-r-\sigma_D\cdot\theta}. \tag{12}$$

Proof. By definition 1, we have that

$$\Psi(t) = D(t)E_t\left(\int_t^T \frac{\Lambda(u)D(u)}{\Lambda(t)D(t)}du\right) \tag{13}$$

Applying change of variable on (13), we have

$$\Psi(t) = D(t)E\left(\int_0^{T-t} \frac{\Lambda(\tau)D(\tau)}{\Lambda(0)D(0)}\mathrm{d}\tau\right) \tag{14}$$

Applying parallelogram law and martingale principles on (14), we have

$$E\left(\frac{\Lambda(\tau)D(\tau)}{\Lambda(0)D(0)}\right) = \exp((k-r-\sigma_D\cdot\theta)\tau).$$

Therefore,

$$\Psi(t) = D(t)\left(\int_0^{T-t}\exp((k-r-\sigma_D\cdot\theta)\tau)\mathrm{d}\tau\right). \tag{15}$$

Integrating, we have

$$\Psi(t) = \frac{D(t)(\exp((k-r-\sigma_D\cdot\theta)(T-t))-1)}{k-r-\sigma_D\cdot\theta}. \tag{16}$$

Figure 2 was obtained by setting $D_0 = 100$, $k = 0.099$, $r = 0.04$, $\sigma_1^D = 0.25$, $\sigma_2^D = 0.36$, $\mu = 0.09$, $\sigma_S = 0.4$, $\sigma_I = 0.3$, $\rho = 0.6$ and $\theta_I = 0.08$.

At $t = 0$, we obtain the present discounted value of future SCI to be

$$\Psi(0) = \Psi_0 = \frac{D_0(\exp((k-r-\sigma_D\cdot\theta)T)-1)}{k-r-\sigma_D\cdot\theta}. \tag{17}$$

If $r+\sigma_D\cdot\theta > k$ and we allow $T\to\infty$ *i.e.*,

$$\lim_{T\to\infty}\Psi_0 = \lim_{T\to\infty}\left[\frac{D_0(\exp((k-r-\sigma_D\cdot\theta)T)-1)}{k-r-\sigma_D\cdot\theta}\right],$$

$$r+\sigma_D\cdot\theta > k$$

$$= \frac{D_0}{r+\sigma_D\cdot\theta-k}, r+\sigma_D\cdot\theta > k.$$

For a deterministic case, we have the present discounted value future deterministic cash inflows to be

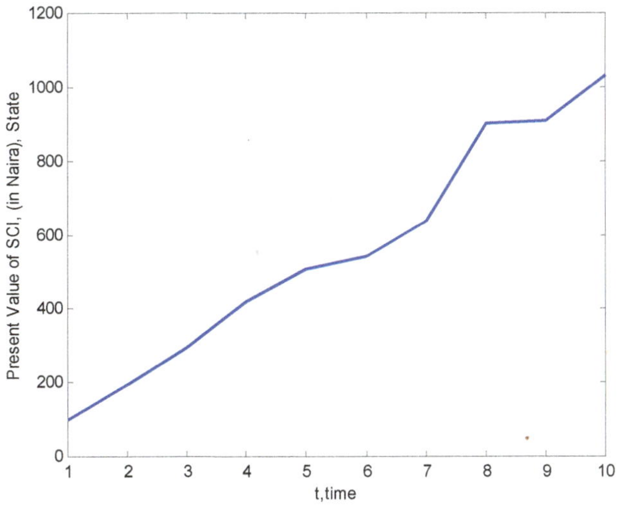

Figure 2. The flow of the discounted value of SCI.

$$\Psi_0 = \frac{D_0\left(\exp\left((k-r)T\right)-1\right)}{k-r}. \tag{18}$$

Hence,

$$\lim_{T\to\infty}\Psi_0 = \lim_{T\to\infty}\left[\frac{D_0\left(\exp\left((k-r)T\right)-1\right)}{k-r}\right], r>k$$

$$=\frac{D_0}{r-k}, r>k.$$

This shows that as $T\to\infty$, Ψ_0 converges to $\frac{D_0}{r+\sigma_D\cdot\theta-k}$, provided $r+\sigma_D\cdot\theta>k$.

For the deterministic case, it shows that as $T\to\infty$, Ψ_0 converges to $\frac{D_0}{r-k}$, provided $r>k$.

Figure 3 was obtained by setting $D_0=100$, $k=0.099$, $r=0.04$, $\sigma_1^D=0.25$, $\sigma_2^D=0.36$, $\mu=0.09$, $\sigma_S=0.4$, $\sigma_I=0.3$, $\rho=0.6$ and $\theta_I=0.08$.

Figure 2 represents the flow of the discounted value of stochastic cash inflow in the investment at time t and **Figure 3** represents the present value of discounted future SCI at time t.

We now consider the sensitivity analysis of Ψ_0. Proposition 2 establishes this fact.

Proposition 2:

Let $\beta=k-r-\sigma_D\cdot\theta$, then

$$\frac{\partial\Psi_0}{\partial T}=D_0\exp(\beta T).$$

Proof. The results follow by taking the partial derivatives of Ψ_0 with respect to T, D_0, r, σ_D and k, respectively.

$$\frac{\partial\Psi_0}{\partial D_0}=\frac{1}{\beta}\left(\frac{1}{D_0}\frac{\partial\Psi_0}{\partial T}-1\right);$$

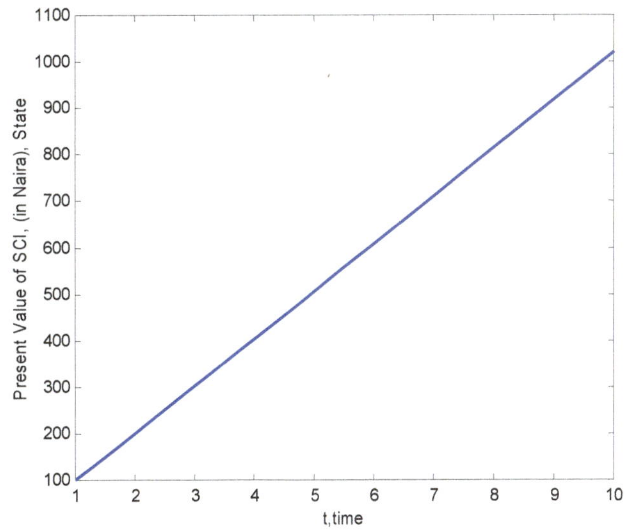

Figure 3. The present discounted value of future SCI.

$$\frac{\partial\Psi_0}{\partial r}=\frac{1}{\beta^2}\left((1-\beta T)\frac{\partial\Psi_0}{\partial T}-D_0\right);$$

$$\frac{\partial\Psi_0}{\partial\sigma_D}=\theta\frac{\partial\Psi_0}{\partial r};$$

$$\frac{\partial\Psi_0}{\partial k}=\frac{1}{\beta^2}\left((\beta T-1)\frac{\partial\Psi_0}{\partial T}+D_0\right)=-\frac{\partial\Psi_0}{\partial r}.$$

Table 1 shows the sensitivity analysis of the discounted value of the SCI.

Proposition 3:

Suppose that Proposition 1 holds, then

$$d\Psi(t)=\Psi(t)\left(\left(r+\sigma_D\cdot\theta\right)dt+\sigma_D'\cdot dW(t)\right) -D(t)dt. \tag{19}$$

Proof. Finding the differential of both sides of (16) and then substitute (7), we have

$$d\Psi(t)=\frac{D(t)\left(\exp\left(\beta(T-t)\right)-1\right)}{\beta}\times\left(kdt+\sigma_D'\cdot dW(t)\right)$$
$$+\frac{D(t)}{\beta}\left(-\beta\exp\left(\beta(T-t)\right)\right)dt$$
$$=\frac{D(t)}{\beta}\Big(\left(\exp\left(\beta(T-t)\right)-1\right)\left(kdt+\sigma_D'\cdot dW(t)\right)$$
$$-\beta\left(\exp\left(\beta(T-t)\right)-1\right)dt\Big)-D(t)dt$$
$$=\frac{D(t)\left(\exp\left(\beta(T-t)\right)-1\right)}{\beta}\left(\left(r+\sigma_D\cdot\theta\right)dt+\sigma_D'\cdot dW(t)\right)$$
$$-D(t)dt$$
$$=\Psi(t)\left(\left(r+\sigma_D\cdot\theta\right)dt+\sigma_D'\cdot dW(t)\right)-D(t)dt.$$

Let $V(t)$ be a value process at time t. We defined

Table 1. Simulation of the sensitivity analysis.

T	$\frac{\partial\Psi_0}{\partial D_0}$	$\frac{\partial\Psi_0}{\partial\sigma_1^D}$	$\frac{\partial\Psi_0}{\partial\sigma_2^D}$	$\frac{\partial\Psi_0}{\partial T}$	$\frac{\partial\Psi_0}{\partial r}$	$\frac{\partial\Psi_0}{\partial\theta_I}$	$\frac{\partial\Psi_0}{\partial\theta_S}$	$\frac{\partial\Psi_0}{\partial k}$
1	1.0022	−16624	−20005	0.4359	−207850	−51962	−74826	207850
2	2.0087	−14857	−17875	0.8738	−185720	−46429	−66858	185720
3	3.0197	−13079	−15736	1.3136	−163490	−40872	−58855	163490
4	4.0350	−11293	−13587	1.7552	−141160	−35290	−50818	141160
5	5.0548	−9499	−11429	2.1988	−118740	−29685	−42746	118740
6	6.0790	−7697	−9261	2.6444	−96220	−24054	−34638	96220
7	7.1077	−5888	−7084	3.0918	−73600	−18400	−26495	73600
8	8.1408	−4070	−4897	3.5413	−50880	−12720	−18317	50880
9	9.1785	−2245	−2701	3.9926	−28060	−7016	−10103	28060
10	10.2207	−412	−495	4.4460	−5150	−1287	−1853	5150

$V(t)$ as

$$V(t) := X(t) + \Psi(t), \tag{20}$$

where, $X(t)$ satisfy (10) and $\Psi(t)$ satisfy (19).

Proposition 4:

Let $V(t)$ satisfy (20), $X(t)$ satisfy (10) and $\Psi(t)$ satisfy (19), then

$$\begin{aligned} &dV(t) \\ &= \left(r\left(X(t)+\Psi\right)+\Psi(t)\sigma_D\cdot\theta+X(t)\lambda\cdot\Delta(t)\right)dt \quad (21) \\ &+\left(X(t)\Sigma\Delta(t)+\Psi(t)\sigma_D\right)'\cdot dW(t). \end{aligned}$$

Proof. Finding the differential of both sides of (20) and then substitute in (10) and (19), the result follows.

6. Optimization of the Value of Wealth Process

We define the general value function

$$J(t,v) = E\left[u\left(V\left(t,X(t),\Psi(t)\right)\right)\middle| X(t)=x, \Psi(t)=\Psi\right]$$

where $u(V(t))$ is the path of $V(t)$. Define Π to be the set of all admissible portfolio strategy that are $\mathcal{F}$-progressively measurable, that satisfy the integrability conditions $E\left[\int_t^T \Delta'(u)\Delta(u)du\right]<\infty$ and let $U(V(t))$ be a concave function in $V(t)$ such that $U(V(t))$ satisfies the HJB equation

$$\begin{aligned} U(t,v) &= \sup_{\Delta\in\Pi} E\left[u\left(V(T)\right)\mid X(t)=x, \Psi(t)=\Psi\right] \\ &= \sup_{\Delta\in\Pi} J(t,v) \end{aligned}$$

Therefore, by applying Itô lemma on (21), we obtain the following HJB equation:

$$U_t(t,v) + \max_{\Delta\in\Pi} HV = 0, \tag{22}$$

subject to:

$$U(T,v) = \frac{v^{1-\gamma}}{1-\gamma},$$

where,

$$\begin{aligned} HV &= r\Psi U_\Psi + rxU_x + \Psi\sigma_D\cdot\theta U_\Psi + x\lambda\cdot\Delta(t)U_x \\ &+ x\Psi\sigma_D\left(\Sigma\Delta(t)\right)U_{x\Psi} + \frac{1}{2}x^2\left(\Sigma\Delta(t)\right)'\Sigma\Delta(t)U_{xx} \\ &+ \frac{1}{2}\Psi^2\sigma_D'\sigma_D U_{\Psi\Psi} \end{aligned} \tag{23}$$

Let $U(t,v)$ be the solution of the HJB equation (22). Since the utility function is concave and the value function is smooth, *i.e.*, $U(t,V)\in C^{1,2}\left(\mathrm{R}\times[0,T]\right)$, then (22) is well-defined. Hence, we have the following:

$$\begin{aligned} \frac{\partial HV}{\partial\Delta(t)} &= \lambda U_x + x\left(\Sigma\Delta^*(t)\right)'\Sigma U_{xx} + \Psi\sigma_D\Sigma U_{X\Psi} \\ &= 0 \end{aligned} \tag{24}$$

from (24), we have

$$\left(\Delta^*(t)\right)' = \left(\Sigma'\Sigma\right)^{-1}\left(\frac{-\lambda U_x}{xU_{xx}}\right) - \frac{\left(\Sigma'\right)^{-1}\sigma_D\Psi U_{x\Psi}}{xU_{xx}}. \tag{25}$$

Substituting (25) into (22), we obtain the following HJB equation:

$$\begin{aligned} &U_t + rxU_x + \left(r+\sigma_D\cdot\theta\right)\Psi U_\Psi + \frac{1}{2}\sigma_D'\sigma_D\Psi^2U_{\Psi\Psi} \\ &-\frac{\lambda'\left(\Sigma^2\right)^{-1}\lambda U_x^2}{2U_{xx}} - \frac{\sigma_D'\sigma_D\Psi^2U_{x\Psi}^2}{2U_{xx}} \\ &-\frac{\sigma_D'\left(\Sigma^{-1}\right)\lambda\Psi U_xU_{x\Psi}}{U_{xx}} = 0. \end{aligned} \tag{26}$$

This is the resulting HJB equation of our problem.

Proposition 5:

The solution of the HJB equation (26) is of the form

$$U(t,v)=\frac{(vA(t))^{1-\gamma}}{1-\gamma},\gamma\neq 0,\gamma>0,$$

with

$$A(t)=\exp\left(\left(r+\frac{\theta'\theta}{2\gamma}\right)(T-t)\right),\qquad A(T)=1. \tag{27}$$

Proof. Finding the partial derivatives of $U(t,v)=\frac{(vA(t))^{1-\gamma}}{1-\gamma}$ with respect to t, x, xx, Ψ, $x\Psi$ and $\Psi\Psi$ and then substitute into (26), we obtain the following:

$$v^{1-\gamma}A(t)^{-\gamma}A'(t)+rv^{1-\gamma}A(t)^{1-\gamma}+\frac{\lambda'(\Sigma^2)^{-1}\lambda v^{1-\gamma}A(t)^{1-\gamma}}{2\gamma}=0. \tag{28}$$

From (28), we obtain

$$A(t)=\exp\left(\left(r+\frac{\theta'\theta}{2\gamma}\right)(T-t)\right),\qquad A(0)=1 \tag{29}$$

Using (29), we obtain

$$U(t,v)=\frac{v^{1-\gamma}}{1-\gamma}\exp\left(\left(r+\frac{\theta'\theta}{2\gamma}\right)(1-\gamma)(T-t)\right),\qquad U(T,v)=\frac{v^{1-\gamma}}{1-\gamma}. \tag{30}$$

Figure 4 was obtained by setting $D_0=100$, $r=0.04$, $k=0.099$, $T=10$, $\sigma_1^D=0.25$, $\sigma_2^D=0.36$, $\rho=0.6$, $\mu=0.09$, $\sigma_S=0.4$, $\sigma_I=0.3$ and $\theta_I=0.08$.

Figure 4 shows the expected value of utility of wealth at time $t\in[0,10]$ for different values of γ. Here, γ measures the level of risk the investor is willing to take. Observe that the smaller the value of γ, the higher the expected value of wealth, and vice versa. Therefore, when $\gamma=0.07$, the expected value of utility of wealth, $U(t,v)=U(10,v)=2780.9$, when $\gamma=0.08$, $U(10,v)=2271.5$, when $\gamma=0.09$, $U(10,v)=1914.1$ and when $\gamma=0.10$, $U(10,v)=1648.7$. Hence, the lower the rate at which investors are risk averse, the more the wealth that will accrue to them, and vice versa, which is an intuitive result.

Proposition 6:

Suppose that $U(t,V)$ is the solution of the HJB Equation (26), then the optimal portfolio in inflation-linked bond, stock and cash account are given by

$$\Delta_I^*(t)=\frac{\theta_I V^*(t)}{\gamma X^*(t)}-\frac{\sigma_1^D\Psi(t)}{\sigma_I X^*(t)}. \tag{31}$$

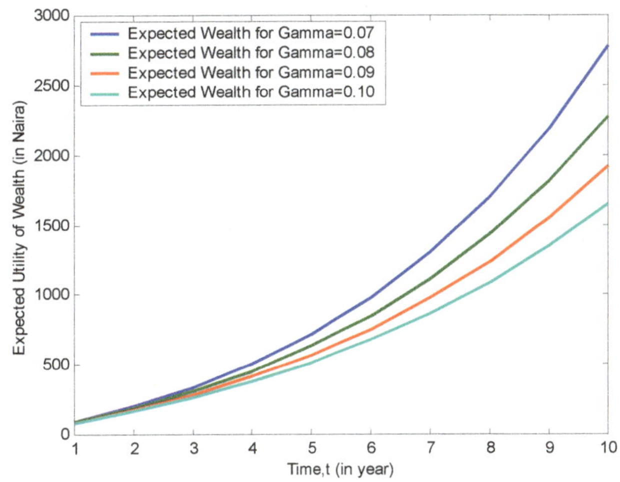

Figure 4. The expected value of utility of wealth for different values of γ.

$$\Delta_S^*(t)=\frac{\left(\sigma_I(\mu-r)+\theta_I\sigma_S\rho\left(\sigma_S\sqrt{1-\rho^2}-\sigma_I\right)\right)V^*(t)}{\gamma(1-\rho^2)\sigma_I\sigma_S^2X^*(t)}-\frac{\left(\sigma_I\sigma_2^D-\sigma_S\sigma_1^D\rho\right)\Psi(t)}{\sigma_I\sigma_S\sqrt{1-\rho^2}X^*(t)}. \tag{32}$$

$$\Delta_0^*(t)=1-\frac{V^*(t)}{X^*(t)}\left(\frac{\theta_I}{\gamma}+\frac{\left(\sigma_I(\mu-r)+\theta_I\sigma_S\rho\left(\sigma_S\sqrt{1-\rho^2}-\sigma_I\right)\right)}{\gamma(1-\rho^2)\sigma_I\sigma_S^2}\right)+\frac{\Psi(t)}{X^*(t)}\left(\frac{\sigma_1^D}{\sigma_I}+\frac{\left(\sigma_I\sigma_2^D-\sigma_S\sigma_1^D\rho\right)}{\sigma_I\sigma_S\sqrt{1-\rho^2}}\right).$$

Proof. From (25), we have that

$$\Delta^*(t)=\frac{(\Sigma^2)^{-1}\lambda V^*(t)}{\gamma X^*(t)}-\frac{\Sigma^{-1}\sigma_D\Psi(t)}{X^*(t)}.$$

But,

$$\Sigma^{-1}\sigma_D=\begin{pmatrix}\dfrac{\sigma_1^D}{\sigma_I}\\[2ex]\dfrac{\sigma_I\sigma_2^D-\sigma_S\sigma_1^D\rho}{\sigma_S\sigma_I\sqrt{1-\rho^2}}\end{pmatrix}$$

$$\Sigma^{-2}\lambda=\begin{pmatrix}\dfrac{\theta_I}{\sigma_I}\\[2ex]\dfrac{\sigma_I(\mu-r)+\sigma_S\theta_I\rho\left(\sigma_S\sqrt{1-\rho^2}-\sigma_I\right)}{\sigma_S^2\sigma_I(1-\rho^2)}\end{pmatrix}$$

Therefore,

$$\Delta^*(t)=\begin{pmatrix}\Delta_I^*(t)\\ \Delta_S^*(t)\end{pmatrix}=\frac{V^*(t)}{\gamma X^*(t)}\begin{pmatrix}\dfrac{\theta_I}{\sigma_I}\\ \dfrac{\sigma_I(\mu-r)+\sigma_S\theta_I\rho\left(\sigma_S\sqrt{1-\rho^2}-\sigma_I\right)}{\sigma_S^2\sigma_I\left(1-\rho^2\right)}\end{pmatrix}-\frac{\Psi(t)}{X^*(t)}\begin{pmatrix}\dfrac{\sigma_1^D}{\sigma_I}\\ \dfrac{\sigma_I\sigma_2^D-\sigma_S\sigma_1^D\rho}{\sigma_S\sigma_I\sqrt{1-\rho^2}}\end{pmatrix}$$

$$=\begin{pmatrix}\dfrac{\theta_I V^*(t)}{\sigma_I\gamma X^*(t)}\\ \dfrac{\left(\sigma_I(\mu-r)+\sigma_S\theta_I\rho\left(\sigma_S\sqrt{1-\rho^2}-\sigma_I\right)\right)V^*(t)}{\sigma_S^2\sigma_I\left(1-\rho^2\right)\gamma X^*(t)}\end{pmatrix}-\begin{pmatrix}\dfrac{\sigma_1^D\Psi(t)}{\sigma_I X^*(t)}\\ \dfrac{\left(\sigma_I\sigma_2^D-\sigma_S\sigma_1^D\rho\right)\Psi(t)}{\sigma_S\sigma_I\sqrt{1-\rho^2}X^*(t)}\end{pmatrix}$$

$$=\begin{pmatrix}\dfrac{\theta_I V^*(t)}{\sigma_I\gamma X^*(t)}-\dfrac{\sigma_1^D\Psi(t)}{\sigma_I X^*(t)}\\ \dfrac{\left(\sigma_I(\mu-r)+\sigma_S\theta_I\rho\left(\sigma_S\sqrt{1-\rho^2}-\sigma_I\right)\right)V^*(t)}{\sigma_S^2\sigma_I\left(1-\rho^2\right)\gamma X^*(t)}-\dfrac{\left(\sigma_I\sigma_2^D-\sigma_S\sigma_1^D\rho\right)\Psi(t)}{\sigma_S\sigma_I\sqrt{1-\rho^2}X^*(t)}\end{pmatrix}$$

It implies that

$$\Delta_I^*(t)=\frac{\theta_I V^*(t)}{\gamma X^*(t)}-\frac{\sigma_1^D\Psi(t)}{\sigma_I X^*(t)}. \quad (33)$$

$$\Delta_S^*(t)=\frac{\left(\sigma_I(\mu-r)+\theta_I\sigma_S\rho\left(\sigma_S\sqrt{1-\rho^2}-\sigma_I\right)\right)V^*(t)}{\gamma\left(1-\rho^2\right)\sigma_I\sigma_S^2X^*(t)}-\frac{\left(\sigma_I\sigma_2^D-\sigma_S\sigma_1^D\rho\right)\Psi(t)}{\sigma_I\sigma_S\sqrt{1-\rho^2}X^*(t)}. \quad (34)$$

$$\Delta_0^*(t)=1-\left(\frac{\theta_I V^*(t)}{\gamma X^*(t)}+\frac{\left(\sigma_I(\mu-r)+\theta_I\sigma_S\rho\left(\sigma_S\sqrt{1-\rho^2}-\sigma_I\right)\right)V^*(t)}{\gamma\left(1-\rho^2\right)\sigma_I\sigma_S^2X^*(t)}\right)+\frac{\sigma_1^D\Psi(t)}{\sigma_I X^*(t)}+\frac{\left(\sigma_I\sigma_2^D-\sigma_S\sigma_1^D\rho\right)\Psi(t)}{\sigma_I\sigma_S\sqrt{1-\rho^2}X^*(t)}. \quad (35)$$

From (33), the first term represents the classical portfolio strategy while the second term represents the intertemporal hedging strategy that offset any shock to the SCI at time *t*. From (34), $\dfrac{\left(\sigma_I(\mu-r)+\theta_I\sigma_S\rho\left(\sigma_S\sqrt{1-\rho^2}-\sigma_I\right)\right)V^*(t)}{\gamma\left(1-\rho^2\right)\sigma_I\sigma_S^2X^*(t)}$ represents the classical portfolio strategy at time t and $\dfrac{\left(\sigma_I\sigma_2^D-\sigma_S\sigma_1^D\rho\right)\Psi(t)}{\sigma_I\sigma_S\sqrt{1-\rho^2}X^*(t)}$ represents the intertemporal hedging term that offset shock resulting from the SCI at time t. From (35), observe that these hedging terms can be transfer to cash account at time t or it can be reinvest in stock and in inflation-linked bond at time t.

Figure 5 was obtained by setting $D_0=100$, $r=0.04$, $k=0.099$, $T=10$, $\sigma_1^D=0.25$, $\sigma_2^D=0.36$, $\rho=0.6$, $\mu=0.09$, $\sigma_S=0.4$, $\sigma_I=0.3$, $\theta_I=0.08$ and $\gamma=0.5$. The optimal portfolio value in inflation-linked bond at time $t=10$ is obtained as 0.16 (or 16%).

Figure 6 was obtained by setting $D_0=100$, $r=0.04$, $k=0.099$, $T=10$, $\sigma_1^D=0.25$, $\sigma_2^D=0.36$, $\rho=0.6$, $\mu=0.09$, $\sigma_S=0.4$, $\sigma_I=0.3$, $\theta_I=0.08$ and $\gamma=0.5$. The optimal portfolio value in stock at time $t=10$ is obtained as 1.001562 (or 100.1562%).

Figure 7 was obtained by setting $D_0=100$, $r=0.04$, $k=0.099$, $T=10$, $\sigma_1^D=0.25$, $\sigma_2^D=0.36$, $\rho=0.6$, $\mu=0.09$, $\sigma_S=0.4$, $\sigma_I=0.3$, $\theta_I=0.08$ and $\gamma=0.5$. The optimal portfolio value in cash account at time $t=10$ is obtained as −0.161562 (or −16.1562%).

In **Figures 5-7**, we set $D_0=100$, $r=0.04$, $k=0.099$, $T=10$, $\sigma_1^D=0.25$, $\sigma_2^D=0.36$, $\rho=0.6$, $\mu=0.09$, $\sigma_S=0.4$, $\sigma_I=0.3$, $\theta_I=0.08$ and $\gamma=0.10$. **Figure 5** shows the portfolio value in inflation-linked bond. We found that the optimal portfolio value in inflation-linked bond at time $t=10$ is 0.16 (or 16%). **Figure 6** shows the portfolio value in stock. We found that the optimal portfolio value in stock at time $t=10$ is 1.001562 (or 100.1562%). **Figure 7** shows the portfolio value in cash

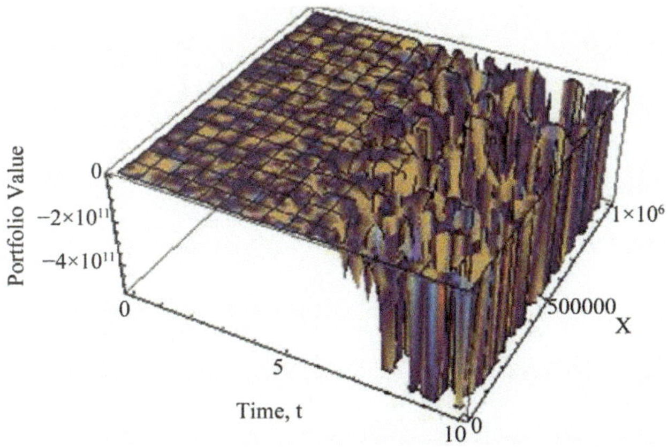

Figure 5. Portfolio value in inflation-linked bond.

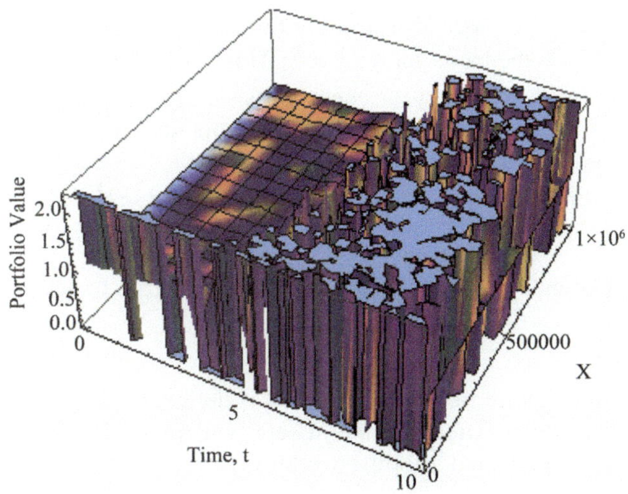

Figure 6. Portfolio value in stock.

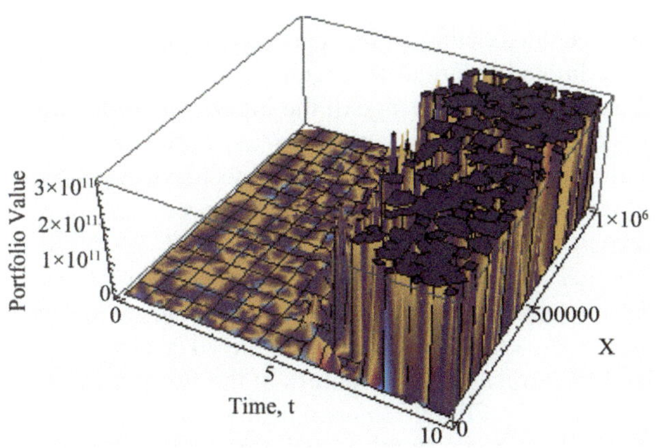

Figure 7. Portfolio value in cash account.

account. We found that the optimal portfolio value in cash account at time $t = 10$ is -0.161562 (or -16.1562%).

7. Conclusion

The optimal portfolio strategy X with discounted stochastic cash inflows was considered. It was assumed that the cash inflow, stock and inflation-linked bond are stochastic and follow a standard geometric Brownian motion. The sensitivity analysis of the present value of the discounted cash inflows was carried out in this paper and the results are presented in **Table 1**. Analytical solution to the resulting HJB equation was obtained. It was found that the smaller the value of γ (which measure the level of risk the investor is willing to take), the higher the expected value of wealth, and vice versa. The optimal portfolio values in stock, inflation-linked bond and cash account were obtained. The resulting optimal portfolio values in stock and inflation-linked bond were found to involve intertemporal hedging terms that offset any shock to the SCI.

REFERENCES

[1] G. Deelstra, M. Grasselli and P. Koehl, "Optimal Investment Strategies in a CIR Framework," *Journal of Applied Probability*, Vol. 37, No. 4, 2000, pp. 936-946.

[2] D. O. Cajueiro and T. Yoneyama, "Optimal Portfolio, Optimal Consumption and the Markowitz Mean-Variance Analysis in a Switching Diffusion Market," 2003. unb.br/face/eco/seminarios/sem0803.pdf

[3] A. Zaks, "Present Value of Annuities under Random Rates of Interest," 2003. http://academic.research.microsoft.com/Publication/6244175/present-value-of-annuities-under-random-rates-of-interest

[4] D. Dentcheva and A. Ruszczynski, "Portfolio Optimization with Stochastic Dominance Constraints," *SIAM Journal on Optimization*, Vol. 14, No. 2, 2003, pp. 548-566.

[5] D. Blake, "Efficiency, Risk Aversion and Portfolio Insurance: An Analysis of Financial Asset Portfolios Held by Investors in the United Kindom," *Economic Journal*, Vol. 106, No. 438, 1996, pp. 1175-1192.

[6] A. Zhang, "Stochastic Optimization in Finance and Life Insurance: Applications of the Martingale Method," Ph.D. Thesis, University of Kaiserslauten, Kaiserslautern, 2007.

[7] J. Mukuddem-Peterson, M. A. Peterson and I. M. Schoeman, "An Application of Stochastic Optimization Theory to Institutional Finance," *Applied Mathematics Sciences*, Vol. 1, No. 28, 2007, pp. 1359-1385.

[8] P. Battocchio, "Optimal Portfolio Strategies with Stochastic Wage Income: The Case of a Defined Contribution Pension Plan," Working Paper, Université Catholique de Louvain, Louvain-la-Neuve, 2002.

[9] B. H. Lim and U. J. Choi, "Optimal Consumption and Portfolio Selection with Portfolio Constraints," *International Sciences*, Vol. 4, 2009, pp. 293-309.

[10] C. I. Nkeki, "On Optimal Portfolio Management of the Accumulation Phase of a Defined Contributory Pension Scheme," Ph.D. Thesis, University of Ibadan, Ibadan, 2011.

[11] C. I. Nkeki and C. R. Nwozo, "Variational Form of Classical Portfolio Strategy and Expected Wealth for a Defined Contributory Pension Scheme," *Journal of Mathematical Finance*, Vol. 2, No. 1, 2012, pp. 132-139.

12

Super-Diffusive Noise Source in Asset Dynamics

Max-Olivier Hongler
Ecole Polytechnique Fédérale de Lausanne (EPFL), IMT/STI/LPM, Lausanne, Switzerland

ABSTRACT

Given an asset with value S_t, we revisit the Black and Scholes dynamics $\mathrm{d}\left[\log(S_t)\right]/\mathrm{d}t = \mu + \xi_t$ when the driving noise ξ_t is a non-Gaussian super-diffusive stochastic process with variance of the type $t + \gamma t^2$. This super-diffusive quadratic variance behavior, synthesizes a ballistic component which would occur in strongly fluctuating environments. When $\gamma > \mu$, the assets can, with high probability, be driven towards the bankruptcy $S = 0$. This extra dynamic feature significantly affects the management of an optimal portfolio. In this context, we focus on basic decisions like: 1) determine the optimal level to sell the asset; 2) determine how to balance a portfolio which incorporates such a high volatility asset; and 3) when facing incertitudes on the asset's growth rate μ, construct an optimal adaptive portfolio control. In all mentioned cases and despite the presence of this highly non-Gaussian noise source, we are able to deliver simple exact and fully explicit optimal control rules.

Keywords: Black-Scholes Dynamics; Non-Gaussian Volatility; Optimal Stopping; Adaptive Optimal Control; Exact Solutions

1. Asset Dynamics Driven by a Super-Diffusive Noise Source

For time $t \in \mathbb{R}^+$, let us consider the basic scalar Black and Schole (BS) type dynamics

$$\dot{S}_t = S_t\left[\mu + \xi_t\right], \quad \mu > 0, S_0 > 0, \tag{1}$$

where the driving process ξ_t is generally a not White Gaussian noise (WGN) stochastic process. In presence of such a general noise source, the solution process S_t Equation (1) is generally not Markovian. Accordingly, besides the initial position S_0, additional information regarding the state of the noise source ξ_t is mandatory to characterize the time-dpendent statistical properties of S_t. Contrary to the "classical" BS driven by the WGN, optimal asset management, based on optimal stopping rules and/or optimal dynamic portfolio composition, cannot be taken based solely on information of the asset's value level at a given initial time. This seems truly natural, indeed decisions taken under random environments often rely not only on S_0 but possibly on additional features characterizing the underlying fluctuation processes, in particular non vanishing correlations. Hence, often actual applications requires that one escapes the pure WGN's world. In finance, this aspect has been essentially pioneered in [1] and subsequently it triggered a strong research activity involving non-Gaussian volatility models. Another, though intimately related, dynamic feature of the environment is definitely played by correlations affecting the assets volatility. This last aspect motivated a former work of ours [2], in which we fully and exactly discuss optimal stopping issues for the dynamics Equation (1) when ξ_t is an alternating Markovian renewal process, (*i.e.* a continuous time two-states Markov chain). In this particular case, besides S_0, the additional information required to construct optimal decisions is the knowledge of the initial state of the noise source, *i.e.* one basically needs to know whether initially the noise tendency is to increase or decrease the nominal growth rate μ. As general noise sources are finitely correlated, contrary to the δ-correlated WGN, they potentially offer a more realistic stylization of actual environment. This general remark contributes to motivate our present note where we shall unveil a class of elementary correlated noise sources in the BS dynamics for which we are still able to analytically master the mathematical description. In the sequel, for $t \geq t_0$, we focus on the dynamics:

$$\begin{cases} dS_t = S_t\left[\mu dt + dZ_t\right], & \mu > 0, S_0 > 0, \\ dZ_t = \gamma \tanh[\gamma Z_t \mid dt + dW_t, & Z_0 = 0, \end{cases} \tag{2}$$

where the dZ_t-noise source obeys the scalar diffusion process

$$dZ_t = \gamma \tanh[\gamma Z_t \mid dt + dW_t, \qquad Z_0 = 0, \tag{3}$$

with $\gamma > 0$ a given constant and W_t a standard Wiener process. For the highly non-Gaussian process defined by Equation (3), one can nevertheless derive the very simple properties of the transition probability density, (see for examples [3] and [4]):

$$P(z,t \mid 0,t_0) = \frac{1}{2}\left[G_+(z,t \mid 0,t_0) + G_-(z,t \mid 0,t_0)\right], \quad (4)$$

with the definition:

$$G_\pm(z,t \mid 0,t_0) = \frac{e^{\frac{-[z \pm \gamma(t-t_0)]^2}{2(t-t_0)}}}{\sqrt{2\pi(t-t_0)}}. \quad (5)$$

The use of Equation (4) implies that the first moment and the covariance respectively read:

$$\begin{cases} \langle Z_t \rangle = 0, \\ \langle Z_t Z_s \rangle = \gamma^2 st + \min\{s,t\}. \end{cases} \quad (6)$$

Besides enjoying the simple moments given in Equation (6), it has been shown in [5], that the process dZ_t is the unique non-Gaussain stochastic process that exhibits Brownian bridges. The superposition of a couple of Gaussian densities appearing in Equation (4), suggests that the process Equation (3) can alternatively be represented in another manner and indeed, as it has been rigorously shown in [6], the Z_t realizations coincide with those obtained from the couple of drifted Brownian motions:

$$dZ_t = (\mathcal{B}\gamma)dt + dW_t, \qquad Z_0 = 0, \quad (7)$$

where $\mathcal{B} \in \{-1,+1\}$ is a W_t-independent Bernoulli random variable (r.v.) taking the values $\pm\{1\}$ with symmetric probability $1/2$. In other words, the process described by Equation (7) should be understood as follows: "*at initial time operate the Bernoulli choice of the drift and then evolve according to the resulting* $\pm\gamma$*-drifted Brownian motion*".

At this stage, we emphasize that the process $(\mathcal{B}, W_t, \ln(S_t))$ is a degenerate Markovian diffusion process on the state space $\{\{-1\},\{+1\}\} \times \mathbb{R}^2$. Using the noise representation given by Equation (4) into the basic dynamics Equation (2), we can directly calculate the marginal probability density $P_m(s,t \mid s_0) := \int_{\mathbb{R}} P(s,z \mid s_0,0)\mathrm{d}z$ and it takes the form:

$$\begin{cases} P_m(s,t \mid s_0)ds = \frac{1}{2}\left[G_+(s,t \mid s_0) + G_-(s,t \mid s_0)\right]ds, \\ G_\pm(s,t \mid s_0)ds = \frac{1}{\sqrt{2\pi t}} e^{\frac{-[\log(s)-\log(s_0)-(\mu\pm\gamma)t]^2}{2t}} d[\log(s)]. \end{cases} \quad (8)$$

Hence, for strong ballistic component occurring when $\gamma > \mu$, the minus part of the $G_-(s,t \mid s_0)$ marginal density converges, in the long run, to the Dirac delta probability mass:

$$\lim_{t\to\infty} G_-(s,t \mid s_0) = \delta(s). \quad (9)$$

Equation (9) therefore shows that even for strictly positive asset's growth rate, (*i.e.* $\mu > 0$), the super-diffusive noise in Equation (2) can actually drive the process towards the bankrupt state $S = 0$ with probability $(1/2)$ given by Equation (8). The possibility to reach a bankrupt state with high probability should prepare us to derive new optimal management policies for such strongly fluctuating assets. At this stage, it should already be clear that the noise source representation in Equation (4) offers a very simple mathematical approach to discuss several non trivial problems in finance and this will be explicitly explored in the next sections.

2. Optimal Level to Sell an Asset

Consider the standard BS dynamics as given by Equation (2) with $\gamma = 0$, (hence $dZ_t = dW_t$). One naturally asks to determine the critical level S^* at which one should optimally sell the asset when the utility function is:

$$\mathbb{E}\left\{e^{-\rho\tau}[S_\tau - a] \mid S_0\right\}. \quad (10)$$

In Equation (10) ρ is a discounting rate, which will be chosen such that $\rho > \mu$ and $a > 0$ is a transaction cost. As it is explicitly discussed in Section 10.2.2 in [7], the exact solution of this optimal stopping problem recommends sale of the asset when its value equals or exceeds the optimal level S^* given by:

$$S^* = a\frac{\lambda}{\lambda - 1} \text{ with}$$
$$\lambda = \left[\left(\frac{1}{2} - \mu\right) + \sqrt{\left(\frac{1}{2} - \mu\right)^2 + 2\rho}\right] > 1. \quad (11)$$

For $\gamma = 0$ in Equation (2), the process S_t alone is Markovian. Hence, only the observation of the asset level enables to take the optimal decision. On the contrary, when $\gamma > 0$, the S_t process alone does not remain Markovian, (due to correlations of the noise source dZ_t), and therefore an optimal selling decision can only be taken if we provide additional information regarding the noise source. The Bernoulli representation in Equation (7) shows that the knowledge of the initial realization of the r.v. $\mathcal{B}$ is here the required additional information. Once this information is available, one is very directly driven to consider separately the following couple of regimes:

- The realization of the Bernoulli variable is $\mathcal{B} = 1$. This implies:

a) $\mu + \gamma > \rho \Rightarrow$ never sell the asset (*i.e* the utility steadily continues to increase leading the stopping time to be $\tau = \infty$).

b) $\mu+\gamma<\rho \Rightarrow$ use directly the result given by Equation (11) with the substitution $\mu \mapsto \mu+\gamma$.

- The realization of the Bernoulli variable is $\mathcal{B}=-1$. This implies:

a) $0<\mu-\gamma<\rho \Rightarrow$ use directly the result given by Equation (11) with the substitution $\mu \mapsto \mu-\gamma$.

b) $\mu-\gamma<0 \Rightarrow$ bankruptcy is reached with probability $(1/2)$ and according to Equation (9) one should sell the asset immediately at time $\tau=0$.

3. Optimal Portfolio Dynamic Balancing

Here, one asks to determine the optimal portfolio proportion between a risky asset $S_{1,t}$ and a fully safe one $S_{2,t}$, in order to ensure that, at a given time horizon T, the maximal utility, say $U(T)$, will be achieved. For the WGN driving noise, this problem is explicitly solved in Example 11.2.5 in [7]. The dynamics of the couple of assets reads:

$$\begin{cases} dS_{1,t}=S_{1,t}\left[adt+dW_t\right], & S_{1,t=0}=s_{1,0}, \\ dS_{2,t}=bS_{2,t}dt, & S_{2,t=0}=s_{2,0}. \end{cases} \quad (12)$$

where $a>b$ are the asset's growth rates. By writing $p(t)$ the proportion of the capital invested in the risky asset at time t, the resulting capital dynamics C_t evolves as

$$dC_t=p(t)C_t\left[adt+dW_t\right]+\left(1-p(t)\right)bC_t. \quad (13)$$

For the specific class of utility functions given by:

$$U(t)=\begin{cases} 0 & \text{for } 0\le t<T, \\ \left(C_T\right)^{\alpha} & \text{for } t=T, \alpha>1, \end{cases} \quad (14)$$

it is established in [7] that the optimal proportion p^* is

$$p^*=\frac{a-b}{\alpha-1}. \quad (15)$$

Accordingly the optimal portfolio balance will be realized by:

$$\begin{cases} p^*>1 & \Rightarrow \text{invest all the capital in asset } S_1, \\ 0<p^*<1 & \Rightarrow \text{compose with fixed proportion} \\ & \quad\ p^* \text{ as in Equation (15),} \\ p^*<0 & \Rightarrow \text{invest all the capital in the fully} \\ & \quad\ \text{safe asset } S_2. \end{cases} \quad (16)$$

When replacing dW_t in Equation (12) with our correlated noise source dZ_t defined in Equation (3), the resulting process $S_{1,t}$ does not remain Markovian. Hence, the optimal portfolio can only be determined provided additional information on the noise Z_t is given. Again this information is contained in the initial value taken by the r.v. $\mathcal{B}$ in Equation (7). Accordingly, the optimal portfolio composition initially given by Equation (15) now has to be modified to take into account the noise correlations. According to the value taken by $\mathcal{B}$, two alternative optimal proportions are found:

$$\begin{cases} p_+^*=\dfrac{a+\gamma-b}{\alpha-1} & \text{when the initial realization is } \mathcal{B}=+1, \\ p_-^*=\dfrac{a-\gamma-b}{\alpha-1} & \text{when the initial realization is } \mathcal{B}=-1. \end{cases} \quad (17)$$

and consequently, the optimal decisions will be given by Equation (16) with the modified proportions given by Equation (17).

4. Adaptive Optimal Control Problem

We have seen in Sections 2 and 3, that, in presence of the ballistic noise source Z_t, the construction of optimal decisions necessarily require knowledge of the initial realization of $\mathcal{B}$. Now, one may wonder, whether only a partial knowledge of Z_t could be compensated by an ad-hoc adaptive control policy enabling, as time evolves, to estimate part of the missing information. Specifically, let us assume that we a priori know the value of γ in Equation (3) but we however ignore the actual realization $\{\{-1\},\{+1\}\}$ initially taken by $\mathcal{B}$. As time evolves, an ad-hoc estimator gains sufficient information on Z_t to enable the construction of optimal stategies. This problematic has been formalized by I. Karatzas [8] for WGN driving noise. In this section, we will extend Karatzas' results for the Z_t noise source. Following the lines exposed in [8], we start by considering the stochastic process:

$$Y_t=W_t+bt, \qquad t\in[0,T]\subset\mathbb{R}, \quad (18)$$

where b is a random variable with known probability density $\Gamma(b)db$. The r.v. b is assumed to be independent of the Wiener process W_t. We further assume that neither the process W_t nor the value of b can be observed directly. Observations can however be made on the process Y_t itself and we define;

$$X_t=x_0+\int_0^T \pi(s)\mathrm{d}Y_s, \quad x_0\in X_t\in\Omega=[0,1]. \quad (19)$$

In Equation (19), we introduce a control process $\pi(\cdot)$ which aims at maximizing the probability to reach the right-endpoint of the interval Ω within a fixed time horizon $t=T$. To fix the ideas, one may for example interpret the process X_t to represent the logarithm of an asset value S_t as in Equation (1). Let us write $V(x_0)$ for the value function of the resulting **adaptive optimal control problem** (AOCP) and therefore we formally express:

$$V(x_0)=\sup_{\pi(\cdot)}\left\{\mathbf{P}\left(X^{x_0,\pi}(T)=1\right)\right\}, \qquad x_0\in[0,1]. \quad (20)$$

Writing $\hat{\pi}$ the corresponding optimal control, Equation (20) therefore reads:

$$V(x_0) = \mathbf{P}\left(X^{x_0,\hat{\pi}}(T) = 1\right) \in [0,1], \qquad x_0 \in [0,1].$$

In a remarkable contribution [8], Karrazas solves the above AOCP for pure BM noise sources. For this case, $V(x_0)$ is shown to obey a dynamic programming equation (DPE) exhibiting the form of a parabolic Monge-Ampère partial differential equation:

$$\begin{cases} 2Q_s(s,x,y)Q_{xx}(s,x,y) \\ = Q_{xx}(s,x,y)Q_{yy}(s,x,y) - \left[Q_{x,y}(s,x,y)\right]^2, \\ Q(T,x_0,0) := V(x_0) \end{cases} \tag{21}$$

and Equation (21) is supplemented by a set of appropriate boundary conditions to be found in [8]. The associated optimal control $\hat{\pi}(t)$ is given by:

$$\hat{\pi}(t) = -\frac{Q_{xy}}{Q_{xx}}\left(T-t, X^{x_0,\hat{\pi}}(t), Y(t)\right), \quad 0 \le t \le T. \tag{22}$$

Let us now consider a fully similar problem by replacing the BM with the super-diffusive noise Equation (3). Thanks to the noise representation given in Equation (7), one concludes that when substituting dZ_t in place of dW_t in Equation (18), the Karatzas' approach and results Equations (18)-(20) can be straight-forwardly used provided one simply modifies the original probability distribution $\Gamma(b)$ by the convolution:

$$\Gamma_\gamma(b) = 1/2\int_{\mathbb{R}}\Gamma(b-u)\left[\delta(u-\gamma)+\delta(u+\gamma)\right]\mathrm{d}u = \frac{\Gamma(\gamma+b)+\Gamma(b-\gamma)}{2}. \tag{23}$$

Hence, invoking [8] together with Equation (23), two possible regimes differentiated by the support of $\Gamma_\gamma(b)$ have to be considered separately:

1) $\Gamma_\gamma(b)$ *has its support strictly lying on either the positive or the negative axis.* In this case, the optimal control policy can be derived and it obeys a *certainty-equivalence principle* (CEP) holds. To briefly explain the CEP mechanism, assume first that the optimal policy holding when the parameter $b = b_d$ is known with certainty in Equation (18) is explicitly known. When b is unknown but drawn from a probability distribution $\Gamma_\gamma(b)$, the CEP ensures that replacing b_d by a suitable optimal time-depend estimator of $\hat{b}(t)$ yields the optimal control.

2) $\Gamma_\gamma(b)$ *has its support simultaneously lying on the positive and negative axis.* In this situation, [8] shows that drastically different optimal control policy holds.

The previous classification therefore depends intimately on the noise amplitude γ in Equation (3) and for both situations 1) and 2) and fully explicit results are available, (see **Appendix**). For large values of γ, *i.e.* highly volatile noise sources, (see Equation (6)), the drastic difference between cases 1) and 2) can be traced back to the possibility to effectively have negative drifts (*i.e.* $\mu-\gamma<0$) with probability $(1/2)$. When such negative drifts occur, the use of the *certainty-equivalence principle* (CEP) is precluded and the resulting optimal control is structurally different.

Explicit illustration. Consider the case where $b = b_d > 0$ is exactly known and therefore $\Gamma(b) = \delta(b-b_d)$ in presence of the Z_t noise source. In this case, Equation (23) reduces to

$$\Gamma_\gamma(b) = 1/2\left[\delta(b+b_d-\gamma)+\delta(b+b_d+\gamma)\right] \tag{24}$$

and let us assume that $b_d > \gamma$, hence we are in case 1). For the WGN, *i.e.* when $\gamma = 0$, it follows from the pioneering work [9], (see Appendix), that the corresponding value function $V(x_0,T)$ and optimal control $\hat{\pi}(t)$ read:

$$\begin{cases} V(x_0,T) = \Phi\left[\Phi^{-1}(x_0)+b_d\sqrt{T}\right], \\ \hat{\pi}(t) = \dfrac{\operatorname{sign}(b_d)}{\sqrt{T-t}}\varphi\left[\dfrac{Y(t)+\sqrt{T}\Phi^{-1}(x_0)}{\sqrt{T-t}}\right]. \end{cases} \tag{25}$$

where the notation are given in Appendix, see Equations (29) and (30). Now in presence of the Z_t noise Equation (3), *i.e.* when $\gamma > 0$ and assuming $0<\gamma<b_d$, the use of Equation (6.5') in [8], (*i.e.* Equation (28) in the Appendix) with Equation (24) implies that Equation (25) has to be modified as:

$$\begin{cases} V(x_0,T) = \dfrac{1}{2}\left\{\Phi\left[\Phi^{-1}(x_0)+(b_d+\gamma)\sqrt{T}\right] + \Phi\left[\Phi^{-1}(x_0)+(b_d-\gamma)\sqrt{T}\right]\right\} \\ \hat{\pi}(t) = \dfrac{\operatorname{sign}\left[\hat{b}(t)\right]}{\sqrt{T-t}}\varphi\left[\dfrac{Y(t)+\sqrt{T}\Phi^{-1}(x_0)}{\sqrt{T-t}}\right] \\ = \dfrac{1}{\sqrt{T-t}}\varphi\left[\dfrac{Y(t)+\sqrt{T}\Phi^{-1}(x_0)}{\sqrt{T-t}}\right]. \end{cases} \tag{26}$$

Equation (26) directly follows from the CEP which holds since $b_d > \gamma$ implies that $\Gamma_\gamma(b)$ has a positive definite support. Hence substituting $\operatorname{sign}(b_d) \mapsto \operatorname{sign}\left[\hat{b}(t)\right]$ yields the optimal control in presence of the super-diffusive noise. Here the explicit form of the estimator $\hat{b}(t)$ can be explicitly found by using of Equation (4.4) of [8] and Equation (24) and for $0 < t \le T$, we have:

$$\begin{cases} \Gamma_\gamma(b) = \dfrac{1}{2}\left[\delta(b+b_d-\gamma)+\delta(b+b_d+\gamma)\right], \\ \hat{b}(t) = \dfrac{\mathrm{d}}{\mathrm{d}y}\log\left\{\displaystyle\int_{\mathbb{R}}\left[\mathrm{e}^{by-\frac{b^2}{2}t}\right]\Gamma_\gamma(b)\mathrm{d}b\right\}\Big|_{y=Y(t)} \\ = b_d + \gamma\tanh\left[\gamma Y(t)\right]. \end{cases} \tag{27}$$

and therefore $\text{sign}\left[\hat{b}(t)\right]=1$ as already written in Equation (26).

Let us close this section by a couple of remarks:

a) For a given fixed drift, when $\Gamma(b)=\delta(b-b_d)$, and with BM driving noise, the optimal control is given by Equation (25) and its form is independent of the volatility amplitude. This is drastically different for non-Gaussian Z_t as the volatility amplitude γ drastically affects the structure of the optimal control;

b) In this model, the information a priori required to construct the optimal control is the volatility amplitude of γ only and not initial knowledge of the initial realization of $\mathcal{B}$. It is the adaptive filtering mechanism which provides the missing information on $\mathcal{B}$. This has therefore to be contrasted with the former situations encountered in sections 2 and 3 where both γ and initial realization of $\mathcal{B}$ are a priori needed.

5. Conclusion

While several dynamical situations involving stochastic differential equations driven by the super-diffusive noise source Equation (3) have recently received attention in physics [3,4] and various optimal control problems [10], the use of this noise source in finance remains yet unexplored and this motivates our present note. As the super-diffusive noise produces a quadratic increase of the variance, (*i.e.* volatility) with time, it may lead the assets towards the bankrupt state with high probability. When bankruptcy becomes highly probable, one observes rather drastic modifications in all optimal stopping decisions and portfolio's compositions. These modifications are easily calculated for the super-diffusive noise source Equation (3). This offers the possibility, in a very simple way, to investigate exactly non-Gaussain and correlation's effects in assets dynamics. The super-diffusive noise source used here provides a simple and quite efficient didactical tool to escape the ubiquitous Gaussian world in which most exactly soluble models belong.

6. Acknowledgements

This work has been partially supported by the Swiss National Foundation for Scientific Research. I benefit from constructive discussions with Dr. R. Filliger and Dr. F. Hashemi.

REFERENCES

[1] O. E. Barndorff-Nielsen and N. Shepard, "Non-Gaussian Ornstein-Uhlenbeck-Based Models and Some of Their Uses in Financial Economics," *Journal of the Royal Statistical Society*, Vol. 63, No. 2, 2001, pp. 167-241.

[2] R. C. Dalang and M.-O. Hongler, "The Right Time to Sell a Stock Whose Price Is Driven by Markovian Noise," *Annals of Applied Probability*, Vol. 14, No. 4, 2004, pp. 2176-2201.

[3] M.-O. Hongler, R. Filliger and P. Blanchard, "Soluble Models for a Dynamics Driven by Super-Diffuisve Noise," *Physica A: Statistical Mechanics and Its Applications*, Vol. 370, No. 2, 2006, pp. 301-315.

[4] M.-O. Hongler, R. Filliger, P. Blanchard and J. Rodriguez, "On Stochastic Processes Driven by Ballistic Noise Sources," In: A. Adhikari, M. R. Adhikari and Y. P. Chaubey, Eds., *Contemporary Topics in Mathematics and Statistics with Applications*, Asian Books Private Ltd., New Delhi, 2003.

[5] I. Benjamini and S. Lee, "Conditional Diffusions Which Are Brownian Bridges," *Journal of Theoretical Probability*, Vol. 10, No. 3, 1997, pp. 733-736.

[6] L. C. G. Rogers and J. W. Pitman, "Markov Functions," *Annals of Probability*, Vol. 9, No. 4, 1981, pp. 573-582.

[7] B. Øksendal, "Stochastic Differential Equations—An Introduction with Applications," Springer, Berlin, 1998.

[8] I. Karatzas, "Adaptive Control of a Diffusion to a Goal and a Parabolic Monge-Ampère Equation," *The Asian Journal of Mathematics*, Vol. 1, No. 2, 1997, pp. 295-313.

[9] M. Kulldorff, "Optimal Control of Favorable Games with a Time Limit," *SIAM Journal on Control and Optimization*, Vol. 31, No. 1, 1993, pp. 52-69.

[10] R. Filliger and M.-O. Hongler, "Explicit Gittins' Indices for a Class of Super-Diffusive Processes," *Journal of Applied Probability*, Vol. 44, No. 2, 2007, pp. 554-559.

Appendix

Here we simply list, some of the results derived in [8]. For $x \in [0,1]$ and $y \in \mathbb{R}$, we have:

Case 1), Probability distribution $\Gamma_\gamma(b)$ has positive support:

$$Q(s,x,y) = \begin{cases} \int_{\mathbb{R}} e^{by - b^2\frac{(T-s)}{2}} \Phi\left[\Phi^{-1}(x_0) + b\sqrt{s}\right]\Gamma_\gamma(b)\,db, \\ 0 < s < T, \\ \left[\int_{\mathbb{R}} e^{\left[by - \frac{b^2 T}{2}\right]}\Gamma_\gamma(b)\,db\right]\mathbb{I}_{\{1\}}(x), \qquad s = 0, \end{cases}$$

$$\hat{\pi}_+(t) = \frac{1}{\sqrt{T-t}} e^{-\frac{\left[Y(t)+\sqrt{T}\left(\Phi^{-1}(x_0)\right)\right]^2}{2(T-t)}} \tag{28}$$

where we use the notation:

$$\Phi(x) = \frac{1}{\sqrt{2\pi}}\int_{-\infty}^{x} e^{-\frac{z^2}{2}}dz = 12\left[1 + \mathrm{Erf}\left(\frac{x}{\sqrt{2}}\right)\right], \tag{29}$$

$$\varphi(x) = \frac{1}{\sqrt{2\pi}} e^{-\frac{x^2}{2}}. \tag{30}$$

For the case probability distribution $\Gamma_\gamma(b)$ with purely negative support, the situation is, up appropriate signs changes, entirely similar and we do not reproduce it here.

Case 2) Support of the probability distribution $\Gamma_\gamma(b)$ without definite sign.

For $x \in [0,1]$ and $y \in \mathbb{R}$ and the notation $A := A(s,y;x)$, $B := B(s,y;x)$:

$$Q(s,x,y) = \begin{cases} \int_{\mathbb{R}} e^{by - b^2\frac{(T-s)}{2}} \left[L(s, y+bs; A, B)\right]\Gamma_\gamma(b)\,db, \\ 0 < s < T, \\ \left[\int_{\mathbb{R}} e^{\left[by - \frac{b^2 T}{2}\right]}\Gamma_\gamma(b)\,db\right]\mathbb{I}_{\{1\}}(x), \quad s = 0, \end{cases}$$

$$\hat{\pi}(t) = \frac{1}{\sqrt{2\pi(T-t)}}\left[e^{-\frac{(Y(t)-A)^2}{2(T-t)}} - e^{-\frac{(Y(t)-B)^2}{2(T-t)}}\right], \tag{31}$$

where:

$$\left[L(s, y+bs; A, B)\right] = 2 - \Phi\left(\frac{A-y}{\sqrt{s}}\right) - \Phi\left(\frac{y-B}{\sqrt{s}}\right) \tag{32}$$

and, for fixed s and y, the quantities $A < B$ are determined by the couple of transcendent equations

$$\begin{cases} L(s,y;A,B) = x, \\ e^{(b+\gamma)A} e^{-\frac{(b+\gamma^2)T}{2}} = e^{(b-\gamma)B} e^{-\frac{(b-\gamma^2)T}{2}} \end{cases} \tag{33}$$

and the optimal value function reads $V(x_0) = Q(T, x_0, 0)$.

13

Sensitivity of the Investments of Sub-Saharan Firms to Financial Constraints

Elie Ngongang
Department of Quantitative Techniques, Faculty of Economic and Management, University of Yaounde II, Yaounde, Cameroon

ABSTRACT

Investment is an important instrument of growth and competitiveness for non financial firms. However, these firms have limited financial resources (or liquidity) at their disposal. The financial constraint is defined as a conditionality to be met in order to have access to liquidity by assuming that the information held by shareholders is perfect, and that financial markets are efficient. We have attempted in this study to analyze empirically the impact of these financial constraint on the investments of Sub-Saharan manufacturing firms. We carried out an empirical analysis of a sample of 73 firms belonging to the different manufacturing sectors listed on the stock market during the period 1998-2009, and by taking inspiration from panel data methodology. The empirical tests emphasize the fact that the manufacturing firms of Sub-Saharan countries, including the smallest ones and those with which financial institutions have no close relations, witness an environment with a strong information asymmetry between borrowers and lenders. These firms are constrained in their access to external indebtedness due to the levelling-off of indebtedness. However, taking account of uncertainty could enrich the extension of this study.

Keywords: Investment; Financial Constraints; Indebtedness; Information Asymmetry; Financial Flows; Sub-Saharan Africa

1. Introduction

Investment is the operation which consists for a firm in increasing its capital stock (machines, equipments of all types, goods of all kinds, etc.) with the prospect of future growth and competitiveness. On the accounting level, it represents an expenditure on a movable, corporeal or incorporeal property acquired or created by the firm, and intended to remain durably in the same form in the firm. On the theoretical level the analyses carried out on the firms' sources of growth, investment takes up a predominant place. Its high volatility contributes to the fluctuations of the firm in a non-negligible way. Its role in the short term and its role in the long term make of investment a key variable for the firm. Understanding the evolution of investment behaviour requires an identification of the main variables which guide this behaviour.

Glesne and Legris [1] assume that investment is the result of the combination: 1) of an opportunity to invest, which may be the occasion of pressure on the firm's demand, added to a shortfall in the production capacity; 2) of the will to invest, which is the direct corollary of the ability of the investment project to satisfy certain requirements of the managers; and 3) of the capacity to invest, which is linked to the possession by the manager of the financial means necessary for the implementation of projects which satisfy the above characteristics. Thus, investment is a particularly decisive variable for non-financial firms. Its degree of aversion to risk is to be taken into account, just as the financing constraint when the firm is set in an environment where it has access to a financial market.

The financial constraint is defined as a conditionality to be met in order to have access to liquidity, by considering the fact that stockholders information is perfect and that financial markets are efficient. The asymmetry of information between stockholders, the banks and executives can modify the structure of financing. It refers to the nature of incentives to the efficiency of the firm's executives.

Investment therefore appears to come under the multiple and complex objectives which must also take account of the influence of long-term programmes that aim at increasing the firms' effectiveness and competitiveness. The investment of manufacturing firms has recently and very often taken the form of external growth, that is, the repurchase of existing firms rather than a physical investment. Generally speaking, these firms increasingly hold securities.

The different financial and econometric approaches to investment collide against the problems of taking account of the financial constraints that keep firms from investing as much as they would wish. Under the assumption of one financial market, Modigliani and Miller [2] demonstrated the absence of interactions between investment and financing.

But during the last twenty five years, the separation between the real sphere and the financial sphere tends to become less pronounced. This situation is due to the development of an abundant theoretical and empirical literature which deals with the impact of financial constraints on the structure of the firm as far as investment is concerned. The study by Fazzari, *et al.* [3] constitutes the point of departure of this empirical literature which is explicitly based on theoretical contributions that deal with the asymmetry of information and its impact on the existence of financial constraints. According to these authors, the firms most likely to be constrained in their external financing are small-sized and young.

Generally speaking, investment is a significant instrument for the growth and competitiveness of non-financial firms. However, they have limited financial resources (liquidities) at their disposal. This problem is recurrent in the non-financial firms of North-American countries (and it increasingly occurs in Sub-Saharan countries) and in the presence of financial constraints due to information asymmetries. The assumption used to detect a financing constraint is that of Fazzari, *et al.* [3]. They distinguished constrained from unconstrained firms through one of the fundamental characteristics of the firm: the availability of internal funds in direct relation with its financial status. But most of the studies do not confirm the results arrived at by these authors. The use of the sensitivity of investment to operating cash flows have generated heterogeneous results, and the most recent studies carried out by Carpenter and Guariglia [4], Gugler, *et al.* [5] have not found definitive answers.

Minton and Schrand [6] used the volatility of internal funds to analyze the impact of the debt or of equity capital on investment. Consequently, the very identification of appropriate criteria to measure the firms' sensitivity to financial ratios gives rise to problems.

One major question emerges from all this development: What is the influence of financial constraints on the investment decisions of Sub-Saharan manufacturing firms? In other words, do financial constraints have an impact on the investments of manufacturing firms in the Sub-Saharan context?

We may envisage several methods for answering these questions. A possible method may consist of specifying a reduced-form model such as Vogt [7], Kaplan and Zingales [8], Heitor and Campello [9] who specify the empirical relationship between Cash-flows, debts, fixed investment capital, and equipment expenditures. Though it is quite interesting, this method become more complex at the level of data, and when there exist variables in first differences in the estimated model, as well as exogenous variables which are lagged one period.

It is for this reason that one may specify an Euler equation (version Whited [10], Bond and Meghir [11]), which is revisited in their recent studies by Daoudand Kammoun [12], with the firm's profit maximization program under different constraints. It has the advantage of taking the recurrent nature of the decisions of firms, information that is necessary to determine the optimal trajectory of investment, to measure the sensitivity of the firms' investment to financial constraints considering the information available at each period. This study fits into this perspective.

The objective of this study is therefore to analyze empirically the impact of this financial constraint on the investment decisions of Sub-Saharan manufacturing entreprises. In other words, our aim is to explain the influence of financial constraints on the investments of manufacturing entreprises in the context of Sub-Saharan countries. To test the hypothesis of the presence of a relationship between financial constraints and investment, it is useful to examine in Section 2 below, the theoretical motivations, then in Section 3 the methodological approach, and lastly in Section 4, the results of the study and their interpretation.

2. Review of the Literature

In the exercise of their daily activities, firms are confronted by certain situations which may paralyze their operation. This is essentially summarized in the problems they face in financing the activities of the firm.

Actually, there exists a multiplicity of choices for a firm when it faces financial problems. But the firm may be incapable of using these alternatives to solve these problems owing, for instance, to the indebtedness clause to be respected. Thus, the firm is limited in its decision making, linked to financial constraints.

In general, under the assumption of a limited control of the managers, the stockholders prefer a distribution of part of the internal gross cash flow to a total re-investment of this liquidity in the projects. However, if external financing becomes imperative when self-financing is insufficient to finance profitable projects, firms have recourse to indebtedness and sometimes to the issuing of new stocks.

2.1. Sensitivity of Investment to Cash Flows: A Measure of the Degree of Financial Constraints

The literature on financial constraints has been an area of research interest for several authors, and each of them has chosen a firm's characteristic which seems to explain this situation better.Fazzari, *et al.* [3] used the dividends distribution criterion to characterize the firms which are financially constrained.

Fazzari, *et al.* [3] have integrated the cash-flow variable among the factors that explain investment. They have analyzed the sensitivity between the cash flow and investment with a view to confirming or invalidating the assumption of the existence of a financial constraint in the presence of market imperfections. These authors used the distribution of dividends as a constraint because it has an informative content. According to this criterion, the firms which distribute more dividends are the most financially constrained, all the more since the managers thus have a reduced internal financing capacity.

These studies open a new debate on the question of the validity of using the sensitivity of investment to cash flows as a measure of the degree of the firms' constraints. This debate takes shape when Kaplan and Zingales ([8,13]) wonder about the effectiveness of using the sensitivity of investment to cash flows to explain the firms' financial constraints. They suggest, for firms that disburse small amounts of dividends, that the sensitivity differences which appear are partially attributable to differences in the firms' rates of growth. Thus, the sensitivity of investment to cash flows may be due to the preferences of managers who prefer financing their investments with internal liquidity (cash flow).

It emerges from previous works that the firms' investment policy is sensitive to the fluctuations of cash flows. In addition, the most financially-constrained firms have higher investment sensitivity to cash flows than those facing weaker financing constraints. Other authors use the indebtedness level to explain the firms' financial constraints.

2.2. Sensitivity of Investment to the Debt: A Risk Linked to the Financial Structure

According to the theory developed byModigliani and Miller [2], the market value of a firm does not depend on its capital structure. External and internal financings are substitutable and the investment decisions of a firm are totally independent of its financing decisions and of financial factors such as liquidity, the indebtedness level or dividends policies. However, some frictions linked to information asymmetry problems, may lead to dependence between the investment and financing decisions. For this reason, in the presence of imperfections on the credit market, a central role is given to financial indebtedness conditions.

In the context of financial theory, Modigliani and Miller [2] show that in the presence of a perfect financial market, the financial structure appears to be neutral on the market value of the firm. These authors suggest a maximal indebtedness to make the most of the advantages brought about by the fiscal economy, and this, when the financial problem is without a distress cost.

According to Modigliani and Miller [2], the firm is indifferent in terms of financing its investment through indebtedness, retention of profits or through the issuance of stocks. This situation leads to some form of equality between the yield required by stockholders and the interest rate of creditors. The initial model of Modiglianiand Miller [2] has been criticized by several researchers, notably the simultaneous introduction of taxation and failure costs. In addition, the deduction of financing costs from profit may reduce the firm's self-financing, and thus facilitate a continuous increase in indebtedness. Furthermore, the increase in indebtedness entails an increased risk of failure: for example, the optimal level of indebtedness is obtained by arbitrage between the fiscal advantage linked to the debt and the cost of the risk of failure.

Several studies, particularly those of Nivoix, *et al.* [14], as well as Daoud and Kammoun [12], show that financeing by issuing new stocks represents a small share of external financing, the effect of financial constraints which are thus associated with it would be significant on the decisions of the firm.

2.3. Sensitivity of Investment to Tobin's q: A Transmission of Financial Shocks (Role of Financial Variables)

According to Tobin [15], firms invest in new projects if the market value of the firm is higher than its accounting value. In other words, if the market increases the value of these beyond what they did cost (or if the market value them beyond what they cost). According to this author, this ratio is the only relevant indicator which can explain the firms' investment decisions. This ratio therefore serves as an incentive indicator to investment. Theoretically, this is due to the uncertainty that weighs on the (market) outlets, and the irreversibility of investment decisions that there exists a relationship between investment and profitability. Thus, the higher Tobin's q is, the more the firms invest and take the risk of overcapacity when facing an uncertain demand (Malinvaud, [16,17]).

Empirical studies on this argument were many and they gave some support to the relationship between investment and Tobin's q. They traditionally use the average q of Tobin which is evaluated with financial market data instead of marginal q. The average q may be measured directly from the value of the firm on the market. The marginal q is the only relevant ratio in theory, which provides the signal in the investment decision of the firm's manager. In effect, one does not observe the marginal q which is the implicit value of a new unit of capital installed relative to the cost of this unit, or which is the same thing at the optimum of the firm's programme, the present value of profit flows which will be reported in the future by a dollar of new investment. The marginal q only coincides with the average q under certain conditions: a financial environment which verifies the theorem of Modigliani and Miller [18], a production function with constant returns to scale, and a homogenous function of costs adjustments of degree one, and the firm is a price-taker (Hayashi, [19]).

Vogt [20] shows through an empirical model the effect of flows of cash flows on the value of Tobin's q under the assumption of high agency costs. The model is then enlarged to appreciate how the dividends (a means of reducing the flow of cash flow and of controlling the managers) affect Tobin's q. Jensen [21] defines the flow of cash flow as the "excess gross margin of self-financing" required to finance all the projects which have the net positive present value discounted at the appropriate cost of capital" In this regard, when the flow of cash flows is present and the control of the stockholder is incomplete, the agency problem of the type of policymaker suddenly appears.

Indeed, the manager tends to over invest (to invest in projects with a negative net present value (NPV) to capture the pecuniary and non-pecuniary advantages (allocations) of the firm's growth Jensen and Meckling [22], whereas the stockholders would prefer the distribution of dividends in order to reduce the flows of cash flows (Langa and Litzenberger, [23]), and hence to control the manager. There exist complicated models which help to test Tobin [15] assumptions. However, they provide little additional insight or perspicacity. Vogt [20] then proposes to use a simple estimation method to test the influence of Tobin's average q on the firms' investments.

Vogt [20] then wonders about whether the importance of cash flows in the investment decisions of firms consists of a waste of cash flows or whether the firms really face up to costly external financings due to the asymmetry of information phenomenon. Two aspects of this situation are then developed: the theoretical implications of cash flows and of Tobin's q.

The study by Vogt [20] shows that investment expenditures financed by cash flows are marginally unproductive for the firms and at the same time, identify the potential sources of their ineffectiveness. Encashed cash flows finance the growth of large firms, whereas firms with small dividends tend to destroy their values. The importance of dividends as a method for attenuating cash-flows agency costs is increasingly confirmed. The policymakers of the firms that are rich in terms liquidity flows, may consider increasing disbursements of dividends as a method for increasing the effectiveness of their investment expenditure decisions. However, a continuous policy of "high dividends disbursement" may also be a signal for shareholders that an additional (costly) control is useless.

The main assumption in the theoretical work on the firm's financial constraints is that these constraints entirely manifest themselves in the costs of external financing which are generally very high. This assumption poses two types of research problems (Heitor and Campello [24]). Firstly, it reduces the comprehension of financial constraints. However, the firms often practically face credit rationing. To explain the phenomenon of credit rationing for example, Jaffee and Modigliani [25] mentioned the effect of uncertainty and of the risk of failure of the firm which give rise to an information cost on the supply of credit. These authors add that the lender undertakes credit rationing in the case where the demand for credit exceeds the supply, for a given interest rate. Secondly, they give rise to the debate on the real implication of financial constraints in the firms' investment decisions. Heitor and Campello [24] develop a theory which explains the relationship between the firm's investment and cash flow when the firms face credit volume constraints. They show that when the firm's investments and the use of external financing are endogenously linked, an increase in the sensitivity of investments to cash flow is expected. In an empirical perspective, their analyses suggest a coherent way of identifying the impact of financial constraints on the investment of the firm. However, their results are manifestly different from theoretical predictions.

In a second approach, Heitor and Campello [9] use the link between financial constraints and the firm's demand for liquidity to develop a new test of the effect of financial constraints on the financing policy of the firm. The effect of financial constraints may be captured by the propensity of a firm to economize on the progressive cash flows of liquid money ("the sensitivity of the cash flow of money"). For this reason, while constrained firms should have a positive sensitivity to economize on liquid cash flow, those that are unconstrained should not be systematically linked to cash flows. They evaluate the cash flow of liquid money by using a large sample of industrial firms during the period 1971-2000. They note that the firms that are more likely to be financially constrained present liquid money cash flow sensitivity significantly positive and different from zero, whereas the firms that are not constrained are not. Also compatible (in agreement) with their argument, they note that the liquid cash flow sensitivity of constrained firms increases during recessions, while that of unconstrained firms remain unchanged thanks to innovations.

2.4. Theoretical Formalization Linking Financial Constraints and Investment

The role of financial variables in the explanation of the firms' investment takes up an important place in the financial theory of the firm. It depends on the value of the firm, hence the use of financial ratios as explanatory variables in order to test the effect of financial constraints on investment.

The approach through Euler's investment equation, integrated by Abel [26,27], empirically tested afterwards by Whited [10], and Bond and Meghir [11], though deriving from the firm's profit maximization program under different constraints, takes into account the recurrent nature of the firms' decisions, but reduces the conditions of information only to those that are important to determine the optimal trajectory of investment, given the information available in each period.

Whited [10], and Bond and Meghir [11] use Euler's equation to test the first order conditions of the firm's profit maximization program. This technique does not require the measurement of Tobin's q. Their approach implies the imposition of an exogenous constraint on external financing, and tests the influence of this constraint on the firms' investment. It emerges from their result that dividends may indeed serve as a signalling mechanism. Their payments are used to separate the firms that have favourable internal information from those that do not. In addition, the firms that exhaust their reserves and hence lack the capacity to distribute dividends are generally obliged to depend on external financing.

According to Azofra and Lopez [28], the use of Euler's equation without financing constraints on panel data has presented a net divergence depending on whether the estimation takes account of the totality of the sample or only the sub-samples of firms which are the most subjected to information problems, whereas the works of Whited [10], and Bond and Meghir [11] present a bad specification. In the work of Azofra and Lopez [28], the result is quite the opposite since the equation must not be rejected as a function describing the investment process of the firms least subjected to the asymmetry of information.

Under the assumption of the existence of imperfect financial markets, this model thus shows the influence of the financial situation of firms on the conditions of access to external financing (cost and availability). Therefore, the expression of our equation will be simply established. It will take into account the impact of financial ratios on the investment decision such as the effect of the debt, Tobin's q, and the cash flows of the firm.

3. The Methodological Approach

We take inspiration in our empirical approach from the model similar to those of Bond and Meghir [11], Jaramillo *et al.* [29], Azofra and Lopez [28], Rosenwald [30], which is revisited by Daoud and Kammoun [12] and which permit to establish an Euler equation of capital accumulation. This approach permits us to build our investment equation, which here is considered as the result of the first order condition of the optimization of the value of the firm under financial constraints. Thus, in this model, the maximization of the value of the firm may be given as follows:

$$\mathrm{MAX}(V_t) = E_t \sum_{i=0}^{\infty} B_t^i \left[\gamma_{t+1} D_{t+i} - S_{t+1}^n \right] \quad (1)$$

For this reason, $\mathrm{Max}(V_t)$ is therefore equal to the expectation (E_t) of the present value of the sum (B_t) of present and future returns (D_t) which take account of taxation (γ_t) and the dilution property rights due to the issue of new stocks (S_t). This maximization of the value of firm is subject to the following which must be respected:

The constraint linked to the dividends of the firm, which is given by:

$$\begin{aligned} D_t = (1-\tau_t)\big[& P_t F_t(K_t, L_t) - G(K_t, I_t) - w_t L_t \\ & - i_t B_{t-1} - A\left(B_{t-1}, P_{t-1}^K, K_{t-1}\right)\big] \\ & - P_t I_t + (B_t - B_{t-1}) + S_t + C_t \end{aligned} \quad (2)$$

where (L_t) and (K_t) are respectively the labour rand capital variables at time *t*, $A(B_{t-1}, P_{t-1}, K_{t-1})$ = informamation asymmetry costs represented here by the agency function, which means, a function of the level of the debt and of capital. (S_t) = new stocks issue; (D_t) = dividends; (C_t) = endowments to amortizations; $(w_t L_t)$ = share of labour; $(i_t B_{-1t})$ = reimbursement of interests; $F(K_t, L_t)$ = function de production which depends on the variables labour (L_t) and capital (K_t); $G(K_t, I_t)$ = adjustment cost function, assumed to be convex to investment; P_t = the level of output prices; P_{t-1}^K = price of capital, and τ_t the rate of the tax on companies.

The classical constraint of capital accumulation *K*

$$K_t = I_t + (1-\delta) K_{t-1} \quad (3)$$

The constraints linked to the issue of stocks, dividends, and debts must be positive:

$$D_t \geq 0, S_t \geq 0 \text{ et } B_t \geq 0 \quad (4)$$

And finally, the constraint linked to setting a ceiling on the level of indebtedness:

$$NE_t \geq \left[\frac{B_t}{P_t^K K_t} \right] \quad (5)$$

The special feature of this model is the presence a new additional constraint in the maximization program which here imposes a ceiling on the firm's level of indebtedness, as well as an agency cost function in the definition of the dividend. This is a special feature of the model that distinguishes the classical approach which does not take the financing constraints into consideration.

For this reason, this agency function depends on two arguments, namely the level of the debts (B), and the capital stock (K). Similarly, we make the assumption that the higher (B) is, the more incentive problems are severe $(A_B \geq 0)$ while the capital stock (K) reflects the guarantee level which the firm gives to its financial institution, in order to promote greater trust and lower agency costs $(A_K \leq 0)$. The specification of functions helps us to obtain the following testable functional form:

Cost function linked to adjustment:

$$G(K_t, I_t) = \left(\frac{c}{2}\right) \cdot \left(\frac{I^2}{K_{t-1}}\right)$$

where, c is a parameter representing the significance of adjustment costs, and $c \geq 0$.

Function linked to agency costs :

$$A(B_{t-1}, P_{t-1}, K_{t-1}) = \left(\frac{r}{2}\right)\left(\frac{B_{t-1}^2}{P_{t-1}^K K_{t-1}}\right)$$

where r is the average rate of investment, and $r \geq 0$.

Generally speaking, the firm does issue new stocks and does not pay dividends simultaneously. It does not finance its debt and does not issue stocks, and the dividend is strictly positive.

With these assumptions, the maximization of Equation **(1)** subject to constraints of Equations **(2)** and **(5)** permits to specify Euler's equation which is given in the following form:

$$\left(\frac{I}{K}\right)_i = a_1\left(\frac{I}{K}\right)_{it-1} + a_2\left(\frac{I}{K}\right)^2_{it-1} + a_3\left(\frac{\Pi}{K}\right)_{it-1} + a_4\left(\frac{Y}{K}\right)_{it-1} + a_5\left(\frac{B}{K}\right)^2_{it-1} + a_6\left(\frac{B}{K}\right)_{it-1} + u_{it} \quad (6)$$

$$i = 1, \cdots, N, t = 1, \cdots, T$$

where, the estimated values of the coefficients (a_5) and (a_6) which respectively capture the presence (or not) of a premium of access to external financing and a level of the debt ceiling.

If $(a_6 = 0)$ and $(a_5 \prec 0)$, then the debt ceiling constraint is absent. The observed ratio of the debt to the capital stock representing the debt ceiling (see constraint (5) of the maximization of the firm's value) does not exist. For this reason, imperfections on the credit market are linked to agency problems. This situation constrains the firm in its access to external indebtedness, which is explained by the premium to be paid in addition to the interest rate set by the financial institution.

On the other hand, if $(a_6 \prec 0)$ and $(a_5 \succ 0)$, then the firm is subject to an indebtedness ceiling constraint, and an increase in the ratio of the debt to the capital stock reduces the advantage of financing through the debt, owing to the premium to be paid in addition to the interest rate without risk (see constraint (2)).

3.1. Econometric Specification

The disturbance term (ε_{it}) of the investment equation, which is considered as being random, contains a variety of specification errors:

The differences between firms (particularly, in the areas of technology, the rate of depreciation, measures used etc.) affects the specification of the model to be estimated. These effects are captured by the presence of individual a_i and temporal a_t, as well as by the term of idiosyncratic errors (the common ε_{it}), $u_{it} = a_t + a_i + \varepsilon_{it}$.

The model to be estimated here is characterized by the presence of lagged endogenous variables among the explanatory variables of the model. This is an autoregressive model with a causality of the bias that must be considered: the correlation between explanatory variables, and individual specific effects. The origin of the bias is due to the fact that the rate of investment, $\left(\frac{I}{K}\right)_{it}$ is a function of a_i, and hence $\left(\frac{I}{K}\right)_{it-1}$ is correlated with individual specific coefficients.

Moreover, the effects may be correlated with other explanatory variables, in particular, the profitability term.

This technique boils down to highlighting, according Arellano and Bond [31], the generalized moments method (GMM) which makes the model appear in first differences. The equation to be estimated is given by:

$$\Delta Y = a\Delta Y_{t-1} + b\Delta X + \Delta u$$

where, Δ is the first difference operator such that $(\Delta X = X_{it} - X_{it-1})$, $Y =$ variable$\left(\frac{I}{K}\right)_{it}$, X= matrix of explanatory variables, except for the lagged endogenous variable, and b = the vector of corresponding parameters.

The data we use in this study show a great variability in individual decisions. They help to capture better the behaviour of investment in its detailed and structural aspects. These data take into consideration the accounting and financial data listed, and extracted from the stock markets of Nigeria, Ghana, and Libreville Gabon).

Note that our sample is composed of a panel of 73 manufacturing firms of different countries (more particularly the synthesis of the firms of Nigeria, Côte d'Ivoire, Ghana, Gabon, etc.), and different activity sectors such as (metallurgy, food processing, chemical, electricity, etc.) over the period 1999-2009.

Our approach carries out an estimation of the Euler investment equation over a ten-year period (1999-2009). In the model, we take account of the existence of variables in first differences, as well as exogenous variables lagged one period. Thus, we are forced to eliminate the first two years (1999 and 2000) of the study period used. In order to decide in favour of the use of the model with a fixed individual effect or with a random effect, we carried out the Hausman [32] test.

The Hausman test is specified in the following manner:

The null hypothesis of the absence of correlation between the characteristics of manufacturing firms and explanatory variables is rejected, if the theoretical χ^2 with k (number of exogenous variables) degrees of freedom is lower than the determined χ^2.

If the theoretical χ^2 with k degrees of freedom is higher than the calculated χ^2, then the null hypothesis Ho is accepted and the specific effects are considered as being random; and furthermore, there are no specification errors.

Generally speaking, our model tests two constraints which may affect the investment decisions of a firm, namely: the setting of a ceiling and the increase in the cost of the debt as a function of the ratio of the debt to the capital stock.

This model may then be written as follows:

$$\Delta\left(\frac{I}{K}\right)_i = a_1\Delta\left(\frac{I}{K}\right)_{it-1} + a_2\Delta\left(\frac{I}{K}\right)^2_{it-1} + a_3\Delta\left(\frac{\Pi}{K}\right)_{it-1} + a_4\Delta\left(\frac{Y}{K}\right)_{it-1} + a_5\Delta\left(\frac{B}{K}\right)^2_{it-1} + a_6\Delta\left(\frac{B}{K}\right)_{it-1} + u_{it} \quad (7)$$

where,

I = investment in equipment or $I_t = IMB_t - IMB_{t-1}$ (or the investment process of the firm = investment expenditure);

K = Stock K or $K_t = (1-\delta)K_{t-1}$; δ = a measure of the stock K; Π = gross operating result of the firm at time t; B = medium and long-term debt;

Y = the turnover of the firm; u_{it} = the error term;

$\left(\frac{I}{K}\right)_t$ = Ratio of investment to the capital stock K = rate of accumulation of K; $\left(\frac{Y}{K}\right)_t$ = Ratio of output to the capital stock K; $\left(\frac{\Pi}{K}\right)_t$ = Ratio of profit to the capital stock; $\Delta\left(\frac{I}{K}\right)^2_{it-1}$ = change in the ratio of investment to the stock of capital lagged 2 periods; $\left(\frac{B}{K}\right)^2_{it-1}$ = change in the ratio of the debt to the capital stock lagged 2 periods.

By generating the model with the synthesis of the available data of different Sub-Saharan countries, the interpretation of the estimated results takes account of two approaches: before the decomposition of the samples, and with the taking account of the dimension (size), and the participative relations of financial institutions.

4. Empirical Results and Interpretations

They concern two aspects:

4.1. Interpretation of the Estimation of the Model before the Decomposition of the Sample

Table 1 presents the results derived from the estimation of model (7) before the decomposition of the sample (the Hausman test). According to the results of the Hausman test, the determined $\chi^{2\text{ is}}$ equal to 11.9287. This value is lower than the theoretical χ^2 (read) at the 5% significance level and 7 degrees of freedom (that is to say, 16.088). The Hausman test does not show the existence of a correlation between the individual effect and the explanatory variables. For this reason, this may be a model with purely random effects.

Moreover, we note that the first two exogenous variables ($\Delta\left(\frac{I}{K}\right)_{it-1}$ and $\Delta\left(\frac{I}{K}\right)^2_{it-1}$) have significant coefficients, but their signs are opposite. The sign of the coefficient of the first variable is negative, while that of the second variable is positive. We note that the investment rate of the previous period negatively affects the present rate at an increasing rate.

In effect, the insignificance of the coefficients of variable $\Delta\left(\frac{\Pi}{K}\right)_{it-1}$ clearly illustrates the fact that the profitability variable is not important enough. Similarly, the estimation result indicates that the capital accumula-

Table 1. Results derived from Equation (7) estimation.

Variables	coefficient	t-statistic	probability
$\Delta\left(\frac{I}{K}\right)_{it-1}$	−3.554	(−7.223)	0.0000***
$\Delta\left(\frac{I}{K}\right)^2_{it-1}$	0.345	(7.765)	0.0000***
$\Delta\left(\frac{\Pi}{K}\right)_{it-1}$	0.418	(0.660)	0.2891
$\Delta\left(\frac{Y}{K}\right)_{it-1}$	0.487	(3.867)	0.0121**
$\Delta\left(\frac{B}{K}\right)_{it-1}$	0.092	(4.451)	0.0008***
$\Delta\left(\frac{B}{K}\right)^2_{it-1}$	−0.842	(−2.334)	0.0044**

***Significant at 5%, **Significant at 1%.

tion behaviour of the activity of the previous year, which is taken into account by the ratio of the turnover to the capital stock $\left(\frac{I}{K}\right)_{it-1}$, has an impact on the rate of investment. This result helps us to distinguish as Daoud and Kammoun [12], the pertinence of the accelerator theory under the imperfections of the capital market assumption. For that reason the accelerator effect, which is taken into account by the explanatory role of demand measured by the turnover, is important.

If we get interested in variables which measure financial constraints, the variable $\Delta\left(\frac{B}{K}\right)_{it-1}$ has a significant coefficient, but it has a negative sign. This demonstrates the effectiveness of setting a ceiling on indebtedness by financial institutions. The increase in the ratio of the debt to the capital stock reduces the advantage of financing through the debt because of the premium to be paid; in addition to the interest rate without risk (an effect which is due to the agency cost which is captured by the ratio $\Delta\left(\frac{B}{K}\right)^2_{it-1}$ and which therefore re duces the firms' investment expenditures.

The coefficient estimate of $\Delta\left(\frac{B}{K}\right)^2_{it-1}$ is positively significant. It also shows the effectiveness of the existence of costs linked to information asymmetries between the firm and the financial institution of credit. On that account, the higher (B) is, the more incentive problems are severe. These results corroborate with the works of Jaramillo *et al.* [29] and Daoud and Kammoun [12].

Therefore, it appears that Sub-Saharan firms are experiencing an environment with quite a strong information asymmetry between the borrowers and lenders. In addition, these firms are constrained in their access to external indebtedness owing to the levelling-off of indebtedness.

4.2. Estimation with Integration of the Dimension and the Participative Relations of Financial Institutions

In order to integrate the heterogeneity of the firms in the analysis of the impact of financial constraints on the investment decisions of manufacturing firms, we have carried out a categorisation of the firms according to two criteria: the dimension and the participative relationship of financial institutions.

The financial literature states the fact that small firms are put at a disadvantage by the banks, either by higher guarantees, or by high borrowing costs.

Ydriss Ziane [33], Guariglia [34], Hovakimian [35,36] Hsiao and Tahmiscioglu [36] and Daoud and Kammoun [12] underline the fact that a participative relation of financial institutions is profitable to the firm, thanks to better terms and conditions of financing. According to these authors, the closeness of the relations between financial institutions and firms has the effect of reducing interest costs and of being less financially constrained.

The dimension of the firm is considered as a factor of differentiation of the impact of financial constraints on the rate of investment. Several criteria are used to appreciate the firm's dimension, namely the number of employees in the firm, the turnover achieved, and total assets.

In the present study, we consider a large firm as any structure making a turnover of higher than 2 billions CFA Francs, and a small firm as a firm whose turnover is lower that this value.

On the basis of this criterion (the participative relations of financial institutions), we have distinguished the firms where financial institutions appear in their property structure, and those where financial institutions do not have participative relations. In order for financial variables to be different according to their dimension (a participative relation of financial institutions), we have defined a dimension control variable (DIME) which is equal to 1 if the firm is large (there exists a relation between firm and financial institution) and zero if not.

For that reason, to estimate the coefficient of $\Delta\left(\frac{B}{K}\right)^2_{it-1}$ for large firms we estimate the coefficient of the variable ($\Delta\left(\frac{B}{K}\right)^2_{it-1}$ × DIME). This has helped us estimate the following equations respectively:

Equation 1

$$\Delta\left(\frac{I}{K}\right)_i = a_1\Delta\left(\frac{I}{K}\right)_{it-1} + a_2\Delta\left(\frac{I}{K}\right)^2_{it-1} + a_3\Delta\left(\frac{\Pi}{K}\right)_{it-1} + a_4\Delta\left(\frac{Y}{K}\right)_{it-1} + a_5\Delta\left(\frac{B}{K}\right)^2_{it-1} \times \text{DIME}$$
$$+ a_5'\Delta\left(\frac{B}{K}\right)^2_{it-1} \times (1-\text{DIME}) + a_6\Delta\left(\frac{B}{K}\right)_{it-1} \times \text{DIME} + a_6'\Delta\left(\frac{B}{K}\right)_{it-1} \times (1-\text{DIME}) + u_{it}$$

Equation 2

$$\Delta\left(\frac{I}{K}\right)_i = a_1\Delta\left(\frac{I}{K}\right)_{it-1} + a_2\Delta\left(\frac{I}{K}\right)^2_{it-1} + a_3\Delta\left(\frac{\Pi}{K}\right)_{it-1} + a_4\Delta\left(\frac{Y}{K}\right)_{it-1} + a_5\Delta\left(\frac{B}{K}\right)^2_{it-1}\times\text{RPIF}$$
$$+ a_5'\Delta\left(\frac{B}{K}\right)^2_{it-1}\times(1-\text{RPIF}) + a_6\Delta\left(\frac{B}{K}\right)_{it-1}\times\text{RPIF} + a_6'\Delta\left(\frac{B}{K}\right)_{it-1}\times(1-\text{RPIF}) + u_{it}$$

According to the Hausman test results, the χ^2 determined by the first and the second equation is equal to 11.989 and 11.402 respectively. These values are lower than that of the theoretical χ^2 which is equal to 17.889 at the 5% significance level.

From the preceding presentation, we can maintain the lack of correlation between the individual effect and explanatory variables. Both models have purely random effects.

The examination of **Table 2** shows that the coefficients of exogenous variables $\Delta\left(\frac{I}{K}\right)^2_{it-1}$, $\Delta\left(\frac{I}{K}\right)_{it-1}$, $\Delta\left(\frac{\Pi}{K}\right)_{it-1}$, $\Delta\left(\frac{Y}{K}\right)_{it-1}$ remain unchanged in the results of both estimations, and the interpretation made previously as to their significance remains the same.

As concerns the variable $\Delta\left(\frac{B}{K}\right)^2_{it-1}$, it has a positive and significant effect on the investment expenditures of small firms. On the other hand, for large firms the coefficient of this variable is negative and insignificant. Similarly for the second variable which represents the indebtedness ceiling constraint, $\Delta\left(\frac{B}{K}\right)_{it-1}$ its coefficient is negative and significant for small firms. Both of these results imply that information problems and the indebtedness ceiling influence the rate of investment.In addition, these results agree with those obtained by Jaramillo *et al.* [29] and Daoud and Kammoun [12] by confirming the results according to which small firms and growth firms are more constrained in their access to external financing, given that they are young and have less time indeed to make themselves known by lenders and to establish relations of trust with the latter. Actually, the estimation which makes a distinction between firms according to their dimensions show that this criterion is relevant

Table 2. Estimation Results of 2 Equations.

Coefficients	Estimation with the taking account of the firms' dimensions.	Estimation with the taking account of the participative relations of financial institutions
a_1	-3.556^{***} (-7.367)	-3.524^{***} (-7.223)
a_2	0.483^{***} (7.777)	0.472^{***} (7.765)
a_3	0.490 (0.677)	0.486 (0.660)
a_4	0.499^{**} (3.658)	0.692^{***} (3.867)
a_5	-0.650 (-0.191)	-0.356 (-0.108)
a_5'	0.092^{***} (4.451)	0.088^{***} (4.430)
a_6	1.490 (0.337)	1.573 (0.879)
a_6'	-0.842^{**} (-3.212)	-0.768^{**} (-2.334)

Sources: The figures between parentheses represent the values of *t*-student statistics.

The effect of these two financial constraints on investment according to the criterion of participative relations of financial investment with the firm presents pertinent results. The firms where financial institutions appear in their property structure are more capable of finding external financial resources there. These pertinent results are brought out by the insignificance of indebtedness coefficients (a_5 and a_6). While these coefficients are significant for the firms with which the financial institutions have no participative relations. These firms are more constrained in obtaining financing on the credit market.

5. Conclusions

The purpose of this paper was to explain the influence of financial constraints on the investments of manufacturing firms in the context of Sub-Saharan countries. In this framework, we empirically tested two constraints which may affect the investment decisions of a firm. These constraints correspond to a levelling-off of the indebtedness level and the increase in the cost of the debt according to the amount borrowed reflecting the asymmetry of information which exists between the lender and the borrower. The estimation results of Euler's capital accumulation equation derived by Jaramillo *et al.* [29] and revisited by Daoud and. Kammoun [12], help us to conclude that the manufacturing firms of Sub-Saharan Africa (belonging to different activity sectors) are witnessing a financial environment made up of a strong information asymmetry between the lenders and the borrowers. The empirical results also add that these firms are subject to constraints in their access to external financing owing to the levelling-off of the debt.

In addition, the effect of information problems and of the levelling-off of indebtedness on the rate of investment according to the dimension criterion, show that small firms are put to a disadvantage by the financial institutions either by high borrowing costs, or by high guarantees. Similarly, the distinction of the effect of two financial constraints on investment according to the criterion of a participative relation of financial institutions indicates that the firms where the financial institutions appear in their property structure are more capable of finding external financial resources there, thanks to the relations of trust between financial institutions and the firms. Generally speaking, the firms are less constrained in obtaining financing on the credit market.

REFERENCES

[1] A. Glesne and G. Legris, "La Décision d'Investissement des Grandes Sociétés Françaises une Approche Econométrique," *Revue économique*, Vol. 25, No. 1, 1974, pp. 49-74.

[2] F. Modigliani and M. Miller, "The Cost of Capital, Corporate Finance, and the Theory of Investment," *American Economic Review*, Vol. 48, No. 3, 1958, pp. 97-261.

[3] S. M. Fazzari, R. G. Hubbard and B. C. Peterson, "Financing Constraints and Corporate Investment," *Brookings Papers on Economic Activity*, Vol. 1, No. 1, 1988, pp. 141-195.

[4] R. Carpenter and A. Guariglia, "Cash Flow, Investment, and Investment Opportunities: New Tests Using UK Panel Data," University of Nottingham Discussion Paper n 03/24, 2003.

[5] K. Gugler, D. C. Mueller and B. B. Yurtoglu, "Marginal *q*, Tobin's *q*, Cash-Flow and Investment," *Southern Economic Journal*, Vol. 70, No. 3, 2004, pp. 512-531.

[6] A. Minton and C. Schrand, "The Impact of Cash Flow Volatility on Discretionary Investment and the Costs of Debt and Equity Financing," *Journal of Financial Economics*, Vol. 54, No. 3, 1999, pp. 423-460.

[7] S. C. Vogt, "The Cash Flow/Investment Relationship: Evidence from U.S. Manufacturing g Firms," *Financial Management*, Vol. 23, No. 2, 1994, pp. 3-20.

[8] S. N. Kaplan and L. Zingales, "Do Financing Constraints Explain Why Investment is Correlated with Cash-Flow?" NBER Working Paper, N5267, 1995.

[9] A. Heitor and M. Campello, "Financial Constraints, Asset Tangibility, and Corporate Investment," *Review of Financial Studies*, Vol. 20, No. 5, 2007, pp. 1429-1460.

[10] M. T. Whited, "Debt, Liquidity Constraints, and Corporate Investment: Evidence from Panel Data," *Journal of Finance*, Vol. 47, No. 4, 1992, pp. 1425-1460.

[11] S. Bond and C. Meghir, "Dynamic Investment Models and the Firm's Financial Policy," *Review of Economic Studies*, Vol. 61, No. 2, 1994, pp. 197-222.

[12] Y. Daoud and A. Kammoun, "Contraintes Financières et Comportement d'Investissement: Le cas des Entreprises Tunisiennes Cotées," *Revue Libanaise de Gestion et d'Économie*, Vol. 1, No. 5, 2011, pp. 1-33.

[13] S. N. Kaplan and L. Zingales, "Do Investment Cash-Flow Sensitivities Provide Useful Measures of Financing Constraints?" *Quarterly Journal of Economics*, Vol. 115, No. 2, 1997, pp. 707-712.

[14] S. Nivoix, J. Faouzzi and W. Saidani, "Sensibilité des Investissements aux Cash-Flows et Degré de Contrainte Financière des Firmes: Le cas des *keiretsu*japonais," Working Paper, Université de Tunis, 2003.

[15] T. Tobin, "A General Equilibrium Approach to Monetary Theory," *Journal of Money*, Vol. 1, No. 1, 1969, pp. 15-29.

[16] E. Malinvaud, "Profitability and Unemployment," Cambridge University Press, Cambridge, 1980.

[17] E. Malinvaud, "The Challenge of Macroeconomic Understanding," *BancoNazionale Del Lavoro Quarterly Review*, Vol. 1, No. 162, 1987, pp. 219-238.

[18] F. Modigliani and M. Miller, "Some Estimates of the Cost of the Capital to the Electric Utility Industry, 1954-1957," *American Economic Review*, Vol. 56, 1957, pp. 333-391.

[19] F. Hayashi, "Tobin's Marginal q and Average q: a Neoclassical Interpretation," *Econometrica*, Vol. 50, No. 1, 1982, pp. 213-224.

[20] E. Malinvaud, "Econometric Methodology at the Cowles Commission: Rise and Maturity," *Econometric Theory*, Vol. 4, No. 2, 1988, pp. 187-209.

[21] M. Jensen, "Agency Cost of Free Cash-Flow, Corporate Finance, and Takeovers," *American Economic Review*, Vol. 76, No. 2, 1986, pp. 323-329.

[22] M. Jensen and W. Meckling, "Theory of the Firm: Managerial Behavior, Agency Costs, and Ownership Structure," *Journal of Financial Economics*, Vol. 3, No. 4, 1976, pp. 305-360.

[23] L. Lang and R. Litzenberger, "Dividend Announcements: Cash Flow Signalling vs. Free Cash Flow Hypothesis," *Journal of Financial Economics*, Vol. 24, No. 1, 1989, pp. 181-191.

[24] A. Heitor and M. Campello, "Financial Constraints and Investment-Cash Flow Sensitivities: New Research Directions," Working Paper at the Utah Winter Finance Conference, 2001.

[25] M. Jaffee and F. Modigliani, "A Theory and Test of Credit Rationing," *The American Economic Review*, Vol. 59, No. 7, 1969, pp. 850-872.

[26] A. B. Abel, "Investment and the Value of Capital," Garland, New-York, 1980.

[27] A. B. Abel and O. Blanchard, "The Present of Profit and Cyclical Movements in Investment," *Econometrica*, Vol. 54, No. 2, 1986, pp. 249-273.

[28] V. P. Azofra and F. J. Lopez, "Déterminants Financiers de l'Investissement en Capital Fixe: Le cas Espagnol," *Revue Économie Industrielle*, Vol. 86, No. 86, 1998, pp, 25-48.

[29] F. Jaramillo, F. Schiantarelli and A. Weiss, "Capital

Market Imperfection before and after Financial Liberalisation: An Euler Equation Approach to Panel Data for Ecuadorian Firm," *Journal of Development Economics*, Vol. 51, No. 2, 1996, pp. 367-386.

[30] F. Rosenwald, "L'Impact des Conditions Financières sur la Décision d'Investissement," Économie et Prévisions, No. 1-2, 2001, pp. 341-342,

[31] M. Arellano and S. Bond, "Some Tests of Specification for Panel Data: Monte Carlo Evidence and an Application to Employment Equations," *The Review of Economic Studies*, Vol. 58, No. 2, 1991, pp. 277-297.

[32] J. A. Hausman, "Specification Tests in Econometrics," Econometrica, Vol. 46, No. 6, 1980, pp. 1251-1271.

[33] Y. Ziane, "Nombre de Banques et Relation de Crédit, une Étude Empirique," *Revue Économique*, Vol. 55, No. 3, 2004, pp. 415-428.

[34] A. Guariglia, "Internal Financial Constraints, External Constraints, and Investment Choice: Evidence from a Panel of UK Firms," *Journal of Management Finance*, Vol. 32, No. 9, 2008, pp. 1795-1809.

[35] G. Hovakimian, "Determinants of Investment Cash-Flow Sensitivity," *Financial Mangement*, Vol. 38, No. 6, 2009, pp. 161-183.

[36] C. Hsiao and A. K. Tahmiscioglu, "A panel Analysis of Liquidity Constraints and Firm Investment," *Journal of the American Statistical Association*, Vol. 92, 1997, pp. 455-465.

Risk Measures and Nonlinear Expectations*

Zengjing Chen[1,2], Kun He[3], Reg Kulperger[4]
[1]School of Mathematics, Shandong University, Jinan, China
[2]Department of Financial Engineering, Ajou University, Suwon, Korea
[3]Department of Mathematics, Donghua University, Shanghai, China
[4]Department of Statistical and Actuarial Science, The University of Western Ontario London, Ontario, Canada

ABSTRACT

Coherent and convex risk measures, Choquet expectation and Peng's g-expectation are all generalizations of mathematical expectation. All have been widely used to assess financial riskiness under uncertainty. In this paper, we investigate differences amongst these risk measures and expectations. For this purpose, we constrain our attention of coherent and convex risk measures, and Choquet expectation to the domain of g-expectation. Some differences among coherent and convex risk measures and Choquet expectations are accounted for in the framework of g-expectations. We show that in the family of convex risk measures, only coherent risk measures satisfy Jensen's inequality. In mathematical finance, risk measures and Choquet expectations are typically used in the pricing of contingent claims over families of measures. The different risk measures will typically yield different pricing. In this paper, we show that the coherent pricing is always less than the corresponding Choquet pricing. This property and inequality fails in general when one uses pricing by convex risk measures. We also discuss the relation between static risk measure and dynamic risk measure in the framework of g-expectations. We show that if g-expectations yield coherent (convex) risk measures then the corresponding conditional g-expectations or equivalently the dynamic risk measure is also coherent (convex). To prove these results, we establish a new converse of the comparison theorem of g-expectations.

Keywords: Risk Measure; Coherent Risk; Convex Risk; Choquet Expectation; g-Expectation; Backward Stochastic Differential Equation; Converse Comparison Theorem; BSDE; Jensen's Inequality

1. Introduction

The choice of financial risk measures is very important in the assessment of the riskiness of financial positions. For this reason, several classes of financial risk measures have been proposed in the literature. Among these are coherent and convex risk measures, Choquet expectations and Peng's g-expectations. Coherent risk measures were first introduced by Artzner, Delbaen, Eber and Heath [1] and Delbaen [2]. As an extension of coherent risk measures, convex risk measures in general probability spaces were introduced by Föllmer & Schied [3] and Frittelli & Rosazza Gianin [4]. g-expectations were introduced by Peng [5] via a class of nonlinear backward stochastic differential equations (BSDEs), this class of nonlinear BSDEs being introduced earlier by Pardoux and Peng [6]. Choquet [7] extended probability measures to nonadditive probability measures (capacity), and introduced the so called Choquet expectation.

Our interest in this paper is to explore the relations among risk measures and expectations. To do so, we restrict our attention of coherent and convex risk measures and Choquet expectations to the domain of g-expectations. The distinctions between coherent risk measure and convex risk measure are accounted for intuitively in the framework of g-expectations. We show that 1) in the family of convex risk measures, only coherent risk measures satisfy Jensen's inequality; 2) coherent risk measures are always bounded by the corresponding Choquet expectation, but such an inequality in general fails for convex risk measures. In finance, coherent and convex risk measures and Choquet expectations are often used in the pricing of a contingent claim. Result 2) implies coherent pricing is always less than Choquet pricing, but the pricing by a convex risk measure no longer has

*This work is supported partly by the National Natural Science Foundation of China (11231005; 11171062) and WCU(World Class University program of the Korea Science and Engineering Foundation (R31-20007 and the NSERC grant of RK.
This work has been supported by grants from the Natural Sciences and Engineering Research Council (NSERC) of Canada.

this property. We also study the relation between static and dynamic risk measures. We establish that if g-expectations are coherent (convex) risk measures, then the same is true for the corresponding conditional g-expectations or dynamic risk. In order to prove these results, we establish in Section 3, Theorem 1, a new converse comparison theorem of g-expectations. Jiang [8] studies g-expectation and shows that some cases give rise to risk measures. Here we are able to show, in the case of g-expectations, that coherent risk measures are bounded by Choquet expectation but this relation fails for convex risk measures; see Theorem 4. Also we show that convex risk measures obey Jensen's inequality; see Theorem 3.

The paper is organized as follows. Section 2 reviews and gives the various definitions needed here. Section 3 gives the main results and proofs. Section 4 gives a summary of the results, putting them into a Table form for convenience of the various relations.

2. Expectations and Risk Measures

In this section, we briefly recall the definitions of g-expectation, Choquet expectation, coherent and convex risk measures.

2.1. g-Expectation

Peng [5] introduced g-expectation via a class of backward stochastic differential equations (BSDE). Some of the relevant definition and notation are given here.

Fix $T\in[0,\infty)$ and let $(W_t)_{0\le t\le T}$ be a d-dimensional standard Brownian motion defined on a completed probability space $(\Omega,\mathcal{F},P)$. Suppose $\{\mathcal{F}_t\}_{0\le t\le T}$ is the natural filtration generated by $(W_t)_{0\le t\le T}$, that is $\mathcal{F}_t=\sigma\{W_s;s\le t\}$. We also assume $\mathcal{F}_T=\mathcal{F}$. Denote

$$L^2(\Omega,\mathcal{F}_t,P)=\left\{\xi:\xi \text{ is } \mathcal{F}_t\text{—measurable random variables with } E|\xi|^2<\infty\right\},\ t\in[0,T];$$

$$L^2(0,T,\mathbb{R}^d)=\left\{X: X \text{ is } \mathbb{R}^d\text{—valued}, \mathcal{F}_t\text{—adapted processes with } E\int_0^T|X_s|^2\,\mathrm{d}s<\infty\right\}$$

Let $g:\ \Omega\times\mathbb{R}\times\mathbb{R}^d\times[0,T]\to\mathbb{R}$ satisfy

(H1) For any $(y,z)\in\mathbb{R}\times\mathbb{R}^d$, $\{g(y,z,t)\}_{t\ge 0}$ is a continuous progressively measurable process with

$$E\left[\int_0^T|g(y,z,s)|^2\,\mathrm{d}s\right]<\infty.$$

(H2) There exists a constant $K\ge 0$ such that for any

$$(y_1,z_1),(y_2,z_2)\in\mathbb{R}\times\mathbb{R}^d$$

$$|g(y_1,z_1,t)-g(y_2,z_2,t)|$$
$$\le K(|y_1-y_2|+|z_1-z_2|),\ t\in[0,T].$$

(H3) $g(y,0,t)=0,\ \forall(y,t)\in\mathbb{R}\times[0,T]$.

In Section 3, Corollary 3 we will consider a special case of $\mathbb{R}^d$ with $d=1$.

Under the assumptions of (H1) and (H2), Pardoux and Peng [6] showed that for any $\xi\in L^2(\Omega,\mathcal{F},P)$, the BSDE

$$y_t=\xi+\int_t^T g(y_s,z_s,s)\,\mathrm{d}s-\int_t^T z_s\,\mathrm{d}W_s,\ 0\le t\le T \qquad (1)$$

has a unique pair solution

$$(y_t,z_t)_{t\ge 0}\in L^2(0,T,\mathbb{R})\times L^2(0,T,\mathbb{R}^d).$$

Using the solution y_t of BSDE (1), which depends on ξ, Peng [5] introduced the notion of g-expectations.

Definition 1 *Assume that* (*H*1), (*H*2) *and* (*H*3) *hold on* g *and* $\xi\in L^2(\Omega,\mathcal{F},P)$. *Let* (y_s,z_s) *be the solution of BSDE* (1).

$\mathcal{E}_g[\xi]$ defined by $\mathcal{E}_g[\xi]:=y_0$ is called the g-expectation of the random variable ξ.

$\mathcal{E}_g[\xi|\mathcal{F}_t]$ defined by $\mathcal{E}_g[\xi|\mathcal{F}_t]:=y_t$ is called the conditional g-expectation of the random variable ξ.

Peng [5] also showed that g-expectation $\mathcal{E}_g[\cdot]$ and conditional g-expectation $\mathcal{E}_g[\cdot|\mathcal{F}_t]$ preserve most of basic properties of mathematical expectation, except for linearity. The basic properties are summarized in the next Lemma.

Lemma 1 (Peng) *Suppose that*

$$\xi,\xi_1,\xi_2\in L^2(\Omega,\mathcal{F},P).$$

1) Preservation of constants: For any constant c, $\mathcal{E}_g[c]=c$.

2) Monotonicity: If $\xi_1\ge\xi_2$, then $\mathcal{E}_g[\xi_1]\ge\mathcal{E}_g[\xi_2]$.

3) Strict monotonicity: If $\xi_1\ge\xi_2$, and $P(\xi_1>\xi_2)>0$, then $\mathcal{E}_g[\xi_1]>\mathcal{E}_g[\xi_2]$.

4) Consistency: For any $t\in[0,T]$,

$$\mathcal{E}_g\left[\mathcal{E}_g[\xi|\mathcal{F}_t]\right]=\mathcal{E}_g[\xi].$$

5) If g does not depend on y, and η is $\mathcal{F}_t$-measurable, then

$$\mathcal{E}_g[\xi+\eta|\mathcal{F}_t]=\mathcal{E}_g[\xi|\mathcal{F}_t]+\eta.$$

In particular, $\mathcal{E}_g\left[\xi-\mathcal{E}_g[\xi|\mathcal{F}_t]\big|\mathcal{F}_t\right]=0$.

6) Continuity: If $\xi_n\to\xi$ as $n\to\infty$ in $L^2(\Omega,\mathcal{F},P)$, then $\lim_{n\to\infty}\mathcal{E}_g[\xi_n]=\mathcal{E}_g[\xi]$.

The following lemma is from Briand *et al.* [9, Theorem 2.1]. We can rewrite it as follows.

Lemma 2 (Briand *et al.*) *Suppose that* $\{X_t\}$ *is of the form* $X_t = x + \int_0^t \sigma_s \mathrm{d}W_s$, $0 \le t \le T$, *where* $\{\sigma_t\}$ *is a continuous bounded process. Then*

$$\lim_{s\downarrow t} \frac{\mathcal{E}_g\left[X_s|\mathcal{F}_t\right] - E\left[X_s|\mathcal{F}_t\right]}{s-t} = g(X_t, \sigma_t, t),\ t \ge 0,$$

where the limit is in the sense of $L^2(\Omega, \mathcal{F}, P)$.

2.2. Choquet Expectation

Choquet [7] extended the notion of a probability measure to nonadditive probability (called capacity) and defined a kind of nonlinear expectation, which is now called Choquet expectation.

Definition 2

1) A real valued set function $V: \mathcal{F} \to [0,1]$ is called a capacity if

a) $V(\varnothing) = 0, V(\Omega) = 1$;

b) $V(A) \le V(B)$, whenever $A, B \in \mathcal{F}$ and $A \subset B$.

2) Let V be a capacity. For any $\xi \in L^2(\Omega, \mathcal{F}, P)$, the Choquet expectation $\mathcal{C}_V(\xi)$ is defined by

$$\mathcal{C}_V(\xi) := \int_{-\infty}^{0}\left[V(\xi \ge t) - 1\right]\mathrm{d}t + \int_0^{\infty} V(\xi \ge t)\mathrm{d}t$$

Remark 1 *A property of Choquet expectation is positive homogeneity, i.e. for any constant* $a \ge 0$,

$$\mathcal{C}_V(a\xi) = a\mathcal{C}_V(\xi).$$

2.3. Risk Measures

A risk measure is a map $\rho: \mathcal{G} \to \mathbb{R}$, where $\mathcal{G}$ is interpreted as the "habitat" of the financial positions whose riskiness has to be quantified. In this paper, we shall consider $\mathcal{G} = L^2(\Omega, \mathcal{F}, P)$.

The following modifications of coherent risk measures (Artzner *et al.*[1]) is from Roorda *et. al.* [10].

Definition 3 *A risk measure* ρ *is said to be coherent if it satisfies*

1) Subadditivity: $\rho(X_1 + X_2) \le \rho(X_1) + \rho(X_2)$, $X_1, X_2 \in \mathcal{G}$;

2) Positive homogeneity: $\rho(\lambda X) = \lambda\rho(X)$, for all real number $\lambda \ge 0$;

3) Monotonicity: $\rho(X) \le \rho(Y)$, whenever $X \le Y$;

4) Translation invariance: $\rho(X + \alpha) = \rho(X) + \alpha$ for all real number α.

As an extension of coherent risk measures, Föllmer and Schied [3] introduced the axiomatic setting for convex risk measures. The following modifications of convex risk measures of Föllmer and Schied [3] is from Frittelli and Rosazza Gianin [4].

Definition 4 *A risk measure is said to be convex if it satisfies*

1) Convexity:

$$\rho(\lambda X_1 + (1-\lambda)X_2) \le \lambda\rho(X_1) + (1-\lambda)\rho(X_2),$$

$\forall \lambda \in [0,1]$, $X_1, X_2 \in \mathcal{G}$;

2) Normality: $\rho(0) = 0$;

3) Properties (3) and (4) in Definition 3.

A functional $\rho(\cdot)$ in Definitions 3 and 4 is usually called a static risk measure. Obviously, a coherent risk measure is a convex risk measure.

As an extension of such a functional $\rho(\cdot)$, Artzner *et al.* [11,12], Frittelli and Rosazza Gianin [13] introduced the notion of dynamic risk measure $\rho_t(\cdot)$, which is random and depends on a time parameter t.

Definition 5 *A dynamic risk measure*

$$\rho_t(\cdot): L^2(\Omega, \mathcal{F}, P) \to L^2(\Omega, \mathcal{F}_t, P)$$

is a random functional which depends on t, *such that for each* t *it is a risk measure. If* $\rho_t(\cdot)$ *satisfies for each* $t \in [0,T]$ *the conditions in Definition* 3, *we say* $\rho_t(\cdot)$ *is a dynamic coherent risk measure. Similarly if* $\rho_t(\cdot)$ *satisfies for each* $t \in [0,T]$ *the conditions in Definition* 4, *we say* $\rho_t(\cdot)$ *is a dynamic convex risk measure.*

3. Main Results

In order to prove our main results, we establish a general converse comparison theorem of *g*-expectation. This theorem plays an important role in this paper.

Theorem 1 *Suppose that* g, g_1 *and* g_2 *satisfy* (*H*1), (*H*2) *and* (*H*3). *Then the following conclusions are equivalent.*

1) For any $\xi, \eta \in L^2(\Omega, \mathcal{F}, P)$,

$$\mathcal{E}_g[\xi + \eta] \le \mathcal{E}_{g_1}[\xi] + \mathcal{E}_{g_2}[\eta].$$

2) For any $(y_1, z_1, t), (y_2, z_2, t) \in \mathbb{R} \times \mathbb{R}^d \times [0,T]$,

$$g(y_1 + y_2, z_1 + z_2, t) \le g_1(y_1, z_1, t) + g_2(y_2, z_2, t). \tag{2}$$

Proof: We first show that inequality (2) implies inequality 3).

Let (y_t^1, z_t^1), (y_t^2, z_t^2) and (Y_t, Z_t) be the solutions of the following BSDE corresponding to the terminal value $X = \xi, \eta$ and $\xi + \eta$, and the generator $\overline{g} = g_1, g_2$ and g, respectively

$$y_t = X + \int_t^T \overline{g}(y_s, z_s, s)\mathrm{d}s - \int_t^T z_s \mathrm{d}W_s. \tag{3}$$

Then $\mathcal{E}_{g_1}[\xi] = y_0^1$, $\mathcal{E}_{g_2}[\eta] = y_0^2$, $\mathcal{E}_g[\xi + \eta] = Y_0$.

For fixed (y_t^1, z_t^1), consider the BSDE

$$y_t = \xi + \eta + \int_t^T\left[g_2(y_s - y_s^1, z_s - z_s^1, s) + g_1(y_s^1, z_s^1, s)\right]\mathrm{d}s - \int_t^T z_s \mathrm{d}W_s. \tag{4}$$

It is easy to check that $\left(y_t^1+y_t^2, z_t^1+z_t^2\right)$ is the solution of the BSDE (4).

Comparing BSDEs (4) and (3) with $X=\xi+\eta$ and $\bar{g}=g$, assumption (2), (2) then yields

$$g\left(y_t^1+y_t^2, z_t^1+z_t^2, t\right) \leq g_1\left(y_t^1, z_t^1, t\right)$$
$$+g_2\left(y_t^2, z_t^2, t\right),\ t \geq 0.$$

Applying the comparison theorem of BSDE in Peng [5], we have $Y_t \leq y_t^1+y_t^2,\ t \geq 0$. Taking $t=0$, thus by the definition of g-expectation, the proof of this part is complete.

We now prove that inequality (1) implies (2). We distinguish two cases: the former where g does not depend on y, the latter where g may depend on y.

Case 1, g does not depend on y. The proof of this case 1 is done in two steps.

Case 1, Step 1: We now show that for any $t \in[0, T]$, we have

$$\mathcal{E}_g\left[\xi+\eta \mid \mathcal{F}_t\right] \leq \mathcal{E}_{g_1}\left[\xi \mid \mathcal{F}_t\right]+\mathcal{E}_{g_2}\left[\eta \mid \mathcal{F}_t\right],$$
$$\forall\, \xi, \eta \in L^2(\Omega, \mathcal{F}, P).$$

Indeed, for $\forall t \in[0, T]$, set

$$A_t=\left\{\omega: \mathcal{E}_g\left[\xi+\eta \mid \mathcal{F}_t\right]>\mathcal{E}_{g_1}\left[\xi \mid \mathcal{F}_t\right]+\mathcal{E}_{g_2}\left[\eta \mid \mathcal{F}_t\right]\right\}.$$

If for all $t \in[0, T]$, we have $P\left(A_t\right)=0$, then we obtain our result.

If not, then there exists $t \in[0, T]$ such that $P\left(A_t\right)>0$. We will now obtain a contradiction.

For this t,

$$I_{A_t} \mathcal{E}_g\left[\xi+\eta \mid \mathcal{F}_t\right]>I_{A_t}\left(\mathcal{E}_{g_1}\left[\xi \mid \mathcal{F}_t\right]+\mathcal{E}_{g_2}\left[\eta \mid \mathcal{F}_t\right]\right).$$

That is

$$I_{A_t}\left(\mathcal{E}_g\left[\xi+\eta \mid \mathcal{F}_t\right]-\mathcal{E}_{g_1}\left[\xi \mid \mathcal{F}_t\right]-\mathcal{E}_{g_2}\left[\eta \mid \mathcal{F}_t\right]\right)>0.$$

Taking g-expectation on both sides of the above inequality, and apply the strict monotonicity of g-expectation in Lemma 1 (3), it follows

$$\mathcal{E}_g\left[I_{A_t}\left(\mathcal{E}_g\left[\xi+\eta \mid \mathcal{F}_t\right]-\mathcal{E}_{g_1}\left[\xi \mid \mathcal{F}_t\right]-\mathcal{E}_{g_2}\left[\eta \mid \mathcal{F}_t\right]\right)\right]>0.$$

But by Lemma 1 (4) and (5),

$$\mathcal{E}_g\left[I_{A_t}\left(\mathcal{E}_g\left[\xi+\eta \mid \mathcal{F}_t\right]-\mathcal{E}_{g_1}\left[\xi \mid \mathcal{F}_t\right]-\mathcal{E}_{g_2}\left[\eta \mid \mathcal{F}_t\right]\right)\right]$$
$$=\mathcal{E}_g\left[I_{A_t}\left((\xi+\eta)-\mathcal{E}_{g_1}\left[I_{A_t} \xi \mid \mathcal{F}_t\right]-\mathcal{E}_{g_2}\left[I_{A_t} \eta \mid \mathcal{F}_t\right]\right)\right].$$

Note that by Lemma 1(v)

$$\mathcal{E}_{g_i}\left[I_{A_t} \xi-\mathcal{E}_{g_i}\left[I_{A_t} \xi \mid \mathcal{F}_t\right]\right]=0,\ i=1,2.$$

Thus

$$\begin{aligned}
0 &<\mathcal{E}_g\left[I_{A_t}(\xi+\eta)-\mathcal{E}_{g_1}\left[I_{A_t} \xi \mid \mathcal{F}_t\right]-\mathcal{E}_{g_2}\left[I_{A_t} \eta \mid \mathcal{F}_t\right]\right] \\
&=\mathcal{E}_g\left[I_{A_t} \xi-\mathcal{E}_{g_1}\left[I_{A_t} \xi \mid \mathcal{F}_t\right]+I_{A_t} \eta-\mathcal{E}_{g_2}\left[I_{A_t} \eta \mid \mathcal{F}_t\right]\right] \\
&\leq \mathcal{E}_{g_1}\left[I_{A_t} \xi-\mathcal{E}_{g_1}\left[I_{A_t} \xi \mid \mathcal{F}_t\right]\right] \\
&\quad+\mathcal{E}_{g_2}\left[I_{A_t} \eta-\mathcal{E}_{g_2}\left[I_{A_t} \eta \mid \mathcal{F}_t\right]\right] \\
&=0
\end{aligned}$$

This induces a contradiction, thus concluding the proof of this Step 1.

Case 1, Step 2: For any $\tau, t \in[0, T]$ with $\tau \geq t$ and $z_i \in \mathbb{R}^d$, let us choose $X_\tau^i=z_i\left(W_\tau-W_t\right),\ i=1,2$. Obviously, $X_\tau^i \in L^2(\Omega, \mathcal{F}, P)$.

By Step 1,

$$\mathcal{E}_g\left[X_\tau^1+X_\tau^2 \mid \mathcal{F}_t\right] \leq \mathcal{E}_{g_1}\left[X_\tau^1 \mid \mathcal{F}_t\right]$$
$$+\mathcal{E}_{g_2}\left[X_\tau^2 \mid \mathcal{F}_t\right],\ t \in[0, T].$$

Thus

$$\begin{aligned}
&\frac{\mathcal{E}_g\left[X_\tau^1+X_\tau^2 \mid \mathcal{F}_t\right]-E\left[X_\tau^1+X_\tau^2 \mid \mathcal{F}_t\right]}{\tau-t} \\
&\leq \frac{\mathcal{E}_{g_1}\left[X_\tau^1 \mid \mathcal{F}_t\right]-E\left[X_\tau^1 \mid \mathcal{F}_t\right]}{\tau-t} \\
&+\frac{\mathcal{E}_{g_2}\left[X_\tau^2 \mid \mathcal{F}_t\right]-E\left[X_\tau^2 \mid \mathcal{F}_t\right]}{\tau-t}.
\end{aligned}$$

Let $\tau \rightarrow t$, applying Lemma 2, since g does not depend on y, we rewrite $g(y, z, t)$ simply as $g(z, t)$, thus $g\left(z_1+z_2, t\right) \leq g_1\left(z_1, t\right)+g_2\left(z_2, t\right),\ t \geq 0$. The proof of Case 1 is complete.

Case 2, g depends on y. The proof is similar to the proof of Theorem 2.1 in Coquet *et al.* [14]. For each $\varepsilon>0$ and $\left(y_1, z_1\right),\left(y_2, z_2\right) \in \mathbb{R} \times \mathbb{R}^d$, define the stopping time

$$\begin{aligned}
\tau_\varepsilon &=\tau_\varepsilon\left(y_1, z_1 ; y_2, z_2\right) \\
&=\inf \left\{t \geq 0 ; g_1\left(y_1, z_1, t\right)+g_2\left(y_2, z_2, t\right)\right. \\
&\quad\left.\leq g\left(y_1+y_2, z_1+z_2, t\right)-\varepsilon\right\} \wedge T.
\end{aligned}$$

Obviously, if for each $\left(y_1, z_1\right),\left(y_2, z_2\right) \in \mathbb{R} \times \mathbb{R}^d$, $P\left(\tau_\varepsilon\left(y_1, z_1 ; y_2, z_2\right)<T\right)=0$, for all ε, then the proof is done. If it is not the case, then there exist $\varepsilon>0$ and

$$\left(y_1, z_1\right),\left(y_2, z_2\right) \in \mathbb{R} \times \mathbb{R}^d,$$

such that

$$P\left(\tau_\varepsilon\left(y_1, z_1 ; y_2, z_2\right)<T\right)>0.$$

Fix $\varepsilon, y_i, z_i,(i=1,2)$, and consider the following (forward) SDEs defined on the interval $\left[\tau_\varepsilon, T\right]$

$$\begin{cases}\mathrm{d} Y^i(t)=-g_i\left(Y^i(t), z_i, t\right) \mathrm{d} t+z_i \mathrm{d} W_t, \\ Y^i\left(\tau_\varepsilon\right)=y_i,\ t \geq \tau_\varepsilon,\ i=1,2\end{cases}$$

and

$$\begin{cases} dY^3(t) = -g\left(Y^3(t), z_1 + z_2, t\right)dt + \left(z_1 + z_2\right)dW_t, \\ Y^3(\tau_\varepsilon) = y_1 + y_2, \quad t \ge \tau_\varepsilon. \end{cases}$$

Obviously, the above equations admit a unique solution Y^i which is progressively measurable with

$$E\left[\sup_{0\le t\le T}\left|Y^i(t)\right|^2\right] < \infty.$$

Define the following stopping time

$$\tau_\delta := \inf\left\{t \ge \tau_\varepsilon; g_1\left(Y^1(t), z_1, t\right) + g_2\left(Y^2(t), z_2, t\right) \ge g\left(Y^3(t), z_1 + z_2, t\right) - \frac{\varepsilon}{2}\right\} \wedge T.$$

It is clear that $\tau_\varepsilon \le \tau_\delta \le T$ and note that $\tau_\delta = T$ whenever $\tau_\varepsilon = T$, thus, $\{\tau_\varepsilon < \tau_\delta\} = \{\tau_\varepsilon < T\}$. Hence $P(\tau_\varepsilon < \tau_\delta) > 0$.

Moreover, we can prove

$$Y^1(\tau_\delta) + Y^2(\tau_\delta) > Y^3(\tau_\delta), \text{ on } \{\tau_\varepsilon < \tau_\delta\}.$$

In fact, setting

$$\hat{Y}(t) = Y^3(t) - Y^1(t) - Y^2(t),$$

then

$$d\hat{Y}(t) = \left[-g\left(Y^3(t), z_1 + z_2, t\right) + g_1\left(Y^1(t), z_1, t\right) + g_2\left(Y^2(t), z_2, t\right)\right]dt.$$

Thus $\dfrac{d\hat{Y}(t)}{dt} \le -\dfrac{\varepsilon}{2}$, $t \in [\tau_\varepsilon, \tau_\delta)$, $\hat{Y}(\tau_\varepsilon) = 0$.

It follows that on $[\tau_\varepsilon, \tau_\delta)$, $\hat{Y}(\tau_\delta) \le -\dfrac{\varepsilon}{2}(\tau_\delta - \tau_\varepsilon) < 0$.

This implies

$$P\left(Y^3(\tau_\delta) < Y^1(\tau_\delta) + Y^2(\tau_\delta)\right) \ge P(\tau_\varepsilon < \tau_\delta) > 0. \quad (5)$$

By the definition of Y^1, Y^2 and Y^3, the pair processes $\left(Y^1(t), z_1\right), \left(Y^2(t), z_2\right)$ and $\left(Y^3(t), z_1 + z_2\right)$ are the solutions of the following BSDEs with terminal values $Y^1(T)$, $Y^2(T)$ and $Y^3(T)$,

$$y_t = Y^i(T) + \int_t^T g_i(y_s, z_i, s)ds - \int_t^T z_i dW_s, \quad i = 1,2$$

and

$$y_t = Y^3(T) + \int_t^T g(y_s, z_1 + z_2, s)ds - \int_t^T (z_1 + z_2)dW_s.$$

Hence,

$$\mathcal{E}_{g_1}\left[Y^1(\tau_\delta)\middle|\mathcal{F}_{\tau_\varepsilon}\right] = \mathcal{E}_{g_1}\left[Y^1(T)\middle|\mathcal{F}_{\tau_\varepsilon}\right] = y_1,$$

$$\mathcal{E}_{g_2}\left[Y^2(\tau_\delta)\middle|\mathcal{F}_{\tau_\varepsilon}\right] = \mathcal{E}_{g_2}\left[Y^2(T)\middle|\mathcal{F}_{\tau_\varepsilon}\right] = y_2$$

and

$$\mathcal{E}_g\left[Y^3(\tau_\delta)\middle|\mathcal{F}_{\tau_\varepsilon}\right] = \mathcal{E}_g\left[Y^3(T)\middle|\mathcal{F}_{\tau_\varepsilon}\right] = y_1 + y_2.$$

Applying the strict comparison theorem of BSDE and inequality (5), by the assumptions of this Theorem, we have

$$y_1 + y_2 = \mathcal{E}_g\left[Y^3(\tau_\delta)\right] < \mathcal{E}_g\left[Y^1(\tau_\delta) + Y^2(\tau_\delta)\right] \le \mathcal{E}_{g_1}\left[Y^1(\tau_\delta)\right] + \mathcal{E}_{g_2}\left[Y^2(\tau_\delta)\right] = y_1 + y_2.$$

This induces a contradiction. The proof is complete.

Lemma 3 *Suppose that g satisfies (H1), (H2) and (H3). For any constant* $c \ne 0$, *let*

$$\overline{g}(y,z,t) = cg\left(\frac{1}{c}y, \frac{1}{c}z, t\right).$$

Then for any $\xi \in L^2(\Omega, \mathcal{F}, P)$, $\mathcal{E}_{\overline{g}}[c\xi] = c\mathcal{E}_g[\xi]$.

Proof: Letting $\overline{y}_t = \mathcal{E}_{\overline{g}}\left[c\xi\middle|\mathcal{F}_t\right]$, then $\overline{y}_t$ is the solution of BSDE

$$\overline{y}_t = c\xi + \int_t^T \overline{g}(\overline{y}_s, \overline{z}_s, s)ds - \int_t^T \overline{z}_s dW_s.$$

Since

$$\overline{g}(y,z,t) = cg\left(\frac{1}{c}y, \frac{1}{c}z, t\right),$$

the above BSDE can be rewritten as

$$\overline{y}_t = c\xi + \int_t^T cg\left(\frac{1}{c}\overline{y}_s, \frac{1}{c}\overline{z}_s, s\right)ds - \int_t^T \overline{z}_s dW_s. \quad (6)$$

Let $y_t = \mathcal{E}_g\left[\xi\middle|\mathcal{F}_t\right]$, then cy_t satisfies

$$cy_t = c\xi + \int_t^T cg(y_s, z_s, s)ds - \int_t^T cz_s dW_s. \quad (7)$$

Comparing with BSDE (6) and BSDE (7), by the uniqueness of the solution of BSDE, we have

$$(cy_t, cz_t) = (\overline{y}_t, \overline{z}_t).$$

Let $t = 0$, then $cy_0 = \overline{y}_0$. The conclusion of the Lemma now follows by the definition of *g*-expectation. This concludes the proof.

Applying Theorem 1 and Lemma 3, immediately, we obtain several relations between *g*-expectation $\mathcal{E}_g[\cdot]$ and g. These are given in the following Corollaries.

Corollary 1 *The g-expectation* $\mathcal{E}_g[\cdot]$ *is the classical mathematical expectation if and only if g does not depend on* y *and is linear in* z.

Proof: Applying Theorem 1, $\mathcal{E}_g[\cdot]$ is linear if and only if $g(y,z,t)$ is linear in (y,z). By assumption (H3), that is $g(y,0,t) = 0$ for all (y,t). Thus g does not depend on y. The proof is complete.

Corollary 2 *The* g*-expectation* $\mathcal{E}_g[\cdot]$ *is a convex risk measure if and only if* g *does not depend on* y *and is convex in* z.

Proof: Obviously, g-expectation $\mathcal{E}_g[\cdot]$ is convex risk measure if and only if for any $\lambda \in (0,1)$

$$\mathcal{E}_g[\lambda\xi+(1-\lambda)\eta]\le\lambda\mathcal{E}_g[\xi]+(1-\lambda)\mathcal{E}_g[\eta],\quad \forall\,\xi,\eta\in L^2(\Omega,\mathcal{F},P). \tag{8}$$

For a fixed $\lambda\in(0,1)$, let

$$g_1(y,z,t)=\lambda g\left(\frac{1}{\lambda}y,\frac{1}{\lambda}z,t\right),$$

$$g_2(y,z,t)=(1-\lambda)g\left(\frac{1}{1-\lambda}y,\frac{1}{1-\lambda}z,t\right).$$

Applying Lemma 3,

$$\mathcal{E}_{g_1}[\lambda\xi]=\lambda\mathcal{E}_g[\xi],\ \mathcal{E}_{g_2}[(1-\lambda)\xi]=(1-\lambda)\mathcal{E}_g[\xi].$$

Inequality (8) becomes

$$\mathcal{E}_g[\lambda\xi+(1-\lambda)\eta]\le\mathcal{E}_{g_1}[\lambda\xi]+\mathcal{E}_{g_2}[(1-\lambda)\eta],\quad \forall\,\xi,\eta\in L^2(\Omega,\mathcal{F},P).$$

Applying Theorem 1, for any

$$(y_i,z_i,t)\in\mathbb{R}\times\mathbb{R}^d\times[0,T],\ i=1,2,$$

$$\begin{aligned}&g(\lambda y_1+(1-\lambda)y_2,\lambda z_1+(1-\lambda)z_2,t)\\ &\le g_1(\lambda y_1,\lambda z_1,t)+g_2((1-\lambda)y_2+(1-\lambda)z_2,t)\\ &=\lambda g(y_1,z_1,t)+(1-\lambda)g(y_2,z_2,t)\end{aligned}$$

which then implies that g is convex. By the explanation of Remark for Lemma 4.5 in Briand *et al.* [9], the convexity of g and the assumption (H3) imply that g does not depend on y. The proof is complete.

The function g is positively homogeneous in z if for any $a\ge 0$, $g(\cdot,az,\cdot)=ag(\cdot,z,\cdot)$.

Corollary 3 *The g-expectation $\mathcal{E}_g[\cdot]$ is a coherent risk measure if and only if g does not depend on y and it is convex and positively homogenous in z. In particular, if $d=1$, g is of the form*

$$g(z,t)=a_t|z|+b_tz \ \text{ with } a\ge 0.$$

Proof: By Corollary 2, the g-expectation $\mathcal{E}_g[\cdot]$ is a convex risk measure if and only if g does not depend on y and is convex in z. Applying Theorem 1 and Lemma 3 again, it is easy to check that g-expectation $\mathcal{E}_g[\cdot]$ is positively homogeneous if and only if g is positively homogeneous (that is for all $a>0$ and ξ, $\mathcal{E}_g[a\xi]=a\mathcal{E}_g[\xi]$ if and only if for any $a\ge 0$, $g(\cdot,az,\cdot)=ag(\cdot,z,\cdot)$.

In particular, if $d=1$, notice the fact that g is convex and positively homogeneous on $\mathbb{R}$, and that g does not depend on y. We write it as $g(z,t)$ then

$$\begin{aligned}g(z,t)&=g(z,t)I_{[z\ge0]}+g(z,t)I_{[z\le0]}\\ &=g(1,t)zI_{[z\ge0]}+g(-1,t)(-z)I_{[z\le0]}.\end{aligned} \tag{9}$$

Note that $zI_{[z\ge0]}=z^+$, $(-z)I_{[z\le0]}=z^-$, but

$$z^+=\frac{|z|+z}{2},\ z^-=\frac{|z|-z}{2}.$$

Thus from (9)

$$g(z,t)=\frac{g(1,t)+g(-1,t)}{2}|z|+\frac{g(1,t)-g(-1,t)}{2}z.$$

Defining

$$a_t:=\frac{g(1,t)+g(-1,t)}{2},\ b_t:=\frac{g(1,t)-g(-1,t)}{2}.$$

Obviously $a\ge 0$, since the convexity of g yields

$$\frac{g(1,t)+g(-1,t)}{2}\ge g(0,t)=0.$$

The proof is complete.

Remark 2 *Corollaries 2 and 3 give us an intuitive explanation for the distinction between coherent and convex risk measures. In the framework of g-expectations, convex risk measures are generated by convex functions, while coherent measures are generated only by convex and positively homogenous functions. In particular, if d = 1, it is generated only by the family $g(z,t)=a_t|z|+b_tz$ with $a\ge 0$. Thus the family of coherent risk measures is much smaller than the family of convex risk measures.*

Jensen's inequality for mathematical inequality is important in probability theory. Chen *et al.* [15] studied Jensen's inequality for *g*-expectation.

We say that g-expectation satisfies Jensen's inequality if for any convex function $\varphi:\mathbb{R}\to\mathbb{R}$, then

$$\varphi(\mathcal{E}_g[\xi])\le\mathcal{E}_g[\varphi(\xi)],\quad \text{whenever } \xi,\varphi(\xi)\in L^2(\Omega,\mathcal{F},P). \tag{10}$$

Lemma 4 [*Chen et al.* [15] *Theorem* 3.1] *Let g be a convex function and satisfy $(H1)$, $(H2)$ and $(H3)$. Then*

1) Jensen's inequality (10) holds for g-expectations if and only if g does not depend on y and is positively homogeneous in z;

2) If $d=1$, the necessary and sufficient condition for Jensen's inequality (10) to hold is that there exist two adapted processes $a\ge 0$ and b such that

$$g(z,t)=a_t|z|+b_tz.$$

Now we can easily obtain our main results. Theorem 2 below shows the relation between static risk measures and dynamic risk measures.

Theorem 2 *If g-expectation $\mathcal{E}_g[\cdot]$ is a static convex (coherent) risk measure, then the corresponding conditional g-expectation $\mathcal{E}_g[\cdot|\mathcal{F}_t]$ is dynamic convex (coherent) risk measure for each $t\in(0,T)$.*

Proof: This follows directly direct from Theorem 1.

Theorem 3 below shows that in the family of convex risk measure, only coherent risk measure satisfies Jensen's inequality.

Theorem 3 *Suppose that* $\mathcal{E}_g[\cdot]$ *is a convex risk measure. Then* $\mathcal{E}_g[\cdot]$ *is a coherent risk measure if and only if* $\mathcal{E}_g[\cdot]$ *satisfies Jensen's inequality.*

Proof: If $\mathcal{E}_g[\cdot]$ is a convex risk measure, then by Corollary 2, g is convex. Applying Lemma 4, $\mathcal{E}_g[\cdot]$ satisfies Jensen's inequality if and only if g is positively homogenous. By Corollary 2, the corresponding $\mathcal{E}_g[\cdot]$ is coherent risk measure. The proof is complete.

Theorem 4 and Counterexample 1 below give the relation between risk measures and Choquet expectation.

Theorem 4 *If* $\mathcal{E}_g[\cdot]$ *is a coherent risk measure, then* $\mathcal{E}_g[\cdot]$ *is bounded by the corresponding Choquet expectation, that is* $\mathcal{E}_g[\xi]\le \mathcal{C}_V(\xi)$, $\xi\in L^2(\Omega,\mathcal{F},P)$ *where* $V(A)=\mathcal{E}_g[I_A]$. *If* $\mathcal{E}_g[\cdot]$ *is a convex risk measure then inequality above fails in general. By construction there exists a convex risk measure and random variables* ξ_1 *and* ξ_2 *such that*

$$\mathcal{E}_g[\xi_1]\le \mathcal{C}_V(\xi_1) \text{ and } \mathcal{E}_g[\xi_2]> \mathcal{C}_V(\xi_2)$$

The prove this theorem uses the following lemma.

Lemma 5 *Suppose that* g *does not depend on* y. *Suppose that the* g *-expectation* $\mathcal{E}_g[\cdot]$ *satisfies* (1) $\mathcal{E}_g[I_A+I_B]\le \mathcal{E}_g[I_A]+\mathcal{E}_g[I_B]$, $\forall A,B\in\mathcal{F}$ (2) *For any positive constant* $a<1$,

$$\mathcal{E}_g[a\xi]\le a\mathcal{E}_g[\xi],\ \xi\in L^2(\Omega,\mathcal{F},P).$$

Then for any $\xi\in L^2(\Omega,\mathcal{F},P)$ the g-expectation $\mathcal{E}_g[\cdot]$ is bounded by the corresponding Choquet expectation, that is

$$\mathcal{E}_g[\xi]\le \int_{-\infty}^{0}\left[\mathcal{E}_g\left[I_{\{\xi\ge x\}}\right]-1\right]\mathrm{d}x+\int_0^{\infty}\mathcal{E}_g\left[I_{\{\xi\ge x\}}\right]\mathrm{d}x. \quad (11)$$

Proof: The proof is done in three steps.

Step 1. We show that if $\xi\ge 0$ is bounded by $N>0$, then inequality (11) holds.

In fact, for the fixed N, denote $\xi^{(n)}$ by

$$\xi^{(n)}:=\sum_{i=0}^{2^n-1}\frac{iN}{2^n}I_{\left\{\frac{iN}{2^n}\le\xi<\frac{(i+1)N}{2^n}\right\}}.$$

Then $\xi^{(n)}\to\xi, n\to\infty$ in $L^2(\Omega,\mathcal{F},P)$.

Moreover, $\xi^{(n)}$ can be rewritten as

$$\xi^{(n)}=\sum_{i=1}^{2^n}\frac{N}{2^n}I_{\left\{\xi\ge\frac{iN}{2^n}\right\}}.$$

But by the assumptions (1) and (2) in this lemma, we have

$$\begin{aligned}\mathcal{E}_g\left[\xi^{(n)}\right]&=\mathcal{E}_g\left[\sum_{i=1}^{2^n}\frac{N}{2^n}I_{\left\{\xi\ge\frac{iN}{2^n}\right\}}\right]\\&\le\sum_{i=1}^{2^n}\frac{N}{2^n}\mathcal{E}_g\left[I_{\left\{\xi\ge\frac{iN}{2^n}\right\}}\right].\end{aligned} \quad (12)$$

Note that

$$\sum_{i=1}^{2^n}\frac{N}{2^n}\mathcal{E}_g\left[I_{\left\{\xi\ge\frac{iN}{2^n}\right\}}\right]\to\int_0^{\infty}\mathcal{E}_g\left[I_{\{\xi\ge x\}}\right]\mathrm{d}x,\ n\to\infty.$$

and $\mathcal{E}_g\left[\xi^{(n)}\right]\to\mathcal{E}_g[\xi],\ n\to\infty.$

Thus, taking limits on both sides of inequality (12), it follows that $\mathcal{E}_g[\xi]\le\int_0^{\infty}\mathcal{E}_g\left[I_{\{\xi\ge x\}}\right]\mathrm{d}x$. The proof of Step 1 is complete.

Step 2. We show that if ξ is bounded by $N>0$, that is $|\xi|\le N$, then inequality (11) holds.

Let $\xi^N=\xi+N$, then $0\le\xi^N\le 2N$. Applying Step 1,

$$\mathcal{E}_g[\xi+N]\le\int_0^{\infty}\mathcal{E}_g\left[I_{\{\xi+N\ge x\}}\right]\mathrm{d}x. \quad (13)$$

But by Lemma 1(v), $\mathcal{E}_g[\xi+N]=\mathcal{E}_g[\xi]+N$. On the other hand,

$$\begin{aligned}\int_0^{\infty}\mathcal{E}_g\left[I_{\{\xi+N\ge x\}}\right]\mathrm{d}x&=\int_0^{2N}\mathcal{E}_g\left[I_{\{\xi\ge x-N\}}\right]\mathrm{d}x\\&=\int_{-N}^{N}\mathcal{E}_g\left[I_{\{\xi\ge x\}}\right]\mathrm{d}x\\&=\int_{-N}^{0}\mathcal{E}_g\left[I_{\{\xi\ge x\}}\right]\mathrm{d}x\\&\quad+\int_0^{N}\mathcal{E}_g\left[I_{\{\xi\ge x\}}\right]\mathrm{d}x.\end{aligned}$$

Thus by (13)

$$\mathcal{E}_g[\xi]+N\le\int_{-N}^{0}\mathcal{E}_g\left[I_{\{\xi\ge x\}}\right]\mathrm{d}x+\int_0^{N}\mathcal{E}_g\left[I_{\{\xi\ge x\}}\right]\mathrm{d}x.$$

Therefore

$$\mathcal{E}_g[\xi]\le\int_{-N}^{0}\left[\mathcal{E}_g\left[I_{\{\xi\ge x\}}\right]-1\right]\mathrm{d}x+\int_0^{N}\mathcal{E}_g\left[I_{\{\xi\ge x\}}\right]\mathrm{d}x.$$

Step 3. For any $\xi\in L^2(\Omega,\mathcal{F},P)$. let $\xi^N=\xi I_{[|\xi|\le N]}$, then $\left|\xi^N\right|\le N$. By Step 2,

$$\mathcal{E}_g\left[\xi^N\right]\le\int_{-N}^{0}\left[\mathcal{E}_g\left[I_{\{\xi\ge x\}}\right]-1\right]\mathrm{d}x+\int_0^{N}\mathcal{E}_g\left[I_{\{\xi\ge x\}}\right]\mathrm{d}x.$$

Letting $N\to\infty$, it follows that

$$\mathcal{E}_g[\xi]\le\int_{-\infty}^{0}\left[\mathcal{E}_g\left[I_{\{\xi\ge x\}}\right]-1\right]\mathrm{d}x+\int_0^{\infty}\mathcal{E}_g\left[I_{\{\xi\ge x\}}\right]\mathrm{d}x.$$

The proof is complete.

Proof of Theorem 4: If the g-expectation $\mathcal{E}_g[\cdot]$ is a coherent risk measure, then it is easy to check that the g-expectation $\mathcal{E}_g[\cdot]$ satisfies the conditions of Lemma 5.

Let $V(A)=\mathcal{E}_g[I_A]\ \forall A\in\mathcal{F}$. By Lemma 5 and the definition of Choquet expectation, we have $\mathcal{E}_g[\xi]\le\mathcal{C}_V[\xi]$. The first part of this theorem is complete.

Counterexample 1 shows that this property of coherent risk measures fails in general for more general convex risk measures. This completes the proof of Theorem 4.

Counterexample 1 *Suppose that* $\{W_t\}$ *is* 1*-dimensional Brownian motion* (*i.e.* $d=1$). *Let* $g(z)=(z-1)^+$ *where* $x^+=\max\{x,0\}$. *Then* $\mathcal{E}_g[\cdot]$ *is a convex risk* *measure. Let* $\xi_1 = \frac{1}{2} I_{\{W_T \ge 1\}}$ *and* $\xi_2 = 2I_{\{W_T \ge 1\}}$. *Then* $\mathcal{E}_g[\xi_1] \le \mathcal{C}_V(\xi_1)$ *However* $\mathcal{E}_g[\xi_2] > \mathcal{C}_V(\xi_2)$. *Here the capacity* V *in the Choquet expectation* $\mathcal{C}_V(\cdot)$ *is given by* $V(A) = \mathcal{E}_g[I_A]$.

Proof of the Inequality in Counterexample 1: The convex function $g(z) = (z-1)^+$ satisfies (H1), (H2) and(H3). Thus, by Corollary 2, g-expectation $\mathcal{E}_g[\cdot]$ is a convex risk measure. This together with the property of Choquet expectation in Remark 1 implies

$$\mathcal{E}_g[\xi_1] = \mathcal{E}_g\left[\frac{1}{2} I_{\{W_T \ge 1\}}\right] \le \frac{1}{2}\mathcal{E}_g\left[I_{\{W_T \ge 1\}}\right] = \frac{1}{2}\mathcal{C}_V\left(I_{\{W_T \ge 1\}}\right) = \mathcal{C}_V\left(\frac{1}{2} I_{\{W_T \ge 1\}}\right) = \mathcal{C}_V(\xi_1).$$

Moreover, since $d = 1$ by Corollary 3, $\mathcal{E}_g[\cdot]$ is a convex risk measure rather than a coherent risk measure. We now prove that $\mathcal{E}_g[\xi_2] > \mathcal{C}_V(\xi_2)$ In fact, since

$$\mathcal{C}_V\left(2I_{\{W_T \ge 1\}}\right) = 2\mathcal{C}_V\left(I_{\{W_T \ge 1\}}\right) = 2\mathcal{E}_g\left[I_{\{W_T \ge 1\}}\right],$$

we only need to show

$$\mathcal{E}_g\left[2I_{\{W_T \ge 1\}}\right] > 2\mathcal{E}_g\left[I_{\{W_T \ge 1\}}\right].$$

Let (y, z) be the solution of the BSDE

$$y_t = 2I_{\{W_T \ge 1\}} + \int_t^T (z_s - 1)^+ \,\mathrm{d}s - \int_t^T z_s \mathrm{d}W_s. \quad (14)$$

First we prove that

$$(L \times P)\left((t, \omega) \in [0, T) \times \Omega : z_t(\omega) > 1\right) > 0, \quad (15)$$

where L is Lebesgue measure on $[0, T]$.

If it is not true, then $z_t \le 1$ a.e. $t \in [0, T]$ and BSDE (14) becomes

$$y_t = 2I_{\{W_T \ge 1\}} - \int_t^T z_s \mathrm{d}W_s.$$

Thus

$$y_t = 2E\left[I_{\{W_T \ge 1\}} \middle| \mathcal{F}_t\right] = 2E\left[I_{\{W_T - W_t \ge 1 - W_t\}} \middle| \mathcal{F}_t\right].$$

By the Markov property,

$$y_t = 2P\left(W_T - W_t \ge 1 - W_t \middle| \sigma(W_t)\right).$$

Recall that $W_T - W_t$ and W_t are independent and $W_T - W_t \sim N(0, T-t)$. Thus

$$y_t = 2\int_{1-x}^{\infty} \varphi(y)\mathrm{d}y\Big|_{x = W_t},$$

where $\varphi(x)$ is the density function of the normal distribution $N(0, T-t)$. Thus $z_t = D_t y_t = 2\varphi(1 - W_t)$, where D_t is the Malliavin derivative. Thus z_t can be greater than 1 whenever t is near 0 and W_t is near 0. Thus (15) holds, which contradicts the assumption $z_t \le 1$ a.e. $t \in [0, T]$.

Secondly we prove that

$$\mathcal{E}_g\left[2I_{\{W_T \ge 1\}}\right] > 2\mathcal{E}_g\left[I_{\{W_T \ge 1\}}\right].$$

Let (Y_t, Z_t) be the solution of the BSDE

$$Y_t = 2I_{\{W_T \ge 1\}} + \int_t^T 2\left(\frac{Z_s}{2} - 1\right)^+ \mathrm{d}s - \int_t^T Z_s \mathrm{d}W_s. \quad (16)$$

Obviously,

$$\frac{Y_t}{2} = I_{\{W_T \ge 1\}} + \int_t^T \left(\frac{Z_s}{2} - 1\right)^+ \mathrm{d}s - \int_t^T \frac{Z_s}{2} \mathrm{d}W_s,$$

which means $\left(\frac{Y_t}{2}, \frac{Z_s}{2}\right)$ is the solution of BSDE

$$\bar{y}_t = I_{\{W_T \ge 1\}} + \int_t^T (\bar{z}_s - 1)^+ \mathrm{d}s - \int_t^T \bar{z}_s \mathrm{d}W_s.$$

But $\bar{y}_t = \mathcal{E}_g\left[I_{\{W_T \ge 1\}} \middle| \mathcal{F}_t\right]$. Thus by the uniqueness of the solution of BSDE, $\frac{Y_t}{2} = \mathcal{E}_g\left[I_{\{W_T \ge 1\}} \middle| \mathcal{F}_t\right]$. On the other hand, let (y_t, z_t) be the solution of the BSDE

$$y_t = 2I_{\{W_T \ge 1\}} + \int_t^T (z_s - 1)^+ \mathrm{d}s - \int_t^T z_s \mathrm{d}W_s. \quad (17)$$

Comparing BSDE(17) with BSDE (16), notice (15) and the fact

$$(z-1)^+ \ge 2\left(\frac{z}{2} - 1\right)^+ \quad \text{and} \quad \begin{matrix} \mathcal{E}_g[\xi] \\ \mathcal{E}_g[\xi] < \mathcal{C}_V(\xi) \end{matrix}$$

whenever $z > 1$. By the strict comparison theorem of BSDE, we have $y_t > Y_t$, $t \in [0, T)$.

Setting $t = 0$, thus

$$\mathcal{E}_g\left[2I_{\{W_T \ge 1\}}\right] > 2\mathcal{E}_g\left[I_{\{W_T \ge 1\}}\right] = \mathcal{C}_V\left(2I_{\{W_T \ge 1\}}\right).$$

The proof is complete.

Remark 3 *In mathematical finance, coherent and convex risk measures and Choquet expectation are used in the pricing of contingent claim. Theorem 4 shows that coherent pricing is always less than Choquet pricing, while Counterexample 1 demonstrates that pricing by a convex risk measure no longer has this property. In fact the convex risk price may be greater than or less than the Choquet expectation.*

4. Summary

Coherent risk measures are a generalization of mathematical expectations, while convex risk measures are a generalization of coherent risk measures. In the framework of g-expectation, the summary of our results is given in **Table 1**. In that Table, the Choquet expectation is $V(A) := \mathcal{E}_g[I_A]$.

Counterexample 1 shows that convex risk may be $\ge$ or $\le$ Choquet expectation. Only in the case of coherent

Table 1. Relations among coherent and convex risk measures $\mathcal{E}_g[\xi]$, choquet expectation and Jensen's inequality.

Risk Measures	Relation to Choquet Expectation	Jensen inequality
	g is linear	
math. expectation	$\mathcal{E}_g[\xi]=\mathcal{C}_V(\xi)$	true
	g is convex and positively homogeneous	
coherent	$\mathcal{E}_g[\xi]<\mathcal{C}_V(\xi)$	true (*)
	g is convex	
convex	Neither $\leq$ nor $\geq$	not true except (*)

risk there is an inequality relation with Choquet expectation.

REFERENCES

[1] P. Artzner, F. Delbaen, J. M. Eber and D. Heath, "Coherent Measures of Risk," *Mathematical Finance*, Vol. 9, No. 3, 1999, pp. 203-228.

[2] F. Delbaen, "Coherent Risk Measures on General Probability," In: K. Sandmann and P. Schonbucher, Eds., *Advances in Finance and Stochastics*, Springer-Verlag, Berlin, 2002, pp. 1-37.

[3] H. Föllmer and A. Schied, "Convex Measures of Risk and Trading Constraints," *Finance and Stochastics*, Vol. 6, No. 4, 2002, pp. 429-447.

[4] M. Frittelli and E. R. Gianin, "Putting Order in Risk Measures," *Journal of Banking Finance*, Vol. 26, No. 7, 2002, pp. 1474-1486.

[5] S. G. Peng, "BSDE and Related *g*-Expectation," *Pitman Research Notes in Mathematics Series*, Vol. 364, 1997, pp. 141-159.

[6] E. Pardoux and S. G. Peng, "Adapted Solution of a Backward Stochastic Differential Equation," *Systems and Control Letters*, Vol. 14, No. 1, 1990, pp. 55-61.

[7] G. Choquet, "Theory of Capacities," *Annales de l'institut Fourier (Grenoble)*, Vol. 5, 1953, pp. 131-195.

[8] L. Jiang, "Convexity, Translation Invariance and Subadditivity for *g*-Expectations and Related Risk Measures," *Annals of Applied Probability*, Vol. 18, No. 1, 2008, pp. 245-258.

[9] P. Briand, F. Coquet, Y. Hu, J. Mémin and S. G. Peng, "A Converse Comparison Theorem for BSDEs and Related Problems of *g*-Expectation," *Electronic Communications in Probability*, Vol. 5, 2000, pp. 101-117.

[10] B. Roorda, J. M. Schumacher and J. Engwerda, "Coherent Acceptability Measures in Multi-Period Models," *Mathematical Finance*, Vol. 15, No. 4, 2005, pp. 589-612.

[11] P. Artzner, F. Delbaen, J. M. Eber, D. Heath and H. Ku, "Multiperiod Risk and Coherent Multiperiod Risk Measurement," E.T.H.Zürich, Preprint, 2002.

[12] P. Artzner, F. Delbaen, J. M. Eber, D. Heath and H. Ku, "Coherent Multiperiod Risk Adjusted Values and Bellman's Principle," *Annals of Operations Research*, Vol. 152, No. 1, 2007, pp. 5-22.

[13] M. Frittelli and E. R. Gianin, "Dynamic Convex Risk Measures," In: G. Szegö, Ed., *Risk Measures for the 21st Century*, John Wiley, Hoboken, 2004, pp. 227-248.

[14] F. Coquet, Y. Hu, J. Mémin and S. G. Peng, "A General Converse Comparison Theorem for Backward Stochastic Differential Equations," *Comptes Rendus de l'Académie des Sciences Paris, Series I*, Vol. 333, 2001, pp. 577-581.

[15] Z. J. Chen, R. Kulperger and L. Jiang, "Jensen's Inequality for *g*-Expectation: Part 1," *Comptes Rendus de l'Académie des Sciences Paris, Series I*, Vol. 337, 2003, pp. 725-730.

15

Contingent Claims in Incomplete Markets: A Case Study

Sure Mataramvura
Division of Actuarial Science, School of Management Studies, University of Cape Town, Cape Town, South Africa

ABSTRACT

In this paper, we revisit pricing contingent claims in incomplete markets. While a lot have been done on pricing in incomplete markets, there is still a gap on the categorization of the payoffs. Some contingent claims are attainable while others will not be attainable. We address the question of which contingent claims belong to each group. We also propose a generalization of the equivalent martingale measures used for pricing, a generalization which includes those studied so far. We also provide some examples of how to price in each class and introduce important definitions.

Keywords: Incomplete Markets; Equivalent Martingale Measure; Admissible Pricing Measure

1. Introduction

In this paper we extend the study of the pricing of contingent claims in incomplete markets. We categorize these contingent claims into those which are attainable and those which are not attainable which has not been fully addressed in previous works. In a market where there are more Brownian motions than number of stocks the market is likely to be incomplete. We refer the reader to [1] for more discussion on incompleteness of markets of this type. The Girsanov theorems give an explicit representation of the market price of risk which induces the equivalent martingale measure used for pricing. In incomplete markets there are infinitely many such equivalent martingale measures, leaving researchers looking for what could be a good candidate measure for pricing. Common examples of these measures $Q^{\circledast}$ are the minimal martingale measure as in [2], the relative entropy minimizer as in [3], the Esscher transform in [4], the minimal f^{q}—divergence as in [5] among others.

One objective for this study is to generalize these measures to include even those measures not yet studied. We call these measures *admissible pricing measures*. We note that the mapping from the set of equivalent martingale measures to the price of contingent claims is a many to one mapping. Therefore there are some contingent claims which have a unique price calculated using different equivalent martingale measures. We do this by means of some simple toy examples that reveal our results. It is in this light that the uniqueness of some of the *admissible pricing measures* suggested before could be brought into question. However, if we introduce an equivalence relation which results in cosets, each containing admissible pricing measures that gives the same price for a given contingent claim, then this mapping becomes an injective function. We have limited this ideas into the idealizations and we leave further scrutny to interested readers.

This paper is organized as follows: the next section gives the preliminaries. In that we also introduce some important definitions. The final chapter deals with the important results where we observe that the pricing measures are not unique after all. This is achieved through some toy examples of European options belonging to the sets of attainable claims and non-attainable claims respectively.

2. Mathematical Preliminaries

Assume that we have a filtered probability space

$$(\Omega, \mathcal{F}, \mathcal{F}_t, P)$$

with the filtration chosen in such a way that asset prices are $\mathcal{F}_t$-adapted. Consider a market

$$X(t) = \left(X_0(t), X_1(t), \cdots, X_m(t)\right)$$

where $X_0(t)$ is the price of the bond at time t and is given by

$$\mathrm{d}X_0(t) = \rho(t) X_0(t)\mathrm{d}t,\ X_0(0) = 1,\ 0 \le t \le T \quad (2.1)$$

where $\rho(t)$ is the interest rate and for $1 \le i \le m$ the price of stock i is given by

$$\mathrm{d}X_i(t) = X_i(t)\left[\alpha_i(t)\mathrm{d}t + \sum_{j=1}^{n}\sigma_{ij}(t)\mathrm{d}B_j(t)\right], \qquad (2.2)$$
$$X_i(0) = x_i,\ 0 \le t \le T$$

where

$$B(t) = \left(B_1(t), B_2(t), \cdots, B_n(t)\right)^*$$

is an n-dimensional P-Brownian motion and $*$ means transposition. We can write (2.2) as

$$\mathrm{d}X(t) = X(t)\left[\alpha(t)\mathrm{d}t + \sigma\mathrm{d}B(t)\right]$$

where

$$\alpha(t) = \left(\alpha_1(t), \cdots, \alpha_m(t)\right)^*$$

is the vector of appreciation rates and

$$\sigma = \begin{pmatrix} \sigma_{11}(t) & \cdots & \sigma_{1m}(t) \\ \vdots & \ddots & \vdots \\ \sigma_{m1}(t) & \cdots & \sigma_{mn}(t) \end{pmatrix}$$

is the volatility matrix. Assume that $m < n$ and rank $\sigma \ne m$ so that σ has no left inverse. It is then clear from this setup that the market of stocks and bonds is incomplete (see [1]).

By the Girsanov theorem for this market (see [1]), the market price of risk is $u(t) = \left(u_1(t), \cdots, u_n(t)\right)^*$ such that

$$\sigma(t)u(t) = \alpha(t) - \rho(t)\mathcal{I}$$

where I is the 1-vector in $\mathbb{R}^m$. The system (2.3) has infinitely many solutions in $u(.)$. By the same Girsanov theorems cited above, the probability measure Q given by

$$\frac{\mathrm{d}Q}{\mathrm{d}P} = M(T)$$

where

$$M(t) = \exp\left(-\int_0^t u(s)\mathrm{d}B(s) - \frac{1}{2}\int_0^t \left\|u(s)\right\|^2 \mathrm{d}s\right)$$

is equivalent to P and is such that

$$\mathrm{e}^{-\int_0^t \rho(s)\mathrm{d}s} X_i(t)$$

is a Q- martingale. In this case $\|.\|$ represents the usual norm in $\mathbb{R}^n$. Moreover $B(t)$ given by

$$\mathrm{d}\tilde{B}(t) = u(t)\mathrm{d}t + \mathrm{d}B(t)$$

is a Q-Brownian motion. Surely there are infinitely many equivalent martingale measures Q. Let $\mathcal{M}_e$ be the set of all equivalent martingale measures Q for this market.

Pricing a contingent T- claim with payoff $F(\omega)$ in such a market has been studied before. The most common ideas include either to complete the market (see [6]) or finding a measure $Q^{\circledast} \in \mathcal{M}_e$ which is "good" enough so that

$$\Pi(t) = E_{Q^{\circledast}}\left[\mathrm{e}^{-\int_t^T \rho(s)\mathrm{d}s} F(\omega) \middle| \mathcal{F}_t\right]$$

is the "best" price admissible to buyers and sellers. It is known (see [1] and references therein) that

$$\Pi^b(t) \le \Pi(t) \le \Pi^s(t)$$

where respectively $\Pi^b(.)$ and $\Pi^s(.)$ represents the buyer's price and seller's price. The interval

$$\left[\Pi^b(.), \Pi^s(.)\right]$$

is the set of admissible prices for both buyers and sellers. Any price charged outside this interval will cause one to create an arbitrage. In [1], the authors give an explicit representation of $\Pi^b(.)$ and $\Pi^s(.)$.

In this paper we aim to characterize and price contingent claims in incomplete markets. We will characterize them into those which are attainable and those which are not and we give an overview of their pricing procedure.

3. Ontingent Claims in Incomplete Markets

We look at the following results:

Proposition 3.1 Let f be a measurable function and T > 0 be a finite time horizon. Any contingent T- claim of the form

$$F(\omega) = f\left(X_i(T)\right),\ 1 \le i \le m$$

is attainable in the market, its price is unique and is independent of the choice of the equivalent martingale measure Q.

Proof:

Without loss of generality, let us assume constant coefficients. With respect to P, we have

$$X_i(t) = X_i(0)\exp\left[\left(\alpha - \frac{1}{2}\sum_{j=1}^{n}\sigma_{ij}^2\right)t + \sum_{j=1}^{n}\sigma_{ij}\mathrm{d}B_j(t)\right]$$

and with respect to Q we have

$$X_i(t) = X_i(0)\exp\left[\left(\rho - \frac{1}{2}\sum_{j=1}^{n}\sigma_{ij}^2\right)t + \sum_{j=1}^{n}\sigma_{ij}d\tilde{B}_j(t)\right]$$

Clearly, $X_i(t)$ is independent of the market price of risk u and thus is independent of the equivalent martingale measure Q, so that the price

$$\Pi(t) = E_Q\left[\mathrm{e}^{-\rho(T-t)} f\left(X_i(T)\right) \middle| \mathcal{F}_t\right] \qquad (3.1)$$

is independent of Q. Thus $\Pi(t)$ is uniquely determined in (3.1). To show that every $F(\omega)$ of this nature is attainable, it is enough to use the martingale representation theorem and also normalize to get a martingale representation of the terminal value of the self-financing portfolio of stocks and bonds. We refer the reader to [1] Chapter 12 for details of this working.

N.B: What the proposition above tells us is that in incomplete markets the set of attainable claims is not empty. So in incomplete markets there are some contingent claims which can be hedged by a portfolio of stocks and bonds. Let $\mathcal{A}_Q^a$ be the set of all T-claims which are attainable in this market. Therefore

$$F(\omega) = f(X_i(T)) \in \mathcal{A}_Q^a.$$

we are not so certain as to what other types of payoff are in $\mathcal{A}_Q^a$ and this remains a good exercise for interested readers.

Proposition 3.2 *Let g be a measurable function, then any T-claim with payoff*

$$F(\omega) = g(B_i(T)),\ i \le i \le n$$

is not attainable in the market.

The proof is in [1] Chapter 12 for a particular case which could easily be generalized. The set of T-claims which are not attainable in the market shall be denoted $\mathcal{A}_Q^n$.

Definition 3.3 *An equivalent martingale measure $Q^{\circledast} \in \mathcal{M}_e$ is called an admissible pricing martingale measure for the T-claim $F(\omega)$ if*

$$\Pi^{\circledast}(t) = E_{Q^{\circledast}}\left[\mathrm{e}^{-\rho(T-t)}F(\omega)\middle|\mathcal{F}_t\right]$$

is admissible to buyers and sellers and there exist utility functions $U_b(.)$, (the buyer's utility) and $U_s(.)$, (the seller's utility) such that

$$U_b(\Pi^{\circledast}) = \sup_{\Pi(t)\in\left[\Pi^b(t),\Pi^s(t)\right]} U^b(\Pi(t)), \text{ and} \quad (3.2)$$

$$U_s(\Pi^{\circledast}) = \sup_{\Pi(t)\in\left[\Pi^b(t),\Pi^s(t)\right]} U^s(\Pi(t)) \quad (3.3)$$

Note that (3.2) and (3.3) can easily be justified through an auction of the contingent claim $F(\omega)$ and the price for this claim obtained through such an auction is $\Pi^{\circledast}(t)$. Therefore for each contingent claim $F(\omega)$ there is a unique price $\Pi^{\circledast}(t)$ admissible to buyers and seller and there exists an admissible pricing measure $Q^{\circledast}$ such that

$$\Pi^{\circledast}(t) = E_{Q^{\circledast}}\left[\mathrm{e}^{-\rho(T-t)}F(\omega)\middle|\mathcal{F}_t\right].$$

what may not be clear for now is whether this admissible pricing measure is unique for each contingent claim. This will be addressed later after looking at the following particular cases.

3.1. Examples of Pricing in $\mathcal{A}_Q^a$ and $\mathcal{A}_Q^n$

We assume constant coefficients and assume $m = 1$ and $n = 2$. We also consider the mean-variance measure as one of the studied admissible pricing measures. The choice of this measure is arbitrary since the results for the other already studied pricing measures will be similar.

The market will now be $X(t) = (X_0(t), X_1(t))$ with

$$\begin{cases} \mathrm{d}X_0(t) = \rho X_0(t)\mathrm{d}t,\ X_0(0) = 1 \\ \mathrm{d}X_1(t) = X_1(t)\left[\alpha \mathrm{d}t + \sigma_1 \mathrm{d}B_1(t) + \sigma_2 \mathrm{d}B_2(t)\right], \\ \qquad X_1(0) = x_1 \end{cases} \quad (3.4)$$

Then by the Girsanov theorem, the market price of risk is $u = (u_1, u_2)^*$ such that

$$\sigma_1 u_1 + \sigma_2 u_2 = \alpha - \rho \quad (3.5)$$

There are infinitely many solutions for u_1 and u_2. The measure Q given by

$$\frac{\mathrm{d}Q}{\mathrm{d}P} = M(T)$$

where

$$M(t) = \exp\left(-u_1 B_1(t) - u_2 B_2(t) - \frac{1}{2}\left(u_1^2 + u_2^2\right)t\right)$$

is an equivalent martingale measure such that $\mathrm{e}^{-\rho t}X_1(t)$ is a Q-martingale. Moreover,

$$\tilde{B}(t) = \left(\tilde{B}_1(t), \tilde{B}_2(t)\right)^*$$

given by

$$\mathrm{d}\tilde{B}_k(t) = u_k \mathrm{d}t + \mathrm{d}B_k(t),\ (k = 1,2)$$

is a two dimensional Brownian motion with respect to Q.

Since u induces Q then there are infinitely many equivalent martingale measures to P. Any payoff $F(\omega) \in \mathcal{A}_Q^n$ will have infinitely possible prices . The challenge is to find the "best" such price admissible to buyers and sellers.

3.1.1. Pricing a Payoff in $\mathcal{A}_Q^n$ by the Mean Variance Martingale Measure

Let us for simplicity consider the European T-claim with payoff

$$F(\omega) = \exp(B_1(T) + B_2(T)).$$

then with respect to Q, we have

$$F(\omega) = \exp\left(\tilde{B}_1(T) + \tilde{B}_2(T) - (u_1 + u_2)T\right).$$

the mean variance equivalent martingale measure $Q^{\circledast}$ is the one which minimizes

$$E_Q\left[V(T) - F(\omega)\right]^2$$

over all $Q \in \mathcal{M}_e$ where $V(T)$ is the terminal value of a self financing portfolio $\Theta = (\theta_0, \theta_1)^*$ of stocks and bonds. We have

$$V(t)=\theta_0 X_0(t)+\theta_1 X_1(t)$$

and

$$\mathrm{d}V(t)=\theta_0\mathrm{d}X_0(t)+\theta_1\mathrm{d}X_1(t).$$

Therefore to get $Q^{\circledast}$ we find

$$u^{\circledast}=\left(u_1^{\circledast},u_2^{\circledast}\right)$$

from

$$\begin{cases}\min\limits_{u_1,u_2} E_Q\left[\mathrm{e}^{\tilde{B}_1(T)+\tilde{B}_2(T)-(u_1+u_2)T}-\theta_0 X_0(T)-\theta_1 X_1(T)\right]^2\\ \text{subject to } \sigma_1 u_1+\sigma_2 u_2=\alpha-\rho\end{cases}$$

Therefore $u^{\circledast}$ is obtained from the following system of equations

$$\begin{cases}a_1\mathrm{e}^{-2(u_1+u_2)T}+a_2 T\mathrm{e}^{-(u_1+u_2)T}+\lambda\sigma_1=0\\ a_1\mathrm{e}^{-2(u_1+u_2)T}+a_2 T\mathrm{e}^{-(u_1+u_2)T}+\lambda\sigma_2=0\\ \sigma_1 u_1+\sigma_2 u_2=\alpha-\rho\end{cases}\qquad(3.6)$$

where $\lambda\in\mathbb{R}$ is the Lagrange multiplier.

Here $a_1=-2T\mathrm{e}^{4T}$ and

$$a_2=2T\theta_0\mathrm{e}^{(1+\rho)T}\left(1+x_1\mathrm{e}^{(\sigma_1+\sigma_2)T}\right)$$

Solving we get

$$\begin{cases}\sigma_1=\sigma_2\\ u_1^{\circledast}+u_2^{\circledast}=\dfrac{\alpha-\rho}{\sigma}\end{cases}\qquad(3.7)$$

where $\sigma=\sigma_1=\sigma_2$

Therefore, with respect to $Q^{\circledast}$, we have

$$F(\omega)=\exp\left(\tilde{B}_1(T)+\tilde{B}_2-\left(\frac{\alpha-\rho}{\sigma}\right)T\right).$$

We see here that $Q^{\circledast}$ is uniquely determined by (3.7). The price of the contingent claim $F(\omega)$ is

$$\begin{aligned}\Pi^{\circledast}(t)&=E_{Q^{\circledast}}\left[\mathrm{e}^{-\rho(T-t)}F(\omega)\middle|\mathcal{F}_t\right]\\&=\exp\left((1-\rho)(T-t)+\tilde{B}_1(t)+\tilde{B}_2(t)\right)\end{aligned}.$$

In particular if $t=0$, then $\Pi^{\circledast}(0)=\mathrm{e}^{(1-\rho)T}$.

Remark 3.4 If instead, we consider

$$F(\omega)=\mathrm{e}^{B_1(T)}$$

then we get the solution

$$\sigma_2=0,\ u_1^{\circledast}=\frac{\alpha-\rho}{\sigma_1},\ u_2^{\circledast}\in\mathbb{R}$$

is arbitrary. Therefore in this case the mean variance measure is not unique since $u_2^{\circledast}$ can take any value in $\mathbb{R}$.

The price for this contingent claim is

$$\begin{aligned}\Pi^{\circledast}(t)&=\exp\left(\left(\frac{1}{2}-\rho\right)(T-t)-u_1^{\circledast}T+\tilde{B}_1(t)\right)\\&=\exp\left(\left(\frac{1}{2}-\rho\right)(T-t)-\left(\frac{\alpha-\rho}{\sigma_1}\right)T+\tilde{B}_1(t)\right)\end{aligned}$$

and is independent of the choice of $u_2^{\circledast}$.

In particular to these toy examples, we see that if $t=0$, then

$$\Pi^{\circledast}(0)=\mathrm{e}^{\left(\frac{1}{2}-\rho\right)T-\left(\frac{\alpha-\rho}{\sigma_1}\right)T}.$$

In conclusion, we see that in $\mathcal{A}_Q^n$, each chosen contingent claim has a unique price calculated using either a unique or infinitely many admissible pricing measures. So the mapping from the set of admissible pricing measures to the set of admissible prices can be a many to one mapping.

3.1.2. Pricing a Payoff in $\mathcal{A}_Q^a$ by the Mean Variance Martingale Measure

Let us now consider a payoff of the form

$$F(\omega)=f\left(X_1(T)\right)$$

and in particular let f be the identity function so that

$$\begin{aligned}F(\omega)=X_1(t)\exp&\left(\left(\alpha-\frac{1}{2}\sigma_1^2-\frac{1}{2}\sigma_2^2\right)T\right.\\&\left.+\sigma_1 B_1(T)+\sigma_2 B_2(T)\right)\end{aligned}.$$

With respect to Q, we have

$$\begin{aligned}F(\omega)=X_1(t)\exp&\left(\left(\rho-\frac{1}{2}\sigma_1^2-\frac{1}{2}\sigma_2^2\right)T\right.\\&\left.\sigma_1 B_1(T)+\sigma_2 B_2(T)\right)\end{aligned}$$

which does not depend on u. Therefore the mean variance measure $Q^{\circledast}$ does not depend on u meaning that any choice of (u_1,u_2) will reult in the same price for F, which price is

$$\Pi(t)=X_1(t)\exp\left(\sigma_1\tilde{B}_1(t)+\sigma_2\tilde{B}_2(t)\right)$$

and if $t=0$, then $\Pi(0)=x_1$, the price of the stock. Therefore a European contingent claim which promises to pay the terminal stock price should charge the current stock price.

Definition 3.5 Two admissible pricing measures Q_1 and Q_2 are **substitutes** with respect to a given payoff $F(\omega)$ if and only if the discounted price of F with respect to Q_1 is the same as that with respect to Q_2

Remark 3.6 The relationship substitutes defined above is an equivalence relation.

The proof of this remark is trivial. Now the equivalence relation would result in the creation of equivalent classes and considering $\mathcal{M}_e$ as a set of these atoms, then the map from $\mathcal{M}_e$ to $\left[\Pi^b(t), \Pi^s(t)\right]$ will be an injective function. We are not interested in pursuing this algebraic reality in this paper and leave it for interested readers to explore further.

In conclusion to this section, we have managed to categorize payoffs which are attainable and those which are not in an incomplete market. Each payoff will be priced using an admissible pricing measure. Our definition of admissible pricing measures shows that any contingent claim in incomplete markets can be priced and the price is unique. However the uniqueness of the price does not imply the uniqueness of the pricing measure. For example, if the payoff is attainable, then all $Q \in \mathcal{M}_e$ yields the same price. The story is different in the case that the claim is not attainable.

4. Conclusion

We have managed to categorize the T-claims which are attainable and those which are not and we have linked each payoff to a price which in turn is linked to a class of *substitutes*. Therefore, given a contingent claim, we should be able to find its price using one of the admissible pricing measures. The price is calculated as the discounted expectation of the payoff with respect to the admissible measure and buyers and sellers would always agree on this price.

REFERENCES

[1] B. Oksendal, "Stochastic Differential Equations," 6th Edition, Springer-Verlag, Berlin, 2007.

[2] M. Schweizer, "On the Minimal Martingale Measure and the Möllmer-Schweizer Decomposition," *Stochastic Analysis and Applications*, Vol. 13, No. 5, 1995, pp. 573-599.

[3] M. Fritelli, "The Minimal Entropy Martingale Measure and the Valuation Problem in Incomplete Markets," *Mathematical Finance*, Vol. 10, No. 1, 2000, pp. 39-52.

[4] H. U. Gerber and E. S. W. Shi, "Option Pricing by Esscher Transforms," *Transactions of the Society of Actuaries*, Vol. 46, 1994, pp. 99-191.

[5] M. Jeanblanc, S. Klöppel and Y. Miyahara, "Minimal f^q-Martingale Measures for Exponential Lévy Processes," *The Annals of Applied Probability*, Vol. 17, No. 5-6, 2007, pp. 1615-1638.

[6] S. Mataramvura, P. Dankemlmann and S. W. Mgobhozi, "Completion of Markets by Variation Processes," Working Paper, 2013.

16

Design of Financial Market Regulations against Large Price Fluctuations Using by Artificial Market Simulations*

Takanobu Mizuta[1,2], Kiyoshi Izumi[2,3], Isao Yagi[4], Shinobu Yoshimura[2]
[1]SPARX Asset Management Co., Ltd., Tokyo, Japan
[2]School of Engineering, The University of Tokyo, Tokyo, Japan
[3]CREST & PRESTO, Japan Science and Technology Agency, Tokyo, Japan
[4]Faculty of Information Technology, Kanagawa Institute of Technology, Kanagawa, Japan

ABSTRACT

We built an artificial market model and compared effects of price variation limits, short selling regulations and up-tick rules. In the case without the regulations, the price fell to below a fundamental value when an economic crush occurred. On the other hand, in the case with the regulations, this overshooting did not occur. However, the short selling regulation and the up-tick rule caused the trading prices to be higher than the fundamental value. We also surveyed an adequate limitation price range and an adequate limitation time span for the price variation limit and found a parameters' condition of the price variation limit to prevent the over-shorts. We also showed the limitation price range should be bigger than a volatility calculated by the limitation time span.

Keywords: Artificial Market; Multi Agent Simulation; Financial Crash; Price Variation Limit; Short Selling Regulation; Up-Tick Rule

1. Introduction

Financial exchanges sometimes employ a "price variation limit", which restrict trades out of certain price ranges within certain time spans to avoid sudden large price fluctuations. For example, Tokyo Stock Exchange employs two kinds of price variation limits that adopt different time spans: one is "daily price limit" which restricts price fluctuations within a single trading day, and the other is "special quote", which restricts within three minutes [1]. Most Asian stock exchanges (Tokyo, Taipei, Shanghai, Shenzhen, Seoul, and so on) employ the price variation limits, but many American and European stock exchanges do not because there is a debate over whether the price variation limit makes financial market more efficient or not. On financial markets, other regulations, "short selling regulation"[1], "up-tick rule"[2] and so on, also are debated over whether makes more efficient or not.

Because so many factors cause price formation in actual markets, an empirical study can not isolate a pure contribution of these regulations to price formation. Therefore, it is very difficult to discuss about a pure effect of these regulations only by results of empirical studies. An artificial market[3] which is a kind of an agent based simulation will help us to discuss about this very well. There are several previous studies to discuss about regulations of financial market using artificial market simulations. Yagi *et al.* investigated effect of short selling regulations induce bubbles [4,5]. Westerhoff discussed effectiveness of transaction taxes, central bank interventions and trading halts [6]. Thurner *et al.* showed that as leverage increases price fluctuation becomes heavy tailed and display clustered volatility [7]. Kobayashi and Hashimoto showed that circuit breakers play an important role in controlling price fluctuations, while they also reduce the trading volume [8]. Yeh and Yang investigated the effectiveness of price variation limits and showed that price variation limits help to reduce volatility and price distortion [9]. Mi-

*It should be noted that the opinions contained herein are solely those of the authors and do not necessarily reflect those of SPARX Asset Management Co., Ltd.

[1]Short selling is the selling of a stock that the seller doesn't own. Short selling regulation is that any short selling is restricted.

[2]Up-tick rule is that short selling except upon an up-tick of last traded price is restricted.

[3]Excellent reviews are [2,3].

zuta *et al.* discussed effectiveness of price variation limits and argued that an artificial market model testing such regulations should be implementing a learning process to replicate bubbles, and showed that a hazard rate enables verification of whether the models can replicate a bubble process or not [10]. However, no simulation studies have investigated up-tick rules, and compared effects of the short selling regulation, the up-tick rule and the price variation limit using an artificial market model. These regulations are expected to be especially effective to prevent bubbles and crushes, so simulation studies investigating these regulations should use artificial market models replicating bubbles and crushes.

We built an artificial market model and compared effects of price variation limits, short selling regulations and up-tick rules. In the case without the regulations, the price fell to below a fundamental value when an economic crush occurred. On the other hand, in the case with the regulations, this overshooting did not occur. However, the short selling regulation and the up-tick rule caused the trading prices to be higher than the fundamental value. We also surveyed an adequate limitation price range and an adequate limitation time span for the price variation limit and found a parameters' condition of the price variation limit to prevent the over-shorts. We also showed the limitation price range should be bigger than a volatility calculated by the limitation time span. The paper is structured as follows; in Section 2, we explain details of our artificial market model. In Section 3, we show results of simulations. The paper's conclusions are presented in Section 4.

2. Artificial Market Model

We built a simple artificial market model on the basis of the model of [11]. The model treats only one risk asset and non-risk asset (cash) and adopts a continuous double auction[4] to determine a market price of the risk asset. The number of agents is n. At first, at time $t=1$, an agent 1 orders to buy or sell the risk asset; after that at $t=2$ an agent 2 orders; at $t=3,4,\cdots,n$, an agent $3,4,\cdots,n$ orders respectively. At $t=n+1$, going back to the first, the agent 1 orders, and at $t=n+2,n+3,\cdots,n+n$, an agent $2,3,\cdots,n$ orders respectively, and this cycle is repeated. Note that time t passes even if no deals are done. An agent j determines an order price and buys or sells by the following process. Agents use a combination of fundamental value and technical rules to form expectations on a risk asset returns. An expected return of the agent j is

$$r_{e,j}^t = \frac{1}{\sum_i w_{i,j}}\left(w_{1,j}\log\frac{P_f}{P^t} + w_{2,j} r_{h,j}^t + w_{3,j}\epsilon_j^t \right), \tag{1}$$

where $w_{i,j}$ is weight of term i of the agent j, and is determined by random variables of uniformly distributed in the interval $(0, w_{i,\max})$ at the start of the simulation independently for each agent. P_f is a fundamental value that is constant. P^t is a market price of the risk asset at time t. (When the dealing is not done at t, P^t remains at the last market price P^{t-1}, and at $t=1$, $P^t = P_f$). ϵ_j^t is a noise determined by random variables of normal distribution with an average 0 and a variance σ_ϵ. $r_{h,j}^t$ is a historical price return inside an agent's time interval τ_j, and $r_{h,j}^t = \log\left(P^t / P^{t-\tau_j}\right)$. τ_j is determined by random variables uniformly distributed in the interval $(1, \tau_{\max})$ at the start of the simulation independently for each agent. The first term of Equation (1) represents a fundamental strategy: an agent expects a positive return when the market price is lower than the fundamental value, and vice verse. The second term of Equation (1) represents a technical strategy: an agent expects a positive return when historical market return is positive, and vice verse. After the expected return has been determined, an expected price is

$$P_{e,j}^t = P^t \exp\left(r_{e,j}^t\right). \tag{2}$$

We modeled an order price $P_{o,j}^t$ by random variables of uniformly distributed in the interval $\left(P_{e,j}^t - P_d, P_{e,j}^t + P_d\right)$, where P_d is a constant. *A* minimum unit of a price change (tick size) is δP, we round off a fraction of less than δP. Buy or sell is determined by a magnitude relation between the expect price $P_{e,j}^t$ and the order price $P_{o,j}^t$, that is,

When $P_{e,j}^t > P_{o,j}^t$, the agent orders to buy one share.

When $P_{e,j}^t < P_{o,j}^t$, the agent orders to sell one share.

Agents always order only one share. Our model adopts the continuous double auction, so when an agent orders to buy (sell), if there is a lower price sell order (a higher price buy order) than the agent's order, dealing is immediately done. If there is not, the agent's order remains in the order book. The remaining order is canceled at t_c after the order time. Agents can short selling freely. The quantity of holding positions is not limited, so agents can take any shares for both long and short positions to infinity.

We also developed a model implementing a learning process of agents. Every agent learns just before every ordering. If there is only the first term (representing a fundamental strategy) or second term (representing a technical strategy) in Equation (1), an expected return $r_{i,j}^t\,(i=1,2)$ at time t of an agent j is

$$r_{1,j}^t = \log P_f / P^t, r_{2,j}^t = r_{h,j}^t, \tag{3}$$

respectively. We define $r_{l,j}^t = \log P^t / P^{t-t_l}$ where t_l is

[4]A continuous double auction is an auction mechanism where multiple buyers and sellers compete to buy and sell some financial assets, respectively, in the market, and where transactions can occur at any time whenever an offer to buy and an offer to sell match [12].

a constant evaluation term. $w_{i,j}$ is changed when both $r_{i,j}^t$ and $r_{l,j}^t$ are the same signs,

$$w_{i,j} \leftarrow w_{i,j} + kr_{l,j}^t u_{i,j}^t \left(w_{i,\max} - w_{i,j}\right), \quad (4)$$

On the other hand, when both $r_{i,j}^t$ and $r_{l,j}^t$ are opposite signs,

$$w_{i,j} \leftarrow w_{i,j} - kr_{l,j}^t u_{i,j}^t w_{i,j}, \quad (5)$$

where $u_{i,j}^t$ is random variables of uniformly distributed in the interval (0,1) for each t, j, i, k is constant. Besides this process, $w_{i,j}$ is reset, random variables of uniformly distributed in the interval $\left(0, w_{i,\max}\right)$, occurring with small probability, m. In this way, agents learn better parameters and switch to the investment strategy that estimates correctly: the fundamental strategy or technical strategy.

We investigated effectiveness of price variation limits, short selling regulations and up-tick rules. In this study, we modeled these regulations as follows. Price variation limits were modeled that any agents can freely order a price from $P^{t-t_{pl}} - \Delta P_{pl}$ to $P^{t-t_{pl}} + \Delta P_{pl}$, where t_{pl} is a constant time span, and ΔP_{pl} is a constant price. Any order prices of buy above $P^{t-t_{pl}} + \Delta P_{pl}$ are changed to $P^{t-t_{pl}} + \Delta P_{pl}$, and any order prices of sell under $P^{t-t_{pl}} - \Delta P_{pl}$ are changed to $P^{t-t_{pl}} - \Delta P_{pl}$. This prevents trading that prices outside $P^{t-t_{pl}} - \Delta P_{pl}, P^{t-t_{pl}} + \Delta P_{pl}$. Short selling regulations were modeled that agents which do not have the risk asset can not order to sell. Any agents have initially one unit risk asset. Up-tick rules were modeled when an agent which do not have the risk asset tries to order to sell a price not greater than P^t, the order price is changed to $P^t + \delta P$.

3. Simulation Result

In this study, we set $n = 1000$, $w_{1,\max} = 1$, $w_{2,\max} = 10$, $w_{3,\max} = 1$, $\tau_{\max} = 10,000$, $\sigma_\epsilon = 0.03$, $P_d = 1000$, $t_c = 10,000$, $\delta P = 1$, $k = 4$, $m = 0.01$, $t_l = 10,000$, $t_{pl} = 50,000$, $\Delta P_{pl} = 1000$. We also investigated two cases: the fundamental value P_f was fixed to 10,000 (constant fundamental value); P_f was 10,000 until $t = 100,000$ and changed to 7000 after $t = 100,000$ (sharp declining fundamental value). We ran simulations to $t =$ 10,000,000.

3.1. Verification the Model

In many previous artificial market studies[5], the models are verified to see whether they can explain the stylized facts such as a fat-tail[6], volatility-clustering[7], and so on.

[5]Excellent reviews are [2,3].

[6]This means that the kurtosis of price returns is positive. There are empirical studies for the fat-tail [13,14].

[7]This means that the square returns have positive autocorrelation, and the autocorrelation slowly decays as its time separation becomes larger There are empirical studies for the volatility-clustering [14-16].

Table 1 lists stylized facts in each case. We used returns for 100 time units' intervals to calculate the statistical values for the stylized facts[8]. In all runs, we can find that both kurtosis and autocorrelation coefficients for square returns with several lags are positive, which means that all runs replicate stylized facts.

In the actual financial markets including bubbles (crushes), the probability that a run, sequence of observations of the same sign, of positive (negative) returns will end should decline with the length of the run i [17,18]. A hazard rate $H(i)$ is used for the test of bubbles or crushes. $H(i)$ represents the conditional probability that a run ends at i, given that it lasts until i. Empirical studies show that $H(i)$ decline with the length of run i if observation data include bubble or crush phenomena [17,18]. This means that the bubble (crush) returns tend to continue to be positive (negative) and this tendency becomes stronger as runs of positive (negative) returns become longer. In the **Table 1**, $H(i)$ represents the conditional probability that a negative return run ends at i, given that it lasts until i. When hazard rates $H(i)$ declined increasing i, the simulation can replicate a significant crush like those occurring in actual markets. In the case of the constant fundamental value with a short selling regulation, $H(i)$ declined. This indicates that some small crushes occurred even though there was no crush-inducing trigger. In the case of the sharp declining fundamental value, except the case of implementing the price variation limit, $H(i)$ declined shallowly. These cases replicated big crushes like those occurring in actual markets.

3.2. Time Evolutions of Prices

Figure 1 shows time evolution of market prices in the case of the constant fundamental value. In the case without regulations and with the price variation limit, the market prices oscillated around the fundamental value, 10,000. This indicates that the market was efficient. On the other hand, in the case with the short selling regulation, bubbles and crushes occurred repetitively, and the prices were almost higher than the fundamental value. This result is consistent with previous studies [4][9]. In the case with the up-tick rule, the prices were almost higher than the fundamental value although the amplitudes are less than those of the case with short selling regulation.

Figure 2 shows time evolution of prices in the fundamental value P_f changed at $t = 100,000$ from 10,000 to 7000, which was the new fundamental value. In the case

[8]In this model, time passes by an agent just ordering even if no dealing is done. Therefore, the returns for one tick (one time) include many zero returns, and they will bias statistical values. This is the reason we use returns for 100 time units.

[9]Yagi *et al.* showed lager amplitudes of bubbles and crushes than those of this study [4]. However, we confirmed the amplitudes were smaller and same as those of this study when initial cash was decreased.

Table 1. Stylized facts in each run.

		Constant Fundamental Value $(=10,000)$				Sharp Declining Fundamental Value $(=10,000 \to 7000)$			
		Non-Regulation	Price Variation Limit	Short Selling Regulation	Up-Tick Rule	Non-Regulation	Price Variation Limit	Short Selling Regulation	Up-Tick Rule
Kurtosis		5.39	5.39	7.28	9.37	4.96	8.15	9.21	9.27
	Lag								
Autocorrelation Coefficient for Square Return	1	0.13	0.12	0.10	0.15	0.24	0.14	0.09	0.18
	2	0.11	0.10	0.09	0.12	0.21	0.13	0.09	0.16
	3	0.09	0.09	0.07	0.10	0.19	0.11	0.07	0.15
	4	0.07	0.07	0.07	0.09	0.18	0.11	0.07	0.14
	5	0.06	0.06	0.06	0.08	0.18	0.10	0.06	0.14
	6	0.05	0.05	0.05	0.07	0.18	0.10	0.06	0.13
	i								
Hazard Rate	1	55%	55%	52%	70%	55%	55%	51%	70%
	2	53%	52%	48%	72%	50%	53%	47%	70%
	3	49%	49%	45%	72%	45%	50%	44%	65%
	4	47%	47%	41%	71%	40%	48%	41%	52%
	5	44%	46%	40%	65%	34%	46%	38%	38%
	6	44%	45%	37%	61%	28%	44%	35%	25%

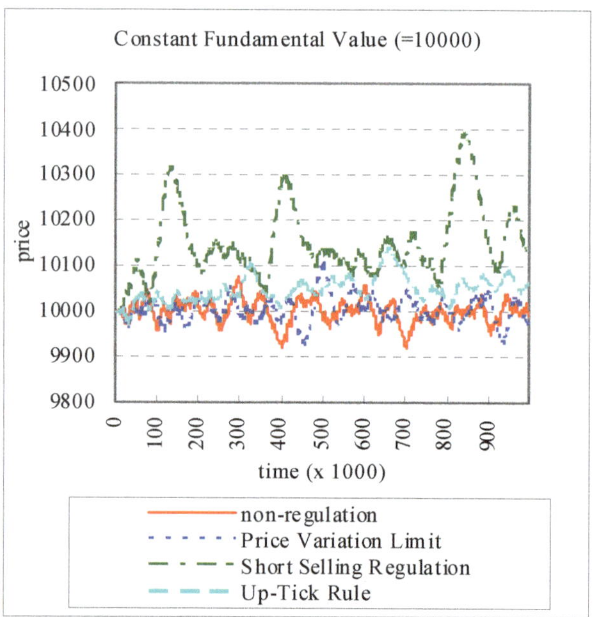

Figure 1. A time evolution of market prices in case that the fundamental value is constant $P_f = 10,000$.

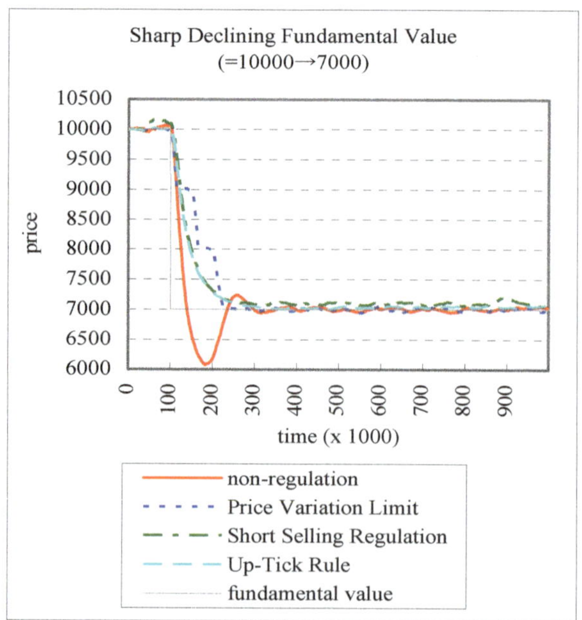

Figure 2. A time evolution of market prices in case that the fundamental value is sharply declining $P_f = 10,000 \to 7000$.

without regulations, the price went far 6000 beyond the new fundamental value, in other words, an overshoot occurred. After this overshoot, the price rebounded to the new fundamental value. Such the overshoots and rebounds were investigated by previous studies [19]. On the other hand, in the case with regulations, the price variation limit, the market price took longer to reach the new fundamental price $(P_f = 7000)$ than in the case without the regulations, but the bubble almost vanished. In the case with the short selling regulation and the up-tick rule, small bubbles and crushes occurred repetitively after the prices converged as same when the fundamental values were constants. The price variation limit prevented both such small bubbles and the overshoots. The most efficient market, an ideal market, prevents overshoots and achieves immediate convergence to the new fundamental value. However, this study shows that no market achieves both at once.

3.3. Switching Strategy

Figures 3 and **4** show a time series of fundamental strategy weights $\left(\sum_j w_{1,j} / \sum_i \sum_j w_{i,j}\right)$ and technical strategy weights $\left(\sum_j w_{2,j} / \sum_i \sum_j w_{i,j}\right)$ in case of the sharp declining fundamental value, without regulations and with the price variation limit, respectively. **Figure 3** shows that, during the crush from about $t = 100,000$ to $t = 200,000$, the technical strategy weight increased and the fundamental strategy weight declined. This is consistent with empirical studies [20,21] that show that investors tend to switch from the fundamental to the technical strategy during a crush because the fundamental strategy looses during an overshoot, declining the price less than the fundamental value. **Figure 4** shows that, in contrast to in the case without regulations, during the crush the technical strategy weight did not increase but the fundamental strategy weight did. The price variation limit restricted agents switching to the technical strategy and sprevented overshoots occurring[10].

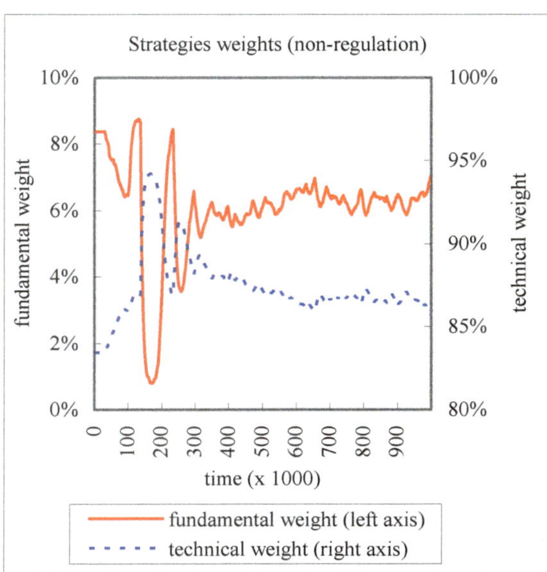

Figure 3. Time series of a fundamental strategy weight and a technical strategy weight in case without any regulations.

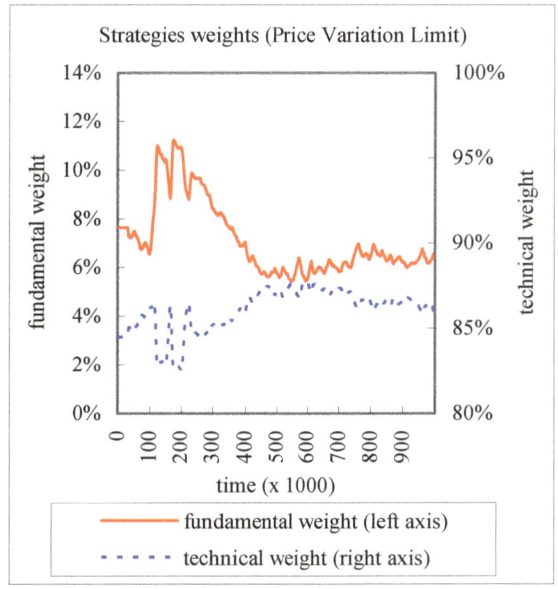

Figure 4. Time series of a fundamental strategy weight and a technical strategy weight in case with the price variation limit.

3.4. Survey Adequate Price Limitation

Next, we investigated optimization of $\Delta P_{pl}, t_{pl}$. The price variation limit prevents overshoots but also causes converging speed of market prices to the fundamental value to go slower. The most efficient market, an ideal market, prevents overshoots and achieves immediate convergence to the new fundamental value. However, no market achieves both at once. To make amplitude of an overshoot smaller, market prices converge to fundamental prices more slowly. On the other hand, if you speed up converging speed of market prices to the new fundamental value, occurrence of an overshoot is unavoidable. Therefore, it is important to search for better parameters, $\Delta P_{pl}, t_{pl}$, preventing overshoots and not trying to make the converging speed much slower.

Table 2 lists minimum prices from new fundamental value (max price minus 7000) for various $\Delta P_{pl}, t_{pl}$, and **Table 3** lists reaching times to new fundamental value divided by 1000 for various $\Delta P_{pl}, t_{pl}$. The reaching times are measured from a time when fundamental value is decreased, $t = 100,000$. "--" shows the case where market price could not reach the new fundamental price until $t = 600,000$. **Table 2** indicates that when t_{pl} is longer and/or ΔP_{pl} is smaller, overshoots are smaller. On the other hand, **Table 3** indicates that when t_{pl} is shorter and/or ΔP_{pl} is larger, converging speed to the fundamental value is faster. These tables suggest that the

[10]In the cases of the short selling regulation and the up-tick rule, the results were same as the case of the price variation.

Table 2. Minimum prices from new fundamental value for various $\Delta P_{pl}, t_{pl}$.

Minimum Price from New Fundamental Value		t_{pl}										
		1000	2000	3000	4000	5000	7000	10000	15000	20000	25000	30000
	100	−1064	−546	−312	−214	−155	−111	−69	−46	—	—	—
	200	−1180	−1141	−835	−540	−405	−234	−149	−88	−66	−53	−40
	300	−1213	−1159	−1136	−908	−702	−441	−258	−144	−105	−73	−51
	400	−1154	−1140	−1169	−1175	−958	−632	−399	−156	−105	−78	−74
	500	−1180	−1198	−1151	−1228	−1094	−820	−528	−282	−195	−137	−65
⊿Ppl	700	−1134	−1148	−1171	−1170	−1135	−1122	−774	−481	−201	−105	−74
	1000	−1141	−1112	−1202	−1169	−1148	−1191	−1199	−726	−561	−361	−132
	1500	−1172	−1196	−1209	−1157	−1181	−1186	−1165	−1189	−841	−755	−379
	2000	−1157	−1135	−1166	−1169	−1157	−1164	−1147	−1143	−1160	−788	−540
	2500	−1137	−1172	−1132	−1156	−1120	−1164	−1158	−1112	−1186	−1144	−910
	3000	−1146	−1188	−1118	−1146	−1160	−1158	−1108	−1126	−1131	−1131	−1149

Table 3. Reaching times to new fundamental value divided by 1000 for various $\Delta P_{pl}, t_{pl}$.

Reach Time to New Fundamental Value (×1000)		tpl										
		1000	2000	3000	4000	5000	7000	10000	15000	20000	25000	30000
	100	40	65	94	126	159	223	325	479	--	--	--
	200	39	39	50	64	78	109	155	231	306	380	455
	300	39	39	39	46	55	73	103	155	204	254	303
	400	39	39	39	39	44	57	78	120	158	198	236
	500	39	39	39	39	39	48	64	95	124	152	180
ΔPpl	700	39	39	39	39	39	39	48	67	92	117	143
	1000	39	39	39	39	39	39	39	50	64	77	91
	1500	39	39	39	39	39	39	39	39	46	53	61
	2000	39	39	39	39	39	39	39	39	39	45	54
	2500	39	39	39	39	39	39	39	39	39	39	41
	3000	39	39	39	39	39	39	39	39	39	39	39

faster convergence to the new fundamental price and the smaller overshoot are not compatible. To make amplitude of a overshoot smaller, market prices converge to fundamental prices more slowly. On the other hand, if you speed up converging speed of market prices to fundamental value, occurrence of an overshoot is unavoidable. In an area of the lower left of **Table 3**, values are very similar, about 39,000. This value is almost the same as the converging speed to the fundamental value without the price variation limit, v. In the case without the price variation limit, it took about 39,000 for a price to rise to 7000 from 10,000, so $v = 3000/39,000 \simeq 0.077\$$. Shadow areas in **Tables 2** and **3** satisfy an inequality constraint,

$$\frac{\Delta P_{pl}}{t_{pl}} < v \simeq 0.077 . \qquad (6)$$

Table 2 shows that overshoots did not occur in this shadow area. Therefore, Equation (6) is a condition for the price variation limit to prevent overshoots. In the left term of Equation (6) (further to upper right in these tables) bubbles are smaller but the converging speed slower. In this sense, the market is less efficient. When we design the price variation limit, it is important that the parameters satisfy Equation (6) and the left term is not much smaller than the right term.

Figure 5 showed that several in the same $\Delta P_{pl}/t_{pl}$, $\Delta P_{pl} = 200, t_{pl} = 5, \Delta P_{pl} = 2000, t_{pl} = 50$ and $\Delta P_{pl} = 20{,}000$, $t_{pl} = 500$. When $\Delta P_{pl}/t_{pl}$ is same, it seemed that the time evolution of market prices tend to be similar from **Tables 2** and **3**. However, in **Figure 5**, only in the case of $\Delta P_{pl} = 200$, $t_{pl} = 5$, the market prices declined a little and did never reach to the new fundamental value by the simulation end time, $t = 500{,}000$. This implicated that even if $\Delta P_{pl}/t_{pl}$ is same, when ΔP_{pl} and t_{pl} are too small, the market become to be inefficient prevented converging to the new fundamental value. **Table 4** showed ratios of reaching to new fundamental value by simulation ends to 100 times simulation runs for various small $\Delta P_{pl}, t_{pl}$, and V_{tpl}, volatilities calculated by t_{pl}[11]. A shadow area satisfies an inequality constraint Equation (6), $\Delta P_{pl}/t_{pl} < v$. **Table 4** shows that the inequality constraint Equation (6) was not related whether or not the price converged to the new fundamental value. An upper right area above the solid line shows $\Delta P_{pl} < V_{tpl}$ is satisfied. In this area, the market price never converged to the new fundamental value. Therefore, not only Equation (6) but also a condition,

$$\Delta P_{pl} > V_{tpl}, \tag{7}$$

is needed to effective price variation limits, which make markets efficiently.

4. Conclusion and Future Study

We built an artificial market model and compared effects of price variation limits, short selling regulations and up-tick rules. In the case without the regulations, the price fell to below a fundamental value when an economic crush occurred. On the other hand, in the case with the regulations, this overshooting did not occur. However, the short selling regulation and the up-tick rule caused the trading prices to be higher than the fundamental value. We also surveyed an adequate limitation price range and an adequate limitation time span for the price variation limit and found a parameters' condition of the price variation limit to prevent the over-shorts. We also showed the limitation price range should be bigger than a volatility calculated by the limitation time span.

One future study is to a find way to recommend actually good parameters of the price variation limit to real

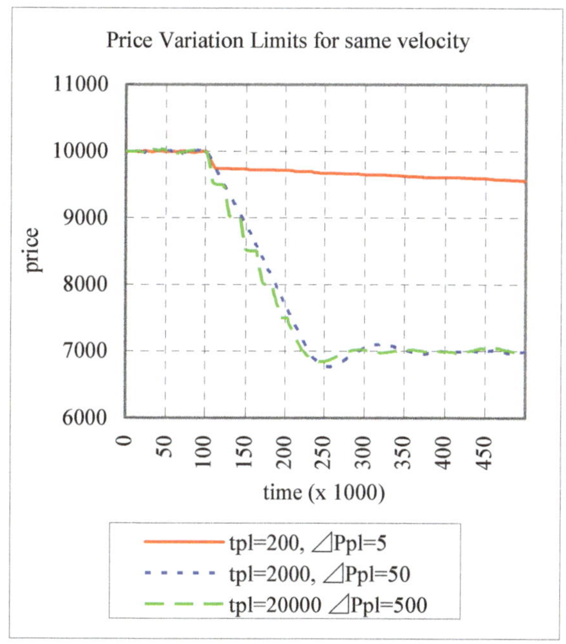

Figure 5. A time evolution of market prices in the same $\Delta P_{pl}/t_{pl}$.

Table 4. Ratios of reaching to new fundamental value by simulation ends to 100 times simulation runs for various small $\Delta P_{pl}, t_{pl}$, and V_{tpl}, volatilities calculated by t_{pl}.

Ratio of Reaching to New Fundamental Value		tpl									
		5	10	20	50	100	200	500	1000	2000	5000
Vtpl (Volatility by tpl)		0.01%	0.01%	0.02%	0.02%	0.04%	0.05%	0.06%	0.08%	0.09%	0.10%
⊿Ppl	1	0%	0%	0%	0%	0%	0%	0%	0%	0%	0%
	2	0%	0%	0%	0%	0%	0%	0%	0%	0%	0%
	5	84%	83%	80%	87%	2%	0%	0%	0%	0%	0%
	10	99%	100%	100%	100%	99%	100%	25%	0%	0%	0%
	20	100%	100%	100%	100%	100%	100%	100%	100%	100%	0%
	50	100%	100%	100%	100%	100%	100%	100%	100%	100%	100%
	100	100%	100%	100%	100%	100%	100%	100%	100%	100%	100%

[11]The volatilities were standard deviation of returns of market prices within t_{pl}.

stock exchanges. We cannot observe actual v shown in Section 3.4. Tokyo Stock Exchange employs two kinds of price variation limits that adopt different time spans: one is "daily price limit", which restricts price fluctuations within a single trading day, and the other is "special quote" which restricts within three minutes [1]. We can interpret that the special quote that has a shorter time span determines v and the daily price limit that has a longer time span prevents bubbles. Thus, where parameters of the daily price limit are $\Delta P_{pl,1}, t_{pl,1}$ and those of the special quote are $\Delta P_{pl,2}, t_{pl,2}$, when these parameters satisfied

$$\frac{\Delta P_{pl,1}}{t_{pl,1}} < \frac{\Delta P_{pl,2}}{t_{pl,2}}, \tag{8}$$

these price variation limits can prevent bubbles. However, the left term of Equation (8) should be not so smaller than the right term as we suggested in Section 3.4. For example, $t_{pl,1} = 300$ minutes, $\Delta P_{pl,1} = 300$ yen, $t_{pl,2} = 3$ minutes, and $\Delta P_{pl,2} = 30$ yen for stocks that have prices from 1000 yen to 1500 yen in Tokyo Stock Exchange. Therefore, Equation (8) is strongly satisfied but the left term of Equation (8) is much smaller than the right term. It is possible that the daily price limit is too tight ($t_{pl,1} = 300$ minutes is too large or $\Delta P_{pl,1} = 300$ yen is too small) or the special quote is too loose ($t_{pl,2} = 3$ minutes is too small or $\Delta P_{pl,2} = 30$ yen is too large). However, this study could not discuss such actual parameters. This is a future work.

REFERENCES

[1] Tokyo Stock Exchange, "Guide to TSE Trading Methodology," 2012.

[2] B. LeBaron, "Agent-Based Computational Finance," *Handbook of Computational Economics*, Vol. 2, 2006, pp. 1187-1233.

[3] S.-H. Chen, C.-L. Chang and Y.-R. Du, "Agent-Based Economic Models and Econometrics," *The Knowledge Engineering Review*, Vol. 27, No. 2, 2009, pp. 187-219.

[4] I. Yagi, T. Mizuta and K. Izumi, "A Study on the Effectiveness of Shortselling Regulation Using Artificial Markets," *Evolutionary and Institutional Economics Review*, Vol. 7, No. 1, 2010, pp. 113-132.

[5] I. Yagi, T. Mizuta and K. Izumi, "A Study on the Market Impact of Short-Selling Regulation Using Artificial Markets," In: Q. Bai and N. Fukuta, Eds., *Advances in Practical Multi-Agent Systems, ser. Studies in Computational Intelligence*, Vol. 325, Springer, Berlin, Heidelberg, 2011, pp. 217-231.

[6] F. Westerhoff, "The Use of Agent-Based Financial Market Models to Test the Effectiveness of Regulatory Policies," *Jahrbucher Fur Nationalokonomie Und Statistik*, Vol. 228, No. 2, 2008, p. 195.

[7] S. Thurner, J. Farmer and J. Geanakoplos, "Leverage Causes Fat Tails and Clustered Volatility," *Quantitative Finance*, Vol. 12, No. 5, 2012, pp. 695-707.

[8] S. Kobayashi and T. Hashimoto, "Benefits and Limits of Circuit Breaker: Institutional Design Using Artificial Futures Market," *Evolutionary and Institutional Economics Review*, Vol. 7, No. 2, 2011, pp. 355-372.

[9] C. Yeh and C. Yang, "Examining the Effectiveness of Price Limits in an Artificial Stock Market," *Journal of Economic Dynamics and Control*, Vol. 34, No. 10, 2010, pp. 2089-2108.

[10] T. Mizuta, K. Izumi and S. Yoshimura, "Price Variation Limits and Financial Market Bubbles: Artificial Market Simulations with Agents' Learning Process," 2013 *IEEE Symposium Series on Computational Intelligence for Financial Engineering Economics*, Singapore City, April 2013, pp. 1-7. http://www.ntu.edu.sg/home/epnsugan/index_files/SSCI2013/index.html

[11] C. Chiarella, G. Iori and J. Perelló, "The Impact of Heterogeneous Trading Rules on the limit order book and Order Flows," *Journal of Economic Dynamics and Control*, Vol. 33, No. 3, 2009, pp. 525-537.

[12] D. Friedman, "The Double Auction Market Institution: A Survey," In: D. Friedman and J. Rust, Eds., *The Double Auction Market: Institutions, Theories, and Evidence*, Addison-Wesley, Boston, 1993, pp. 3-25.

[13] B. Mandelbrot, "The Variation of Certain Speculative Prices," *The Journal of Business*, Vol. 36, No. 4, 1963, pp. 394-419.

[14] R. Cont, "Empirical Properties of Asset Returns: Stylized Facts and Statistical Issues," *Quantitative Finance*, Vol. 1, 2001, pp. 223-236.

[15] B. Mandelbrot, "Statistical Methodology for Nonperiodic Cycles: From the Covariance to R/S Analysis," *Annals of Economic and Social Measurement*, Vol. 1, No. 3, 1972, pp. 259-290.

[16] M. Sewell, "Characterization of Financial Time Series," 2006.

[17] G. McQueen and S. Thorley, "Bubbles, Stock Returns, and Duration Dependence," *Journal of Financial and Quantitative Analysis*, Vol. 29, No. 3, 1994, pp. 379-401.

[18] K. Chan, G. McQueen and S. Thorley, "Are There Rational Speculative Bubbles in Asian Stock Markets?" *Pacific-Basin Finance Journal*, Vol. 6, No. 1-2, 1998, pp. 125-151.

[19] I. Yagi, T. Mizuta and K. Izumi, "A Study on the Reversal Mechanism for Large Stock Price Declines Using Artificial Markets," 2012 *IEEE Conference on Computational Intelligence for Financial Engineering Economics*, New York, March 2012, pp. 1-7. http://www.ieee-cifer.org/2012/index.html

[20] J. Frankel and K. Froot, "Chartists, Fundamentalists, and Trading in the Foreign Exchange Market," *The American Economic Review*, Vol. 80, No. 2, 1990, pp. 181-185.

[21] R. Yamamoto and H. Hirata, "Strategy Switching in the Japanese Stock Market," *Japan Center for Economic Research Discussion Paper*, No. 135, 2012.

17

The Hidden Risk Factor

J. H. Witte, D. Ples, J. Corominas
Record Currency Management, Windsor, UK

ABSTRACT

To achieve maximum returns consistent with an investor's appetite for risk, the correct identification and estimation of all relevant risk factors in a portfolio are necessary. In this paper, we identify the role of foreign currency as an important risk factor from an international investor's point of view.

Keywords: Currency Risk; Risk Premium; Risk Factor; FX Hedge; Currency Overlay

1. Introduction

It has been noted repeatedly (cf. [1]) that, since the start of the financial crisis in 2007, global asset correlation has been increased steadily. This effect has made it much harder for portfolio managers to achieve performance *alpha* by skillfully selecting superior investment opportunities. In order to outperform in such a world (cf. [2]), investors have to correctly identify and characterise the available risk premia, and build a portfolio that matches their appetite for risk while attempting maximum diversification (cf. [3,4]).

A risk factor is usually understood to be any variable that contributes to explaining the composition of the total portfolio risk. This means that if we can decompose the total portfolio risk into different components, *i.e.*, the different risk factors, then this will give us a clearer understanding of where our existing risk originates. More importantly, it allows us to analyse the risk premia of the different risk factors, and enables us to make sure that these are consistent with our overall requirements for diversification and appetite for risk.

In a sense, a risk factor analysis reverses the view taken by Markowitz's modern portfolio theory (cf. [5,6]). In a Markowitz setting, an investor makes his investment decisions *ex ante*, based on his expectations about the statistical properties of the individual assets under consideration. In contrast, in a risk factor analysis, we look at the portfolio *ex post*, attempting to describe the total portfolio risk as accurately as possible by decomposing it into the different drivers of risk, the main risk factors. This enables us to observe effects that show a big impact only if considered in aggregate in a large portfolio.

In this paper, we show that currency is an important risk factor to an international investor, and we emphasise that any change in an investor's international currency position may increase or decrease the total portfolio risk, depending on market circumstances. Therefore, the reward/risk ratio induced by currency, in line with classic risk factors such as equities, inflation, and credit, has to be regarded as indicative for investment performance. In particular, we attempt to quantify the extent to which such change would impact portfolio risk.

The effect of currency on international investments has been widely studied in the literature. In [7], it is discussed how country factors affect stock prices far more than, e.g., market sectors and industries, and most of this difference can be attributed to currency (see also [8]). In [9], the currency risk premium is compared to market risk premium, and the interaction between the two is analysed; in some ways, this is a first step towards the more recent studies on the marginal contribution of specific risk factors.

Over the past decade, we have also seen an expansion in the literature on risk factors and the calculation of marginal risk contributions to portfolio risk, as investors have become increasingly concerned with downside management (see for example [1,2,10-12]) and have recognised the need for an improved understanding of the impact of risk factors.

This paper is structured as follows. In Section 2, we introduce our definitions of risk and a risk factor. In Section 3, we introduce our approach to risk factor analysis. In particular, we introduce the notion of risk factor decomposition and risk factor impact. In Section 4, we discuss in detail how an elevated risk factor is to be interpreted in our framework. In Section 5, we apply our methodology to a representative international portfolio, and we compare the risk factor impacts of the most commonly studied risk factors. We demonstrate that, empirically, currency is an important risk factor to an international investor. We conclude by summarising our findings in Section 6.

2. Defining a Risk Factor

Consider a portfolio of return sources, and consider an investor who is holding this portfolio with the aim of maintaining or increasing its value over some future time horizon. In this setting, we define *risk* as follows.

Definition 1. *Risk is the* (*exposure to*) *the possibility of unpredicted portfolio moves*; *every chance or situation involving such a possibility.*[1]

Hence, risk is defined based on unexpected changes to our portfolio value. We then move on to very generally defining a *risk factor* as anything providing us with information about our portfolio risk.

Definition 2. *A risk factor is a variable associated with the magnitude of portfolio risk.*[2]

We emphasise the following corollary, which is at times overlooked.

Corollary 1. *Risk factors are correlational, not necessarily causal. Correlation does not imply causation.*

For example, a fund manager who is fully invested in shares of a single company will not necessarily underperform in a group of more diversified managers. He is merely more likely to underperform due to higher volatility, but his lack of diversification does not imply underperformance (e.g., imagine he had bought shares in Apple or Google early on).

3. The Risk Factor Challenge

In the previous section, we have very generally introduced the notion of *risk* and *risk factor*. We will now explain how portfolio risk can be analysed by studying a portfolio's risk factors.

3.1. Risk Factor Decomposition

We start by introducing what we understand to be a *risk factor decomposition* of a given portfolio.

Definition 3. *Suppose our portfolio return is described by the random variable* X. *A risk factor decomposition is any finite number of random variables* $X_1,\cdots,X_N$ *and scalar values* $\alpha_1,\cdots,\alpha_N$ *such that*

$$X=\sum_{i=1}^{N}\alpha_i X_i. \tag{1}$$

[1]See also [13].
[2]See also [14].

In this case, the portfolio variance is given by

$$\sigma_X^2=\sum_i \alpha_i^2\sigma_{X_i}^2+2\sum_{i,k;i<k}\alpha_i\alpha_k\sigma_{X_i}\sigma_{X_k}\rho_{ik},$$

where ρ_{ik} *is the correlation coefficient of* X_i *and* X_k, *and* σ_{X_i} *is the standard deviation of* X_i. *We denote the portfolio risk by* σ_X.

Remark 1. *One way of constructing a risk factor decomposition as given in Equation* (1) *is to consider* $X_1,\cdots,X_N$ *as the returns of the individual assets in our portfolio, with* $\alpha_1,\cdots,\alpha_N$ *denoting the respective weights of the exposure. However, this is by no means a unique decomposition of* X.

In Section 5, we will explain how to also analyse other risk factors, such as inflation and credit. Any decomposition into return sources can form a foundation for a risk factor analysis.

Remark 2. *By Equation* (1), *a risk factor decomposition does not allow for any purely correlational risk factors, as these do not add to the information contained in the causational factors. Put differently, this means that a risk factor which has no impact on portfolio volatility will not be admitted in the decomposition.*

3.2. Risk Factor Impact

To measure the particular effects of the different risk factors on our total portfolio risk, we come to define what we understand to be the *risk factor impact*.

We aim to measure risk impact of a factor X_k by taking into account the following three aspects.

1) Weight α_k: exposure to X_k.
2) Volatility σ_{X_k}: volatility of X_k.
3) Correlation $\rho_{ik}, i\neq k$: relationship to the other factors $X_i, i\neq k$.

In detail: we want the risk factor impact to **increase/decrease** in accordance with **weight** or **volatility**; and we want the risk factor impact to **increase** and **decrease**, respectively, with **positive** and **negative** cumulative **correlation** to the other risk factors. Our mathematical definition is as follows.

Definition 4: *Consider the risk factor decomposition* (1). *We define the impact of risk factor* X_k *to be*

$$\theta_k:=\frac{\partial\sigma_X}{\partial\alpha_k}=\frac{1}{\sigma_X}\left(\alpha_k\sigma_{X_k}^2+\sum_{i\neq k}\alpha_i\sigma_{X_i}\sigma_{X_k}\rho_{ik}\right). \tag{2}$$

From Equation (2), we see how θ_k generally respects the desired characteristics listed in 1), 2), and 3).

More specifically, since θ_k is the partial derivative of σ_X by α_k, **it measures the rate of change of the portfolio volatility** σ_X **in response to small changes in the weight** α_k. In other words, it is the marginal risk contribution of factor X_k. We will clarify this property in Section 4.

3.3. A Two Asset Portfolio

Consider a portfolio return $X = \alpha_1 X_1 + \alpha_2 X_2$, consisting of the returns X_1 and X_2 of two assets, with weights α_1 and $\alpha_2 = 1-\alpha_1$, respectively. The portfolio variance is given by

$$\sigma_X^2 = \mathrm{Var}(\alpha_1 X_1 + \alpha_2 X_2) = \alpha_1^2\sigma_{X_1}^2 + \alpha_2^2\sigma_{X_2}^2 + 2\rho\alpha_1\alpha_2\sigma_{X_1}\sigma_{X_2},$$

where ρ denotes the correlation coefficient of X_1 and X_2, and we have

$$\theta_i = \frac{\sigma_{X_i}}{\sigma_X}\left(\alpha_i\sigma_{X_i} + \rho\alpha_k\sigma_{X_k}\right) \quad (3)$$

for $(i,k)\in\{1,2\}$, $i\neq k$.

Example 1. *Suppose* $\rho = 1$ *and* $\sigma_{X_1} = \sigma_{X_2}$. *We have*

$$\theta_1 = \theta_2.$$

Hence, for equally volatile and perfectly correlated risk factors, the risk factor impacts are identical.

Suppose $\rho = -1$. *In this case, we have*

$$\theta_1 - \theta_2 = \alpha_1\frac{4\sigma_{X_1}^2}{\sigma_X} - \frac{\sigma_{X_1}^2}{\sigma_X}.$$

Hence, in a portfolio with two perfectly anticorrelated assets, the difference between the risk factor impacts scales linearly with the weight α_1.

Suppose $\rho = 0$. *In this case, Equation* (3) *becomes*

$$\theta_1 - \theta_2 = \alpha_1\frac{2\sigma_{X_1}^2}{\sigma_X} - \frac{\sigma_{X_1}^2}{\sigma_X}. \quad (4)$$

In a portfolio with two perfectly independent assets that are equally volatile, the allocation α_1 *between the two assets linearly determines which of the two has the higher impact.*

Suppose X_3 *is a third asset with weight* $\alpha_3 = \alpha_1$. *Suppose* X_3 *is independent of* X_1 *and* X_2. *Suppose that* X_1 *and* X_2 *are correlated by* $\rho > 0$, *and that* $\sigma_{X_1} = \sigma_{X_2} = \sigma_{X_3}$. *In this case, we have*

$$\theta_3 = \alpha_1\frac{\sigma_{X_1}^2}{\sigma_X} < \frac{1}{\sigma_X}\left(\alpha_1\sigma_{X_1}^2 + \rho\alpha_2\sigma_{X_1}^2\right) = \theta_1.$$

We observe that, because X_1 *is correlated with* X_2, *the risk factor impact of* X_1 *is greater than that of* X_3.

In other words, if we add a third asset to our portfolio which is strongly correlated with one of the two we already have, then the third asset will have a higher risk impact than if it was slightly correlated or independent.

Example 2. *Suppose* $\alpha_1 = \alpha_2$. *We have*

$$\theta_1 - \theta_2 = \frac{\alpha_1}{\sigma_X}\left(\sigma_{X_1}^2 - \sigma_{X_2}^2\right). \quad (5)$$

Hence, for two equally weighted assets, the difference between the risk factor impacts scales linearly with the difference in variance, independently of the correlation coefficient.

Suppose, in addition, that $\sigma_{X_1} = \sigma_{X_2}$. *We have*

$$\theta_1 = \theta_2.$$

Hence, for two equally volatile assets with equal weights, the risk factor impacts are identical, independently of the correlation coefficient. This is desireable since, all else being equal, the correlation coefficient contains no information that can be used to measure the relative impacts of the individual risk factors.

4. What a High Risk Factor Impact Means

Suppose our portfolio return is described by the random variable X. Suppose we have a risk factor decomposition

$$X = \sum_{i=1}^{N}\alpha_i X_i.$$

Remark 3. *Consider two risk factors* X_i *and* X_k *with impacts* θ_i *and* θ_k, *respectively. Suppose* $\theta_i > \theta_k$. *In this case, adding a small quantity to the weight of* X_i *will add more risk to our portfolio than increasing the weight of* X_k *by the same quantity. The opposite effect holds when decreasing the weight by small quantities.*

We present this property more rigorously in the following theorem.

Theorem 1. *Consider two risk factors* X_i *and* X_k *with impacts* θ_i *and* θ_k, *respectively. Suppose* $\theta_i > \theta_k$. *Then, there exists a threshold* $h^* > 0$ *such hat*

$$\sigma_{X,\alpha_i+h} > \sigma_{X,\alpha_k+h} \text{ and } \sigma_{X,\alpha_i-h} < \sigma_{X,\alpha_k-h} \quad (6)$$

for all $0 < h < h^*$, *where* σ_{X,α_k+h} *denotes the standard deviation of*

$$X = \sum_{i\neq k}\alpha_i X_i + (\alpha_k + h)X_k.$$

Proof. *Suppose* σ_X *is differentiable with respect to* α_i *and* α_k, *respectively. We have*

$$\theta_i = \frac{\partial\sigma_X}{\partial\alpha_i} = \lim_{h\to 0}\frac{\sigma_{X,\alpha_i+h} - \sigma_X}{h} > \lim_{h\to 0}\frac{\sigma_{X,\alpha_k+h} - \sigma_X}{h} = \frac{\partial\sigma_X}{\partial\alpha_k} = \theta_k.$$

Let $\varepsilon > 0$ *such that* $\theta_i - \theta_k > 2\varepsilon > 0$. *There exists* $h^* > 0$ *such that*

$$\frac{\sigma_{X,\alpha_i+h} - \sigma_X}{h} > \frac{\sigma_{X,\alpha_k+h} - \sigma_X}{h},$$

for all $0 < h < h^*$ *and* $-h^* < h < 0$, *which is equivalent to Equation* (6), *which proves the theorem.* ■

5. Analysis of an International Portfolio

We now come to apply the risk factor methodology introduced in this paper to an actual investment scenario. We study two sample portfolios as outlined below; in **Tables 1** and **2**, we indicate return sources, data sources, and weights.

For each of the two sample portfolios, we derive a risk factor decomposition and compute the marginal risk contributions of a series of pre-defined risk factors. We proceed as follows.

We analyse the following risk factors; our choice is driven by the risk premia we believe investors are seeking to exploit[3].

- International Equity
- Currency
- Cash
- Domestic Equity
- Inflation (Duration + Term Premium)
- Credit
- Commodities

Certain risk factors are not directly investible in the sense that they depend on two or more carrier assets to be identified. This is the case with *inflation*, *credit*, and *currency*. Still, they are important risk factors when making forward looking judgements about markets within a Global Tactical Asset Allocation (GTAA) framework, for instance. We capture these by rewriting the equations as

Currency = Int. Equities − Hedged Int. Equities
Inflation = Government Bonds − Cash
Credit = Corporate Bonds − Government Bonds

This decomposition helps bring to light certain risk factors which would otherwise not be directly observable and quantifiable in an appropriate manner since they are embedded in other asset classes, yet can represent a substantial risk to the portfolio. Currency is our main example here.

Based on the monthly returns of the listed indices, we compute a rolling standard deviation and correlation for all factors, using a 12 months look back window. In other words, for every month, we estimate σ_k and ρ_{ik} from the previous 12 data points, $1 \le i,k \le 9$. Together with the weights α_k, $1 \le k \le 9$, indicated in **Tables 1** and **2**, we then have all required information to calculate the risk factor impacts θ_k, $1 \le k \le 9$, on a monthly basis, following Equation (2).

Our monthly data set starts in January 1994 and ends in June 2012. We rebalance our sample portfolio monthly to maintain the constant weights given in **Tables 1** and **2**.

How to interpret each risk factor? To make the decomposition intelligible in a single framework, **Figures 1** and **2** illustrate the size of each risk factor relative to the total size of all risk factors: it shows the absolute marginal risk contribution of each risk factor relative to the aggregate measure of such absolute marginal risk contributions (see also **Table 3**).

In mathematical terms, **Figures 1** and **2** show our monthly values for

$$\frac{|\theta_k|}{\sum_{1\le i\le 9}|\theta_i|}, \quad 1 \le k \le 9, \tag{7}$$

describing the evolution of the relative absolute magnitude of all risk factor impacts over time.

Remark 4. *Unlike the notion of risk factor impact* θ_k, *introduced in Section* 3.2, *the absolute values* $|\theta_k|$ *shown in* ***Figures*** 1 *and* 2 *do not contain any directional*

[3]It is important to note that there is no single unique risk factor decomposition for any given portfolio. That is, risk factors can be defined and analysed depending on what is intended to be shown.

Table 1. Allocation and data source. Aggressive sample portfolio.

Aggressive Portfolio		
Asset	Data Source	Weight %
Cash	J.P. Morgan, CMI, Index, 1 Year	3
US Government Bonds	J.P. Morgan, CMI, Index, 7 Year	15
US Corporate Bonds	ML, Broad Market, Corporates 5 - 10 Years	15
US Equities	S&P 500 Composite	20
International Equities	ACWI ex-US Index	35
Commodities	S&P GSCI Total Return Index	12

Table 2. Allocation and data source. Defensive sample portfolio.

Defensive Portfolio		
Asset	Data Source	Weight %
Cash	J.P. Morgan, CMI, Index, 1 Year	5
US Government Bonds	J.P. Morgan, CMI, Index, 7 Year	35
US Corporate Bonds	ML, Broad Market, Corporates 5 - 10 Years	15
US Equities	S&P 500 Composite	20
International Equities	ACWI ex-US Index	20
Commodities	S&P GSCI Total Return Index	5

Table 3. Based on monthly returns, we compute a rolling standard deviation and correlation for all factors, using a 12 months look back window. We then compute the risk factor impacts on a monthly basis. In the table below, we see the June 2012 values for the defensive sample portholio.

Risk Factor	σ	θ	$\|\theta\|$	$\|\theta_k\|/\sum_{1\le i\le 9}\|\theta_i\|$
Hedged Int. Equity	7.49%	0.0028	0.0028	44.38%
Currency	2.65%	−0.0003	0.0003	4.9%
Domestic Equity	5.83%	0.0021	0.0021	32.96%
Inflation	3.12%	−0.0006	0.0006	8.91%
Credit	1.14%	0.00004	0.00004	0.7%
Commodities	3.42%	0.0005	0.0005	8.11%

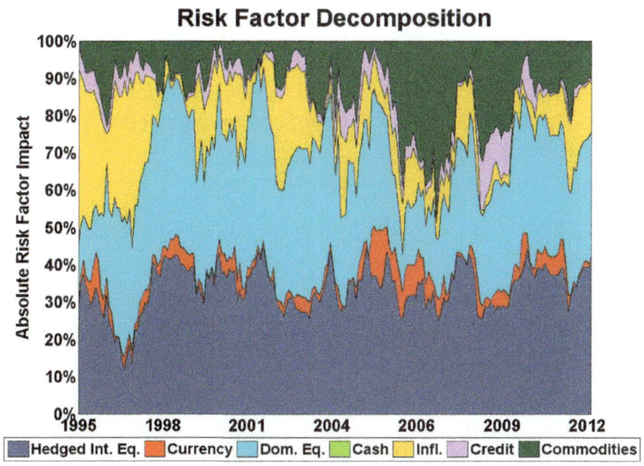

Figure 1. Risk factor impacts. Aggressive sample portfolio.

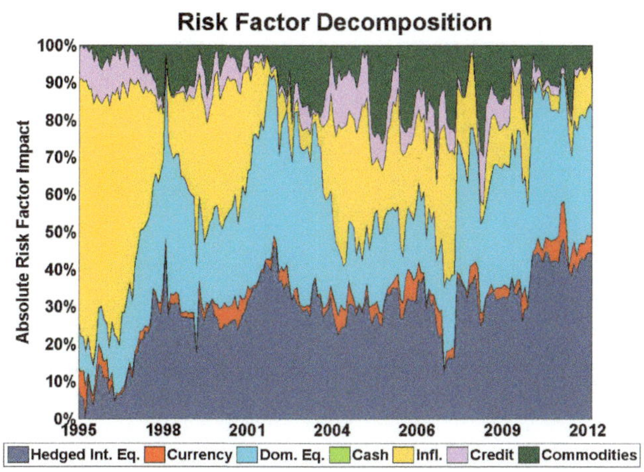

Figure 2. Risk factor impacts. Defensive sample portfolio.

information.

The absolute values in Equation (7) indicate the **magnitude to which changes in the exposure to different risk factors affect the total volatility** of investment performance. It serves as an index of **risk relevance**.

The directionality says whether an increased exposure to a risk factor results in an increased or decreased overall volatility. It can only be meaningfully evaluated when studying the risk factor impact in conjunction with the expected returns of the different factors. In that case, the risk factor impacts can serve as a starting point for recalibration of portfolio weights.

6. Conclusions

In this paper, we have introduced a theoretical framework for risk factor analysis. We have introduced the *risk factor impact* as

$$\theta_k = \frac{\text{change in portfolio risk}}{\text{change in weight of factor } k},$$

which presents a unique way of understanding the effects of risk factor weights on the total portfolio risk. Our measure of risk factor impact is identical to the marginal risk contribution, and we provide a rigorous account why this measure is of relevance and how to interpret it.

By studying a representative global portfolio, we have empirically analysed the different risk factor impacts with particular focus on currency. We find that an international investor's currency exposure is one of the most impactful risk factors. This suggests that currency exposure, in line with classic risk factors as domestic and international equities, inflation, credit, and commodities, is indicative of future investment performance. Hence, currency exposure, together with all assets in a portfolio, should be given thoughtful and prudent risk and return analysis to help guide an investor's expectations.

REFERENCES

[1] S. Page and M. Taborsky, "The Myth of Diversification: Risk Factors versus Asset Classes," *Journal of Portfolio Management*, Vol. 37, No. 4, 2011, pp. 1-2.

[2] D. Rosen and D. Saunders, "Risk Factor Contributions in Portfolio Credit Risk Models," *Journal of Banking and Finance*, Vol. 34, No. 2, 2010, pp. 336-349.

[3] J. Lintner, "The Valuation of Risk Assets and the Selection of Risky Investments in Stock Portfolios and Capital Budgets," *The Review of Economics and Statistics*, Vol. 47, No. 1, 1965, pp. 13-39.

[4] O. Ruban and D. Melas, "Risk Parity Portfolios: Rebalance, Leverage, Or Both?" *The Journal of Investing*, Vol. 20, No. 1, 2011, pp. 99-108.

[5] H. M. Markowitz, "Portfolio Selection," *The Journal of Finance*, Vol. 7, No. 1, 1952, pp. 77-91.

[6] H. M. Markowitz, "Portfolio Selection: Efficient Diversification of Investments," John Wiley & Sons, New York, 1958.

[7] J. Diermeier and B. Solnik, "Global Pricing of Equity," *Financial Analysts Journal*, Vol. 57, No. 4, 2001, pp. 37-47.

[8] J.-F. L'Her, O. Sy and M. Y. Tnan, "Country, Industry, and Risk Factor Loadings in Portfolio Management," *The Journal of Portfolio Management*, Vol. 28, No. 4, 2002, pp. 70-79.

[9] G. De Santis and B. Gerard, "How Big Is the Premium for Currency Risk?" *Journal of Financial Economics*, Vol. 49, No. 3, 1998, pp. 375-412.

[10] A. S. Cherny and D. B. Madan, "Coherent Measurement of Factor Risks," 2006. http://arxiv.org/abs/math/0605062v1

[11] J. Bender, R. Briand, F. Nielsen and D. Stefek, "Portfolio of Risk Premia: A New Approach to Diversification," *The*

Journal of Portfolio Management, Vol. 36, No. 2, 2010, pp. 17-25.

[12] S. Maillard, T. Roncalli and J. Teiletche, "On the Properties of Equally-Weighted Risk Contributions Portfolios," *The Journal of Portfolio Management*, Vol. 36, No. 4, 2010, pp. 60-70.

[13] MSCI Barra, "Barra Risk Model Handbook," 2007.

[14] C. R. Harvey, "The Risk Exposure of Emerging Equity Markets," *The World Bank Economic Review*, Vol. 9, No. 1, 1993, pp. 19-50.

18

Assessing the Risks of Trading Strategies Using Acceptability Indices

Masimba E. Sonono[1], Hopolang P. Mashele[2]
[1]Unit for Business Mathematics and Informatics, North-West University, Potchefstroom, South Africa
[2]Centre for Business Mathematics and Informatics, North-West University, Potchefstroom, South Africa

ABSTRACT

The paper looks at the quantification of risks of trading strategies in incomplete markets. We realized that the no-arbitrage price intervals are unacceptably large. From a risk management point of view, we are concerned with finding prices that are acceptable to the market. The acceptability of the prices is assessed by risk measures. Plausible risk measures give price bounds that are suitable for use as bid-ask prices. Furthermore, the risk measures should be able to compensate for the unhedgeable risk to an extent. Conic finance provides plausible bid-ask prices that are determined by the probability distribution of the cash flows only. We apply the theory to obtain bid-ask prices in the assessment of the risks of trading strategies. We analyze two popular trading strategies—bull call the spread strategy and bear call spread strategy. Comparison of risk profiles for the strategies is done between the Variance Gamma Scalable Self Decomposable model and the Black-Scholes model. The findings indicate that using bid-ask prices compensates for the unhedgeable risk and reduces the spread between bid-ask prices.

Keywords: Conic Finance; Coherent Risk Measure; Acceptability Indices; Incomplete Markets; Bid-Ask Prices; Continuous Time Models

1. Introduction

The paper focuses on the quantification of risks of trading strategies, particularly when the market is incomplete. The incompleteness of the market gives rise to many martingales, each of which produces a no-arbitrage price. Thus there is no exact replication so as to obtain a unique price. Furthermore, the no-arbitrage price intervals are unacceptably large. From a risk management point of view, we are concerned with finding the prices which are acceptable. The acceptability of these prices is assessed by risk measures.

In the financial literature, two major classes of risk measures have gained ground in assessing the risks of financial positions. Foremost, we have coherent measures introduced by [1]. Since then, the theory of coherent risk measures has been applied to several problems in finance. Secondly, there is the grounding work of [2], in which they proposed a new class of performance measures known as acceptability indices. The acceptability indices can be considered as an extension of coherent risk measures. Under the acceptability framework, a financial position is acceptable if its distribution function withstands high levels of stress, or in other words, a stressed sampling of the financial position has a positive expectation. In this paper, our contribution is assessing the risk profiles of trading strategies using the acceptability framework.

The rest of the paper is organized as follows: Section 2 looks at the problem of pricing in incomplete markets. Section 3 gives an overview of risk measures and presents new acceptability indices based on the family of distortion functions. Section 4 presents a brief detail on conic finance and provides closed form expressions for the bid-ask prices. Section 5 presents the models that are used in this work. Section 6 presents numerical tests on assessing the risks of two trading strategies. Section 7 is the conclusion.

2. Problem of Pricing in Incomplete Markets

We start by motivating the problem through explaining the mathematical structure of good deal bounds by [3], also found in [4]. The good deal bounds determine the range of values of a risky position payoff. Let R be the set of replicable payoffs, $\Pi(Y)$ be the market price to replicate a payoff $Y \in R$, and A be an acceptance set of payoffs that are acceptable to the situation. The lower good deal bound for a payoff X is:

$$b(X) = \sup_{Y \in R}\left\{-\Pi(Y) \middle| Y + X \in A\right\}. \quad (1)$$

This payoff might be interpreted as a bid price. Equation (1) tells us that if X can be bought for less than $b(X)$, then there is a Y that can be bought for $\Pi(Y)$ such that a cost $b(X)+\Pi(Y)<0$. The upper good deal bound, which might be interpreted as the ask price for X, is given by:

$$a(X) = -b(-x) = \inf_{Y \in R}\left\{\Pi(Y) \middle| Y - X \in A\right\}. \quad (2)$$

Equation (2) tells us that selling X or buying $-X$ yields the same effect. The interpretation of $-b(X)$ is the cost that renders X to be acceptable. As [5] propose: any valuation principle that gives price bounds induces a risk measure and vice versa. The acceptance set A must include the set of riskless payoffs, $\{Z | Z \geq 0\}$, which is the acceptance set that generates no-arbitrage bounds. The set A does not intersect with the set $\{Z | Z < 0\}$ of pure losses. The acceptance set A must be consistent with market prices, Π, or arbitrage occurs.

Now, an incomplete market is one in which there are many martingale measures Q. The price bounds in Equations (1) and (2) form an interval of arbitrage-free prices for X:

$$I = \left(\inf_{Q \in \mathcal{M}} E^Q[X], \sup_{Q \in \mathcal{M}} E^Q[X]\right) \quad (3)$$

where $\mathcal{M}$ is a set of equivalent martingale measures. The problem with the interval of the arbitrage-free prices for X is that it is usually too wide for the no-arbitrage bounds to serve as useful bid-ask prices.

In practice, derivatives traders are aware of the incompleteness of the markets and after making trades on certain positions, they are not able to hedge away all the risk. Instead, they must bear the risk associated with the trade. To cover their business expenses and to earn compensation for bearing the risk they are not able to hedge, traders establish bid-ask intervals around the expected discounted payoff.

Now, in constructing the bid-ask prices, the difficulty posed by incomplete markets is very significant because of adverse selection. For instance, if the ask price is too high, few potential investors will be willing to pay so much and the result is foregone profits. If the ask price is too low, the resulting trade is bad for a trader and entails likely losses. So, to ensure that trades made at bid and ask prices are beneficial, it helps to use methods that produce bounds for the prices that are suitable for use as bid-ask prices and are adequate to minimize unhedgeable risk to an extent. In the process, we will be able to quantify risk since any valuation method that yields price bounds also induces a risk measure [5].

3. Risk Performance Measures

In this section, we give a brief overview of the risk measures. In general, a risk measure, $\rho: X \to \mathbb{R}$, is a functional that assigns a numerical value to a random variable representing an uncertain payoff.

3.1. Coherent Risk Measure

Definition Coherent Risk Measure

A risk measure ρ is coherent if it satisfies the following axioms:

- Translation Invariance:

$$\rho(X + \alpha r) = \rho(X) - \alpha,$$

for all $X \in \mathcal{G}, \alpha \in \mathbb{R}$.
- Monotonicity: $\rho(X) \leq \rho(Y)$ if $X \geq Y$ a.s.
- Positive Homogeneity:

$$\rho(\lambda X) = \lambda \rho(X),$$

for $\lambda \geq 0$.
- Subadditivity:

$$\rho(X + Y) \leq \rho(X) + \rho(Y),$$

for all $X, Y \in \mathcal{G}$
- Relevance: $\rho(X) > 0$ if $X \leq 0$ and $X \neq 0$.

The last property is included although it is not a determinant of coherency. Translation invariance axiom implies that by adding a fixed amount α to the initial position and investing it in a reference instrument, the risk $\rho(X)$ decreases by α. The monotonicity axiom postulates that if $X(\omega) > Y(\omega)$ for every state of nature ω, Y is more risk because it has higher risk potential.

The positive homogeneity axiom implies that risk linearly increases with size of the position, that is to say that the size of the risk of a position should scale with the size of the position. This is just a natural requirement, though this condition may not be satisfied in the real world since markets may be illiquid. The subadditivity axiom implies that the risk of a portfolio is always less than the sum of the risks of its subparts. This axiom ensures that diversification decreases the risk.

According to the basic representation theorem proved by [1] for a finite Ω, any coherent risk measure admits a representation of the form:

$$\rho(X) = -\inf_{Q \in \mathcal{D}} E^Q[X], \quad (4)$$

with a certain set $\mathcal{D}$ of probability measures with respect to P. A cash flow X is acceptable if it has negative risk, that is $\rho(X) < 0$.

3.2. Acceptability Indices

Cherny and Madan, defined a subclass of risk measures called acceptability indices, defined formally as:

3.3. Definition. Index of Acceptability

The acceptability index is as a mapping α from the set of bounded random variables to the extended half-line $[0,\infty]$. The index satisfies the following four properties:

- **Monotonicity**
  If Y dominates X, that is $X \leq Y$, then
  $$\alpha(X) \leq \alpha(Y).$$
- **Scale invariance**
  $\alpha(X)$ stays the same when X is scaled by a positive number, that is $\alpha(cX) = \alpha(X)$ for $c > 0$.
- **Quasi-concavity**
  If $\alpha(X) \geq Y$ and $\alpha(Y) \geq Y$, then
  $$\alpha(\lambda X + (1-\lambda)Y) \geq Y,$$
  for any $\lambda \in [0,1]$.
- **Fatou Property (Convergence)**
  Let $\{X_n\}$ be a sequence of random variable. $|X_n| \leq 1$ and X_n converges in probability to a random variable *X*. If $\alpha(X_n) \geq x$, then $\alpha(X) \geq x$.

The acceptability indices are constructed by replacing the cumulative distribution function of X, $F_X(x)$, by a risk adjusted distribution, $\Psi_X(F_X(x))$. The corresponding risk measure is the negative expectation of the zero cost cash flow under the distorted distribution function:

$$\rho_\gamma(X) = -\int_{\mathbb{R}} x d(\Psi_\gamma(F_X(x))), \gamma \in \mathbb{R}_+ \quad (5)$$

where Ψ_γ is a family of concave distortion functions on [0,1] increasing pointwise in the stress level parameter γ. A higher value of γ results in severe distortion of the distribution function of X. Then, the acceptability index, $\alpha(X)$, is the largest stress level γ such that the expectation of X remains positive under the distortion or in other words the distorted cash flow remains acceptable:

$$\alpha(X) = \sup\{\gamma \in \mathbb{R}_+ : \rho_\gamma(X) \leq 0\}. \quad (6)$$

Cherny and Madan introduced four acceptability indices based on the family of distortion functions which are namely: AIMIN, AIMAX, AIMINMAX, AIMAXMIN.

- AIMIN is the largest number x such that the expectation of the minimum of $x+1$ draws from cash flow distribution is still positive. Let
  $$Y \overset{law}{=} \min X_1, \cdots, X_{x+1},$$
  where $X_1, \cdots, X_{x+1}$ are independent draws from X. The concave distortion function is given by:
  $$\Psi_x(y) = 1-(1-y)^{x+1}, x \in \mathbb{R}^+, y \in [0,1] \quad (7)$$
- AIMAX constructs a distribution from which one draws numerous times and takes the maximum to get the cash flow distribution being evaluated. Let,
  $$\max\{Y_1, \cdots, Y_{x+1}\} \overset{law}{=} X,$$
  where $Y_1, \cdots, Y_{x+1}$ are independent draws of Y. The concave distortion function is given by:
  $$\Psi_x(y) = y^{\frac{1}{x+1}}, x \in \mathbb{R}^+, y \in [0,1] \quad (8)$$
- AIMAXMIN is constructed by first using the MINVAR and then followed by the MAXVAR to create worst case scenarios.
  Let
  $$\max\{Y_1, \cdots, Y_{x+1}\} \overset{law}{=} \min\{X_1, \cdots, X_{x+1}\},$$
  where $X_1, \cdots, X_{x+1}$ are independent draws of X and $Y_1, \cdots, Y_{x+1}$ are independent draws of Y. Combining the MINVAR and MAXVAR, we have the distortion function:
  $$\Psi_x(y) = \left(1-(1-y)^{x+1}\right)^{\frac{1}{x+1}}, x \in \mathbb{R}^+, y \in [0,1] \quad (9)$$
- AIMAXMIN is constructed by first using the MAXVAR and then followed by the MINVAR to create worst case scenarios. Let
  $$Y \overset{law}{=} \min Z_1, \cdots, Z_{x+1},$$
  $$\max Z_1, \cdots, Z_{x+1} \overset{law}{=} X,$$
  where $Z_1, \cdots, Z_{x+1}$ are independent draws of Z. Combining the MINVAR and MAXVAR, we have the distortion function:
  $$\Psi_x(y) = 1-\left(1-y^{\frac{1}{x+1}}\right)^{x+1}, x \in \mathbb{R}^+, y \in [0,1] \quad (10)$$

The acceptability indices are more plausible in assessing the risks of financial positions. The acceptability indices have been used heavily in the theory of conic finance, which we review next.

4. Conic Finance Theory

We look at the principles of conic finance as set out in [6]. The market serves a passive counterparty accepting the opposite side of zero cost trades proposed by market participants. The departure of conic finance from the traditional one price economy is that trade now depends on the direction of trade, with the market buying at bid price and selling at ask price. Cash flows to trade are modeled as bounded random variables on a fixed probability space $(\Omega, \mathcal{F}, P)$ for a base probability measure selected by the economy.

Now, for a risk with a cash flow outcome denoted by

the random variable X with a distribution $F(x)$ at a fixed period, we develop bid-ask prices at which the cash flow is bought and sold such that the net cash flow is an acceptable risk. The set of acceptable risks is defined by a convex cone of random variables that contains the non-negative cash flows. [1] showed that any acceptable set (cone) $\mathcal{A}$ of acceptable risks, there exists a convex set $\mathcal{M}$ of probability measures $Q \in \mathcal{M}$, Q equivalent to P, with the property that $X \in \mathcal{A}$ if and only if:

$$E^Q[X] \geq 0, \text{ all } Q \in \mathcal{M}. \tag{11}$$

The acceptability of a cash flow can then be completely determined by its distribution function. Acceptability of cash flows is linked to positive expectation via concave distortion. So for some concave distribution function $\Psi(u)$, $0 \leq u \leq 1$ the cash flow distribution function $F(x) = P(X \leq x)$ is acceptable if:

$$\int_{-\infty}^{\infty} x\mathrm{d}\Psi(F(x)) \geq 0. \tag{12}$$

[6] show that the bid price, $b(x)$, for the cash flow X is given by:

$$b(x) = \int_{-\infty}^{\infty} x\mathrm{d}\Psi(F(x)) \geq 0 = \inf_{Q\in\mathcal{M}} E^Q[X], \tag{13}$$

and the ask price is given by:

$$a(x) = -\int_{-\infty}^{\infty} x\mathrm{d}\Psi(1 - F(-x)) \geq 0 = \sup_{Q\in\mathcal{M}} E^Q[X]. \tag{14}$$

The bid and ask prices for call and put options can be obtained by using closed formulas which are obtained on integration by parts. Let S be the random variable at time T of an underlying asset. The call option $C = (S-K)^+$ and put option $P = (K-S)^+$, where K is the strike price. The following are the closed bid and ask prices expressions:

$$a_\gamma(C) = \int_K^{\infty} \Psi^\gamma(1 - F_S(x))\mathrm{d}x, \tag{14}$$

$$b_\gamma(C) = \int_K^{\infty} (1 - \Psi^\gamma(F_S(x)))\mathrm{d}x, \tag{15}$$

$$a_\gamma(P) = \int_0^K \Psi^\gamma(F_S(x))\mathrm{d}x, \tag{16}$$

$$b_\gamma(P) = \int_0^K (1 - \Psi^\gamma(1 - F_S(x)))\mathrm{d}x. \tag{17}$$

F_s is the distribution function of S and is important because the bid and ask prices are determined completely by this distribution.

5. Continuous Time Models for Option Pricing

This section looks at the models that are used for option pricing. It is acknowledged that the relatively most liquid traded assets with market information are quoted vanilla options. In practice, trades mark to market their models to quoted vanilla options before they can price non-quoted options. As a result, this has led to demands for models that are capable of synthesizing the surface of vanilla options. It is well known that the geometric Brownian model is not capable of synthesizing the surface of vanilla options, although it remains a standard quoting model in the markets. Improvements on this model are offered by Lévy processes, which were found to be successful in synthesizing across strikes for a given maturity. The following is a brief overview of the models.

5.1. Black-Scholes Model

The log-normal process models continuously compounded returns using the general Brownian motion so that:

$$X(t) = \nu t + \sigma W(t), \tag{18}$$

where $W(t)$ is a standard Weiner process, ν is the instantaneous drift and σ is the instantaneous volatility of returns. The stochastic differential equation of the stock price is:

$$\mathrm{d}S(t) = S(t)(\mu\mathrm{d}t + \sigma\mathrm{d}W(t)), \tag{19}$$

where μ is the growth rate of the stock and is related to ν as follows $\nu = \mu - 1/2\sigma^2$. The stochastic differential equation can be solved to give the following dynamics of the stock price:

$$S(t) = S(0)\exp\left\{\left(\mu - \frac{1}{2}\sigma^2\right)t + \sigma W(t)\right\}. \tag{20}$$

The characteristic function for the logarithm of the stock price is:

$$E\left[\mathrm{e}^{iu\ln(S(t))}\right] = \exp\left\{iu\left[\ln S(0) + \left(\mu - \frac{1}{2}\sigma^2\right)\right]t - \frac{1}{2}\sigma^2u^2t\right\} \tag{21}$$

5.2. Variance Gamma Model

[7] define a Variance Gamma process, $X(t,\nu,\sigma,\theta)$, as a time changed Brownian motion as follows:

$$X(t,\nu,\sigma,\theta) = \theta\gamma(t) + \sigma W(\gamma(t)), \tag{22}$$

where $\gamma(t)$ is a Gamma process with parameters a and b, that is, $\gamma(t) \sim Gamma(at,b)$ where the gamma probability density function $\gamma(a,b)$ is given by:

$$f_\gamma(x,a,b) = \frac{b^a x^{a-1}}{\Gamma(a)}\mathrm{e}^{-bx}, x > 0. \tag{23}$$

θ and σ are respectively the instantaneous drift and volatility and $W(t)$ is a standard Brownian motion. The Variance Gamma process uses a gamma process to time change a Brownian motion. The density function of a Variance Gamma process is known in closed form and requires the computation of the modified Bessel function of the second kind which can be time consuming. Thus we resort to using the characteristic function, which is found by the conditioning on the jump $\gamma(t)$ as in many Lévy processes and is given by:

$$\Phi_{X(t)}(u) = \left(1 - iu\nu\theta + \frac{1}{2}u^2\nu\sigma^2\right)^{-t/\nu}. \quad (24)$$

The dynamics of the stock price are given by:

$$S(t) = S(0)\exp\{(\mu+\omega)t + X(t,\nu,\sigma,\theta)\}, \quad (25)$$

where μ is the instantaneous expected return of the stock evaluated at calendar time and ω is a compensator term The characteristic function for the logarithm of stock price is:

$$E\left[e^{iu\ln(S(t))}\right] = \exp\{iu[\ln S(0) + (\mu+\omega)t]\}\Phi_{X(t)}(u). \quad (26)$$

The compensator term can be found from the characteristic function and is given by:

$$\omega = \frac{-1}{t}\ln\left(\Phi_{X(t)}(-i)\right).$$

5.3. Variance Gamma Scalable Self Decomposable (VGSSD) Model

Sato process model was first introduced by [8]. The Sato process was shown to be effective in synthesizing many options on numerous underliers at the same time. The idea behind the model was to construct stochastic processes that had inhomogeneous independent increments from Lévy processes with homogeneous independent increments such that the higher moments are constant over the time horizon.

The starting point for the construction of the Sato model is the self-decomposable law. Loosely speaking, the self-decomposable law describes random variables that decompose into the sum of a scaled down version of themselves and an independent residual term. The scaling property means the distribution of increments of various time scales can be obtained from that of other time scale by rescaling the random variable at that time scale. Thus the distribution at larger time scales are derived from those at smaller time scales, which are easier to estimate as the data are sufficient. [9] proposed that the self-decomposable law is associated with the unit time distribution of self-similar additive process whose increments are independent, but not necessarily stationary.

It is known that stock prices are moved by many pieces of information. If the pieces of information are considered as a sequence of independent random variables $(Z_i : i = 1,2,\cdots)$, then the price changes are consequences of the impacts from all Z_i. Now, let $S_n = \sum_{i=1}^{n} Z_i$ denote their sum. Suppose that there exist centering constants c_n and scaling constants b_n such that the distribution of $b_n S_n + c_n$ converges to the distribution of the random variable X, which belongs to a family law "class L". Then the random variable X is said to have the class L property. So, the price change over the time horizon is the outcome of many independent random variables which can be approximated as a random variable X that has the law of "class L". [10] define the self-decomposable law as follows.

5.4. Definition Self Decomposable Law

A random variable X is self-decomposable if for all $c \in (0,1)$,

$$X \overset{law}{=} cX + X^c, \quad (27)$$

where X^c is a random variable independent of X.

The self-decomposable random variable X can be decomposed into a partial of itself and another independent random variable. [10] also shows that one may associate with such a self-decomposable law at unit time a process with independent but inhomogeneous increments by defining the marginal law of the process at time points t upon scaling the law at unit time. Therefore we have that:

$$X(t) = t^{\gamma}X, t > 0. \quad (28)$$

Thus we can study the price changes easily using self-decomposable laws, which are easier to handle than class L.

Self-decomposable laws are an important sub-class of the class of infinitely divisible laws [11]. The characteristic function of the self-decomposable laws has the form (see [10])

$$E\left[e^{iux}\right] = \exp\left\{iru - \frac{1}{2}\sigma^2u^2 + \int_R \left(e^{iux} - 1 - iux1_{|x|\le 1}\frac{g(x)}{|x|}dx\right)\right\}, \quad (29)$$

where r, σ are constants, $\sigma^2 \ge 0$,

$$\int_R \left(|x|^2 \wedge 1\right)\frac{g(x)}{|x|}dx < \infty,$$

and $g(x)$ is an increasing function when $x < 0$ and decreasing function when $x > 0$. An infinitely divisible law is self-decomposable if the corresponding Lévy density has the form

$$\frac{g(x)}{|x|},$$

where $g(x)$ is increasing for negative x and decreasing for positive x.

The dynamics of the stock price is defined as:

$$S(t)=S(0)\exp\{r(t)+X(t)+\omega(t)\}, \quad (30)$$

where $\omega(t)$ is a compensator term. The Sato process used in this work is the one constructed from the variance gamma process and is known as the Variance Gamma Scalable Self Decomposable (VGSSD) process. The variance gamma process is defined by time changing an arithmetic Brownian motion with drift θ and volatility σ by an independent gamma process with unit mean rate and variance rate ν. Let $G(t;\nu)$ be the gamma process, then the variance gamma process is written as:

$$X_{VG}(t,\sigma,\nu,\theta)=\theta G(t;\nu)+\sigma W(G(t;\nu)), \quad (31)$$

where $W(t)$ is an independent standard Brownian motion.

The gamma process is an increasing pure jump Lévy process with independent identically distributed increments over regular non overlapping intervals of length h that are gamma distributed with density $f_h(g)$ where:

$$f_h(g)=\frac{g^{\frac{h}{\nu}-1}e^{-\frac{g}{\nu}}}{\nu^{\frac{h}{\nu}}\Gamma\left(\frac{h}{\nu}\right)}, g>0. \quad (32)$$

The VGSSD is constructed from the variance gamma process by defining the scaled stochastic process $X(t)$ such that it is equal in law to $t^{\gamma}X_{VG}(1)$ where $X_{VG}(1)$ is a variance gamma random variable at unit time. It follows that the characteristic function of $X(t)$ is given by [7]

$$\Phi_{X(t)}(u)=\Phi_{X_{VG}(1)}=\left(1-iut^{\gamma}\nu\theta+\frac{1}{2}u^2t^{2\gamma}\nu\sigma\right). \quad (33)$$

Since the VGSSD is a scaled stochastic process, its higher moments remain constant over time.

6. Numerical Tests

Next, focus is shifted to analyzing the risk profiles of option investing strategies. We examine two option strategies which are namely bull call spread strategy and bear call spread strategy. We determine the maximum risk, maximum reward and breakeven price for each of the strategies. Comparison of risk profiles is done between the VGSSD model and the Black-Scholes model. The Black-Scholes model is considered here since it is the one that is mostly used by industrial practioners. So, the Black-Scholes is a proxy for market prices. The theory of conic finance provides bid-ask prices, which depend on the risk appetite of investors. For evaluation of bid-ask prices, we use acceptability indices based on the MAXMINVAR. The options used in the strategies are of European type and are applied to Single Stocks Futures (SSF) options offered in the South African financial markets.

A bull call spread is a bullish strategy formed by buying an "in-the-money call option" (lower strike) and selling "out-of-the-money" (higher strike). Both call options must be on the same underlying and expiration date. The strategy's net effect is to bring down the cost and breakeven (long call strike price + net debt) on a buy call (long call) strategy.

A bear call spread is a bearish strategy formed by buying an "out-of-the-money" call option (higher strike) and selling an "in-the-money" call option (lower strike). Both call options must be on the same underlying security and expiration date. The strategy's concept is to protect the downside of the sold call option by buying a call option of higher strike price. Then, the investor receives a net credit since the call option which has been bought has a higher strike price than the sold option. The breakeven will be the sum of the strike price of the short call option plus the premium received.

For numerical illustration purposes, we used names of two large South African banks—ABSA and Standard Bank. Note that, the illustrations do not pertain to any real positions on the banks. The bid-ask prices were computed at various theoretical prices of the underlying on the expiration date. The 3-month JIBAR is used as a proxy for the risk-free interest rate. To realize model calibration, we need market prices. Simulated data set of bid-ask options at different strikes maturing on the same date were generated using the models introduced in the previous Section.

The illustrations that follow merely suggest what an investor can do given the different risk appetites on an investor. The illustrations are implemented at stress (risk) level of 0.01, 0.05 and 0.10.

6.1. Bull Call Spread Risk Profile

6.1.1. Scenario

An investor owns 100 shares in ABSA Bank (ASAQ), which in early July are trading at a Single Stock Future (SSF) fair value of R140. The investor believes the market will be bullish in the coming 6 months and decided to create a bull call spread. So the investor buys a DEC ASAQ 140 call option and sells a DEC ASAQ call option with a higher strike price, so as to create the bull call spread strategy. The concern for the investor is on the appropriate higher strike which can create an attractive strategy.

1) At different stress (risk) levels, the investor determines the bid-ask prices for the range of strike prices.

2) The investor analyzes the risk profiles at each strike price choice so as to create an appropriate trade.

3) The investor finally assesses the performance of the

strategy, given a range of possible values of the underlying at expiration for the appropriate strike price from step 2 at a stress level of 0.01.

In addition, the investor gathers the following information:

$$3\text{month JIBAR rate } = 5.01\%$$

$$\text{Time to expiration } = 6/12 \text{ yr}$$

$$\text{Dividend yield } = 0\% \text{ (assumption)}.$$

In order to create the strategy appropriately, the investor implemented the following steps.

1) Bid-Ask Prices at Different Stress (γ) Levels

The calibrated parameters used for this strategy are $\sigma = 0.240$ in the Black-Scholes model and

$$\sigma = 0.226, \theta = -0.131, \nu = 0.08, \gamma = 0.480$$

in the VGSSD model. An attractive bull call spread is created when an investor buys a lower strike call and sells a higher strike call. In the scenario presented above, the investor has the choices shown in **Table 1**. **Table 2** shows the bid-ask prices for the options using both the Black-Scholes model and VGSSD model.

2) Risk Profile Analysis

Next, we look at the risk profiles for each of the choices using bid-ask prices provided in step 1 at a stress level of 0.01. Under the Black-Scholes model, an attractive strategy can be created by choice 4) as shown in **Table 3**. The reason is that the risk and breakeven point is lower whilst maximum reward and maximum Return on Investment (ROI) are high enough to be attractive.

Also under the VGSSD model, an attractive strategy can be created using choice 4) as shown in **Table 4**. The reason being again that the risk and breakeven is lower whilst the maximum reward and maximum Return on Investment (ROI) are high enough to be attractive.

3) Scenario Analysis at the Expiration Date

After choosing an attractive choice from step 2, we now look at the profit/loss of the strategy at expiration for a range of prices for the underlying. We compare the profit/loss under the two models—Black-Scholes model and VGSSD model. **Table 5** shows the profit/loss of the strategy under the two models. **Figure 1** shows the plot of the profit/loss of the strategy for a range of prices of the underlying at expiration. From **Figure 1**, it can be observed that the breakeven point is lower using the VGSSD model than the Black-Scholes model. A lower breakeven point is ideal for a strategy which intends to reduce risk.

6.1.2. Comment on the Strategy

The spread was observed to be lower in the VGSSD model than in the Black-Scholes model. Reduced spread can minimize the unhedgeable risk, which can be a major boost for option trading strategies. As a result, the cost of trade is lowered as the sold options can offset the cost of the bought option. In conclusion, the strategy becomes less risky in terms of lower risk and lower breakeven point but offers limited potential reward, which can still be highly attractive.

Table 1. Bull call spread investor choices.

Step 1	Long Call	Buy R140 Strike Call
Step 2	**1) Short Call**	Sell R141 Strike Call
Or	**2) Short Call**	Sell R142 Strike Call
Or	**3) Short Call**	Sell R143 Strike Call
Or	**4) Short Call**	Sell R144 Strike Call
Or	**5) Short Call**	Sell R145 Strike Call

6.2. Bear Call Spread Risk Profile

6.2.1. Scenario

In early July an investor believes the SSF fair price of Standard Bank (SBKQ) is going to fall from the current levels of R120 to around R117.50. The investor wants to create an attractive bear call spread. So the investor writes a SEP SBKQ 119 call option and buys a higher SEP SBKQ strike call, so as to create a bear call strategy. A little bit of concern to the investor is on the appropriate higher strike to choose so as to create an attractive strategy.

1) Now at different stress (risk) levels, the investor determines the bid-ask prices for the range of higher strike prices.

2) The investor analyzes the risk profiles at each of strike price choices so as to create an appropriate trade.

3) Finally, the investor accesses the performance of the strategy for the appropriate strike price in step 2 at a stress level of 0.01 given a range of possible values of the underlying at expiration.

1) Bid-Ask Prices at Different Stress (γ) Levels

The calibrated parameters used for this strategy are $\sigma = 0.306$ in the Black-Scholes model and

$$\sigma = 0.285, \theta = -0.070, \nu = 0.060, \gamma = 0.510$$

in the VGSSD model. An attractive bear call spread is created when an investor sells a lower strike call and buys a higher strike call. In the scenario presented here, the investor has the choices shown in **Table 6**. **Table 7** shows the bid-ask prices for the options using both the Black-Scholes model and VGSSD model.

2) Risk Profile Analysis

We now look at the risk profiles for each of the choices using bid-ask prices provided in step 1 at a stress level of 0.01. In **Table 8** a potential strategy can be created using a strike which provides reduced risk and a lower breakeven point. In addition, the gain on this strategy is the net credit received upon entering the trade. As

Table 2. Bull call spread bid-ask prices at different stress levels.

Stress Level	Black-Scholes Model					VGSSD Model				
	S	K	Bid	Ask	Spread	S	K	Bid	Ask	Spread
0.01	140	140	11.05	11.83	0.78	140	140	11.04	11.77	0.73
		141	10.56	11.32	0.76		141	10.54	11.25	0.71
		142	10.07	10.81	0.74		142	10.04	10.73	0.69
		143	9.62	10.33	0.71		143	9.59	10.26	0.67
		144	9.16	9.85	0.69		144	9.15	9.79	0.64
		145	8.71	9.37	0.66		145	8.70	9.32	0.62
0.05	140	140	10.50	14.59	4.09	140	140	10.49	14.28	3.79
		141	10.03	14.00	3.79		141	10.01	13.68	3.67
		142	9.56	13.40	3.84		142	9.53	13.09	3.56
		143	9.09	12.80	3.71		143	9.07	12.52	3.45
		144	8.67	12.28	3.61		144	8.66	12.01	3.35
		145	8.24	11.72	3.48		145	8.23	11.47	3.24
0.10	140	140	9.85	18.45	8.60	140	140	9.81	17.67	7.86
		141	9.38	17.72	8.34		141	9.35	16.99	7.64
		142	8.93	17.03	8.10		142	8.92	16.35	7.43
		143	8.49	16.33	7.84		143	8.46	15.67	7.21
		144	8.07	15.67	7.60		144	8.05	15.05	7.00
		145	7.68	15.05	7.37		145	7.67	14.46	6.79

Table 3. Bull call spread risk profile using Black-Scholes model.

Step 1	Long Call				
	Buy R140 Strike Call@R11.77				
Step 2	**Short Call**	**Risk**	**Reward**	**Breakeven**	**Max ROI**
1)	Sell R141 Strike Call@R10.54	R1.23	-R0.23	R141.23	−18.70%
2)	Sell R142 Strike Call@R10.04	R1.73	R0.27	R141.73	15.61%
3)	Sell R143 Strike Call@R9.59	R2.18	R0.82	R142.18	37.61%
4)	Sell R144 Strike Call@R9.15	R2.62	R1.38	R142.62	52.67%
5)	Sell R145 Strike Call@8.70	R3.07	R1.93	R143.07	62.87%

Table 4. Bull call spread risk profile using VGSSD model.

Step 1	Long Call				
	Buy R140 Strike Call@R11.83				
Step 2	**Short Call**	**Risk**	**Reward**	**Breakeven**	**Max ROI**
1)	Sell R141 Strike Call@R10.56	R1.27	−R0.27	R141.27	−21.26%
2)	Sell R142 Strike Call@R10.07	R1.76	R0.24	R141.76	13.64%
3)	Sell R143 Strike Call@R9.62	R2.21	R0.79	R142.21	35.75%
4)	Sell R144 Strike Call@R9.16	R2.67	R1.33	R142.67	49.81%
5)	Sell R145 Strike Call@R8.71	R3.12	R1.88	R143.12	60.26%

a result choice 4) is attractive to create the strategy since the net credit is fairly high, and the breakeven point as well as the risk are reduced.

In **Table 9** a potential strategy again can be created using a strike which provides reduced risk and lower breakeven. Also, the gain on this strategy is the net credit received upon entering the trade. As a result choice 4) is attractive to create the strategy since the net credit is fairly high, and the breakeven point is reduced and the risk is fairly low.

3) Scenario Analysis at the Expiration Date

Next, we look at the profit/loss of the strategy at expiration for a range of prices for the underlying using the choice selected in Step 2. We compare the profit/loss under the two models—Black-Scholes model and VGSSD model. **Table 10** shows the profit/loss of the strategy under the

Table 5. Bull call spread profit/loss under Black-Scholes and VGSSD models.

Black-Scholes Model		VGSSD Model	
ASAQ@expiry	Profit/Loss	ASAQ@expiry	Profit/Loss
135	−2.67	135	−2.62
136	−2.67	136	−2.62
137	−2.67	137	−2.62
138	−2.67	138	−2.62
139	−2.67	139	−2.62
140	−2.67	140	−2.62
141	−1.67	141	−1.62
142	−0.67	142	−0.62
142.67	0.00	142.62	0.00
143	0.33	143	0.38
144	1.33	144	1.38
145	1.33	145	1.38
146	1.33	146	1.38
147	1.33	147	1.38
148	1.33	148	1.38
149	1.33	149	1.38
150	1.33	150	1.38

Table 6. Bear call spread investor choices.

Step 1	Short Call	Sell R119 Strike Call
Step 2	1) Long Call	Buy R120 Strike Call
Or	2) Long Call	Buy R121 Strike Call
Or	3) Long Call	Buy R122 Strike Call
Or	4) Long Call	Buy R123 Strike Call
Or	5) Long Call	Buy R124 Strike Call

Table 7. Bear call spread bid-ask prices at different stress levels.

Stress Level	Black-Scholes Model					VGSSD Model				
	S	K	Bid	Ask	Spread	S	K	Bid	Ask	Spread
0.01	120	119	6.91	7.45	0.54	120	119	6.87	7.40	0.73
		120	6.40	6.90	0.50		120	6.37	6.86	0.71
		121	5.92	6.40	0.48		121	5.88	6.35	0.69
		122	5.47	5.93	0.46		122	5.43	5.89	0.67
		123	5.02	5.45	0.43		123	5.01	5.43	0.64
		124	4.62	5.03	0.41		124	4.61	5.02	0.41
0.05	120	119	6.57	9.42	2.85	120	119	6.55	9.34	2.79
		120	6.06	8.76	2.70		120	6.04	8.67	2.63
		121	5.61	8.16	2.55		121	5.59	8.09	2.50
		122	5.18	7.61	2.43		122	5.17	7.53	2.36
		123	4.75	7.03	2.28		123	4.73	6.95	2.22
		124	4.35	6.50	2.15		124	4.33	6.42	2.09
0.10	120	119	6.16	12.25	6.09	120	119	6.14	12.05	5.91
		120	5.67	11.44	5.77		120	5.66	11.28	5.62
		121	5.25	10.74	5.49		121	5.23	10.56	5.33
		122	4.81	10.00	5.19		122	4.80	9.85	5.05
		123	4.42	9.33	4.91		123	4.41	9.19	4.78
		124	3.71	8.08	4.37		124	3.69	7.94	4.25

Table 8. Bear call spread risk profile using Black-Scholes model.

Step 1	Short Call				
	Sell R119 Strike Call@R6.91				
Step 2	**Long Call**	**Risk**	**Reward**	**Breakeven**	**Max ROI**
1)	Buy R120 Strike Call@R6.90	R0.99	R0.01	R119.01	1.01%
2)	Buy R121 Strike Call@R6.40	R1.49	R0.51	R119.51	34.23%
3)	Buy R122 Strike Call@R5.93	R2.02	R0.98	R119.98	48.51%
4)	Buy R123 Strike Call@R5.45	R2.54	R1.46	R120.46	57.48%
5)	Buy R124 Strike Call@5.03	R3.12	R1.88	R120.88	60.26%

Table 9. Bear call spread risk profile using VGSSD model.

Step 1	Short Call				
	Sell R119 Strike Call@R6.87				
Step 2	**Long Call**	**Risk**	**Reward**	**Breakeven**	**Max ROI**
1)	Buy R120 Strike Call@R6.86	R0.99	R0.01	R119.01	1.01%
2)	Buy R121 Strike Call@R6.35	R1.48	R0.52	R119.52	35.14%
3)	Buy R122 Strike Call@R5.89	R2.02	R0.98	R119.98	48.51%
4)	Buy R123 Strike Call@R5.43	R2.56	R1.44	R120.44	56.25%
5)	Buy R124 Strike Call@5.02	R3.15	R1.85	R120.85	58.73%

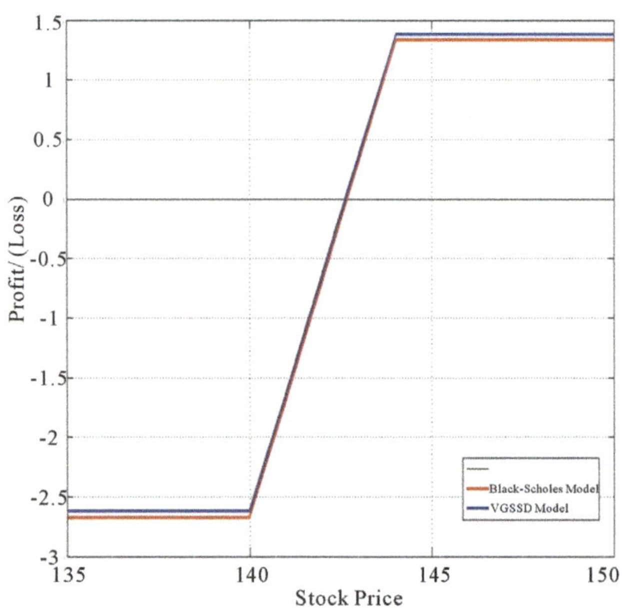

Figure 1. Plot of bull call spread profit/loss.

Table 10. Bull call spread profit/loss under the Black-Scholes and VGSSD models.

Black-Scholes Model		VGSSD Model	
SBKQ@expiry	**Profit/Loss**	**SBKQ@expiry**	**Profit/Loss**
125	−2.54	125	-2.56
124	−2.54	124	-2.56
123	−2.54	123	-2.56
122	−1.54	122	-1.56
121	−0.54	121	-0.56
120.46	0.00	120.44	0.00
120	0.46	120	0.44
119	1.46	119	1.44
118	1.46	118	1.44
117	1.46	117	1.44
116	1.46	116	1.44
115	1.46	115	1.44

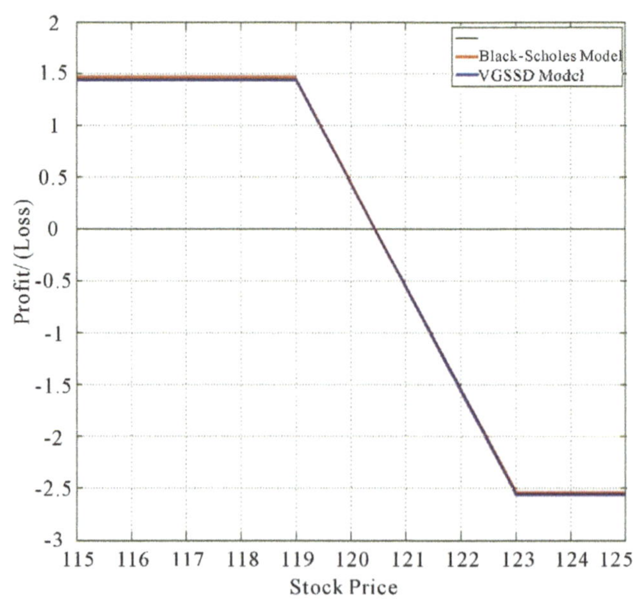

Figure 2. Plot of bear call spread profit/loss.

two models. **Figure 2** shows the plot of the profit/loss of the strategy for a range of prices of the underlying at expiration. The breakeven point is lower in the VGSSD model than the Black-Scholes model, which is ideal in creating a strategy with reduced risk.

6.2.2. Comment on the Strategy

Under this strategy, the spread is reduced under the VGSSD model than the Black-Scholes model. The lower spread implies reduced cost of risk and lower breakeven point. However, in this strategy reducing the risk impacts on the potential reward under the VGSSD model as compared to the Black-Scholes model.

7. Conclusions

In this paper, we have looked at the quantification of risks of trading strategies in incomplete markets. We established that the no-arbitrage price intervals are unacceptably large. We need intervals with prices which are acceptable to the market. The acceptability of the prices is assessed by risk measures. Ideal risk measures are those that produce price bounds that are suitable for use as bid-ask prices and are able to compensate for unhedgeable risk. Plausible risk measures we look at are coherent risk measure and acceptability indices. Acceptability indices are heavily used in the theory of conic finance, which we used to assess the risk of trading strategies. Conic finance provides plausible bid-ask prices which are determined only by the probability distribution of the cash flow.

We assess the risks of financial positions using two strategies-bull call spread and bear call spread. Comparison of the risk profiles for the trading strategies is done between the VGSSD model and the Black-Scholes model. The findings showed that the spread was reduced, especially using the VGSSD model as compared to the Black-Scholes model. In addition, the findings showed that the bid-ask price intervals are able to compensate for the unhedgeable risk. Ultimately, reward from the strategies had a potential of increasing.

REFERENCES

[1] P. Artzner, F. Delbaen, J. Eber and D. Heath, "Definition of Coherent Measure of Risk," *Mathematical Finance*, Vol. 9, No. 3, 1999, pp. 203-228.

[2] A. Cherny and D. Madan, "New Measure of Performance Evaluation," *Review of Financial Studies*, Vol. 22, No. 7, 2009, pp. 2571-2606.

[3] J. N. Cochrane and J. Saá-Requejo, "Beyond Arbitrage: 'Good Deal' Asset Price Bounds in Incomplete Markets," *Journal of Political Economy*, Vol. 108, No. 1, 2000, pp. 79-11.

[4] J. Staum, "Incomplete Markets," In: J. R. Birge and V. Linetsky, *Handbook in Operations Research and Management Science*, Vol. 15, Chapter 12, Elsevier, Berlin, 2008, pp. 511-563.

[5] S. Jaschke and K. Küchler, "Coherent Risk Measures and Good Deal Bounds," *Finance and Stochastics*, Vol. 5, No. 2, 2001, pp. 181-200.

[6] A. Cherny and D. Madan, "Markets as a Counterparty: An Introduction to Conic Finance," *International Journal of Theoretical and Applied Finance*, Vol. 13, No. 8, 2010, pp. 1149-1177.

[7] D. Madan, P. Carr and E. Chang, "The Variance Gamma Process and Option Pricing," *European Finance Review*, Vol. 2, No. 1, 1998, pp. 79-105.

[8] P. Carr, H. Geman, D. Madan, and M. Yor, "Self Decomposability and Option Pricing," *Mathematical Finance*, Vol. 17, No. 1, 2007, pp. 31-57.

[9] K. Sato, "Self Similar Processes with Independent Increments," *Probability Theory and Related Fields*, Vol. 89, No. 3, 1991, pp. 285-300.

[10] K. Sato, "Lévy Processes and Infinitely Divisible Distributions," Cambridge University, Cambridge, 1999.

[11] P. Carr, H. Geman, D. Madan and M. Yor, "Pricing Options on Realized Variance," *Finance and Stochastics*, Vol. 9, No. 4, 2005, pp. 453-475.

Mixed Band Control of Mutual Proportional Reinsurance*

Michael Taksar[1], John Liu[2], Jiguang Yuan[3#]
[1]Department of Mathematics, University of Missouri, Columbia, USA
[2]College of Business, City University of Hong Kong, Hong Kong, China
[3]Center for Transport, Trade and Financial Studies, City University of Hong Kong, Hong Kong, China

ABSTRACT

In this paper, we investigate the optimization of mutual proportional reinsurance—a mutual reserve system that is intended for the collective reinsurance needs of homogeneous mutual members, such as P&I Clubs in marine mutual insurance and reserve banks in the US Federal Reserve, where a mutual member is both an insurer and an insured. Compared to general (non-mutual) insurance models, which involve one-sided impulse control (*i.e.*, either downside or upside impulse) of the underlying insurance reserve process that is required to be positive, a mutual insurance differs in allowing two-sided impulse control (*i.e.*, both downside and upside impulse), coupled with the classical proportional control of reinsurance. We prove that a special band-type impulse control (a, A, B, b) with $a = 0$ and $a < A < B < b$, coupled with a proportional reinsurance policy (classical control), is optimal when the objective is to minimize the total maintenance cost. That is, when the reserve position reaches a lower boundary of $a = 0$, the reserve should immediately be raised to level A; when the reserve reaches an upper boundary of b, it should immediately be reduced to a level B. An interesting finding produced by the study reported in this paper is that there exists a situation such that if the upside fixed cost is relatively large in comparison to a finite threshold, then the optimal band control is reduced to a downside only (*i.e.*, dividend payment only) control in the form of $(0, 0; B, b)$ with $a = A = 0$. In this case, it is optimal for the mutual insurance firm to go bankrupt as soon as its reserve level reaches zero, rather than to jump restart by calling for additional contingent funds. This finding partially explains why many mutual insurance companies, that were once quite popular in the financial markets, are either disappeared or converted to non-mutual ones.

Keywords: Insurance and Risk Management; Dynamic Programming and Control

1. Introduction

This study is motivated by the long lasting while still strong-going success of marine mutual insurance (e.g., a P&I club of ship owners), the longest in the insurance business with a history of over 200 years; and by the still unanswered question why the once popular mutual insurance firms almost disappeared after 1990's, either went bankrupt or converted to commercial (non-mutual) insurance business. A client of a mutual insurance is both insurer and insured, under a unique contingent regulation scheme of two-way impulse control (termed band control) which we give a brief description as follows. A mutual insurance firm is allowed: 1) to make calls for contingent injection from its clients once the reserve level is considered too low, as opposed to a commercial (non-mutual) insurance firm which would go bankrupt once its reserve becomes depleted; 2) or to make refunds (pay dividends) to its clients if the reserve is considered too high. We shall note that it is also permissible to adjust premium rate and liability policy in the continuous time horizon in conjunction of the band control as just mentioned, which in this case is referred to as a mixed band control of insurance reserves (*i.e.*, a band type impulse control mixed with time-continuous classical control of a reserve process). Although in practice, mutual insurance engages mixed band control, most studies in the current literature are focused on the band control only, without classical control (e.g., with given constant premium rate, see [1,2]

*This work was initiated by and is completed in memory of the late Professor Taksar.
This work is support in part by Hong Kong GRF522507E.
#Corresponding author.

for reference). In this paper we consider mixed band control of mutual reinsurance which provides insurance to other mutual insurance firms, such as P&I clubs, of which each insures a number of ship-owners.

Reinsurance has been long investigated as an intrinsic part of commercial insurance, of which the mainstream modeling framework is profit maximization with the one-sided impulse control of an underlying reserve process. There are two types of one-sided impulse control: downside-only impulse control (such as a dividend payment) with a fixed cost K^- (e.g., Cadenillas *et al.* [3], Hojgaard and Taksar [4]) and upside-only impulse control (such as inventory ordering) with a fixed cost K^+ (e.g., Bensoussan *et al.* [2], Eisenberg and Schmidli [5], Sulem [6]). In this paper, we examine mutual proportional reinsurance—a mutual reserve system that is intended for the collective reinsurance needs of homogeneous mutual members, such as the P&I Clubs in marine mutual insurance (e.g., Yuan [7]) and the reserve banks in the US Federal Reserve (e.g., Dawande *et al.* [8]). A mutual insurance differs from a general (non-mutual) insurance in two key dimensions: 1) a mutual system is not for profit, and 2) a mutual reserve involves two-sided impulse control (*i.e.*, both a dividend refund as a downside impulse to decrease the reserve with cost K^- and a call for funds as an upside impulse to increase the reserve with cost K^+). It should be noted that the reserve process for a general insurance must always be positive (above zero), and the insurance firm is considered bankrupt as soon as its reserve falls to zero.

The mutual proportional reinsurance model developed in this paper is a generalization of the proportional reinsurance models (e.g., Cadenillas *et al.* [3], Hojgaard and Taksar [4], Eisenberg and Schmidli [5], Løkka and Zervos [9]) and is modified with the two differing characteristics noted above. More specifically, the proportional reinsurance rate can be adjusted in continuous time, and the underlying mutual reserve process is regulated by a two-sided impulse control in terms of a contingent dividend payment (*i.e.*, a downside impulse control to decrease the mutual reserve level) and contingent call for contributions (*i.e.*, an upside impulse control to increase the mutual reserve level). The corresponding mathematical problem for mutual proportional reinsurance becomes a two-sided impulse control system combined with a classical rate control in continuous time, a problem yet to be posed in insurance research. A problem that involves a mix of impulse control and classical control is termed a hybrid control problem in control theory, of which the difficulty has been well noted (e.g., Bensoussanand Menaldi [10], Branicky, Borkarand Mitter [11], Abate *et al.* [12]).

A pure two-sided impulse control problem (*i.e.*, without a classical rate control) was investigated by Constantinides [13] in the form of cash management. Constantinides and Richard [1] showed an optimal two-sided impulse control policy to exist in the form of a band control, denoted with four parameters as $(a,A;B,b)$ with $a<A\le B<b$. In other words, when the reserve position reaches a lower boundary *a*, then the reserve should immediately be raised to level *A*; when the reserve reaches upper boundary *b*, it should immediately be reduced to level *B*. For our mutual proportional reinsurance problem, we specify the corresponding Hamilton-Jacobi-Bellman (HJB) equation and the associated quasi-variational inequalities (QVI), from which we analytically solve the optimal value function. We then prove that a special band-type impulse control $(0,A,B,b)$ with $a=0$, combined with a proportional reinsurance policy (classical control), is optimal when the objective is to minimize the total maintenance cost. An interesting finding reported here is that there exists a situation such that if the upside fixed cost K^+ is relatively large in comparison to a finite threshold K^+, then the optimal band control is reduced to a downside only (*i.e.*, a dividend payment only) control in the form of $(0,0;B,b)$ with $a=A=0$. In this case, it is optimal for the mutual insurance to go bankrupt as soon as its reserve level falls to zero, rather than to restart by calling for additional contingent funds. This finding partially explains why many mutual insurance companies, that were once quite popular in the financial markets, are either disappeared or converted to non-mutual ones.

The remainder of the paper is organized as follows. In Section 2, we formulate the mathematical model and specify the HJB equation and the QVI of the corresponding stochastic control problem. We solve the QVI for the optimal value function in Section 3. In Section 3.2, we characterize and analyze the threshold K^+. In Section 4, we prove the verification theorem and verify the optimal control. Finally, we make concluding remarks in Section 5.

2. The Model

2.1. Feasible Control

The classical Cramer-Lundberg model of an insurance reserve (surplus) is described via a compound Poisson process:

$$D(t)=D(0)+pt-\sum_{i=0}^{N(t)}Y_i,$$

where $D(t)$ is the amount of the surplus available at time t, quantity p represents the premium rate, $N(t)$ is the Poisson process of incoming claims and Y_i is the size of the *i*th claim. This surplus process can be approximated by a diffusion process with drift $\mu=p-\lambda E[Y]$ and diffusion coefficient $\sigma=\sqrt{\lambda EY^2}$, where λ is the intensity of the Poisson process $N(t)$. We assume that the insurer always sets $p > \lambda E[Y]$ (*i.e.* $\mu > 0$). Thus, with no control, the reserve process $X(t)$ is described by

$$X(t) = X(0) + \int_0^t \mu \mathrm{d}s + \int_0^t \sigma \mathrm{d}W_s, \tag{2.1}$$

where W_t is a standard Brownian motion.

We start with a probability space $(\Omega, \mathcal{F}, P)$, that is endowed with *information filtration* $\mathcal{F}_t$ and a standard Brownian motion W_t on Ω adapted to $\mathcal{F}_t$. Two types of controls are used in this model. The first is related to the ability to directly control its reserve by raising cash from or making refunds to members at any particular time. The second is related to the mutual insurance firm's ability to delegate all or part of its risk to a reinsurance company, simultaneously reducing the incoming premium (all or part of which is in this case channeled to the reinsurance company). In this model, we consider a *proportional reinsurance* scheme. This type of scheme corresponds to the original insurer paying u fraction of the original claim. The premium rate coming to the original insurer is simultaneously reduced by the same fraction. The reinsurance rate can be chosen dynamically depending on the situation.

Mathematically, control U takes a triple form:

$$U = \{u(t), (\tau_1, \tau_2, \cdots), (\xi_1, \xi_2, \cdots)\}, \tag{2.2}$$

where $0 \le u(t) \le 1$ is a predictable process with respect to $\mathcal{F}_t$, the random variables $\tau_1 < \tau_2 < \cdots$ constitute an increasing sequence of stopping times with respect to $\mathcal{F}_t$, and ξ_i is a sequence of $\mathcal{F}_{\tau_i}$-measurable random variables, $i = 1, 2, \cdots$.

The meaning of these controls is as follows. The quantity $u(t)$ represents the fraction (reinsurance share) of the premium and risk (loss) incurred by the mutual insurance at time t. Suppose that $u(t) = u$ is chosen at time t. Then, in the diffusion approximation (2.1), drift μ and diffusion coefficient σ are reduced by factor u (see Cadenillas *et al.* [14], Hojgaard and Taksar [4]).

The fact that the process $u(t)$ is adapted to information filtration means that any decision has to be made on the basis of past rather than the future information. The stopping times τ_i represent the times when the *i*th intervention to change the reserve level is made. If $\xi_i > 0$, then the decision is to raise cash by calling the members/clients. If $\xi_i < 0$, then the decision is to make a refund. The fact that τ_i is a stopping time and ξ_i is $\mathcal{F}_{\tau_i}$ measurable also indicates that the decisions concerning when to make a contingent call and how much cash to raise are made on the basis of only past information. The same applies to the refund decisions.

Once control U is chosen, the dynamics of the reserve process becomes:

$$X(t) = X(0) + \int_0^t u(s) \mu \mathrm{d}s + \int_0^t u(s) \sigma \mathrm{d}W_s + \sum_{\tau_i \le t} \xi_i. \tag{2.3}$$

Define the ruin time as

$$\tau = \inf\{t : X(t) < 0\}. \tag{2.4}$$

Control U is called admissible for initial position x if, for $X(0) = x$ for any $\tau_i \le \tau$,

$$X(\tau_i) \ge 0; \tag{2.5}$$

and if

$$E \sum_{\tau_i < \tau} \mathrm{e}^{-r\tau_i} |\xi_i| < \infty. \tag{2.6}$$

We denote the set of all admissible controls by $\mathcal{U}$.

The meaning of admissibility is as follows. At any time the decision to make a refund is made, the refund amount cannot exceed the available reserve. As can be seen in the following, if this condition is not satisfied, then one can always achieve a cost equal to $-\infty$, simply by making an infinitely large refund. The second condition of admissibility is a rather natural technical condition of integrability.

2.2. Cost Structure and Value Function

The objective in this model is to minimize the operational cost and the lost opportunity to invest the money in the market. Cost function g is defined as

$$g(\xi) = K^+ 1_{\xi > 0} + c^+ \xi^+ + K^- 1_{\xi < 0} - c^- \xi^-. \tag{2.7}$$

Here, ξ^+ and ξ^- denote the positive and negative components of ξ, that is, $\xi^+ = \max(\xi, 0)$ and $\xi^- = -\min(\xi, 0)$. The costs associated with refunds are of a different nature. A contingent call always increases the total cost, whereas a refund decreases it. However fixed set-up costs $K^+ > 0$ and $K^- > 0$ are incurred regardless of of the size of a contingent call or a refund. In addition, when the call is made and the cash is raised, there is a proportional cost associated with the amount raised. The constant $c^+ > 1$ represents the amount of cash that needs to be raised in order for one dollar to be added to the reserve. If the reserve is used for a refund, then a part of it may be charged as tax. The constant $0 < c^- < 1$ represents the amount actually received by the shareholders for each dollar taken from the reserve.

Given a discount rate r, the cost functional associated with the control U is defined as

$$C(x; U) = E_x \left\{ \sum_{i=1}^{\infty} g(\xi_i) \mathrm{e}^{-r\tau_i} 1_{\tau_i \le \tau} \right\}. \tag{2.8}$$

The objective is to find the value function,

$$V(x)=\inf_{U\in\mathcal{U}} C(x;U), \quad (2.9)$$

and *optimal control* U^*, such that

$$C(x,U^*)=V(x).$$

2.3. Variational Inequalities for the Optimal Value Function

For each $0\le u\le 1$, define the infinitesimal generator $\mathcal{L}^u$. For any twice continuously differentiable function $\phi:[0,\infty)\mapsto\mathbb{R}$

$$(\mathcal{L}^u\phi)(x)=\frac{1}{2}u^2\sigma^2\frac{d^2\phi(x)}{dx^2}+u\mu\frac{d\phi(x)}{dx}. \quad (2.10)$$

Let M be the *inf-convolution operator*, defined as

$$\mathcal{M}\phi(x)=\inf_{\xi\neq 0}\left[g(\xi)+\phi(x+\xi)\right]. \quad (2.11)$$

Definition 2.1. The QVI of the control problem are

$$\mathcal{L}^uV-rV\ge 0, \quad (2.12)$$

and

$$\mathcal{M}V\ge V, \quad (2.13)$$

together with the tightness condition

$$(\mathcal{M}V-V)\left(\min_{u\in[0,1]}\left(\mathcal{L}^uV-rV\right)\right)=0. \quad (2.14)$$

3. Solution of the QVI

Before you begin to format your paper, first write and save the content as a separate text file. Keep your text and graphic files separate until after the text has been formatted and styled. Do not use hard tabs, and limit use of hard returns to only one return at the end of a paragraph. Do not add any kind of pagination anywhere in the paper. Do not number text heads—the template will do that for you.

Finally, complete content and organizational editing before formatting. Please take note of the following items when proofreading spelling and grammar:

3.1. The HJB Equation in the Continuation Region

In this model, the application of the control that is related to calls and refunds results in a jump in the reserve process. This type of model is considered in the framework of the so-called *impulse control*. Because we also have a control whose application changes the drift and the diffusion coefficient of the controlled process, the resulting mathematical problem becomes a mixed regular-impulse control problem (e.g., Cadenillas *et al.* [14]). In the case of a pure impulse control, the optimal policy is of the (a,A,B,b) type, where the four parameters used to construct the optimal control must be computed as a part of a solution to the problem (see Cadenillas and Zapatero [15], Constantinides and Richard [10], Harrison and Taylor [16], and Paulsen [17]). Parameters a and b represent the levels at which the intervention (application of impulses) must be made, whereas A and B stand for the positions that the controlled process must be in after the intervention is made. This is a so-called *band-type* policy, with (a,A) and (B,b) understood as the two bands that determine the nature of the optimal control. The interval $[a,b]$ is called the *continuation region*. When the process falls inside the continuation region, no interventions/impulses are applied. When an intervention is initiated, the time when the process reaches one of the boundaries of the continuation region corresponds to one of τ_i.

We conjecture that, in our case, the optimal intervention (impulse control) component of the problem is also of the band type. Moreover, as the following analysis implicitly shows, we can narrow our search for the optimal policy to a special band-type control $(0,A,B,b)$, where the level a associated with the contingent calls is set to zero. Therefore, only three of the four band-type policy parameters remain unknown. After finding these parameters (and determining the optimal drift/diffusion control in the continuation region), we will see that the cost function associated with this policy satisfies the QVI.

The derivation of the value function is similar to [3] and [14].Suppose that $V(x)$ satisfies all of the QVI conditions: (2.12), (2.13) and (2.14). First note that the function $V(x)$ is a decreasing function of x, and thus $V'\le 0$. To satisfy (2.14), for any $x\ge 0$, at least one of the two functions on the left side of the equation should be equal to zero. We conjecture that the value function has the following structure.

$$V-\mathcal{M}V=0 \quad (3.15)$$

for $x\in 0\cup[b,+\infty)$. Also

$$\min_{u\in[0,1]}\left(\mathcal{L}^uV-rV\right)=0 \quad (3.16)$$

for $x\in(0,b)$.

Assume that $u^*\in[0,1]$ minimizes the function $\mathcal{L}^uV-rV$ in foregoing equation. If $V''>0$ then

$$u^*=-\frac{\mu V'}{\sigma^2V''}, \quad (3.17)$$

provided that the right-hand side of (3.17) belongs to $(0,1)$. (Note that if $V''(x)=0$, then (3.16) cannot be satisfied and we exclude $V''(x)=0$ from consideration).

Substituting (3.17) into (3.16), we get

$$2r\sigma^2V_1V_1''+\mu^2(V_1')^2=0. \quad (3.18)$$

The general solution for (3.18) is

$$V_1(x) = -C_1(x+C_2)^{\gamma}, \tag{3.19}$$

where C_1 and C_2 are free constants to be determined later, and

$$\gamma = \frac{1}{1+\dfrac{\mu^2}{2r\sigma^2}}. \tag{3.20}$$

It is easy to see that $0<\gamma<1$. From (3.17), we obtain the expression for $u^*(x)$ (provided that $C_1>0$, which will be verified later):

$$u^*(x) = \frac{\mu(x+C_2)}{\sigma^2(1-\gamma)}. \tag{3.21}$$

Note that the solution of (3.18) coincides with the solution of (3.16) only in the region where

$$0 < \frac{\mu}{\sigma^2(1-\gamma)}(x+C_2) < 1.$$

From this expression, we conjecture that there is a switching point x_0 such that $u(x)=1$ when $x>x_0$. As $u^*(x_0)=1$, by virtue of the equation (3.21), we obtain the following expression for x_0:

$$x_0 = \frac{\sigma^2(1-\gamma)}{\mu} - C_2. \tag{3.22}$$

For $x>x_0$, $u^*(x)=1$; and the corresponding differential equation becomes

$$\frac{1}{2}\sigma^2 V_2'' + \mu V_2' - rV_2 = 0. \tag{3.23}$$

The general solution for (3.23) is

$$V_2(x) = C_3 e^{\rho_1(x-x_0)} + C_4 e^{-\rho_2(x-x_0)}, \tag{3.24}$$

where

$$\rho_1 = \frac{\sqrt{\mu^2+2r\sigma^2}-\mu}{\sigma^2} \tag{3.25}$$

$$\rho_2 = \frac{\sqrt{\mu^2+2r\sigma^2}+\mu}{\sigma^2}, \tag{3.26}$$

with $0<\rho_1<\rho_2$. Standard arguments show that

$$V'(x) = -c^- \tag{3.27}$$

For $x \ge b$ (see e.g., Cadenillas *et al.* [14]). The boundary conditions for the equation are rather tricky. If 0 and b are the points at which the impulse control (intervention) is initiated then the boundary conditions at these points become

$$V(0) = V(A) + K^+ + c^+A \tag{3.28}$$

$$V'(A) = -c^+ \tag{3.29}$$

$$V(b) = V(B) + K^- - c^-(b-B) \tag{3.30}$$

$$V'(B) = -c^-. \tag{3.31}$$

However, if bankruptcy is allowed and no intervention is initiated when the process reaches 0, then the boundary condition at 0 becomes straightforward: $V(0)=0$ (see Cadenillas and Zapatero [3] and Cadenillas, *et al.* [14]). In our case, whether 0 is the point that corresponds to the intervention in the form of a contingent call or whether it corresponds to bankruptcy is not given a priori; rather it is part of the solution to the problem.

We seek the solution by finding a function V such that

$$V(x) = V_1(x), 0 \le x \le x_0, \tag{3.32}$$

$$V(x) = V_2(x), x_0 < x < b, \text{ and} \tag{3.33}$$

$$V(x) = V(b) - c^-(x-b), x \ge b. \tag{3.34}$$

To find the free constants in the expressions for V_1 an V_2 and to paste different pieces of the solution together we apply the *principle of smooth fit* by making the value and the first derivatives to be continuous at the switching points x_0 and b,

$$V_1(x_0) = V_2(x_0), \tag{3.35}$$

$$V_1'(x_0) = V_2'(x_0), \tag{3.36}$$

$$V_2'(b) = -c^-, \tag{3.37}$$

where x_0 is defined by (3.22).

(It should be noted that the function V, which is constructed from (3.32)-(3.34) subject to conditions (3.28)-(3.31) and (3.35)-(3.37), corresponds to the case in which the optimal policy leads to $\tau=\infty$). We begin by constructing such a function. The main technique is not to consider the function V itself, but rather first to construct V'.

The form of $V'(x)$ is shown in **Figure 1**.

From $u^*(x_0)=1$ and (3.17), we have

$V_1''(x_0) = -\frac{\mu}{\sigma^2}V_1'(x_0)$. By the continuity on V and V' at x_0, and by (3.23), we have $\frac{\mu}{2r}V_2'(x_0) = V_2(x_0)$. From this relation and (3.24), we have

$$C_4 = \frac{\rho_1\dfrac{\mu}{2r}-1}{\rho_2\dfrac{\mu}{2r}+1}C_3.$$

Let $\beta = \dfrac{\rho_1\cdot\dfrac{\mu}{2r}-1}{\rho_2\cdot\dfrac{\mu}{2r}+1}$. Then, $C_4=\beta C_3$, and we can write

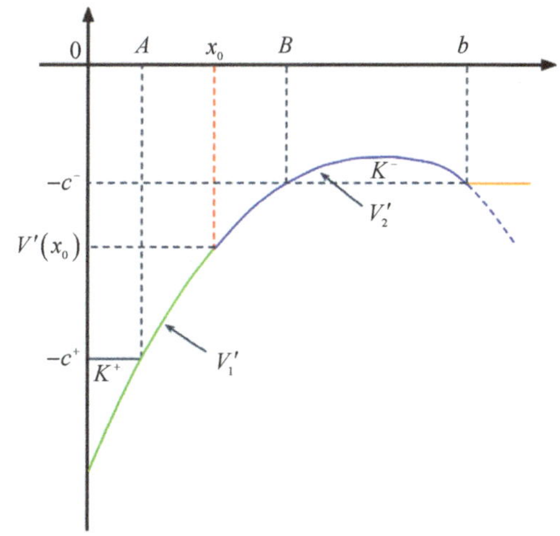

Figure 1. Optimal policy parameters.

$$V_2(x;C_3) = C_3 e^{\rho_1(x-x_0)} + \beta C_3 e^{-\rho_2(x-x_0)}.$$

We can easily get the inequalities:

$$-1 < \beta < 0. \tag{3.38}$$

From (3.22), we get

$$V_1(x_0) = -C_1(x_0 + C_2)^\gamma = -C_1\left(\frac{\sigma^2(1-\gamma)}{\mu}\right)^\gamma.$$

From $V_2(x_0) = C_3 + \beta C_3$, and from the continuity of V at x_0, we obtain the expression for C_1:

$$C_1 = -(1+\beta)\left(\frac{\sigma^2(1-\gamma)}{\mu}\right)^{-\gamma} C_3.$$

Let $\lambda = -(1+\beta)\left(\frac{\sigma^2(1-\gamma)}{\mu}\right)^{-\gamma}$. (Obviously, $\lambda < 0$ since $\beta > -1$.) Now, we can write V_1 in terms of C_2 and C_3:

$$V_1(x;C_2,C_3) = -\lambda C_3(x+C_2)^\gamma.$$

What remains is to determine C_2 and C_3. Once these constants are found, we have $V_1(x)$ and $V_2(x)$, and thus $V(x)$. Let

$$V(x,C_2,C_3) = \begin{cases} V_1(x;C_2,C_3) = -\lambda C_3(x+C_2)^\gamma, & \text{for } 0 < x \le x_0 \\ V_2(x;C_3) = C_3 e^{\rho_1(x-x_0)} + \beta C_3 e^{-\rho_2(x-x_0)}, & \text{for } x \ge x_0 \end{cases}$$

where $x_0 = \frac{\sigma^2(1-\gamma)}{\mu} - C_2$.

Note that if $C_2 \ge 0$ and $C_3 < 0$, then it is easy to show that for $x > 0$, $V_1'(x;C_2,C_3) < 0$, $V_1'''(x;C_2,C_3) < 0$ and $V_2'(x;C_2,C_3) < 0$, $V_2'''(x;C_2,C_3) < 0$. Therefore, $V(x,C_2,C_3)$ is decreasing on $x > 0$ and $V'(x,C_2,C_3)$ is concave on $x > 0$. In the remainder of this section, we find C_2 and C_3 and complete the construction of the function V. We do this in an implicit manner by adopting an auxiliary problem in which no contingent calls are allowed and by using the optimal value function of that problem to construct the function V.

Let's consider a slightly different problem in which only those controls U for which ξ_i on the right-hand side of (2.2) are negative allowed. This problem is similar to that considered in Cadenillas *et al.* [14]. Let $v(x)$ be the optimal value function for this problem. As was shown in [14], the function v satisfies the same HJB equation, except for boundary conditions (3.28) and (3.29). These conditions are replaced by $v(0) = 0$.

The same arguments as those above show that we can make the conjecture that the function v should be sought as a solution to (3.39)-(3.44) below.

$$2r\sigma^2 v(x)v''(x) + \mu^2(v'(x))^2 = 0 \quad \text{for } 0 \le x \le \tilde{x}_0 \tag{3.39}$$

$$\frac{1}{2}\sigma^2 v''(x) + \mu v'(x) - rv(x) = 0 \quad \text{for } \tilde{x}_0 < x \le \tilde{b} \tag{3.40}$$

$$v(0) = 0 \tag{3.41}$$

$$v'(\tilde{b}) = -c^- \tag{3.42}$$

$$v'(\tilde{B}) = -c^- \tag{3.43}$$

$$v(\tilde{b}) = v(\tilde{B}) + K^- - c^-(\tilde{b} - \tilde{B}), \tag{3.44}$$

where $\tilde{x}_0 = \frac{\sigma^2(1-\gamma)}{\mu}$.

A Solution to the Auxiliary Problem

First note that a general solution to (3.39), (3.41) is $-cx^\gamma$, where γ is the same as in (3.20) and c is a free constant, and a general solution to (3.40) is $-a_1 e^{\rho_1(x-\tilde{x}_0)} - a_2 e^{\rho_2(x-\tilde{x}_0)}$, where ρ_1 and ρ_2 are the same as in (3.25), (3.26).

To solve our auxiliary problem we apply the same technique as that used in Cadenillas *et al.* [14]. We begin with $H(x)$, which is defined as follows.

$$H(x) = \begin{cases} -\gamma x^{\gamma-1}, & \text{for } 0 < x \le \tilde{x}_0 \\ -a_1\rho_1 e^{\rho_1(x-\tilde{x}_0)} + a_2\rho_2 e^{-\rho_2(x-\tilde{x}_0)}, & \text{for } x \ge \tilde{x}_0. \end{cases} \tag{3.45}$$

this expression, constants a_1 and a_2 are chosen in such a way that $-a_1\rho_1 + a_2\rho_2 = -\gamma\tilde{x}_0^{\gamma-1}$ and $-a_1\rho_1^2 + a_2\rho_2^2 = -\gamma(\gamma-1)\tilde{x}_0^{\gamma-2}$. That is, the functions H and H' are continuous at $\tilde{x}_0$. (Note that $H(x)$ is a derivative of $-x^\gamma$ on $[0,\tilde{x}_0]$ and $H(x)$ is a derivative of $-a_1 e^{\rho_1(x-\tilde{x}_0)} - a_2 e^{\rho_2(x-\tilde{x}_0)}$ on $[\tilde{x}_0, \infty)$.) We next examine the family of functions $MH(x)$, where $M > 0$. We seek M^* such that $M^* H(x)$ becomes the derivative of the optimal value function v.

To this end, we start by finding points $\tilde{b}_M$ and $\tilde{B}_M$ such that $\tilde{b}_M = \max\{x : MH(x) = -c^-\}$ and $\tilde{B}_M = \min\{x : MH(x) = -c^-\}$. Note that H is a concave function, which is easily checked by differentiation. Let $\bar{x} = \arg\max H(x)$, the point at which the maximum of H is achieved (it is easy to see that $H'(0) > 0$, whereas $\lim_{x\to\infty} H'(x) = -\infty$, which shows that $\bar{x}$ exists; in view of the fact that $H''(x) < 0$, it is unique). It is obvious by virtue of the concavity of H that, for any $M \le -c^-/H(\bar{x})$, $\tilde{b}_M$ and $\tilde{B}_M$ exist.

We now consider $I(M) = \int_{\tilde{B}^M}^{\tilde{b}^M} \left(MH(x) + c^-\right) \mathrm{d}x$. Informally, $I(M)$ is the area under the graph of $MH(x)$ and above the horizontal line $= -c^-$. It is obvious that $I(M)$ is a continuous function of M. For $M = -c^-/H(\bar{x})$, we have $\tilde{b}_M = \tilde{B}_M$; Let

$$H^*(x) = \begin{cases} M^* H(x), & x \le \bar{b}, \\ -c^-, & x \ge \bar{b}. \end{cases}$$

Then,

$$v(x) = \int_0^x H^*(y)\mathrm{d}y \tag{3.46}$$

is the optimal value function of the auxiliary problem (see **Figure 2**). The proof here is identical to that of a similar statement in Cadenillas *et al.* [14] and thus we omit it.

3.2. The Optimal Value Function for the Original Problem

We employ the function H^* obtained in the previous subsection to construct the derivative of the optimal value function V. The main idea is to consider $H^*(x+S)$ and try to find S such that $V'(x) = H^*(x+S)$. The optimal value function V will then be sought in the form of $v(x+S)$. To this end, we need the following proposition.

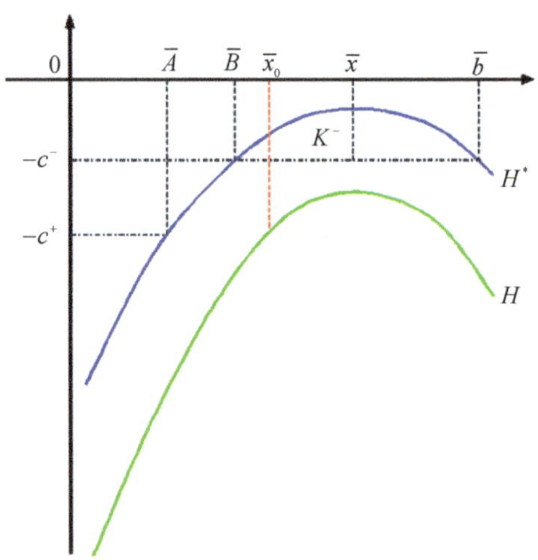

Figure 2. Solution to the auxiliary problem.

Proposition 3.1. Suppose that $f(x)$ satisfies (3.39) (satisfies (3.40)); then, for any *S*, the function $f(x+S)$ satisfies the same equation on the interval shifted by *S* to the left.

The proof of this proposition is straightforward.

From (3.45), we can see that H^* has a singularity at 0 with $\lim_{x\downarrow 0} H^*(x) = -\infty$. The concavity of H^* on $[0, \bar{b}]$ implies that H^* is increasing on $(0, \bar{x}]$ and decreasing on $[\bar{x}, \infty)$ (recall that $H^*(x)$ is constant on $[\bar{b}, \infty)$). Therefore, there exists unique $0 < \bar{A} < \bar{B}$ such that $H^*(\bar{A}) = -c^+$. Define

$$\overline{K^+} = \int_0^{\bar{A}} \left(-c^+ - H^*(x)\right) \mathrm{d}x. \tag{3.47}$$

Note that H^* decreases to $-\infty$ at 0 at the order of $x^{\gamma-1}$ (see (3.45)); therefore, H^* is integrable at 0 and, as a result, $K^+ < \infty$.

The qualitative nature of the solution to the original problem depends on the relationship between K^+ and K^+; hence, we divide our analysis into two cases.

3.2.1. The Case of $K^+ \le \overline{K^+}$

Consider the following integral

$$\mathcal{J}(S) = \int_S^{\bar{A}} \left(-c^+ - H^*(y)\right) \mathrm{d}y$$

Geometrically this integral represents the area of a curvilinear triangle bounded by the lines $y = -c^+$, $x = S$ and the graph of the function $H^*(x)$. Obviously, $\mathcal{J}(S)$ is a continuous function of S. Because $\mathcal{J}(0) = \overline{K^+}$ and $\mathcal{J}(\bar{A}) = 0$, there exists an S^* (see **Figure 3**) such that

$$\mathcal{J}(S^*) = K^+. \tag{3.48}$$

In what follows, we show that $H^*(x+S^*)$ is the derivative of the solution V to the QVI, inequalities (2.12)-(2.14).

Let

$$V(x) = v(x+S^*). \tag{3.49}$$

Also let

$$A = \bar{A} - S^*, \tag{3.50}$$

$$b = \bar{b} - S^*, \tag{3.51}$$

$$B = \bar{B} - S^*, \tag{3.52}$$

$$x_0 = \tilde{x}_0 - S^*, \tag{3.53}$$

$$x^* = \bar{x} - S^*. \tag{3.54}$$

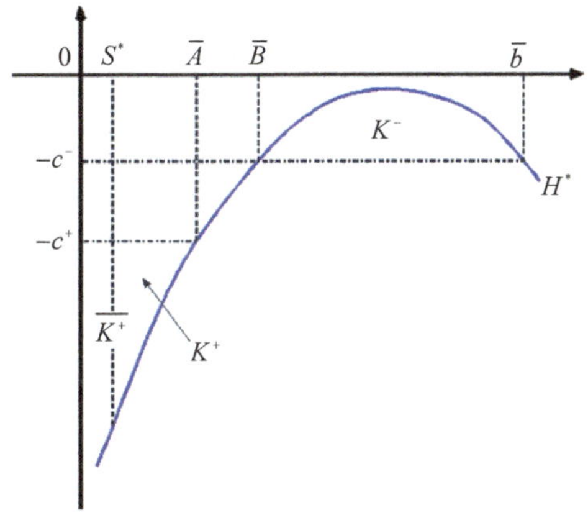

Figure 3. Determining the parameters for the value function $V(x)$ by utilizing the solution of the auxiliary problem $H^*(x)$ when $K^+ \le \overline{K^+}$.

By virtue of Proposition 3.1, the function V satisfies (3.18) on $(0,x_0]$, as well as (3.23) on $[x_0,b)$. In addition, from (3.48), we can see that

$$V(0)-V(A)\equiv -\int_{S^*}^{\bar{A}} H^*(y)\mathrm{d}y = c^+A+K^+. \quad (3.55)$$

From the construction of the function v, we can also see that

$$\begin{aligned} V(b)-V(B) &\equiv v(\bar{b})-v(\bar{B}) \\ &= -c^-(b-B)+K^-. \end{aligned} \quad (3.56)$$

We also have $V'(A)=v'(\bar{A})=H^*(\bar{A})=-c^+$ and similarly $V'(B)=-c^-$, so $V(x)$ satisfies all the conditions (3.28)-(3.31).

Theorem 3.1. The function V given by (3.56) is a solution to the QVI (2.12)-(2.14).

The proof of this theorem is divided into several propositions.

Proposition 3.2. The function V satisfies (3.16) on $[0,b)$.

Proof. 1) From the construction of the function v, we have $-\frac{\mu v'}{\sigma^2 v''}\le 1$ on $(0,\tilde{x}_0]$. Consequently,

$$-\frac{\mu V'}{\sigma^2 V''}<1 \quad (3.57)$$

on $(0,x_0]$. As V satisfies (3.18), it also satisfies (3.16) because these two equations are equivalent whenever (3.16) holds.

2) To prove that (3.16) holds for $x\ge x_0$, it is sufficient to show that for each $0\le u\le 1$,

$$\mathcal{L}^u V - rV \equiv \frac{1}{2}\sigma^2u^2V_2'' + \mu u V_2' - rV_2 = 0 \ge 0 \quad (3.58)$$

because, in view of Proposition 3.1, the function V satisfies (3.23) (that is, $\mathcal{L}^1 V - rV = 0$). By subtracting (3.58) from the left hand side of (3.23), we can see that (3.58) is equivalent to

$$\frac{1}{2}\sigma^2\left(1-u^2\right)V_2''(x)+\mu(1-u)V_2'(x)\le 0 \quad (3.59)$$

for $x\in[x_0,b)$. In view of the continuity of the first and second derivatives, and in view of the fact that (3.16) holds on $(0,x_0]$, we know that (3.59) is true for $x=x_0$. As both $V'<0$ and $V''<0$ on the left-hand side of (3.59) are decreasing, therefore is nonpositive for all $x\ge x_0$. □

Note that $\mathcal{M}\phi(x)=\min\left(\mathcal{M}_1\phi(x),\mathcal{M}_2\phi(x)\right)$, where

$$\mathcal{M}_1\phi(x)=\inf_{\xi>0}\left[K^+ + c^+\xi+\phi(x+\xi)\right];$$

$$\mathcal{M}_2\phi(x)=\inf_{\xi>0}\left[K^- + c^-\xi+\phi(x-\xi)\right].$$

Proposition 3.3. For each $x\ge 0$, we have

$$\mathcal{M}V(x)\ge V(x). \quad (3.60)$$

If $x=0$, or if $x\ge b$, then

$$\mathcal{M}V(x)=V(x). \quad (3.61)$$

Proof. 1) We first prove, that $\mathcal{M}_1V(x)\ge V(x)$. Supposethat $x<A$. The function $V(x+\xi)+c^+\xi$ is continuously differentiable. By construction,
$V'(x)=H^*(x+S^*)$ is increasing on $(0,x^*)$ and decreasing on $[x^*,\infty)$ with $V'(x)\equiv -c^-$ for $x\ge b$. Therefore, the point A is the only point y such that $V'(y)\equiv H^*(A)=-c^+$. Because $(H^*)'(A)<0$, we can see that $A=\arg\min_x V(x+\xi)+c^+\xi$. Therefore, for $x\le A$,

$$\mathcal{M}_1V(x)=V(A)+c^+(A-x)+K^+.$$

Also,

$$\mathcal{M}_1V(x)-V(x)=V(A)-V(x)+c^+(A-x)+K^+\ge 0$$

if

$$\begin{aligned} &-c^+(A-x)-V(A)-V(x) \\ &\equiv \int_x^A\left[-c^+-V(y)\right]\mathrm{d}y\le K^+. \end{aligned}$$

However,

$$\begin{aligned} \int_x^A\left[-c^+-V(y)\right]\mathrm{d}y &\le \int_0^A\left[-c^+-V'(y)\right]\mathrm{d}y \\ &\equiv \int_{S^*}^{\bar{A}}\left[-c^+-H^*(z)\right]\mathrm{d}z = K^+. \end{aligned}$$

This proves that $M_1V(x)\ge V(x)$ for all $x\le A$ and also shows that

$$\mathcal{M}_1V(0)=V(0). \quad (3.62)$$

Because $V'(y)>-c^+$ for $y>A$, we know that for any $x>A$ the function $V(x+\xi)+c^+\xi$ is an increasing function of $\xi>0$. Therefore, the minimum in the expression for $\mathcal{M}_1$ is attained for $\xi = 0$; as a result, $\mathcal{M}_1(x) = V(x) + K^+ > V(x)$.

2) Consider $V(x-\xi) - c^-\xi$ for $b > x \ge B$. Because $V'(y) > -c^-$ for $y > B$ and $V'(y) < c^-$ for $y < B$, we can see that $V(x-\xi) - c^-\xi$ has a unique minimum at $x - \xi = B$. Therefore, $\mathcal{M}_2 V(x) = V(B) - c^-(x-B) + K^-$. Thus, $\mathcal{M}_2 V(x) - V(x) \ge 0$ if

$$V(x) - V(B) + c^-(x-B) \equiv \int_B^x \left[V'(y) + c^-\right] \mathrm{d}y \le K^-.$$

The foregoing inequality always holds true because, by construction,

$$K^- = \int_{\bar{B}}^{\bar{b}} \left[H^*(y) + c^-\right] \mathrm{d}y \equiv \int_B^b V'(y) + c^- \mathrm{d}y.$$

For $x \ge b$, we note, that $V(x) - V(b) = -c^-(x-b)$, and hence

$$\begin{aligned} \mathcal{M}_2 V(x) - V(x) &= \mathcal{M}_2 V(b) - V(b) \\ &= V(B) - V(b) - c^-(b-B) + K^- = 0. \end{aligned} \quad (3.63)$$

To complete the proof of Theorem 3.1, we need only show the following.

Proposition 3.4. If $x > b$, then (2.12) holds.

Proof. It is sufficient to show that for any $0 \le u \le 1$ and any $x > b$,

$$\begin{aligned} f(x) \equiv \frac{1}{2} u^2 \sigma^2 \frac{\mathrm{d}^2 V(x)(x)}{\mathrm{d}x^2} \\ + u\mu \frac{\mathrm{d}V(x)(x)}{\mathrm{d}x} - rV(x) \ge 0. \end{aligned} \quad (3.64)$$

From Proposition 3.2 we know that (3.64) is true for $x = b-$. As $V''(b-) < 0$, we obtain

$$(\mathcal{L}^u V)(b+) - rV(b+) = u\mu c^- - rV(b) \ge 0.$$

For any $x > b$, we have

$$(\mathcal{L}^u V)(x) - rV(x) = u\mu c^- - rV(x) > c^- - V(b)$$

because V is a decreasing function. □

This completes the proof of Theorem 3.1.

3.2.2. The Case of $K^+ > \overline{K^+}$

When $K^+ > K^+$ we cannot find any S^* such that (3.48) is satisfied. In this case, we set $V(x) = v(x)$ (that is, we have $S^* = 0$, which corresponds to $A = 0$).

Theorem 3.2. If $K^+ > K^+$, then $V(x) = v(x)$ is a solution to the QVI (2.12)-(2.14).

To prove this theorem, it is sufficient to prove Propositions 3.2-3.4. The proofs of Propositions 3.2 and 3.4 are identical to the case of $K^+ \le K^+$, whereas that of Proposition 3.3 requires a slight modification.

Proposition 3.5. For each $x \ge 0$,

$$\mathcal{M}V(x) \ge V(x). \quad (3.65)$$

If $x \ge b$, then

$$\mathcal{M}V(x) = V(x). \quad (3.66)$$

Proof. The proof that $\mathcal{M}_2 V(x) \ge V(x)$ for all x and that $\mathcal{M}_2 V(x) = V(x)$ for $x \ge b$ is the same as that in Proposition 3.3.

If $x \le A$, then $\mathcal{M}_1 V(x) \ge V(x)$ is equivalent to

$$-c^+(A-x) - V(A) - V(x) \equiv \int_x^A \left[-c^+ - V(y)\right] \mathrm{d}y \le K^+.$$

The foregoing inequality is always true because

$$\int_x^A \left[-c^+ - V(y)\right] \mathrm{d}y \le \int_0^A \left[-c^+ - V(y)\right] \mathrm{d}y = \overline{K^+} < K^+$$

by assumption.

If $x > A$, then $\mathcal{M}_1 V(x) \ge V(x)$ still holds, due to the same argument as that in Proposition 3.3. □

Remark 3.1. In the case of $K^+ > K^+$ we have $\mathcal{M}V(x) = V(x)$ only for $x \ge b$, whereas $\mathcal{M}V(0) > V(0)$ in contrast to the case when $K^+ \le \overline{K^+}$. Also, when $K^+ > \underline{K^+}$, we have $V(0) = 0$, whereas $V(0) < 0$ if $K^+ \le K^+$. Equivalently, in the case that the fixed cost to call for additional funds is relatively large (*i.e.*, $K^+ > K^+$), the optimal band control is reduced to $(0, 0; B, b)$ with $a = A = 0$. That is, as soon as the reserve reaches zero, it becomes optimal for the mutual insurance firm to go bankrupt, rather than to be restarted by calling for additional funds.

4. Verification Theorem and the Optimal Control

Theorem 4.1. If V is a solution to QVI (2.12)-(2.14), then for any control U,

$$V(x) \le C(x, U). \quad (4.67)$$

Proof. We prove this inequality when $K^+ \le \overline{K^+}$. In this case, $V'(0) = v'(S^*) > -\infty$. Let U be any admissible control defined by (2.2) and process $X(t)$ be the corresponding surplus process (2.3), with $X(0) = x$. Let τ be its ruin time given by (2.4). Let $\tau(t) = \tau \wedge t$ and $\tau_i(t) = \tau_i \wedge \tau \wedge t$. Then,

$$\begin{aligned} &\mathrm{e}^{-r\tau(t)} V(X(\tau(t))) - V(x) \\ &= \sum_{i=1}^{\infty} \left[\mathrm{e}^{-r\tau_i(t)} V(X(\tau_i(t)-)) - \mathrm{e}^{-r\tau_{i-1}}(t) V(X(\tau_{i-1}(t)))\right] \\ &+ \sum_{i=1}^{\infty} \mathrm{e}^{-r\tau_i(t)} \left[V(X((\tau_i(t)))) - V(X(\tau_i(t)-))\right]. \end{aligned} \quad (4.68)$$

By convention, $\tau_0 = 0$. In view of (2.13), we have

$$\begin{aligned} &|V(x) - V(y)| \\ &\le \left(c^+|y-x| + K^+\right) 1_{y<x} + \left(K^- - c^-|y-x|\right) 1_{y>x}. \end{aligned}$$

Therefore,

$$\left|V\left(X\left(\tau_i(t)\right)\right)-V\left(X\left(\tau_i(t)-\right)\right)\right|$$
$$\leq\left(c^+\xi_i^+ + K^+\right)1_{\xi_i>0}+\left(K^- - c^-\xi_i^-\right)1I_{\xi<0}$$

and

$$\begin{aligned}&\left|\sum_{i=1}^{\infty}\mathrm{e}^{-r\tau_i(t)}\left[V\left(X\left(\tau_i(t)\right)\right)-V\left(X\left(\tau_i(t)-\right)\right)\right]\right|\\&\leq\sum_{i=1}^{\infty}\mathrm{e}^{-r\tau_i(t)}\left|V\left(X\left(\tau_i(t)\right)\right)-V\left(X\left(\tau_i(t)-\right)\right)\right|\\&\leq\sum_{i=1}^{\infty}\mathrm{e}^{-r\tau_i(t)}\left[\left(c^+\xi_i^+ + K^+\right)1_{\xi_i>0}+\left(K^- - c^-\xi_i^-\right)1_{\xi_i<0}\right]\\&\leq\sum_{\tau_i\leq\tau}\mathrm{e}^{-r\tau_i}\left[\left(c^+\xi_i^+ + K^+\right)1_{\xi_i>0}+\left(K^- - c^-\xi_i^-\right)1_{\xi_i<0}\right]\end{aligned}\tag{4.69}$$

In view of (2.6), this implies that for any t the second sum in (4.68) is bounded by the same integrable random variable independent of t.

On $[\tau_{i-1},\tau_i]$, process $X(t)$ is continuous, and we can apply Ito's formula to get

$$\begin{aligned}&\mathrm{e}^{-r\tau_i(t)}V\left(X\left(\tau_i(t)-\right)\right)-\mathrm{e}^{-r\tau_{i-1}}(t)V\left(X\left(\tau_{i-1}(t)\right)\right)\\&=\int_{\tau_{i-1}(t)}^{\tau_i(t)}\mathrm{e}^{-rs}\left[\mathcal{L}^{u(s)}V\left(X(s)\right)-rV\left(X(s)\right)\right]\mathrm{d}s\\&+\int_{\tau_{i-1}(t)}^{\tau_i(t)}\mathrm{e}^{-rs}V'\left(X(s)\right)u(s)\sigma\mathrm{d}W(s).\end{aligned}\tag{4.70}$$

From this equation, using (2.6) and standard but rather tedious arguments, we can deduce that the first sum in (4.69) for all t is also bounded by the same integrable random variable. Similar arguments show that

$$\lim_{t\to\infty}E\left[\mathrm{e}^{-r\tau(t)}V\left(X\left(\tau(t)\right)\right)1_{\tau=\infty}\right]=0\tag{4.71}$$

and

$$\lim_{t\to\infty}E\left[\mathrm{e}^{-r\tau(t)}V\left(X\left(\tau(t)\right)\right)\right]=E\left[\mathrm{e}^{-r\tau}V\left(X(\tau)\right)1_{\tau<\infty}\right].\tag{4.72}$$

(see Cadenillas *et al.* [7]). Note that the second integral on the right-hand side of (4.70) is a martingale whose expectation vanishes. However, in view of (2.12), the integrand in the first integral of (4.70) is nonnegative. Therefore,

$$E\left[\mathrm{e}^{-r\tau_i(t)}V\left(X\left(\tau_i(t)-\right)\right)-\mathrm{e}^{-r\tau_{i-1}}(t)V\left(X\left(\tau_{i-1}(t)\right)\right)\right]\geq 0,\tag{4.73}$$

and, taking into account the dominated convergence theorem, we can see that the expectation of the first sum on the right-hand side of (4.68) is nonnegative.

From (2.13), we can see that

$$\begin{aligned}&V\left(X(\tau_i)\right)-V\left(X(\tau_i-)\right)\\&\equiv V\left(X(\tau_i-)+\xi_i\right)-V\left(X(\tau_i-)\right)\\&\geq-\left[\left(K^+ + c^+\xi_i\right)1_{\xi_i>0}+\left(K^- - c^-\xi_i\right)1_{\xi_i<0}\right].\end{aligned}$$

Substituting this inequality into (4.2) and taking expectations of both sides, we obtain

$$\begin{aligned}&E\left[\mathrm{e}^{-r\tau(t)}V\left(X\left(\tau(t)\right)\right)\right]-V(x)\\&\geq-E\sum_{\tau_i\leq\tau,\tau_i\leq t}\mathrm{e}^{-r\tau_i}\left[\left(K^+ + c^+\xi_i^+\right)1_{\xi_i>0}+\left(K^- - c^-\xi_i^-\right)1_{\xi_i<0}\right]\end{aligned}\tag{4.74}$$

Letting $t\to\infty$, and employing (4.72) and the monotone convergence theorem on, we get

$$\begin{aligned}&E\left[\mathrm{e}^{-r\tau}V\left(X(\tau)\right)1_{\tau<\infty}\right]-V(x)\\&\geq-E\sum_{\tau_i\leq\tau}\mathrm{e}^{-r\tau_i}\left[\left(K^+ + c^+\xi_i^+\right)1_{\xi_i>0}+\left(K^- - c^-\xi_i^-\right)1\backslash_{\xi_i<0}\right]\\&=-C(x,U)\end{aligned}\tag{4.75}$$

As $V\left(X(\tau)\right)\leq 0$, on $\{\tau<\infty\}$, the inequality (4.75) implies (4.67).

Remark 4.1. For the expectation of the stochastic integral on the right hand side of (4.70) to vanish, it is sufficient for its integrand to be bounded. In particular, it is sufficient for V' to be bounded. This is the case when $K^+ < K^+$. When $K^+\geq K^+$, the function V' has a singularity at 0. We can, however, apply the same technique, first replacing τ by $\tau^\epsilon=\inf\{t:X(t)<\epsilon\}$ and then passing to a limit as $\epsilon\to 0$. This will yield inequality (4.74), which is all we need for the proof of Theorem 4.1

Let $\mathcal{H}^*(x)=\arg\min_u\{\mathcal{L}^uV(x)-rV(x)\}$, that is

$$\mathcal{L}^{\mathcal{H}^*(x)}V(x)-rV(x)=0\tag{4.76}$$

From (3.46), (3.45), (3.49), and (3.53), we can see that

$$\mathcal{H}^*(x)=\min\left\{x/\left(x_0+S^*\right),1\right\}.$$

Consider the process defined as

$$\begin{aligned}X^*(t)&=X\left(\tau_{\tau_i}\right)+\int_{\tau_i}^t\mu\mathcal{H}^*\left(X^*(s)\right)\mathrm{d}s\\&+\int_{\tau_i}^t\sigma\mathcal{H}^*\left(X^*(s)\right)\mathrm{d}W_s\end{aligned}\tag{4.77}$$

$i=0,1,\cdots$, with $\tau_0\equiv 0$, $X(\tau_0)\equiv X(0)=x$, and τ_i and $X(\tau_i)$ are defined below sequentially.

If $K^+ < K^+$ (that is, no S^* exists, such that (3.48) holds), then

$$X^*(\tau_i)=B,\ \xi_i=b-B,\tag{4.78}$$

where

$$\tau_i=\inf\left\{t:X^*(t)\geq b\right\}.\tag{4.79}$$

If $\overline{K^+}\geq K^*$ (that is, there exists an S^*, such that (3.48) holds), then

$$X^*(\tau_i)=\begin{cases}B, & \xi_i=b-B\quad X^*(\tau_i-)=b\\ A, & \xi_i=A\quad X^*(\tau_i-)=0.\end{cases}\tag{4.80}$$

where

$$\tau_i = \inf\{t : X^*(t) \notin [0,b]\} \quad (4.81)$$

Remark 4.2. Informally, if $\overline{K^+} < K^+$, then process $X^*(s)$ is a continuous diffusion process with a drift and diffusion coefficient of, $\mu\mathcal{H}^*(X^*(s))$ and $\sigma\mathcal{H}^*(X^*(s))$, respectively, until the times of intervenetion. The times of intervention in this case are the times at which this diffusion process hits the level b, which are associated with the refunds of the constant amount of $b-B$. The time when 0 is hit is the ruin time.

When $K^+ \geq K^+$, the process $X^*(s)$ is a continuous diffusion process with the same drift and diffusion coefficients as above, between the times of intervention. The intervention times are the times at which this process reaches either 0 or b. At point 0, the control is set to displace the process to point A, which corresponds to raising cash (making a call to shareholders) in the amount of A. Reaching the level b results in the displacement of the process to the point B which, corresponds to making a refund in the amount of $b-B$.

Theorem 4.2. (The verification theorem) Let U^* be the control described by (4.76) and (4.79)-(4.80). Then,

$$C(x,U^*) = V(x) = \inf_{U\in\mathcal{U}} C(x,U)$$

Proof. In view of (4.67), it is sufficient to show that

$$C(x,U^*) = V(x). \quad (4.82)$$

Equality (4.76) shows that

$$\mathcal{L}^{\mathcal{H}^*(X^*(s))}V(X^*(s)) - rV(X^*(s)) = 0. \quad (4.83)$$

From Propositions 3.3 and 3.5, we know that $V(b)-V(B) = K^- - c^-(b-B)$ and if $K^+ \geq K^+$ then $V(0)-V(A) = K^+ + c^+A$. Thus, we can repeat the arguments in the proof of Theorem 3.2 and see that, for $U = U^*$, all of the inequalities are tight. As a result, we obtain

$$\begin{aligned} &E\left[e^{-r\tau}V(X(\tau))1_{\tau<\infty}\right] - V(x) \\ &= -E\sum_{\tau_i\leq\tau} e^{-r\tau_i}\left[(K^+ + c^+\xi^+)1_{\xi_i>0} + (K^- - c^-\xi^-)1_{\xi_i<0}\right] \\ &= C(x,U^*). \end{aligned} \quad (4.84)$$

Because we know that, when $\overline{K^+} \geq K^+$, we have $1_{\tau<\infty} = 0$ and, when $K^+ < K^+$, the function V satisfies $V(0) \equiv v(0) = 0$, the first term on the left-hand side of (4.84) vanishes, and we get (4.82). □

5. Conclusions

The optimal policy in this model has several interesting nontrivial features. The fact that calls should be made only when there is no possibility of waiting any longer (that is when the reserve reaches zero) is supported by intuition. However, the qualitative structure of the optimal policy and its dependence on the model parameters are not as obvious.

It turns out that it is always optimal to pay dividends, no matter what the costs associated with such payments are. However, raising cash may not be optimal when the initial set-up cost is too high. Quantity K^+, which determines the threshold for set-up cost K^+, such that if the cost is higher than this threshold then it is optimal to allow ruin, is in itself determined via an auxiliary problem with a one-sided impulse control. Although there is no closed-form expression for the quantity $\overline{K^+}$, it can be determined in an algorithmic manner prior to solving the optimal control problem for the mutual insurance company.

There is one rather curious feature of the optimal solution when $K^+ = K^+$. As our analysis shows, in this case, $S^* = 0$ and $V = v$, the same as is the case when $K^+ > K^+$. However, from the construction of the optimal policy, we can see that the two band-type policy is optimal in this case as well. In this borderline case, we thus have two optimal policies, one for which $\tau = \infty$ with the lower band equal to $(0, A)$ and one for which reaching 0 corresponds to ruin and for which $\tau < \infty$. This is a rather unique feature of this particular problem that has not been observed previously.

A natural question arises: what if ruin is explicitly disallowed, and we must find an optimal policy from among those for which $\tau = \infty$. As can be seen from our analysis, we find a solution to this problem for the case of $\overline{K^+} \geq K^+$. However, when this inequality does not hold, then of the stochastic control technique and the HJB equation used in this paper do not work. Another approach should be developed, as can be seen indirectly in the work of Eisenberg [18] and Eisenberg and Schmidli [5], where a similar (although not identical) problem is considered for the case of a surplus process modeled via the classical Cramer-Lundberg model. This constitutes an interesting and challenging problem for future study, the nature of whose solution is not obvious at this time.

REFERENCES

[1] G. M. Constantinides, and S. F. Richard, "Existence of Optimal Simple Policies for Discounted-cost Inventory and Cash Management in Continuous Time," *Operations Research*, Vol. 26, No. 4, 1978, pp. 620-636.

[2] A. Bensoussan, R. H. Liu and S. P. Sethi, "Optimality of an (s, S) Policy with Compound Poisson and Diffusion Demands: AQuasi-variationalInequalities Approach,"

SIAM Journal on Control and Optimization. Vol. 44, No. 5, 2006, pp. 1650-1676.

[3] A. Cadenillas and F. Zapatero, "Classical and Impulse Stochastic Control of the Exchange Rate Using Interest Rate and Reserves," *Mathematical Finance*, Vol. 10, No. 2, 2000, pp. 141-156.

[4] B. M. Hojgaard and M. Taksar, "Optimal Dynamic Portfolio Selection for a Corporation with Controllable Risk and Dividend Distribution Policy," *Quantitative Finance*, Vol. 4, No. 3, 2004, pp. 256-265.

[5] J. Eisenberg and H. Schmidli,"Minimizing Expected Discounted Capital Injections by Reinsurance in a Classical Risk Model," *Scandinavian Actuarial Journal*, No. 3, 2011,pp. 155-176.

[6] A. Sulem, "A Solvable One-dimensional Model of A Diffusion Inventory System," *Mathematics of Operations Research*, Vol. 11, No. 1, 1986, pp. 125-133.

[7] J. Yuan, J, "Computational Optimization of Mutual Insurance Systems: A Quasi-variational Inequality Approach," Ph.D. Thesis, The Hong Kong Polytechnic University, 2008.

[8] M. Dawande, M. Mehrotra, V. Mookerjee and C. Srikandarajah, "An Analysis of Coordination Mechanism for the U.S. Cash Supply Chain," *Management Science*, Vol. 56, No. 3, 2010, pp. 553-570.

[9] A. Løkka and A. M. Zervos, "Optimal Dividend and Issuance of Equity Policies in the Presence of Proportional Costs," *Insurance*: *Mathematics and Economics*, Vol. 42, No. 3, 2008, pp. 954-961.

[10] A. Bensoussan and J. L. Menaldi, "Stochastic Hybrid-Control," *Journal of Mathematical Analysis and Applications*, Vol. 249, No. 1, 2000, pp. 261-288.

[11] M. S. Branicky, V. S. Borkar and S. K. Mitter, "A Unified Framework for Hybrid Control: Model and Optimal Control Theory," *IEEE Transactions on Automatic Control*, Vol. 43, No. 1, 1998, pp. 31-45.

[12] A. Abate, A. D. Ames and S. Sastry, "Stochastic Approximations for Hybrid Systems," *Proceedings of the 24th American Control Conference*, Portland, 2005, pp. 1557-1562.

[13] G. M. Constantinides, "Stochastic Cash Management with Fixed and Proportional Transaction Costs," *Management Science*, Vol. 22, No. 12, 1976, pp. 1320-1331.

[14] A. Cadenillas, T. Choulli, M. Taksar and L. Zhang, "Classical and Impulse Stochastic Control for the Optimization of the Dividend and Risk Policies of an Insurance Firm," *Mathematical Finance*, Vol. 16, No. 1, 2006, pp. 181-202.

[15] A. Cadenillas and F. Zapatero, "Optimal Central Bank Intervention in the Foreign Exchange Market," *Journal of Economic Theory*, Vol. 87, No. 1, 1999, pp. 218-242.

[16] J. M. Harrison, T. M. Sellke and A. J. Taylor, "Impulse control of Brownian Motion," *Mathematics of Operations Research*, Vol. 8, No. 3,1983, pp. 454-466.

[17] J. Paulsen, "Optimal Dividend Payments and Reinvestments of Diffusion Processes with Both Fixed and Proportional Costs," *SIAM Journal on Control and Optimization*, Vol. 47, No. 5, 2008, pp. 2201-2226.

[18] J. Eisenberg, "Optimal Control of Capital Injections by Reinsurance and Investments," *Blätter der DGVFM*, Vol. 31, No. 2, 2010, pp. 329-345.

Intra-Business Group Transactions for Inducing Relationships between Network and Performance: Can the Network Be Optimized?

Hsien-Chang Kuo[1], Lie-Huey Wang[2]
[1]Department of Accounting, and Department of Finance, Shih Chien University, Taipei, Taiwan
[2]Department of Finance, Ming Chuan University, Taipei, Taiwan

ABSTRACT

This paper analyzes the relation between network linkage and firm performance through the intra-business group related-party transactions, and also explores whether the network linkage could be optimized. It is listed on the Taiwan Stock Exchange over 2006-2008 by using financial information for business groups. For whole samples, we find a U-shaped relation between ROA and related-party purchases network linkage, and there is an inverted-U-shaped association between related-party receivable-payable network linkages and debt ratio. We also find the sales expenses ratio is positively correlated with the number of related-party buyers, but negatively correlated with the related-party sales ratio. Moreover, for high related-party sales and high related-party purchases group, it demonstrates an inverted-U-shaped association between related-party sales and ROA, and the related-party receivable-payable gap ratio is negatively correlated with debt ratio. While for low related-party sales and low related-party purchases group, related-party purchases network linkage and ROA display a U-shaped characteristic, and there is a U-shaped association between total receivable-payable gap ratio and debt ratio.

Keywords: Intra-Business Group; Network Linkage; Return on Assets; Related-Party Transactions

1. Introduction

As the economic environment changes with time, firms can no longer rely on their own resources to compete in the market. Thus, firms are gradually turning away from the self-production models in the past, toward cooperation among supply chain firms, resulting in close interactions between the firms. Moreover, for the purpose of diversification and resource sharing, a firm usually has multiple and diverse cooperating firms.

Since Johanson and Mattsson [1] proposed the concept of network linkage, to explain the foundation of cooperation between firms. This issue has already been widely discussed. From the perspective of exchange, the main motivation for the linkage between dissimilar organizations is to acquire external resources (Echols and Tsai [2]; McEvily and Marcus [3]), such as market channels (Chen and Chen, [4]), technology and R&D (Burgers *et al.* [5]; Pittaway *et al.* [6]), different knowledge pools (Burt [7]), pooling of cooperation (Uzzi [8]), third-party endorsements (Stuart *et al.* [9]), and innovation (Pittaway *et al.* [6]; Zaheer and Bell [10]). From the perspective of homophily, the main purpose of the linkage between similar organizations is to pursue joint goals through cooperation (Wholey and Huonket [11]). In addition, based on social network theory, network relationship is an important social capital for a firm to create value (Tsai [12]).

Extensive studies on the firm performance have already been made. Dyer [13] and Rowley *et al.* [14] posed that closer links and sound cooperation can enhance the competitive advantage of firms. Kim [15] found the direct and indirect effects of supply chain integration increase firm performance. Zeng *et al.* [16] found access to customers and suppliers on the upstream and downstream network connection can improve the innovation of SMEs. Dyer and Hatch [17] stated buyers gain knowledge assets through a supplier network. Gulati *et al.* [18] and Rowley *et al.* [14] argued the firm performance is significantly influenced by inter-firm ties and strategic networks. Goerzen and Beamish [19] found a more dispersed multinational enterprise alliance network that decreases firm performance. However, Goerzen [20] found if a firm continues to maintain an equity-based cooperative partnership will help improve firm performance. In addition, access to resources and improvements in operating capability gained through alliance networks are considered unique and irreplaceable assets (Gulati [21]). Therefore, network linkage is the foundation for a firm to gain strategic advantages (Gulati *et al.* [18]; Hagedoorn and Duysters [22]; Koka and Prescott [23]), and development and investment in the relationships between network partners will significantly influence a firm's performance and value (Blankenburg *et al.* [24]; Gulati *et al.* [18]; Tsai [25]; Kuo [26]; Kim [15]; Zeng *et al.* [16]). Exploring the network linkage of a firm not only allows further analysis of performance and an optimal network, but also leads to the extension of firm value related studies. Previous literatures discussed network relationships from different aspects, such as human relations network, knowledge network, alliance network, business network, and social network (Johanson and Mattsson [1]; Uzzi [27]). In this paper, we test the network linkage through related-party sales and purchases transactions for business group.

Under the trend of liberalization and internationalization, firms are facing harsher competition pressure; to expand production scale, diversify risk, expand the market, and increase economic efficiency and competitive advantages, they strengthen the linkage between firms through mergers, investments and cross holdings, to form affiliated enterprises or large business groups; and, through the cooperative relationship between related-parties, they can gain beneficial resources and decrease transaction costs, thereby increasing the firm's asset allocation efficiency and this, in turn, maximize the firms' profit and value (Yeh *et al.* [28]; Gordon *et al.* [29]; Cheung *et al.* [30]). For many developed countries and emerging market countries, business groups are major enterprises influencing the national economy (Hoshi *et al.* [31]; Chung [32]), and they have different characteristics. For example, American syndicates are monopolistic institutions formed by a small number of large companies in the same production sector for vast profits, whose integration is mainly dominated by horizontal merger. Japanese keiretsu groups are often formed by a group of companies horizontally or vertically (Lincoln *et al.* [33]). The horizontal keiretsus are formed by merger of banking Industry, e.g. Sumitomo Mistsui financial group, Mitsubishi UFJ financial group, and Mizuho financial group. The vertical keiretsus follow the supply chain to vertically integrate upstream and downstream firms, e.g. Toyota group, Nissan group, Honda group, Matsushita group, Hitachi group, Toshiba group, SONY group, and Nikon group. The Korean Chaebol groups are formed by the vertical integration of a family group (Kim [34]). In Taiwan, most of the business groups are formed by the growth, division, and evolution of family business (Hmailton and Kao [35]; Chung [32]), and therefore can be seen as derivatives of a family relatives or interpersonal network (Wong [36]). In addition, the ownership is highly concentrated on family members and the board of directors is also mainly controlled by the family shareholders (Yeh *et al.* [37]; Lin and Hu [38]).

Since business groups are integrated by a group of legally independent entities that formed network relationships by embedding equities in subsidiaries, a business group can be called the collective body of a network. The characteristic of "kinship" in Taiwanese family groups highlights the traits of a network relationship. Due to Taiwanese business groups generally have supply chain cooperation between group members through related-party sales and purchases to gain the resources, and through exchange of payables and receivables in the groups to get the funds. In this paper, we use the numbers of related-party buyer and supplier, the ratios of related-party sales and purchase, and the gap between accounts of payable and receivable as indicators of network linkage in the groups. And then, we analyze the relation between network linkage and firm performance through the intra-business group related-party transactions, and also explore whether the network linkage could be optimized. In addition, we also use the sales expenses ratio to measure the running costs generated from establishing a network linkage relationship, and to capture its negative effects on network linkage.

The organization of the reminder of this paper is as follows. Section 2 describes the data and our empirical models. Section 3 reports and discusses the outcomes of empirical analysis. Section 4 offers the conclusions.

2. Methodology

2.1. Data

Definitions of business groups are many and varied (Chung [32]; Khanna and Rivkin [39]). In our empirical analysis we employ the definition of Taiwan Economic Journal (TEJ) to define a business group as composed of companies having the same ultimate shareholder and fulfilling the following criteria: 1) most of the primary shareholders come from the same family (primary shareholder refers to the top ten largest shareholders or shareholders with more than 5% of shares); 2) at least one third of the board of directors are the same; 3) the identical primary management (*i.e.* with the same director or CEO); 4) existing a controlling or subordinate relationship (*i.e.* with actual controlling power); 5) existing a mutual investment relationship.

We collected data for listed business groups over 2006-2008 from TEJ financial statement database, TEJ corporate governance database, Taiwan Stock Exchange Market Observation Post System (MOPS), and companies' annual reports. First, the 600 core companies of business groups are taken as main objects. Second, based on related-party data disclosed by MOPS and the core companies' annual reports, we check the names of related-party companies and related-party transactions one by one. This is the first level of related-party sales and purchases linkage. And then, according to the companies of the first level linkage, we continually repeat the same process to check the names of related-party companies and related-party transactions. This is the second level of related-party sales and purchases linkage. All the related supplier and buyer firms are placed in one group. The previous process will be repeated until a firm has already appeared in the linkage or the firm is another core company.

To analyze the influence of the related-party sales and purchases network linkage on firm performance, we divide the samples into four sub-groups based on the median of the three years average related-party sales (purchases) for the whole samples, *i.e.* high related-party sales and high related-party purchases (abbreviated HH), high related-party sales and low related-party purchases (HL), low related-party sales and high related-party purchases (LH), and low related-party sales and low related-party purchases (LL). A firm has the sales (purchases) over 100 million NT dollars or greater than 20% paid-in capital with related-party buyer (supplier) is to be related-party sales (purchases). In addition, we also divide the samples into information technology (IT) and non-IT firms[1], large and small firms based on the median of total assets for the whole samples, family and non-family firms according to the criteria of a family shareholding ratio greater than 20% is considered to be a family firm (La Porta *et al.* [40]). We use the Pearson's Chi-square test to explore the association among related-party sales and purchases, industry, firm size, and family control. The results are given in **Table 1**.

As shown in **Table 1 Panel A**, approximately 61% ~

Table 1. Results of Pearson's Chi-square.

	High related-party sales & High related-party purchases (HH)	High related-party sales & Low related-party purchases (HL)	Low related-party sales & High related-party purchases (LH)	Low related-party sales & Low related-party purchases (LL)	Number of Firms (%)
		Panel A: Industry v.s. related-party transactions			
Information Technology	26firms (81.3%)	66 firms (61.7%)	28 firms (63.6%)	66 firms (50.0%)	186 firms (59.0%)
Non-IT	6 firms (18.8%)	41 firms (38.3%)	16 firms (36.4%)	66 firms (51.2%)	129 firms (41.0%)
		Pearson χ^2 35.046*** Cramer's V 0.193***			
		Panel B: Firm size v.s. related-party transactions			
Large size	16 firms (50.0%)	57 firms (53.3%)	17 firms (37.9%)	68 firms (51.35%)	158 firms (50.1%)
Small size	16 firms (50.0%)	50 firms (46.7%)	27 firms (62.1%)	64 firms (48.7%)	157 firms (49.1%)
		Pearson χ^2 9.383***** Cramer's V 0.100**			
		Panel C: Family firms v.s. related-party transactions			
Family	14firms (43.8%)	52 firms (48.6%)	26 firms (59.1%)	85 firms (64.4%)	177 firms (56.2%)
Non-Family	18 firms (56.3%)	55 firms (51.4%)	18 firms (40.9%)	47 firms (35.6%)	138 firms (43.8%)
		Pearson χ^2 24.829*** Cramer's V 0.162**			
Number of firms (observation)	32 firms (96)	107 firms (321)	44 firms (132)	132 firms (396)	315 firms (945)

Note: The tests of Pearson χ^2 and Cramer's V are used to examine the relation among related-party sales and purchases network linkage, industry; firm size; and family control. **Panel A** reports the results of test for relation between industry and related-party transactions; **Panel B** reports the results of test for relation between firm size and related-party transactions; **Panel C** reports the results of test for relation between family control and related-party transactions. We divide the samples into four sub-groups based on the median of the three years average related-party sales (or purchases) for the whole samples, *i.e.* high related-party sales and high related-party purchase firms (HH), high related-party sales and low related-party purchase firms (HL), low related-party sales and high related-party purchase firms (LH), and low related-party sales and low related-party purchases firms (LL). The samples also are categorized into information technology (IT) firms and non-IT firms, large and small firms based on the median of total assets for the whole samples, family and non-family firms according to the criteria of a family shareholding ratio greater than 20% is considered to be a family firm (proposed by La Porta *et al.* [40]). Statistical significance is denoted by ***, **, * for 1%, 5%, and 10% levels, respectively.

[1]The information technology (IT) industry includes semi-conductor, computer and peripherals, optical electronics, communication networks, components, electronics vendors, and information service firms. The non-IT industry includes cement, food, plastics, textile, machinery, chemistry, biotechnology and medicine, steel, rubber, automobile, construction and material, transportation, and retailer firms.

81% of the firms in three sub-groups (including HH, HL, and LH) are IT firms, which suggest that IT firms appear to utilize the network linkage of intra-business groups, and to obtain resources of technology, innovation, as well as market channels. **Table 1 Panel B** shows there are 53.3% of large firms in the HL group and 62.1% of small firms in the LH group, this indicates large firms appear to use the network linkage of related-party sales to integrate marketing resources and channels and this, in turn, obtains favorable income benefits from sales network linkage, while small firms prefer using the network linkage of related-party purchase to integrate production and R&D resources and this, in turn, obtains advantageous cost benefits from production network linkage. Further, **Table 1 Panel C** shows, approximately 51% ~ 56% of the firms in HH and HL groups are non-family firms, while about 59% ~ 64% of firms in LH and LL groups are family firms, indicating non-family firms prefer the network linkage of related-party sales, while family firms prefer the network linkage of related-party purchase. **Tables 1 Panel B** and **Panel C** show the network linkage of intra-group related-party sales and purchases are not unique to large firms or family firms. Finally, the results of Pearson χ^2 and Cramer's V indicate there is a significant association among related-party transaction network linkage, industry, firm size, and family control.

In summary, we find that information technology groups tend to maximize their profit by related-party sales-purchase linkage. Large groups gain favorable revenue effects through related-party sales network linkage; however, small groups obtain favorable cost effects through related-party purchase network linkage. Furthermore, non-family groups prefer related-party sales network linkage, but family groups favor related-party purchase network linkage.

2.2. Research Variables

In this study, the firm performance is measured by return on assets (ROA). Concerning the phenomena generally existing in Taiwanese business groups, of supply chain cooperation through related-party transactions and of funding by related-party accounts of receivable and payable, we use the number of related-party buyers and suppliers and the ratios of related-party sales and purchases to proxy the transaction network linkage of intra-business group, and measure the funding network linkage of intra-business group by calculating the ratio of the spread between related-party accounts and notes payable and related-party accounts and notes receivable to total revenue (named related-party receivable-payable gap ratio). Meanwhile, this study also uses the total receivable-payable gap ratio and net receivable-payable gap ratio to measure the whole financial network linkage and external receivable-payable network linkage of the business groups. The total receivable-payable gap ratio is the ratio of the spread between accounts and notes payable and accounts and notes receivable to total revenue. The net receivable-payable gap ratio is the total receivable-payable gap ratio minus the related-party receivable-payable gap ratio.

In addition, we also take the negative effect of operating cost derived from building network linkage into account, which is measured by the sales expenses ratio. Since a firm's performance is also influenced by other factors such as firm size and financial leverage (Fama and Frehnch [41]; Sharma [42]), we uses the number of group member firms (*i.e.* group size), total asset (*i.e.* total asset size), and total revenue (*i.e.* revenue size) as proxies for firm size, and also use the ratio of total debt to total assets (*i.e.* debt ratio) as a proxy for financial leverage (or capital structure). The definition of variables is presented in **Table 2**.

2.3. Empirical Model

In our empirical analysis, we use square term to capture a U-shaped (non-linear) relation, and estimate the panel data regression models. Equations (1) and (2) are the main models for our analysis of relation between transaction (or financial) network linkage and firm performance.

$$ROA_{it} = \alpha_i + \beta_1 Sale\_ratio_{it} + \beta_2 Sale\_ratio_{it}^2 + \beta_3 Purchase\_ratio_{it} + \beta_4 Purchase\_ratio_{it}^2 + \beta_5 SaleExp_{it} + \beta_6 LnTA_{it} + \beta_7 Debt_{it} + \varepsilon_{it} \quad (1)$$

$$ROA_{it} = \alpha_i + \beta_1 RGAP_{it} + \beta_2 RGAP_{it}^2 + \beta_3 NGAP_{it} + \beta_4 NGAP_{it}^2 + \beta_5 LnTA_{it} + \beta_6 Debt_{it} + \varepsilon_{it} \quad (2)$$

Since Kuo [26] found network linkage and financial leverage are negatively correlated, we further take into account the effect of the related-party receivable-payable financial network linkage on capital structure. The Equation (3a) is the empirical model for HH, HL, and LH groups. Due to LL group has a lower related-party transaction and financial network linkages, the Equation (3b) is the empirical model for LL group.

$$Debt_{it} = \alpha_i + \beta_1 RGAP_{it} + \beta_2 RGAP_{it}^2 + \beta_3 NGAP_{it} + \beta_4 NGAP_{it}^2 + \beta_5 LnTA_{it} + \varepsilon_{it} \quad (3a)$$

$$Debt_{it} = \alpha_i + \beta_1 TGAP_{it} + \beta_2 TGAP_{it}^2 + \beta_3 LnTA_{it} + \varepsilon_{it} \quad (3b)$$

Moreover, we also employ Equations (4a), (4b) and (5) to examine the relation between network linkage and related-party transactions.

$$Sale\_ratio_{it} = \alpha_i + \beta_1 Sale\_No_{it} + \beta_2 Sale\_No_{it}^2 + \beta_3 LnSale_{it} + \beta_4 GpSize_{it} + \beta_5 IND_{it} + \varepsilon_{it} \quad (4a)$$

Table 2. Variable definitions.

Variables (Abbreviation)	Definition
Return on assets (*ROA*)	Return on assets = [Net earnings after tax/average total assets] × 100%.
Number of related-party buyers (*Sale_No*)	Number of related-party buyer firms having transaction amounts of over one hundred million NT dollars or above 20% of paid-in capital with the related-party.
Number of related-party suppliers (*Supply_No*)	Number of related-party supplier firms having transaction amounts of over one hundred million NT dollars or above 20% of paid-in capital with the related-party.
Related-party sales ratio (*Sale_ratio*)	Related-party sales ratio = [related-party sales/total sales] × 100%; in which related-party sales is the sales of over one hundred million NT dollars or above 20% paid-in capital with the related-party buyer.
Related-party purchases ratio (*Purchase_ratio*)	Related-party purchase ratio = [related-party purchases/total purchases] × 100%; in which related-party purchases is purchase of over one hundred million NT dollars or above 20% paid-in capital with the related-party supplier.
Total receivable-payable gap ratio (*TGAP*)	Total receivable-payable gap ratio = [(total accounts and notes receivable − total accounts and notes payable)/total revenue] × 100%.
Related-party receivable-payable gap ratio (*RGAP*)	Related-party receivable-payable gap ratio = [(related-party accounts and notes receivable − related-party accounts and notes payable)/total revenue] × 100%.
Net receivable-payable gap ratio (*NGAP*)	Net receivable-payable gap ratio = [(total accounts and notes receivable − total accounts and notes payables) − (related-party accounts and notes receivable − related-party accounts and notes payable)/total revenue] × 100%.
Sales expenses ratio (*SaleExp*)	Sales expenses ratio = [sales expenses/total revenue] × 100%.
Group size (*GpSize*)	Number of group member firms.
Total asset size (*LnTA*)	Total asset size = natural logarithm of total assets.
Revenue size (*LnSale*)	Revenue size = natural logarithm of total revenues.
Debt ratio (*Debt*)	Debt ratio = [total debts/total assets] × 100%.
Industry (*IND*)	We use dummy variables to divide the samples into information technology (IT) firms and non-information technology (non-IT) firms. If it is an IT firm, IND = 1; if it is a non-IT firm, IND = 0.

$$Purchase\_ratio_{it} = \alpha_i + \beta_1 Supply\_No_{it} + \beta_2 Supply\_No_{it}^2 + \beta_3 LnSale_{it} + \beta_4 GpSize_{it} + \beta_5 IND_{it} + \varepsilon_{it} \quad (4b)$$

$$\begin{aligned} RGAP_{it} &= \alpha_i + \beta_1 Sale\_No_{it} + \beta_2 Sale\_No_{it}^2 \\ &+ \beta_3 Supply\_No_{it} + \beta_4 Supply\_No_{it}^2 + \beta_5 Sale\_ratio_{it} \\ &+ \beta_6 Sale\_ratio_{it}^2 + \beta_7 Purchase\_ratio_{it} \\ &+ \beta_8 Purchase\_ratio_{it}^2 + \beta_9 GpSize_{it} + \beta_{10} IND_{it} + \varepsilon_{it} \end{aligned} \quad (5)$$

Finally, we use Equation (6) to perform additional analysis on the relation between the related-party purchases network linkage and operating costs.

$$\begin{aligned} SaleExp_{it} &= \alpha_i + \beta_1 Sale\_No_{it} + \beta_2 Sale\_ratio_{it} \\ &+ \beta_3 LnSale_{it} + \beta_4 GpSize_{it} + \beta_5 IND_{it} + \varepsilon_{it} \end{aligned} \quad (6)$$

The variables in Equations (1)-(6) are defined earlier and given in **Table 2**.

3. Results

3.1. Data Analysis

In this sub-section, we examine the descriptive statistics of the variables mentioned earlier and the tests of four sub-groups are given in **Table 3**. **Table 3 Panel A** shows that for the number of related-party buyers and suppliers, on average, are about 2.68 and 1.74, and the standard deviation are 3.54 and 2.08, which means that the related-party buyers are more dispersed. For related-party sales and purchases ratios, on average, are 21.98% and 29.81%, and the standard deviation are 31.93% and 23.73%, indicating the related-party purchases has a higher variability. For receivable-payable gap ratio and net receivable-payable gap ratio, on average, are −0.36 and 4.91, indicating intra-group related-party receivable-payable is a negative gap, while the extra-group receivable-payable is a positive gap. This means business groups can obtain spontaneous financing through internal financial network linkage, while external financial network linkage might be a financial pressure of the firm's working capital. For sales expenses ratio, on average, is 4.79%, the maximum and minimum, from 0% to 83.26%, display high variability.

Table 3 Panel B shows HH group has the highest ROA (6.82%), while the HL group has the lowest ROA (1.50%), however, from **Table 3 Panel C**, the ANOVA-test of ROA does not differ significantly among four groups, and the t-test of ROA does not differ significant between HH and LL groups. As shown in **Table 3 Panel C**, the ROA, related-party sales ratio, and related-party purchases ratio of HH group are significantly greater than HL, LH, and HL groups, respectively. This means that HH group appear to use related-party sales and purchases to create positive income effects (*i.e.* increasing income) and positive cost effects (*i.e.* decreasing costs), thereby increasing the firm's ROA. Furthermore, both

Table 3. Descriptive statistics and variance analysis.

	ROA	*Sale_No*	*Supply_No*	*Sale_ratio*	*Purchase_ratio*	*RGAP*	*NGAP*	*SaleExp*	*Total assets (thousand)*	*GpSize*	*Debt*
					Panel A: Descriptive statistics						
Mean	5.22	2.68	1.74	21.98	29.81	−0.36	4.91	4.79	31,300,793	6.85	37.44
Maximum	53.1	29.00	17.00	100.00	100.00	191.70	39.27	83.26	648,633,988	36.00	86.86
Minimum	−47.38	0	0	0	0	−1761.02	−188.70	0	186,148	1	0.31
Standard Dev.	9.61	3.54	2.08	23.43	31.93	58.44	11.43	6.15	78,428,102	8.02	15.77
					Panel B: Mean of sub-groups						
HH	6.82	3.92	2.80	37.51	76.27	−0.56	5.57	4.46	55,802,076	10.22	33.09
HL	1.50	4.00	1.50	42.54	12.32	7.37	−0.36	4.44	29,092,877	7.13	37.33
LH	4.78	1.48	2.05	5.24	78.30	−20.36	12.33	5.13	23,488,205	5.70	37.70
LL	5.57	1.71	1.56	7.15	16.56	0.10	6.55	5.03	29,755,033	6.14	38.50
					Panel C: Variance analysis						
ANOVA-test	1.760	37.361***	11.998***	376.886***	775.842***	7.177***	51.083***	0.785	3.728**	7.730***	3.063**
t-test											
LL v.s. HH	−1.229	−5.389***	−5.295***	−15.913***	−28.865***	0.782	1.088	0.813	−2.301**	−4.125***	3.025***
LL v.s. LH	0.758	0.784	−2.957***	2.557**	−37.983***	1.534	−5.529***	−0.156	0.817	0.474	0.495
LL v.s. HL	1.518	−9.331***	0.361	−26.212***	3.298***	−9.175**	8.394***	1.586	0.120	−1.648	1.002
HH v.s. LH	1.495	4.615***	3.021***	16.013***	−0.906	1.264	−5.737***	−0.576	2.405**	3.930***	−2.107**
HH v.s. HL	1.967**	−0.194	5.079***	−2.203**	32.952***	−5.469***	4.119***	0.030	2.103**	2.982***	−2.382**
LH v.s. HL	0.266	−6.093***	3.050***	−24.901***	39.954***	−2.076**	9.505***	0.869	−0.841	−1.658*	0.228

Note: **Panel A** reports the descriptive statistics of variables; **Panel B** reports the mean of variables for the four sub-groups; **Panel C** reports the results of ANOVA analysis and T-test for the four sub-groups. *ROA* is return on assets = [Net earnings after tax/average total assets] × 100%. *Sale_No* is number of related-party buyer firms having transaction amounts of over one hundred million NT dollars or above 20% of paid-in capital with the related-party. *Supply_No* is number of related-party supplier firms having transaction amounts of over one hundred million NT dollars or above 20% of paid-in capital with the related-party. *Sale_ratio* is related-party sales ratio = [related-party sales/total sales] × 100%; in which related-party sales is the transaction amount of over one hundred million NT dollars or above 20% paid-in capital with the related-party buyer. *Purchase_ratio* is the related-party purchase ratio = [related-party purchases/total purchases] × 100%; in which related-party purchases are a transaction amount of over one hundred million NT dollars or above 20% paid-in capital with the related-party supplier. *RGAP* is the related-party receivable-payable gap ratio = [(related-party accounts and notes receivable − related-party accounts and notes payable)/total revenue] × 100%. *NGAP* is the net receivable-payable gap ratio = [(total accounts and notes receivable − total accounts and notes payables) − (related-party accounts and notes receivable − related-party accounts and notes payable)/total revenue] × 100%. *SaleExp* is the Sales expenses ratio = [sales expenses/total revenue] × 100%. Total assets are the amount of total assets. *GpSize* is the number of group member firms. *Debt* is equal to total debts/total assets × 100%. The four sub-sample groups include high related-party sales and high related-party purchases (HH), high related-party sales and low related-party purchases (HL), low related-party sales and high related-party purchases (LH), and low related-party sales and low related-party purchases (LL). Statistical significance is denoted by ***, **, * for 1%, 5%, and 10% levels, respectively.

ANOVA-test and t-test of related-party sales network linkage and intra- and extra-group receivable-payable network linkage show significant differences among four groups. However, the ANOVA-tests and t-tests of the sales expenses ratio do not differ significantly among four groups.

3.2. Results of Relationship between Related-Party Transaction Network Linkage and Performance

Table 4 Panel A shows a significantly positive linear relation between related-party sales ratio and ROA, indicating related-party sales create positive revenue effects and thus increase a firm's ROA. However, the association between related-party purchases ratio and ROA is U-shaped, and the related-party purchases ratio is negatively associated with ROA (*i.e.* the coefficient of $Purchase\_ratio^2$ is 0.001, $p < 0.05$ and the coefficient of *Purchase_ratio* is −0.112, $p < 0.10$). It demonstrates a non-linear characteristic. The ROA is differentiated with respect to the related-party purchases ratio, the critical value of the related-party purchases ratio is 56%. It means that when the related-party purchases ratio is lower than 56%, ROA is decreased the increase in related-party purchases ratio because of factors such as diseconomies of scale, illegal transfer of benefits and tunneling. However, when the related-party purchases ratio is greater than 56%, it might increase ROA with an increased related-party purchases ratio, because of positive cost effects such as securing resources of upstream supply-chain.

From **Table 4 Panel B**, we observe a non-linear inverted-U-shaped association between the related-party sales ratio and ROA (*i.e.* the coefficient of $Sale\_ratio^2$ is −0.009, $p < 0.10$) for HH group. The ROA is differentiated with respect to the related-party sales ratio, the critical value of related-party sales ratio is 29.67%. It means that when the related-party sales ratio is lower than 29.67%,

Table 4. Results of relationship between related-party transaction network linkage and performance.

Variables	Panel A	Panel B			
	All	HH	HL	LH	LL
Sale_ratio	0.135* (1.901)	0.534 (1.647)	0.191* (1.870)	−0.311 (−0.959)	0.212 (0.978)
$Sale\_ratio^2$	−0.001 (−1.169)	−0.009* (−1.938)	−0.001 (−1.102)	0.007 (1.193)	−0.004 (−0.691)
Purchase_ratio	−0.112* (−1.789)	−0.257 (−1.098)	−0.185 (−1.243)	0.884 (1.437)	−0.118 (−1.139)
$Purchase\_ratio^2$	0.001** (2.169)	0.003 (1.252)	0.0008 (0.300)	−0.006 (−1.397)	0.002* (1.693)
SaleExp	−0.292*** (−3.448)	−0.350 (−1.270)	−1.136*** (−2.876)	−0.103 (−0.928)	−0.558*** (−2.957)
LnTA	9.064*** (5.931)	8.439 (1.198)	7.783*** (2.987)	15.489*** (4.096)	6.302** (2.583)
Debt	−0.216*** (−5.474)	−0.241** (−2.325)	−0.224*** (−3.264)	−0.225** (−2.097)	−0.226*** (−3.358)
F-test	4.44***	4.06***	4.60***	5.88***	3.63***
LM-test	196.39***	11.74***	58.74***	30.45***	71.67***
Hausman-test	44.77***	15.69**	21.28***	16.18**	18.71***
Adj. R^2	0.5389	0.5502	0.5595	0.6505	0.4791

Note: **Panel A** reports the results of whole samples. **Panel B** reports the results of the four sub-sample groups (*i.e.* high related-party sales and high related-party purchases (HH), high related-party sales and low elated-party purchases (HL), low related-party sales and high related-party purchases (LH), and low related-party sales and low related-party purchases (LL)). The dependent variable is *ROA*, which is return on assets = [Net earnings after tax/average total assets] × 100%. *Sale_ratio* is related-party sales ratio = [related-party sales/total sales] × 100%; in which related-party sales is the transaction amount of over one hundred million NT dollars or above 20% paid-in capital with the related-party buyer. *Purchse_ratio* is the related-party purchase ratio = [related-party purchases/total purchases] × 100%; in which related-party purchases are a transaction amount of over one hundred million NT dollars or above 20% paid-in capital with the related-party supplier. *SaleExp* is the sales expenses ratio = [sales expenses/total revenue] × 100%. *LnTA* is the natural logarithm of total assets. *Debt* is equal to total debts/total assets × 100%. Statistical significance is denoted by ***, **, * for 1%, 5%, and 10% levels, respectively.

ROA is improved with the increase in related-party sales ratio because of factors such as advantageous market channels, positive income effects from strategic alliance, or higher intra-group transfer pricing. However, when the related-party sales ratio is higher than 29.67%, negative income effects such as the illegal transfer of benefits or tunneling may exist in related-party transactions, causing ROA to decrease with the increase in related-party sales ratio. For LL group, the related-party purchases ratio and ROA display a non-linear U-shaped association (*i.e.* the coefficient of $Purchase\_ratio^2$ is 0.002, $p < 0.10$). The ROA is differentiated with respect to the related-party purchases ratio, the critical value of related-party purchases ratio is 29.50%.

As findings earlier indicate a U-shaped relation between ROA and related-party purchases network linkage for Taiwanese business groups. This finding is in line with the view of past studies (Dyer [13]; Mowery *et al.* [43]; Uzzi [27]; Dyer and Singh [44]; Tsai and Ghoshal [45]; Gulati [21]; Gulati *et al.* [18]; Rowey *et al.* [14]; Tsai [12]; Hagedoorn and Duysters [22]; Koka and Prescott [23]) indicating that the network can contribute to firm performance. Moreover, for HH group, it demonstrates an inverted-U-shaped association between related-party sales and ROA, it displays that related-party sales network linkage can generate a positive income effect and this, in turn, increase the ROA of business group. While for LL group, related-party purchases network linkage and ROA display a U-shaped characteristic.

3.3. Results of Relationship between Financial Network Linkage and Performance

From **Table 5 Panel A**, it seems that related-party receivable-payable gap does not significantly affect the ROA, but it indicates a U-shaped relation between net receivable-payable gap ratio and ROA (*i.e.* the coefficient of $NGAP^2$ is 0.011, $p < 0.05$). The ROA is differentiated with respect to the net receivable-payable gap ratio, the critical value of net receivable-payable gap ratio is a negative gap −3.81%.

Table 5 Panel B shows that for HH group, the net receivable-payable gap ratio is positively correlated with ROA. For HL group, the finding does not offer a significant correlation between the net receivable-payable gap ratio and ROA. For LH group, the association between related-party receivable-payable gap ratio and ROA is a U-shaped, and related-party receivable-payable gap ratio is positively associated with ROA (*i.e.* the coefficient of $RGAP^2$ is 0.0008, $p < 0.05$ and the coefficient of *RGAP* is 0.154, $p < 0.05$). The ROA is differentiated with respect to related-party receivable-payable gap ratio, the critical value of related-party receivable-payable gap ratio is a negative gap −96.25%. For LL group, it shows a

Table 5. Results of relationship between financial network linkage and performance.

Variables	Panel A	Panel B			
	All	HH	HL	LH	LL
RGAP	0.044 (0.253)	−0.069 (−0.452)	0.066 (0.631)	0.154** (2.355)	0.044 (0.253)
$RGAP^2$	0.003 (0.486)	−0.002 (−0.205)	0.001 (0.441)	0.0008** (2.251)	0.003 (0.486)
NGAP	0.084 (0.604)	0.467** (2.504)	−0.067 (−0.503)	0.188 (0.916)	0.084 (0.604)
$NGAP^2$	0.011** (2.100)	−0.005 (−0.383)	−0.002 (−0.773)	−0.002 (−0.297)	0.011** (2.100)
LnTA	7.999*** (3.320)	1.039 (1.377)	7.707*** (2.981)	18.343*** (4.629)	7.999*** (3.320)
Debt	−0.211*** (−3.157)	−0.221*** (−3.042)	−0.219*** (−3.204)	−0.226** (−2.179)	−0.211*** (−3.157)
Intercept		−4.878 (−0.402)			
F-test	3.59***	4.13***	4.20***	6.30***	3.59***
LM-test	67.70***	20.71***	53.39***	26.27***	67.70***
Hausman-test	17.16***	20.71	15.16***	24.47***	17.16***
Adj. R^2	0.4730	0.5491	0.5282	0.6647	0.4730

Note: **Panel A** reports the results of whole samples. **Panel B** reports the results of the four sub-sample groups (*i.e.* high related-party sales and high related-party purchases (HH), high related-party sales and low related-party purchases (HL), low related-party sales and high related-party purchases (LH), and low related-party sales and low related-party purchases (LL)). The dependent variable is *ROA*, which is return on assets = [Net earnings after tax/average total assets] × 100%. *RGAP* is the related-party receivable-payable gap ratio = [(related-party accounts and notes receivable − related-party accounts and notes payable)/total revenue] × 100%. *NGAP* is the net receivable-payable gap ratio = [(total accounts and notes receivable − total accounts and notes payables) − (related-party accounts and notes receivable − related-party accounts and notes payable)/total revenue] × 100%. *LnTA* is the natural logarithm of total assets. *Debt* is equal to total debts/total assets × 100%. Statistical significance is denoted by ***, **, * for 1%, 5%, and 10% levels, respectively.

U-shaped association between the related-party receivable-payable gap ratio and ROA. The ROA is differentiated respect to related-party receivable-payable gap ratio, the critical value of related-party receivable-payable gap ratio is a negative gap −3.81%.

In summary, the findings present the critical values of both intra-group and extra-group receivable-payable gaps are negative gaps, indicating that while a negative gap can contribute to self-financing and ROA improvement.

According to the findings of Kuo [26], we perform additional analysis on the relation between receivable-payable financial network linkage and capital structure. **Table 6 Panel A** shows an inverted-U-shaped relation between the related-party receivables payable gap ratio and debt ratio and related-party receivable-payable gap ratio is negatively associated with debt ratio (*i.e.* the coefficient of $RGAP^2$ is −0.0007, $p < 0.01$ and the coefficient of *RGAP* is −0.133, $p < 0.01$). The debt ratio is differentiated with respect to the related-party receivable-payable gap ratio, the critical value of related-party receivable-payable gap ratio is a negative gap −95%. For HH group, the related-party receivable-payable gap ratio is negatively correlated with debt ratio. For HL group, both the related-party receivable-payable gap ratio and extra-group receivable-payable gap ratio are negatively correlated with debt ratio. For LH group, the finding does not offer a significant relation between financial network linkage and debt ratio. For LL group, there is a U-shaped association between total receivable-payable gap ratio (*TGAP*) and debt ratio (*i.e.* the coefficient of $TGAP^2$ is 0.010, $p < 0.05$). The debt ratio is differentiated with respect to the total receivable-payable gap ratio, the critical value of total receivable-payable gap ratio is a positive gap 8.05%.

As findings of **Tables 5** and **6**, which demonstrate an inverted-U-shaped association between intra-group related-party receivable-payable network linkages and debt ratio. Moreover, from **Table 3 Panel A**, it shows a negative related-party receivable-payable gap, indicating self-financing from related-party payables might decrease the cost of capital, and therefore increasing a firm's ROA. In addition, a positive extra-group receivable-payable gap, indicating the higher demands of working capital might increase the cost of capital, and therefore decreasing a firm's ROA.

3.4. Results of Relationship between Network Linkage and Related-Party Transaction

In this sub-section, we take into an industry dummy account to control the effect of industry, and estimate the industry random effects model.

Tables 7 Panel A and **Panel B** present an inverted-U-shaped between related-party sales (purchases) ratio and the number of related-party buyers (suppliers), and

Table 6. Results of relationship between financial network linkage and capital structure.

Variables	Panel A	Panel B			
	All	HH	HL	LH	LL
RGAP	-0.133^{***} (−2.715)	-0.435^{**} (−2.051)	-0.269^{***} (−3.024)	−0.006 (0.094)	
RGAP^2	-0.0007^{***} (−2.744)	0.004 (0.375)	−0.0005 (−0.260)	−0.00007 (−0.193)	
NGAP	−0.008 (−0.133)	−0.058 (−0.227)	-0.239^{**} (−2.215)	−0.199 (−0.918)	
NGAP^2	0.0002 (0.603)	0.019 (1.236)	0.0002 (0.082)	0.004 (0.903)	
TGAP					−0.161 (−1.334)
TGAP^2					0.010^{**} (2.190)
LnTA	4.611^{***} (2.981)	2.709^{**} (2.080)	0.932 (1.131)	14.361^{***} (3.687)	0.384 (0.424)
Intercept		−12.331 (−0.576)	24.435^{*} (1.836)		32.269^{**} (2.193)
F-test	14.61^{***}	8.12^{***}	11.42^{***}	17.24^{***}	19.55^{***}
LM-test	618.98^{***}	47.56^{***}	182.64^{***}	81.73^{***}	291.23^{***}
Hausman-test	9.83^{*}	1.55	4.66	12.69^{**}	3.24
Adj. R^2	0.8214	0.7295	0.7832	0.8561	0.8628

Note: **Panel A** reports the results of whole samples. **Panel B** reports the results of the four sub-sample groups (*i.e.* high related-party sales and high related-party purchases (HH), high related-party sales and low related-party purchases (HL), low related-party sales and high related-party purchases (LH), and low related-party sales and low related-party purchases (LL)). The dependent variable is *Debt Ratio*, which is equal to total debts/total assets ×100%. *RGAP* is the related-party receivable-payable gap ratio = [(related-party accounts and notes receivable − related-party accounts and notes payable)/total revenue] × 100%. *NGAP* is the net receivable-payable gap ratio = [(total accounts and notes receivable − total accounts and notes payables) − (related-party accounts and notes receivable − related-party accounts and notes payable)/total revenue] × 100%. *TGAP* the total receivable-payable gap ratio = [(total accounts and notes receivable − total accounts and notes payable)/total revenue] × 100%. *LnTA* is natural logarithms of total assets. Statistical significance is denoted by ***, **, * for 1%, 5%, and 10% levels, respectively.

the number of related-party buyers (suppliers) is positively related with related-party sales (purchases) ratio (*i.e.* the coefficient of *Sale_No*^{2} is −0.173, $p < 0.01$ and the coefficient of *Sale_No* is 6.014, $p < 0.01$; the coefficient of *Supply_No*^{2} is −0.621, $p < 0.01$ and the coefficient of *Supply_No* is 10.841, $p < 0.01$). As **Table 7 Panel C** shows the association between number of related-party suppliers (buyers) and related-party receivable-payable gap ratio is U-shaped and number of related-party suppliers (buyers) is negatively associated with related-party receivable-payable gap ratio (*i.e.* the coefficient of *Sale_No*^{2} is 0.165, $p < 0.05$ and the coefficient of *Sale_No* is −5.702, $p < 0.01$; the coefficient of *Supply_No*^{2} is 0.381, $p < 0.10$ and the coefficient of *Supply_No* is −7.518, $p < 0.01$). Moreover, it also presents an inverted-U-shaped between related-party receivable-payable gap ratio and related-party purchases ratio, and related-party purchases ratio is positively related with related-party receivable-payable gap ratio (*i.e.*, the coefficient of *Purchase_ratio*^{2} is −0.12, $p < 0.01$ and the coefficient of *Purchase_ratio* is 0.929, $p < 0.01$). In addition, we also find the IT firms appear to have higher related-party sales and purchases.

As results report that the sales expenses ratio is negatively correlated with ROA. Therefore, we perform additional analysis on the relation between the sales expenses ratio and related-party transactions. **Table 7 Panel D** shows sales expenses ratio is positively correlated with the number of related-party buyers, but negatively correlated with the related-party sales ratio. This means that the larger related-party transactions might decrease the costs of network linkage because of the scale economy from network linkage, but the more number of related-party buyers (or the dispersion of related-party buyers) might increase the firm's operating costs. In addition, we also find IT firms appear to have lower sales expenses ratios than those of non-IT firms. For 186 IT firms, about 66 firms are attributed to low related-party sales and purchases (see **Table 1**). This indicates IT firms appear to use related-party upstream and downstream network linkage and this, in turn, might decrease a firm's operating costs.

4. Conclusions

This paper analyzes the relation between network linkage and performance through the intra-business group related-party transaction, and examine whether the network linkage could be optimized for a sample of business

Table 7. Results of relationship between network linkage and related-party transactions.

Variables	Panel A *Sale ratio*	Panel B *Purchase ratio*	Panel C *RGAP*	Panel D *SaleExp*
Sale_No	6.014*** (13.451)		−5.702*** (−3.127)	0.255*** (3.002)
Sale_No^2	−0.173*** (−7.936)		0.165** (2.078)	
Supply_No		10.841*** (13.539)	−7.518*** (−2.585)	
Supply_No^2		−0.621*** (−9.936)	0.381* (1.726)	
Sale_ratio			0.863*** (2.938)	−0.021** (−2.163)
Sale_ratio^2			−0.005 (−1.464)	
Purchase_ratio			0.929*** (3.408)	
Purchase_ratio^2			−0.12*** (6.690)	
LnSale	−4.671*** (−6.689)	−3.371*** (−3.805)	13.846*** (6.690)	−2.154*** (−10.145)
GpSize	0.206 (1.461)	0.256 (1.318)	−0.291 (−0.919)	0.083** (2.006)
IND	5.646*** (2.687)	11.740*** (3.980)	3.828 (0.823)	−1.850*** (−2.981)
Intercept	78.229*** (7.428)	60.040*** (4.462)	−215.422*** (−6.882)	39.068*** (11.921)
Lagrange Multiplier test	601.93***	701.95***	4.16**	502.82***
Adj R^2	0.8691	0.9198	0.2627	0.7969

Note: **Panels A** and **B** report the results of Equation (4). **Panel C** reports the results of Equation (5). **Panel D** reports the results of Equation (6). The four sub-sample groups include high related-party sales and high related-party purchases (HH), high related-party sales and low related-party purchases (HL), low related-party sales and high related-party purchases (LH), and low related-party sales and low related-party purchases (LL). *Sale_ratio* is related-party sales ratio = [related-party sales/total sales] × 100%; in which related-party sales is the transaction amount of over one hundred million NT dollars or above 20% paid-in capital with the related-party buyer. *Purchase_ratio* is the related-party purchase ratio = [related-party purchases/ total purchases] × 100%; in which related-party purchases are a transaction amount of over one hundred million NT dollars or above 20% paid-in capital with the related-party supplier. *RGAP* is the related-party receivable-payable gap ratio = [(related-party accounts and notes receivable − related-party accounts and notes payable)/total revenue] × 100%. *SaleExp* is the sales expenses ratio = [sales expenses/total revenue] × 100%. *Sale_No* is number of related-party buyer firms having transaction amounts of over one hundred million NT dollars or above 20% of paid-in capital with the related-party. *Supply_No* is number of related-party supplier firms having transaction amounts of over one hundred million NT dollars or above 20% of paid-in capital with the related-party. *LnSale* is the natural logarithm of total revenues. *GSize* is the number of group member firms. *IND* is a dummy variable, an information technology firm, IND = 1; a non-information technology firm, IND = 0. Statistical significance is denoted by ***, **, * for 1%, 5%, and 10% levels, respectively.

groups listed on the Taiwan Stock Exchange over 2006-2008. For whole samples, we find a U-shaped relation between ROA and related-party purchases network linkage, and there is an inverted-U-shaped association between intra-group related-party receivable-payable network linkages and debt ratio. Moreover, we also find the sales expenses ratio is positively correlated with the number of related-party buyers, but negatively correlated with the related-party sales ratio. For HH group, it demonstrates an inverted-U-shaped association between related-party sales and ROA, and the related-party receivable-payable gap ratio is negatively correlated with debt ratio. While for LL group, related-party purchases network linkage and ROA display a U-shaped characteristic, and there is a U-shaped association between total receivable-payable gap ratio and debt ratio.

The results reported in this study can contribute to our understanding of the relation between intra-business group related-party transaction and performance. First, unlike previous studies, this study discusses the issue from the perspectives of related-party transaction network linkage, and uses the numbers of related-party buyer and supplier, the ratios of related-party sales and purchases, and the gap between accounts of payable and receivable as indicators of the network linkage in the groups. Our analysis provides a more insightful prediction of the interplay between network linkage and performance for business groups. Second, most Taiwanese conglomerates are developed from family or personal relationship networks, with strong "family ties" that highlight their characteristics of network linkage. Third, this study empirically supports the related-party network linkage could be optimized. Future studies can take corporate government into account, such as agency problems and earning management on related-party transactions.

5. Acknowledgements

This study was completed thanks to the funding and support from the research grants of National Science Council, project number: NSC 98-2410-H-147-011-MY2.

REFERENCES

[1] J. Johanson and L. G. Mattsson, "Interorganization Relation in Industrial Systems: A Network Approach Compared with the Transaction-Cost Approach," *International Studies of Management and Organization*, Vol. 17, No. 1, 1987, pp. 34-48.

[2] A. Echols and W. Tsai, "Niche and Performance: The Moderating Role of Network Embeddedness," *Strategic Management Journal*, Vol. 26, No. 3, 2005, pp. 219-238.

[3] B. McEvily and A. Marcus, "Embedded Ties and the Acquisition of Competitive Capabilities," *Strategic Management Journal*, Vol. 26, No. 11, 2005, pp. 1033-1055.

[4] H. Chen and T-J. Chen, "Network Linkages and Location Choice in Foreign Direct Investment," *Journal of Interna-*

tional Business Studies, Vol. 29, No. 3, 1998, pp. 445-467.

[5] W. Burgers, C. Hill and C. Kim, "A Theory of Global Strategic Alliances: The Case of the Global Auto Industry," *Strategic Management Journal*, Vol. 14, No. 6, 1999, pp. 419-432.

[6] L. Pittaway, M. Robertson, K. Munir, D. Denyer and A. Neely, "Networking and Innovation: A Systematic Review of the Evidence," *International Journal of Management Review*, Vol. 5/6, No. 3/4, 2004, pp. 137-168.

[7] R. S. Burt, "Structural Holes," Harvard University Press, Cambridge, 1992.

[8] B. Uzzi, "The Sources and Consequences of Embeddedness for the Economic Performance of Organizations: The Network Effect," *American Sociological Review*, Vol. 61, No. 4, 1996, pp. 674-698.

[9] T. E. Stuart, H. Hoang and R. C. Hybels, "Interorganizational Endorsements and the Performance of Entrepreneurial Ventures," *Administrative Science Quarterly*, Vol. 44, No. 2, 1999, pp. 315-349.

[10] A. Zaheer and G. G. Bell, "Benefiting from Network Position: Firm Capabilities, Structural Holes, and Performance," *Strategic Management Journal*, Vol. 26, No. 9, 2005, pp. 809-825.

[11] D. R. Wholey and J. W. Huonker, "Effects of Generalism and Niche Overlap on Network Linkages among Youth Service Agencies," *Academy of Management Journal*, Vol. 36, No. 2, 1993, pp. 349-371.

[12] W. Tsai, "Social Capital, Strategic Relatedness, and the Formation of Intra-Organizational Strategic Linkages," *Strategic Management Journal*, Vol. 21, No. 9, 2000, pp. 925-939.

[13] J. Dyer, "Specialized Supplier Networks as a Source of Competitive Advantage: Evidence from Auto Industry," *Strategic Management Journal*, Vol. 17, No. 4, 1996, pp. 271-291.

[14] T. Rowley, D. Behrens, and D. Krackhardt, "Redundant Governance Structures: An Analysis of Structural and Relational Embeddedness in the Steel and Semiconductor Industries," *Strategic Management Journal*, Vol. 21, No. 3, 2000, pp. 369-386.

[15] S. W. Kim, "An Investigation on the Direct and Indirect Effect of Supply Chain Integration on Firm Performance," *International Journal of Production Economics*, Vol. 119, No. 2, 2009, pp. 328-346.

[16] S. X. Zeng, X. M. Xie and C. M. Tam, "Relationship between Cooperation Networks and Innovation Performance of SMEs," *Technovation*, Vol. 30, No. 3, 2010, pp. 181-194.

[17] J. H. Dyer and N. W. Hatch, "Relation-Specific Capabilities and Barriers to Knowledge Transfers: Creating Advantage through Network Relationships," *Strategic Management Journal*, Vol. 27, No. 8, 2006, pp. 701-719.

[18] R. Gulati, N. Nohria and A. Zaheer, "Strategic Networks," *Strategic Management Journal*, Vol. 21, No. 3, 2000, pp. 203-215.

[19] A. Goerzen and P. W. Beamish, "The Effect of Alliance Network Diversity on Multinational Enterprise Performance," *Strategic Management Journal*, Vol. 26, No. 4, 2005, pp. 333-354.

[20] A. Goerzen, "Alliance Networks and Firm Performance: The Impact of Repeated Partnerships," *Strategic Management Journal*, Vol. 28, No. 5, 2007, pp. 487-509.

[21] R. Gulati, "Network Location and Learning: The Influence of Network Resources and Firm Capabilities on Alliance Formation," *Strategic Management Journal*, Vol. 20, No. 5, 1999, pp. 397-420.

[22] J. Hagedoorn and G. Duysters, "External Sources of Innovative Capabilities: The Preference for Strategic Alliances or Mergers and Acquisitions," *Journal of Management Studies*, Vol. 39, No. 2, 2002, pp. 167-188.

[23] B. Koka and J. Prescott, "Strategic Alliances as Social Capital: A Multidimensional View," *Strategic Management Journal*, Vol. 23, No. 9, 2002, pp. 795-816.

[24] H. D. Blankenburg, K. Eriksson and J. Johanson, "Creating Value through Mutual Commitment to Business Network Relations," *Strategic Management Journal*, Vol. 20, No. 5, 1999, pp. 467-486.

[25] W. Tsai, "Knowledge Transfer in Intra-Organizational Networks: Effects of Network Position and Absorptive Capacity on Business Unit Innovation and Performance," *Academy of Management Journal*, Vol. 44, No. 5, 2001, pp. 996-1004.

[26] H. C. Kuo, "Network Linkage and Financial Leverage," *Journal of Financial Studies*, Vol. 14, No. 1, 2006, pp. 95-123.

[27] B. Uzzi, "Social Structure and Competition in Interfirm Networks: The Paradox of Embeddedness," *Administrative Science Quarterly*, Vol. 42, No. 1, 1997, pp. 35-67.

[28] Y. H. Yeh, Y. H. Su, C. E. Ko and T. K. Lee, "Influences of Corporate Governance Mechanism on Related-Party Transactions," *Review of Securities and Futures Markets*, Vol. 15, No. 4, 2003, pp. 69-106.

[29] E. A. Gordon, E. Henry and D. Palia, "Related-Party Transactions and Corporate Governance," *Advances in*

Financial Economics, Vol. 9, No. 1, 2004, pp. 1-27.

[30] Y. Cheung, P. R. Rau, and A. Stouraitis, "Tunneling, Propping, and Expropriation: Evidence from Connected Party Transactions in Hong Kong," *Journal of Financial Economics*, Vol. 82, No. 2, 2006, pp. 343-386.

[31] T. Hoshi, A. Kashyap and D. Scharfstein, "The Role of Banks in Reducing the Costs of Financial Distress in Japan," *Journal of Financial Economics*, Vol. 27, No. 1, 1990, pp. 67-88.

[32] C. N. Chung, "Markets, Culture and Institutions: The Emergence of Large Business Groups in Taiwan," *Journal of Management Studies*, Vol. 38, No. 5, 2001, pp. 719-745.

[33] J. R. Lincoln, M. L. Gerlach and C. L. Ahmadjian, "Keiretsu Networks and Corporate Performance in Japan," *American Sociological Review*, Vol. 61, No. 1, 1996, pp. 67-88.

[34] E. M. Kim, "The Industrial Organization and Growth of the Korean Chaebol: Integrating Development and Organizational Theories," In: G. Hamilton, Ed., *Business Networks and Economic Development in East and Southeast Asia*, *Hong Kong*: *Centre of Asian Studies*, University of Hong Kong, 1991, pp. 272-299.

[35] G. G. Hamilton and C. S. Kao, "The Institutional Foundations of Chinese Business: The Family Firm in Taiwan," *Comparative Social Research*, Vol. 12, No. 1, 1990, pp. 135-151.

[36] S. L. Wong, "The Chinese Family Firm: A Model," *The British Journal of Sociology*, Vol. 36, No. 1, 1985, pp. 58-72.

[37] Y. H. Yeh, T. S. Lee and T. Woidtke, "Family Control and Corporate Governance: Evidence for Taiwan," *International Review of Finance*, Vol. 2, No. 1-2, 2001, pp. 21-48.

[38] S. H. Lin and S. Y. Hu, "A Family Member or Professional Management? The Choice of a CEO and Its Impact on Performance," *Corporate Governance*: *An International Review*, Vol. 15, No. 6, 2007, pp. 1348-1362.

[39] T. Khanna and J. W. Rivkin, "Estimating the Performance Effects of Business Groups in Emerging Markets," *Strategic Management Journal*, Vol. 22, No. 1, 2001, pp. 45-74.

[40] R. La Porta, F. Lopez-de-Silanes and A. Shleifer, "Corporate Ownership around the World," *Journal of Finance*, Vol. 54, No. 2, 1999, pp. 471-517.

[41] E. Fama and K. French, "Testing Trade-Off and Pecking Order Predictions about Dividends and Debt," *The Review of Financial Studies*, Vol. 15, No. 1, 2002, pp. 1-33.

[42] A. K. Sharma, "Financial Leverage and Firm's Value: A Study of Capital Structure of Selected Manufacturing Sector Firms in India," *The Business Review*, Vol. 6, No. 2, 2006, pp. 70-76.

[43] D. C. Mowery, J. E. Oxley and B. S. Silverman, "Strategic Alliances and Interfirm Knowledge Transfer," *Strategic Management Journal*, Vol. 17, No. 1, 1996, pp. 77-91.

[44] J. Dyer and H. Singh, "The Relational View: Cooperative Strategy and Sources of Interorganizational Competitive Advantage," *Academy of Management Review*, Vol. 23, No. 4, 1998, pp. 660-679.

[45] W. Tsai and S. Ghoshal, "Social Capital and Value Creation: The Role of Intra-Firm Networks," *Academy of Management Journal*, Vol. 41, No. 4, 1998, pp. 464-476.

Leverage and the Maturity Structure of Debt in Emerging Markets

Cesario Mateus[1], Paulo Terra[2]
[1]Department of Accounting and Finance, University of Greenwich Business School, London, United Kingdom
[2]Escola de Administracao, Universidade Federal do Rio Grande do Sul (UFRGS), Porto Alegre, Brazil

ABSTRACT

The aim of this paper is to analyse for a multi-country large emerging market sample the choice between debt and equity simultaneously with the decision between short- and long-term debts. In order to investigate the joint decision among leverage and maturity, we examine an unique sample of 986 firms and 13,490 firm-year observations from Latin America and 686 firms and 7919 firm-year observations from Eastern Europe for the period 1990-2003. We employ dynamic panel data analysis using Generalized Method of moments. The empirical results support three main findings. First, the cross-effects between leverage and maturity behave exactly the opposite between Latin America and Eastern Europe sub-samples. Capital structure and debt maturity are policy complements in Latin America and substitutes in Eastern Europe. Second, there is a significant dynamic effects component in the determination of leverage and maturity. Finally, adjustment to the target maturity is by no means costless and instantaneous with firm facing moderate adjustment costs.

Keywords: Capital Structure; Debt Maturity; Dynamic Panel Data Analysis; Latin America; Eastern Europe

1. Introduction

Most of the empirical research on capital structure has focused on a single decision at a time, that is, each financial decision is taken as independent of the other decisions. It may be the case that most of these decisions are not independent but actually complements or substitutes among each other. If that is the case, a further investigation should be undertaken whether there is interdependence among them or not.

In this paper, we investigate the choice between debt and equity simultaneously with the decision between short-and long-term debt for a large sample of emerging markets from Latin America and Eastern Europe. In order to investigate the joint decision among leverage and maturity, we examine an unique sample of 986 firms and 13,490 firm-year observations from Latin America and 686 firms and 7919 firm-year observations from Eastern Europe for the period 1990-2003. These two regions are ideal for our purposes because they contain a larger number of countries that have gone through extensive privatization during the time period analysed but still in different stages in the transition to capitalism systems and markets development. In fact, Latin America has experienced hyperinflation and economic instability over the 1980s and profound economic reforms in the 1990s, and Eastern Europe has made the transition from centralized to market economies during the 1990s as well.

This paper has several objectives: First, we examine whether in an emerging countries context, the theory of joint capital structure and debt maturity determination, attempts to understand country and regions specific differences. Second, we test whether there is a substantial dynamic component in the determination of the endogenous variables. Third, we analyse whether there are differences in the adjustment costs towards optimal capital structure and debt maturity.

The paper proceeds as follows: Section 2 is dedicated to the literature review. Section 3 presents the data sources and discusses sample selection, macro and firm-level financial information. In Section 4, the model and specification tests are presented. Results are presented in Section 5; Section 6 concludes.

2. Background on Capital Structure and Debt Maturity

Theories in capital structure and debt maturity as well as

subsequent empirical work mainly focused in a single decision at a time. The main theories of capital structure can be classified into three groups: tax based, agency cost and asymmetric information theories. Trade-off theory argues that firms establish a debt target and strive to reach it through time. In the theoretical framework firms pursue an optimal capital structure determined by a trade-off between the tax benefits of increasing debt financing (interest tax shield) and bankruptcy costs that arise from higher debt levels. As imperfections such taxes (corporate and personal), a variable interest rate, credit constraints, and bankruptcy costs are introduced in the model, the trade-off results (*i.e.* [1-3]).

A second group of the literature encompasses all those explanations that are based on imperfect information assumptions. In his seminal paper [4], argues that the value of the firm depends on its assets in place (whose value do not depend on future investment) as well as growth opportunities (whose value depends on future investment strategy). The implication is that this real option characteristic of the firm induces a transfer of wealth between shareholders and bondholders that may prevent the firm to undertake positive NPV projects (the debt overhand- or underinvestment problem). [5] realizes that managers have privileged information regarding both tangible (assets in place) and intangible (growth opportunities) assets and investors are aware of this fact. In light of such imperfect information there may be wealth transfers between old and new shareholders when the firm decides to issue new securities. This information asymmetry affects the firm's financing-investment decision in a way that causes managers to pass up valuable investment opportunities in order to preserve (old) shareholders' interests: the underinvestment problem. Other stream of literature suggests the agency theory framework to study the optimal leverage ratio [6,7]. In their perspective, too little debt can lead to an overinvestment problem, as managers seek to sustain growth at the expense of profitability.

Theoretical arguments for the choice of corporate debt maturity can be divided in trade-off considerations and, asymmetric information problems as well. Arguments based on trade-off considerations rely on the proposition that the optimal maturity of debt is determined by the trade-off between the costs of rollover short-term debt *vis-à-vis* the usually higher interest rate bore by long-term debt. In many senses the arguments rely on explicit transaction costs of different kinds of debt such as flotation and rollover costs as well as tax-shield benefits and implicit bankruptcy costs. The tax-based explanation suggested by [8,9] are perhaps the best known examples. Other hypothesis derives from asymmetric information. In this case, the maturity structure is yet another instrument that firms can use in order to solve the agency problems faced by the various stakeholders of the firm. These agency approaches suggest that firms choose the optimal debt maturity in order to solve information asymmetry that gives rise to the underinvestment and/or over-investment problems.

Most of the existing literature on capital structure comes from single country analysis. These studies use primarily large listed firms as in [10], for the United States, [11-13] for the United Kingdom, [14] for Spain and [15] for Portugal. A few studies focus on international samples ([16-20]) and more recently [21-23]. However, all of these studies focus on large listed firms. In [16] the sample was from large listed firms for the G7 countries. They found that the determinants of capital structure in the United States are the same for the other countries. They also find that debt levels do not differ among bank-oriented countries and market-oriented ones. [17] finds for a sample of G5 countries that the mean leverage among countries appears to be similar. However, he highlights that some of the differences can occur because of the differences in tax policies, agency problems, and information asymmetries and shareholder/creditors conflicts. [18] finds for 10 developing countries that capital structure choices are affected by the same variables as in developed countries. [19], using the same sample as [16] but with more recent data found that the overall leverage in 2001 is lower than in 1991 and the determinants of capital structure is the United States lose some of the explanatory power overseas. [20] using a sample of listed firms provided evidence that neither the trade-off nor pecking order model offer a suitable description of the capital structure policies in Europe. They also document that the notional environment do matter for capital structure decisions. [21] uses a large sample of listed firms for 42 countries equally divided between developed and developing countries covering the years from 1997 to 2001. They stated that country-specific factors do matter in determining and affecting the leverage choice around the countries analysed. [22] analyses how firms operating in capital market-oriented economies (United States and United Kingdom) and bank-oriented economies (France, Germany and Japan) determine their capital structure. They find that leverage is affected by the market conditions in which the firm operates and overall the capital structure of a firm is heavily influenced by corporate governance, tax systems and the level of investor protection. Finally [23], using a sample of 39 developed and developing countries for the period 1991 to 2006 suggest that a firm's capital structure is determined more by the country in which it is located than by its industry affiliation. They find as well that country's legal and tax systems, level of corruption explain a significant portion of the variation in leverage.

Regarding debt maturity, most empirical studies have concentrated on the United States. [24,25] pioneer studies have taken different empirical approaches to the problem. While [25] investigates the maturity structure of firm's total indebtedness, [24] focuses on the maturity of single bond issues. These are the two most common empirical approaches in the literature. The first approach is followed by [26-32]. The second approach is preferred by [33-35] who also investigate bond issues finding evidence of market timing of bond issues. Few studies investigate debt maturity in an international setting. [36] investigates the maturity structure of 604 and 750 non-financial firms from the United Kingdom and Italy, respectively. They find support for the hypothesis that firm chooses the maturity of their liabilities to match those in their assets. Their results are in line with those of [37,38] and find that debt maturity depends on both firm-specific and country-specific factors, opening the question of the degree of influence of each group of factors on the maturity structure. Larger sets of countries are studied by [39] who explored the hypothesis that the financial development of a country determines the maturity of its firms' debt. They find support for the hypothesis that legal and institutional differences among countries explain a large part of the leverage and debt maturity choices of firms. [23] also studies the subject for 11 industries in 39 countries and their results largely support [39] findings.

In a joint determination of capital structure and debt maturity perspective [40] build the argument that a firm chooses leverage and debt maturity to maximize its value given a set of exogenous firm characteristics. Their empirical results suggest that capital structure and debt maturity are substitutes in addressing financial problems.

3. Data, Variables and Methodology

3.1. Macro Financial Data

This study focus in emerging markets countries that have gone through substantial changes in the past couple of decades. Two geographic distinguish groups are studied: Latin America, which has experienced hyperinflation and economic instability over the 1980s and profound economic reforms in the 1990s and, Eastern Europe that have made the transition from centralized to market economies about the same period of time. Both groups of countries have gone through extensive privatization as documented in [41,42] in the case of Latin America and [43,44] for Eastern Europe.

In **Table 1** is provided a country-level summary statistics on key economic indicators and financial indicators for these countries for the period 1990 to 2003[1]. The countries sampled are Argentina, Brazil, Chile, Colombia, Mexico, Peru and Venezuela (henceforth called "Latin America 7" or simply "LA-7") and Bulgaria, Czech Republic, Latvia, Lithuania, Poland, Romania and the Russian Federation (henceforth called "Eastern Europe 7" or simply "EE-7").

In both groups of countries is observed highly inflationary environments in the period 1990-2003, although the high average annual inflation is influenced by the hyper-inflationary early 1990s in some countries (e.g. Argentina, Bulgaria, Brazil and Mexico). In addition, inflation has been more resilient in Romania and Russian Federation (henceforth simply "Russia") during the same period. Due to this inflationary environment, countries in the sample display depressing growth, particularly in Eastern Europe. The average annualized growth rates are often negative for the EE-7, and generally below 3 percent in Latin America[2]. The economies in the sample are in general small, with three large outliers: Brazil, Mexico and Russia, which have GDPs above US$300 billion in constant US dollars (2000). In terms of financial structure, Latin American economies showed in general a more developed stage than Eastern European ones. The EE-7 has a larger ratio of liquid liabilities to GDP than the LA-7 that might be reflect of the higher inflation rate, since central bank assets are proportionally bigger in the LA-7. In both groups the credit to the private sector is similar, but EE-7 countries seem to be more bank-based than the LA-7 given the larger bank deposits to GDP and bank concentration. Interestingly, the net interest margin is higher for the LA-7 indicating a less competitive bank market. Private bond markets are equally incipient for both groups of countries, while public bond markets are at least three times larger. This might suggest that the government crowds out private issuers in such markets. Stock markets are greater in Latin America, in both absolute and relative terms, although Eastern European markets are relatively more actively traded. In all other aspects, Latin American stock markets seem more developed: they trade a larger number of companies and those companies have larger market capitalization than their counterparts in the EE-7. This is not a surprise since stock markets in Latin America date from the beginning of the 20th century while in Eastern Europe such markets have just begun trading about two decades ago.

In summary, these are economies that have a recent history of unstable economies, combining higher inflation with lower growth. These economies are predominantly bank-based, although the LA-7 has comparatively more developed stock markets, and public bond markets are much larger than private ones moving towards market based more quickly than eastern European countries.

3.2. Firm-Level Data and Variables

The primary data sources are from the Economatica Pro

[1]These indicators are collected from World Bank's World Development Indicators and World Bank's Financial Structure Database.

[2]Chile has been an exception with a growth rate of more than 5 percent a year over the sample period.

Table 1. Macro financial data. The table presents key economic and financial indicators from the financial structure database (World Bank, 2005a) and World Development Indicators Online (World Bank, 2005b). The sample consists of yearly observations for each country over the period 1990 to 2003 (unless indicated otherwise), depending on data availability. EE-7 refers to the simple average of country-level data for Bulgaria, Czech Republic, Latvia, Lithuania, Poland, Romania and the Russia, and "LA-7" refers to the simple average of country-level data for Argentina, Brazil, Chile, Colombia, Mexico, Peru and Venezuela.

Panel (a) Latin America

Country			Argentina	Brazil	Chile	Colombia	Mexico	Peru	Venezuela	LA-7
Variable	Unit	Period								
Annual Inflation Rate	Percentage	1990-2003 Average	13.21	123.63	7.30	15.65	14.04	26.31	34.91	33.58
Real GDP (constant 2000 US$)	US$ Millions	2003	263,469	624,490	81,955	90,131	593,551	57,862	101,878	259,048
Real GDP growth	Percentage	1990-2003 Average	2.67	2.18	5.21	2.32	2.61	3.45	0.48	2.70
GDP per capita	US$	2003	6957	3536	5196	2022	5803	2131	3968	4230
GDP per capita growth	Percentage	1990-2003 Average	1.51	0.90	3.82	0.56	1.11	1.76	−1.38	1.18
Deposit money bank vs central bank assets	Percentage	1990-2003 Average	83.99	73.16	76.64	92.66	93.65	98.47	70.07	84.09
Liquid Liabilities (M3) to GDP	Percentage	1990-2003 Average	21.70	25.66	37.14	28.86	26.81	23.03	23.98	26.74
Central bank assets to GDP	Percentage	1990-2003 Average	5.25	14.14	16.06	1.50	2.67	0.28	6.87	6.68
Private credit by deposit money banks to GDP	Percentage	1990-2003 Average	18.03	25.80	49.76	16.83	20.99	16.62	11.06	22.73
Private credit by deposit money banks and other financial institutions to GDP	Percentage	1990-2003 Average	18.39	31.53	60.29	26.82	21.70	17.34	14.36	27.20
Bank deposits to GDP	Percentage	1990-2003 Average	17.60	22.65	33.38	16.60	23.59	18.66	17.55	21.43
Bank Concentration (share of 3 largest banks in total deposits)	Percentage	1990-2003 Average	44.34	45.47	60.95	37.38	62.60	71.74	60.32	54.69
Net Interest Margin	Percentage	1990-2003 Average	7.64	12.16	5.53	7.06	6.48	10.63	17.52	9.57
Stock market capitalization to GDP	Percentage	1990-2003 Average	28.44	24.97	79.64	13.19	27.82	17.25	9.78	28.73
Stock market total value traded to GDP	Percentage	1990-2003 Average	3.03	12.94	7.56	1.01	9.88	3.71	2.15	5.89
Stock market turnover ratio	Percentage	1990-2003 Average	27.18	51.18	9.18	7.51	34.94	22.31	18.19	24.36
Private bond market capitalization to GDP	Percentage	1990-2003 Average	3.90	9.93	15.52	0.47	2.14	2.49	NA	5.74
Public bond market capitalization to GDP	Percentage	1990-2003 Average	8.42	30.15	27.85	10.13	12.32	1.63	NA	15.08
Listed domestic companies, total	Number	1990-2003 Median	142	540	261	118	192	238	87	192
Market capitalization of listed companies	US$ Millions	1990-2002 Average	65,636	149,069	52,354	11,254	119,715	9104	7766	59,271

Panel (b) Eastern Europe

Variable	Unit	Period	Bulgaria	Czech Republic	Latvia	Lithuania	Poland	Romania	Russia	EE-7
Annual Inflation Rate	Percentage	1990-2003 Average	71.10	5.36	25.09	27.16	19.30	75.35	76.56	42.84
Real GDP (constant 2000 US$)	US$ Millions	2003	14,380	60,186	9553	14,179	177,016	42,688	306,690	89,242
Real GDP growth	Percentage	1990-2003 Average	−0.31	0.73	−0.62	−0.85	3.04	−0.32	−1.63	0.00
GDP per capita	US$	2003	1838	5899	4116	4105	4634	1963	2138	3528
GDP per capita growth	Percentage	1990-2003 Average	0.46	0.84	0.38	−037	3.30	0.14	−1.39	0.44
Deposit money bank vs central bank assets	Percentage	1990-2003 Average	80.10	96.68	93.54	99.81	89.39	91.38	71.55	88.92
Liquid Liabilities (M3) to GDP	Percentage	1990-2003 Average	46.08	65.70	26.09	21.33	34.47	21.81	NA	35.91
Central bank assets to GDP	Percentage	1990-2003 Average	8.50	2.01	1.29	0.03	3.76	1.70	NA	2.88
Private credit by deposit money banks to GDP	Percentage	1990-2003 Average	48.33	62.86	21.18	16.90	29.70	19.34	NA	33.05
Private credit by deposit money banks and other financial institutions to GDP	Percentage	1990-2003 Average	29.37	54.58	15.02	12.22	20.89	7.60	NA	23.28
Bank deposits to GDP	Percentage	1990-2003 Average	37.28	57.57	17.37	15.01	28.74	18.99	NA	29.16
Bank Concentration (share of 3 largest banks in total deposits)	Percentage	1990-2003 Average	60.58	76.72	55.35	89.09	55.30	76.44	38.98	64.64
Net Interest Margin	Percentage	1990-2003 Average	5.27	3.12	4.66	4.92	5.13	9.25	8.47	5.83
Stock market capitalization to GDP	Percentage	1990-2003 Average	3.14	20.61	5.69	9.99	8.91	3.17	15.94	9.64
Stock market total value traded to GDP	Percentage	1990-2003 Average	0.40	8.59	1.39	1.42	3.98	0.60	5.47	3.12
Stock market turnover ratio	Percentage	1990-2003 Average	9.78	44.20	24.33	17.76	72.85	28.54	54.74	36.03
Private bond market capitalization to GDP	Percentage	1990-2003 Average	NA	4.17	NA	NA	NA	NA	NA	4.17
Public bond market capitalization to GDP	Percentage	1990-2003 Average	NA	21.51	NA	NA	27.98	NA	3.62	17.70
Listed domestic companies, total	Number	1990-2003 Median	355	213	62	54	143	93	196	143
Market capitalization of listed companies	US$ Millions	1990-2002 Average	453	12,488	404	1151	13,932	1052	42,803	10,326

database for the Latin America countries (Economatica 2003) and from the 2004 version of Amadeus (Analyse major Database from European Sources) Database by Bureau Van Dijk for the Eastern European countries. We only considered listed firms, the level of analysis is each firm and observations are yearly during the period 1990-2002 for Latin America and 1994-2003 to Eastern Europe. The database contains 1242 unique firms for the LA-7 and 693 industrial firms for the EE-7 over the period covered. After excluding financial firms as well as firms with missing data for key variables (discussed later), the sample is reduced to 986 firms and 13,490 firm-year observations from Latin America and 686 firms and 7,919 firm-year observations from Eastern Europe[3]. **Table 2** presents the distribution of firms by country and region.

The dependent variables in our study are proxies for leverage and maturity of debt and measured as long-term debt over book equity (*i.e.* the debt-equity-to-ratio "Leverage") and long-tern financial debt over short-term loans plus long-term financial debt (*i.e.* "Maturity")[4].

Table 3 panels **(a)** and **(b)** shows the summary statistics of *Leverage* and *Maturity*for the LA-7 and EE-7 countries, respectively. One can highlight that Brazil heavily influences the Latin America sample while the most influential countries in Eastern Europe are Poland, Russia and Bulgaria. On the other hand, Venezuela has little impact on the Latin America sample as well as Latvia in the Eastern Europe group of firms. There is evidence of substantially higher maturity ratios for EE-7 compared with LA-7 (0.59 and 0.48, respectively), being Mexico and Poland the countries with larger values in each sub-sample (0.54 and 0.76, respectively). In terms of *Leverage*, long term debt corresponds to 105 percent and 19 percent of equity to LA-7 and EE-7 countries, respectively. Brazil has the highest level of leverage for the whole 14 countries (170 percent) while Poland has the lowest level (8 percent).

Table 2. Firms by country and region. The sample consists of 986 firms from Argentina, Brazil, Chile, Colombia, Mexico, Peru and Venezuela (Economatica Pro database, 2003) over the period 1990-2002 and 686 firms from Bulgaria, Czech Republic, Latvia, Lithuania, Poland, Romania and Russia (Amadeus database, 2004) over the period 1994-2003.

Latin America LA-7		Eastern Europe EE-7	
Argentina	76	Bulgaria	148
Brazil	395	Czech Republic	48
Chile	169	Latvia	21
Colombia	47	Lithuania	27
Mexico	145	Poland	146
Peru	126	Romania	48
Venezuela	28	Russia	134
LA-7	986	EE-7	686

Table 3. Summary statistics. The sample consists of 13,490 firm-year observations from Argentina, Brazil, Chile, Colombia, Mexico, Peru and Venezuela (Economatica Pro database, 2003) over the period 1990-2002 and 7919 firm-year observations from Bulgaria, Czech Republic, Latvia, Lithuania, Poland, Romania and Russia (Amadeus database, 2004) over the period 1994-2003. *Leverage* is calculated as the book value of long-term debt over book value of equity. *Maturity* is the book value of long-term financial debt over book value of short-term loans plus book value of long-term financial debt. "LA-7" refers to the pooling together of all firm-level data from Argentina, Brazil, Chile, Colombia, Mexico, Peru and Venezuela, while "EE-7" refers to the pooling of firm level data for Bulgaria, Czech Republic, Latvia, Lithuania, Poland, Romania and Russia.

Panel (a) Dependent Variables: Latin America

		Leverage				**Maturity**	
Countries	Observations	Mean	Std. Dev.	*Countries*	Observations	Mean	Std. Dev.
Argentina	614	0.9552	6.7349	Argentina	538	0.4184	0.3283
Brazil	3270	1.6999	15.1451	Brazil	2850	0.4645	0.3078
Chile	1742	0.3266	0.6098	Chile	1518	0.4997	0.3540
Colombia	280	0.4687	1.7781	Colombia	241	0.4617	0.3410
Mexico	1324	0.6869	1.2427	Mexico	1204	0.5431	0.3227
Peru	1012	1.0447	19.5014	Peru	142	0.4012	0.3392
Venezuela	175	0.2757	0.3367	Venezuela	146	0.4292	0.3112
LA-7	8417	1.0527	11.7826	LA-7	6639	0.4808	0.3272

Panel (b) Dependent Variables: Eastern Europe

		Leverage				**Maturity**	
Countries	Observations	Mean	Std. Dev.	*Countries*	Observations	Mean	Std. Dev.
Bulgaria	633	0.3324	1.0155	Bulgaria	540	0.5249	0.4283
Czech Republic	417	0.1441	0.2046	Czech Republic	364	0.3684	0.3582
Latvia	115	0.1465	0.2330	Latvia	87	0.4337	0.3559
Lithuania	190	0.1902	0.2543	Lithuania	161	0.5181	0.3374
Poland	755	0.0808	0.3462	Poland	234	0.7640	0.2964
Romania	421	0.0945	0.4080	Romania	267	0.7116	0.3663
Russia	655	0.2777	2.0953	Russia	603	0.6952	0.3692
EE-7	3186	0.1903	1.0852	EE-7	2256	0.5881	0.3960

[3]In order to reduce the survival bias, firms are allowed to leave and enter the dataset over time. The final sample is an unbalanced panel.

[4]We choose book values instead of market values because the reliability of market based figures for emerging markets for the studied time period is questionable (in particular with respect to debt valuation), due secondary markets are thin, trade is often infrequent and data availability is difficult.

Firm-specific determinant factors for the debt maturity structure are chosen from those often suggested in the literature. The set of firm-specific variables consists of the following: size, growth opportunities, profitability, liquidity, tangibility, tax effects and business risk. In detail the variables are calculated as: 1) *size* is measured by the natural logarithm of sales; 2) *growth opportunities* of the firm are assessed by the market-to-book ratio for Latin America firms[5] calculated as book value liabilities plus market capitalization over total book value assets; for Eastern Europe firms *growth opportunities* are measure as the ratio of intangible fixed assets to total fixed assets[6]; 3) *profitability*, a proxy for firm and credit quality, is calculated according to the usual return-on-assets ratio by operating income over total book assets; 4) *business risk* is measured by the degree of operational leverage and calculated as sales divided by operating income; 5) the degree of *liquidity* as an indicator of cash constraints is given by the current liquidity ratio and measured as current assets over current liabilities; 6) the *degree of tangibility* of assets as an indicator of collateral value is given by the degree of asset immobilization and measured as net fixed assets over total book assets and finally; 7) the tax effects are measured by the effective average tax rate of the firm the ratio of total taxes charges divided by taxable earnings[7]. Additionally, we also define a binary variable to control for regulated industries. This variable assumes the value of one if the firm's main industrial activity belongs to one of the following Industries: Contraction, Electricity, Gas and Oil, Mining, Telecommunications, Transport and Logistics. These Industries are subject to closer government scrutiny even when pursued solely by private companies, and are submitted to stricter regulations than other industries.

Table 4 panels **(a)** and **(b)** reports summary statistics for the independent variables of Latin America and Eastern European firms, respectively. We can highlight that LA-7 firms are larger, with more growth opportunities, are less profitable, have lower business risk and pay less taxes, on average. However, some variables have a larger dispersion around their average. That is the case for example for the business Risk proxy with a standard deviation of 218.00 and 507.45 for LA-7 and EE-7, respectively. Therefore, the average values should be analysed with some concerns suggesting the presence of large outliers that may inflate the standard deviation for this variable and others[8].

In **Table 5** (Panels **(a)** and **(b)**) it is presented the correlation matrix for the independent variables (firm's characteristics). We can highlight that larger firms tend to be more profitable, with more growth opportunities, have less liquidity, are riskier and have more fixed assets as a proportion of total assets in the case of LA-7 and less so for the EE-7 countries[9].

Besides the above variables, we employ a set of dummy variables as instruments. First, the sector where each firm operates is included, given the possible systematic effects that the nature of the firm's businesses may have over its leverage, in particular the total leverage measures. The different sectors[10] are represented by a set of dummy variables based on their classification provided in the databases. The sector "Food and Beverages" is chosen as the base-case so that the instrument set may include an intercept. Similarly, country dummies are used to account for any country-specific variation such as the institutional framework, business environment, and macroeconomic conditions. For this situation "Brazil" is chosen as the base case for Latin America and "Bulgaria" for Eastern Europe.

4. Model and Specification Tests

4.1. The Empirical Model

A panel data analysis is performed according to the following general (static) model:

$$\text{Leverage}_{i,t} = \beta_{0,i} + \beta_{0,t} + \sum_{k=1}^{K} \beta_{1,k} Y_{i,k,t} + \sum_{l=1}^{L} \beta_{2,l} Z_{i,l,t} + \upsilon_i + \varepsilon_{i,t}$$

(Equation (1))

$$\text{Maturity}_{i,t} = \beta_{0,i} + \beta_{0,t} + \sum_{k=1}^{K} \beta_{1,k} \Delta Y_{i,k,t} + \sum_{l=1}^{L} \beta_{2,l} Z_{i,l,t} + \upsilon_i + \varepsilon_{i,t}$$

where, $\text{Leverage}_{i,t}$ and $\text{Maturity}_{i,t}$ are the stacked vec-

[5]Nevertheless book values are chosen in this study, we use a market based variable in this case since stock markets in Latin America are much more liquid than debt markets. Therefore, the use of the market-to-book ratio here seems reasonable.

[6]The majority of Eastern European firms in our sample did not have stock market data available in the database used (Amadeus by Bureau Van Dijk) therefore we choose this variable with an alternative measure.

[7]The more correct way to measure the effect of taxes on maturity structure would be calculating the Miller Tax Term, *i.e.* $1-\left(\frac{(1-T_c)\times(1-T_e)}{(1-T_i)}\right)$, where T_c is the corporate tax rate, T_i is the personal tax rate and T_e is the tax rate on equity income. However, obtaining reliable tax rates over several years for seven different countries can prove difficult. In this study, we choose the average effective tax rate as a substitute, following [18].

[8]In order to account for such cases in the Business Risk variable and others, in the data analyses that follows we take appropriate remedial measures.

[9]Since the correlations are generally low in our sample, there are no multicollinearity problems among the independent variables.

[10]Firms are classified in one of the following 19 sectors, according to their primary NAICS (Latin America) or NACE (Eastern Europe) codes: Agriculture, Chemical, Construction, Electricity, Electronic, Food and Beverages, Gas and Oil, Machinery, Manufacturing, Mining, Pulp and Paper, Retailing and Wholesaling, Services, Software, Steel, Telecommunications, Textile, Transport and Logistics, and Vehicles and Parts.

Table 4. Summary statistics for independent variables. (a) The sample consists of 13,490 firm-year observations from Argentina, Brazil, Chile, Colombia, Mexico, Peru and Venezuela (Economatica Pro database, 2003) over the period 1990-2002. *Size* is the natural logarithm of total sales. *Growth opportunities* are equal to the book value of liabilities plus market capitalization over book value of total assets. *Profitability* is equal to operating income over book value of total assets. *Business Risk* is calculated as sales over operating income. *Liquidity* is book value of current assets over book value of current liabilities. *Tangibility* is defined as net fixed assets over book value of total assets. *Tax Effects* is equal to taxes over taxable earnings. "*Latin America*" refers to the pooling together of all firm-level data from Argentina, Brazil, Chile, Colombia, Mexico, Peru and Venezuela; (b) The sample consists of 7919 firm-year observations from Bulgaria, Czech Republic, Latvia, Lithuania, Poland, Romania and Russia (Amadeus database, 2004) over the period 1994-2003. *Size* is the natural logarithm of total sales. *Growth Opportunities* are the ratio of intangible fixed assets to total fixed assets. *Profitability* is equal to operating income over book value of total assets. *Business Risk* is calculated as sales over operating income. *Liquidity* is book value of current assets over book value of current liabilities. *Tangibility* is defined as net fixed assets over book value of total assets. *Tax Effects* is equal to taxes over taxable earnings. "*Eastern Europe*" refers to the pooling together of all firm-level data from Bulgaria, Czech Republic, Latvia, Lithuania, Poland, Romania and Russia.

Panel (a) Latin America

Countries	Argentina			Brazil			Chile			Colombia		
Variables	*Obs.*	*Mean*	*Std. Dev.*	*Obs.*	*Mean*	*Std. Dev.*	*Obs.*	*Mean*	*Std. Dev.*	*Obs.*	*Mean*	*Std. Dev.*
Size	582	11.3880	1.8235	2896	11.5804	1.8322	1580	10.2488	1.8960	297	11.0402	1.5650
Growth Opportunities	497	0.9887	0.4354	2813	0.8115	0.4786	1320	2.1829	8.6707	201	0.8253	0.4274
Profitability	614	0.3538	0.0711	3262	0.0308	0.8922	1748	0.0587	0.1025	287	0.0303	0.0781
Business Risk	594	0.8755	155.6350	3253	1.2234	155.8223	1633	12.7145	125.3976	286	31.1815	725.7262
Liquidity	614	1.6938	2.7358	3263	2.5267	22.5466	1738	5.0646	43.2245	281	1.6976	1.1712
Tangibility	597	0.4597	0.2619	3265	0.3578	0.2621	1719	0.4111	0.2879	274	0.2494	0.1894
Tax Effects	344	0.1399	1.0425	3260	0.4042	12.4357	1482	0.0295	0.8842	287	0.1107	1.5110

Countries	Mexico			Peru			Venezuela			Latin America		
Variables	*Obs.*	*Mean*	*Std. Dev.*	*Obs.*	*Mean*	*Std. Dev.*	*Obs.*	*Mean*	*Std. Dev.*	*Obs.*	*Mean*	*Std. Dev.*
Size	1335	12.2981	1.7981	1005	10.2201	1.2713	166	10.9196	1.8189	7861	11.2121	1.9207
Growth Opportunities	873	1.2778	0.6577	633	1.1085	0.7247	140	0.7463	0.3507	6477	1.1955	3.9775
Profitability	1339	0.0756	0.7630	1010	0.0597	0.1178	175	0.0346	0.0659	8435	0.0475	0.0938
Business Risk	1339	16.8693	196.8102	1006	14.8608	267.0739	171	2.1902	51.4443	8282	8.7048	218.0081
Liquidity	1340	5.2687	99.4697	1012	2.0033	4.2355	175	2.1203	2.8290	8423	3.3263	46.4780
Tangibility	1340	0.5120	0.2716	1012	0.4771	0.2220	175	0.5355	0.2263	8382	0.4152	0.2705
Tax Effects	1339	−4.1846	137.5319	1009	0.3121	3.9597	174	0.0971	1.5772	7895	−0.4851	57.2277

Panel (b) Eastern Europe

Countries	Bulgaria			Czech Republic			Latvia			Lithuania		
Variables	*Obs.*	*Mean*	*Std. Dev.*	*Obs.*	*Mean*	*Std. Dev.*	*Obs.*	*Mean*	*Std. Dev.*	*Obs.*	*Mean*	*Std. Dev.*
Size	1434	6.8570	4.3720	480	16.0723	6.4678	206	9.1521	8.2399	270	11.7904	7.9011
Growth Opportunities	633	0.1066	0.0622	417	0.0122	0.0200	115	0.0280	0.0640	190	0.0058	0.0107
Profitability	633	0.0030	0.0223	417	0.0548	0.0790	115	1.3005	13.3508	190	0.0670	0.0911
Business Risk	628	30.5194	122.325	402	12.6361	232.3752	115	18.3172	75.8044	187	11.2720	112.5914
Liquidity	633	2.2747	3.1276	417	1.9586	2.1405	114	5.3497	8.2373	188	2.7688	3.2459
Tangibility	633	0.5637	0.2133	417	0.6444	0.1962	115	0.5370	0.1797	190	0.5829	0.1353
Tax Effects	628	−0.7088	1.1245	403	0.0891	0.3397	115	0.1540	0.4990	186	0.0858	0.1412

Countries	Poland			Romania			Russia			Eastern Europe		
Variables	*Obs.*	*Mean*	*Std. Dev.*	*Obs.*	*Mean*	*Std. Dev.*	*Obs.*	*Mean*	*Std. Dev.*	*Obs.*	*Mean*	*Std. Dev.*
Size	1443	9.1656	8.7902	473	15.0243	5.4213	1325	8.8765	9.3132	5631	9.7159	8.6823
Growth Opportunities	757	0.5502	0.0907	421	0.0095	0.0312	655	0.0309	0.1116	3188	0.0257	0.0750
Profitability	758	0.0630	0.1190	421	0.1117	0.1317	655	0.0915	0.1952	3189	0.1072	2.5387
Business Risk	750	11.0998	181.9291	421	22.0645	181.7592	654	2.9837	158.3979	3157	15.2124	507.4524
Liquidity	746	1.7289	1.9473	421	1.6851	1.2560	655	1.7785	2.2589	3174	2.0640	2.8004
Tangibility	758	0.4416	0.2056	421	0.5459	0.1578	655	0.5501	0.2012	3189	0.5403	0.2002
Tax Effects	750	0.1595	2.3871	421	0.2524	0.2372	654	1.0830	19.0344	3157	0.1769	12.0275

Table 5. Correlation matrices. (a) The sample consists of 13,490 firm-year observations from Argentina, Brazil, Chile, Colombia, Mexico, Peru and Venezuela (Economatica Pro database, 2003) over the period 1990-2002; (b) The sample consists of 7919 firm-year observations from Bulgaria, Czech Republic, Latvia, Lithuania, Poland, Romania and Russia (Amadeus database, 2004) over the period 1994-2003.

Panel (a) Latin America

	Size	Growth Opportunities	Profitability	Business Risk	Liquidity	Tangibility	Tax Effects
Size	1.0000						
Growth Opportunities	0.0696	1.0000					
Profitability	0.2085	0.0233	1.0000				
Business Risk	0.0116	−0.0016	0.0110	1.0000			
Liquidity	−0.0060	−0.0243	−0.0177	−0.1498	1.0000		
Tangibility	0.1652	0.0568	0.1169	0.0070	−0.0505	1.0000	
Tax Effects	−0.0200	−0.0008	0.0039	−0.0028	0.0003	−0.0028	1.0000

Panel (b) Eastern Europe

	Size	Growth Opportunities	Profitability	Business Risk	Liquidity	Tangibility	Tax Effects
Size	1.0000						
Growth Opportunities	0.0937	1.0000					
Profitability	0.0312	0.0642	1.0000				
Business Risk	0.0024	−0.0221	−0.0003	1.0000			
Liquidity	−0.1053	0.0164	0.0554	−0.0089	1.0000		
Tangibility	−0.0166	−0.1819	0.0028	−0.0138	−0.0602	1.0000	
Tax Effects	0.0293	−0.0040	0.0005	−0.0017	0.0122	−0.0330	1.0000

tors of the dependent (endogenous) variables ((the ith-firm leverage and maturity ratios on the tth-period), $Y_{i,k,t}$ is the matrix of K firm-specific independent (explanatory) variables (including industry dummies in the simple pooling and random-effects models), $Z_{i,l,t}$ is the matrix of L country dummies (in the simple pooling and random-effects models), $\beta_{0,i}$ is the firm-specific intercept in the fixed-effects model, $\beta_{0,t}$ is the period-specific intercept, $\beta_{1,k}$ and $\beta_{2,l}$ are the matrices of coefficients, υ_i is the firm-specific error term in the random-effects model, and $\varepsilon_{i,t}$ is a vector of error terms. Due to the nature of the data (panel data) we test the model for fixed and random effects. Once it is established that the fixed-effects model provides a good fit for the model then the lagged endogenous variable is added to Equation (1), which is then first-differenced yielding the dynamic system below:

$$\Delta\text{Leverage}_{i,t} = \beta_{0'i}\Delta\text{Leverage}_{i,t-1} + \sum_{k=1}^{k}\beta_{1,k}\Delta Y_{i,k,t} + \varepsilon_{i,t}$$

(Equation (2))

$$\Delta\text{Maturity}_{i,t} = \beta_{0'i}\Delta\text{Maturity}_{i,t-1} + \sum_{k=1}^{k}\beta_{1,k}\Delta Y_{i,k,t} + \varepsilon_{i,t}$$

One advantage of this specification is that the rate of adjustment of the firm towards its optimal capital structure and maturity (assuming that the optimal capital and maturity structures are determined by the exogenous variables $\Delta Y_{i,k,t}$) can be estimated as $\lambda = (1-\beta_{0'i})$. If adjustment costs are high, the rate of adjustment is expected to be small (λ approaching zero), while a very high rate of adjustment (λ approaching one) suggests the presence of negligible adjustment costs.

4.2. Preliminary Specification Tests

Our analysis starts to determine which model (simple polling, fixed-effects, or random-effects) is more appropriate to the sample data. We perform two independent specification tests: The F-test of Simple Pooling *versus* Fixed-effects model and the Hausman test of random-effects *versus* fixed effects. The results are shown in **Table 6** (Panels **(a)** and **(b)**). The results (Panel **(a)**) strongly reject the single intercept hypothesis, both for the LA-7 and for the EE-7. In panel **(b)** the Hausman specification test is performed to test which model of variable intercepts across firms better fits the data. This test is particularly appropriated in situations wher N (the number of cross-sectional units) is large relative to T (the number of time periods) which is precisely the case of our sample. The test rejects the random-effects specification for the leverage equation in the LA-7 and the maturity equation for the EE-7. However, for the remaining cases it cannot reject such specification for both groups of countries.

5. Results

5.1. Dynamic Panel Data Estimation Results

Preliminary runs of the fixed-effects model of Equation (1) revealed a substantial presence of autocorrelation in the residuals. This finding raises the question that the maturity choice of the firm may be dynamic, *i.e.*, current

Table 6. Specification tests. (a) This test statistic is for testing the null hypothesis that firms' intercept in the basic fixed-effects panel data model are all equal, against the alternative hypothesis that each firm has its own (distinct intercept). The test assumes identical slopes for all independent variables across all firms, and it is distributed $F(df_1, df_2)$. "All" refers to the pooling together of all firm-level data for Argentina, Brazil, Chile, Colombia, Mexico, Peru, Venezuela, Bulgaria, Czech Republic, Latvia, Lithuania, Poland, Romania and Russia. "LA-7" refers to the polling together of all firm-level data for Argentina, Brazil, Chile, Colombia, Mexico, Peru, Venezuela while "EE-7" refers to the polling of firm-level data for Bulgaria, Czech Republic, Latvia, Lithuania, Poland, Romania and Russia. The data covers the period 1990-2003. Endogenous variables are: *Leverage* is equal to long-term book liabilities divided by book value of equity and *Maturity* is equal to long term debt divided by total debt. *P-values* are in parenthesis. *, ** and * represents significant at the 1%, 5% and 10% levels; (b) This test statistic is for testing the null hypothesis of the random-effects specification against the alternative hypothesis of the fixed-effects specification in the basic panel data model, and it is distributed X^2 (*df*). "All" refers to the pooling together of all firm-level data for Argentina, Brazil, Chile, Colombia, Mexico, Peru, Venezuela, Bulgaria, Czech Republic, Latvia, Lithuania, Poland, Romania and Russia. "LA-7" refers to the polling together of all firm-level data for Argentina, Brazil, Chile, Colombia, Mexico, Peru, Venezuela while "EE-7" refers to the polling of firm-level data for Bulgaria, Czech Republic, Latvia, Lithuania, Poland, Romania and Russia. The data covers the period 1990-2003. Endogenous variables are: *Leverage* is equal to long-term book liabilities divided by book value of equity and *Maturity* is equal to long term debt divided by total debt. *P-values* are in parenthesis. ***, ** and * represents significant at the 1%, 5% and 10% levels.**

Panel (a) F-Test of a Simple pooled OLS against a Fixed Effects Specification

Region	Period	Leverage	Maturity
ALL	1990-2003	F (1205; 5637) 2.7088*** (0.000)	F (1205; 5637) 4.9346*** (0.000)
LA-7	1990-2002	F (714; 3908) 2.0101*** (0.000)	F(714; 3908) 4.9446 (0.000)
EE-7	1994-2003	F (490; 1696) 2.4474*** (0.000)	F (490; 1696) 3.5822*** (0.000)

Panel (b) Hausman Specification Test of Random-effects against Fixed-effects Specification

Region	Period	Leverage	Maturity
ALL	1990-2003	X^2 (6) 11.170* (0.083)	X^2 (11) 14.230 (0.221)
LA-7	1990-2002	X^2 (4) 101.960*** (0.000)	X^2 (13) 16.864* (0.221)
EE-7	1994-2003	X^2 (2) 1.985 (0.3706)	X^2 (10) 45.418*** (0.000)

maturity may depend on past maturity. [22] explicitly models such possibility, and suggest that a dynamic rather than static panel data analysis may be adequate. However, the usual OLS and GLS estimators are biased and inconsistent when the lagged dependent variable is included in the right-hand side of the panel data model[11]. In order to overcome this problem, GMM estimation is used instead. Therefore, Equation (2) is estimated by Generalized Method of Moments (GMM) using as instruments first-order lagged values of the levels of explanatory variables, sector dummies, country dummies, and a constant. Standard errors are heteroskedasticity robust according to the method proposed by [49] and are also robust to autocorrelation. **Table 7** reports the results for all countries pooled together and **Table 8** for each region separately[12].

One major result is that maturity equations perform slightly better than the leverage ones. When all countries are polled together (in **Table 7**) the dummy variable used to signal the difference between the two regions, becomes significant for the leverage equation but not for the maturity one. This result indicates that the level of debt is different between the two samples. Another interesting result is that it is easier for the firm to change the maturity of its debt than to adjust its leverage ratio. At the same time, adjustment to the target maturity is by no means costless and instantaneous. The estimated rate of adjustment to an optimal capital structure ranges between 0.55 and 0.64 an indication that firms in the sample face moderate adjustment costs, being these adjustments costs in general higher for capital structure than for debt maturity, and this is a pattern between the LA-7 and the EE-7 samples. The cross-effects between leverage and maturity behave exactly the opposite between the LA-7 and the EE-7 (**Table 8**). While maturity has a significant positive contemporaneous effect on leverage (and vice versa) for the LA-7, it has a significant negative effect in the EE-7. This finding indicates that these policy variables are complements in Latin America and substitutes in Eastern Europe. One possible explanation for this difference in results for each group of countries is their particular institutional and economic environments differences for the period of the analysis. Latin America stock markets seem more developed (trade more companies and have larger market capitalization than their counterparts in Eastern Europe) and therefore Latin American firms obtained a financial advantage that allows them use financing alternatives in their favour, reinforcing each other. Regarding the explanatory variables, it is worth to underscore that the two variables pointed out by [27] as the

[11]See [45-48] for further discussion.

[12]One important issue when estimating via GMM is to make sure that the instrument set is adequate. We report in **Tables 7** and **8** the Sargan's test statistic for the null hypothesis that moment restrictions are orthogonal.

Table 7. Panel data analysis of maturity ratios for Pooled Countries. First-differences model so that idiosyncratic firm-effects constant through time are eliminated. The following model are estimated $\Delta\text{Leverage}_{i,t} = \beta_{0,1}\Delta\text{Leverage}_{i,t-1} + \sum_{k=1}^{k} \beta_{1,k}\Delta Y_{1,k,t} + \varepsilon_{i,t}$ and $\Delta\text{Maturity}_{i,t} = \beta_{0,1}\Delta\text{Maturity}_{i,t-1} + \sum_{k=1}^{k} \beta_{1,k}\Delta Y_{1,k,t} + \varepsilon_{i,t}$ by Generalized Method of Moments (GMM) using as instruments first order lagged values of the levels of explanatory variables, industry and country dummies and constant. Estimation period is from 1990 to 2003. The sample refers to the polling together of all firm-level data for Argentina, Brazil, Chile, Colombia, Mexico, Peru, Venezuela, Bulgaria, Czech Republic, Latvia, Lithuania, Poland, Romania and Russia. Dependent variables are *Leverage* equal to long-term book liabilities divided by book value of equity and Maturity is equal to Long-term debt divided by total debt. Reported t-statistics are calculated using heteroskedasticity-robust standard errors (White) and are also robust for autocorrelation (Bartlett Kernel); t-statistics in parenthesis and ***, ** and * represents significant at the 1%, 5% and 10% levels.

Variables	Leverage	Maturity
$\Delta Leverage_t$		0.0062(0.7951)
$\Delta Maturity_t$	1.2707(1.3585)	
$\Delta Leverage_{t-1}$	$0.4646^{**}(2.3833)$	0.0010(0.2540)
$\Delta Maturity_{t-1}$	−0.6379(−1.4060)	$0.3262^{***}(9.6831)$
$\Delta Size_t$	−0.0191(−0.2080)	−0.0123(−1.4663)
$\Delta Growth\ Opportunities_t$	0.1767(1.5220)	0.0038(0.1622)
$\Delta Profitability_t$	0.1898(0.1895)	0.1379(.3297)
$\Delta Business\ Risk_t$	0.0000(0.0791)	0.0000(−1.7631)
$\Delta Liquidity_t$	−0.0231(−0.4335)	$0.0169^{**}(1.9758)$
$\Delta Tangibility_t$	1.0902(0.6615)	−0.0544(−0.2651)
$\Delta TaxEffects_t$	0.0001(1.2487)	$-0.0001^{***}(-3.8930)$
Regulation Dummy	−0.0229(−0.6052)	0.0021(0.2518)
Latin America Dummy	$0.0919^{***}(2.9976)$	−0.0039(−0.6183)
Number of Observations	4436	4436
F-statistic	0.1570	3.0127^{***}
$F(df_1; df_2)$	(11; 4424)	(11; 4424)
Sargan's Test Statistic (p-value) X^2 (df)	(38.8082) 0.969	(57)

Table 8. Panel data analysis of maturity ratios for Latin America and Eastern Europe. First-differences model so that idiosyncratic firm-effects constant through time are eliminated. The following model are estimated $\Delta\text{Leverage}_{i,t} = \beta_{0,1}\Delta\text{Leverage}_{i,t-1} + \sum_{k=1}^{k} \beta_{1,k}\Delta Y_{1,k,t} + \varepsilon_{i,t}$ and $\Delta\text{Maturity}_{i,t} = \beta_{0,1}\Delta\text{Maturity}_{i,t-1} + \sum_{k=1}^{k} \beta_{1,k}\Delta Y_{1,k,t} + \varepsilon_{i,t}$ by Generalized Method of Moments (GMM) using as instruments first order lagged values of the levels of explanatory variables, industry and country dummies and constant. Estimation period is from 1990 to 2003. "Latin America" refers to the pooling together of all firm-level data for Argentina, Brazil, Chile, Colombia, Mexico, Peru and Venezuela. "Eastern Europe" refers to the polling together of all firm-level data for Bulgaria, Czech Republic, Latvia, Lithuania, Poland, Romania and Russia. The sample refers to the polling together of all firm-level data for,. Dependent variables are *Leverage* equal to long-term book liabilities divided by book value of equity and Maturity is equal to Long-term debt divided by total debt. Reported t-statistics are calculated using heteroskedasticity-robust standard errors (White) and are also robust for autocorrelation (Bartlett Kernel); t-statistics in parenthesis and ***, ** and * represents significant at the 1%, 5% and 10% levels.

	Latin America		Eastern Europe	
Variables	Leverage	Maturity	Leverage	Maturity
$\Delta Leverage_t$		$0.0262^{***}(6.9861)$		$-0.4109^{***}(-11.0160)$
$\Delta Maturity_t$	$15.8237^{***}(8.9450)$		$-1.9181^{***}(-16.9139)$	
$\Delta Leverage_{t-1}$	0.3281(1.2109)	−0.0039(−0.6735)	$0.4543^{**}(2.2236)$	$0.2067^{**}(2.0843)$
$\Delta Maturity_{t-1}$	$-5.8078^{***}(-6.0183)$	$0.3679^{***}(8.8230)$	$0.6808^{***}(5.5210)$	$0.3629^{***}(5.6040)$
$\Delta Size_t$	$2.0609^{**}(2.5093)$	$-0.1089^{***}(-2.6423)$	−0.0114(−1.1196)	−0.0057(−0.9155)
$\Delta Growth\ Opportunities_t$	0.3043(0.7780)	−0.0153(−0.6760)	0.3296(0.4204)	0.2233(0.7125)
$\Delta Profitability_t$	−1.2305(−0.3338)	0.1477(0.8179)	0.1597(0.9369)	0.0627(0.6947)
$\Delta Business\ Risk_t$	0.0005(1.3408)	0.0000(−1.5770)	0.0000(−0.1483)	0.0000(−0.2950)
$\Delta Liquidity_t$	$-0.5759^{***}(-3.1660)$	$0.0329^{***}(2.5854)$	$-0.0668^{**}(-2.4803)$	$-0.0383^{**}(-2.3800)$
$\Delta Tangibility_t$	−5.6540(−1.3894)	0.2333(1.1477)	0.6023(1.0268)	0.3167(1.0093)
$\Delta TaxEffects_t$	$0.0015^{***}(3.5933)$	$-0.0001^{***}(-3.9366)$	$0.0080^{***}(1.9943)$	$0.0038^{**}(2.3653)$
Regulation Dummy	−0.0238(−0.1707)	0.0018(0.2446)	−0.0163(−0.5778)	−0.0086(−0.5024)
Number of Observations	3305	3305	1131	1131
F-statistic	0.1145	2.7712^{***}	1.1492	2.3916^{***}
$F(df_1; df_2)$	(10; 3294)	(10; 3294)	(10; 1120)	(10; 1120)
Sargan's Test Statistic (p-value) X^2 (df)	26.7493 (0.986)	(45)	21.9077 (0.998)	(44)

major theoretical determinants of the joint decision, *Growth Opportunities* and the *Regulation* dummy, are not significant in any equation and sample. Additionally, *Size* is found significant in Latin America, but not in Eastern Europe; *Liquidity* is significant in both samples and for all equations, being in general positive (more liquid firms choose less and shorter debt); Tax Effects are also significant and positive (except for the leverage equation of the EE-7), indicating that more heavily taxed firms choose a higher level of indebtedness and longer maturity.

5.2. Sensitivity Analyses

One question that emerges from the cross-country approach chosen in this paper is whether a single country may be driving the results. In order to check for the robustness of the findings, we apply [50] global sensitivity analysis approach. We therefore re-estimate Equation (2) by dropping all observations of a given country at a time. We also check for the influence of any single year over the results by dropping all observations of a given year at a time and that of a single industry by dropping all firms of an industry at a time. Results of these sensitivity analyses support the robustness of the previous findings. The average coefficients for independent variables are similar to the results reported above, and so are the t-statistics. In particular, the significance is in general confirmed in the [50] histograms for those variables that are significant in the whole sample analysis presented in **Table 8** (lagged leverage and lagged maturity, contemporaneous leverage and maturity, size, liquidity, and tax effects).

6. Conclusions

This paper investigates the choice between debt and equity simultaneously with the decision between short-and long-term debt for a large sample of emerging markets from Latin America and Eastern Europe. This was done by using a unique sample of 986 firms and 13,490 firm-year observations from Latin America and 686 firms and 7919 firm-year observations from Eastern Europe for the period 1990-2003. The paper sets out to address three research questions: are capital structure and debt maturity decisions taken simultaneously? Secondly, is there a dynamic component in the determination of the optimal capital structure and debt maturity? Thirdly, are adjustments costs towards optimal capital structure and debt maturity important?

The empirical results support three main findings: first, the cross-effects between leverage and maturity behave exactly the opposite between Latin America and Eastern Europe sub-samples. Capital structure and debt maturity are policy complements in Latin America and substitutes in Eastern Europe; secondly, there is a significant dynamic effects component in the determination of leverage and maturity; finally, adjustment to the target maturity is by no means costless and instantaneous with firm's facing moderate adjustment costs.

REFERENCES

[1] F. Modigliani and M. Miller, "Corporate Income Taxes and the Cost of Capital: A Correction," *American Economic Review*, Vol. 53, No. 3, 1963, pp. 433-443.

[2] M. H. Miller, "Debt and Taxes," *Journal of Finance*, Vol. 32, No. 2, 1977, pp. 261-275.

[3] H. DeAngelo and R. W. Masulis, "Optimal Capital Structure under Corporate and Personal Taxation," *Journal of Financial Economics*, Vol. 8, No. 1, 1980, pp. 3-29.

[4] S. Myers, "Determinants of Corporate Borrowing," *Journal of Financial Economics*, Vol. 5, No. 2, 1977 pp. 147-175

[5] S. Myers and S. Majluf, "Corporate Financing and Investment Decisions When Firms Have Information That Investors Do Not Have," *Journal of Financial Economics*, Vol. 13, No. 2, 1984, pp. 187-221.

[6] M. C. Jensen and W. H. Meckling, "Theory of the Firm: Managerial Behaviour, Agency Costs and Ownership Structure," *Journal of Financial Economics*, Vol. 3, No. 4, 1976, pp. 305-360.

[7] M. C. Jensen, "Agency Costs of Free Cash Flow, Corporate Finance and Takeovers," *American Economic Review*, Vol. 76, 1986, pp. 323-339.

[8] I. E. Brick and A. Ravid, "On the Relevance of Debt Maturity Structure," *Journal of Finance*, Vol. 40, No. 5, 1985, pp. 1423-1437.

[9] I. E. Brick and A. Ravid, "Interest Rate Uncertainty and the Optimal Debt Maturity Structure," *Journal of Financial and Quantitative Analysis*, Vol. 26, No. 1, 1991, pp. 63-81.

[10] S. Titman and R. Wessels, "The Determinants of Capital Structure Choices," *The Journal of Finance*, Vol. 43, 1988, pp. 1-19.

[11] A. Bevan and J. Danbolt, "Capital Structure and Its Determinants in the UK: A Decompositional Analysis," *Applied Financial Economics*, Vol. 12, No. 3, 2002, pp. 159-170.

[12] A. Ozkan, "Determinants of Capital Structure and Adjustment to Long Run Target: Evidence from UK Company Panel Data," *Journal of Business Finance and Accounting*, Vol. 28, No. 1-2, 2001, pp. 175-198.

[13] M. Bennet and R. Donnelly, "The Determinants of Capital Structure: Some UK Evidence," *British Accounting Review*, Vol. 25, No. 1, 1993, pp. 43-59.

[14] A. Miguel and J. Pindado, "Determinants of Capital

Structure: New Evidence from Spanish Panel Data," *Journal of Corporate Finance*, Vol. 7, No. 1, 2001, pp. 77-99.

[15] J. Bartholdy and C. Mateus, "Debt and Taxes for Private Firms," *International Review of Financial Analysis*, Vol. 20, No. 3, 2011, pp. 177-189.

[16] R R. ajan and L. Zingales, "What Do We Know about Capital Structure? Some Evidence from International Data," *The Journal of Finance*, Vol. 50, No. 5, 1995, pp. 1421-1460.

[17] J. Wald, "How Firm Characteristics Affect Capital Structure: An International Comparison," *Journal of Financial Research*, Vol. 22, 1999, pp. 161-187.

[18] L. Both, V. Aivazian, A. Demirguc-Kunt and V. Maksimovic, "Capital Structures in Developing Countries," *The Journal of Finance*, Vol. 56, No. 1, 2001, pp. 87-130.

[19] R. Aggarwal and S. Jamdee, "Determinants of Capital Structure: Evidence from the G-7 Countries," Working Paper, 2003.

[20] P. Gaud, M. Hoesli and A. Bender, "Debt-Equity Choice in Europe," Fame Research Paper Series, 2005, p. 152.

[21] A. De Jong, R. Kabir and T. Nguyen, "Capital Structure around the World: The Roles of Firm- and Country-Specific Determinants," *Journal of Banking and Finance*, Vol. 32, No. 9, 2008, pp. 1954-1969.

[22] A. Antoniou, Y. Guney and K. Paudyal, "The Determinants of Capital Structure: Capital Market-Oriented versus Bank-Oriented Institutions," *Journal of Financial and Quantitative Analysis*, Vol. 43, No. 1, 2008, pp. 59-92.

[23] J. Fan, S. Titman and G. Twite, "An International Comparison of Capital Structures of Debt and Maturity Choices," *Journal of Financial and Quantitative Analysis*, Vol. 47, No. 1, 2012, pp. 23-56.

[24] K. Mitchell, "The Call, Sinking Fund and Term-To-Maturity Features of Corporate Bonds: An Empirical Investigation," *Journal of Financial and Quantitative Analysis*, Vol. 26, No. 2, 1991, pp. 201-222.

[25] J. Morris, "Factors Affecting the Maturity Structure of Corporate Debt," Working Paper, University of Colorado, Denver, 1992.

[26] J. C. Easterwood and P. R. Kadapakkam, "Agency Conflicts, Issue Costs and Debt Maturity," *Quarterly Journal of Business and Economics*, Vol. 33, No. 3, 1994, pp. 69-80.

[27] M. J. Barclay and C. W. Smith Jr., "The Maturity Structure of Corporate Debt," *Journal of Finance*, Vol. 50, No. 2, 1995, pp. 609-631.

[28] M. J. Barclay and C. W. Smith Jr., "On Financial Architecture: Leverage, Maturity and Priority," *Journal of Applied Corporate Finance*, Vol. 8, No. 1, 1996, pp. 4-17.

[29] M. Stohs and D. Mauer, "The Determinants of Corporate Debt Maturity Structure," *Journal of Business*, Vol. 69, No. 3, 1996, pp. 279-312.

[30] S. A. Johnson, "An Empirical Analysis of the Determination of Corporate Debt Ownership Structure," *Journal of Financial and Quantitative Analysis*, Vol. 32, No. 1, 1997, pp. 47-69.

[31] F. Scherr and H. Hulburt, "The Debt Maturity Structure of Small Firms," *Financial Management*, Vol. 30, No. 1, 2001, pp. 85-111.

[32] E. Lyandres and A. Zhdanov, "Underinvestment or Over-Investment? The Effect of Debt Maturity on Investment," William E. Simon Graduate School of Business Administration Working Paper, 2003.

[33] K. Mitchell, "The Debt Maturity Choice: An Empirical Investigation," *Journal of Financial Research*, Vol. 16, No. 4, 1993, pp. 309-320.

[34] J. Guedes and T. Opler, "The Determinants of the Maturity of Corporate Debt Issues," *Journal of Finance*, Vol. 51, No. 1, 1996, pp. 1809-1833.

[35] M. Baker, R. Greenwood and J. Wurgler, "The Maturity of Debt Issues and Predictable Variation in Bomd Returns," Harvard Business School Working Paper, 2002.

[36] F. Schiantarelli and A. Sembenelli, "The Maturity Structure of Debt: Determinants and Effects on Firms' Performance," World Bank Policy Research Working Paper, 1997.

[37] D. Heyman, M. Deloof and H. Ooghe, "The Debt Maturity Structure of Small Firms in a Creditor Oriented Environment," Universiteit Gent Working Paper, 2003.

[38] A. Antoniou, Y. Guney and K. Paudyal, "The Determinants of Debt Maturity Structure: Evidence from France, Germany and the UK," *European Financial Management*, Vol. 12, No. 2, 2006, pp. 161-194.

[39] A. Demirguc-Kunt and V. Maksimovic, "Institutions, Financial Markets and Firm Debt Maturity," *Journal of Financial Economics*, Vol. 54, No. 3, 1999, pp. 295-336.

[40] M. J. Barclay, L. M. Marx and C. W. Smith Jr., "The Joint Determination of Leverage and Maturity," *Journal of Corporate Finance*, Vol. 9, No. 2, 2003, pp. 149-167.

[41] W. Glade and R. Corona, "Bigger Economies, Smaller governments: Privatization in Latin America," Westview Press, Boulder, 1996.

[42] L. Manzetti, "Regulatory Policy in Latin America: Post-Privatization Realities," Lynne Rienner Publishers, Boulder, 2000.

[43] R. Frydman, A. Rapczynski and J. Earle, "The Privatization process in Central America," Central European University Press, Budapest, 1993.

[44] T. Boeri and G. Perasso, "Privatisation and Corporate Governance: Some Lessons from the Experience of Tran-

sitional Economies," In: M. Balling, E. Hennessy and R. O'Brien, Eds., *Corporate Governance, Financial Markets and Global Convergence*, Kluwer Academic Press, Alphen aan den Rijn, 1998, pp. 77-86.

[45] T. W. Anderson and C. Hsiao, "Estimation of dynamic models with error components," *Journal of the American Statistical Association*, Vol. 76, No. 375, 1981, pp. 598-606.

[46] L. P. Hansen, "Large sample properties of generalized method of moments estimators," *Econometrica*, Vol. 50, No. 4, 1982, pp. 1029-1054.

[47] M. Arellano and S. R. Bond, "Some tests of specification for panel data: Monte Carlo evidence and an application to employment equations," *Review of Economic Studies*, Vol. 58, No. 2, 1991, pp. 277-297.

[48] B. H. Baltagi, "Econometric Analysis of Panel Data," John Wiley & Sons, Hoboken, 1995.

[49] H. White, "A Heteroskedasticity-Consistent Covariance Matrix Estimator and a Direct Test for Heteroskedasticity," *Econometrica*, Vol. 48, No. 4, 1980, pp. 817-838.

[50] E. Leamer, "Sensitivity Analyses Would Help," *The American Economic Review*, Vol. 75, No. 3, 1985, pp. 308-313.

Permissions

The contributors of this book come from diverse backgrounds, making this book a truly international effort. This book will bring forth new frontiers with its revolutionizing research information and detailed analysis of the nascent developments around the world.

We would like to thank all the contributing authors for lending their expertise to make the book truly unique. They have played a crucial role in the development of this book. Without their invaluable contributions this book wouldn't have been possible. They have made vital efforts to compile up to date information on the varied aspects of this subject to make this book a valuable addition to the collection of many professionals and students.

This book was conceptualized with the vision of imparting up-to-date information and advanced data in this field. To ensure the same, a matchless editorial board was set up. Every individual on the board went through rigorous rounds of assessment to prove their worth. After which they invested a large part of their time researching and compiling the most relevant data for our readers. Conferences and sessions were held from time to time between the editorial board and the contributing authors to present the data in the most comprehensible form. The editorial team has worked tirelessly to provide valuable and valid information to help people across the globe.

Every chapter published in this book has been scrutinized by our experts. Their significance has been extensively debated. The topics covered herein carry significant findings which will fuel the growth of the discipline. They may even be implemented as practical applications or may be referred to as a beginning point for another development. Chapters in this book were first published by Scientific Research Publishing Inc.; hereby published with permission under the Creative Commons Attribution License or equivalent.

The editorial board has been involved in producing this book since its inception. They have spent rigorous hours researching and exploring the diverse topics which have resulted in the successful publishing of this book. They have passed on their knowledge of decades through this book. To expedite this challenging task, the publisher supported the team at every step. A small team of assistant editors was also appointed to further simplify the editing procedure and attain best results for the readers.

Our editorial team has been hand-picked from every corner of the world. Their multi-ethnicity adds dynamic inputs to the discussions which result in innovative outcomes. These outcomes are then further discussed with the researchers and contributors who give their valuable feedback and opinion regarding the same. The feedback is then collaborated with the researches and they are edited in a comprehensive manner to aid the understanding of the subject.

Apart from the editorial board, the designing team has also invested a significant amount of their time in understanding the subject and creating the most relevant covers. They scrutinized every image to scout for the most suitable representation of the subject and create an appropriate cover for the book.

The publishing team has been involved in this book since its early stages. They were actively engaged in every process, be it collecting the data, connecting with the contributors or procuring relevant information. The team has been an ardent support to the editorial, designing and production team. Their endless efforts to recruit the best for this project, has resulted in the accomplishment of this book. They are a veteran in the field of academics and their pool of knowledge is as vast as their experience in printing. Their expertise and guidance has proved useful at every step. Their uncompromising quality standards have made this book an exceptional effort. Their encouragement from time to time has been an inspiration for everyone.

The publisher and the editorial board hope that this book will prove to be a valuable piece of knowledge for researchers, students, practitioners and scholars across the globe.

List of Contributors

Alessandro Ramponi
Department of Economics and Finance, University of Roma Tor Vergata, Roma, Italy

Jinwu Huang
School of Finance, Shanghai University of Finance and Economics, Shanghai, China

Hideki Iwaki
Faculty of Business Administration, Kyoto Sangyo University, Kyoto, Japan

Lei Luo
Finance Division, Citigroup Global Markets Japan, Tokyo, Japan

Petter N. Kolm
Courant Institute of Mathematical Sciences, New York University, New York, USA

Xinbing Kong
School of Management, Fudan University, Shanghai, China

Bingyi Jing
Department of Mathematics, Hong Kong University of Science and Technology, Hong Kong, China
School of Mathematics and Statistics, Lanzhou University, Lanzhou, China

Cuixia Li
School of Mathematics and Statistics, Lanzhou University, Lanzhou, China

Annamaria Barbagallo
Department of Mathematics and Applications "R. Caccioppoli", University of Naples "Federico II", Naples, Italy

Patrizia Daniele, Mariagrazia Lorino, Antonino Maugeri and Cristina Mirabella
Department of Mathematics and Computer Science, University of Catania, Catania, Italy

Anatoliy Swishchuk and Kaijie Cui
Department of Mathematics and Statistics, University of Calgary, Calgary, Canada

George Tzagkarakis
Eonos Investment Technologies, Paris, France

Juliana Caicedo-Llano
Eonos Investment Technologies, Paris, France
University of Evry-Val-d Essone, Evry, France

Thomas Dionysopoulos
Axianta Research, Nicosia, Cyprus

Yi-Long Hsiao
Department of Finance, National Dong Hwa University, Hualien, Chinese Taipei

Romar Correa
Department of Economics, University of Mumbai, Mumbai, India

Charles I. Nkeki
Department of Mathematics, Faculty of Physical Sciences, University of Benin, Benin City, Nigeria

Max-Olivier Hongler
Ecole Polytechnique Fédérale de Lausanne (EPFL), IMT/STI/LPM, Lausanne, Switzerland

Elie Ngongang
Department of Quantitative Techniques, Faculty of Economic and Management, University of Yaounde II, Yaounde, Cameroon

Zengjing Chen
School of Mathematics, Shandong University, Jinan, China
Department of Financial Engineering, Ajou University, Suwon, Korea

Kun He
Department of Mathematics, Donghua University, Shanghai, China

Reg Kulperger
Department of Statistical and Actuarial Science, The University of Western Ontario London, Ontario, Canada

Sure Mataramvura
Division of Actuarial Science, School of Management Studies, University of Cape Town, Cape Town, South Africa

Takanobu Mizuta
SPARX Asset Management Co., Ltd., Tokyo, Japan
School of Engineering, The University of Tokyo, Tokyo, Japan

Shinobu Yoshimura
School of Engineering, The University of Tokyo, Tokyo, Japan

Kiyoshi Izumi
School of Engineering, The University of Tokyo, Tokyo, Japan
CREST & PRESTO, Japan Science and Technology Agency, Tokyo, Japan

Isao Yagi
Faculty of Information Technology, Kanagawa Institute of Technology, Kanagawa, Japan

J. H. Witte, D. Ples and J. Corominas
Record Currency Management, Windsor, UK

Masimba E. Sonono
Unit for Business Mathematics and Informatics, North-West University, Potchefstroom, South Africa

Hopolang P. Mashele
Centre for Business Mathematics and Informatics, North-West University, Potchefstroom, South Africa

Michael Taksar
Department of Mathematics, University of Missouri, Columbia, USA

John Liu
College of Business, City University of Hong Kong, Hong Kong, China

Jiguang Yuan
Center for Transport, Trade and Financial Studies, City University of Hong Kong, Hong Kong, China

Hsien-Chang Kuo
Department of Accounting, and Department of Finance, Shih Chien University, Taipei, Taiwan

Lie-Huey Wang
Department of Finance, Ming Chuan University, Taipei, Taiwan

Cesario Mateus
Department of Accounting and Finance, University of Greenwich Business School, London, United Kingdom

Paulo Terra
Escola de Administracao, Universidade Federal do Rio Grande do Sul (UFRGS), Porto Alegre, Brazil